PART ONE

The Complete Works of
WASHINGTON IRVING

Richard Dilworth Rust
General Editor

THE CRAYON
MISCELLANY

Washington Irving

1828

WASHINGTON IRVING

THE CRAYON MISCELLANY

Edited by
Dahlia Kirby Terrell

Twayne Publishers
Boston
1979

Published by Twayne Publishers

A Division of G. K. Hall & Co.

Copyright © 1979 by

G. K. Hall & Co.

All Rights Reserved

The Complete Works of Washington Irving

Volume XXII

CENTER FOR EDITIONS OF
AMERICAN AUTHORS

AN APPROVED TEXT

MODERN LANGUAGE
ASSOCIATION OF AMERICA

®

Library of Congress Cataloging in Publication Data

Irving, Washington, 1783–1859.
The Crayon miscellany.

(The Complete works of Washington Irving; v. 22)
Includes index.
CONTENTS: A tour on the prairies.—Abbotsford, and
Newstead Abbey.—Legends of the conquest of Spain.
1. Irving, Washington, 1783–1859—Journeys.
2. The West—Description and travel—To 1848.
3. Authors, American—19th century—Biography.
4. Scott, Walter, Sir, bart., 1771–1832—Biography.
5. Authors, Scottish—19th century—Biography.
6. Byron, George Gordon Noël Byron, Baron, 1788–1824—
Homes and haunts—England—Nottinghamshire.
7. Poets, English—19th century—Biography.
8. Spain—History—711–1516. I. Terrell, Dahlia,
1919–   II. Title.
PS2060.A1   1979   818'.2'07   79–11432
ISBN 0-8057-8518-3

Manufactured in the United States of America

ACKNOWLEDGMENTS

My indebtedness extends to many individuals, institutions, and libraries for assistance in the preparation of this volume. For permission to use the various manuscripts I am grateful to Irving B. Kingsford; Helen Kingsford Preston; Lola L. Szladits, Curator of the Berg Collection, and John P. Baker, Executive Assistant, The Research Libraries, the New York Public Library; John Murray Publishers, Ltd.; June Moll and the staff of Miriam Lutcher Stark Library at the University of Texas; and Edmund Berkeley, Jr., Curator of Manuscripts, Manuscripts Division, the University of Virginia Library. Professors Ben Harris McClary and Ralph Aderman deserve thanks for their help in procuring materials from England, and numerous libraries in the United States and Canada, acknowledged in the Textual Commentary and notes, for sending first edition copies of *A Tour on the Prairies*, *Abbotsford and Newstead Abbey*, and *Legends of the Conquest of Spain* through inter-library loan to Texas Tech University for examination and collation. The Historical Society of Pennsylvania, Sleepy Hollow Restorations at Tarrytown, New York, and the National Archives provided valuable records and letters; the map libraries of the University of New Mexico, Kansas State University at Manhattan, Southern Methodist University, and the Geosciences Map Collection at Texas Tech University furnished materials which were helpful in the preparation of the map for this volume. My sincere gratitude goes to Barbara Geyer for her fine, meticulous work in the preparation of the map showing Irving's route in Oklahoma. For their invaluable assistance with various historical and textual problems, especially in relation to *A Tour on the Prairies*, I am indebted to the late Professor Henry Pochman and to Professor Edwin T. Bowden.

Generous financial aid has come from The Center for Editions of American Authors of the Modern Language Association for materials, travel, and free working time and from Texas Tech University for clerical assistance, work-study aid, and working time through a summer grant, a year's research grant, and a semester's development leave.

D.K.T.

Texas Tech University

CONTENTS

CONTENTS

CONTENTS

EDITORIAL APPARATUS

ILLUSTRATIONS

FRONTISPIECE

Washington Irving
after the drawing by David Wilkie, in Seville,
1828

MAP

Irving's Route on the Prairies of Oklahoma
(following page 3)

INTERIOR ILLUSTRATIONS

The Abbotsford Family in 1817
(page 124)

Newstead Abbey—West Front
(page 170)

Malaga
(page 240)

INTRODUCTION

When he published *A Tour on the Prairies* in the spring of 1835, Washington Irving designated it as the first in a planned series of sketches about America and Europe. As he had written in a letter to his brother Peter in January, 1835, he meant to "clear off all manuscripts" he had on hand, in a plan which would enable him to "throw off single volumes which would not be of sufficient importance to stand by themselves."[1] In the same year which saw the publication of *A Tour* there also appeared *Abbotsford and Newstead Abbey* in one volume and *Legends of the Conquest of Spain* in another. At the outset, Irving intended, as his letter had said, "when once launched," to "keep going," but other plans diverted his attention. Even before the first number came out, he had committed himself to examining John Jacob Astor's papers and materials, with his nephew Pierre Munro Irving's help, and to writing *Astoria*. Following *Astoria*'s appearance in two volumes in 1836, the next year Irving published *The Adventures of Captain Bonneville*, the story of another Western figure whom he first met at Astor's home. These works engrossed Irving's full energies and on completion were substantial enough to require no bolstering as a part of a series. No record shows that Irving ever considered a fourth number for *The Crayon Miscellany* series.

In 1849 when George P. Putnam published the revised edition, Irving used *The Crayon Miscellany* as title for the volume including *A Tour on the Prairies*, *Abbotsford*, and *Newstead Abbey*. *Legends of the Conquest of Spain* was withheld, Pierre Irving surmised, to be published later with other Spanish narratives which still lay in Irving's trunks.[2] Such plans never materialized, and the third number did not see publication again until 1866, seven years after Irving's death, when Pierre included it in the first volume of *Spanish Papers*.

Irving's decision to present his materials as a medley or collection was a natural one for him. Since his boyhood he had written sketches and articles which he contributed, sometimes anonymously, to the *New York Morning Chronicle* edited from 1802 to 1805 by his elder

---

1. From a letter dated New York, January 8, 1835, quoted in Pierre M. Irving, *The Life and Letters of Washington Irving* (New York: G. P. Putnam, 1863), III, 65; hereafter cited as PMI.

2. PMI, III, 76.

brother Peter,[3] to a political newspaper entitled *The Corrector*,[4] and at least on one occasion to the *New York Evening Post*.[5] As he had stated in 1824, he "preferred adopting the mode of sketches and short tales rather than long works."[6] Several earlier writings, including *Letters of Jonathan Oldstyle, Gentleman* (1802–1803), *Salmagundi* (1805), and *The Sketch Book* (1819) had presented an assortment of subjects. Furthermore, his reason for deciding on the 1835 miscellany, his reticence concerning *A Tour on the Prairies* as a single volume once he had finished writing it,[7] was more nearly characteristic than unusual for the author. He consistently doubted his own efforts.[8] When the 1833 assurance that he was again "at home upon American themes"[9] gave way to doubts two years later at the prospect of sending his book before the American public, the solution was to make it a part of a larger plan. He would include "writings relative to Spain &c., so that the series [would] form a kind of gallery of varied works."[10]

Though the series ceased after three numbers, its diversity of contents justifies "Miscellany" in the title. Settings of time and place vary from the current American West still unsettled by the white man in the first number, to the English countryside and Scottish Highlands decades earlier in the second, and to the ancient days of the Moslems

3. In addition to the nine *Letters of Jonathan Oldstyle, Gentleman* appearing in the *Chronicle* between November 15, 1802, and April 28, 1803, and reprinted (all but the first) in 1824 by William H. Clayton in New York, see also two Irving letters identified in Wayne R. Kime, "An Actor Among the Albanians: Two Rediscovered Sketches of Albany by Washington Irving," *New York History* 56 (1975), 409–25.

4. See Martin Roth, ed., *Washington Irving's Contributions to "The Corrector"* (Minneapolis: University of Minnesota Press, 1968).

5. See Wayne R. Kime, "Washington Irving and the 'Extension of the Empire of Freedom': An Unrecorded Contribution to the Evening Post May 14, 1804," *Bulletin of the New York Public Library* 76 (1972), 220–30.

6. From a letter to Henry Brevoort, dated Paris, Rue Richelieu, No. 89, December 11, 1824, quoted in PMI, II, 227.

7. Stanley T. Williams in *The Life of Washington Irving* (New York: Oxford University Press, 1935), II, 72–74 and 79–83 emphasizes (perhaps in unnecessarily critical language) Irving's sense of opportunism and "timidity" in falling "back on his old stratagem" to fill *The Crayon Miscellany* with the "refuse of Geoffrey Crayon's old notebooks." Hereafter Williams' biography will be cited as STW.

8. Irving's letters to his friend Henry Brevoort, for example, repeatedly express his anxiety about his "imperfections," and, in the case of *The Sketch Book*, request Brevoort's opinion and his judgment in omitting any number considered unworthy. (See PMI, I, 414–28 for quotations from letters written in 1819.)

9. Irving's expression in a letter to Peter dated New York, October 28, 1833, quoted in PMI, III, 57.

10. From a letter to Peter dated New York, January 8, 1835, quoted in PMI, III, 65.

in the old country of the Iberian Peninsula in the third. *A Tour on the Prairies* and *Abbotsford and Newstead Abbey* both record personal experiences and have a basis in Irving's journals, but one volume is a short travelogue and the other is made up of two separate narratives, one about his visit with Scott in 1817 and the other about his visit to Byron's home in 1832 seven years after Byron's death. Furthermore, *A Tour on the Prairies* was conceived and written entirely in America, whereas some of the work for the other two was done while Irving was still in Europe. The last of the series recounts three Spanish legends reminiscent of *The Conquest of Granada* (1829) and, like that book, is based on chronicles in Spanish sources. It, too, was begun—and nearly completed—some time before Irving returned from abroad. No thread of narrative or preconceived order links the three numbers. They are a small, but diverse, "gallery."

The characteristic the series shares with Irving's writings in general is pointed up in the "Crayon" in its title. Each of the title pages indicates the volume is "By the Author of The Sketch Book"; Irving's name does not appear on the 1835 editions. The writer presents sketches, and in *The Crayon Miscellany*, as through most of his literary career,[11] he finds the Geoffrey Crayon image a useful one in portraying his Western scenes, in recalling the visits to Abbotsford and to Newstead Abbey, and in telling the narratives of early Spain.

A Tour on the Prairies

The first publication in the series, *A Tour on the Prairies* (1835), deals with Irving's native land and tells of a brief expedition he made in the fall of 1832 upon returning to America after a seventeen-year absence in Europe. The volume covers only a small part of the traveling he did within a seven-month period after arrival in New York on May 21. Usually with his two companions on the voyage across the Atlantic, the Englishman Charles Joseph Latrobe and the young Swiss Count de Pourtalés, the Englishman's charge, and part of the time with his American friend James Kirke Paulding, he visited parts of New York, Ohio, Pennsylvania, and New Hampshire before he met Indian Commissioner Henry L. Ellsworth on a Lake Erie steamer. Accepting Ellsworth's invitation to make a jaunt into the West, Irving, with Latrobe and Pourtalés, accompanied him across Ohio and Kentucky and into Missouri and Kansas to reach the Oklahoma area. *A Tour on the Prairies* tells only of the month's horseback trip he made through the Indian

11. The pseudonym Geoffrey Crayon was first assumed in May, 1819, with the publishing of the first number of *The Sketch Book of Geoffrey Crayon, Gent.* simultaneously in New York, Boston, Philadelphia, and Baltimore.

territory of Eastern Oklahoma with his friends and a military group of rangers, setting out from Fort Gibson on October 10, 1832, and returning on November 8 to the same point. Based on the journal Irving kept, the book presents vivid sketches of people, landscape, and activities on the tour, reflecting much of the personal attitude and reaction of the Eastern literary traveler.

With the strong interest in the West in 1832 it seemed inevitable that America's most popular author should associate himself with that interest as a part of his rediscovery of his homeland.[12] Furthermore, he had been curious about the Indians and the American frontier since boyhood visits to Canada as early as 1803; he had asked his friend, Henry Brevoort, Jr., to send him books about Indians while he was abroad; and his literary interest had been heightened through acquaintance with the first of James Fenimore Cooper's three Leather-stocking books which had appeared before the tour.[13]

Irving was excited when the accidental meeting with Henry Ellsworth in late August, 1832, brought the invitation to join an expedition into the country set aside for the emigrating Indians by the Indian Removal Act of 1830.[14] Recalling the incident in December, 1832, in a letter to his brother Peter, Irving described his enthusiasm:

> The offer was too tempting to be resisted: I should have an opportunity of seeing the remnants of those great Indian tribes, which are now about to disappear as independent nations, or to be amalgamated under some new form of government. I should see those fine countries of the "far west," while still in a state of pristine wilderness, and behold herds of buffaloes scouring their native prairies, before they are driven beyond the reach of a civilized tourist.[15]

Irving, Latrobe, and Pourtalés traveled the long journey to Fort Gibson most of the time with Ellsworth, where they were to meet the

12. See Edgeley W. Todd's discussion of the significance of Irving's trip in "Washington Irving Discovers the Frontier," *Western Humanities Review* 11 (1957), 29–39.

13. *The Pioneers* (1823), *The Last of the Mohicans* (1826), and *The Prairie* (1827) had all been published, but Irving had read only *The Pioneers*. (See his letter to Brevoort quoted in PMI, II, 261.)

14. A statute approved on May 28, 1830, by the Twenty-first Congress provided for the removal of all Indians residing in any of the states and territories to an area west of the Mississippi River.

15. A portion of Irving's letter dated Washington City, December 18, 1832, is quoted in John Francis McDermott's introduction to *The Western Journals of Washington Irving* (Norman: University of Oklahoma Press, 1944), p. 10. Irving's

other two Indian commissioners and where the expedition was to begin. When they discovered on arrival that Commissioners Montfort Stokes and John F. Schermerhorn were not expected for at least two weeks, and that the rangers they had understood Colonel Matthew Arbuckle was to provide for them had departed two days earlier, Ellsworth requested that the rangers be detained and he and his friends made preparation to follow them. His decision was to set out on a three weeks' exploration in order "to employ [his] time to the best advantage."[16] When the secretary assigned to the expedition, Colonel Samuel C. Stambaugh, also failed to appear, Ellsworth gave Irving official status in the group by asking him to serve as secretary during the brief tour,[17] a fact Irving never mentioned in his letters, in his notebooks, or in *A Tour on the Prairies.*

The delight Irving had felt during his months of travel continued as he moved further westward. A letter to his sister Mrs. Paris mailed from Fort Gibson on October 9, the day after their arrival, reflected Irving's high spirits as he anticipated the journey: "You see, I am completely launched in savage life, and am likely to continue in it for some weeks to come. I am extremely excited and interested by this wild country, and the wild scenes and people by which I am surrounded."[18] Nine days later another letter to Mrs. Paris, written on the trail and returned by some rangers escorting two or three sick men back to camp, told of their being "on the borders of the Pawnee country" and of Irving's excitement at "the idea of exploring a wild country."[19] Finally, after their return to Fort Gibson he could write her proudly of the completion of "a very rough" but "very interesting and gratifying" tour.[20]

During the thirty-one-day expedition Irving kept day by day notations as was his custom throughout his life on his travels. Ellsworth

---

popularity and the wide publicity given to his Western trip in America and abroad are exemplified by the publication of this letter during 1833 in the London *Athenaeum,* the *New York Commercial Advertiser,* the *Arkansas Gazette,* and the *Missouri Intelligencer.*

16. From Henry L. Ellsworth's letter to Secretary of War Lewis Cass, dated Fort Gibson, October 9, 1832, now in *Senate Document* 512, III, 481. The complete letter is quoted in McDermott's Introduction to *The Western Journals of Washington Irving,* pp. 24–25.

17. Letter from Ellsworth to the secretary of war dated Fort Gibson, November 18, 1832 (Office of Indian Affairs, National Archives, Washington, D.C.).

18. Quoted in PMI, III, 40.

19. Quoted in PMI, III, 41, 42.

20. From a letter dated Montgomery's Point, Mouth of the Arkansas, Mississippi River, November 16, 1832, quoted in PMI, III, 42.

noted that Irving's "mode of recording events [was] not to confide much to the memory, but to sketch in a little book every occurence [*sic*] worthy of remembrance and especially dates & facts."[21] His journal entries reflect his eager response to the new experience and record various details about landscape and activity that were to serve later as a nucleus for the literary account. For the period from the October 9 departure from Fort Gibson through the events of October 17 and for the last days of the journey, October 31 through November 9, Irving's notes still survive.[22] In addition, there are several pages of undated notes where Irving reversed his notebooks and scribbled additional comments and recorded snatches of narrative and dialogue, some of which later would be incorporated in *A Tour on the Prairies*. Unfortunately no journal has been found for October 18–30 to reveal what he wrote at the time about the trek through the Cross Timber or about such events as the fire in the camp, the false Pawnee scare, the ringing of the wild horse, or the hunting of buffaloes and his own experience in bringing down one of the herd himself.

Irving had known even before the Oklahoma trip began that he was expected to use his materials and to write of his experiences. The popularity of the well-known author required something from his pen. Before the travelers reached Fort Gibson, the *Missouri Intelligencer* on September 29, ten days after their brief stop in Columbia, printed comments on Irving's visit and ended with the prediction that he would "no doubt acquire a valuable fund of materials in his progress, for interesting works or Sketches, which, ere long, we may have the gratification of perusing." If we are to believe Pourtalés, Irving had mentioned plans for writing of his travels even before their stop in Columbia. The young count wrote his mother on September 26, "Our nomadic period will end brilliantly. Mr. Irving will publish two works on this summer's trip. He has spoken to us of the plan and the form of the

21. Henry Leavitt Ellsworth, *Washington Irving on the Prairie or A Narrative of a Tour of the Southwest in the Year 1832*, ed. S. T. Williams and Barbara D. Simison (New York: American Book Company, 1937), p. 71; hereafter referred to as *Narrative*.

22. The jottings for the period of the journey (October 10–November 8) occupy only a portion of the five volumes known as the Western journals now located in New York Public Library: Journal I Cincinnati, September 3–St Louis, September 14; Journal II Independence, September 26–Cabin Creek, October 6; Journal III Cabin Creek, October 6–On the Red Fork, October 17; Journal IV On the Little River, October 31–Fort Gibson, November 10; Journal V Fort Gibson, November 11–Stack Island, November 17. The text of the journals was published in the Trent-Hellman edition by the Bibliophile Society of Boston in 1919 and is readily available in *The Western Journals of Washington Irving*, edited and annotated by John Francis McDermott (Norman: University of Oklahoma Press, 1944).

work and has told us, in confidence, some of the anecdotes which he will include. That is the very great advantage of traveling in such company!"[23] Though Irving must have been less confident about his publishing plans than Pourtalés' statements indicate, he no doubt looked forward to utilizing the notes he made as he traveled.

After the tour Irving had difficulty finding time to write. Until early December he continued to travel—to New Orleans and through Alabama, Georgia, South Carolina, North Carolina, and Virginia to Washington, where he was to stay until March, 1833. Society and politics absorbed his time and attention. Back in New York he continued "the rounds of dinners, &c." and, as he wrote Peter, was "harassed by the claims of society."[24] It is doubtful that he did any work at all on his writing until the latter part of 1833.[25] On October 7 he wrote his brother Ebenezer, apparently in response to the latter's chiding him for leaving his pen idle for so long, "I want to get to work as much as you can wish me to do so, but God knows my mind and time are so cut up and engrossed, that I am almost in despair of ever getting quiet again."[26]

Furthermore, he apparently did not consider his reorientation in the American setting completed. It was not until October 28, 1833 (three weeks after the letter to Ebenezer), that he could write Peter, "I am now getting at home upon American themes, and the scenes and characters I have noticed since my return begin to assume a proper tone and form and grouping in my mind and to take a tinge from my imagination."[27] The anxiety he had felt over the months of delay had only been intensified by the urging and expectations of family, friends, and the American public that he would write of his experiences in a manner that would "be in every way gratifying."[28]

23. *On the Western Tour With Washington Irving: The Journal and Letters of Count de Pourtalés*, ed. George F. Spaulding, trans. Seymour Feiler (Norman: University of Oklahoma Press, 1968), pp. 35–36; hereafter referred to as *Pourtalés*.

24. Letter dated New York, April 15, quoted in PMI, III, 50–51. Philip Hone, New York mayor, noted Irving's appearance at various gatherings and commented on the fine intellect and sociability of the accomplished author. *The Diary of Philip Hone, 1828–1851*, ed. Bayard Tuckerman (New York, 1889), I, 72, 116, 140, 143, 194, 198, 205, 207.

25. On April 1, 1833, he wrote Peter from New York: "I have been so completely bewildered by the variety of scenes, circumstances, and persons crowding upon my attention, that for months past I have lost all command of my time or my thoughts. . . . excitement still continues, and unfits me for any calm application," quoted in PMI, III, 49–50.

26. Quoted in PMI, III, 55.

27. Quoted in PMI, III, 57.

28. The prediction printed January 30, 1833, in the *Arkansas Gazette* is generally

During the final months of 1833 the "scenes and characters" he had recently met began to "assume proper form and grouping" for Irving as he managed to relate them to the brief Oklahoma tour. Of all his travels to reacquaint himself with America, only the Western trip with Ellsworth constituted a unit with a defined mission and the promise of activity and drama of the kind that would interest readers. As he looked at his journals, Irving recognized the month's excursion as "an episode complete as far as it goes."[29] With his notebooks before him he began to recreate the personages in his mind and to relive the scenes of a year earlier in an effort to organize his material. The historic mission headed by the lone Indian Commissioner Henry L. Ellsworth whom he and his two companions, Latrobe and Pourtalés, had joined and whom Captain Jesse Bean and his rangers had escorted would serve as the focus for his tale. The day by day notations he made would provide all the materials his memory and creative imagination needed. Since he had an official position as secretary on the tour and served on the advisory council with Ellsworth, Bean, and the surgeon Doctor Holt, his store of knowledge of the affairs of the traveling group would be sufficient.

At no time apparently, either on the tour or later, did Irving have access to anyone else's notes about activities on the tour. He knew Latrobe would write about the experience and was anxious to precede him into publication,[30] but no record shows that the two friends exchanged information.[31] If Ellsworth made an official report to Secretary of War Lewis Cass or if Captain Jesse Bean submitted one to Colonel Matthew Arbuckle following the expedition,[32] no evidence

---

representative of those in newspapers all over the country as they anticipated Irving's work. (See, for example, those listed in note 15.)

29. Introduction, *A Tour on the Prairies*, Twayne edition, page 9 line 10.

30. Letter from Irving to his London literary agent Colonel Aspinwall on December 29, 1834, warned, "Be on your guard . . . say nothing on the subject" (quoted by STW, II, 74, from a letter in the possession of Marston Drake, New York City). Latrobe's account appeared in 1835 in his two-volume work *The Rambler in North America* (New York: Harper and Brothers) with a dedication to Irving.

31. See earlier reference, however, to Pourtalés' letter of September 26, 1832, prior to the journey indicating that Irving discussed his plans for writing with the travellers. The incident, if not entirely the imagining of the young count, was doubtless only a casual reference or Irving's answer to a question rather than sharing of information.

32. Neither report is in the National Archives. Colonel Arbuckle's letter to Bean dated Fort Gibson, October 5, 1832, instructed him to keep a journal to "note the course and distance of each day's march, the character of the soil, timber, water minerals and whatever else you may judge worthy of particular

indicates that Irving saw their reports. Nor was he aware, so far as anyone knows, of Ellsworth's 116–page personal letter to his wife which gave details of the events on the trail in journal fashion and which was to be published more than a century later under the title *Washington Irving on the Prairie or a Narrative of a Tour of the Southwest in the Year 1832.*[33] If Irving knew of the diary the young Count Pourtalés kept in French or of the letters he wrote about the trip,[34] he did not consider the fact worth mentioning. Irving was considered to be the writer among the travelers; perhaps no one would have presumed to offer him any materials.[35]

Essentially the dates and incidents of Irving's narrative agree with those in the accounts of Latrobe, Ellsworth, and Pourtalés; yet it is not accurate to say that what Irving did in writing *A Tour on the Prairies* was simply to "expand" the journal of 1832 to create a "log book of the tour."[36] On the journey he made each entry the record of a day's activities; in writing the narrative he alluded to specific dates in only nine instances even though he followed the chronology of events as they had occurred. Overall he managed to exercise the writer's prerogative of selecting, of adding, and even of arranging some materials to tell a unified story.[37]

---

remark." The complete letter, now located in the National Archives, Washington, D.C. (Arbuckle Letters 1830–1836), is reprinted in McDermott's introduction to *The Western Journals of Washington Irving*, pp. 31–33.

33. Yale University owns the manuscript transcribed by editors Stanley T. Williams and Barbara D. Simison and printed by the American Book Company in 1937. Included is a valuable intimate description of Irving and various comments on Irving's writings and the activities on the tour.

34. George F. Spaulding's discovery of the 133-year-old manuscripts in 1965 in Munich at the home of Pourtalés' great-granddaughter led to the 1968 publication of a fourth contemporary account of the historic tour. (See footnote 23.)

35. Ellsworth wrote in detail of Irving's observation of men and landscape and of his "filling his little sketch book" with information as "foundations" for "additional rooms when he builds his fabric and adds the rest" (*Narrative*, pp. 42, 71). Pourtalés' admiration for Irving revealed in his letters and journals caused Spaulding to conclude that the "heavy, grandiose style" of his early recordings is an attempt to emulate the famous author (Editor's Introduction, *Pourtalés*, p. 12).

36. In STW, II, 80 these phrases appear in a discussion of Irving's catering to "popular taste."

37. See Wayne R. Kime, "The Completeness of Washington Irving's *A Tour on the Prairies*," *Western American Literature*, 8 (Spring and Summer 1973), 55–65 for a perceptive and well-reasoned scholarly discussion of *Tour* as a unified narrative revealing Irving's personal growth in understanding of the West as it was and of himself as an Easterner separated from it. Professor Kime's article shows how the author selected and arranged his materials in accord with a "sense of the design of the original experience."

First of all, the story required the addition of details in the first chapter to describe setting and characters, to show where the journey took place and who the traveling companions closest to Irving were, in order to establish overall a tone of expectancy of adventure and possible danger. Succeeding chapters continued the chronological account with frequent additions of personal impressions and opinions as the journey began and progressed along the trail. Notations apparently served to revive the writer's memory of the sense of expectancy and the excitement he felt as they moved into the unexplored area. Choice of material and additions seem to have been directed largely by Irving's decision to sketch a personal experience, not to record history. Such added details as the reference to their "going on a long and rough tour" which necessitated their being well mounted "in case of meeting with hostile savages" describe accurately their dread and anticipation as they prepared to leave Fort Gibson. Likewise Irving's added allusion to his dislike of Pierre Beatte the guide recalls an uneasiness that was part of the atmosphere at the beginning before experience and understanding relieved the tension. His own responses, as he reflected, provided further material. By recalling his enthusiasm for the independence and freedom on the prairie in the "savage state," his delight at seeing real-life Indians in contrast to poetic drawings, and his experiencing of loneliness and of the thrills and agonies of the buffalo hunt, Irving made his account personal reminiscence rather than either travelogue or history.

In *A Tour on the Prairies,* as in all of his writing, Irving's interest lay in people,[38] in scenery and landscape, and in legend. He filled his story not only with descriptions of his companions, of their servants, and of Indians, but also with descriptions of numerous scenes of merriment, of boisterous activity, of weary travel, of varied hunting, of feasting and scarcity, and of quiet repose. Bits of legend and folktales and snatches of conversation scattered through his journals were developed and interspersed appropriately within the narrative. Through recollection Irving added vignettes and sketches utilizing much of what he recorded during the first days of the journey and less of what he recorded during the last nine days following the climactic buffalo hunt.

As Irving worked with his materials, it was as natural for him to use literary allusions and to construct a literary narrative as it was for him to compare what he saw with European scenes he had witnessed

---

38. Ellsworth wrote, "With the great, he feels sufficiently acquainted—He desires most to ramble among the natural actions of men—He watches every spring and looks with microscopic eye into the hidden wheels that move men along, on the common walks of life" (*Narrative,* p. 71).

for seventeen years prior to the tour[39] or to portray vignettes reflecting a lifelong interest in visual art and longstanding friendships with artists.[40] His drawing of the hunter "Old Ryan," for example, shows the literary propensity. He made three brief references to Ryan in the portion of the journal still extant. Two of them served as the basis for the literary picture: (1) "old huntsman in rifle shirt of leather asks permission to go hunting—"[41] and (2) "Capt ['] I should send to look after them [missing hunters] but Old Ryans with them, and he knows how to take care of himself & them. If it were not for him I would not give much for the rest. He's quite at home—never lost in the woods—[']."[42] Reminded of Cooper's Natty Bumppo, Irving called Ryan a "real old Leatherstocking" in *A Tour on the Prairies* and intermittently through several chapters showed him as meat provider, scout, and teacher for the younger rangers.[43]

The story of the tour was not easy for Irving to write. His own high expectations, in addition to distractions and public pressure, combined with his usual distrust of his abilities to plague him as he wrote. It was difficult to recapture his sense of expectation and discovery on an "interesting and gratifying" journey a year earlier. He had difficulty writing anything that would "satisfy" himself.[44] It was in late November, 1834, more than a year after he began work on it, before he completed the first draft of his narrative. He was not pleased with the three hundred and fifty pages he had written and did not wish "to let it go before the public."[45] During the last weeks of the year he worked to revise and strengthen the tale he considered "extremely simple, and

39. From 1815 to 1818 he represented family business interests in Liverpool; in August, 1818, he took up residence in London and thereafter at various times traveled in Scotland, France, Germany, and Spain before his return to America in May, 1832.

40. Washington Allston, David Wilkie, C. R. Leslie, Stuart Newton, and Benjamin West were among Irving's friends. While he was enjoying the companionship of Allston in Italy in 1805, the twenty-two-year-old Irving briefly considered becoming a painter.

41. *The Western Journals of Washington Irving*, ed. McDermott, pp. 118–119. See footnote 22.

42. *Ibid.*, p. 128.

43. See *A Tour on the Prairies* (Chapters VIII, X, XIII, XIV, XV, XVI, XXII, XXIII, and XXVIII) for references to the ranger "Old Ryan" whom Irving made into a minor hero. Though both John Ryan (Irving's "Old Ryan") and his son, William Ryan, were on the tour, Irving included only the older man in his notations and in his literary account.

44. From a letter to Peter dated New York, January 8, 1835, quoted in PMI, III, 65.

45. From a letter to Peter dated November 24, 1834, quoted in PMI, III, 64.

by no means striking in its details." By January, 1835, he had decided
to publish and to make the story the first of a series under the "Miscellany" title with the second title *A Tour on the Prairies* to designate
the particular contents of the volume.[46]

Eager to precede Latrobe's book which was about to be published,
he set to work to prepare manuscripts to be sent as printer's copy to
London and to Philadelphia. Hoping for simultaneous publication in
England and in America,[47] he had to send the materials to England
some time ahead of the copy to be printed at home. Therefore he
engaged several copyists to transcribe the English manuscript while he
continued revisions. Frequently on the copied pages he made the
same corrections he had decided on for the American copy, at times
adding a whole paragraph, as he did in Chapter XX to describe the
effect of the introduction of the horse on the life of the Indian in the
Far West, or in some instances substituting a specific word for a more
general one, as in the phrase "singularly wild" rather than "regularly
wild" to describe the scene when Beatte tamed a wild horse. By such
means he worked to achieve the "proper tone." By January 8, 1835, the
four hundred and twenty-four pages of English manuscript had been
completed and mailed to Irving's London literary agent, Colonel Thomas
Aspinwall.

In spite of the author's strained relations with John Murray which
had developed in 1831[48] and his own resolution in 1832 "to have nothing
more to do with him,"[49] Irving now turned to the prestigious firm
which had already published a half dozen books for him (*The Sketch
Book*, 1820; *Bracebridge Hall*, 1822; *Tales of a Traveller*, 1824; *Life
of Columbus*, 1828; *The Conquest of Granada*, 1829; and *Companions
of Columbus*, 1830). On February 2 he wrote to Aspinwall suggesting
that he approach John Murray. Irving hoped for five hundred guineas,

46. From a letter to Peter dated New York, January 8, 1835, quoted in PMI,
III, 65.

47. Irving's notes prepared in 1850 answering the questions of John Murray
III about *Tour* (now in the Yale University Library) state that he intended
simultaneous publication. He wanted to protect himself from piracy in both countries. On April 8, a month after the London edition was out, he wrote Henry Carey
at Philadelphia, "Are you not endangering my copyright here by keeping the
work back[?]" (From a letter in the Henry E. Huntington Library and Art Gallery).

48. See Ben Harris McClary, *Washington Irving and the House of Murray:
Geoffrey Crayon Charms the British, 1817–1856* (Knoxville: University of Tennessee
Press, 1969) for a discussion of the Irving-Murray relationship, especially pages
157–168 relating to negotiations concerning *Mahomet*.

49. From a letter to C. R. Leslie, January, 1832 (Manuscript Division, New
York Public Library).

but he asked Aspinwall "to make such bargain as you can."[50] On February 5 Aspinwall rejected Murray's offer to assume all of the risks and to grant Irving two-thirds of the net profit. Shortly afterward John Murray bought the copyright, agreeing to pay the author four hundred pounds within four months.[51] The volume was published March 2, 1835. Spottiswoode printed two thousand copies at first and then one thousand additional for Murray.[52] In a letter to Peter on April 11 Irving wrote that he was "well satisfied with the terms of sale."[53] The book went through the press without his assistance and with only editorial proofreading.

For more than a month after he mailed the British copy, Irving continued to revise and make additions in the American printer's copy he was preparing. By the middle of February he was almost finished, and his brother Ebenezer, Irving's agent for his books in America, so informed Carey, Lea, and Blanchard in Philadelphia, publishers of *Tales of a Traveller* in 1824 and Irving's publisher since 1829.[54] A letter from the firm requested "some idea of the price per copy and time for disposal of five thousand copies," suggesting that the arrangements for the printing also be left to them.[55] Before the middle of March Irving had A. Chandler prepare the stereotyped plates and sent them to Carey, Lea, and Blanchard.[56] For publishing and vending rights the firm agreed to pay fifteen hundred dollars for five thousand copies in equal notes at six, nine, and twelve months, and three hundred dollars for every additional thousand.[57] The book was put to press before March 16, 1835, by C. Sherman and Co. for Carey but apparently

50. From a letter dated New York, February 2, 1835 (Sleepy Hollow Restorations, Sunnyside, Tarrytown, New York).

51. The promissory note in Murray Archives indicates that the amount was paid in full on July 5.

52. Ledger C, p. 120 (Murray Archives).

53. Quoted in PMI, III, 66.

54. The British copy went to Aspinwall before January 8. A letter from the Carey, Lea, and Blanchard firm to Ebenezer Irving, dated February 17, 1835, expresses pleasure at finding Irving "so nearly ready to publish his Tour" (Carey and Lea manuscript letter books, Historical Society of Pennsylvania; hereafter cited as LB). For a discussion of Irving's relationship with the Carey firm, see David Kaser's *Messrs. Carey and Lea of Philadelphia* (Philadelphia: University of Pennsylvania Press, 1957), pp. 82–86 and William Charvat's *Literary Publishing in America 1790–1850* (Philadelphia: University of Pennsylvania Press, 1959), pp. 44, 49, 50, 54.

55. From a letter dated February 17, 1835 (LB).

56. A letter to Ebenezer Irving dated March 16, 1835, acknowledged receipt of the first plates and advised that the book was "progressing rapidly through the press" (LB).

57. PMI, III, 67.

moved more slowly than Irving thought it should. On April 8 he wrote to Henry Carey, fearful that the delay of more than a month after the Murray edition was out would endanger his copyright.[58] An immediate reply on April 10, for someone writing for Henry Carey who was out of town, promised publication the following day with copies "forwarded to the New York booksellers at every part of the country."[59] Carey's cost book listed April 10 as the publication date;[60] and the book went out on the 11. By November 10, 1835, the firm had paid Irving for the eighth thousand.[61]

While the work was in the press, Washington Irving continued what he referred to as "re-dressing" of his narrative. For the American edition he also wrote a separate notation labeled "Advertisement" stating his intention for The Crayon Miscellany and a new "Introduction" in which he included a personal explanation of his long absence from his native country and a public declaration of his love for his countrymen and his homeland. This last portion, the basis later for insinuations of "duplicity" on Irving's part in courting favor both in England and in America,[62] was not to be printed again until the twentieth century when it would be included for its historical interest.

Public expectations were not disappointed either in America or abroad when the volume came out. The New York Mirror had printed two chapters, "The Honey Camp" and "A Bee Hunt" in the issue of April 4, 1835, one week before the American edition was distributed. Within a seven-month period Carey had to have three thousand extra copies printed, beyond the original five thousand, in order to meet the demands of his booksellers.[63] Murray added another thousand to his original two thousand. In the month in which the American publication appeared, Dr. Francis Lieber, the political scientist and writer, wrote Irving complimenting the work and requesting permission to do

58. See footnote 47.

59. Letter to Washington Irving dated April 10, 1835 (LB).

60. David Kaser, The Cost Book of Carey & Lea 1825–1838 (Philadelphia: University of Pennsylvania Press, 1963), p. 169, entry 484.

61. PMI, III, 68.

62. See PMI, III, 102–9 for a discussion of the "attack" on Irving by the editor of the Plaindealer, Mr. Leggett, in the issue of January 28, 1837, and for Irving's letter explaining the circumstances of his writing the Introduction.

63. Stanley T. Williams and Mary Ellen Edge, A Bibliography of the Writings of Washington Irving: A Check List (New York: Oxford University Press, 1936), p. 56, lists an 1836 printing of A Tour on the Prairies by Carey, Lea and Blanchard which they did not see. Apparently their listing is in error. Library of Congress catalogs have no 1836 Carey listing, the cost book of the firm for 1825–1838 has no entry for an 1836 printing, and no copy has been located in an extensive survey of major libraries in the United States and Canada.

an abridgement, an offer which Irving graciously but firmly declined.[64] American newspapers and periodicals all over the country praised the publication, agreeing with the sentiment expressed by Irving's friend Philip Hone who called it "the very best kind of light reading."[65] Edward Everett in the *North American Review* commended both its style and content in which, he said, "nearly all the elements of several different kinds of writing are beautifully and gayly blended into a production almost *sui generis*." The *Southern Literary Messenger* in May, 1835, commended the author's accomplishment, saying that he abandoned "romance for reality."[66] Irving need not have worried about the reception of his volume.

Though the response in England was understandably less strong than in America, considering Irving's subject matter, approval of the work there was certain.[67] Its immediate popularity on the Continent is evidenced also by the appearance of two editions in Paris (published by Galignani and Baudry) from the English text and by 1835 translations into Dutch, French, and German, the latter being published by four separate firms. An extract also appeared in the Berlin periodical *Magazin für die Literatur des Auslandes*. Within two years Russian and Italian translations had appeared, and French translations continued to be printed through the nineteenth century.[68] In 1850 in London both H. G. Bohn and G. Routledge, in an effort to pirate Murray's book, came out with cheap reprints.

In May, 1849, *A Tour on the Prairies* with *Abbotsford and Newstead Abbey* comprised *The Crayon Miscellany*, published by Putnam as Volume IX of the Author's Revised Edition of *The Works of Washington Irving*. The editor of the *Literary World* praised "its unique, finished character" and predicted that it probably would "be read as long as

64. Irving's three-page letter dated New York, April 22, 1835, declining Dr. Lieber's offer was advertised in Catalog no. 70 February, 1972, by Paul C. Richards, Bridgewater, Massachusetts. Irving felt "much flattered" but feared an abridgment would delete "its most striking features" and "interfere with its circulation."

65. Bayard Tuckerman, ed., *The Diary of Philip Hone* (New York: Dodd, Mead, 1889), entry for April 14, 1835.

66. For other comments and reviews in 1835 see *Metropolitan Magazine* (April), *Eclectic Review* (April), *American Monthly Magazine* (May), *Knickerbocker Magazine* (May), *American Ladies' Magazine* (June), *New York Mirror* (July 4), *Southern Literary Journal* (September), *American Quarterly Review* (December).

67. C. R. Leslie wrote Irving from London on May 11, 1835, of the favorable reception of his work and of the approval of the poet Samuel Rogers. See C. R. Leslie, *Autobiographical Recollections* (Boston, 1860), p. 300.

68. For further details on the various printings of *A Tour on the Prairies* see Stanley T. Williams and Mary Ellen Edge, pp. 55–60.

any of [Irving's] writings."[69] Following 1849 (except for Bohn's and Routledge's pirated editions), the revised edition text has usually been the one used. During the nineteenth century *A Tour* was seldom out of print, being usually included as a part of *The Crayon Miscellany* or in one of the various collected editions. Following its reissue in 1851 as a part of the works of Irving by Putnam, it appeared in 1865 in the Riverside edition produced cooperatively by Putnam, Hurd, and Houghton and in such Putnam impressions as the Kinderhook edition (ca. 1868), the Riverside edition (1869), and the Hudson edition (1882 and again in 1902), in addition to several reissues of these and various separate Putnam editions. J. B Lippincott of Philadelphia brought out at least two printings of collected works (1871 and 1874) in which *A Tour* was included, and through the rest of the century smaller companies such as P. F. Collier, J. W. Lovell, John B. Alden, and Belford printed it either separately or in a volume with other Irving works.

In the twentieth century *A Tour on the Prairies* has been printed less frequently and its reputation generally has fallen to a level lower than that of Irving's earlier works.[70] Though his biographer Stanley T. Williams praised Irving on the one hand for his "power of description" as a "natural stylist,"[71] he criticized him on the other hand for his "prettifying of buffalo, wild horses, and the customs of the Osage Indians."[72] Williams emphasized what he called Irving's answering "the popular outcry" to write on an American theme and concluded, "Posterity has since forgotten Irving in Arkansas."[73] Yet the status of *A Tour on the Prairies* as a minor classic seems assured as attested by its continued classroom use[74] and by intermittent critical attention.[75] Historically

69. Quoted in PMI, IV, 51.
70. See, for example, William L. Hedges, *Washington Irving: An American Study 1802–1832* (Baltimore: Johns Hopkins Press, 1965) which deals with "the relevance of Irving" whose reputation, the study assumes, rests on work completed before his return to America in 1832.
71. See STW, pp. 80–83.
72. See "Washington Irving," in *Literary History of the United States*, ed. Robert E. Spiller et al. (New York: The Macmillan Company, 1963), p. 250.
73. STW, 78.
74. See, for example, selected chapters in college anthologies: *Major Writers of America*, ed., Perry Miller (New York: Harcourt, Brace and World, 1962); *American Poetry and Prose*, ed., Foerster et al. (Boston: Houghton Mifflin, 1970); and *The American Tradition in Literature*, I, ed., Bradley et al. (New York: Grosset and Dunlap, 1974).
75. See, for example, articles in the Irving issue of the *Emerson Society Quarterly* (First Quarter, 1970); Edgeley W. Todd's article cited in footnote 12; and Wayne R. Kime's article cited in footnote 37; see also twentieth-century editions of the work.

the Washington Irving trail in Oklahoma has become well known, celebrated during the centennial anniversary in 1932 and defined by markers
and monuments along the route.[76] As a literary work, his story of the
trip receives favorable comment in two annotated, widely distributed
editions, one by George C. Wells and Joseph B. Thoburn (1926, 1927,
and 1955),[77] and the other by John Francis McDermott, printed in
August, 1956, and again in October, 1962.[78] Both include maps of
Irving's route[79] and extensive geographical and historical details. Wells
and Thoburn compliment Irving's "delineation of the characters" in a
narrative that "reveal[s] the true Irving in a manner not found in his
other works." McDermott alters his original disparagement of A Tour
expressed in 1944 in his edition of the Western journals[80] to recognize
Irving as a genre painter whose "masterful handling of composition and
color still charms us."

These estimates, in the same favorable vein with the evaluation given
by Wayne R. Kime in his recent article,[81] call for a new consideration
of A Tour on the Prairies as a thematic whole and as a work of some
stature. Though Irving certainly did not achieve in A Tour a quality to
rival his greatest works, as New York Mirror, the Arkansas Gazette, and
others predicted he would, the reviewer in Knickerbocker in May, 1835,
may not have been too inaccurate in concluding that the work "sustains
the brilliant reputation heretofore acquired by the immortal author
of Knickerbocker's History."

76. See Joseph B. Thoburn, "Centennial of the Tour on the Prairies by Washington Irving (1832–1932)," Chronicles of Oklahoma 10 (1932), 425–33 and George
H. Shirk, "A Tour on the Prairies Along the Washington Irving Trail in Oklahoma,"
Chronicles of Oklahoma 45 (1967), 312–31.

77. Washington Irving, A Tour on the Prairies, ed. George C. Wells and Joseph
B. Thoburn (Oklahoma City: Harlow Publishing Co., 1926, 1927, 1955). An
introduction and glossary were added in 1955.

78. Washington Irving, A Tour on the Prairies, ed. John Francis McDermott
(Norman: University of Oklahoma Press, 1956; reprinted 1962). This is no. 7 in
the Western Frontier Library Series; an introductory essay is included.

79. In 1832 surveys of the territory had not been made and specific distances
and boundaries were not known. Only frontier maps (see Chapter X in A Tour)
drawn from information supplied by trappers and by military explorers existed.
One of the earliest maps of the Indian Territory was drawn by Asa Hitchcock
in 1834 (now in the Oklahoma State Historical Society). Josiah Gregg's map, copyrighted 1844, is one of the best known. No edition of A Tour in Irving's lifetime
included a map, but in this century several editors, prior to this edition, have
reconstructed the route the group followed. In some instances, locations can
be only approximate.

80. See footnote 15.

81. See footnote 37.

Abbotsford and Newstead Abbey

The manuscript for the second number of *The Crayon Miscellany* went to England several weeks before the first number came out in America.[82] On the day the American *Tour* appeared Irving wrote Peter that the second in the series was "nearly stereotyped"[83] and six days later reported that it would go to press in Philadelphia "within a fortnight."[84] It consisted of two works, both inspired by what might be called literary pilgrimages, fifteen years apart, and both filled with poetry quotations and literary references. The first is an essay about Irving's four-day visit with Walter Scott and his family at Abbotsford in 1817; the other is an eleven-chapter narrative written as the result of his three weeks' residence in 1832 at Newstead Abbey, Lord Byron's ancestral home, seven years after the poet's death. *Abbotsford*, far more than *Newstead Abbey*, seems a personal recording directed to "you" (the reader).[85] *Newstead* uses the present only to recall the past and is largely a third-person description of the history of the Abbey, its surroundings, and its legends.

Abbotsford

Abbotsford is Washington Irving's tribute to Scott whom he considered equal to Shakespeare. In addition to narrating the circumstances and events of the short visit Irving had enjoyed in Scott's home and in the neighborhood in the late summer of 1817, the essay commemorates Scott's kindness to his family, to his pets, and to other human beings and recalls with delight his numerous anecdotes and constant geniality.

Irving had long admired the popular Scottish poet and novelist before he made the trip to Scotland. In 1810, before *The Lady of the Lake* was printed in America, Irving had borrowed the English copy from Inskeep and Bradford and had stolen away secretly to read it under a tree at the Hoffman's retreat on the Hudson.[86] He had been gratified in 1813 when Scott had complimented his *History of New York*, comparing his style to Swift's and Sterne's and remarking that on reading the

---

82. From a letter to Irving from Colonel Aspinwall, dated London, April 14, 1835, gave the terms he had made with Murray, quoted in PMI, III, 70.

83. From a letter dated April 11, 1835, quoted in PMI, III, 66.

84. From a letter dated April 17, 1835, quoted in PMI, III, 69.

85. The manuscript for Murray and the English edition printed from it have the inscription "To _____" above the first line as if Irving were following the epistolary style for his narrative.

86. PMI, I, 254.

book his sides had become "absolutely sore with laughing."[87] Finally in 1817, two years after he had gone to Europe for the second time, Irving planned an excursion to Scotland and determined to see Scott. He carried a letter of introduction from Thomas Campbell, the poet for whose works he had written a preface and a brief biographical sketch in 1810 and with whom he had become personally acquainted shortly after he arrived in England in 1815.

The four days he spent at Abbotsford, beginning on the morning of August 30, 1817 must have left an indelible impression on Irving's memory. Irving was thirty-four and Scott forty-six, not yet having received the baronetcy, but well established in his community as sheriff and famous as "laird" and author. The two men walked over the countryside, talking of scenery, of literature, and of Scottish legends. In the evenings they visited around the family dining table or sat in the drawing room where Scott sometimes read aloud or his daughter Sophia sang simple Scottish songs. Visitors came, and everyone was welcomed and entertained.

Irving made few notes during this period, recording only the event of his arrival at Abbotsford with the alarm it gave "to a legion of dogs that garrison Scotts [sic] castle" and the response Scott made to the delivery of Irving's card by his immediate appearance "limping up the hill."[88] In two letters to Peter, one from Abbotsford on September 1 and the other from Edinburgh on September 6, Irving told of his visit.[89] The hours passed too quickly for him to commit much of the magic to his journal. On the second day he wrote Peter, "I have rambled about the hills with Scott; visited the haunts of Thomas the Rhymer, and other spots rendered classic by border tale and witching song, and have been in a kind of dream or delirium." He could have been thinking of future literary plans as well as of conversation when he promised Peter to "say more of [Scott] hereafter, for," he continued, "[Scott] is a theme on which I shall love to dwell."

Almost two decades passed, however, before Irving wrote of his

87. Henry Brevoort, who had sent Scott a copy of the second edition, had reported Scott's response to Irving. Scott's letter to Brevoort, dated Abbotsford, April 2, 1813, quoted in PMI, I, 240.

88. The text of Irving's notes made during the Scotland tour from August 25 to September 21 or 22 is readily available in *Tour in Scotland 1817*, ed. with a critical introduction by Stanley T. Williams (New Haven: Yale University Press, 1927). The two notebooks from which the information came were listed as property of Mr. Preston Davie of Tuxedo Park, New York. Photostats of the notebooks are in the Yale University Library. The entry relating to Abbotsford constitutes only eighteen lines in Williams' book (pp. 39–40).

89. Quoted in PMI, I, 380–84.

experience. He had tried to see Scott again on September 23 as he
returned from the Highlands but did not find him at home, and in
intervening years their friendship had continued until Scott's death in
1832.[90] Presumably Irving did not care to write about Scott during his
lifetime. After Scott died in September following Irving's return to
America four months earlier, Irving probably felt again the urge to
speak about his friend and to add his eulogy to those offered in 1832.
His plans for *The Crayon Miscellany* enabled him to turn that desire
into reality. He decided to make it a part of his second number.

The work on *Abbotsford* began in New York in 1834—probably late
in the year but almost certainly before *A Tour on the Prairies* was
finished.[91] The notebooks were too sketchy to offer much more than
suggestions. He made direct use of the entry about his arrival at
Abbotsford and probably glanced at the brief notes on his later visit to
Ayr, birthplace of Robert Burns,[92] before recalling it in a paragraph in
the essay. Notations or phrases about people he saw, occasional snatches
of conversation overheard, and allusions to places associated with Scott's
fiction and poetry found their way here and there into his discussion,
sometimes removed, however, from the time sequence or the context in
which he recorded them in his notebook.[93] For the rest Irving had to
rely upon Scott's poems and some of his novels which he must have
had before him as he wrote, and upon his own memory, perhaps
strengthened by repeated allusions through the years to the visit and to
the legends and anecdotes associated with it.

Having finished a rough draft, Irving revised his pages and engaged
copyists, as he had done for *Tour* and would do almost at once for
Newstead, to prepare a manuscript to send to England. In late February
he wrote his London agent, Colonel Aspinwall,[94] and negotiations with
Murray for the volume containing both *Abbotsford* and *Newstead Abbey*

90. For discussions of their relationship see STW, I, chap. 7; J. G. Lockhart,
Memoirs of the Life of Sir Walter Scott, Bart. (Edinburgh, 1837), chap. 4; PMI,
I, 386–87, 438–44, 456, 457; Edgar Johnson, *Sir Walter Scott: The Great Unknown*
(New York: The Macmillan Company, 1970), passim.

91. Irving's "Notes Used in the Preparation of Letter 64" to John Murray III
in 1850, now in Yale University Library and printed in an appendix in McClary's
Washington Irving and the House of Murray, simply state that the work was composed in New York in 1834. McClary's book (See footnote 48) is hereafter cited
as *Irving and Murray*.

92. *Tour in Scotland 1817*, pp. 70–71.

93. For example, an anecdote attributed in the notebook to a man named
Willie Symes becomes one told by Scott's caretaker, Johnny Bower, in the essay.
See *A Tour in Scotland 1817*, pp. 23–24.

94. STW, II, 320–21 refers to Irving's letter dated February 24, 1835, listed as
in the possesion of Mrs. Irwin Strasburger, New York City.

were completed before the middle of April. Irving had hoped to get
five hundred guineas for the volume since both essays related to British
writers and environment. Instead, Murray agreed to pay four hundred
pounds at six and nine months for three thousand copies and an additional
two hundred pounds at six and nine months after a second edition was
published.[95] Irving was satisfied with the terms and the volume was published on May 1. The copyright was registered on May 4 at Stationers
Hall. Promissory notes dated May 4, 1835, now in the Murray Archives
show that the amount of two hundred pounds was paid on November 7,
1835, and another two hundred on February 7, 1836. A second edition
never came out; therefore four hundred pounds was the total Irving
realized from the British sale of this volume.[96]

Work on the printer's copy for the Carey, Lea, and Blanchard printing of *Abbotsford* was finished before Aspinwall completed arrangements in England. At the end of March, manuscript for *Abbotsford* and
for *Newstead Abbey* went to A. Chandler for stereotyping and then
some time after April 10 to Carey, Lea, and Blanchard for printing and
distribution.[97] The book came out on May 30, almost a month after
the British edition. The Philadelphia firm again paid Irving fifteen
hundred dollars for five thousand copies at six, nine, and twelve months.[98]

The second number of *The Crayon Miscellany*, like the first, appeared
at once on the Continent and in translations. In 1835 Galignani and
Baudry brought out editions based on Murray's printing, and both
French and German translations appeared.[99] A number of magazines,
including *The Casket* (April, 1836), printed extracts from *Abbotsford*.
In the 1850's both Bohn and Routledge published the volume. Through
the 1870's and 1880's the essays appeared in various editions of the
collected works with *A Tour on the Prairies* and occasionally in a single
volume (by J. W. Lovell and J. B. Alden in 1883 in America and Bell
and Daldy in 1884 in London, for example).

Both Scott's family and the reading public in America and abroad
liked *Abbotsford* at once. Scott's son-in-law, J. G. Lockhart, had read

95. Irving quoted the terms from Aspinwall's letter of April 14, 1835, in his
letter to Peter dated May 25, 1835 (see PMI, III, 70–71).

96. PMI, IV, 410.

97. A letter from Carey to Irving dated April 10, 1835, urged him to send
"in the plates of No. 2 Miscellanies as far as they are prepared" (LB).

98. PMI, III, 71–72. Carey's *Cost Book* (See footnote 60 for bibliographical information) shows (entry 495) that the firm paid for the plates of No. 2 but apparently not for Nos. 1 and 3.

99. Williams and Edge, *Bibliography*, p. 57, lists a German publication of
Abbotsford as late as 1886 in an English author's series for classroom use.

the manuscript and had urged Murray to publish it.[100] Irving's friend
David Wilkie wrote from London to tell of the popularity of the essay
there.[101] Compliments from New York friends and sales in America
encouraged Irving about the whole series. He sent a copy of *Abbotsford
and Newstead Abbey* to Peter in Havre and wrote, "It takes with the
public; indeed the two numbers of the Miscellany are doing admirably,
and give promise that the plan of a series of similar light volumes will
be very popular and profitable."[102] No doubt its timeliness in appearing
three years after Scott's death and the personal quality of *Abbotsford*
contributed to the appeal the narrative held.

In the twentieth century there has been no separate edition of *Abbotsford* or of *Abbotsford and Newstead Abbey*. Critical attention has been
sparse, though in 1935 Irving's biographer Stanley Williams predicted
Abbotsford "would outlive" *A Tour on the Prairies*.[103] Perhaps Irving
was accurate in calling his essay on Scott a "humble stone upon his
cairn"; yet it provides a portrait only he could have drawn and helps
to complete the story of Scott's life.[104] As a literary sketch it rambles
and is sentimental but, as Williams said, "It is a sensible, gracious
record . . . and it may well remain an honest source of knowledge."[105]

Newstead Abbey

Irving never met Lord Byron but was a personal friend of his biographer
Thomas Moore and an admirer of his works. In 1824 in Paris he also met
Byron's friend Captain Medwin, with whom he had long talks about
Byron only two months before the poet's death in Greece.[106] According
to Pierre, Irving read the memoirs which Byron had given Moore and
which were later destroyed at the family's request.[107] As early as 1813–
1814 Irving, as editor of *Analectic Magazine*, had written a review of
Byron's works; and in 1820 he had been particularly pleased to learn

100. Samuel Smiles, *A Publisher and His Friends: Memoir and Correspondence
of the Late John Murray* (London, John Murray, 1891), II, 261. See also J. G.
Lockhart's *Memoirs of the Life of Sir Walter Scott, Bart.* (Edinburgh, 1837), chap. 4.

101. From a letter from Wilkie to Irving dated London, May 8, 1835 (Yale
University Library).

102. From a letter dated New York, June 10, 1835, quoted in PMI, III, 72–73.

103. STW, II, 78.

104. Irving's essay has served to some degree as a source for Scott biographies
from the time of Lockhart's *Memoirs* in 1837 to Edgar J. Johnson's two-volume
work in 1970. (See footnote 90 for bibliographical information on these works.)

105. STW, II, 321.

106. See PMI, II, 184, for Irving's journal recordings about Byron on February 1,
1824, from his conversation with Captain Medwin.

107. PMI, II, 68–69.

from Murray that Byron liked his writing and thought Geoffrey Crayon "very good."[108] Both his friendship with Moore and his high regard for Byron caused him in 1829 to work to get Moore's *Life of Byron* published in America.[109]

Two years later Irving was pleased when the opportunity came to visit Byron's former home, Newstead Abbey, while he was away from London visiting in Birmingham, in Sheffield, and in Nottinghamshire. He made the first excursion with his host at Barlborough Hall, the Reverend C. R. Reaston Rodes, and wrote about it on October 28, 1831, to his sister Mrs. Paris, using some of the same descriptive details he would include later in his essay.[110] Late in the year he stopped at the Abbey briefly with former Secretary of State Van Buren and his son with whom he was on a tour; and the three of them returned in January for a longer visit at the invitation of the current owner, Colonel Wildman, who was engaged in a vast project of restoring and preserving the Abbey. The other two remained only two days, but Irving extended his visit into the "three weeks sojourn" that became the inspiration for *Newstead Abbey*.

At Newstead, Irving occupied Byron's room and slept in his bed; he explored the ancient mansion, its grounds, and the surrounding countryside; he talked with Colonel Wildman, the servants, and neighbors. He had keen interest, as his letters to Peter and to Mrs. Paris clearly reveal, in the "old building . . . more than usually favored by ghosts."[111] He made copious notes[112] and wrote long letters full of details he would repeat later in his essay. Colonel and Mrs. Wildman supplied him with whatever information and materials they could, including the story of the ghostly little White Lady who is the subject of the final chapter of *Newstead Abbey*.[113]

When Irving left Newstead to return to London late in January, 1832, the notes and materials went into his trunks and in April and May made the journey with him to America. Nearly three years later when he

108. See PMI, II, 25–26 and *Irving and Murray*, p. 31.
109. See PMI, II, 418–22 for the exchange of letters between Irving and his brother Ebenezer and between Irving and Thomas Moore.
110. Quoted in PMI, II, 462–63.
111. From a letter to Mrs. Paris dated Newstead Abbey, January 20, 1832, quoted in PMI, II, 465–69.
112. Some of these dated notes with details of what Irving did at Newstead are among what appears to be first draft pages of his writing of the essay (approximately 104 pages in all) now in the possession of the Clifton Waller Barrett Library at the University of Virginia.
113. With the notes for *Newstead Abbey* at the University of Virginia are four letters signed by Sophia Hyatt and dated Weir Mill Farm, Newstead, June 22, July 4, July 13, and September 20, 1825, respectively, the first three to Colonel

decided to bring out a series of volumes, this was part of the material he referred to as lying "dormant" in his trunks. An essay on Newstead would provide an appropriate companion piece for *Abbotsford* in the second number of the *Miscellany*. Many of his notes required little additional work, except for arrangement and final polishing, for example, the material on Robin Hood, information about Nanny Smith, and many of the legends and superstitions. Before him as he wrote, in addition to his notes and journal entries, he had Byron's poetry which related to Newstead Abbey and to his youthful love for Mary Anne Chaworth, and he had Moore's *Life of Byron*. He organized his material into eleven chapters associating the history of the Abbey and various places within it and its environs with Lord Byron. From the reference to events during his visit which he took from his journal, he omitted all dates, even in the chapter entitled "Arrival at the Abbey," permitting the emphasis to be on the past. His personal experiences allowed him to move from one topic to another as he went from place to place and too frequently, at least for twentieth-century taste, provided the means for his emotional response to past events or traditions. Neither his activities nor those of any of the people then in the Newstead area were the real topics of his essay. The present visit was only a reminder of what he called "poetical associations," a means of paying sentimental homage to those qualities in Byron which he admired.[114]

The publication record of *Newstead* through the nineteenth century (already discussed with *Abbotsford*) indicates acceptance of the work by contemporary readers. Interest in Byron and in such mystery as Irving created in the story of "The Little White Lady" guaranteed a reading audience and accounted for its extreme popularity in Germany.[115] In London the *Athenaeum* (May 9, 1835) commented on Irving's interest in supernatural legend. Poe's *Southern Literary Messenger* (July, 1835) complimented Irving's recording of a real "instance of monomania" calling the essay the greatest display Irving had ever made of his "peculiar faculty of imparting to all he touches the coloring of his genius." In 1855 Irving was still answering inquiries about the authen-

---

Wildman and the last to Mrs. Wildman. Written in a clear, even hand on large pages both sides of which are covered with writing, they give the details of the woman's plight. The letters are respectively 6, 4 1/2, 3 1/2, and 10 pages in length.

114. Though *Newstead* is only one third longer than *Abbotsford*, it contains three times as many lines of poetry quotations, almost six hundred in all.

115. See STW, II, 320 for a discussion of the nineteenth-century interest in mysterious legend and of its reflection in current magazines.

ticity of the Sophia Hyatt story and declaring the account *"strictly according to facts* furnished me by Colonel and Mrs. Wildman."[116] At that time the 1849 reviewer in the *Literary World* had not been proved wrong in his comparison of *Newstead Abbey* with "the best of the Sketch Book or Bracebridge Hall."[117]

The twentieth century has generally ignored *Newstead Abbey*. Stanley Williams noted Irving's successful use of the popular literary device but probably reflected the attitude of his age in concluding that "Few studies of Byron are more commonplace or, as in the account of Mary Ann Chaworth, more lachrymose."[118] The reader misses the light touches and flashes of humor found intermittently through *Abbotsford* and frequently in many of Irving's writings. In may require another era less affected by the kind of romantic sentiment to which this century reacts unfavorably to look beneath it for particulars of sketches and legends worth noting.

Legends of the Conquest of Spain

Irving knew from the time of his decision to publish a *Miscellany* that it would include his Spanish legends. Some had been finished since 1829 when he left the Alhambra; these were manuscripts he had on hand. Others, he must have thought, would require little effort in preparation beyond what had been done during his years in Spain. It probably was the timeliness of the Scott and Byron topics and his suspicion of their greater favor in America that caused him to make *Legends* third instead of second in the series. At any rate after the disappointing "slightness" in the size of the first two numbers, he knew that with his Spanish manuscripts he could produce a volume ample in size. He wrote Peter on July 8, 1835, that it would include "The Legend of Don Roderick," "The Legend of the Subjugation of Spain," "The Legend of Pelayo," and "The Legend of the Family of Count Julian."[119] For some reason, however, "Pelayo" was omitted from the volume; perhaps it was large enough with the other three legends and Irving decided to withhold "Pelayo" to publish with other Spanish legends still on hand. According to Pierre, it was these larger plans for publication of his "Spanish and Moorish themes" that caused

116. From a letter from Irving to E. H. Munday, dated Sunnyside, December 5, 1855, quoted in STW, II, 320.
117. Quoted in PMI, IV, 51.
118. STW, II, 320.
119. Quoted in PMI, III, 74.

Irving fourteen years later not to include *Legends* in the collected edition of his works.[120]

Irving's interest in Spain and in Spanish literature had developed strongly from the time of his residence in Paris in December, 1824, when he began to study Spanish, which he came to know within a year or two better than he knew French, German, or Italian.[121] He considered the language "full of power, magnificence and melody" and was delighted with old Spanish history and literature.[122] Through 1825 he studied faithfully, recording in his notebook excerpts and references which substantiate a developing skill and growing interest.[123] In February, 1826, when he went to Madrid to hold a minor position at the American legation and ultimately to begin his work on Columbus, he was fortunate in obtaining living quarters at the home of the American consul, Obadiah Rich, whose library was filled with Spanish materials. Through the year as he worked at his biography of Columbus, he also read a great deal and made frequent allusions in his journal to Moorish history and Moorish themes. Through a part of the year he put Columbus aside and worked on a rough sketch of *The Conquest of Granada*. In 1827 he again spent long hours at writing on Columbus but also was busy early and late at research, as shown by daily journal references to "Kings Library" and "Jesuits Library."[124] By the time he was ready to send his work on Columbus to John Murray at the end of July, 1827, he could write him that he also had "other writings in preparation."[125] These included the rough draft of *The Conquest of Granada*, which was to come out in 1829, and notes for a number of other Moorish chronicles, several of which would not appear in book

120. PMI, III, 76.

121. See *Washington Irving: Journals and Notebooks Volume III 1819–1827*, ed. Walter A. Reichart (Madison: University of Wisconsin Press, 1970), especially entries from December 9, 1824, through September 17, 1825, for references to his serious study of Spanish. The manuscript of Irving's journal is in the Seligman Collection in the New York Public Library.

122. See Irving's letter to his nephew Pierre Paris Irving, dated Paris, March 29, 1825, quoted in PMI, II, 233–38.

123. See STW, I, chap. 13 and footnote reference to Notebook, 1825, property of the late Dr. Roderick Terry, Newport, Rhode Island.

124. PMI, II, chap. 15 gives some of the details of his activities, quoting from his correspondence and his journal entries. Manuscripts for this period have been printed in *The Journals of Washington Irving* [February 10, 1826–April 30, 1827], ed. W. T. Trent and G. S. Hellman (Boston, 1919) and in "Washington Irving's Madrid Journal 1827–1828 and Related Letters" [May 1, 1827–February 29, 1828], ed. Andrew Breen Myers, *Bulletin of the New York Public Library* 62, nos. 5, 6, 8, 9 (May, 1958).

125. From a letter dated Madrid, July 29, 1827, quoted in PMI, II, 262–64.

form until 1866 when Pierre published them in Volume 1 of *Spanish Papers.* Referring to this period of his life later, Irving wrote, "When I was in Madrid, in 1826–27, just after I had finished Columbus, I commenced a series of Chronicles illustrative of the wars between the Spaniards and the Moors; to be given as the productions of a monk, Fray Antonio Agapida. *The Conquest of Granada* was the only one I finished, though I roughly sketched out parts of some others."[126]

In October, 1827, Irving left Madrid and took brief excursions to the Escorial and to the city of Toledo, legendary site of the cave of Hercules, one of his "Illustrations" of "The Legend of Don Roderick." Through the first months of 1828 he continued to spend mornings at the library of the Jesuits' College of St. Isidoro before he left on March 1 for a tour through the southern parts of Spain with visits to Granada and to the Alhambra, examining antiquities and recalling more of the history related to the scenery he was observing.[127] In Seville he worked on a second edition and an abridgement of *Columbus* and completed *The Conquest of Granada.* Before the year ended he had again picked up Don Roderick on which he had begun writing in June of 1827, eighteen months earlier.[128] The succeeding year, 1829, brought further "laboring at Don Roderick"[129] during February and March and Irving's residence before the middle of May at the Alhambra where, according to Pierre, he put "finishing touches to *The Legends of the Conquest of Spain.*"[130] Actually, however, only the first legend was near completion. On June 11, 1829, Irving wrote in his diary, "Finished Don Roderick."[131] Years later, though, he would rewrite the last pages of that narrative, work further on the second one, and add the short "Legend of Count Julian and His Family."

When Irving left Granada on July 29, 1829, to serve as secretary of

---

126. From a letter to Pierre M. Irving dated Sunnyside, April 14, 1847, quoted in PMI, IV, 14–16.

127. The manuscript of Irving's diary from April 7, 1828, through February 28, 1829, now in the possession of The Hispanic Society of America, New York, gives many of the details of his activities and observations. The text is available in the Society's publication, *Washington Irving Diary, Spain 1828–1829,* ed. C. L. Penney (New York, 1926).

128. See entries in Irving's journal for June, 1827 (bibliographical information in footnote 121).

129. See Irving's letter to Peter dated Seville, March 3, 1829, and diary entries for March, quoted in PMI, II, 371–74.

130. PMI, II, 389.

131. PMI, II, 389, n. The quotation given by Pierre M. Irving is from a portion of Irving's diary apparently no longer extant, a lacuna of five months (March 1, 1829–July 27, 1829) being the only one remaining to cover Irving's first residence in Spain from 1826 to 1829.

legation at London, he packed his notes and manuscripts for *Legends* along with materials for *Mahomet* prepared in Madrid and various other Spanish notes and materials. Only *The Voyages and Discoveries of the Companions of Columbus* in 1831 and *The Alhambra* early in 1832 would come to publication before he returned to America. The greater part of his Spanish notes and sketches would remain in his trunks to make the return journey to New York; these were a part of "the materials in hand for easy arrangement" which he had mentioned to Peter in March, 1829, in a letter referring to his desire to go home. At that time he had determined to go as soon as he could "arrange [his] papers, so as to have materials to work upon for some few months without the necessity of much invention or planning."[132] Six years later it seemed logical for these materials, long on hand already, to be included in *The Crayon Miscellany.* Perhaps other volumes of Spanish legends might have appeared later in the series had Irving not had the distractions of work on *Astoria* and *Bonneville* immediately and had he not continued to hold in mind the plan for a larger work comprised of his Spanish sketches.[133]

The notes he made from books in Rich's library and even more from libraries of Madrid and Seville and various other places he visited gave Irving the history and anecdotes he used in *Legends of the Conquest of Spain.* He read from a number of writers, some of whose names appear in his footnotes: Fray Jaime Bleda, Fray Esteban de Salazar, Ambrosio de Morales, Juan de Mariana, Luis del Mármol, Florian de Ocampo, José Antonio Conde, Pedro Abarca, and several others. All of these had based their works on that of the Moor Rasis in the tenth century, though none of them, with the possible exception of Morales, had seen the Moor's history in anything but translated and unauthorized versions.[134] Irving was mistaken in believing that the copy of *Crónica del Rey Don*

132. From a letter dated Seville, March 3, 1829, quoted in PMI, II, 371–73.

133. The idea persisted for more than two decades. Pierre Irving points out that Irving's diary in 1827 indicates that he was "engaged in taking notes for a suite of works he had projected, illustrative of the domination of the Arabs in Spain" (PMI, II, 270). Twenty years later (April 14, 1847) in a letter to Pierre, Washington Irving told how Peter had always favored such a plan and how at that time he had taken up the chronicles again with sufficient materials already to "make a couple of volumes" (PMI, IV, 14–16). The revised edition (1848–1851) required Irving's attention later, and during his last years he had to work on *Life of Washington.*

134. See Ramón Menéndez Pidal, *Crónicas Generales de España Descritas,* 3d ed. (Madrid, 1918) for a discussion of manuscripts of Rasis (one possessed by Morales, another kept at the Cathedral of Toledo, and one at La Real Biblioteca) and of the defective modern copies made of them. See also D. Eduardo Saavedra, *Estudio Sobre La Invasión De Los Arabes En España* (Madrid, 1892), p. 8.

Rodrigo which he used and which he listed in his footnotes was a translation from Rasis; instead the work was that of Pedro del Corral in the middle of the fifteenth century.[135] The general history of the conquest of Spain by the Arabs contained in the *Crónica* of Rasis y Atariji had been known since antiquity; varying additions and alterations made in events and in attitudes toward them through the years Irving sometimes recorded in his notes and included later in his narratives. Several of the sources Irving followed have been called "imposters" in their adding to the historical facts—as Corral (Irving's unacknowledged source) is accused of doing—or "false historians" in pretending to translate earlier works—as Miguel de Luna pretended to translate from a wise Moor named Abulcásim Tarif Abentarique, one of the sources Irving gave in his footnotes.[136]

In addition to such historical sources, Irving also was aware of Lope de Vega's *comedia, El Ultimo Rey Godo,* and of his trilogy relating to Rodrigo, Count Julian, and Don Pelayo, and of the episode of Don Rodrigo and *la cava* in the sixth book of *Jerusalén Conquistada.* He also must have known such nineteenth-century works as Scott's poem, *The Vision of Don Roderick* (1811), Landor's five-act tragedy *Count Julian* (1812), and Southey's poem *Roderick, the Last of the Goths,* a copy of which he is said to have had beside him as he wrote.[137] His allusion to Roderick's heroic attitude of penitence could have been influenced by Southey's development of the narrative.

Irving found the writing of *Legends* difficult, having begun with *Don Roderick* as early as June 28, 1827,[138] and struggled rather frequently for long hours before that legend was completed in 1829. It was almost two years after he began before he felt that he had the narrative in hand. On February 7, 1829, he informed Peter that he had "written a few of the early chapters of Don Roderick but feebly and

135. D. Eduardo Saavedra in *Estudio Sobre La Invasión De Los Arabes En España,* p. 60, discusses Irving's use both of Miguel de Luna's *Historia Verdadera Del Rey Don Rodrigo* (1589) which he does not acknowledge and of Pedro del Corral's 1430 book which he always cited under the name of Rasis, doubtless from his having seen it inscribed with red ink in the frontispiece as a copy of the *Crónica Del Rey Don Rodrigo* that is kept in the Biblioteca Nacional of Madrid.

136. See the discussion of "imposters" and "fabricated" history in the various accounts of early Spanish history in Ramón Menéndez Pidal, *El Rey Rodrigo En La Literatura* (Madrid, 1925), pp. 81, 125–32.

137. STW, I, 357. Note also the following sentence in Irving's letter to Peter (March 3, 1829) expressing concern about "the manner" in which his Spanish narrative could be executed: "It also has been so much harped upon by Scott and Southey as not to possess novelty with literary persons" (PMI, II, 371).

138. He recorded in his diary for that day, "try at Don Roderick."

unsatisfactorily."[139] Part of his problem was solved with the decision to "reduce the whole to a chronicle or legend" rather than writing Moorish history. Considering his materials "too coldly extravagant and flimsy to please as romance," and without "merit as history," he resolved to write "a short chronicle or legend, containing the most striking scenes at full length and with full effect."[140] Finally, the "flimsy" story of Roderick, by this means, could be "brought to a sound, substantial form, which [he could] expand and ornament and render attractive," and it could be supported by succeeding chronicles. Irving's personal travel experiences in Spain got into the three legends only in one or two references to his traveling companions, David Wilkie and Lord Mahon, and in the use of the single journal entry relating to his visit to Toledo which is the source for his literary reference to the visit later and for "The Cave of Hercules" in the "Illustrations" to "The Legend of Don Roderick." Irving usually translated freely from his sources with "ornamentation" of his own, though an exception in the more nearly literal translation of "Story of the Marvellous and Portentous Tower" may be worth mentioning. He credits the "minute account" from ancient sources to the fictitious Fray Antonio Agapida, his narrator in *The Conquest of Granada*, whom he mentions for the first time and without introduction at this point in Chapter VII of the Roderick legend. In four instances in the same legend and twice in "Legend of the Subjugation of Spain" he alludes to the "discreet" or "venerable" friar but almost at once seems to forget him and to insist instead on the authority of his historical sources. The vein in which he should cast the narratives bothered Irving from the beginning to the end of his work on *Legends*. The seriousness of his style worried the author even after he had finished the work at the Alhambra. He wrote Peter on June 13, 1829: "The Chronicle of the Conquest of Spain is grave throughout; perhaps in one or two places there is a gleam of humor; but I thought it misplaced in such a subject, and likely to displease the reader. Nothing has a more trivial or indeed heartless appearance than a jest introduced amidst scenes of real dignity and distress."[141]

Irving put "the finishing touches" to *Legends of the Conquest of Spain* in June, 1835, exactly six years after he left the Alhambra, in preparation for making it the third number in *The Crayon Miscellany*.[142] He rewrote most of the last chapter of "Don Roderick" and added "Legend of Count Julian and His Family." His manuscript of 396 pages went to A. Chandler in Philadelphia for stereotyping, and by the middle

139. From a letter dated Seville, February 7, 1829, quoted in PMI, II, 367.
140. From a letter to Peter dated Seville, March 3, 1829, quoted in PMI, II, 371.
141. Quoted in PMI, II, 392.
142. From a letter to Peter dated June 10, 1835, quoted in PMI, II, 72–73.

of July proof sheets had been mailed to Aspinwall in Liverpool for publication in London by John Murray. The plan again was to publish volumes simultaneously in England and in America, but for some reason there was a delay in forwarding the proof sheets to London. As a result the work came out in America from Carey, Lea, and Blanchard in October and did not appear in London until December with the copyright registered at Stationers' Hall on December 15, 1835. John Murray declined paying the price Irving asked[143] but had Spottiswoode print two thousand copies in December, 1835, and January, 1836, with the understanding that the author would receive half of the profits. Sales in the next three and a half years earned for the author one hundred pounds. Carey, Lea, and Blanchard agreed to pay fifteen hundred dollars for five thousand copies at six, nine, and twelve months.[144] The Philadelphia company had hoped to receive the plates as soon as they were prepared and had been eager to begin publication as soon as possible. They wrote Ebenezer in July stating the terms and finally on August 28 informed him that the plates had arrived and that the volume would go to press at once.[145]

Like the first two numbers of the *Miscellany*, *Legends of the Conquest of Spain* had an immediate success, though Irving's friend, former New York mayor Philip Hone, believed that "if any other person than Irving had written the book, the publishers would not have sold fifty copies."[146] It was published in Paris in 1836 by Galignani and by Baudry and in the same year appeared in German translations with an excerpt in the Berlin periodical *Magazin für die Literatur des Auslandes*.[147] The strong interest in Spanish tales accounted for its wide acceptance and for praise of its style and subject matter in such journals as *Albion* (October 10, 1835), the *Southern Literary Messenger* (December, 1835), *Fraser's Literary Chronicle* (January 23, 1836), and the *Metropolitan Magazine* (February 23, 1836).[148] The *New York Mirror* for February 6, 1836, gave the volume the highest praise and called it "a gem of the purest water." Its reputation since the initial reception has fallen to a much lower level, with subsequent printings in the nineteenth cen-

143. From a letter to Peter, February 16, 1836, mentioned in PMI, III, 76.
144. PMI, III, 76.
145. Letters in LB dated July 11, July 27, and August 28, 1835. The latter requested, "Please inform us when it is to be published in London."
146. Entry for October 19, 1835, in *The Diary of Philip Hone, 1828–1851*, ed. Allan Nevins (New York, 1927).
147. Williams and Edge, *Bibliography*, p. 59.
148. See the discussion of the current interest in Spanish stories in America and of its reflection in magazines and books in STW, p. 323.

tury, other than Pierre's in 1866 in *Spanish Papers,* only by such small houses as J. B. Alden and J. W. Lovell as part of a series.

Williams' and Edge's *Bibliography of Washington Irving* lists only one publication of *Legends* in the twentieth century, José F. Godoy's Spanish version entitled *Leyendas Espanolas* by D. Appleton in 1919. Irving criticism has paid little attention to *Legends.* Historians and Spanish critics sometimes point out Irving's errors in facts or allude to his imperfect understanding of the Castilian language.[149] Stanley Williams acknowledges the occasional dramatic quality in the tales but points out the inferiority of workmanship and unevenness in comparison to the more carefully written *Conquest of Granada.*[150] Far from being "a *chef-d'oeuvre*" of the author as the *New York Mirror* claimed it was in 1835, *Legends of the Conquest of Spain* nevertheless has some importance among the Spanish volumes in reflecting Irving's continuing interest in Spanish sketches and in being a literary representative of a longer project he was never able to finish.

149. See, for example, S. P. Scott's discussion in Volume 1 of *History of the Moorish Empire in Europe* (Philadelphia: J. B. Lippincott, 1904) and references to Irving in Ramón Menéndez Pidal, *El Rey Rodrigo en la Literatura* (Madrid, 1924).

150. STW, pp. 321–23.

THE CRAYON
MISCELLANY

A TOUR ON THE PRAIRIES

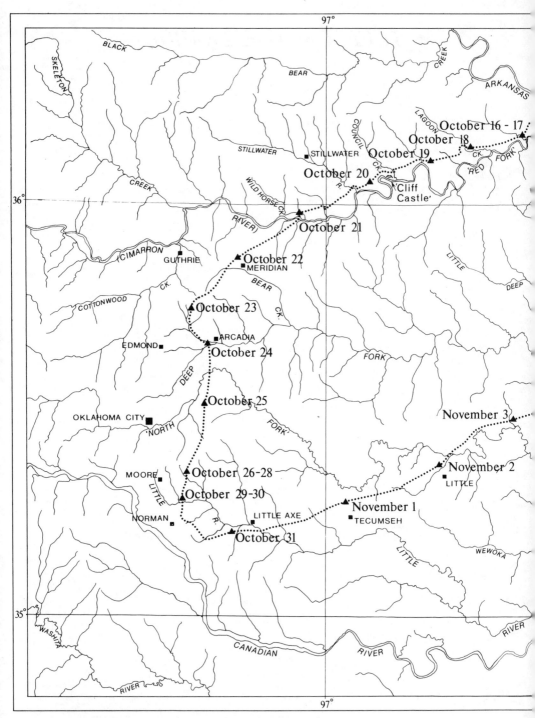

A map showing Irving's route on the prairies of Oklahoma
October 8 through November 9, 1832.

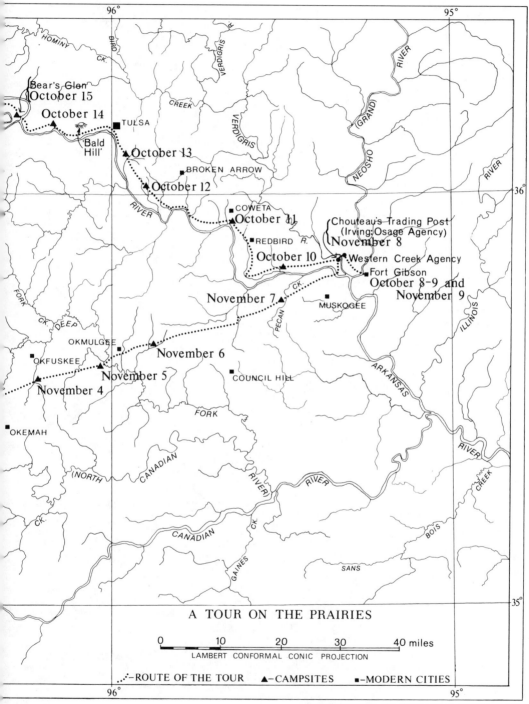

Bear's Glen
October 15
October 14
'Bald
Hill'
TULSA
October 13
BROKEN ARROW
October 12
COWETA
October 11
Chouteau's Trading Post
(Irving Osage Agency)
November 8
REDBIRD R.
October 10
Western Creek Agency
Fort Gibson
October 8-9 and
November 9
November 7
MUSKOGEE
OKMULGEE
November 6
OKFUSKEE
November 5
COUNCIL HILL
November 4
OKEMAH

A TOUR ON THE PRAIRIES

0   10   20   30   40 miles

LAMBERT CONFORMAL CONIC PROJECTION

⋯-ROUTE OF THE TOUR   ▲-CAMPSITES   ■-MODERN CITIES

CARTOGRAPHY BY BARBARA L. GEYER — 1977

INTRODUCTION

"As I saw the last blue line of my native land fade away, like a cloud in the horizon, it seemed as if I had closed one volume of the world and its concerns, and had time for meditation, before I opened another. That land, too, now vanishing from my view, which contained all that was most dear to me in life; what vicissitudes might occur in it—what changes might take place in me, before I should visit it again! Who can tell, when he sets forth to wander, whither he may be driven by the uncertain currents of existence; or when he may return; or whether it may ever be his lot to revisit the scenes of his childhood!"*

Such were the dubious thoughts that passed like a shade across my mind many years since, as I lost sight of my native land, on my voyage to Europe. Yet, I had every reason for bright anticipations. I was buoyant with health, had enough of the "world's geer" for all my wants, was on my way to visit the fairest scenes of Europe, with the prospect of returning home in a couple of years, stored with recollections for the remainder of my life.

The boding doubts, however, which had beclouded my mind at the moment of departure, threatened to prove prophetic. Years and years elapsed, yet I remained a voluntary exile from my home. Why did I so?—The question has often been asked; for once I will make a brief reply.

It was my lot, almost on landing in Europe, to experience a reverse of fortune, which cast me down in spirit, and altered the whole tenor of my life. In the midst of perplexities and humiliations, I turned to my pen for solace and support. I had hitherto exercised it for amusement; I now looked to it as my main dependence, resolving, if successful, never to abandon it for any prospect of worldly gain, nor to return to my friends, until, by my literary exertions, I had placed myself above their pity, or assistance.

Such are the main reasons that unexpectedly beguiled me into a long protracted absence. How and why that absence was thus protracted, would involve a story of baffled plans and deferred hopes, which led me on from month to month, and year to year, and left me where they found me; would involve, in short, the checquered story of my humble concerns and precarious feelings—and I have a shrinking repugnance to such an exposure.

Suffice it to say, that my path, which many are apt to think was a flowery one, was too often beset by thorns; and that at times when I was

*Sketch Book, Vol. I.

supposed beguiled by the pleasures and splendours of Europe, and "treading the primrose path of dalliance," I was in fact shut up from society, battling with cares and perplexities, and almost struggling for subsistence.

In the mean time, my lengthened exile subjected me to painful doubts and surmises. Some, who really valued me, supposed that I was dazzled by the factitious splendours around me, and was leading a life of epicurean indulgence. Others, who knew me not, or chose to judge harshly, accused me of a want of affection for my native land; I met with imputations of the kind in the public papers, and I received anonymous letters, reiterating them, and basely endeavouring to persuade me that I had lost the good will of my countrymen.

I should have treated these imputations with little regard, but they reached me in desponding moments, when other circumstances had produced a morbid state of feelings, and they sunk deeply in my mind. The literary undertakings in which I was engaged, and on which I depended for my maintainance, required a further absence from my country, yet I found that absence attributed to motives abhorrent to my feelings, and wounding to my pride.

By degrees I was led to doubt the entire sentiment of my countrymen towards me. Perhaps I was rendered more sensitive on this head by the indulgent good will I had ever experienced from them. They had always cherished me beyond my deserts, excusing my many deficiencies, taking my humours and errors in good part, and exaggerating every merit. Their cordial kindness had in a manner become necessary to me. I was like a spoiled child, that could not bear the glance of an altered eye. I cared even less for their good opinion than their good will, and felt indignant at being elbowed into a position with respect to them, from which my soul revolted.

I was repeatedly urged by those who knew the workings of my feelings, to lay them before my countrymen, and to repel the doubts that had been cast upon my patriotism. I declined to follow their advice. I have generally been content, in all matters relating to myself, to suffer the truth to work its own way to light. If the conduct and concerns of an individual are worthy of public attention, they will sooner or later be accurately known and appreciated; and it is that ultimate opinion that alone constitutes true reputation: all transient popularity is little worth struggling for.

Beside, what was I asked to vindicate myself from—a want of affection to my native country? I should as soon think of vindicating myself from the charge of a want of love to the mother that bore me! I could not reply to such an imputation;—my heart would swell in my throat, and keep me silent.

Yet I will confess, that the arrow which had been planted in my heart, rankled and festered there. The corroding doubt that had been infused in my waking thoughts, affected my sleeping fancies. The return to my country, so long anticipated, became the constant subject of harassing dreams. I would fancy myself arrived in my native city, but the place would be so changed that I could not recognize it. I would wander through strange streets, meet with strange faces, and find every thing strange around me: or, what was worse, I would meet with those I loved, with my kindred, and the companions of my youth, but they no longer knew me, or passed me by with neglect. I cannot tell how often I have awakened from such dreary dreams, and felt a sadness at heart for hours afterwards.

At length the long anticipated moment arrived. I again saw the "blue line of my native land" rising like a cloud in that horizon where, so many years before, I had seen it fade away. I again saw the bright city of my birth rising out of its beautiful bay; its multiplied fanes and spires, and its prolonged forest of masts, proclaiming its augmented grandeur. My heart throbbed with pride and admiration as I gazed upon it—I gloried in being its son.

But how was the wanderer to be received, after such an absence? Was he to be taken, as a favoured child, to its bosom; or repulsed as a stranger, and a changeling?

My old doubts recurred as I stepped upon land. I could scarcely realize that I was indeed in my native city, among the haunts of my childhood. Might not this be another of those dreams that had so often beguiled me? There were circumstances enough to warrant such a surmise. I passed through places that ought to be familiar to me, but all were changed. Huge edifices and lofty piles had sprung up in the place of lowly tenements; the old landmarks of the city were gone; the very streets were altered.

As I passed on, I looked wistfully in every face: not one was known to me—not one! Yet I was in haunts where every visage was once familiar to me. I read the names over the door: all were new. They were unassociated with any early recollection. The saddening conviction stole over my heart that I was a stranger in my own home! Alas! thought I, what had I to expect after such an absence!

Let not the reader be mistaken. I have no doleful picture to draw; no sorrowful demand to make upon his sympathies. It has been the lot of many a wanderer, returning after a shorter lapse of years, to find the scenes of his youth gone to ruin and decay. If I had any thing to deplore, it was the improvement of my home. It had outgrown my recollection from its very prosperity, and strangers had crowded into it from every clime, to participate in its overflowing abundance. A little while was sufficient to reconcile me to a change, the result of prosperity. My friends, too, once clustered in neighboring contiguity, in a moderate community, now scattered widely asunder, over a splendid metropolis, soon gathered together to welcome me; and never did wanderer, after such an absence, experience such a greeting. Then it was that every doubt vanished from my mind. Then it was that I felt I was indeed at home—and that it was a home of the heart! I thanked my stars that I had been born among such friends; I thanked my stars, that had conducted me back to dwell among them while I had yet the capacity to enjoy their fellowship.

It is the very reception I met with that has drawn from me these confessions. Had I experienced coldness or distrust—had I been treated as an alien from the sympathies of my countrymen, I should have buried my wounded feelings in my bosom, and remained silent. But they have welcomed me home with their old indulgence; they have shown that, notwithstanding my long absence, and the doubts and suggestions to which it had given rise, they still believe and trust in me. And now, let them feel assured, that I am heart and soul among them.

I make no boast of my patriotism; I can only say, that, as far as it goes, it is no blind attachment. I have sojourned in various countries; have been treated in them above my deserts; and the remembrance of them is grateful and pleasant to me. I have seen what is brightest and best in foreign lands, and have found, in every nation, enough to love and honour; yet, with all these recollections living in my imagination and kindling in my heart, I look round with delightful exultation upon my native land, and feel that, after all my ramblings about the world, I can be happiest at home.

And now a word or two with respect to the volume here presented to the reader. Having, since my return to the United States, made a wide and varied tour, for the gratification of my curiosity, it has been supposed that I did it for the purpose of writing a book; and it has more than once been intimated in the papers, that such a work was actually in the press, containing scenes and sketches of the Far West.

These announcements, gratuitously made for me, before I had put pen to paper, or even contemplated any thing of the kind, have embarrassed me exceedingly. I have been like a poor actor, who finds himself announced for a part he had no thought of playing, and his appearance expected on the stage before he has committed a line to memory.

I have always had a repugnance, amounting almost to disability, to write in the face of expectation; and, in the present instance, I was expected to write about a region fruitful of wonders and adventures, and which had already been made the theme of spirit-stirring narratives from able pens; yet about which I had nothing wonderful or adventurous to offer.

Since such, however, seems to be the desire of the public, and that they take sufficient interest in my wanderings to deem them worthy of recital, I have hastened, as promptly as possible, to meet in some degree, the expectation which others have excited. For this purpose, I have, as it were, plucked a few leaves out of my memorandum book, containing a month's foray beyond the outposts of human habitation, into the wilderness of the Far West. It forms, indeed, but a small portion of an extensive tour; but it is an episode, complete as far as it goes. As such, I offer it to the public, with great diffidence. It is a simple narrative of every day occurrences; such as happen to every one who travels the prairies. I have no wonders to describe, nor any moving accidents by flood or field to narrate; and as to those who look for a marvellous or adventurous story at my hands, I can only reply in the words of the weary knife-grinder: "Story! God bless you, I have none to tell, sir."

CHAPTER I

The Pawnee hunting grounds—Travelling companions—A commissioner —A virtuoso—A seeker of adventures—A Gil Blas of the frontier—A young man's anticipations of pleasure.

In the often vaunted regions of the Far West, several hundred miles beyond the Mississippi, extends a vast tract of uninhabited country, where there is neither to be seen the log house of the white man, nor the wigwam of the Indian. It consists of great grassy plains, interspersed with forests and groves and clumps of trees, and watered by the Arkansas, the grand Canadian, the Red River, and all their tributary streams. Over these fertile and verdant wastes still roam the Elk, the Buffalo, and the wild horse in all their native freedom. These, in fact, are the hunting grounds of the various tribes of the Far West. Thither repair the Osage, the Creek, the Delaware, and other tribes that have linked themselves with civilization, and live within the vicinity of the white settlements. Here resort also the Pawnees, the Comanches, and other fierce and as yet independent tribes, the nomades of the prairies, or the inhabitants of the skirts of the Rocky Mountains. The region I have mentioned forms a debateable ground of these warring and vindictive tribes. None of them presume to erect a permanent habitation within its borders. Their hunters and "braves" repair thither in numerous bodies during the season of game, throw up their transient hunting camps, consisting of light bowers, covered with bark and skins, commit sad havoc among the innumerable herds that graze the prairies, and having loaded themselves with venison and Buffalo meat, warily retire from the dangerous neighborhood. These expeditions partake, always, of a warlike character; the hunters are all armed for action offensive and defensive, and are bound to incessant vigilance. Should they in their excursions meet the hunters of an adverse tribe, savage conflicts take place. Their encampments too are always subject to be surprised by wandering war parties, and their hunters when scattered in pursuit of game, to be captured or massacred by lurking foes. Mouldering skulls and skeletons bleaching in some dark ravine, or near the traces of a hunting camp, occasionally mark the scene of a foregone act of blood, and let the wanderer know the dangerous nature of the region he is traversing. It is the purport of the following pages to narrate a month's excursion to these noted hunting grounds through a tract of country which had not, as yet, been explored by white men.

It was early in October 1832, that I arrived at Fort Gibson, a frontier post of the Far West, situated on the Neosho, or Grand River, near its confluence with the Arkansas. I had been travelling for a month past with a small party, from St. Louis, up the banks of the Missouri, and along the frontier line of agencies and missions, that extends from the Missouri to the Arkansas. Our party was headed by one of the commissioners appointed by the government of the United States to superintend the settlement of the Indian tribes migrating from the East to the West of the Mississippi. In the discharge of his duties he was thus visiting the various outposts of civilization.

And here let me bear testimony to the merits of this worthy leader of our little band. He was a native of one of the towns of Connecticut, a man in whom a course of legal practice and political life had not been able to vitiate an innate simplicity and benevolence of heart. The greater part of his days had been passed in the bosom of his family and the society of deacons, elders and select men, on the peaceful banks of the Connecticut; when suddenly he had been called to mount his steed, shoulder his rifle and mingle among stark hunters, back woodsmen and naked savages, on the trackless wilds of the Far West.

Another of my fellow travellers was Mr. L——, an Englishman by birth, but descended from a foreign stock; and who had all the buoyancy and accommodating spirit of a native of the Continent. Having rambled over many countries he had become, to a certain degree, a citizen of the world, easily adapting himself to any change. He was a man of a thousand occupations; a botanist, a geologist, a hunter of beetles and butterflies, a musical amateur, a sketcher of no mean pretensions, in short a complete virtuoso; added to which he was a very indefatigable, if not always a very successful sportsman. Never had a man more irons in the fire, and, consequently, never was man more busy or more cheerful.

My third fellow traveller was one who had accompanied the former from Europe, and travelled with him as his Telemachus; being apt, like his prototype, to give occasional perplexity and disquiet to his mentor. He was a young Swiss Count, scarce twenty one years of age, full of talent and spirit, but galliard in the extreme, and prone to every kind of wild adventure.

Having made this mention of my comrades, I must not pass over unnoticed a personage of inferior rank, but of all pervading and all prevalent importance: the squire, the groom, the cook, the tent man, in a word the factotum, and I may add the universal meddler and marplot of our party. This was a little swarthy, meagre, wiry French Creole, named Antoine, but familiarly dubbed Tonish: a kind of Gil Blas of the frontiers, who had passed a scrambling life sometimes among white men, sometimes among Indians. Sometimes in the employ of traders, missionaries and Indian agents; sometimes mingling with the Osage hunters. We picked him up at St. Louis, near which he has a small farm, an Indian wife and a brood of half blood children. According to his own account, however, he had a wife in every tribe: in fact, if all this little vagabond said of himself were to be believed, he was without morals, without caste, without creed, without country, and even without language; for he spoke a jargon of mingled French, English and Osage. He was, withal, a notorious braggart and a liar of the first water. It was amusing to hear him vapour and gasconade about his terrible exploits and hair breadth escapes in war and hunting. In the midst of his volubility, he was prone to be seized by a spasmodic gasping, as if the springs of his jaws were suddenly unhinged, but I am apt to think it was caused by some falsehood that stuck in his throat, for I generally remarked that immediately afterwards there bolted forth a lie of the first magnitude.

Our route had been a pleasant one, quartering ourselves occasionally at the widely separated establishments of the Indian missionaries, but in general camping out in the fine groves that border the streams, and sleeping under cover of a tent. During the latter part of our tour we had pressed forward in hopes of arriving in time at Fort Gibson to accompany the Osage hunters on their autumnal visit to the Buffalo prairies. Indeed the imagination of the young Count had become completely excited on the subject. The grand scenery and wild habits of the prairies had set his spirits madding, and the stories that little Tonish told him of Indian braves and Indian beauties, of hunting buffaloes and catching wild horses, had set him all agog for a dash into savage life. He was a bold and hard rider, and longed to be scouring the hunting grounds. It was amusing to hear his youthful anticipations of all that he was to see, and do, and enjoy, when mingling among the Indians and participating in their hardy adventures; and it was still more amusing to listen to the gasconadings of little Tonish, who volunteered to be his faithful squire in all his perilous undertakings: to teach him how to catch the wild horse, bring down the buffalo, and win the smiles of Indian princesses:—"And if we can only get sight of a prairie on fire!" said the young Count—"By gar—I'll set one on fire myself!" cried the little Frenchman.

CHAPTER II

Anticipations disappointed—New plans—Preparations to join an exploring party—Departure from Fort Gibson—Fording of the Verdigris—An Indian cavalier.

The anticipations of a young man are prone to meet with disappointment. Unfortunately for the Count's scheme of wild campaigning, before we reached the end of our journey we heard that the Osage hunters had set forth upon their expedition to the buffalo grounds. The young Count still determined, if possible, to follow on their track and overtake them; and, for this purpose stopped short at the Osage Agency, a few miles distant from Fort Gibson, to make enquiries and preparations. His travelling companion Mr. L. stopped with him; while the Commissioner and myself proceeded to Fort Gibson, followed by the faithful and veracious Tonish. I hinted to him his promises to follow the count in his campaignings, but I found the little varlet had a keen eye to self interest. He was aware that the Commissioner, from his official duties, would remain for a long time in the country, and be likely to give him permanent employment, while the sojourn of the count would but be transient. The gasconading of the little braggart, was suddenly, therefore, at an end. He spake not another word to the young count about Indians, Buffalos and wild horses, but putting himself tacitly in the train of the commissioner, jogged silently after us to the garrison.

On arriving at the fort, however, a new chance presented itself for a cruise on the prairies. We learnt that a company of mounted rangers, or riflemen had departed but three days previous, to make a wide exploring tour, from the Arkansas to the Red river, including a part of the Pawnee hunting grounds where no party of white men had as yet penetrated. Here, then, was an opportunity of ranging over those dangerous and interesting regions under the safeguard of a powerful escort; protected too by privilege, for the Commissioner in virtue of his office, could claim the service of this newly raised corps of riflemen, and the very country they were to explore, was destined for the settlement of some of the migrating tribes connected with his mission.

Our plan was promptly formed and put into execution. A couple of Creek Indians were sent off express by the commander of Fort Gibson to overtake the rangers and bring them to a halt until the Commissioner and his party should be able to join them. As we should have a march of three or four days through a wild country, before we could overtake the company of rangers, an escort of fourteen mounted riflemen, under the command of a lieutenant, was assigned us.

We sent word to the young count and Mr. L. at the Osage Agency, of our new plan and prospects, and invited them to accompany us. The Count, however, could not forego the delights he had promised himself in mingling with absolutely savage life. In reply he agreed to keep with us until we should come upon the trail of the Osage hunters, when, it was his fixed resolve to strike off into the wilderness in pursuit of them; and his faithful mentor, though he grieved at the madness of the scheme was too staunch a friend to desert him. A general rendezvous of our party and escort was appointed, for the following morning, at the Agency.

We now made all arrangements for prompt departure. Our baggage had hitherto been transported on a light waggon, but we were now to break our way through an untravelled country, cut up by rivers, ravines and thickets, where a vehicle of the kind would be a complete impediment. We were to travel on horseback, in hunters' style, and with as little encumbrance as possible. Our baggage, therefore, underwent a rigid and most abstemious reduction. A pair of saddlebags, and those by no means crammed, sufficed for each man's scanty wardrobe, and, with his great coat, were to be carried upon the steed he rode. The rest of the luggage was placed on pack horses. Each one had a bear skin and a couple of blankets for bedding, and there was a tent to shelter us in case of sickness or bad weather. We took care to provide ourselves with flour, coffee, and sugar, together with a small supply of salt pork for emergencies; for our main subsistence we were to depend upon the chase.

Such of our horses as had not been tired out in our recent journey, were taken with us as pack horses, or supernumeraries: but as we were going on a long and rough tour, where there would be occasional hunting, and where, in case of meeting with hostile savages, the safety of the rider might depend upon the goodness of his steed, we took care to be well mounted. I procured a stout silver grey; somewhat rough, but staunch and powerful; and retained a hardy pony, which

I had hitherto ridden, and which, being somewhat jaded, was suffered
to ramble along with the pack horses, to be mounted only in case of
emergency.

All these arrangements being made we left Fort Gibson on the morning
of the tenth of October, and crossing the river in the front of it, set off
for the rendezvous at the Agency. A ride of a few miles brought us to
the ford of the Verdigris, a wild rocky scene overhung with forest trees.
We descended to the bank of the river and crossed in straggling file,
the horses stepping cautiously from rock to rock, and in a manner feeling
about for a foothold beneath the rushing and brawling stream.

Our little Frenchman Tonish brought up the rear with the pack
horses. He was in high glee having experienced a kind of promotion.
In our journey hitherto he had driven the waggon, which he seemed
to consider a very inferior employ; now he was master of the horse.
He sat perched like a monkey behind the pack on one of the horses;
he sang, he shouted, he yelped like an Indian and ever and anon
blasphemed the loitering pack horses in his jargon of mingled French,
English and Osage, which not one of them could understand.

As we were crossing the ford we saw on the opposite shore a Creek
Indian on horseback. He had paused to reconnoitre us from the brow
of a rock, and formed a picturesque object, in unison with the wild
scenery around him. He wore a bright blue hunting shirt trimmed with
scarlet fringe; a gaily coloured handkerchief was bound round his head
something like a turban, with one end hanging down beside his ear;
he held a long rifle in his hand and looked like a wild Arab on the
prowl. Our loquacious and ever meddling little Frenchman called out
to him in his Babylonish jargon, but the savage having satisfied his
curiosity tossed his hand in the air, turned the head of his steed, and
gallopping along the shore soon disappeared among the trees.

CHAPTER III

*An Indian agency—Riflemen—Osages, Creeks, trappers, dogs, horses,
half breeds—Beatte the huntsman.*

Having crossed the ford we soon reached the Osage Agency where
Col. Choteau has his offices and magazines for the despatch of Indian
affairs, and the distribution of presents and supplies. It consisted of a
few loghouses on the banks of the river, and presented a motley
frontier scene. Here was our escort awaiting our arrival—some were
on horseback, some on foot, some seated on the trunks of fallen trees,

some shooting at a mark. They were a heterogeneous crew, some in frock coats made of green blankets; others in leathern hunting shirts, but the most part in marvellously ill cut garments, much the worse for wear, and evidently put on for rugged service.

Near by these was a groupe of Osages: stately fellows; stern and simple in garb and aspect. They wore no ornaments, and their dress consisted merely of blankets, leathern leggings, and moccasins. Their heads were bare, their hair was cropped close excepting a bristling ridge on top like the crest of a helmet, with a long scalp lock hanging behind. They had fine Roman countenances, and broad deep chests, and, as they generally wore their blankets wrapped round their loins, so as to leave the bust and arms bare, they looked like so many noble bronze figures. The Osages are the finest looking Indians I have ever seen in the West. They have not yielded sufficiently, as yet, to the influence of civilization to lay by their simple Indian garb, or to lose the habits of the hunter and the warrior, and their poverty prevents their indulging in much luxury of apparel.

In contrast to these was a gaily dressed party of Creeks. There is something, at the first glance, quite oriental in the appearance of this tribe. They dress in calico hunting shirts of various brilliant colours, decorated with bright fringes: and belted with broad girdles embroidered with beads: they have leggings of dressed deer skins or of green or scarlet cloth, with embroidered knee bands and tassels: their moccasins are fancifully wrought and ornamented, and they wear gaudy handkerchiefs tastefully bound round their heads.

Beside these there was a sprinkling of trappers, hunters, half breeds, creoles, negroes of every hue; and all that other rabble rout of nondescript beings that keep about the frontiers, between civilized and savage life, as those equivocal birds the bats, hover about the confines of light and darkness.

The little hamlet of the agency was in a complete bustle; the blacksmith's shed in particular was a scene of preparation. A strapping negro was shoeing a horse; two half breeds were fabricating iron spoons in which to melt lead for bullets. An old trapper in leathern hunting frock and moccasins, had placed his rifle against a work bench, while he superintended the operation and gossipped about his hunting exploits; several large dogs were lounging in and out of the shop or sleeping in the sunshine, while a little cur, with head cocked on one side and one ear erect, was watching, with that curiosity common to little dogs, the process of shoeing the horse, as if studying the art, or waiting for his turn to be shod.

We found the Count and his companion the Virtuoso ready for the march. As they intended to overtake the Osages and pass some time in hunting the Buffalo and the wild horse, they had provided themselves accordingly; having, in addition to the steeds which they used for travelling, others of prime quality, which were to be led when on the march, and only to be mounted for the chase.

They had, moreover, engaged the services of a young man named Antoine, a half breed of French and Osage origin. He was to be a kind of jack of all work; to cook, to hunt, and to take care of the horses, but he had a vehement propensity to do nothing, being one of the worthless brood engendered and brought up among the missions. He was, moreover, a little spoiled by being really a handsome young fellow, an Adonis of the frontier, and still worse by fancying himself highly connected, his sister being concubine to an opulent white trader!

For our own parts, the commissioner and myself were desirous, before setting out, to procure another attendant well versed in wood craft, who might serve us as a hunter; for our little Frenchman would have his hands full when in camp, in cooking, and on the march, in taking care of the pack horses. Such a one presented himself, or rather was recommended to us, in Pierre Beatte, a half breed of French and Osage parentage. We were assured that he was acquainted with all parts of the country, having traversed it in all directions, both in hunting and war parties; that he would be of use both as guide and interpreter, and that he was a first rate hunter.

I confess I did not like his looks when he was first presented to me. He was lounging about, in an old hunting frock and metasses or leggings, of deer skin, soiled and greased and almost japanned by constant use. He was apparently about thirty six years of age, square and strongly built. His features were not bad, being shaped not unlike those of Napoleon, but sharpened up, with high Indian cheek bones. Perhaps the dusky greenish hue of his complexion aided his resemblance to an old bronze bust I had seen of the Emperor. He had, however, a sullen saturnine expression, set off by a slouched woolen hat, and elf locks that hung about his ears.

Such was the appearance of the man, and his manners were equally unprepossessing. He was cold and laconic; made no promises nor professions; stated the terms he required for the services of himself and his horse, which we thought rather high, but shewed no disposition to abate them, nor any anxiety to secure our employ. He had altogether more of the red than the whiteman in his composition; and, as I had been taught to look upon all half breeds with distrust, as an uncertain and faithless race, I would gladly have dispensed with the services of Pierre Beatte. We had no time, however, to look about for any one more to our taste, and had to make an arrangement with him on the spot. He then set about making his preparations for the journey, promising to join us at our evenings encampment.

One thing was yet wanting to fit me out for the prairies: a thoroughly trust worthy steed. I was not yet mounted to my mind. The grey I had bought, though strong and serviceable, was rough. At the last moment I succeeded in getting an excellent animal; a dark bay; powerful, active, generous spirited, and in capital condition. I mounted him with exultation and transferred the silver grey to Tonish who was in such extacies at finding himself so completely *en Cavalier,* that I feared he might realize the ancient and well known proverb of "a beggar on horseback."

CHAPTER IV

The departure

The long drawn notes of a bugle at length gave the signal for departure. The rangers filed off in a straggling line of march through the woods: we were soon on horseback and following on, but were detained by the irregularity of the pack horses. They were unaccustomed to keep the line and straggled from side to side among the thickets, in spite of all the pesting and bedevilling of Tonish; who, mounted on his gallant grey, with a long rifle on his shoulder, worried after them, bestowing a superabundance of dry blows and curses.

We soon, therefore, lost sight of our escort, but managed to keep on their track, thridding lofty forests and entangled thickets, and passing by Indian wigwams, and negro huts until towards dusk we arrived at a frontier farm house, owned by a settler of the name of Berryhill. It was situated on a hill, below which the rangers had encamped in a circular grove, on the margin of a stream. The master of the house received us civilly, but could offer us no accommodation, for sickness prevailed in his family. He appeared, himself, to be in no very thriving condition for though bulky in frame, he had a sallow unhealthy complexion, and had a whiffling double voice, shifting abruptly from a treble to a thorough bass.

Finding his log house was a mere hospital, crowded with invalids, we ordered our tent to be pitched in the farm yard.

We had not been longed encamped when our recently engaged attendant, Beatte, the Osage half breed, made his appearance. He came mounted on one horse and leading another which seemed to be well packed with supplies for the expedition. Beatte was evidently an "old soldier," as to the art of taking care of himself and looking out for emergencies. Finding that he was in government employ, being engaged by the commissioner, he had drawn rations of flour and bacon, and put them up so as to be weather proof. In addition to the horse for the road, and for ordinary service, which was a rough hardy animal, he had another for hunting. This was of a mixed breed like himself, being a cross of the domestic stock with the wild horse of the prairies; and a noble steed it was, of generous spirit, fine action and admirable bottom. He had taken care to have his horses well shod at the Agency. He came prepared at all points for war or hunting: his rifle on his shoulder, his powder horn and bullet pouch at his side, his hunting knife stuck in his belt, and coils of cordage at his saddle bow, which we were told were lariats, or noosed cords, used in catching the wild horse.

Thus equipped and provided, an Indian hunter on a prairie, is like a cruiser on the ocean, perfectly independent of the world, and competent to self protection and self maintenance. He can cast himself loose from every one, shape his own course, and take care of his own fortunes. I thought Beatte seemed to feel his independence, and to consider himself superior to us all, now that we were launching into the wilderness. He maintained a half proud, half sullen look, and a great taciturnity; and his first care was to unpack his horses, and put them in safe quarters for the night. His whole demeanour was in perfect contrast to our vapouring, chattering, bustling little Frenchman. The latter, too, seemed jealous of this new comer. He whispered to us that these half breeds were a touchy, capricious people, little to be depended upon. That Beatte had evidently come prepared to take care of himself, and that, at any moment in the course of our tour, he would be liable to take some sudden disgust or affront, and abandon us at a moments warning: having the means of shifting for himself, and being perfectly at home on the prairies.

CHAPTER V

Frontier scenes—A Lycurgus of the border—Lynch's law—The danger of finding a horse—The young Osage.

On the following morning (Oct. 11) we were on the march by half past seven o'clock, and rode through deep rich bottoms of alluvial soil, overgrown with redundant vegetation, and trees of an enormous size. Our route lay parallel to the west bank of the Arkansas, on the borders of which river, near the confluence of the Red Fork, we expected to overtake the main body of Rangers. For some miles the country was sprinkled with Creek villages and farm houses; the inhabitants of which appeared to have adopted, with considerable facility, the rudiments of civilization, and to have thriven in consequence. Their farms were well stocked and their houses had a look of comfort and abundance.

We met with numbers of them returning from one of their grand games of ball, for which their nation is celebrated. Some were on foot, some on horseback; the latter, occasionally, with gaily dressed females behind them. They are a well made race, muscular and closely knit, with well turned thighs and legs. They have a gipsey fondness for brilliant colours, and gay decorations, and are bright and fanciful objects when seen at a distance on the prairies. One had a scarlet handkerchief bound round his head surmounted with a tuft of black feathers like a cock's tail. Another had a white handkerchief, with red feathers; while a third, for want of a plume, had stuck in his turban a brilliant bunch of sumach.

On the verge of the wilderness we paused to enquire our way at a log house, owned by a white settler or squatter, a tall raw boned old fellow, with red hair, a lank lanthorn visage, and an inveterate habit of winking with one eye, as if every thing he said was of knowing import. He was in a towering passion. One of his horses was missing, he was sure it had been stolen in the night by a straggling party of Osages encamped in a neighboring swamp—but he would have satisfaction! He would make an example of the villains. He had accordingly caught down his rifle from the wall, that invariable enforcer of right or wrong upon the frontiers, and having saddled his steed was about to sally forth on a foray into the swamp; while a brother squatter, with rifle in hand, stood ready to accompany him.

We endeavored to calm the old campaigner of the prairies, by suggesting that his horse might have strayed into the neighboring woods; but he had the frontier propensity to charge every thing to the Indians, and nothing could dissuade him from carrying fire and sword into the swamp.

After riding a few miles further we lost the trail of the main body of rangers, and became perplexed by a variety of tracks made by the Indians and settlers. At length coming to a log house, inhabited by a white man, the very last on the frontier, we found that we had wandered from our true course. Taking us back for some distance he again brought us to the right trail; putting ourselves upon which, we took our final departure and launched into the broad wilderness.

The trail kept on like a straggling foot path, over hill and dale, through bush and brake, and tangled thicket, and open prairie. In traversing the wilds it is customary for a party either of horse or foot to follow each other in single file like the Indians: so that the leaders break the way for those who follow and lessen their labour and fatigue. In this way, also, the number of a party is concealed, the whole leaving but one narrow well trampled track to mark their course.

We had not long regained the trail, when, on emerging from a forest, we beheld our raw boned, hard winking, hard riding knight errant of the frontier, descending the slope of a hill, followed by his companion in arms. As he drew near to us the gauntness of his figure and ruefulness of his aspect, reminded me of the descriptions of the hero of La Mancha, and he was equally bent on affairs of doughty enterprise, being about to penetrate the thickets of the perilous swamp, within which the enemy lay ensconced.

While we were holding a parley with him on the slope of the hill, we descried an Osage on horseback, issuing out of a skirt of wood about half a mile off, and leading a horse by a halter. The latter was immediately recognized by our hard winking friend as the steed of which he was in quest. As the Osage drew near I was struck with his appearance. He was about nineteen or twenty years of age but well grown; with the fine Roman countenance common to his tribe, and as he rode with his blanket wrapped round his loins his naked bust would have furnished a model for a statuary. He was mounted on a beautiful pie bald horse, a mottled white and brown, of the wild breed of the prairies, decorated with a broad collar from which hung in front a tuft of horse hair dyed of a bright scarlet.

The youth rode slowly up to us with a frank open air, and signified, by means of our interpreter Beatte, that the horse he was leading had wandered to their camp and he was now on his way to conduct him back to his owner.

I had expected to witness an expression of gratitude on the part of our hard favoured cavalier, but to my surprize the old fellow broke out into a furious passion. He declared that the Indians had carried off his horse in the night, with the intention of bringing him home in the morning, and claiming a reward for finding him; a common practice, as he affirmed, among the Indians. He was, therefore, for tying the young Indian to a tree and giving him a sound lashing; and was quite surprized at the burst of indignation which this novel mode of requiting a service drew from us. Such, however, is too often the administration of law on the frontier, "Lynch's law," as it is technically termed, in which the plaintiff is apt to be witness, jury, judge and executioner, and the defendant to be convicted and punished on mere presumption: and in this way I am convinced, are occasioned many of those heart burnings and resentments among the Indians, which lead to retaliation, and end in Indian wars. When I compared the open, noble countenance and frank demeanour of the young Osage, with the sinister visage and high handed conduct of the frontiers-man, I felt little doubt on whose back a lash would be most meritoriously bestowed.

Being thus obliged to content himself with the recovery of his horse, without the pleasure of flogging the finder into the bargain, the old Lycurgus, or rather Draco, of the frontier set off growling on his return homeward, followed by his brother squatter.

As for the youthful Osage, we were all prepossessed in his favour; the young count especially, with the sympathies proper to his age and incident to his character, had taken quite a fancy to him. Nothing would suit but he must have the young Osage as a companion and squire in his expedition into the wilderness. The youth was easily tempted, and, with the prospect of a safe range over the buffalo prairies and the promise of a new blanket, he turned his bridle, left the swamp and the encampment of his friends behind him, and set off to follow the count in his wanderings in quest of the Osage hunters. Such is the glorious independence of man in a savage state. This youth with his rifle, his blanket and his horse was ready at a moments warning to rove the world; he carried all his worldly effects with him; and in the absence of artificial wants, possessed the great secret of personal freedom. We of society are slaves not so much to others, as to ourselves; our superfluities are the chains that bind us, impeding every movement of our bodies and thwarting every impulse of our souls. Such at least were my speculations at the time though I am not sure but that they took their tone from the enthusiasm of the young Count, who seemed more enchanted than ever with the wild chivalry of the prairies, and talked of putting on the Indian dress and adopting the Indian habits during the time he hoped to pass with the Osages.

CHAPTER VI

Trail of the Osage hunters—Departure of the Count and his party—
A deserted war camp—A vagrant dog—The encampment.

In the course of the morning the trail we were pursuing was crossed by another, which struck off through the forest to the west in a direct course for the Arkansas river. Beatte, our half breed, after considering it for a moment, pronounced it the trail of the Osage Hunters; and that it must lead to the place where they had forded the river on their way to the hunting grounds.

Here then the young Count and his companion came to a halt and prepared to take leave of us. The most experienced frontiers men in the troop remonstrated on the hazard of the undertaking. They were about to throw themselves loose in the wilderness, with no other guides, guards or attendants than a young, ignorant half breed and a still younger Indian. They were embarrassed by a pack horse and two led horses, with which they would have to make their way through matted forests, and across rivers and morasses. The Osages and Pawnees were at war and they might fall in with some warrior party of the latter, who are ferocious foes; besides, their small number, and their valuable horses would form a great temptation to some of the straggling bands of Osages loitering about the frontier, who might rob them of their horses in the night, and leave them destitute and on foot in the midst of the prairies.

Nothing, however, could restrain the romantic ardour of the Count for a campaign of Buffalo hunting with the Osages, and he had a game spirit that seemed always stimulated by the idea of danger. His travelling companion, of discreeter age and calmer temperament, was convinced of the rashness of the enterprize, but he could not control the impetuous zeal of his youthful friend, and he was too loyal to leave him to pursue his hazardous scheme alone. To our great regret, therefore, we saw them abandon the protection of our escort, and strike off on their haphazard expedition. The old hunters of our party shook their heads, and our half breed Beatte predicted all kinds of trouble to them; my only hope, was that they would soon meet with perplexities enough to cool the impetuosity of the young count, and induce him to rejoin us. With this idea we travelled slowly and made a considerable halt at noon. After resuming our march we came in sight of the Arkansas. It presented a broad and rapid stream bordered by a beach of fine sand, overgrown with willows and cotton wood trees. Beyond the river the eye wandered over a beautiful champaign country, of flowery plains and sloping uplands, diversified by groves and clumps of trees, and long screens of woodland; the whole wearing the aspect of complete, and even ornamental cultivation, instead of native wildness. Not far from the river, on an open eminence, we passed through the recently deserted camping place of an Osage war party. The frames of the tents or wigwams remained, consisting of poles bent into an arch with each end stuck into the ground: these are intertwined with twigs and branches, and covered with bark, and skins. Those experienced in Indian lore can ascertain the tribe, and whether on a hunting, or a warlike expedition, by the shape and disposition of the wigwams. Beatte pointed out to us, in the present skeleton camp, the wigwam in which the chiefs had held their consultations round the council fire; and an open area, well trampled down, on which the grand war dance had been performed.

Pursuing our journey, as we were passing through a forest we were met by a forlorn half famished dog, who came rambling along the trial, with inflamed eyes, and bewildered look. Though nearly trampled upon by the foremost rangers he took notice of no one, but rambled heedlessly among the horses. The cry of "mad dog" was immediately raised, and one of the rangers levelled his rifle, but was stayed by the ever ready humanity of the Commissioner. "He is blind!" said he, "it is the dog of some poor Indian, following his master by the scent. It would be a shame to kill so faithful an animal." The ranger shouldered his rifle, the dog blundered blindly through the cavalcade unhurt; and, keeping his nose to the ground continued his course along the trail, affording a rare instance of a dog surviving a bad name.

About three o'clock we came to a recent camping place of the company of rangers: the brands of one of their fires were still smoking; so that, according to the opinion of Beatte, they could not have passed on above a day previously. As there was a fine stream of water close by, and plenty of pea vine for the horses, we encamped here for the night.

We had not been here long when we heard a halloo from a distance and beheld the young count and his party advancing through the forest. We welcomed them to the camp with heartfelt satisfaction; for their departure upon so hazardous an expedition had caused us great uneasiness. A short experiment had convinced them of the toil and difficulty of inexperienced travellers like themselves making their way through the wilderness with such a train of horses, and such slender attendance. Fortunately they determined to rejoin us before nightfall; one night's camping out might have cost them their horses. The Count had prevailed upon his protegee and esquire the young Osage to continue with him, and still calculated upon achieving great exploits with his assistance, on the Buffalo prairies.

CHAPTER VII

News of the rangers—The count and his Indian squire—Halt in the woods—Woodland scene—Osage village—Osage visitors at our evening camp.

In the morning early (Oct. 12) the two Creeks who had been sent express by the Commander of Fort Gibson, to stop the Company of rangers, arrived at our encampment on their return. They had left the company encamped about fifty miles distant in a fine place on the Arkansas abounding in game, where they intended to await our arrival. This news spread animation throughout our party and we set out on our march at sunrise, with renewed spirit.

In mounting our steeds the young Osage attempted to throw a blanket upon his wild horse. The fine, sensitive animal took fright, reared and recoiled. The attitudes of the wild horse and the almost naked savage would have formed studies for a painter or a statuary.

I often pleased myself in the course of our march with noticing the appearance of the young count, and his newly enlisted follower, as they rode before me. Never was preux chevalier better suited with an esquire. The count was well mounted, and, as I have before observed, was a bold and graceful rider. He was fond too of caracolling his horse, and dashing about in the buoyancy of youthful spirits. His dress was a gay Indian hunting frock of dressed deer skin, setting well to the shape, dyed of a beautiful purple and fancifully embroidered with silks of various colours; as if it had been the work of some Indian beauty to decorate a favorite chief. With this he wore leathern pantaloons and moccasins, a foraging cap, and a double barrelled gun slung by a bandaleer athwart his back: so that he was quite a picturesque figure as he managed gracefully his spirited steed.

The young Osage would ride close behind him on his wild and beautifully mottled horse, which was decorated with crimson tufts of hair. He rode with his finely shaped head and bust naked; his blanket being girt round his waist. He carried his rifle in one hand and managed his horse with the other, and seemed ready to dash off at a moments warning, with his youthful leader on any mad cap foray or scamper. The count, with the sanguine anticipations of youth, promised himself many hardy adventures and exploits in company with his youthful "brave," when we should get among the buffaloes, in the Pawnee hunting grounds.

After riding some distance we crossed a narrow deep stream upon a solid bridge, the remains of an old beaver dam; the industrious community which had constructed it had all been destroyed. Above us a streaming flight of wild geese, high in air, and making a vociferous noise, gave note of the waning year.

About half past ten o'clock we made a halt in a forest where there was abundance of the pea vine. Here we turned the horses loose to graze. A fire was made, water procured from an adjacent spring, and in a short time our little Frenchman Tonish had a pot of coffee prepared, for our refreshment. While partaking of it we were joined by an old Osage, one of a small hunting party who had recently passed this way. He was in search of his horse which had wandered away or been stolen. Our half breed Beatte made a wry face on hearing of Osage hunters in this direction. "Until we pass those hunters," said he, "we shall see no buffalos. They frighten away every thing, like a prairie on fire."

The morning repast being over the party amused themselves in various ways. Some shot with their rifles at a mark, others lay asleep half buried in the deep bed of foliage, with their heads resting on their saddles; others gossipped round the fire at the foot of a tree, which sent up wreaths of blue smoke among the branches. The horses banquetted luxuriously on the pea vine, and some lay down and rolled amongst them.

We were overshadowed by lofty trees, with straight smooth trunks, like stately columns, and as the glancing rays of the sun shone through the transparent leaves, tinted with the many coloured hues of autumn, I was reminded of the effect of sunshine among the stained windows and clustering columns of a Gothic cathedral. Indeed there is a grandeur and solemnity in some of our spacious forests of the West that awaken in me the same feeling I have experienced in those vast and venerable piles, and the sound of the wind sweeping through them, supplies occasionally the deep breathings of the organ.

About noon the bugle sounded to horse, and we were again on the march, hoping to arrive at the encampment of the rangers before night, as the old Osage had assured us it was not above ten or twelve miles distant. In our course through a forest we passed by a lonely pool covered with the most magnificent water lilies that I had ever beheld; among which swam several wood ducks, one of the most beautiful of water fowl, remarkable for the gracefulness and brilliancy of its plumage.

After proceeding some distance farther we came down upon the banks of the Arkansas at a place where tracks of numerous horses all entering the water, shewed where a party of Osage hunters had recently crossed the river on their way to the buffalo range. After letting our horses drink in the river we continued along its bank for a space, and then across prairies where we saw a distant smoke, which we hoped might proceed from the encampment of the rangers. Following what we supposed to be their trail we came to a meadow in which were a number of horses grazing. They were not, however, the horses of the troop. A little further on, we reached a straggling Osage village on the banks of the Arkansas. Our arrival created quite a sensation. A number of old men came forward and shook hands with us all severally: while the women and children huddled together in groupes, staring at us wildly, chattering and laughing among themselves. We found that all the young men of the village had departed on a hunting expedition, leaving the women and children and old men behind. Here the Commissioner made a speech from horseback; informing his hearers of the purport of his mission to promote a general peace among the tribes of the West, and urging them to lay aside all warlike and bloodthirsty notions and not to make any wanton attacks upon the Pawnees. This speech being interpreted by Beatte, seemed to have a most pacifying effect upon the multitude who promised faithfully that as far as in them lay, the peace should not be disturbed;

and indeed their age and sex gave some reason to hope that they would keep their word.

Still hoping to reach the encampment of the rangers before nightfall, we pushed on until twilight, when we were obliged to halt on the borders of a ravine. The rangers bivouacked under trees, at the bottom of the dell, while we pitched our tent on a rocky knoll near a running stream. The night came on dark and overcast, with flying clouds, and much appearance of rain. The fires of the rangers burnt brightly in the dell, and threw strong masses of light upon the robber looking groups that were cooking, eating and drinking around them. To add to the wildness of the scene, several Osage Indians, visitors from the village we had passed, were mingled among the men. Three of them came and seated themselves by our fire. They watched every thing that was going on round them in silence, and looked like figures of monumental bronze. We gave them food, and, what they most relished, coffee: for the Indians partake in the universal fondness for this beverage which pervades the West. When they had made their supper they stretched themselves, side by side, before the fire and began a low nasal chaunt, drumming with their hands upon their breasts by way of accompanyment. Their chaunt seemed to consist of regular staves, every one terminating, not in a melodious cadence, but in the abrupt interjection huh! uttered almost like a hiccup. This chaunt, we were told by our interpreter Beatte related to ourselves; our appearance, our treatment of them, and all that they knew of our plans. In one part they spoke of the young count, whose animated character and eagerness for Indian enterprize had struck their fancy, and they indulged in some waggery about him and the young Indian beauties that produced great merryment among our half breeds.

This mode of improvising is common throughout the savage tribes; and in this way with a few simple inflections of the voice, they chaunt all their exploits in war and hunting, and occasionally indulge in a vein of comic humour and dry satire, to which the Indians appear to me much more prone than is generally imagined.

In fact the Indians that I have had an opportunity of seeing in real life are quite different from those described in poetry. They are by no means the stoics that they are represented; taciturn, unbending, without a tear or a smile. Taciturn they are, it is true, when in company with white men, whose good will they distrust, and whose language they do not understand; but the white man is equally taciturn under like circumstances. When the Indians are among themselves, however, there cannot be greater gossips. Half their time is taken up in talking over their adventures in war and hunting, and in telling whimsical stories. They are great mimics and buffoons, also, and entertain themselves excessively at the expense of the whites, with whom they have associated, and who have supposed them impressed with profound respect for their grandeur and dignity. They are curious observers, noting every thing in silence, but with a keen and watchful eye; occasionally exchanging a glance or a grunt with each other, when any thing particularly strikes them: but reserving all comments until they are alone. Then it is that they give full scope to criticism, satire, mimicry and mirth.

In the course of my journey along the frontier I have had repeated opportunities of noticing their excitability and boisterous merryment at their games, and have occasionally noticed a groupe of Osages sitting round a fire until a late hour of the night, engaged in the most animated and lively conversation, and at times making the woods resound with peals of laughter.

As to tears, they have them in abundance both real and affected; for at times they make a merit of them. No one weeps more bitterly or profusely at the death of a relative or friend: and they have stated times when they repair to howl and lament at their graves. I have heard doleful wailings at daybreak in the neighborhood of Indian villages, made by some of the inhabitants, who go out at that hour into the fields, to mourn and weep for the dead: at such times, I am told, the tears will stream down their cheeks in torrents.

As far as I can judge, the Indian of poetical fiction is like the shepherd of pastoral romance, a mere personification of imaginary attributes.

The nasal chaunt of our Osage guests gradually died away, they covered their heads with their blankets and fell fast asleep and in a little while all was silent, excepting the pattering of scattered rain drops upon our tent.

In the morning our Indian visitors breakfasted with us, but the young Osage, who was to act as esquire to the Count in his knight errantry on the prairies, was no where to be found. His wild horse too was missing, and, after many conjectures we came to the conclusion that he had taken "Indian leave" of us in the night. We afterwards ascertained that he had been persuaded so to do by the Osages we had recently met with, who had represented to him the perils that would attend him on an expedition to the Pawnee hunting grounds, where he might fall into the hands of the implacable enemies of his tribe; and, what was scarcely less to be apprehended, the annoyances to which he would be subjected from the capricious and overbearing conduct of the white men; who, as I have witnessed in my own short experience, are prone to treat the poor Indians as little better than brute animals. Indeed he had had a specimen of it himself in the narrow escape he made from the infliction of Lynch's law, by the hard winking worthy of the frontier, for the flagitious crime of finding a stray horse.

The disappearance of the youth was generally regretted by our party, for we had all taken a great fancy to him from his handsome, frank and manly appearance, and the easy grace of his deportment. He was indeed a native born gentleman. By none, however, was he so much lamented as by the young count, who thus suddenly found himself deprived of his esquire. I regretted the departure of the Osage for his own sake, for we should have cherished him throughout the expedition, and I am convinced from the munificent spirit of his patron, he would have returned to his tribe laden with wealth of beads and trinkets and Indian blankets.

CHAPTER VIII

The honey camp.

The weather, which had been rainy in the night, having held up, we resumed our march at seven o'clock in the morning, in confident hope of soon arriving at the encampment of the rangers. We had not ridden above three or four miles when we came to a large tree, which had recently been felled by an axe, for the wild honey contained in the hollow of its trunk, several broken flakes of which still remained. We now felt sure that the camp could not be far distant. About a couple of miles further some of the rangers set up a shout and pointed to a number of horses grazing in a woody bottom. A few paces brought us to the brow of an elevated ridge whence we looked down upon the encampment. It was a wild bandit, or Robin Hood scene. In a beautiful open forest, traversed by a running stream, were booths of bark and branches, and tents of blankets, temporary shelters from the recent rain, for the rangers commonly bivouack in the open air. There were groupes of rangers in every kind of uncouth garb. Some were cooking at huge fires made at the feet of trees; some were stretching and dressing deer skins; some were shooting at a mark and some lying about on the grass. Venison jerked, and hung on frames—was drying over the embers in one place; in another lay carcasses recently brought in by the hunters. Stacks of rifles were leaning against the trunks of the trees and saddles bridles and powder horns hanging above them, while horses were grazing here and there among the thickets.

Our arrival was greeted with acclamation. The rangers crowded about their comrades to enquire the news from the fort: for our own part, we were received in frank simple hunter's style by Capt. Bean the commander of the company; a man about forty years of age, vigorous and active. His life had been chiefly passed on the frontier, occasionally in Indian warfare, so that he was a thorough woodsman, and a first rate hunter. He was equipped in character; in leathern hunting shirt and leggings, and a leathern foraging cap.

While we were conversing with the Captain a veteran huntsman approached whose whole appearance struck me. He was of the middle size, but tough and weather proved; a head partly bald and garnished with loose iron grey locks, and a fine black eye, beaming with youthful spirit. His dress was similar to that of the Captain, a rifle shirt and leggings of dressed deer skin, that had evidently seen service; a powder horn was slung by his side, a hunting knife stuck in his belt, and in his hand was an ancient and trusty rifle, doubtless as dear to him as a bosom friend. He asked permission to go hunting which was readily granted. "That's Old Ryan," said the captain, when he had gone. "There's not a better hunter in the camp. He's sure to bring in game."

In a little while our pack horses were unloaded and turned loose to revel among the pea vines. Our tent was pitched; our fire made; the half of a deer had been sent to us from the Captain's lodge; Beatte brought in a couple of wild turkeys; the spits were laden and the camp kettle crammed with meat, and to crown our luxuries, a basin filled with great flakes of delicious honey, the spoils of a plundered bee tree, was given us by one of the rangers. Our little Frenchman Tonish was in an extacy, and tucking up his sleeves to the elbows, set to work to make a display of his culinary skill, on which he prided himself almost as much as upon his hunting, his riding and his warlike prowess.

CHAPTER IX

A bee hunt.

The beautiful forest in which we were encamped abounded in bee trees; that is to say trees in the decayed trunks of which wild bees had established their hives. It is surprizing in what countless swarms the bees have overspread the Far West within but a moderate number of years. The Indians consider them the harbinger of the white man, as the Buffalo is of the red man; and say that, in proportion as the bee advances, the Indian and the Buffalo retire. We are always accustomed to associate the hum of the bee hive with the farm house and the flower garden, and to consider those industrious little animals as connected with the busy haunts of man, and I am told that the wild bee is seldom to be met with at any great distance from the frontier. They have been the heralds of civilization, steadfastly preceding it as it advanced from

the Atlantic borders, and some of the ancient settlers of the West
pretend to give the very year when the honey bee first crossed the Mississippi. The Indians with surprize found the mouldering trees of their
forests suddenly teeming with ambrosial sweets, and nothing, I am told,
can exceed the greedy relish with which they banquet for the first time
upon this unbought luxury of the wilderness.

At present the honey bee swarms in myriads in the noble groves and
forests that skirt and intersect the prairies and extend along the
alluvial bottoms of the rivers. It seems to me as if these beautiful
regions answer literally to the description of the land of promise,
"a land flowing with milk and honey;" for the rich pasturage of the
prairies is calculated to sustain herds of cattle as countless as the
sands upon the sea shore, while the flowers with which they are
enamelled render them a very paradise for the nectar seeking bee.

We had not been long in the camp when a party set out in quest
of a bee tree: and, being curious to witness the sport, I gladly
accepted an invitation to accompany them. The party was headed
by a veteran bee hunter, a tall lank fellow, in homespun garb that
hung loosely about his limbs, and a straw hat shaped not unlike a
bee hive; a comrade, equally uncouth in garb, and without a hat,
straddled along at his heels, with a long rifle on his shoulder. To
these succeeded half a dozen others, some with axes and some with
rifles, for no one stirs far from the camp without fire arms, so as to
be ready either for wild deer or wild Indian.

After proceeding some distance we came to an open glade on the
skirts of the forest. Here our leader halted, and then advanced quietly
to a low bush on the top of which I perceived a piece of honey comb.
This I found was the bait or lure for the wild bees. Several were hum-
ming about it, and diving into its cells. When they had laden themselves
with honey they would rise into the air, and dart off in a straight line,
almost with the velocity of a bullet. The hunters watched attentively
the course they took, and then set off in the same direction, stumbling
along over twisted roots and fallen trees, with their eyes turned up to
the sky. In this way they traced the honey laden bees to their hive, in
the hollow trunk of a blasted oak, where after buzzing about for a
moment they entered a hole about sixty feet from the ground.

Two of the Bee hunters now plied their axes vigorously at the foot
of the tree to level it with the ground. The mere spectators and amateurs,
in the mean time, drew off to a cautious distance, to be out of the way
of the falling of the tree and the vengeance of its inmates. The jarring
blows of the axe seemed to have no effect in alarming or disturbing this
most industrious community. They continued to ply at their usual
occupations, some arriving full freighted into port, others sallying forth

on new expeditions, like so many merchantmen in a money making metropolis, little suspicious of impending bankruptcy and downfall. Even a loud crack which announced the disrupture of the trunk failed to divert their attention from the intense pursuit of gain; at length down came the tree with a tremendous crash, bursting open from end to end, and displaying all the hoarded treasures of the commonwealth.

One of the hunters immediately ran up with a whisp of lighted hay as a defence against the bees. The latter, however, made no attack and sought no revenge; they seemed stupified by the catastrophe and unsuspicious of its cause, and remained crawling and buzzing about the ruins without offering us any molestation. Every one of the party now fell to, with spoon and hunting knife, to scoop out the flakes of honey comb with which the hollow trunk was stored. Some of them were of old date and a deep brown colour, others were beautifully white, and the honey in their cells was almost limpid. Such of the combs as were entire were placed in camp kettles to be conveyed to the encampment; those which had been shivered in the fall were devoured upon the spot. Every stark bee hunter was to be seen with a rich morsel in his hand, dripping about his fingers, and disappearing as rapidly as a cream tart before the holyday appetite of a schoolboy.

Nor was it the bee hunters alone that profited by the downfall of this industrious community; as if the bees would carry through the similitude of their habits with those of laborious and gainful man, I beheld numbers from rival hives, arriving on eager wing, to enrich themselves with the ruins of their neighbors. These busied themselves as eagerly and cheerily as so many wreckers on an Indiaman that has been driven on shore: plunging into the cells of the broken honey combs, banquetting greedily on the spoil, and then winging their way full freighted to their homes. As to the poor proprietors of the ruin they seemed to have no heart to do any thing, not even to taste the nectar that flowed around them; but crawled backwards and forwards, in vacant desolation, as I have seen a poor fellow with his hands in his breeches pocket, whistling vacantly and despondingly about the ruins of his house that had been burnt.

It is difficult to describe the bewilderment and confusion of the bees of the bankrupt hive who had been absent at the time of the catastrophe, and who arrived from time to time, with full cargoes from abroad. At first they wheeled about in the air, in the place where the fallen tree had once reared its head, astonished at finding it all a vacuum. At length, as if comprehending their disaster, they settled down in clusters on a dry branch of a neighboring tree, whence they seemed to contemplate the prostrate ruin and to buzz forth doleful lamentations over the downfall of their republic. It was a scene on which the "Melancholy Jacques" might have moralized by the hour.

We now abandoned the place, leaving much honey in the hollow of the tree. "It will be all cleared off by varmint," said one of the rangers.

"What vermin?" asked I.

"Oh Bears, and skunks, and raccoons and 'possums. The bears is the knowingest varmint for finding out a bee tree in the world. They'll gnaw for days together at the trunk till they make a hole big enough to get in their paws, and then they'll haul out honey, bees and all."

CHAPTER X

Amusements in the camp—Consultations—Hunters' fare and feasting—Evening scenes—Camp melody—The fate of an amateur owl.

On returning to the camp we found it a scene of the greatest hilarity. Some of the rangers were shooting at a mark, others were leaping, wrestling and playing at prison bars. They were mostly young men, on their first expedition, in high health and vigour, and buoyant with anticipations; and I can conceive nothing more likely to set the youthful blood into a flow than a wild wood life of the kind and the range of a magnificent wilderness abounding with game and fruitful of adventure. We send our youth abroad to grow luxurious and effeminate in Europe; it appears to me that a previous tour on the prairies would be more likely to produce that manliness, simplicity and self dependence most in unison with our political institutions.

While the young men were engaged in these boisterous amusements a graver set, composed of the Captain the Doctor and other sages and leaders of the camp were seated or stretched out on the grass, round a frontier map, holding a consultation about our position, and the course we were to pursue.

Our plan was to cross the Arkansas just above where the Red Fork falls into it then to keep westerly, until we should pass through a grand belt of open forest, called the Cross Timber, which ranges nearly north and south from the Arkansas to Red river, after which we were to keep a southerly course towards the latter river.

Our half breed Beatte, being an experienced Osage hunter, was called into the consultation. "Have you ever hunted in this direction?" said the Captain.

"Yes," was the laconic reply.

"Perhaps then you can tell us in which direction lies the Red Fork."

"If you keep along yonder, by the edge of the prairie you will come to a bald hill, with a pile of stones upon it."

"I have noticed that hill as I was hunting," said the Captain.

"Well! those stones were set up by the Osages as a land mark: from that spot you may have a sight of the Red Fork."

"In that case," cried the Captain, "we shall reach the Red Fork tomorrow; then cross the Arkansas above it, into the Pawnee country, and then in two days we shall crack Buffalo bones!"

The idea of arriving at the adventurous hunting grounds of the Pawnees and of coming upon the traces of the buffaloes, made every eye sparkle with animation. Our further conversation was interrupted by the sharp report of a rifle at no great distance from the camp.

"That's Old Ryan's rifle," exclaimed the Captain, "there's a buck down I'll warrant." Nor was he mistaken, for, before long, the veteran made his appearance, calling upon one of the younger rangers to return with him and aid in bringing home the carcass.

The surrounding country in fact, abounded with game, so that the camp was overstocked with provisions, and, as no less than twenty bee trees had been cut down in the vicinity every one revelled in luxury. With the wasteful prodigality of hunters there was a continual feasting, and scarce any one put by provision for the morrow. The cooking was conducted in hunters' style. The meat was stuck upon tapering spits of dog wood, which were thrust perpendicularly into the ground, so as to sustain the joint before the fire, where it was roasted or broiled with all its juices retained in it in a manner that would have tickled the palate of the most experienced gourmand. As much could not be said in favour of the bread. It was little more than a paste made of flour and water and fried like fritters, in lard; though some adopted a ruder style, twisting it round the ends of sticks and thus roasting it before the fire. In either way I have found it extremely palatable on the prairies. No one knows the true relish of food until he has a hunter's appetite.

Before sunset we were summoned by little Tonish to a sumptuous repast. Blankets had been spread on the ground near to the fire, upon which we took our seats. A large dish or bowl, made from the root of a maple tree, and which we had purchased at the Indian village, was placed on the ground before us, and into it were emptied the contents of one of the camp kettles, consisting of a wild turkey hashed, together with slips of bacon and lumps of dough. Beside it was placed another bowl of similar ware, containing an ample supply of fritters. After we had discussed the hash, two wooden spits, on which the ribs of a fat buck were broiling before the fire, were removed and planted in the ground before us, with a triumphant air, by little Tonish. Having no dishes we had to proceed in hunters' style, cutting off strips and slices with our

hunting knives, and dipping them in salt and pepper. To do justice
to Tonish's cookery, however, and to the keen sauce of the prairies,
never have I tasted venison so delicious. With all this our beverage was
coffee, boiled in a camp kettle sweetened with brown sugar, and drank
out of tin cups: and such was the style of our banquetting throughout this
expedition, whenever provisions were plenty, and as long as flour and
coffee and sugar held out.

As the twilight thickened into night the centinels were marched forth
to their stations around the camp, an indispensable precaution in a country
infested by Indians. The encampment now presented a picturesque
appearance. Camp fires were blazing and smouldering here and there
among the trees, with groups of rangers around them; some seated or
lying on the ground, others standing in the ruddy glare of the flames, or
in shadowy relief.

At some of the fires there was much boisterous mirth, where peals of
laughter were mingled with loud ribald jokes and uncouth exclamations,
for the troop was evidently a raw undisciplined band; levied among the
wild youngsters of the frontier, who had enlisted, some for the sake of
roving adventure, and some for the purpose of getting a knowledge
of the country. Many of them were the neighbors of their officers and
accustomed to regard them with the familiarity of equals and companions. None of them had any idea of the restraint and decorum of a
camp, or ambition to acquire a name for exactness in a profession in
which they had no intention of continuing.

While this boisterous merriment prevailed at one of the fires, there
suddenly rose a strain of nasal melody from another, at which a choir of
"vocalists" were uniting their voices in a most lugubrious psalm tune.
This was led by one of the lieutenants; a tall spare man, who we were informed had officiated as schoolmaster, singing master and occasionally
as methodist preacher in one of the villages of the frontier. The chaunt
rose solemnly and sadly in the night air, and reminded me of the
description of similar canticles in the camps of the Covenanters; and,
indeed, the strange medley of figures and faces and uncouth garbs con-
gregated together in our troop would not have disgraced the banners of
Praise God Barebones.

In one of the intervals of this nasal psalmody, an amateur owl, as if
in competition, began his dreary hooting. Immediately there was a cry
throughout the camp of "Charley's owl! Charley's owl!" It seems this
"obscure bird" had visited the camp every night and had been fired at by
one of the centinels, a half witted lad, named Charley, who on being
called up for firing when on duty, excused himself by saying that he
understood that owls made uncommonly good soup.

One of the young rangers mimicked the cry of this bird of wisdom, who, with a simplicity little consonant with his character, came hovering within sight and alighted on the naked branch of a tree lit up by the blaze of our fire. The young Count immediately seized his fowling piece, took fatal aim and in a twinkling the poor bird of ill omen came fluttering to the ground. Charley was now called upon to make and eat his dish of owl soup, but declined as he had not shot the bird.

In the course of the evening I paid a visit to the Captain's fire. It was composed of huge trunks of trees and of sufficient magnitude to roast a buffalo whole. Here were a number of the prime hunters and leaders of the camp, some sitting, some standing, and others lying on skins or blankets before the fire, telling old frontier stories about hunting and Indian warfare.

As the night advanced we perceived above the trees to the west, a ruddy glow flushing up the sky.

"That must be a prairie set on fire by the Osage hunters," said the Captain.

"It is at the Red Fork," said Beatte, regarding the sky. "It seems but three miles distant, yet it perhaps is twenty."

About half past eight o'clock a beautiful pale light gradually sprang up in the East, a precursor of the rising moon. Drawing off from the captain's lodge I now prepared for the nights repose. I had determined to abandon the shelter of the tent and henceforth to bivouack like the rangers. A bear skin spread at the foot of a tree was my bed, with a pair of saddle bags for a pillow. Wrapping myself in blankets I stretched myself on this hunter's couch, and soon fell into a sound and sweet sleep, from which I did not awake until the bugle sounded at day break.

CHAPTER XI

Breaking up of the encampment—Picturesque march—Game—Camp scenes—Triumph of a young hunter—Ill success of old hunters—Foul murder of a pole cat.

Oct. 14. At the signal note of the bugle the sentinels and patrols marched in from their stations around the camp and were dismissed. The rangers were roused from their nights repose and soon a bustling scene took place. While some cut wood, made fires and prepared the mornings meal others struck their foul weather shelters of blankets, and made every preparation for departure while others dashed about, through brush and brake catching the horses and leading or driving them into camp.

During all this bustle the forest rang with whoops, and shouts, and peals of laughter. When all had breakfasted, packed up their effects and camp equipage and loaded the pack horses, the bugle sounded to saddle and mount. By eight o'clock the whole troop set off in a long straggling line, with whoop and halloo, intermingled with many an oath at the loitering pack horses, and in a little while the forest which for several days had been the scene of such unwonted bustle and uproar relapsed into its primeval solitude and silence. It was a bright sunny morning with that pure transparent atmosphere that seems to bathe the very heart with gladness. Our march continued parallel to the Arkansas, through a rich and varied country; sometimes we had to break our way through alluvial bottoms matted with redundant vegetation where the gigantic trees were entangled with grape vines, hanging like cordage from their branches. Sometimes we coasted along sluggish brooks whose feebly trickling current just served to link together a succession of glassy pools, embedded like mirrors in the quiet bosom of the forest, reflecting its autumnal foliage, and patches of the clear blue sky. Sometimes we scrambled up broken and rocky hills from the summits of which we had wide views stretching on one side over distant prairies diversified by groves and forests and on the other ranging along a line of blue and shadowy hills beyond the waters of the Arkansas.

The appearance of our troop was suited to the country; stretching along in a line of upwards of half a mile in length, winding among brakes and bushes, and up and down the defiles of the hills: the men in every kind of uncouth garb, with long rifles on their shoulders, and mounted on horses of every colour. The pack horses too would incessantly wander from the line of march to crop the surrounding herbage and were banged and beaten back by Tonish and his half breed compeers, with vollies of mongrel oaths. Every now and then the notes of the bugle from the head of the column, would echo through the woodlands and along the hollow glens, summoning up stragglers and announcing the line of march. The whole scene reminded me of the descriptions given of bands of buccaneers penetrating the wilds of South America on their plundering expeditions against the Spanish settlements.

At one time we passed through a luxuriant bottom or meadow bordered by thickets where the tall grass was pressed down into numerous "deer beds," where those animals had couched the preceding night. Some oak trees also bore signs of having been clambered by bears, in quest of acorns, the marks of their claws being visible in the bark. As we opened a glade of this sheltered meadow we beheld several deer bounding away in wild affright, until, having gained some distance, they would stop and gaze back, with the curiosity common to this animal, at the strange intruders into their solitudes. There was immediately a sharp report of rifles in every direction, from the young huntsmen of the troop, but they were too eager to aim surely, and the deer, unharmed, bounded away into the depths of the forest.

In the course of our march we struck the Arkansas but found ourselves still below the Red Fork, and, as the river made deep bends, we again left its banks and continued through the woods until nearly three o'clock, when we encamped in a beautiful basin bordered by a fine stream, and shaded by clumps of lofty oaks.

The horses were now "hobbled," that is to say their fore legs were fettered with cords or leathern straps, so as to impede their movements, and prevent their wandering far from the camp; they were then turned loose to graze. A number of rangers, prime hunters, started off in different directions in search of game. There was no whooping or laughing about the camp as in the morning; all were either busy about the fires preparing the evenings repast or reposing upon the grass. Shots were soon heard in various directions. After a time a huntsman rode into the camp with the carcass of a fine buck hanging across his horse. Shortly after came in a couple of stripling hunters on foot, one of whom bore on his shoulders the body of a doe. He was evidently proud of his spoil, being probably one of his first achievements, though he and his companion were much bantered by their comrades, as young beginners who hunted in partnership.

Just as the night set in there was a great shouting at one end of the camp, and immediately afterwards a body of young rangers came parading round the various fires bearing one of their comrades in triumph on their shoulders. He had shot an elk for the first time in his life, and it was the first animal of the kind that had been killed on this expedition. The young huntsman, whose name was M'Lellan, was the hero of the camp for the night, and was the "father of the feast" into the bargain; for portions of his Elk were soon roasting at every fire.

The other hunters returned without success. The Captain had observed the tracks of a buffalo, which must have passed within a few days, and had tracked a bear for some distance until the foot prints had disappeared. He had seen an Elk too on the banks of the Arkansas, which walked out on a sand bar of the river, but before he could steal round through the bushes to get a shot it had re entered the woods.

Our own hunter Beatte returned, silent and sulky, from an unsuccessful hunt. As yet he had brought us in nothing, and we had depended for our supplies of venison upon the captain's mess. Beatte was evidently mortified, for he looked down with contempt upon the rangers, as raw and inexperienced woodmen, but little skilled in hunting lore. They, on the other hand, regarded Beatte with no very complacent eye, as one of an evil breed, and always spoke of him as "the Indian."

Our little Frenchman Tonish also, by his incessant boasting and chattering and gasconading, in his balderdashed dialect, had drawn upon himself the ridicule of many of the wags of the troop, who amused themselves at his expense in a vein of raillery by no means remarkable for its delicacy; but the little varlet was so completely fortified by vanity and self conceit that he was invulnerable to every joke. I must confess, however, that I felt a little mortified at the sorry figure our retainers were making among these moss troopers of the frontier. Even our very equipments came in for a share of unpopularity, and I heard many sneers at the double barreled guns with which we were provided against smaller game; the lads of the West holding "shot guns" as they call them in great contempt, thinking grouse, partridges, and even wild turkeys as beneath their serious attention, and the rifle the only fire arm worthy of a hunter.

I was awakened before daybreak the next morning by the mournful howling of a wolf, who was skulking about the purlieus of the camp attracted by the scent of venison. Scarcely had the first grey streak of dawn appeared when a youngster at one of the distant lodges, shaking off his sleep crowed in imitation of a cock with a loud clear note and prolonged cadence that would have done credit to the most veteran chanticleer. He was immediately answered from another quarter, as if from a rival rooster. The chaunt was echoed from lodge to lodge, and followed by the cackling of hens, quacking of ducks, gobbling of turkeys and grunting of swine, until we seemed to have been transported into the midst of a farm yard, with all its inmates in full concert around us.

After riding a short distance this morning we came upon a well worn Indian track and following it scrambled to the summit of a hill, whence we had a wide prospect over a country diversified by rocky ridges and waving lines of upland, and enriched by groves and clumps of trees of varied tint and foliage. At a distance to the west, to our great satisfaction we beheld the Red Fork rolling its ruddy current to the Arkansas, and found that we were above the point of junction. We now descended and pushed forward, with much difficulty, through the rich alluvial bottom that borders the Arkansas. Here the trees were interwoven with enormous grapevines, forming a kind of cordage, from trunk to trunk and limb to limb; there was a thick undergrowth also of bush and bramble, and such an abundance of hops, fit for gathering, that it was difficult for our horses to force their way through.

The soil was imprinted in many places with the tracks of deer, and the claws of bears were to be traced on various trees. Every one was on the look out in the hope of starting some game, when suddenly there was a bustle and a clamour of voices in a distant part of the line. A bear! A bear! was the cry. We all pressed forward to be present at the sport, when, to my infinite, though whimsical chagrin, I found it to be our two worthies Beatte and Tonish, perpetrating a foul murder on a pole cat, or skunk! The animal had ensconced itself beneath the trunk of a fallen tree, whence it kept up a vigorous defence in its peculiar style, until the surrounding forest was in a high state of fragrance.

Gibes and jeers now broke out on all sides at the expense of the Indian hunter and he was advised to wear the scalp of the skunk as the only trophy of his prowess. When they found, however, that he and Tonish were absolutely bent upon bearing off the carcass as a peculiar dainty there was a universal expression of disgust; and they were regarded as little better than cannibals.

Mortified at this ignominious debut of our two hunters, I insisted upon their abandoning their prize and resuming their march. Beatte complied, with a dogged discontented air, and lagged behind muttering to himself. Tonish, however, with his usual buoyancy consoled himself by vociferous eulogies on the richness and delicacy of a roasted pole cat, which he swore was considered the daintiest of dishes by all experienced Indian gourmands. It was with difficulty I could silence his loquacity by repeated and peremptory commands. A Frenchman's vivacity however, if repressed in one way will break out in another, and Tonish now eased off his spleen by bestowing vollies of oaths and dry blows on the pack horses. I was likely to be no gainer in the end by my opposition to the humours of these varlets, for after a time Beatte, who had lagged behind, rode up to the head of the line to resume his station as a guide, and I had the vexation to see the carcass of his prize, stripped of its skin, and looking like a fat sucking pig, dangling behind his saddle. I made a solemn vow, however, in secret that our fire should not be disgraced by the cooking of that pole cat.

CHAPTER XII

The crossing of the Arkansas.

We had now arrived at the river about a quarter of a mile above the junction of the Red Fork, but the banks were steep and crumbling, and the current was deep and rapid. It was impossible, therefore, to cross at this place, and we resumed our painful course through the forest, despatching Beatte ahead in search of a fording place. We had proceeded about a mile further when he rejoined us bringing intelligence of a place hard by, where the river, for a great part of its breadth, was rendered fordable by sand bars, and the remainder might easily be swam by the horses.

Here then we made a halt. Some of the rangers set to work vigorously with their axes felling trees on the edge of the river, wherewith to form rafts for the transportation of the baggage and camp equipage. Others patrolled the banks of the river farther up, in hopes of finding a better fording place; being unwilling to risk their horses in the deep channel.

It was now that our worthies Beatte and Tonish had an opportunity of displaying their Indian adroitness and resource. At the Osage village which we had passed a day or two before, they had procured a dried buffalo skin. This was now produced; cords were passed through a number of small eyelet holes with which it was bordered, and it was drawn up until it formed a kind of deep trough. Sticks were then placed athwart it on the inside to keep it in shape; our camp equipage and a part of our baggage were placed within and the singular bark was carried down the bank and set afloat. A cord was attached to the prow which Beatte took between his teeth and, throwing himself into the water, went ahead towing the bark after him, while Tonish followed behind, to keep it steady and to propel it. Part of the way they had foot hold and were enabled to wade, but in the main current they were obliged to swim. The whole way they whooped and yelled in the Indian style until they landed safely on the opposite shore.

The commissioner and myself were so well pleased with this Indian mode of ferriage that we determined to trust ourselves in the buffalo hide. Our companions the Count and Mr. L. had proceeded with the horses along the river bank, in search of a ford which some of the rangers had discovered about a mile and a half distant. While we were waiting for the return of our ferry men, I happened to cast my eyes upon a heap of luggage under a bush, and descried the sleek carcass of the pole cat, snugly trussed up and ready for roasting before the evening fire. I could not resist the temptation to plump it into the river, where it sank to the bottom like a lump of lead, and thus our lodge was relieved from the bad odour which this savoury viand had threatened to bring upon it.

Our men having recrossed with their cockleshell bark, it was drawn on shore, half filled with saddles, saddle bags and other luggage amounting to at least a hundred weight and being again placed in the water I was invited to take my seat. It appeared to me pretty much like the embarcation of the wise men of Gotham who went to sea in a bowl: I stepped in, however, without hesitation, though as cautiously as possible, and sat down on top of the luggage, the margin of the hide sinking to within a hands breadth of the water's edge. Rifles, fowling pieces and other articles of small bulk were then handed in until I protested against receiving any more freight. We then launched forth upon the stream, the bark being towed and propelled as before.

It was with a sensation half serious half comic that I found myself

thus afloat, on the skin of a buffalo, in the midst of a wild river, surrounded by wilderness and towed along by a half savage whooping and
yelling like a devil incarnate. To please the vanity of little Tonish I discharged the double barrelled gun to the right and left when in the centre
of the stream. The report echoed along the woody shores and was
answered by shouts from some of the rangers to the great exultation of
the little Frenchman, who took to himself the whole glory of this Indian mode of navigation.

Our voyage was accomplished happily; the Commissioner was ferried
across with equal success, and all our effects were brought over in the
same manner. Nothing could equal the vain glorious vapouring of little
Tonish, as he strutted about the shore and exulted in his superior skill
and knowledge to the rangers. Beatte, however, kept his proud saturnine
look, without a smile. He had a vast contempt for the ignorance of the
rangers and felt that he had been undervalued by them. His only
observation was, "Dey now see de Indian good for someting—any how!"

The broad sandy shore where we had landed was intersected by innumerable tracks of elk, deer, bears, raccoons, turkeys and waterfowl.
The river scenery at this place was beautifully diversified presenting long
shining reaches bordered by willows and cotton wood trees; rich bottoms with lofty forests among which towered enormous plane trees, and
the distance was closed in by high embowered promontories. The foliage
had a yellow autumnal tint which gave to the sunny landscape the golden
tone of one of the landscapes of Claude Lorraine. There was animation
given to the scene by a raft of logs and branches on which the Captain,
and his prime companion the Doctor were ferrying their effects across
the stream, and by a long line of rangers on horseback fording the river
obliquely along a series of sand bars about a mile and a half distant.

CHAPTER XIII

THE CAMP OF THE GLEN

*Camp gossip—Pawnees and their habits—A hunter's adventure—
Horses found and men lost.*

Being joined by the Captain and some of the rangers, we struck into the
woods for about half a mile and then entered a wild rocky dell, bordered
by two lofty ridges of lime stone which narrowed as we advanced, until
they met and united making almost an angle. Here a fine spring of water
rose from among the rocks and fed a silver rill that ran the whole length
of the dell freshening the grass with which it was carpeted.

In this rocky nook we encamped among tall trees. The rangers gradually joined us; straggling through the forest singly or in groupes; some on horseback, some on foot driving their horses before them heavily laden with baggage some dripping wet, having fallen into the river; for they had experienced much fatigue and trouble from the length of the ford, and the depth and rapidity of the stream. They looked not unlike banditti returning with their plunder, and the wild dell was a retreat worthy to receive them. The effect was heightened after dark, when the light of the fires was cast upon rugged looking groupes of men and horses; with baggage tumbled in heaps, rifles piled against the trees and saddles, bridles and powderhorns hanging about their trunks.

At the encampment we were joined by the young count, and his companion and the young half breed Antoine, who had all passed successfully by the ford. To my annoyance, however, I discovered that both of my horses were missing. I had supposed them in the charge of Antoine, but he with characteristic carelessness, had paid no heed to them and they had probably wandered from the line on the opposite side of the river. It was arranged that Beatte and Antoine should recross the river at an early hour of the morning in search of them.

A fat buck and a number of wild turkeys being brought into the camp, we managed, with the addition of a cup of coffee to make a comfortable supper: after which I repaired to the captain's lodge, which was a kind of council fire and gossipping place for the veterans of the camp.

As we were conversing together we observed, as on former nights, a dusky red glow in the west, above the summits of the surrounding cliffs; it was again attributed to Indian fires on the prairies; and supposed to be on the western side of the Arkansas. If so it was thought they must be made by some party of Pawnees, as the Osage hunters seldom ventured in that quarter. Our half breeds, however, pronounced them Osage fires, and that they were on the opposite side of the Arkansas.

The conversation now turned upon the Pawnees, into whose hunting grounds we were about entering. There is always some wild untamed tribe of Indians who form for a time the terror of a frontier, and about whom all kinds of fearful stories are told. Such at present was the case with the Pawnees who rove the regions between the Arkansas and the Red River, and the prairies of Texas. They were represented as admirable horsemen, and always on horseback; mounted on fleet and hardy steeds, the wild race of the prairies. With these they roam the great plains that extend about the Arkansas, the Red River, and through Texas to the Rocky Mountains, sometimes engaged in hunting the deer and buffalo, sometimes in warlike and predatory expeditions, for like their counterparts, the sons of Ishmael their hand is against every one, and every one's hand against them. Some of them have no fixed habitation, but dwell in tents of skins, easily packed up and transported so that they are here to day and away, no one knows where, tomorrow.

One of the veteran hunters gave several anecdotes of their mode of fighting. Luckless, according to his account, is the band of weary traders or hunters descried by them in the midst of a prairie. Sometimes they will steal upon them by stratagem hanging with one leg over the saddle and their bodies concealed, so that their troop at a distance has the appearance of a gang of wild horses. When they have thus gained sufficiently upon the enemy they will suddenly raise themselves in their saddles and come like a rushing blast all fluttering with feathers, shaking their mantles, brandishing their weapons and making hideous yells. In this way they seek to strike a panic into the horses and put them to the scamper, when they will pursue and carry them off in triumph.

The best mode of defence, according to this veteran woodman, is to get into the covert of some wood or thicket, or if there be none at hand, to dismount, tie the horses firmly head to head in a circle, so that they cannot break away and scatter, and resort to the shelter of a ravine, or make a hollow in the sand, where they may be screened from the shafts of the Pawnees. The latter chiefly use the bow and arrow and are dexterous archers, circling round and round their enemy and launching their arrows when at full speed. They are chiefly formidable on the prairies where they have free career for their horses and no trees to turn aside their arrows. They will rarely follow a flying enemy into the forest.

Several anecdotes also were given of the secrecy and caution with which they will follow and hang about the camp of an enemy, seeking a favorable moment for plunder or attack.

"We must now begin to keep a sharp look out," said the captain. "I must issue written orders that no man shall hunt without leave or fire off a gun, on pain of riding a wooden horse with a sharp back. I have a wild crew of young fellows, unaccustomed to frontier service. It will be difficult to teach them caution. We are now in the land of a silent, watchful, crafty people, who, when we least suspect it may be around us spying out all our movements and ready to pounce upon all stragglers."

"How will you be able to keep your men from firing, if they see game while strolling round the camp?" asked one of the rangers.

"They must not take their guns with them, unless they are on duty or have permission."

"Ah Captain!" cried the ranger, "that will never do for me. Where I go my rifle goes. I never like to leave it behind. It's like a part of myself. There's no one will take such care of it as I, and there's nothing will take such care of me as my rifle."

"There's truth in all that," said the captain touched by a true hunter's sympathy. "I've had my rifle pretty nigh as long as I have had my wife, and a faithful friend it has been to me."

Here the Doctor, who is as keen a hunter as the Captain, joined in the conversation. "A neighbor of mine says, next to my rifle I'd as leave lend you my wife."

"There's few," observed the Captain, "that take care of their rifles as they ought to be taken care of."

"Or of their wives either," replied the Doctor, with a wink.

"That's a fact," rejoined the Captain.

Word was now brought that a party of four rangers headed by "Old Ryan" were missing. They had separated from the main body, on the opposite side of the river, when searching for a ford, and had straggled off no body knew whither. Many conjectures were made about them and some apprehensions expressed for their safety.

"I should send to look after them," said the Captain, "but Old Ryan is with them and he knows how to take care of himself and of them too. If it were not for him I would not give much for the rest, but he is as much at home in the woods or on a prairie as he would be in his own farm yard. He's never lost wherever he is. There's a good gang of them to stand by one another; four to watch and one to take care of the fire."

"It's a dismal thing to get lost at night in a strange and wild country," said one of the younger rangers.

"Not if you have one or two in company," said an older one. "For my part I could feel as cheerful in this hollow as in my own home if I had but one comrade to take turns to watch and keep the fire going. I could lie here for hours and gaze up to that blazing star there, that seems to look down into the camp as if it were keeping guard over it."

"Aye, the stars are a kind of company to one, when you have to keep watch alone. That's a cheerful star too, some how, that's the evening star, the planet Venus they call it, I think."

"If that's the planet Venus," said one of the council, who I believe was the psalm singing school master, "it bodes us no good, for I recollect reading in some book that the Pawnees worship that star and sacrifice their prisoners to it. So I should not feel the better for the sight of that star in this part of the country."

"Well," said the sergeant, a thorough bred woodman, "star or no star, I have passed many a night alone in a wilder place than this, and slept sound too, I'll warrant you. Once however I had rather an uneasy time of it. I was belated in passing through a tract of wood near the Tombigbee river; so I struck a light, made a fire, and turned my horse loose while I stretched myself to sleep. By and bye I heard the wolves howl. My horse came crowding near me for protection; for he was terribly frightened. I drove him off but he returned, and drew nearer and nearer, and stood looking at me and at the fire, and dozing and nodding and tottering on his fore feet, for he was powerful tired. After a while I heard a strange dismal cry. I thought at first it might be an owl. I heard it again, and then I knew it was not an owl but must be a panther. I felt rather awkward, for I had no weapon but a double bladed pen knife. I, however, prepared for defence in the best way I could, and piled up small brands from the fire, to pepper him with should he come nigh. The company of my horse now seemed a comfort to me; the poor creature laid down beside me and soon fell asleep, being so tired. I kept watch and nodded and dozed, and started awake, and looked round expecting to see the glaring eyes of the panther close upon me; but some how or other fatigue got the better of me and I fell asleep outright. In the morning I found the tracks of a panther within sixty paces. They were as large as my two fists. He had evidently been walking backwards and forwards, trying to make up his mind to attack me: but luckily he had not courage."

Oct. 16. I awoke before day break. The moon was shining feebly down into the glen from among light drifting clouds, the camp fires were nearly burnt out, and the men lying about them, wrapped in blankets. With the first streak of day our huntsman Beatte, with Antoine the young half breed set off to recross the river in search of the stray horses, in company with several rangers who had left their rifles and baggage on the opposite shore. As the ford was deep and they were obliged to cross in a diagonal line, against a rapid current, they had to be mounted on the tallest and strongest horses.

By eight o'clock Beatte returned. He had found both horses but had lost Antoine. The latter he said was a boy, a green horn, that knew nothing of the woods. He had wandered out of sight of him and got lost. However there were plenty more for him to fall in company with, as some of the rangers had gone astray also, and Old Ryan and his party had not returned.

We waited until the morning was somewhat advanced, in hopes of being rejoined by the stragglers but they did not make their appearance. The Captain observed that the Indians on the opposite side of the river were all well disposed to the whites, so that no serious apprehensions need be entertained for the safety of the missing; the greatest danger was that their horses might be stolen in the night by straggling Osages. He determined, therefore, to proceed leaving a rear guard in the camp to await their arrival.

I sat on a rock that overhung the spring at the upper part of the dell, and amused myself by watching the changing scene before me. First the preparations for departure. Horses driven in from the purlieus of the camp; rangers riding about among rocks and bushes in quest of others that had strayed to a distance; the bustle of packing up camp equipage and the clamour after kettles and frying pans borrowed by one mess from another, mixed up with oaths and exclamations at restive horses, or others that had wandered away to graze after being packed: among which the voice of our little Frenchman Tonish was particularly to be distinguished.

The bugle sounded the signal to mount and march. The troop filed off in irregular line down the glen and through the open forest, winding and gradually disappearing among the trees, though the clamour of voices, and the notes of the bugle could be heard for some time afterwards. The rear guard remained under the trees in the lower part of the dell, some on horseback with their rifles on their shoulders; others seated by the fire or lying on the ground gossipping in a low lazy tone of voice, their horses unsaddled, standing and dozing around: while one of the rangers profiting by this interval of leisure, was shaving himself before a pocket mirror stuck against the trunk of a tree.

The clamour of voices and the notes of the bugle at length died away, and the glen relapsed into quiet and silence, broken occasionally by the low murmuring tones of the groupe around the fire, the pensive whistle of some laggard among the trees, or the rustling of the yellow leaves which the lightest breath of air brought down in wavering showers; a sign of the departing glories of the year.

CHAPTER XIV

Deer shooting—Life on the prairies—Beautiful encampment—Hunter's luck—Anecdotes of the Delawares and their superstitions.

Having passed through the skirt of woodland bordering the river, we ascended the hills, taking a westerly course through an undulating country, of "oak openings" where the eye stretched at times over wide tracts of hill and dale, diversified by forests, groves, and clumps of trees. As we were proceeding at a slow pace those who were at the head of the line descried four deer grazing on a grassy slope about half a mile distant. They apparently had not perceived our approach and continued to graze in perfect tranquility. A young ranger obtained permission from the Captain to go in pursuit of them, and the troop halted in lengthened line, watching him in silence. Walking his horse slowly and cautiously he made a circuit until a skreen of wood intervened between him and the deer. Dismounting then he left his horse among the trees, and creeping round a knoll, was hidden from our view. We now kept our eyes intently fixed on the deer, which continued grazing, unconscious of their danger. Presently there was the sharp report of a rifle; a fine buck made a convulsive bound and fell to the earth, his companions scampered off. Immediately our whole line of march was broken; there was a helter skelter gallopping of the youngsters of the troop, eager to get a shot at the fugitives; and one of the most conspicuous personages in the chase was our little Frenchman, Tonish, on his silver grey; having abandoned his pack horses at the first sight of the deer. It was some time before our scattered forces could be recalled by the bugle and our march resumed.

Two or three times in the course of the day we were interrupted by hurry scurry scenes of the kind. The young men of the troop were full of excitement on entering an unexplored country abounding in game, and they were too little accustomed to discipline or restraint to be kept in order. No one, however, was more unmanageable than Tonish. Having an intense conceit of his skill as a hunter and an irrepressible passion for display he was continually sallying forth, like an ill broken hound, whenever any game was started, and had as often to be whipped back.

At length his curiosity got a salutary check. A fat doe came bounding along in full sight of the whole line. Tonish dismounted, levelled his rifle and had a fair shot. The doe kept on. He sprang upon his horse, stood up on the saddle like a posture master and continued gazing after the animal as if certain to see it fall. The doe, however, kept on its way rejoicing: a laugh broke out along the line, the little Frenchman slipt quietly into his saddle, began to belabour and blaspheme the wandering pack horses, as if they had been to blame, and for some time we were relieved from his vaunting and vapouring.

In one part of our march we came to the remains of an old Indian encampment, on the banks of a fine stream, with the moss grown sculls of deer lying here and there, about it. As we were in the Pawnee country it was supposed, of course, to have been a camp of those formidable rovers; the Doctor, however, after considering the shape and disposition of the lodges pronounced it the camp of some bold Delawares, who had probably made a brief and dashing excursion into these dangerous hunting grounds.

Having proceeded some distance further we observed a couple of figures on horseback, slowly moving parallel to us along the edge of a naked hill about two miles distant; and apparently reconnoitering us. There was a halt and much gazing and conjecturing. Were they Indians? If Indians, were they Pawnees? There is something exciting to the imagination and stirring to the feelings, while traversing these hostile plains, in seeing a horseman prowling along the horizon. It is like descrying a sail at sea in time of war, when it may be either a privateer or a pirate. Our conjectures were soon set at rest by reconnoitering the two horsemen through a small spy glass when they proved to be two of the men we had left at the camp, who had set out to rejoin us and had wandered from the track.

Our march this day was animating and delightful. We were in a region of adventure; breaking our way through a country hitherto untrodden by white men, excepting perchance by some solitary trapper. The weather was in its perfection, temperate, genial and enlivening; a deep blue sky with a few light feathery clouds; an atmosphere of perfect transparency, an air pure and bland, and a glorious country spreading out far and wide in the golden sunshine of an autumnal day; but all silent, lifeless, without a human habitation and apparently without a human inhabitant!

It was as if a ban hung over this fair but fated region. The very Indians dared not abide here but made it a mere scene of perilous enterprize, to hunt for a few days and then away.

After a march of about fifteen miles west we encamped in a beautiful peninsula made by the windings and doublings of a deep, clear and almost motionless brook, and covered by an open grove of lofty and magnificent trees. Several hunters immediately started forth in quest of game before the noise of the camp should frighten it from the vicinity. Our man Beatte also took his rifle and went forth alone, in a different course from the rest.

For my own part, I laid on the grass under the trees, and built castles in the clouds, and indulged in the very luxury of rural repose. Indeed I can scarcely conceive a kind of life more calculated to put both mind and body in a healthful tone. A mornings ride of several hours diversified by hunting incidents, an encampment in the afternoon under some noble grove on the borders of a stream; an evening banquet of venison fresh killed; roasted, or broiled on the coals; turkeys just from the thickets and wild honey from the trees: and all relished with an appetite unknown to the gourmets of the cities. And then at night—such sweet sleeping in the open air; or waking and gazing at the moon and stars, shining between the branches of the trees!

On the present occasion, however, we had not much reason to boast of our larder. But one deer had been killed during the day, and none of that had reached our lodge. We were fain, therefore, to stay our keen appetites by some scraps of turkey brought from the last encampment, eked out with a slice or two of salt pork. This scarcity, however, did not continue long. Before dark a young hunter returned well laden with spoil. He had shot a deer, cut it up in an artist like style, and, putting the meat in a kind of sack made of the hide, had slung it across his shoulder and trudged with it to camp.

Not long after, Beatte made his appearance with a fat doe across his horse. It was the first game he had brought in, and I was glad to see him with a trophy that might efface the memory of the pole cat. He laid the carcass down by our fire without saying a word, and then turned to unsaddle his horse: nor could any questions from us about his hunting draw from him more than laconic replies. If Beatte however observed this Indian taciturnity about what he had done, Tonish made up for it by boasting of what he meant to do. Now that we were in a good hunting country he meant to take the field, and, if we would take his word for it, our lodge would henceforth be overwhelmed with game. Luckily his talking did not prevent his working, the doe was skilfully dissected, several fat ribs roasted before the fire, the coffee kettle replenished, and in a little while we were enabled to indemnify ourselves luxuriously for our late meagre repast.

The Captain did not return until late and he returned empty handed. He had been in pursuit of his usual game the deer, when he came upon the tracks of a gang of about sixty Elk. Having never killed an animal of the kind, and the elk being at this moment an object of ambition among all the veteran hunters of the camp, he abandoned his pursuit of the deer, and followed the newly discovered track. After some time he came in sight of the elk and had several fair chances of a shot, but was anxious to bring down a large buck which kept in the advance. Finding at length, that there was danger of the whole gang escaping him he fired at a doe. The shot took effect, but the animal had sufficient strength to keep on for a time with its companions. From the tracks of blood he felt confident it was mortally wounded, but evening came on, he could not keep the trail and had to give up the search until morning.

Old Ryan and his little band had not yet rejoined us, neither had our young half breed Antoine made his appearance. It was determined therefore to remain at our encampment for the following day, to give time for all stragglers to arrive.

The conversation, this evening, among the old huntsmen turned upon the Delaware tribe, one of whose encampments we had passed in the course of the day; and anecdotes were given of their prowess in war and dexterity in hunting. They used to be deadly foes of the Osages who stood in great awe of their desperate valour though they were apt to attribute it to a whimsical cause. "Look at dem Delawares," would they say, "dey got short leg—no can run—must stand and fight a great heap." In fact the Delawares are rather short legged while the Osages are remarkable for length of limb.

The expeditions of the Delawares whether of war or hunting are wide and fearless; a small band of them will penetrate far into these dangerous and hostile wilds, and will push their encampments even to the Rocky

Mountains. This daring temper may be in some measure encouraged by one of the superstitions of their creed. They believe that a guardian spirit, in the form of a great eagle, watches over them, hovering in the sky, far out of sight. Sometimes, when well pleased with them, he wheels down into the lower regions and may be seen circling with wide spread wings against the white clouds: at such times the seasons are propitious the corn grows finely, and they have great success in hunting. Sometimes however, he is angry, and then he vents his rage in the thunder, which is his voice, and the lightning, which is the flashing of his eye, and strikes dead the object of his displeasure.

The Delawares make sacrifices to this spirit, who occasionally lets drop a feather from his wing in token of satisfaction. These feathers render the wearer invincible, and invulnerable. Indeed the Indians generally consider the feathers of the eagle possessed of occult and sovereign virtues.

At one time a party of Delawares, in the course of a bold incursion into the Pawnee hunting grounds were surrounded on one of the great plains, and nearly destroyed. The remnant took refuge on the summit of one of those isolated and conical hills that rise almost like artificial mounds, from the midst of the prairies. Here the chief warrior, driven almost to despair, sacrificed his horse to the tutelar spirit. Suddenly an enormous eagle rushing down from the sky bore off the victim in his talons and mounting into the air, dropped a quill feather from his wing. The chief caught it up with joy, bound it to his forehead and, leading his followers down the hill, cut his way through the enemy with great slaughter, and without any one of his party receiving a wound.

CHAPTER XV

THE ELK CAMP

The search for the elk—Pawnee stories.

With the morning dawn the prime hunters of the camp were all on the alert, and set off in different directions to beat up the country for game. The Captain's brother, Sergeant Bean, was among the first, and returned before breakfast with success, having killed a fat doe almost within the purlieus of the camp.

When breakfast was over the Captain mounted his horse to go in quest of the Elk which he had wounded on the preceding evening, and which, he was persuaded, had received its death wound. I determined to join him in the search and we accordingly sallied forth together, accompanied also by his brother the sergeant and a lieutenant. Two rangers followed on foot, to bring home the carcass of the doe which the sergeant had killed. We had not ridden far when we came to where it lay on the side of a hill, in the midst of a beautiful woodland scene. The two rangers immediately fell to work, with true hunters' skill, to dismember it, and prepare it for transportation to the camp, while we continued on our course. We passed along sloping hill sides, among skirts of thicket and scattered forest trees until we came to a place where the long herbage was pressed down with numerous elk beds. Here the captain had first roused the gang of elks, and, after looking about diligently for a little while, he pointed out their "trail," the foot prints of which were as large as those of horned cattle. He now put himself upon the track and went quietly forward, the rest of us following him in Indian file. At length he halted at the place where the elk had been when shot at. Spots of blood on the surrounding herbage shewed that the shot had been effective. The wounded animal had evidently kept for some distance with the rest of the herd, as could be seen by sprinklings of blood here and there on the shrubs and weeds bordering the trail. These at length suddenly disappeared. "Somewhere hereabout," said the Captain, "the elk must have turned off from the gang. Whenever they feel themselves mortally wounded they will turn aside, and seek some out of the way place to die alone."

There was something in this picture of the last moments of a wounded deer to touch the sympathies of one not hardened to the gentle disports of the chase; such sympathies, however, are but transient. Man is naturally an animal of prey, and, however changed by civilization, will readily relapse into his instinct for destruction. I found my ravenous and sanguinary propensities daily growing stronger upon the prairies.

After looking about for a little while the captain succeeded in finding the separate trail of the wounded elk, which turned off almost at right angles from that of the herd and entered an open forest of scattered trees. The traces of blood became more faint and rare, and occurred at greater distances: at length they ceased altogether, and the ground was so hard and the herbage so much parched and withered, that the foot prints of the animal could no longer be perceived.

"The elk must lie some where in this neighborhood," said the Captain, "as you may know by those turkey buzzards wheeling about in the air: for they always hover in that way above some carcass. However, the dead elk cannot get away, so let us follow the trail of the living ones: they may have halted at no great distance and we may find them grazing and get another crack at them."

We accordingly returned and resumed the trail of the Elks which led us a straggling course over hill and dale covered with scattered oaks.

Every now and then we would catch a glimpse of a deer bounding away across some glade of the forest, but the Captain was not to be diverted from his elk hunt by such inferior game. A large flock of wild turkeys too were roused by the trampling of our horses, some scampered off as fast as their long legs could carry them: others fluttered up into the trees, where they remained with outstretched necks, gazing at us. The Captain would not allow a rifle to be discharged at them, lest it should alarm the elk which he hoped to find in the vicinity. At length we came to where the forest ended in a steep bank, and the Red Fork wound its way below us, between broad sandy shores. The trail descended the bank and we could trace it, with our eyes, across the level sands until it terminated in the river, which, it was evident, the gang had forded on the preceding evening.

"It is needless to follow on any further," said the Captain. "The elk must have been much frightened, and, after crossing the river may have kept on for twenty miles without stopping."

Our little party now divided, the lieutenant and sergeant making a circuit in quest of game, and the Captain and myself taking the direction of the camp. On our way we came to a buffalo track more than a year old. It was not wider than an ordinary foot path and worn deep into the soil; for these animals follow each other in single file. Shortly afterwards we met two rangers on foot, hunting. They had wounded an elk, but he had escaped; and in pursuing him had found the one shot by the captain on the preceding evening. They turned back and conducted us to it. It was a noble animal, as large as a yearling heifer, and lay in an open part of the forest about a mile and a half distant from the place where it had been shot. The turkey buzzards which we had previously noticed were wheeling in the air above it. The observation of the captain seemed verified. The poor animal, as life was ebbing away, had apparently abandoned its unhurt companions, and turned aside to die alone.

The Captain and the two rangers forthwith fell to work, with their hunting knives, to flay and cut up the carcass. It was already tainted on the inside, but ample collops were cut from the ribs and haunches, and laid in a heap on the outstretched hide. Holes were then cut along the border of the hide, raw thongs were passed through them, and the whole drawn up like a sack, which was swung behind the Captain's saddle. All this while the turkey buzzards were soaring over head, waiting for our departure, to swoop down and banquet on the carcass.

The wreck of the poor Elk being thus dismantled the captain and myself mounted our horses and jogged back to the camp, while the two rangers resumed their hunting.

On reaching the camp I found there our young half breed Antoine.

After separating from Beatte, in the search after the stray horses on the other side of the Arkansas, he had fallen upon a wrong track which he followed for several miles; when he overtook Old Ryan and his party and found he had been following their traces.

They all forded the Arkansas about eight miles above our crossing place, and found their way to our late encampment in the glen, where the rear guard we had left behind was waiting for them. Antoine being well mounted and somewhat impatient to rejoin us had pushed on alone following our trail to our present encampment, and bringing the carcass of a young bear which he had killed.

Our camp during the residue of the day presented a mingled picture of bustle and repose. Some of the men were busy round the fires jerking and roasting venison and bear's meat, to be packed up as a future supply. Some were stretching and dressing the skins of the animals they had killed, others were washing their clothes in the brook and hanging them on the bushes to dry, while many were lying on the grass and lazily gossipping in the shade. Every now and then a hunter would return, on horseback or on foot, laden with game, or empty handed. Those who brought home any spoil deposited it at the captain's fire, and then filed off to their respective messes to relate their days exploits to their companions. The game killed at this camp consisted of six deer, one elk, two bears and six or eight turkeys.

During the last two or three days, since their wild Indian achievement in navigating the river, our retainers had risen in consequence among the rangers, and now I found Tonish making himself a complete oracle among some of the raw and inexperienced recruits, who had never been in the wilderness. He had continually a knot hanging about him and listening to his extravagant tales about the Pawnees, with whom he pretended to have often had fearful encounters. His representations, in fact, were calculated to inspire his hearers with an awful idea of the foe into whose lands they were intruding. According to his accounts the rifle of the white man was no match for the bow and arrow of the Pawnee. When the rifle was once discharged, it took time and trouble to load it again, and in the mean time the enemy could keep on launching his shafts as fast as he could draw his bow. Then the Pawnee, according to Tonish, could shoot with unerring aim three hundred yards, and send his arrow clean through and through a buffalo; nay he had known a Pawnee shaft pass through one buffalo and wound another. And then the way the Pawnees sheltered themselves from the shots of their enemy: they would hang with one leg over the saddle crouching their bodies along the opposite side of their horse, and would shoot their arrows from under his neck, while at full speed!

If Tonish was to be believed there was peril at every step in these debateable grounds of the Indian tribes. Pawnees lurked unseen among the thickets and ravines. They had their scouts and sentinels on the summit of the mounds which command a view over the prairies, where they lay crouched in the tall grass only now and then raising their heads to watch the movements of any war or hunting party that might be passing in lengthened line below. At night they would lurk round an encampment; crawling through the grass, and imitating the movements of a wolf, so as to deceive the centinel on the outpost, until, having arrived sufficently near, they would speed an arrow through his heart, and retreat undiscovered. In telling his stories Tonish would appeal from time to time to Beatte for the truth of what he said; the only reply would be a nod or shrug of the shoulders; the latter being divided in mind between a distaste for the gasconading spirit of his comrade, and a sovereign contempt for the inexperience of the young rangers in all that he considered true knowledge.

CHAPTER XVI

A sick camp—The march—The disabled horse—Old Ryan and the stragglers—Symptoms of change of weather and change of humours.

Oct. 18. We prepared to march at the usual hour but word was brought to the Captain that three of the rangers, who had been attacked with the meazles, were unable to proceed, and that another one was missing. The last was an old frontiers man, by the name of Sawyer, who had gained years without experience; and having sallied forth to hunt on the preceding day, had probably lost his way on the prairies. A guard of ten men was, therefore, left to take care of the sick, and wait for the straggler. If the former recovered sufficiently in the course of two or three days they were to rejoin the main body, other wise to be escorted back to the garrison.

Taking our leave of the sick camp we shaped our course westward along the heads of small streams, all wandering, in deep ravines, towards the Red Fork. The land was high and undulating, or "rolling" as it is termed in the West; with a poor hungry soil mingled with the sandstone, which is universal in this part of the country, and checquered with harsh forests of post oak and black jack.

In the course of the morning I received a lesson on the importance of being chary of one's steed on the prairies. The one I rode surpassed in action most horses of the troop, and was of great mettle and a generous spirit. In crossing the deep ravines he would scramble up the steep banks like a cat, and was always for leaping the narrow runs of water. I was not aware of the imprudence of indulging him in such exertions, until, in leaping him across a small brook, I felt him immediately falter beneath me. He limped forward a short distance but soon fell stark lame, having sprained his shoulder. What was to be done? He could not keep up with the troop, and was too valuable to be abandoned on the prairie. The only alternative was to send him back to join the invalids in the sick camp, and, to share their fortunes. Nobody, however, seemed disposed to lead him back, although I offered a liberal reward. Either the stories of Tonish about the Pawnees had spread an apprehension of lurking foes, and imminent perils on the prairies; or there was a fear of missing the trail and getting lost. At length two young men stepped forward and agreed to go in company, so that, should they be benighted on the prairies, there might be one to watch while the other slept.

The horse was accordingly consigned to their care, and I looked after him with a rueful eye as he limped off, for it seemed as if, with him, all strength and buoyancy had departed from me.

I looked round for a steed to supply his place and fixed my eye upon the gallant grey which I had transferred at the Agency to Tonish. The moment, however, that I hinted about his dismounting and taking up with the supernumerary pony the little varlet broke out into vociferous remonstrances and lamentations, gasping and almost strangling, in his eagerness to give vent to them. I saw that to unhorse him would be to prostrate his spirit and cut his vanity to the quick. I had not the heart to inflict such a wound, or to bring down the poor devil from his transient vain glory: so I left him in possession of his gallant grey; and contented myself with shifting my saddle to the jaded pony.

I was now sensible of the complete reverse to which a horseman is exposed on the prairies. I felt how completely the spirit of the rider depends upon his steed. I had hitherto been able to make excursions at will from the line, and to gallop in pursuit of any object of interest or curiosity. I was now reduced to the tone of the jaded animal I bestrode, and doomed to plod on patiently and slowly after my file leader. Above all, I was made conscious how unwise it is, in expeditions of the kind, where a man's life may depend upon the strength and speed, and freshness of his horse, to task the generous animal by any unnecessary exertion of his powers.

I have observed that the wary and experienced huntsman and traveller of the prairies is always sparing of his horse, when on a journey; never, except in emergency, putting him off of a walk. The regular journeyings of frontiers men and Indians when on a long march seldom exceed above fifteen miles a day, and are generally about ten or twelve, and they never indulge in capricious galloping. Many of those, however, with whom I was travelling, were young and inexperienced and full of excitement at finding themselves in a country abounding with game. It was impossible to retain them in the sobriety of a march, or to keep them to the line. As we broke our way through the coverts and ravines, and the deer started up and scampered off to the right and left, the rifle balls would whiz after them and our young hunters dash off in pursuit. At one time they made a grand burst after what they supposed to be a gang of bears, but soon pulled up on discovering them to be black wolves, prowling in company.

After a march of about twelve miles we encamped, a little after mid day, on the borders of a brook which loitered through a deep ravine. In the course of the afternoon "Old Ryan" the Nestor of the camp made his appearance followed by his little band of stragglers. He was greeted with joyful acclamations, which shewed the estimation in which he was held by his brother woodmen. The little band came laden with venison; a fine haunch of which the veteran hunter laid, as a present, by the Captain's fire.

Our men Beatte and Tonish both sallied forth early in the afternoon, to hunt. Towards evening the former returned with a fine buck across his horse. He laid it down, as usual, in silence, and proceeded to unsaddle and turn his horse loose. Tonish came back without any game, but with much more glory; having made several capital shots, though unluckily the wounded deer had all escaped him.

There was an abundant supply of meat in the camp; for, beside other game, three elk had been killed. The wary and veteran woodmen were all busy jerking meat against a time of scarcity; the less experienced revelled in present abundance leaving the morrow to provide for itself.

On the following morning (Oct. 19) I succeeded in changing my pony and a reasonable sum of money for a strong and active horse. It was a great satisfaction to find myself once more tolerably well mounted. I perceived, however, that there would be little difficulty in making a selection from among the troop, for the rangers had all that propensity for "swapping" or, as they term it "trading" which pervades the West. In the course of our expedition, there was scarce a horse, rifle, powder horn, or blanket that did not change owners several times; and one keen "trader" boasted of having by dint of frequent bargains changed a bad horse into a good one and put a hundred dollars in his pocket.

The morning was lowering and sultry with low muttering of distant thunder. The change of weather had its effect upon the spirits of the troop. The camp was unusually sober and quiet; there was none of the accustomed farm yard melody of crowing and cackling at day break; none of the bursts of merriment, the loud jokes and banterings that had commonly prevailed during the bustle of equipment. Now and then might be heard a short strain of a song, a faint laugh or a solitary whistle, but in general every one went silently and doggedly about the duties of the camp, or the preparations for departure.

When the time arrived to saddle and mount five horses were reported as missing although all the woods and thickets had been beaten up for some distance round the camp. Several rangers were despatched to "skir" the country round in quest of them. In the mean time the thunder continued to growl and we had a passing shower. The horses, like their riders, were affected by the change of weather. They stood here and there about the camp, some saddled and bridled, others loose, but all spiritless and dozing, with stooping head, one hind leg partly drawn up so as to rest on the point of the hoof, and the whole hide reeking with the rain and sending up wreaths of vapour. The men, too, waited in listless groupes the return of their comrades who had gone in quest of the horses, now and then turning up an anxious eye to the drifting clouds, which boded an approaching storm. Gloomy weather inspires gloomy thoughts. Some expressed fears that we were dogged by some party of Indians who had stolen the horses in the night. The most prevalent apprehension, however, was, that they had returned on their traces to our last encampment, or had started off on a direct line for Fort Gibson. In this respect the instinct of horses is said to resemble that of the pigeon. They will strike for home by a direct course, passing through tracts of wilderness which they have never before traversed.

After delaying until the morning was somewhat advanced, a lieutenant with a guard was appointed to await the return of the rangers and we set off on our days journey; considerably reduced in numbers, much as I thought to the discomposure of some of the troop who intimated that we might prove too weak handed in case of an encounter with the Pawnees.

CHAPTER XVII

Thunder storm on the prairies—The storm encampment—Night scene —Indian stories—A frightened horse.

Our march for a part of the day, lay a little to the south of west, through straggling forests of the kind of low scrubbed trees already mentioned, called "post oaks" and "black jacks." The soil of these "oak barrens" is loose and unsound, being little better at times than a mere quicksand in which, in rainy weather the horse's hoof slips from side to side, and now and then sinks in a rotten spongy turf to the fetlock. Such was the case at present in consequence of successive thundershowers, through which we draggled along in dogged silence. Several deer were roused by our approach and scudded across the forest glades, but no one, as formerly, broke the line of march to pursue them. At one time we passed the bones and horns of a buffalo, and at another time a Buffalo track, not above three days old. These signs of the vicinity of this grand game of the prairies had a reviving effect on the spirits of our huntsmen, but it was of transient duration.

In crossing a prairie of moderate extent, rendered little better than a slippery bog by the recent showers, we were overtaken by a violent thundergust. The rain came rattling upon us in torrents and spattered up like steam along the ground; the whole landscape was suddenly wrapped in gloom that gave a vivid effect to the intense sheets of lightning, while the thunder seemed to burst over our very heads, and was reverberated by the groves and forests that checquered and skirted the prairie. Man and beast were so pelted, drenched and confounded that the line was thrown in complete confusion; some of the horses were so frightened as to be almost unmanageable, and our scattered cavalcade looked like a tempest tost fleet, driven hither and thither at the mercy of wind and wave.

At length, at half past two o'clock, we came to a halt, and, gathering together our forces, encamped in an open and lofty grove with a prairie on one side and a stream on the other. The forest immediately rung with the sound of the axe, and the crash of falling trees. Huge fires were soon blazing; blankets were stretched before them by way of tents; booths were hastily reared of bark and skins; every fire had its groupe drawn close round it, drying and warming themselves or perparing a comforting meal. Some of the rangers were discharging and cleaning their rifles which had been exposed to the rain, while the horses, relieved from their saddles and burthens, rolled in the wet grass.

The showers continued from time to time until late in the evening. Before dark our horses were gathered in and tethered about the skirts of the camp, within the outposts through fear of Indian prowlers; who are apt to take advantage of stormy nights for their depredations and assaults. As the night thickened the huge fires became more and more luminous lighting up masses of the overhanging foliage, and leaving other parts of the grove in deep gloom. Every fire had its goblin groupe around it, while tethered horses were dimly seen, like spectres, among the thickets excepting that here and there a grey one stood out in bright relief.

The grove thus fitfully lighted up by the ruddy glare of the fires resembled a vast leafy dome, walled in by opaque darkness; but every now and then two or three quivering flashes of lightning in quick succession would suddenly reveal a vast champaign country where fields and forests and running streams, would start as it were into existence for a few brief seconds, and, before the eye could ascertain them, vanish again into gloom.

A thunder storm on a prairie as upon the ocean, derives grandeur and sublimity from the wild and boundless waste over which it rages and bellows. It is not surprizing that these awful phenomena of nature should be objects of superstitious reverence to the poor savages, and that they should consider the thunder the angry voice of the great spirit. As our half breeds sat gossipping round the fire, I drew from them some of the notions entertained on the subject by their Indian friends. The latter declare that extinguished thunder bolts are sometimes picked up by hunters on the prairies, who use them for the heads of arrows and lances, and that any warrior, thus armed, is invincible. Should a thunder storm occur, however, during battle he is liable to be carried away by the thunder and never heard of more.

A warrior of the Konza tribe, hunting on a prairie was overtaken by a storm, and struck down senseless by the thunder. On recovering he beheld the thunder bolt lying on the ground and a horse standing beside it. Snatching up the bolt he sprang upon the horse but found, too late that he was astride of the lightning. In an instant he was whisked away over prairies, and forests, and streams, and deserts until he was flung senseless at the foot of the Rocky Mountains, whence, on recovering, it took him several months to return to his own people.

This story reminded me of an Indian tradition, related by a traveller, of the fate of a warrior who saw the thunder lying upon the ground with a beautifully wrought moccasin on each side of it. Thinking he had found a prize he put on the moccasins; but they bore him away to the land of spirits, whence he never returned.

These are simple and artless tales, but they had a wild and romantic interest heard from the lips of half savage narrators, round a hunter's fire, in a stormy night with a forest on one side and a howling waste on the other: and, where peradventure savage foes might be lurking in the outer darkness.

Our conversation was interrupted by a loud clap of thunder, followed immediately by the sound of a horse galloping off madly into the waste. Every one listened in mute silence. The hoofs resounded vigorously for a time but grew fainter and fainter, until they died away in remote distance.

When the sound was no longer to be heard the listeners turned to conjecture what could have caused this sudden scamper. Some thought the horse had been startled by the thunder; others that some lurking Indian had mounted and gallopped off with him. To this it was objected, that the usual mode with the Indians is to steal quietly upon the horse, take off his fetters, mount him gently, and walk him off as silently as possible, leading off others, without any unusual stir or noise to disturb the camp.

On the other hand, it was stated as a common practice with the Indians to creep among a troop of horses when grazing at night, mount one quietly and then start off suddenly at full speed. Nothing is so contagious among horses as a panic, one sudden break away of this kind will sometimes alarm the whole troop, and they will set off, helter skelter, after the leader.

Every one who had a horse grazing on the skirts of the camp was uneasy lest his should be the fugitive, but it was impossible to ascertain the fact until morning. Those who had tethered their horses felt more secure, though horses thus tied up and limited to a short range at night are apt to fall off in flesh and strength, during a long march; and many of the horses of the troop already gave signs of being way worn.

After a gloomy and unruly night the morning dawned bright and clear, and a glorious sunrise transformed the whole landscape, as if by magic. The late dreary wilderness brightened into a fine open country with stately groves and clumps of oaks of a gigantic size, some of which stood singly as if planted for ornament and shade in the midst of rich meadows, while our horses scattered about and grazing under them gave to the whole the air of a noble park. It was difficult to realize the fact that we were so far in the wilds beyond the residence of man. Our encampment, alone, had a savage appearance; with its rude tents of skins and blankets; and its columns of blue smoke rising among the trees.

The first care in the morning was to look after our horses. Some of them had wandered to a distance but all were fortunately found: even the one whose clattering hoofs had caused such uneasiness in the night. He had come to a halt about a mile from the camp and was found quietly grazing near a brook.

The Bugle sounded for departure about half past eight. As we were in greater risk of Indian molestation the farther we advanced, our line was formed with more precision than heretofore. Every one had his station assigned him and was forbidden to leave it in pursuit of game without special permission. The pack horses were placed in the centre of the line and a strong guard in the rear.

CHAPTER XVIII

*A grand prairie—Cliff Castle—Buffalo tracks—Deer hunted by wolves
—Cross Timber.*

After a toilsome march of some distance through a country cut up by
ravines and brooks, and entangled by thickets, we emerged upon a
grand prairie. Here one of the characteristic scenes of the Far West
broke upon us. An immense extent of grassy undulating, or as it is
termed, rolling country with here and there a clump of trees, dimly seen
in the distance like a ship at sea; the landscape deriving sublimity from
its vastness and simplicity. To the south west on the summit of a hill
was a singular crest of broken rocks resembling a ruined fortress. It
reminded me of the ruin of some Moorish castle crowning a height in
the midst of a lonely Spanish landscape. To this hill we gave the name
of Cliff Castle.

The prairies of these great hunting regions differed in the character
of their vegetation from those through which I had hitherto passed. Instead of a profusion of tall flowering plants and long flaunting grasses,
they were covered with a shorter growth of herbage called Buffalo grass,
somewhat coarse, but, at the proper seasons, affording excellent and
abundant pasturage. At present it was growing wiry, and in many places
was too much parched for grazing.

The weather was verging into that serene but somewhat arid season
called The Indian Summer. There was a smoky haze in the atmosphere
that tempered the brightness of the sunshine into a golden tint, softening
the features of the landscape and giving a vagueness to the outlines of
distant objects. This haziness was daily increasing and was attributed
to the burning of distant prairies by the Indian hunting parties.

We had not gone far upon the prairie before we came to where deeply
worn footpaths were seen traversing the country: sometimes two or
three would keep on parallel to each other and but a few paces apart.
These were pronounced to be traces of buffalos, where large droves had
passed. There were tracks also of horses, which were observed with some
attention by our experienced hunters. They could not be the tracks of
wild horses, as there were no prints of the hoofs of colts, all were full
grown. As the horses evidently were not shod, it was concluded they
must belong to some hunting party of Pawnees. In the course of the
morning the tracks of a single horse, with shoes, were discovered. This
might be the horse of a Cherokee hunter; or perhaps a horse stolen from
the whites of the frontier. Thus in traversing these perilous wastes every
foot print and dint of hoof becomes matter of cautious inspection and
shrewd surmise; and the question continually is, whether it be the trace

of friend or foe; whether of recent or ancient date, and whether the being that made it be out of reach, or liable to be encountered.

We were getting more and more into the game country: as we proceeded we repeatedly saw deer to the right and left, bounding off for the coverts; but their appearance no longer excited the same eagerness to pursue. In passing along a slope of the prairie between two rolling swells of land we came in sight of a genuine natural hunting match. A pack of seven black wolves and one white one were in full chase of a buck which they had nearly tired down. They crossed the line of our march without apparently perceiving us; we saw them have a fair run of nearly a mile, gaining upon the buck until they were leaping upon his haunches when he plunged down a ravine. Some of our party gallopped to a rising ground commanding a view of the ravine. The poor buck was completely beset, some on his flanks, some at his throat: he made two or three struggles and desperate bounds but was dragged down, overpowered and torn to pieces. The black wolves in their ravenous hunger and fury took no notice of the distant group of horsemen, but the white wolf, apparently less game, abandoned the prey and scampered over hill and dale, rousing various deer that were crouched in the hollows, and which bounded off likewise in different directions. It was altogether a wild scene, worthy of the "hunting grounds."

We now came once more in sight of the Red Fork, winding its turbid course between well wooded hills and through a vast and magnificent landscape. The prairies, bordering on the rivers, are always varied, in this way, with woodland, so beautifully interspersed as to appear to have been laid out by the hand of taste; and they only want here and there a village spire, the battlements of a castle, or the turrets of an old family mansion rising from among the trees, to rival the most ornamented scenery of Europe.

About midday we reached the edge of that scattered belt of forest land, about forty miles in width, which stretches across the country from north to south, from the Arkansas to the Red River, separating the upper from the lower prairies, and commonly called the "Cross Timber." On the skirts of this forest land, just on the edge of a prairie, we found traces of a Pawnee Encampment of between one and two hundred lodges, shewing that the party must have been numerous. The scull of a buffalo lay near the camp, and the moss which had gathered on it shewed that the encampment was at least a year old. About half a mile off we encamped in a beautiful grove watered by a fine spring and rivulet. Our days journey had been about fourteen miles.

In the course of the afternoon we were rejoined by two of Lieutenant King's party which we had left behind a few days before, to look after stray horses. All the horses had been found, though some had wandered to the distance of several miles. The lieutenant, with seventeen of his companions, had remained at our last nights encampment to hunt, having come upon recent traces of buffalo. They had also seen a fine wild horse which, however, had gallopped off with a speed that defied pursuit.

Confident anticipations were now indulged that on the following day we should meet with buffalo, and perhaps with wild horses, and every one was in spirits. We needed some excitement of the kind, for our young men were growing weary of marching and encamping under restraint, and provisions this day were scanty. The captain and several of the rangers went out hunting but brought home nothing but a small deer and a few turkeys. Our two men Beatte and Tonish likewise went out. The former returned with a deer athwart his horse, which as usual he laid down by our lodge and said nothing: Tonish returned with no game but with his customary budget of wonderful tales. Both he and the deer had done marvels. Not one had come within the level of his rifle without being hit in a mortal part, yet strange to say every one had kept on his way without flinching. We all determined that from the wonderful accuracy of his aim Tonish must have shot with charmed balls, but that every deer had a charmed life. The most important intelligence brought by him, however, was, that he had seen the fresh tracks of several wild horses. He now considered himself upon the eve of great exploits, for there was nothing upon which he glorified himself more than his skill in horse catching.

CHAPTER XIX

Hunters' anticipations—The rugged ford—A wild horse.

Oct. 21. This morning the camp was in a bustle at an early hour: the expectation of falling in with buffalo in the course of the day roused every one's spirit. There was a continual cracking off of rifles, that they might be reloaded: the shot was drawn off from double barrelled guns and balls were substituted. Tonish, however, prepared chiefly for a campaign against wild horses.

He took the field with a coil of cordage hung at his saddle bow, and a couple of white wands something like fishing rods, eight or ten feet in length, with forked ends. The coil of cordage thus used in hunting the wild horse, is called a lariat, and answers to the laso of South America. It is not flung, however, in the graceful and dexterous Spanish style. The hunter after a hard chase, when he succeeds in getting almost head and head with the wild horse, hitches the running noose of the lariat over his head by means of the forked stick, then letting him have the full length of the cord, plays him like a fish, and chokes him into subjection.

All this Tonish promised to exemplify to our full satisfaction; we had not much confidence in his success, and feared he might knock up a good horse for us, in a headlong gallop after a bad one, for, like all the French Creoles, he was a merciless hard rider. It was determined, therefore, to keep a sharp eye upon him and check his sallying propensities.

We had not proceeded far on our mornings march when we were checked by a deep stream, running along the bottom of a thickly wooded ravine. After coasting it for a couple of miles we came to a fording place; but to get down to it was the difficulty, for the banks were steep and crumbling, and overgrown with forest trees, mingled with thickets, brambles and grape vines. At length the leading horseman broke his way through the thicket, and his horse putting his feet together, slid down the black crumbling bank, to the narrow margin of the stream; then floundering across, with mud and water up to the saddle girths, he scrambled up the opposite bank and arrived safe on level ground. The whole line followed pell mell after the leader, and pushing forward in close order, Indian file, they crowded each other down the bank and into the stream. Some of the horsemen missed the ford and were soused over head and ears; one was unhorsed and plumped head foremost into the middle of the stream; for my own part, while pressed forward and hurried over the bank by those behind me I was interrupted by a grape vine, as thick as a cable, which hung in a festoon as low as the saddle bow, and, dragging me from the saddle, threw me among the feet of the trampling horses. Fortunately I escaped without injury, regained my steed, crossed the stream without further difficulty, and was enabled to join in the merriment occasioned by the ludicrous disasters of the fording.

It is at passes like this that occur the most dangerous ambuscades and sanguinary surprises of Indian warfare. A party of savages, well placed among the thickets, might have made sad havoc among our men while entangled in the ravine.

We now came out upon a vast and glorious prairie, spreading out beneath the golden beams of an autumnal sun. The deep and frequent traces of buffalo shewed it to be one of their favorite grazing grounds yet none were to be seen. In the course of the morning we were overtaken by the lieutenant and seventeen men who had remained behind, and who came laden with the spoils of buffalos having killed three on the preceding day. One of the rangers, however, had little luck to boast of, his

horse having taken fright at sight of the buffalos, thrown his rider, and
escaped into the woods.

The excitement of our hunters both young and old, now rose almost
to fever height, scarce any of them having ever encountered any of
this farfamed game of the prairies. Accordingly, when in the course of
the day, the cry of Buffalo! Buffalo! rose from one part of the line, the
whole troop were thrown in agitation. We were just then passing through
a beautiful part of the prairie, finely diversified by hills and slopes, and
woody dells, and high stately groves. Those who had given the alarm
pointed out a large black looking animal, slowly moving along the side
of a rising ground about two miles off. The ever ready Tonish jumped up
and stood with his feet on the saddle, and his forked sticks in his hands,
like a posture master or scaramouch at a circus just ready for a feat of
horsemanship. After gazing at the animal for a moment, which he could
have seen full as well without rising from his stirrups he pronounced it
a wild horse, and dropping again into his saddle, was about to dash off
full tilt in pursuit, when, to his inexpressible chagrin, he was called back,
and ordered to keep to his post in rear of the baggage horses.

The captain and two of his officers now set off to reconnoitre the
game. It was the intention of the captain, who was an admirable marksman, to endeavour to crease the horse; that is to say, to hit him with a
rifle ball in the ridge of the neck. A wound of this kind paralyzes a horse
for a moment, he falls to the ground, and may be secured before he
recovers. It is a cruel expedient however, for an ill directed shot may
kill or maim the noble animal.

As the Captain and his companions moved off laterally and slowly, in
the direction of the horse we continued our course forward; watching
intently, however, the movements of the game. The horse moved quietly
over the profile of the rising ground and disappeared behind it. The
Captain and his party were likewise soon hidden by an intervening hill.

After a time the horse suddenly made his appearance to our right, just
a head of the line emerging out of a small valley on a brisk trot, having
evidently taken the alarm. At sight of us he stopped short, gazed at us
for an instant with surprize, then tossing up his head trotted off in fine
style, glancing at us first over one shoulder then over the other, his ample
mane and tail streaming in the wind. Having dashed through a skirt
of thicket that looked like a hedge row, he paused in the open field
beyond, glanced back as us again with a beautiful bend of the neck,
snuffed the air and then, tossing his head again, broke into a gallop and
took refuge in a wood.

It was the first time I had ever seen a horse scouring his native wilderness in all the pride and freedom of his nature. How different from the

poor, mutilated, harnessed, checked, reined-up victim of luxury, caprice and avarice in our cities!

After travelling about fifteen miles we encamped about one o'clock, that our hunters might have time to procure a supply of provisions. Our encampment was in a spacious grove of lofty oaks and walnuts, free from underwood, on the border of a brook. While unloading the pack horses our little Frenchman was loud in his complaints at having been prevented from pursuing the wild horse, which he would certainly have taken. In the mean time I saw our halfbreed Beatte quietly saddle his best horse, a powerful steed of a half savage race, hang a lariat at the saddle bow, take a rifle and forked stick in hand, and, mounting, depart from the camp without saying a word. It was evident he was going off in quest of the wild horse, but was disposed to hunt alone.

CHAPTER XX

THE CAMP OF THE WILD HORSE

Hunters' stories—Habits of the wild horse—The half breed and his prize—A horse chase—A wild spirit tamed.

We had encamped in a good neighborhood for game, as the reports of rifles in various directions speedily gave notice. One of our hunters soon returned with the meat of a doe tied up in the skin and slung across his shoulders. Another brought a fat buck across his horse. Two other deer were brought in and a number of turkeys. All the game was thrown down in front of the captain's fire to be portioned out among the various messes. The spits and camp kettles were soon in full employ and throughout the evening there was a scene of hunters' feasting and profusion.

We had been disappointed this day in our hopes of meeting with buffalo, but the sight of the wild horse had been a great novelty and gave a turn to the conversation of the camp for the evening. There were several anecdotes told of a famous grey horse that has ranged the prairies of this neighborhood for six or seven years setting at naught every attempt of the hunters to capture him. They say he can pace and rack (or amble) faster than the fleetest horses can run. Equally marvellous accounts were given of a black horse on the Brasis, who grazed the prairies on that river's banks in the Texas. For years he outstripped all pursuit. His fame spread far and wide; offers were made for him to the amount of a thousand dollars; the boldest and most hard riding hunters tried incessantly to make prize of him but in vain. At length he fell a victim to his gallantry, being decoyed under a tree by a tame mare, and a noose dropped over his head by a boy perched among the branches.

The capture of the wild horse is one of the most favorite achievements of the prairie tribes, and indeed it is from this source that the Indian hunters chiefly supply themselves. The wild horses which range those vast grassy plains extending from the Arkansas to the. Spanish settlements are of various forms and colours, betraying their various descents. Some resemble the common English stock, and are probably descended from horses which have escaped from our border settlements. Others are of a low but strong make, and are supposed to be of the Andalusian breed, brought out by the Spanish discoverers.

Some fanciful speculatists have seen in them descendants of the Arab stock brought into Spain from Africa and thence transferred to this country, and have pleased themselves with the idea, that their sires may have been of the pure coursers of the desert, that once bore Mahomet and his warlike disciples across the sandy plains of Arabia.

The habits of the Arab seem to have come with the steed. The introduction of the horse on the boundless prairies of the Far West changed the whole mode of living of their inhabitants. It gave them that facility of rapid motion and of sudden and distant change of place so dear to the roving propensities of man. Instead of lurking in the depths of gloomy forests, and patiently threading the mazes of a tangled wilderness on foot, like his brethren of the North, the Indian of the West is a rover of the plain; he leads a brighter and more sunshiny life, almost always on horseback, on vast flowery prairies and under cloudless skies.

I was lying by the Captain's fire late in the evening, listening to stories about these coursers of the prairies, and weaving speculations of my own, when there was a clamour of voices and a loud cheering at the other end of the camp, and word was passed that Beatte the half breed had brought in a wild horse.

In an instant every fire was deserted; the whole camp crowded to see the Indian and his prize. It was a colt about two years old, well grown, finely limbed, with bright prominent eyes and a spirited yet gentle demeanour. He gazed about him with an air of mingled stupefaction and surprize, at the men the horses and the camp fires; while the Indian stood before him with folded arms, having hold of the other end of the cord which noosed his captive, and gazing on him with a most imperturbable aspect. Beatte as I have before observed has a greenish olive complexion, with a strongly marked countenance not unlike the bronze casts of Napoleon; and as he stood before his captive horse, with folded arms and fixed aspect, he looked more like a statue than a man.

If the horse, however, manifested the least restiveness Beatte would immediately worry him with the lariat, jerking him first on one side, then on the other so as almost to throw him on the ground; when he had thus rendered him passive he would resume his statue like attitude and gaze at him in silence.

The whole scene was singularly wild; the tall grove partially illumined by the flashing fires of the camp, the horses tethered here and there among the trees; the carcasses of deer hanging around; and in the midst of all, the wild huntsman and his wild horse, with an admiring throng of rangers, almost as wild.

In the eagerness of their excitement several of the young rangers sought to get the horse by purchase or barter, and even offered extravagant terms, but Beatte declined all their offers. "You give great price now," said he—"tomorrow you be sorry, and take back—and say d—d Indian!"

The young men importuned him with questions about the mode in which he took the horse, but his answers were dry and laconic; he evidently retained some pique at having been undervalued and sneered at by them, and at the same time looked down upon them with contempt as green horns; little versed in the noble science of wood craft.

Afterwards, however, when he was seated by our fire I readily drew from him an account of his exploit, for, though taciturn among strangers, and little prone to boast of his actions, yet his taciturnity like that of all Indians, had its times of relaxation.

He informed me that on leaving the camp he had returned to the place where we had lost sight of the wild horse. Soon getting upon its track he followed it to the banks of the river. Here, the prints being more distinct in the sand, he perceived that one of the hoofs was broken and defective, so he gave up the pursuit.

As he was returning to the camp he came upon a gang of six horses, which immediately made for the river. He pursued them across the stream, left his rifle on the river bank, and putting his horse to full speed, soon came up with the fugitives. He attempted to noose one of them, but the lariat hitched on one of his ears and he shook it off. The horses dashed up a hill, he followed hard at their heels, when, of a sudden, he saw their tails whisking in the air and they plunging down a precipice. It was too late to stop. He shut his eyes, held in his breath and went over with them—neck or nothing. The descent was between twenty and thirty feet but they all came down safe upon a sandy bottom.

He now succeeded in throwing his noose round a fine young horse. As he galloped along side of him the two horses passed each side of a sapling and the end of the lariat was jerked out of his hand. He regained it, but an intervening tree obliged him again to let it go. Having once more caught it, and coming to a more open country, he was enabled to

play the young horse with the line until he gradually checked and subdued him, so as to lead him to the place where he had left his rifle.

He had another formidable difficulty in getting him across the river,
where both horses stuck for a time in the mire and Beatte was nearly
unseated from his saddle by the force of the current and the struggles of
his captive. After much toil and trouble, however, he got across the
stream and brought his prize safe into the camp.

For the remainder of the evening the camp remained in a high state
of excitement; nothing was talked of but the capture of wild horses;
every youngster of the troop was for this harum scarum kind of chase;
every one promised himself to return from the campaign in triumph,
bestriding one of these wild coursers of the prairies. Beatte had suddenly
risen to great importance; he was the prime hunter, the hero of the day;
offers were made him by the best mounted rangers to let him ride their
horses in the chase provided he would give them a share of the spoil.
Beatte bore his honours in silence and closed with none of the offers. Our
stammering, chattering, gasconading little Frenchman however, made
up for his taciturnity by vaunting as much upon the subject as if it were
he that had caught the horse. Indeed he held forth so learnedly in the
matter, and boasted so much of the many horses he had taken, that he
began to be considered an oracle and some of the youngsters were inclined to doubt whether he were not superior even to the taciturn Beatte.

The excitement kept the camp awake later than usual. The hum of
voices, interrupted by occasional peals of laughter was heard from the
groupes around the various fires, and the night was considerably advanced before all had sunk to sleep.

With the morning dawn the excitement revived and Beatte and his
wild horse were again the gaze and talk of the camp. The captive had
been tied all night to a tree among the other horses. He was again led
forth by Beatte by a long halter or lariat, and, on his manifesting the least
restiveness, was, as before, jerked and worried into passive submission.
He appeared to be gentle and docile by nature and had a beautifully
mild expression of the eye. In his strange and forlorn situation the poor
animal seemed to seek protection and companionship in the very horse
which had aided to capture him.

Seeing him thus gentle and tractable, Beatte, just as we were about to
march, strapped a light pack upon his back, by way of giving him the
first lesson in servitude. The native pride and independence of the
animal took fire at this indignity. He reared, and plunged and kicked,
and tried in every way to get rid of the degrading burthen. The Indian
was too potent for him. At every paroxysm he renewed the discipline of
the halter, until the poor animal, driven to despair, threw himself
prostrate on the ground, and lay motionless, as if acknowledging himself

vanquished. A stage hero, representing the despair of a captive prince,
could not have played his part more dramatically. There was absolutely
a moral grandeur in it.

The imperturbable Beatte folded his arms and stood for a time
looking down in silence upon his captive; until, seeing him perfectly
subdued, he nodded his head slowly, screwed his mouth into a sardonic
smile of triumph, and, with a jerk of the halter, ordered him to rise. He
obeyed and, from that time forward, offered no resistance. During that
day he bore his pack patiently and was led by the halter, but in two
days he followed voluntarily at large among the supernumerary horses
of the troop.

I could not but look with compassion upon this fine young animal
whose whole course of existence had been so suddenly reversed. From
being a denizen of these vast pastures, ranging at will from plain to
plain and mead to mead, cropping of every herb and flower and drinking
of every stream, he was suddenly reduced to perpetual and painful
servitude, to pass his life under the harness and the curb amid, perhaps
the din and dust and drudgery of cities. The transition in his lot was such
as sometimes takes place in human affairs, and in the fortunes of towering individuals.—One day a prince of the prairies—the next day a pack
horse!

CHAPTER XXI

*The fording of the Red Fork—The dreary forests of the "Cross
Timber"—Buffalo!*

We left the Camp of the Wild Horse about a quarter before eight and,
after steering nearly south for three or four miles, arrived on the banks
of the Red Fork at as we supposed about seventy five miles above
its mouth. The river was about three hundred yards wide, wandering
among sand bars and shoals. Its shores, and the long sandy banks that
stretched out into the stream, were printed, as usual, with the traces of
various animals that had come down to cross it, or to drink its waters.

Here we came to a halt and there was much consultation about the
possibility of fording the river with safety as there was an apprehension
of quicksands. Beatte, who had been somewhat in the rear came up
while we were debating. He was mounted on his horse of the half
wild breed, and leading his captive by the bridle. He gave the latter
in charge to Tonish and, without saying a word, urged his horse into
the stream, and crossed it in safety. Every thing was done by this man

in a similar way, promptly, resolutely and silently, without a previous promise or an after vaunt.

The troop now followed the lead of Beatte and reached the opposite shore without any mishap, though one of the pack horses wandering a little from the track, came near being swallowed up in a quicksand, and was with difficulty dragged to land.

After crossing the river we had to force our way, for nearly a mile, through a thick cane brake, which, at first sight, appeared an impervious mass of reeds and brambles. It was a hard struggle, our horses were often to the saddle girths in mire and water, and both horse and horseman harassed and torn by bush and briar. Falling however, upon a Buffalo track we at length extricated ourselves from this morass and ascended a ridge of land, where we beheld a beautiful open country before us; while to our right the belt of forest land called The Cross Timber, continued stretching away to the southward, as far as the eye could reach. We soon abandoned the open country and struck into the forest land. It was the intention of the Captain to keep on south west by south and traverse the Cross Timber diagonally, so as to come out upon the edge of the great Western Prairie. By thus maintaining something of a southerly direction he trusted, while he crossed the belt of forest, he would at the same time approach the Red River.

The plan of the Captain was judicious, but he erred from not being informed of the nature of the country. Had he kept directly west a couple of days would have carried us through the forest land, and we might then have had an easy course along the skirts of the upper prairies to Red River, by going diagonally we were kept for many weary days toiling through a dismal series of rugged forests.

The cross timber is about forty miles in breadth, and stretches over a rough country of rolling hills, covered with scattered tracts of post oak and black jack; with some intervening valleys that at proper seasons would afford good pasturage. It is very much cut up by deep ravines, which, in the rainy seasons, are the beds of temporary streams, tributary to the main rivers, and thence called "branches." The whole tract may present a pleasant aspect in the fresh time of the year when the ground is covered with herbage; when the trees are in their green leaf, and the glens are enlivened by running streams. Unfortunately we entered it too late in the season. The herbage was parched; the foliage of the scrubby forests was withered, the whole woodland prospect, as far as the eye could reach, had a brown and arid hue. The fires made on the prairies by the Indian hunters had frequently penetrated these forests, sweeping in light transient flames along the dry grass, scorching and calcining the lower twigs and branches of the trees, and leaving them black and hard, so as to tear the flesh of man and horse that had

to scramble through them. I shall not easily forget the mortal toil, and
the vexations of flesh and spirit that we underwent occasionally, in our
wanderings through the cross timber. It was like struggling through
forests of cast iron.

After a tedious ride of several miles we came out upon an open tract
of hill and dale interspersed with woodland. Here we were roused by
the cry of Buffalo! Buffalo! The effect was something like that of the
cry of a sail! a sail! at sea. It was not a false alarm. Three or four of
those enormous animals were visible to our right, grazing on the slope
of a distant hill.

There was a general movement to set off in pursuit and it was
with some difficulty that the vivacity of the younger men of the troop
could be restrained. Leaving orders that the line of march should be
preserved, the Captain and two of his officers departed at a quiet pace
accompanied by Beatte, and by the ever forward Tonish, for it was
impossible any longer to keep the little Frenchman in check, being
half crazy to prove his skill and prowess in hunting the Buffalo.

The intervening hills soon hid from us both the game and the
huntsmen. We kept on our course in quest of a camping place, which
was difficult to be found, almost all the channels of the streams being
dry, and the country being destitute of fountain heads.

After proceeding some distance there was again a cry of Buffalo,
and two were pointed out on a hill to the left. The Captain being
absent it was no longer possible to restrain the ardour of the young
hunters. Away several of them dashed full speed and soon disappeared
among the ravines. The rest kept on, anxious to find a proper place
for encampment.

Indeed we now began to experience the disadvantages of the season.
The pasturage of the prairies was scanty and parched; the pea vines
which grew in the woody bottoms were withered, and most of the
"branches" or streams were dried up. While wandering in this perplexity
we were overtaken by the Captain and all his party except Tonish.
They had pursued the Buffalo for some distance without getting within
shot, and had given up the chase, being fearful of fatiguing their
horses, or being led off too far from camp. The little Frenchman, however had gallopped after them at headlong speed, and the last they
saw of him—he was engaged, as it were, yard arm and yard arm with
a great Buffalo bull, firing broadsides into him. "I tink dat little man
crazy—some how," observed Beatte dryly.

CHAPTER XXII

The alarm camp.

We now came to a halt and had to content ourselves with an indifferent encampment. It was in a grove of scrub oaks, on the borders of a deep ravine, at the bottom of which were a few scanty pools of water. We were just at the foot of a gradually sloping hill covered with half withered grass that afforded meagre pasturage. In the spot where we had encamped the grass was high and parched. The view around us was circumscribed and much shut in by gently swelling hills.

Just as we were encamping Tonish arrived all glorious from his hunting match, his white horse hung all round with buffalo meat. According to his own account he had laid low two mighty bulls. As usual we deducted one half from his boastings; but now that he had something real to vaunt about, there was no restraining the valour of his tongue.

After having in some measure appeased his vanity by boasting of his exploit, he informed us that he had observed the fresh track of horses, which, from various circumstances he suspected to have been made by some roving band of Pawnees. This caused some little uneasiness. The young men who had left the line of march in pursuit of the two buffalo had not yet rejoined us. Apprehensions were expressed that they might be waylayed and attacked. Our veteran hunter "Old Ryan" also, immediately on our halting to encamp had gone off on foot in company with a young disciple. "Dat old man will have his brains knocked out by de Pawnees yet," said Beatte. "He tink he know every ting, but he don't know Pawnees—any how."

Taking his rifle, the Captain repaired on foot to reconnoitre the country from the naked summit of one of the neighboring hills. In the mean time the horses were hobbled and turned loose to graze in the adjacent fields; and wood was cut, and fires made, to prepare the evenings repast.

Suddenly there was an alarm of fire in the camp! The flame from one of the kindling fires had caught to the tall dry grass: a breeze was blowing; there was danger that the camp would soon be wrapped in a light blaze. "Look to the horses!" cried one; "drag away the baggage!" cried another. "Take care of the rifles and powder horns!" cried a third. All was hurry scurry and uproar. The horses dashed wildly about—some of the men snatched away rifles and powder horns, others dragged off saddles and saddle bags: mean time no one thought of quelling the fire, nor indeed knew how to quell it. Beatte, however, and his comrades attacked it in the Indian mode, beating down the edges of the fire, with blankets and horse cloths, and endeavoring to prevent its spreading among the grass; the rangers followed their example, and in a little while the flames were happily quelled.

The fires were now properly kindled on places from which the dry grass had been cleared away. The horses were scattered about a small valley and on the sloping hill side, cropping the scanty herbage. Tonish was preparing a sumptuous evenings meal from his buffalo meat, promising us a rich soup and a prime piece of roast beef: but we were doomed to experience another and more serious alarm.

There was an indistinct cry from some rangers on the summit of the hill of which we could only distinguish the words, "The horses! the horses! get in the horses!"

Immediately a clamour of voices arose; shouts, enquiries, replies were all mingled together so that nothing could be clearly understood, and every one drew his own inference.

"The Captain has started buffalos," cried one, "and wants horses for the chase." Immediately a number of rangers seized their rifles and scampered for the hill top. "The prairie is on fire beyond the hill," cried another. "I see the smoke—the captain means we shall drive the horses beyond the brook."

By this time a ranger from the hill had reached the skirts of the camp. He was almost breathless and could only say that the Captain had seen Indians at a distance.

"Pawnees! Pawnees!" was now the cry among our wild headed youngsters. "Drive the horses into the camp!" cried one. "Saddle the horses!" cried another. "Form the line!" cried a third. There was now a scene of clamour and confusion that baffles all description. The rangers were scampering about the adjacent field in pursuit of their horses. One might be seen tugging his steed along by a halter, another, without a hat, riding bare backed; another driving a hobbled horse before him that made awkward leaps like a Kangaroo.

The alarm increased. Word was brought from the lower end of the camp that there was a band of Pawnees in a neighboring valley. They had shot Old Ryan through the head, and were chasing his companion! "No, it was not Old Ryan that was killed—it was one of the hunters that had been after the two buffalos." "There are three hundred Pawnees just beyond the hill," cried one voice. "More—more!" cried another.

Our situation shut in among hills prevented our seeing to any distance and left us a prey to all these rumours. A cruel enemy was supposed to be at hand; and an immediate attack apprehended. The horses by this time were driven into the camp and were dashing about among the fires and trampling upon the baggage. Every one endeavored to prepare for action; but here was the perplexity. During the late alarm of fire the saddles, bridles, rifles, powder horns and other equipments had been snatched out of their places and thrown helter skelter among the trees.

"Where is my saddle?" cried one. "Has any one seen my rifle?" cried another.

"Who will lend me a ball?" cried a third who was loading his piece. "I have lost my bullet pouch."

"For God's sake help me to girth this horse!" cried another, "he's so restive I can do nothing with him."—In his hurry and worry he had put on the saddle the hind part before!

Some affected to swagger and talk bold. Others said nothing, but went on steadily preparing their horses and weapons, and on these I felt the most reliance. Some were evidently excited and elated with the idea of an encounter with Indians, and none more so than my young Swiss fellow traveller, who had a passion for wild adventure. Our man, Beatte, led his horses in the rear of the camp, placed his rifle against a tree, then seated himself by the fire in perfect silence. On the other hand little Tonish, who was busy cooking, stopped every moment from his work to play the fanfaron, singing, swearing, and affecting an unusual hilarity, which made me strongly suspect that there was some little fright at bottom, to cause all this effervescence.

About a dozen of the rangers, as soon as they could saddle their horses, dashed off in the direction in which the Pawnees were said to have attacked the hunters. It was now determined, in case our camp should be assailed, to put our horses in the ravine in rear, where they would be out of danger from arrow or rifle ball, and to take our stand within the edge of the ravine. This would serve as a trench, and the trees and thickets with which it was bordered would be sufficient to turn aside any shaft of the enemy. The Pawnees, beside, are wary of attacking any covert of the kind; their warfare, as I have already observed, lies in the open prairies where mounted upon their fleet horses they can swoop like hawks upon their enemy or wheel about him and discharge their arrows. Still I could not but perceive, that, in case of being attacked by such a number of these well mounted and warlike savages as were said to be at hand, we should be exposed to considerable risk from the inexperience and want of discipline of our newly raised rangers, and from the very courage of many of the younger ones, who seemed bent on adventure and exploit.

By this time the Captain reached the camp and every one crowded round him for information. He informed us that he had proceeded some distance on his reconnoitering expedition and was slowly returning towards the camp, along the brow of a naked hill, when he saw something on the edge of a parallel hill that looked like a man. He paused and watched it, but it remained so perfectly motionless that he supposed it a bush, or the top of some tree beyond the hill. He resumed his course, when it likewise began to move in a parallel direction. Another form now rose beside it, of some one who had either been lying down, or had just ascended the other side of the hill. The captain stopped and regarded them; they likewise stopped. He then lay down upon the grass and they began to walk. On his rising they again stopped, as if watching him. Knowing that the Indians are apt to have their spies and centinels thus posted on the summit of naked hills, commanding extensive prospects, his doubts were increased by the suspicious movements of these men. He now put his foraging cap on the end of his rifle and waved it in the air. They took no notice of the signal. He then walked on until he entered the edge of a wood which concealed him from their view. Stepping out of sight for a moment, he again looked forth, when he saw the two men passing swiftly forward. As the hill on which they were walking made a curve toward that on which he stood, it seemed as if they were endeavouring to head him before he should reach the camp. Doubting whether they might not belong to some large party of Indians either in ambush, or moving along the valley beyond the hill, the Captain hastened his steps homeward, and descrying some rangers on an eminence between him and the camp he called out to them to pass the word to have the horses driven in, as these are generally the first objects of Indian depredation.

Such was the origin of the alarm which had thrown the camp in commotion. Some of those who heard the Captain's narrative had no doubt that the men on the hill were Pawnee scouts, belonging to the band that had waylaid the hunters. Distant shots were heard at intervals, which were supposed to be fired by those who had sallied out to rescue their comrades. Several more rangers, having completed their equipments, now rode forth in the direction of the firing; others looked anxious and uneasy.

"If they are as numerous as they are said to be," said one, "and as well mounted as they generally are, we shall be a bad match for them with our jaded horses."

"Well," replied the captain, "we have a strong encampment and can stand a siege."

"Aye, but they may set fire to the prairie in the night and burn us out of our encampment."

"We will then set up a counter fire."

The word was now passed that a man on horseback approached the camp.

"It is one of the hunters!"—"It is Clements!"—"He brings buffalo meat!" was announced by several voices as the horseman drew near.

It was, in fact, one of the rangers who had set off in the morning in pursuit of the two buffaloes. He rode into the camp with the spoils of the chase hanging round his horse and followed by his companions, all sound and unharmed and equally well laden. They proceeded to give an account of a grand gallop they had had after the two buffalos, and how many shots it had cost them to bring one to the ground—

"Well, but the Pawnees—the Pawnees—where are the Pawnees?"

"What Pawnees—?"

"The Pawnees that attacked you—?"

"No one attacked us."

"But have you seen no Indians on your way?"

"Oh yes, two of us got to the top of a hill to look out for the camp, and saw a fellow on an opposite hill cutting queer antics, who seemed to be an Indian."

"Pshaw! that was I!" cried the captain.

Here the bubble burst. The whole alarm had risen from this mutual mistake of the Captain and the two rangers. As to the report of the three hundred Pawnees and their attack on the hunters, it proved to be a wanton fabrication, of which no further notice was taken; though the author deserved to have been sought out and severely punished.

There being no longer any prospect of fighting every one now thought of eating; and here the stomachs throughout the camp were in unison. Tonish served up to us his promised regale of Buffalo soup and Buffalo beef. The soup was peppered most horribly, and the roast beef proved the Bull to have been one of the patriarchs of the prairies: never did I have to deal with a tougher morsel. However, it was our first repast on buffalo meat, so we ate it with a lively faith, nor would our little Frenchman allow us any rest until he had extorted from us an acknowledgment of the excellence of his cookery; though the pepper gave us the lie in our throats.

The night closed in without the return of Old Ryan and his companion; we had become accustomed, however, to the aberrations of this old Cock of the Woods and no further solicitude was expressed on his account.

After the fatigues and agitations of the day the camp soon sunk into a profound sleep, excepting those on guard; who were more than usually on the alert, for the traces recently seen of Pawnees, and the certainty that we were in the midst of their hunting grounds excited to constant vigilance. About half past ten o'clock we were all startled from sleep by a new alarm. A centinel had fired off his rifle and run into camp, crying that there were Indians at hand.

Every one was on his legs in an instant. Some seized their rifles; some were about to saddle their horses; some hastened to the captain's lodge, but were ordered back to their respective fires. The centinel was examined. He declared he had seen an Indian approach, crawling along the ground; whereupon he had fired upon him and run into camp. The captain gave it as his opinion that the supposed Indian was a wolf, he reprimanded the centinel for deserting his post and obliged him to return to it. Many seemed inclined to give credit to the story of the sentinel; for the events of the day had predisposed them to apprehend lurking foes and sudden assaults during the darkness of the night. For a long time they sat round their fires, with rifle in hand, carrying on low murmuring conversations and listening for some new alarm. Nothing further, however, occurred; the voices gradually died away; the gossippers nodded and dozed and sunk to rest, and by degrees silence and sleep once more stole over the camp.

CHAPTER XXIII

Beaver dam—Buffalo and horse tracks—A Pawnee trail—Wild horses— The young hunter and the bear—Change of route.

On mustering our forces in the morning (Oct. 23) Old Ryan and his comrade were still missing, but the captain had such perfect reliance on the skill and resources of the veteran woodsman that he did not think it necessary to take any measures with respect to him.

Our march this day lay through the same kind of rough rolling country checquered by brown dreary forests of post oak, and cut up by deep dry ravines. The distant fires were evidently increasing on the prairies: the wind had been at north west for several days, and the atmosphere had become so smoky, as in the height of Indian summer, that it was difficult to distinguish objects at any distance.

In the course of the morning we crossed a deep stream with a complete beaver dam above three feet high making a large pond, and doubtless containing several families of that industrious animal, though not one shewed his nose above water. The Captain would not permit this amphibious commonwealth to be disturbed.

We now were continually coming upon the tracks of buffalos and wild horses, those of the former tended invariably to the south, as we could perceive by the direction of the trampled grass. It was evident we were on the great high way of these migratory herds but that they had chiefly passed to the southward.

Beatte, who generally kept a parallel course several hundred yards distant from our line of march, to be on the look out for game, and who regarded every track with the knowing eye of an Indian, reported that he had come upon a very suspicious "trail." There were the tracks of men who wore Pawnee moccasins. He had scented the smoke of mingled sumach and tobacco, such as the Indians use. He had observed tracks of horses, mingled with those of a dog; and a mark in the dust where a cord had been trailed along, probably the long bridle one end of which the Indian horsemen suffer to trail after them on the ground. It was evident, they were not the tracks of wild horses.

My anxiety began to revive about the safety of our veteran hunter Ryan, for I had taken a great fancy to this real old Leatherstocking; every one expressed a confidence, however, that wherever Ryan was, he was safe, and knew how to take care of himself.

We had accomplished the greater part of a weary days march and were passing through a glade of the oak openings when we came in sight of six wild horses, among which I especially noticed two very handsome ones, a grey and a roan. They pranced about, with heads erect and long flaunting tails, offering a proud contrast to our poor, spiritless, travel tired steeds. Having reconnoitered us for a moment they set off at a gallop, passed through a woody dingle, and in a little while emerged once more to view trotting up a slope about a mile distant.

The sight of these horses was again a sore trial to the vapouring Tonish, who had his lariat and forked stick ready, and was on the point of launching forth in pursuit, on his jaded horse, when he was again ordered back to the pack horses.

After a days journey of fourteen miles in a southwest direction, we encamped on the banks of a small clear stream, on the northern border of the Cross Timbers, and on the edge of those vast prairies that extend away to the foot of the Rocky Mountains. In turning loose the horses to graze their bells were stuffed with grass to prevent their tinkling, lest it might be heard by some wandering horde of Pawnees.

Our hunters now went out in different directions but without much success as but one deer was brought into the camp. A young ranger had a long story to tell of his adventures. In skirting the thickets of a deep ravine he had wounded a buck which he plainly heard to fall among the bushes. He stopped to fix the lock of his rifle, which was out of order, and to reload it: then advancing to the edge of the thicket in quest of his game he heard a low growling. Putting the branches aside, and stealing silently forward he looked down into the ravine and beheld a huge bear dragging the carcass of the deer along the dry channel of a brook and growling and snarling at four or five officious wolves who seemed to have dropped in to take supper with him.

The ranger fired at the bear, but missed him. Bruin maintained his ground and his prize and seemed disposed to make battle. The wolves too, who were evidently sharp set, drew off to but a small distance. As night was coming on the young hunter felt dismayed at the wildness and darkness of the place, and the strange company he had fallen in with, so he quietly withdrew and returned empty handed to the camp, where having told his story, he was heartily bantered by his more experienced comrades.

In the course of the evening Old Ryan came straggling into the camp followed by his disciple, and as usual was received with hearty gratulations. He had lost himself yesterday when hunting and camped out all night, but had found our trail in the morning and followed it up. He had passed some time at the beaver dam admiring the skill and solidity with which it had been constructed. "These beavers," said he, "are industrious little fellows. They are the knowingest varment as I know; and I'll warrant the pond was stocked with them."

"Aye," said the captain, "I have no doubt most of the small rivers we have passed are full of beaver. I should like to come and trap on these waters all winter."

"But would you not run the chance of being attacked by Indians?" asked one of the company.

"Oh, as to that, it would be safe enough here in the winter time. There would be no Indians here until spring. I should want no more than two companions. Three persons are safer than a larger number for trapping beaver. They can keep quiet and need seldom fire a gun. A Bear would serve them for food for two months, taking care to turn every part of it to advantage."

A consultation was now held as to our future progress. We had thus far pursued a western course, and, having traversed the Cross Timber, were on the skirts of the Great Western Prairie. We were still, however, in a very rough country where food was scarce. The season was so far advanced that the grass was withered and the prairies yielded no pasturage. The peavines of the bottoms, also, which had sustained our horses for some part of the journey, were nearly gone, and for several days past the poor animals had fallen off woefully both in flesh and spirit. The Indian fires on the prairies were approaching us from north and south, and west; they might spread also from the east, and leave a scorched desert between us and the frontier, in which our horses might be famished.

It was determined, therefore, to advance no further to the westward, but to shape our course more to the east so as to strike the north fork of the Canadian as soon as possible where we hoped to find abundance of young cane; which, at this season of the year affords the most nutritious pasturage for the horses, and, at the same time, attracts immense quantities of game. Here then we fixed the limits of our tour to the Far West, being within little more than a days march of the boundary line of Texas.

CHAPTER XXIV

Scarcity of bread—Rencontre with buffalos—Wild turkeys—Fall of a buffalo bull.

The morning broke bright and clear, but the camp had nothing of its usual gaiety. The concert of the farm yard was at an end; not a cock crew nor dog barked; nor was there either singing or laughing; every one pursued his avocations quietly and gravely. The novelty of the expedition was wearing off; some of the young men were getting as way worn as their horses, and most of them unaccustomed to the hunter's life, began to repine at its privations. What they most felt was the want of bread, their rations of flour having been exhausted for several days. The old hunters, who had often experienced this want, made light of it: and Beatte, accustomed when among the Indians to live for months without it, considered it a mere article of luxury. "Bread," he would say scornfully, "is only fit for a child."

About a quarter before eight o'clock we turned our backs upon the Far West, and set off in a south east course, along a gentle valley. After riding a few miles Beatte, who kept parallel with us along the ridge of a naked hill to our right called out and made signals, as if something was coming round the hill to intercept us. Some who were near me cried out that it was a party of Pawnees. A skirt of thickets hid the approach of the supposed enemy from our view. We heard a trampling among the brush wood. My horse looked toward the place, snorted and pricked up his ears, when presently a couple of huge Buffalo bulls who had been alarmed by Beatte came crashing through the brake and making directly towards us. At sight of us they wheeled round and scuttled along a narrow defile of the hills. In an instant half a score of rifles cracked off; there was a universal whoop and halloo, and away went half the troop helter skelter in pursuit, and myself among the number. The most of us soon pulled up and gave over a chase which led through bush and briar and break neck ravines. Some few of the rangers persisted for a time; but eventually rejoined the line slowly lagging one after another. One of them returned on foot, he had been thrown while in full chase; his rifle had been broken in the fall, and his horse, retaining the spirit of the rider, had kept on after the buffalo. It was a melancholy predicament to be reduced to; to be without horse or weapon in the midst of the Pawnee hunting grounds.

For my own part—I had been fortunate enough recently by a further exchange to get possession of the best horse in the troop; a full blooded sorrel, of excellent bottom, beautiful form and most generous qualities. In such a situation it almost seems as if a man changes his nature with his horse. I felt quite like another being now that I had an animal under me spirited yet gentle, docile to a remarkable degree, and easy, elastic and rapid in all his movements. In a few days he became almost as much attached to me as a dog; would follow me when I dismounted, would come to me in the morning to be noticed and caressed; and would put his muzzle between me and my book as I sat reading at the foot of a tree. The feeling I had for this my dumb companion of the prairies gave me some faint idea of that attachment the Arab is said to entertain for the horse that has borne him about the deserts.

After riding a few miles further we came to a fine meadow with a broad clear stream winding through it, on the banks of which there was excellent pasturage. Here we at once came to a halt, in a beautiful grove of elms, on the site of an old Osage encampment. Scarcely had we dismounted when a universal firing of rifles took place upon a large flock of turkeys scattered about the grove, which proved to be a favorite roosting place for these simple birds. They flew to the trees and sat perched upon their branches stretching out their long necks and gazing in stupid astonishment until eighteen of them were shot down.

In the height of the carnage word was brought that there were four buffaloes in a neighboring meadow. The turkeys were now abandoned for nobler game. The tired horses were again mounted and urged to the chase. In a little while we came in sight of the Buffaloes, looking like brown hillocks among the long green herbage. Beatte endeavored to get ahead of them and turn them towards us, that the inexperienced hunters might have a chance. They ran round the base of a rocky hill that hid us from the sight. Some of us endeavored to cut across the hill but became entrapped in a thick wood, matted with grape vines. My horse who, under his former rider had hunted the buffalo, seemed as much excited as myself and endeavoured to force his way through the bushes. At length we extricated ourselves, and, gallopping over the hill, I found our little Frenchman Tonish curvetting on horseback round a great buffalo which he had wounded too severely to fly, and which he was keeping employed until we should come up. There was a mixture of the grand and the comic in beholding this tremendous animal and his fantastic assailant. The Buffalo stood with his shagged front always presented to his foe, his mouth open, his tongue parched, his eyes like coals of fire and his tail erect with rage; every now and then he would make a

faint rush upon his foe, who easily evaded his attack, capering and
cutting all kinds of antics before him.

We now made repeated shots at the Buffalo, but they glanced into
his mountain of flesh without proving mortal. He made a slow and grand
retreat into the shallow river, turning upon his assailants whenever they
pressed upon him; and when in the water took his stand there as if prepared to sustain a siege. A rifle ball, however, more fatally lodged, sent
a tremour through his frame. He turned and attempted to wade across
the stream but, after tottering a few paces, slowly fell upon his side and
expired. It was the fall of a hero, and we felt somewhat ashamed of the
butchery that had effected it; but, after the first shot or two, we had
reconciled it to our feelings by the old plea of putting the poor animal
out of his misery.

Two other buffalos were killed this evening, but they were all bulls,
the flesh of which is meagre and hard at this season of the year. A fat
buck yielded us much more savory meat for our evenings repast.

CHAPTER XXV

Ringing the wild horse.

We left the Buffalo Camp about eight o'clock, and had a toilsome and
harassing march of two hours over ridges of hills covered with a ragged
meagre forest of scrub oaks and broken by deep gullies. Among the oaks
I observed many of the most diminutive size, some not above a foot
high, yet bearing abundance of small acorns. The whole of the cross
timbers, in fact, abound with mast. There is a pine oak which produces
an acorn pleasant to the taste, and ripening early in the season.

About ten o'clock in the morning we came to where this line of rugged
hills swept down into a valley through which flowed the north fork of
the Red river. A beautiful meadow about half a mile wide, enameled
with yellow autumnal flowers, stretched for two or three miles along the
foot of the hills, bordered on the opposite side by the river, whose banks
were fringed with cotton wood trees, the bright foliage of which refreshed and delighted the eye, after being wearied by the contemplation of monotonous wastes of brown forest.

The meadow was finely diversified by groves and clumps of trees, so
happily disposed that they seemed as if set out by the hand of art. As
we cast our eyes over this fresh and delightful valley we beheld a troop
of wild horses quietly grazing on a green lawn about a mile distant to
our right, while to our left at nearly the same distance, were several

buffaloes, some feeding, others reposing and ruminating among the high
rich herbage, under the shade of a clump of cotton wood trees. The
whole had the appearance of a broad beautiful tract of pasture land, on
the highly ornamented estate of some gentleman farmer, with his cattle
grazing about the lawns and meadows.

A council of war was now held, and it was determined to profit by the
present favorable opportunity, and try our hand at the grand hunting
maneuvre which is called ringing the wild horse. This requires a large
party of horsemen well mounted. They extend themselves in each direction singly at certain distances apart, and gradually form a ring of two
or three miles in circumference, so as to surround the game. This has
to be done with extreme care, for the wild horse is the most readily
alarmed inhabitant of the prairie and can scent a hunter at a great distance if to windward.

The ring being formed, two or three hunters ride towards the horses
who start off in an opposite direction. Wherever they approach the
bounds of the ring, however, a huntsman presents himself and turns
them from their course. In this way they are checked and driven back
at every point, and kept gallopping round and round this magic circle
until being completely tired down, it is easy for the hunters to ride up
beside them and throw the lariat over their heads. The prime horses
of most speed, courage and bottom, however, are apt to break through
and escape so that, in general, it is the second rate horses that are taken.

Preparations were now made for a hunt of the kind. The pack horses
were taken into the woods and firmly tied to trees lest, in a rush of the
wild horses, they should break away with them. Twenty five men were
then sent, under the command of a lieutenant, to steal along the edge
of the valley within the strip of woods that skirted the hills. They were
to station themselves about fifty yards apart within the edge of the
woods, and not to advance or shew themselves, until the horses dashed
in that direction. Twenty five men were sent across the valley to steal
in like manner, along the river bank that bordered the opposite side,
and to station themselves among the trees. A third party of about the
same number, was to form a line stretching across the lower part of
the valley, so as to connect the two wings. Beatte and our other half
breed Antoine, together with the ever officious Tonish, were to make a
circuit through the woods so as to get to the upper part of the valley
in the rear of the horses, and to drive them forward into the kind of
sack that we had formed, while the two wings should join behind
them and make a complete circle.

The flanking parties were quietly extending themselves, out of sight,
on each side of the valley and the residue were stretching themselves,
like the links of a chain, across it, when the wild horses gave signs that

they scented an enemy: snuffing the air, snorting and looking about. At length they pranced off slowly toward the river and disappeared behind a green bank. Here, had the regulations of the chase been observed, they would have been quietly checked and turned back by the advance of a hunter from among the trees: unluckily, however, we had our wild fire Jack o lantern little Frenchman to deal with. Instead of keeping quietly up the right side of the valley, to get above the horses, the moment he saw them move toward the river he broke out of the covert of woods and dashed furiously across the plain in pursuit of them; being mounted on one of the led horses belonging to the Count. This put an end to all system. The half breeds and half a score of rangers joined in the chase. Away they all went over the green bank; in a moment or two the wild horses reappeared and came thundering down the valley with Frenchman, half breeds and rangers galloping and yelling like devils behind them. It was in vain that the line drawn across the valley attempted to check and turn back the fugitives. They were too hotly pressed by their pursuers; in their panic they dashed through the line and clattered down the plain. The whole troop joined in the headlong chase, some of the rangers without hats or caps, their hair flying about their ears, others with handkerchiefs tied round their heads. The Buffalos who had been calmly ruminating among the herbage heaved up their huge forms, gazed for a moment with astonishment at the tempest that came scouring down the meadow, then turned and took to heavy rolling flight. They were soon overtaken, the promiscuous throng were pressed together by the contracting sides of the valley, and away they went pell mell—hurry scurry—wild buffalo, wild horse, wild huntsman, with clang and clatter and whoop and halloo that made the forests ring.

At length the Buffalos turned into a green brake on the river bank, while the horses dashed up a narrow defile of the hills with their pursuers close at their heels. Beatte passed several of them having fixed his eye upon a fine Pawnee horse that had his ears slit and saddle marks on his back. He pressed him gallantly, but lost him in the woods. Among the wild horses was a fine black mare far gone with foal. In scrambling up the defile she tripped and fell. A young ranger sprang from his horse and seized her by the mane and muzzle. Another ranger dismounted and came to his assistance. The mare struggled fiercely, kicking and biting and striking with her forefeet, but a noose was slipped over her head and her struggles were in vain. It was some time, however, before she gave over rearing and plunging and lashing out with her feet on every side. The two rangers then led her along the valley by two long lariats, which enabled them to keep at a sufficient distance on each side to be out of the reach of her hoofs, and whenever she struck out in one direction she was jerked in the other. In this way her spirit was gradually subdued.

As to little Scaramouch Tonish, who had marred the whole scheme by his precipitancy, he had been more successful than he deserved, having managed to catch a beautiful cream coloured colt, about seven months old, which had not strength to keep up with its companions. The mercurial little Frenchman was beside himself with exultation. It was amusing to see him with his prize. The colt would rear and kick, and struggle to get free, while Tonish would take him about the neck, wrestle with him, jump on his back, and cut as many antics as a monkey with a kitten. Nothing surprized me more, however, than to witness how soon these poor animals, thus taken from the unbounded freedom of the prairie, yielded to the dominion of man. In the course of two or three days the mare and colt went with the led horses and became quite docile.

CHAPTER XXVI

*Fording of the North Fork—Dreary scenery of the Cross Timber—
Scamper of horses in the night—Osage war party—Effects of a peace
harangue—Buffalo—Wild horse.*

Resuming our march we forded the North Fork, a rapid stream, and of a purity seldom to be found in the rivers of the prairies. It evidently had its sources in high land, well supplied with springs. After crossing the river we again ascended among hills, from one of which we had an extensive view over this belt of cross timber, and a cheerless prospect it was, hill beyond hill, forest beyond forest, all of one sad russet hue, excepting that here and there a line of green cotton wood trees, sycamores and willows marked the course of some streamlet through a valley. A procession of buffalos moving slowly up the profile of one of those distant hills, formed a characteristic object in the savage scene. To the left the eye stretched beyond this rugged wilderness of hills, and ravines and ragged forests, to a prairie about ten miles off, extending in a clear blue line along the horizon. It was like looking from among rocks and breakers upon a distant tract of tranquil ocean. Unluckily our route did not lie in that direction, we still had to traverse many a weary mile of the "cross timber."

We encamped towards evening in a valley beside a scanty pool, under a scattered grove of elms the upper branches of which were fringed with tufts of the mystic mistletoe. In the course of the night the wild colt whinnied repeatedly; and about two hours before day there was a sudden *stampedo*, or rush of horses along the purlieus of the camp, with a snorting and neighing, and a clattering of hoofs, that startled most of the rangers from their sleep, who listened in silence until the sound died away like the rushing of a blast. As usual the noise was at first attributed to some party of marauding Indians: but as the day dawned a couple of wild horses were seen in a neighboring meadow, which scoured off on being approached. It was now supposed that a gang of them had dashed through our camp in the night. A general mustering of our horses took place, many were found scattered to a considerable distance and several were not to be found. The prints of their hoofs, however, appeared deeply dinted in the soil, leading off at full speed into the waste, and their owners, putting themselves on the trail, set off in weary search of them.

We had a ruddy day break, but the morning gathered up grey and lowering with indications of an autumnal storm. We resumed our march silently and seriously, through a rough and cheerless country, from the highest points of which we could descry large prairies stretching indefinitely westward. After travelling for two or three hours, as we were traversing a withered prairie, resembling a great brown heath, we beheld seven Osage warriors approaching at a distance. The sight of any human being in this lonely wilderness was interesting; it was like speaking a ship at sea. One of the Indians took the lead of his companions and advanced towards us with head erect, chest thrown forward, and a free and noble mien. He was a fine looking fellow, dressed in scarlet frock and fringed leggings of deer skin; his head was decorated with a white tuft and he stepped forward with something of a martial air, swaying his bow and arrows in one hand.

We held some conversation with him through our interpreter Beatte, and found that he and his companions had been with the main part of their tribe hunting the buffalo and had met with great success, and he informed us that in the course of another days march we would reach the prairies on the banks of the Grand Canadian and find plenty of game. He added that, as their hunt was over, and the hunters on their return homeward, he and his comrades had set out on a war party, to waylay and hover about some Pawnee camp, in hopes of carrying off scalps or horses.

By this time his companions, who at first stood aloof, joined him. Three of them had indifferent fowling pieces the rest were armed with bows and arrows. I could not but admire the finely shaped heads and busts of these savages, and their graceful attitudes and expressive gestures, as they stood conversing with our interpreter and surrounded by a cavalcade of rangers. We endeavoured to get one of them to join us, as we were desirous of seeing him hunt the buffalo with his bow and arrow. He seemed at first somewhat inclined to do so, but was dissuaded by his companions.

The worthy Commissioner now remembered his mission as Pacificator and made a speech, exhorting them to abstain from all offensive acts against the Pawnees; informing them of the plan of their Father at Washington to put an end to all war among his Red children; and assuring them that he was sent to the frontier to establish a universal peace. He told them therefore to return quietly to their homes with the certainty that the Pawnees would no longer molest them, but would soon regard them as brothers.

The Indians listened to the speech with their customary silence and decorum: after which exchanging a few words among themselves they bade us farewell and pursued their way across the prairie.

Fancying that I saw a lurking smile in the countenance of our interpreter Beatte I privately enquired what the Indians had said to each other after hearing the speech. The leader he said had observed to his companions, that, as their great Father intended so soon to put an end to all warfare, it behooved them to make the most of the little time that was left them. So they had departed with redoubled zeal to pursue their project of horse stealing!

We had not long parted from the Indians before we discovered three Buffalos among the thickets of a marshy valley to our left. I set off with the captain and several rangers in pursuit of them. Stealing through a straggling grove the captain, who took the lead, got within rifle shot and wounded one of them in the flank. They, all three, made off in headlong panic, through thickets and brush wood, and swamp and mire, bearing down every obstacle by their immense weight. The captain and rangers soon gave up a chase which threatened to knock up their horses; I had got upon the traces of the wounded bull, however, and was in hopes of getting near enough to use my pistols, the only weapons with which I was provided; but before I could effect it, he reached the foot of a rocky hill covered with post oak and brambles, and plunged forward, dashing and crashing along with neck or nothing fury, where it would have been madness to follow him.

The chase had led me so far on one side that it was some time before I regained the trail of our troop. As I was slowly ascending a hill a fine black mare came prancing round the summit and was close to me before she was aware. At sight of me she started back, then turning, swept at full speed down into the valley and up the opposite hill, with flowing mane and tail and action free as air. I gazed after her as long as she was in sight, and breathed a wish that so glorious an animal might never come under the degrading thraldom of whip and curb, but remain a free rover of the prairies.

CHAPTER XXVII

*Foul weather encampment—Anecdotes of bear hunting—Indian notions
about omens—Scruples respecting the dead.*

On overtaking the troop I found it encamping in a rich bottom of wood
land, traversed by a small stream, running between deep crumbling
banks. A sharp cracking off of rifles was kept up for some time in various
directions, upon a numerous flock of turkeys, scampering among the
thickets, or perched upon the trees. We had not been long at a halt when
a drizzling rain ushered in the autumnal storm that had been brewing.
Preparations were immediately made to weather it. Our tent was
pitched, and our saddles, saddlebags, packages of coffee, sugar, salt and
every thing else that could be damaged by the rain were gathered under
its shelter. Our men Beatte, Tonish and Antoine drove stakes with forked
ends into the ground, laid poles across them for rafters, and thus
made a shed or penthouse, covered with bark and skins, sloping towards
the wind, and open towards the fire. The rangers formed similar shelters
of bark and skins, or of blankets stretched on poles, supported by forked
stakes, with great fires in front.

These precautions were well timed. The rain set in sullenly and steadily
and kept on, with slight intermissions, for two days. The brook which
flowed peaceably on our arrival swelled into a turbid and boiling torrent, and the forest became little better than a mere swamp. The men
gathered under their shelters of skins and blankets, or sat cowering round
their fires; while columns of smoke curling up among the trees, and
diffusing themselves in the air, spread a blue haze through the woodland. Our poor way worn horses, reduced by weary travel and scanty
pasturage, lost all remaining spirit, and stood, with drooping head,
flagging ears and half closed eyes, dozing and steaming in the rain;
while the yellow autumnal leaves, at every shaking of the breeze, came
wavering down around them.

Notwithstanding the bad weather, however our hunters were not
idle, but during the intervals of the rain, sallied forth on horseback to
prowl through the woodland. Every now and then the sharp report of
a distant rifle boded the death of a deer. Venison in abundance was
brought in. Some busied themselves under the sheds flaying and cutting
up the carcasses, or round the fires with spits and camp kettles, and a
rude kind of feasting or rather gormandizing prevailed throughout the
camp. The axe was continually at work and wearied the forest with its
echoes. Crash! some mighty tree would come down; in a few minutes
its limbs would be blazing and crackling on the huge camp fires, with
some luckless deer roasting before it, that had once sported beneath its
shade.

The change of weather had taken sharp hold of our little Frenchman. His meagre frame composed of bones and whip cord, was racked with rheumatic pains and twinges. He had the tooth ache—the ear ache, his face was tied up, he had shooting pains in every limb: yet all seemed but to increase his restless activity and he was in an incessant fidget about the fire, roasting and stewing, and groaning and scolding and swearing.

Our man Beatte returned grim and mortified from hunting. He had come upon a bear of formidable dimensions and wounded him with a rifle shot. The bear took to the brook which was swollen and rapid. Beatte dashed in after him and assailed him in the rear with his hunting knife. At every blow the bear turned furiously upon him, with a terrific display of white teeth. Beatte, having a foot hold in the brook, was enabled to push him off with his rifle, and when he turned to swim would flounder after, and attempt to hamstring him. The bear, however, succeeded in scrambling off among the thickets, and Beatte had to give up the chase.

His adventure, if it produced no game, brought up at least several anecdotes round the evening fire, relative to bear hunting, in which the grizzly bear figured conspicuously. This powerful and ferocious animal, is a favorite theme of hunters' story, both among red and white men; and his enormous claws are worn round the neck of an Indian brave as a trophy more honorable than a human scalp. He is now rarely seen below the upper prairies and the skirts of the Rocky Mountains. Other bears are formidable when wounded and provoked, but seldom make battle when allowed to escape. The grizzly bear alone, of all the animals of our western wilds, is prone to unprovoked hostility. His prodigious size and strength make him a formidable opponent, and his great tenacity of life often baffles the skill of the hunter, withstanding repeated shots of the rifle and wounds of the hunting knife.

One of the anecdotes related on this occasion gave a picture of the accidents and hard shifts to which our frontier rovers are enured. A hunter while in pursuit of a deer fell into one of those deep funnel shaped pits formed on the prairies by the settling of the waters after heavy rains, and known by the name of sink holes. To his great horror he came in contact, at the bottom, with a huge grizzly bear. The monster grappled him; a deadly contest ensued in which the poor hunter was severely torn and bitten and had a leg and an arm broken, but succeeded in killing his rugged foe. For several days he remained at the bottom of the pit, too much crippled to move, and subsisting on the raw flesh of the bear, during which time he kept his wounds open that they might heal gradually and effectually. He was at length enabled to scramble to the top of the pit and so out upon the open prairie. With great difficulty he crawled to a ravine formed by a stream, then nearly dry. Here he took a delicious draught of water, which infused new life into him; then dragging himself along from pool to pool, he supported himself by small fish and frogs.

One day he saw a wolf hunt down and kill a deer in the neighboring prairie. He immediately crawled forth from the ravine, drove off the wolf, and, lying down beside the carcass of the deer remained there until he had made several hearty meals, by which his strength was much recruited.

Returning to the ravine he pursued the course of the brook until it grew to be a considerable stream. Down this he floated until he came to where it emptied into the Mississippi. Just at the mouth of the stream he found a forked tree which he launched with some difficulty, and, getting astride of it, committed himself to the current of the mighty river. In this way he floated along until he arrived opposite the fort at Council Bluffs. Fortunately he arrived there in the day time, otherwise he might have floated unnoticed past this solitary post and perished in the idle waste of waters. Being descried from the fort a canoe was sent to his relief and he was brought to shore more dead than alive, where he soon recovered from his wounds, but remained maimed for life.

Our man Beatte had come out of his contest with the bear, very much worsted and discomfited. His drenching in the brook, together with the recent change of weather had brought on rheumatic pains in his limbs to which he is subject. Though ordinarily a fellow of undaunted spirit, and above all hardship, yet he now sat down by the fire gloomy and dejected and for once gave way to repining. Though in the prime of life, and of a robust frame and apparently iron constitution yet, by his own account he was little better than a mere wreck. He was, in fact, a living monument of the hardships of wild frontier life. Baring his arm, he shewed it warped and contracted by a former attack of rheumatism; a malady with which the Indians are often afflicted; for their exposure to the vicissitudes of the elements, does not produce that perfect hardihood and insensibility to the changes of the seasons that many are apt to imagine. He bore the scars of various maims and bruizes, some received in hunting, some in Indian warfare. His right arm had been broken by a fall from his horse, at another time his steed had fallen with him, and crushed his left leg.

"I am all broke to pieces and good for nothing;" said he—"I no care now what happen to me any more—" "However," added he, after a moments pause, "for all that—it would take a pretty strong man to put me down—any how."

I drew from him various particulars concerning himself which served to raise him in my estimation. His residence was on the Neosho, in an Osage hamlet or neighborhood, under the superintendence of a worthy missionary from the banks of the Hudson, by the name of Requa who was endeavoring to instruct the savages in the art of agriculture, and to make husbandmen and herdsmen of them. I had visited this agricultural mission of Requa in the course of my recent tour along the frontier, and had considered it more likely to produce solid advantages to the poor Indians, than any of the mere praying and preaching missions along the border.

In this neighborhood Pierre Beatte had his little farm, his Indian wife, and his halfbreed children: and aided Mr. Requa in his endeavors to civilize the habits and meliorate the condition of the Osage tribe. Beatte had been brought up a Catholic, and was inflexible in his religious faith; he could not pray with Mr. Requa, he said, but he could work with him, and he evinced a great zeal for the good of his savage relatives and neighbors. Indeed, though his father had been French, and he himself, had been brought up in communion with the whites, he evidently was more of an Indian in his tastes, and his heart yearned towards his mother's nation. When he talked to me of the wrongs and insults that the poor Indians suffered in their intercourse with the rough settlers on the frontiers; when he described the precarious and degraded state of the Osage tribe, diminished in numbers, broken in spirit, and almost living on sufferance in the land where they once figured so heroically, I could see his veins swell and his nostrils distend with indignation: but he would check the feeling with a strong exertion of Indian self command, and, in a manner, drive it back into his bosom.

He did not hesitate to relate an instance wherein he had joined his kindred Osages, in pursuing and avenging themselves on a party of white men who had committed a flagrant outrage upon them; and I found, in the encounter that took place, Beatte had shown himself the complete Indian.

He had more than once accompanied his Osage relatives in their wars with the Pawnees, and related a skirmish which took place on the borders of these very hunting grounds, in which several Pawnees were killed. We should pass near the place, he said, in the course of our tour, and the unburied bones and sculls of the slain were still to be seen there.

The Surgeon of the troop, who was present at our conversation, pricked up his ears at this intelligence. He was something of a phrenologist, and offered Beatte a handsome reward if he would procure him one of the sculls.

Beatte regarded him for a moment with a look of stern surprize.

"No!" said he at length—"Dat too bad! I have heart strong enough—I no care kill—but—*let the dead alone!*"

He added that once in travelling with a party of white men he had slept in the same tent with a Doctor and found that he had a Pawnee scull among his baggage: he at once renounced the Doctor's tent, and his fellowship. "He try to coax me," said Beatte—"but I say no—we must part—I no keep such company."

In the temporary depression of his spirits Beatte gave way to those superstitious forebodings to which Indians are prone. He had sat for some time, with his cheek upon his hand, gazing into the fire. I found his thoughts were wandering back to his humble home on the banks of the Neosho; he was sure, he said, that he should find some one of his family ill, or dead, on his return: his left eye had twitched and twinkled for two days past; an omen which always boded some misfortune of the kind. Such are the trivial circumstances which, when magnified into omens, will shake the souls of these men of iron. The least sign of mystic and sinister portent is sufficient to turn a hunter or a warrior from his course, or to fill his mind with apprehensions of impending evil. It is this superstitious propensity, common to the solitary and savage rovers of the wilderness that gives such powerful influence to the prophet and the dreamer.

The Osages with whom Beatte had passed much of his life, retain these superstitious fancies and rites in much of their original force. They all believe in the existence of the soul after its separation from the body, and that it carries with it all its mortal tastes and habitudes. At an Osage village in the neighborhood of Beatte, one of the chief warriors lost an only child a beautiful girl of a very tender age. All her play things were buried with her. Her favorite little horse, also, was killed and laid in the grave beside her, that she might have it to ride in the land of spirits.

I will here add a little story which I picked up in the course of my tour through Beatte's country, and which illustrates the superstitions of his Osage kindred. A large party of Osages had been encamped for some time on the borders of a fine stream, called the Nick a nansa. Among them was a young hunter one of the bravest and most graceful of the tribe, who was to be married to an Osage girl, who for her beauty was called the Flower of the Prairies. The young hunter left her for a time among her relatives in the encampment and went to St. Louis to dispose of the products of his hunting, and purchase ornaments for his bride.

After an absence of some weeks he returned to the banks of the Nickanansa, but the camp was no longer there: the bare frames of the lodges and the brands of extinguished fires alone marked the place. At a distance he beheld a female seated, as if weeping, by the side of the stream. It was his affianced bride. He ran to embrace her but she turned mournfully away. He dreaded lest some evil had befallen the camp.

"Where are our people?" cried he.

"They are gone to the banks of the Wagrushka."

"And what art thou doing here alone?"

"Waiting for thee."

"Then let us hasten to join our people on the banks of the Wagrushka."

He gave her his pack to carry, and walked ahead, according to Indian custom.

They came to where the smoke of the distant camp was seen rising from the woody margin of the stream. The girl seated herself at the foot of a tree. "It is not proper for us to return together;" said she. "I will wait here."

The young hunter proceeded to the camp alone, and was received by his relatives with gloomy countenances.

"What evil has happened," said he, "that ye are all so sad."

No one replied.

He turned to his favorite sister, and bade her go forth, seek his bride and conduct her to the camp.

"Alas!" cried she, "how shall I seek her? She died a few days since."

The relatives of the young girl now surrounded him weeping and wailing; but he refused to believe the dismal tidings. "But a few moments since," cried he, "I left her alive and in health—Come with me and I will conduct you to her."

He led the way to the tree where she had seated herself, but she was no longer there, and his pack lay on the ground. The fatal truth struck him to the heart: he fell to the ground dead.

I give this simple little story almost in the words in which it was related to me as I lay by the fire in an evening encampment on the banks of the haunted stream where it is said to have happened.

CHAPTER XXVIII

A secret expedition—Deer bleating—Magic balls.

On the following morning we were rejoined by the rangers who had remained at the last encampment to seek for the stray horses. They had tracked them for a considerable distance through bush and brake and across streams, until they found them cropping the herbage on the edge of a prairie. Their heads were in the direction of the fort and they were evidently grazing their way homewards, heedless of the unbounded freedom of the prairie so suddenly laid open to them.

About noon the weather held up and I observed a mysterious consultation going on between our half breeds and Tonish: it ended in a request that we would dispense with the services of the latter for a few

hours, and permit him to join his comrades in a grand foray. We objected
that Tonish was too much disabled by aches and pains for such an undertaking; but he was wild with eagerness for the mysterious enterprize,
and, when permission was given him, seemed to forget all his ailments
in an instant.

In a short time the trio were equipped and on horseback; with rifles on
their shoulders and handkerchiefs twisted round their heads, evidently
bound for a grand scamper. As they passed by the different lodges of the
camp, the vainglorious little Frenchman could not help boasting to the
right and left, of the great things he was about to achieve; though the
taciturn Beatte, who rode in advance, would every now and then check
his horse, and look back at him with an air of stern rebuke. It was hard,
however, to make the loquacious Tonish play "Indian."

Several of the hunters likewise sallied forth, and the prime old woodman Ryan came back early in the afternoon with ample spoil, having
killed a buck and two fat does. I drew near to a groupe of rangers that
had gathered round him as he stood by the spoil, and found they were
discussing the merits of a stratagem sometimes used in deer hunting.
This consists in imitating, with a small instrument called a bleat, the
cry of the faun, so as to lure the doe within reach of the rifle. There are
bleats of various kinds, suited to calm or windy weather, and to the age
of the faun. The poor animal, deluded by them, in its anxiety about its
young, will sometimes advance close up to the hunter. "I once bleated
a doe," said a young hunter, "until it came within twenty yards of me and
presented a sure mark. I levelled my rifle three times, but had not the
heart to shoot, for the poor doe looked so wistfully that it in a manner
made my heart yearn. I thought of my own mother and how anxious she
used to be about me when I was a child; so to put an end to the matter,
I gave a halloo and started the doe out of rifle shot in a moment."

"And you did right," cried honest Old Ryan: "for my part I never
could bring myself to bleating deer. I've been with hunters who had
bleats, and have made them throw them away. It is a rascally trick to
take advantage of a mother's love for her young."

Towards evening our three worthies returned from their mysterious
foray. The tongue of Tonish gave notice of their approach long before
they came in sight; for he was vociferating at the top of his lungs, and
rousing the attention of the whole camp. The lagging gait and reeking
flanks of their horses gave evidence of hard riding, and on nearer approach we found them hung round with meat like a butcher's shambles.
In fact they had been scouring an immense prairie that extended beyond
the forest, and which was covered with herds of buffalo. Of this prairie,
and the animals upon it, Beatte had received intelligence a few days
before, in his conversation with the Osages; but had kept the information

a secret from the rangers, that he and his comrades might have the first dash at the game. They had contented themselves with killing four, though, if Tonish might be believed, they might have slain them by scores.

These tidings, and the buffalo meat brought home in evidence, spread exultation through the camp, and every one looked forward with joy to a Buffalo hunt on the prairies. Tonish was again the oracle of the camp and held forth by the hour to a knot of listeners, crouched round the fire with their shoulders up to their ears. He was now more boastful than ever of his skill as a marksman. All his want of success in the early part of our march he attributed to being "out of luck," if not "spell bound," and finding himself listened to with apparent credulity, gave an instance of the kind, which he declared had happened to himself, but which was evidently a tale picked up among his relatives the Osages.

According to this account, when about fourteen years of age, as he was one day hunting he saw a white deer come out from a ravine. Crawling near to get a shot, he beheld another, and another, come forth until there were seven, all as white as snow. Having crept sufficiently near he singled one out and fired but without effect; the deer remained unfrightened. He loaded and fired again, and again he missed. Thus he continued firing and missing until all his ammunition was expended, and the deer remained without a wound. He returned home despairing of his skill as a marksman but was consoled by an old Osage hunter. "These white deer," said he, "have a charmed life and can only be killed by bullets of a particular kind."

The old Indian cast several balls for Tonish, but would not suffer him to be present on the occasion, nor inform him of the ingredients and mystic ceremonials.

Provided with these balls Tonish again set out in quest of the white deer and succeeded in finding them. He tried at first with ordinary balls, but missed as before. A magic ball, however, immediately brought a fine buck to the ground. Whereupon the rest of the herd immediately disappeared and were never seen again.

Oct. 29.th The morning opened gloomy and lowering; but, towards eight o'clock the sun struggled forth and lighted up the forest, and the notes of the bugle gave signal to prepare for marching. Now began a scene of bustle and clamour and gaiety. Some were scampering and bawling after their horses, some were riding in bare backed, and driving in the horses of their comrades. Some were stripping the poles of the wet blankets that had served for shelters, others packing up with all possible despatch, and loading the baggage horses as they arrived, while others were cracking off their damp rifles and charging them afresh, to be ready for the sport.

About ten o'clock we began our march. I loitered in the rear of the troop as it forded the turbid brook and defiled through the labyrinths of the forest. I always felt disposed to linger until the last straggler disappeared among the trees and the distant note of the bugle died upon the ear, that I might behold the wilderness relapsing into silence and solitude. In the present instance the deserted scene of our late bustling encampment had a forlorn and desolate appearance. The surrounding forest had been in many places trampled into a quagmire. Trees felled and partly hewn in pieces and scattered in huge fragments; tent poles stripped of their covering; smouldering fires, with great morsels of roasted venison and Buffalo meat, standing on wooden spits before them, hacked and slashed by the knives of hungry hunters; while around were strewed the hides, the horns, the antlers and bones of buffalos and deer, with uncooked joints and unplucked turkeys, left behind with that reckless improvidence and wastefulness which young hunters are apt to indulge when in a neighborhood where game abounds. In the mean time a score or two of turkey buzzards, or vultures, were already on the wing, wheeling their magnificent flight high in the air, and preparing for a descent upon the camp as soon as it should be abandoned.

CHAPTER XXIX

The Grand Prairie—A buffalo hunt.

After proceeding about two hours, in a southerly direction, we emerged towards midday from the dreary belt of the Cross Timber, and to our infinite delight beheld "The Great Prairie" stretching to the right and left before us. We could distinctly trace the meandering course of the Main Canadian and various smaller streams, by the strips of green forest that bordered them. The landscape was vast and beautiful. There is always an expansion of feeling in looking upon these boundless and fertile wastes; but I was doubly conscious of it after emerging from our "close dungeon of innumerous boughs."

From a rising ground Beatte pointed out to us the place where he and his comrades had killed the Buffaloes; and we beheld several black objects moving in the distance, which he said were part of the herd. The Captain determined to shape his course to a woody bottom about a mile distant and to encamp there, for a day or two by way of having a regular buffalo hunt and getting a supply of provisions. As the troop defiled along the slope of the hill towards the camping ground, Beatte proposed to my mess mates and myself that we should put ourselves under his guidance, promising to take us where we should have plenty of sport. Leaving the line of march, therefore, we diverged towards the prairie; traversing a small valley and ascending a gentle swell of land. As we reached the summit we beheld a gang of wild horses about a mile off. Beatte was immediately on the alert, and no longer thought of buffalo hunting. He was mounted on his powerful, half wild horse, with a lariat coiled at the saddle bow, and set off in pursuit: while we remained on a rising ground watching his maneuvres with great solicitude. Taking advantage of a strip of wood land he stole quietly along so as to get close to them before he was perceived. The moment they caught sight of him a grand scamper took place. We watched him skirting along the horizon like a privateer in full chase of a merchantman; at length he passed over the brow of a ridge and down into a shallow valley; in a few moments he was on the opposite hill and close upon one of the horses. He was soon head and head, and appeared to be trying to noose his prey, but they both disappeared again below the hill and we saw no more of them. It turned out afterwards that he had noosed a powerful horse but could not hold him, and had lost his lariat in the attempt.

While we were waiting for his return we perceived two buffalo bulls descending a slope towards a stream which wound through a ravine fringed with trees. The young count and myself endeavored to get near them under covert of the trees. They discovered us while we were yet three or four hundred yards off, and, turning about, retreated up the rising ground. We urged our horses across the ravine and gave chase. The immense weight of head and shoulders causes the buffalo to labour heavily up hill, but it accelerates his descent. We had the advantage, therefore, and gained rapidly upon the fugitives, though it was difficult to get our horses to approach them, their very scent inspiring them with terror. The Count, who had a double barrelled gun loaded with ball, fired but missed. The bulls now altered their course, and gallopped down hill with headlong rapidity. As they ran in different directions we each singled one and separated. I was provided with a brace of veteran brass barrelled pistols which I had borrowed at Fort Gibson, and which had evidently seen some service. Pistols are very effective in Buffalo hunting, as the hunter can ride up close to the animal and fire at it while at full speed; whereas the long heavy rifles used on the frontier cannot be easily managed, nor discharged with accurate aim from horseback. My object, therefore, was to get within pistolshot of the Buffalo. This was no very easy matter. I was well mounted, on a horse of excellent speed and bottom, that seemed eager for the chase and soon overtook the game, but the moment he came nearly parallel he would keep sheering off with ears forked and pricked forward, and every symptom of aversion and alarm. It was no wonder. Of all animals a Buffalo, when close pressed by the hunter, has an aspect the most diabolical. His two short black horns curve out of a huge frontlet of shaggy hair, his eyes glow like coals; his mouth is open, his tongue parched and drawn up into a half crescent, his tail is erect and the tufted end whisking about in the air, he is a perfect picture of mingled rage and terror.

It was with difficulty I urged my horse sufficiently near, when taking aim, to my chagrin both pistols missed fire. Unfortunately the locks of these veteran weapons were so much worn that, in the gallop, the priming had been shaken out of the pans. At the snapping of the last pistol I was close upon the buffalo when, in his despair he turned round with a sudden snort and rushed upon me. My horse wheeled about as if on a pivot, made a convulsive spring, and as I had been leaning on one side with pistol extended I came near being thrown at the feet of the buffalo.

Three or four bounds of the horses carried us out of reach of the enemy, who, having merely turned in desperate self defence, quickly resumed his flight. As soon as I could gather in my panic stricken horse, and prime the pistols afresh, I again spurred in pursuit of the Buffalo, who had slackened his speed to take breath. On my approach he again set off full tilt, heaving himself forward with a heavy rolling gallop, dashing with headlong precipitation through brakes and ravines, while several deer and wolves startled from their coverts by his thundering career ran helter skelter to right and left across the waste.

A gallop across the prairies in pursuit of game is by no means so smooth a career as those may imagine, who have only the idea of an open level plain. It is true the prairies of the hunting grounds are not so much entangled with flowering plants and long herbage as the lower prairies, and are principally covered with short buffalo grass; but they are diversified by hill and dale, and where most level are apt to be cut up by deep rifts and ravines, made by torrents after rains, and which, yawning from an even surface, are almost like pitfalls in the way of the hunter, checking him suddenly, when in full career, or subjecting him to the risk of limb and life. The plains, too, are beset by burrowing holes of small animals, in which the horse is apt to sink to the fet lock, and throw both himself and his rider. The late rain had covered some parts of the prairie, where the ground was hard, with a thin sheet of water, through which the horse had to splash his way. In other parts there were innumerable shallow hollows, eight or ten feet in diameter, made by the buffalos, who wallow in sand and mud like swine. These being filled with water shone like mirrors, so that the horse was continually leaping over them or springing on one side. We had reached, too, a rough part of the prairie, very much broken and cut up; the buffalo, who was running for life, took no heed to his course plunging down break neck ravines, where it was necessary to skirt the borders in search of a safer descent. At length he came to where a winter stream had torn a deep chasm across the whole prairie; laying open jagged rocks and forming a long glen bordered by steep crumbling cliffs of mingled stone and clay. Down one of these the buffalo flung himself half tumbling half leaping, and then scuttled off along the bottom, while I, seeing all further pursuit useless, pulled up, and gazed quietly after him from the border of the cliff, until he disappeared amidst the windings of the ravine.

Nothing now remained but to turn my steed and rejoin my companions. Here at first was some little difficulty. The ardour of the chase had betrayed me into a long heedless gallop. I now found myself in the midst of a lonely waste in which the prospect was bounded by undulating swells of land, naked and uniform, where, from the deficiency of land marks and distinct features an inexperienced man may become bewildered and lose his way as readily as in the wastes of the ocean. The day too was overcast, so that I could not guide myself by the sun; my only mode was to retrace the track my horse had made in coming, though this I would often lose sight of, where the ground was covered with parched herbage.

To one unaccustomed to it there is something inexpressibly lonely in the solitude of a prairie. The loneliness of a forest seems nothing to it. There the view is shut in by trees, and the imagination is left free to picture some livelier scene beyond. But here we have an immense extent of landscape without a sign of human existence. We have the consciousness of being far, far beyond the bounds of human habitation; we feel as if moving in the midst of a desert world. As my horse lagged slowly back over the scenes of our late scamper, and the delirium of the chase had passed away, I was peculiarly sensible to these circumstances. The silence of the waste was now and then broken by the cry of a distant flock of pelicans stalking like spectres about a shallow pool. Sometimes by the sinister croaking of a raven in the air, while occasionally a scoundrel wolf would scour off from before me and having attained a safe distance, would sit down and howl and whine with tones that gave a dreariness to the surrounding solitude.

After pursuing my way for some time I descried a horseman on the edge of a distant hill and soon recognized him to be the Count. He had been equally unsuccessful with myself; we were shortly afterwards rejoined by our worthy comrade the Virtuoso, who, with spectacles on nose, had made two or three ineffectual shots from horseback.

We determined not to seek the camp until we had made one more effort. Casting our eyes about the surrounding waste we descried a herd of buffalo about two miles distant, scattered apart and quietly grazing near a small strip of trees and bushes. It required but little stretch of fancy to picture them so many cattle grazing on the edge of a common and that the grove might shelter some lowly farmhouse.

We now formed our plan to circumvent the herd, and by getting on the other side of them to hunt them in the direction where we knew our camp to be situated: otherwise the pursuit might take us to such a distance as to render it impossible for us to find our way back before nightfall. Taking a wide circuit therefore, we moved slowly and cautiously, pausing occasionally, when we saw any of the herd desist from grazing. The wind fortunately set from them, otherwise they might have scented us and have taken the alarm. In this way we succeeded in getting round the herd without disturbing it. It consisted of about forty head, bulls, cows and calves. Separating to some distance from each other, we now approached slowly in a parallel line, hoping by degrees to steal near without exciting attention. They began however to move off quietly, stopping at every step or two to graze, when suddenly a bull that, unobserved by us, had been taking his siesta under a clump of trees to our left, roused himself from his lair, and hastened to join his companions. We were still at a considerable distance but the game had taken the alarm. We quickened our pace, they broke into a gallop and now commenced a full chase.

As the ground was level they shouldered along with great speed, following each other in a line; two or three bulls bringing up the rear, the last of whom, from his enormous size and venerable frontlet and beard of sunburnt hair, looked like the patriarch of the herd and as if he might long have reigned the monarch of the prairie.

There is a mixture of the awful and the comic in the look of these huge animals as they heave their great bulk forwards, with an up and down motion of the unwieldy head and shoulders; their tail cocked up like the queue of pantaloon in a pantomime, the end whisking about in a fierce yet whimsical style, and their eyes glaring venomously with an expression of fright and fury.

For some time I kept parallel with the line without being able to force my horse within pistolshot, so much had he been alarmed by the assault of the Buffalo in the preceding chase. At length I succeeded, but was again balked by my pistols missing fire. My companions, whose horses were less fleet, and more way worn, could not overtake the herd; at length Mr. L—, who was in the rear of the line, and losing ground levelled his double barrelled gun and fired a long raking shot. It struck a buffalo just above the loins, broke its back bone and brought it to the ground. He stopped and alighted to despatch his prey, when borrowing his gun which had yet a charge remaining in it, I put my horse to his speed, again overtook the herd which was thundering along pursued by the Count. With my present weapon there was no need of urging my horse to such close quarters; gallopping along parallel, therefore, I singled out a buffalo and by a fortunate shot brought it down on the spot. The ball had struck a vital part; it could not move from the place where it fell but lay there struggling in mortal agony: while the rest of the herd kept on their headlong career across the prairie.

Dismounting I now fettered my horse to prevent his straying and advanced to contemplate my victim. I am nothing of a sportsman: I had been prompted to this unwonted exploit by the magnitude of the game and the excitement of an adventurous chase. Now that the excitement was over I could not but look with commiseration upon the poor animal that lay struggling and bleeding at my feet. His very size and importance, which had before inspired me with eagerness, now increased my compunction. It seemed as if I had inflicted pain in proportion to the bulk of my victim, and as if there were a hundred fold greater waste of life than there would have been in the destruction of an animal of inferior size.

To add to these after qualms of conscience the poor animal lingered in his agony. He had evidently received a mortal wound, but death might be long in coming. It would not do to leave him here to be torn piece meal while yet alive, by the wolves that had already snuffed his blood, and were skulking and howling at a distance and waiting for my departure and by the ravens that were flapping about and croaking dismally in the air. It became now an act of mercy to give him his quietus, and put him out of his misery. I primed one of the pistols therefore and advanced close up to the buffalo. To inflict a wound thus in cool blood I found a totally different thing from firing in the heat of the chase. Taking aim, however, just behind the foreshoulder my pistol for once proved true; the ball must have passed through the heart, for the animal gave one convulsive throe and expired.

While I stood meditating and moralizing over the wreck I had so wantonly produced, with my horse grazing near me I was rejoined by my fellow sportsman the Virtuoso, who, being a man of universal adroitness and withal more experienced and hardened in the gentle art of "venerie," soon managed to carve out the tongue of the buffalo, and delivered it to me to bear back to the camp as a trophy.

CHAPTER XXX

A comrade lost—A search for the camp—The commissioner, the wild horse and the buffalo—A wolf serenade.

Our solicitude was now awakened for the young Count. With his usual eagerness and impetuosity he had persisted in urging his jaded horse in pursuit of the herd, unwilling to return without having likewise killed a buffalo. In this way he had kept on following them hither and thither, and occasionally firing an ineffectual shot, until by degrees horseman and herd became indistinct in the distance, and at length swelling ground and strips of trees and thickets hid them entirely from sight.

By the time my friend the Amateur joined me the young count had been long lost to view. We held a consultation on the matter. Evening was drawing on. Were we to pursue him it would be dark before we should overtake him granting we did not entirely lose trace of him in the gloom. We should then be too much bewildered to find our way back to the encampment; even now our return would be difficult. We determined, therefore, to hasten to the camp as speedily as possible and send out our half breeds and some of the veteran hunters, skilled in cruizing about the prairies, to search for our companion.

We accordingly set forward in what we supposed to be the direction of the camp. Our weary horses could hardly be urged beyond a walk. The twilight thickened upon us; the landscape grew gradually indistinct; we tried in vain to recognize various land marks which we had noted in the morning. The features of the prairies are so similar as to baffle the eye of any but an Indian or a practised woodsman. At length night closed in. We hoped to see the distant glare of camp fires; we listened to catch the sound of the bells about the necks of the grazing horses. Once or twice we thought we distinguished them. We were mistaken. Nothing was to be heard but a monotonous concert of insects, with now and then the dismal howl of wolves mingling with the night breeze. We began to think of halting for the night and bivouacking under the lea of some thicket. We had implements to strike a light; there was plenty of fire wood at hand, and the tongues of our buffaloes would furnish us with a repast.

Just as we were preparing to dismount we heard the report of a rifle, and shortly after the notes of the bugle calling up the night guard. Pushing forward in that direction the camp fires soon broke upon our sight, gleaming at a distance from among the thick groves of an alluvial bottom.

As we entered the camp we found it a scene of rude hunters' revelry and wassail. There had been a grand days sport in which all had taken a part. Eight buffaloes had been killed. Roaring fires were blazing on every side; all hands were feasting upon roasted joints, broiled marrow bones, and the juicy hump, farfamed among the epicures of the prairies. Right glad were we to dismount and partake of the sturdy cheer, for we had been on our weary horses since morning without tasting food.

As to our worthy friend the commissioner, with whom we had parted company at the outset of this eventful day, we found him lying in a corner of the tent, much the worse for wear in the course of a successful hunting match.

It seems that our man Beatte, in his zeal to give the Commissioner an opportunity of distinguishing himself and gratifying his hunting propensities, had mounted him upon his half wild horse, and started him in pursuit of a huge buffalo bull that had already been frightened by the hunters. The horse, which was fearless as his owner, and like him had a considerable spice of devil in his composition, and who, beside, had been made familiar with the game, no sooner came in sight and scent of the buffalo, than he set off at full speed, bearing the involuntary hunter hither and thither and whither he would not—up hill, and down hill, leaping pools and brooks, dashing through glens and gullies; until he came up with the game. Instead of sheering off he crowded upon the buffalo. The Commissioner almost in self defence, discharged both barrels of a double barrelled gun into the enemy. The broad side took effect, but was not mortal. The Buffalo turned furiously upon his pursuer. The horse as he had been taught by his owner, wheeled off. The Buffalo plunged after him. The worthy commissioner, in great extremity, drew his sole pistol from his holster, fired it off as a stern chaser, shot the buffalo full in the breast, and brought him lumbering forward to the earth.

The commissioner returned to camp, lauded on all sides for his signal exploit; but grievously battered and way worn. He had been a hard rider per force, and a victor in spite of himself. He turned a deaf ear to all compliments and congratulations; had but little stomach for the hunter's fare placed before him and soon retreated to stretch his limbs in the tent, declaring that nothing should tempt him again to mount that half devil Indian horse, and that he had enough of buffalo hunting for the rest of his life.

It was too dark now to send any one in search of the young count. Guns, however, were fired and the bugle sounded from time to time, to guide him to the camp, if by chance he should straggle within hearing, but the night advanced without his making his appearance; there was not a star visible to guide him, and we concluded that, wherever he was, he would give up wandering in the dark and bivouack until day break.

It was a raw overcast night. The carcasses of the buffaloes killed in the vicinity of the camp had drawn about it an unusual number of wolves, who kept up the most forlorn concert of whining yells prolonged into dismal cadences and inflexions, literally converting the surrounding waste into a howling wilderness. Nothing is more melancholy than the midnight howl of a wolf on a prairie. What rendered the gloom and wildness of the night and the savage concert of the neighboring waste the more dreary to us, was the idea of the lonely and exposed situation of our young and inexperienced comrade. We trusted, however, that on the return of daylight he would find his way back to the camp, and then all the events of the night would be remembered only as so many savoury gratifications of his passion for adventure.

CHAPTER XXXI

A hunt for a lost comrade.

The morning dawned and an hour or two passed without any tidings of the Count. We began to feel uneasiness lest, having no compass to aid him, he might perplex himself and wander in some opposite direction. Stragglers are thus often lost for days; what made us the more anxious about him was, that he had no provisions with him, was totally unversed in "wood craft," and liable to fall into the hands of some lurking or straggling party of savages.

As soon as our people, therefore, had made their breakfast we beat up for volunteers for a cruize in search of the count. A dozen of the rangers, mounted on some of the best and freshest horses, and armed with rifles were soon ready to start; our half breeds Beatte and Antoine also, with our little mongrel Frenchman were zealous in the cause, so Mr. L— and myself, taking the lead, to shew the way to the scene of our late hunt, where we had parted company with the count, we all set out across the prairie.

A ride of a couple of miles brought us to the carcasses of the two buffalos we had killed. A legion of ravenous wolves were already gorging upon them. At our approach they reluctantly drew off, skulking with a caitiff look to the distance of a few hundred yards, and there awaiting our departure that they might return to their banquet.

I conducted Beatte and Antoine to the spot whence the young count had continued the chase alone. It was like putting hounds upon the scent. They immediately distinguished the track of his horse amidst the trampings of the buffalos, and set off at a round pace, following with the

eye in nearly a straight course, for upwards of a mile when they came
to where the herd had divided and run hither and thither about a
meadow. Here the track of the horse's hoofs wandered, and doubled and
often crossed each other; our half breeds were like hounds at fault.
While we were all at a halt, waiting until they should unravel the maze,
Beatte suddenly gave a short Indian whoop or rather yelp, and pointed
to a distant hill. On regarding it attentively we perceived a horseman on
the summit. "It is the Count!" cried Beatte, and set off at full gallop,
followed by the whole company. In a few moments he checked his horse.
Another figure on horseback had appeared on the brow of the hill.
This completely altered the case. The count had wandered off alone; no
other person had been missing from the camp. If one of these horsemen
was indeed the count, the other must be an Indian. If an Indian, in all
probability a Pawnee. Perhaps they were both Indians; scouts of some
party lurking in the vicinity. While these and other suggestions were
hastily discussed, the two horsemen glided down from the profile of
the hill and we lost sight of them. One of the rangers suggested that
there might be a straggling party of Pawnees behind the hill, and that
the count might have fallen into their hands. The idea had an electric
effect upon the little troop. In an instant every horse was at full speed,
the half breeds leading the way; the young rangers as they rode set up
wild yelps of exultation at the thoughts of having a brush with
Indians. A neck or nothing gallop brought us to the skirts of the hill,
and revealed our mistake. In a ravine we found the two horsemen
standing by the carcass of a buffalo which they had killed. They proved
to be two rangers who, unperceived, had left the camp a little before
us, and had come here in a direct line, while we had made a wide circuit
about the prairie.

This episode being at an end and the sudden excitement being over,
we slowly and cooly retraced our steps to the meadow, but it was some
time before our halfbreeds could again get on the track of the count.
Having at length found it, they succeeded in following it through all its
doublings, until they came to where it was no longer mingled with the
tramp of buffalos, but became single and separate, wandering here and
there about the prairies, but always tending in a direction opposite to
that of the camp. Here the count had evidently given up the pursuit of
the herd and had endeavored to find his way to the encampment, but
had become bewildered as the evening shades thickened around him,
and had completely mistaken the points of the compass.

In all this quest our halfbreeds displayed that quickness of eye, in following up a track, for which Indians are so noted. Beatte especially,
was as staunch as a veteran hound. Sometimes he would keep forward
on an easy trot, his eyes fixed on the ground a little a head of his horse,

clearly distinguishing prints in the herbage, which to me were invisible excepting on the closest inspection. Sometimes he would pull up and walk his horse slowly, regarding the ground intensely, where, to my eye nothing was apparent. Then he would dismount, lead his horse by the bridle and advance cautiously, step by step, with his face bent towards the earth, just catching, here and there, a casual indication of the vaguest kind to guide him onward. In some places where the soil was hard and the grass withered, he would lose the track entirely and wander backwards and forwards and right and left in search of it; returning occasionally to the place where he had lost sight of it, to take a new departure. If this failed he would examine the banks of the neighboring streams, or the sandy bottoms of the ravines, in hopes of finding tracks where the count had crossed. When he again came upon the track he would remount his horse and resume his onward course. At length, after crossing a stream, in the crumbling banks of which the hoofs of the horse were deeply dinted we came upon a high dry prairie, where our halfbreeds were completely baffled. Not a foot print was to be discerned, though they searched in every direction, and Beatte at length coming to a pause, shook his head most despondingly.

Just then a small herd of deer, roused from a neighboring ravine came bounding by us. Beatte sprang from his horse, levelled his rifle and wounded one slightly, but without bringing it to the ground. The report of the rifle was almost immediately followed by a long halloo from a distance. We looked around but could see nothing. Another long halloo was heard and at length a horseman was descried emerging out of a skirt of forest. A single glance shewed him to be the young count; there was a universal shout and scamper, every one setting off full gallop to greet him. It was a joyful meeting to both parties, for much anxiety had been felt by us all on account of his youth and inexperience, and for his part, with all his love of adventure, he seemed right glad to be once more among his friends.

As we supposed, he had completely mistaken his course on the preceding evening, and had wandered about until dark, when he thought of bivouacking. The night was cool yet he feared to make a fire lest it might betray him to some lurking party of Indians. Hobbling his horse with his pockethandkerchief, and leaving him to graze on the margin of the prairie, he clambered into a tree, fixed his saddle in the fork of the branches, and, placing himself securely with his back against the trunk, prepared to pass a dreary and anxious night, regaled occasionally with the howlings of the wolves. He was agreeably disappointed. The fatigue of the day soon brought on a sound sleep; he had delightful dreams about his home in Switzerland, nor did he awake until it was broad day light.

He then descended from his roosting place, mounted his horse and rode to the naked summit of a hill, whence he beheld a trackless wilderness around him, but at no great distance the Grand Canadian, winding its way between borders of forest land. The sight of this river consoled him with the idea that, should he fail in finding his way back to the camp, or in being found by some party of his comrades, he might follow the course of the stream which could not fail to conduct him to some frontier post or Indian hamlet.

So closed the events of our haphazard buffalo hunt.

CHAPTER XXXII

A republic of prairie dogs.

On returning from our expedition in quest of the young Count I learned that a burrow, or village, as it is termed, of prairie dogs had been discovered on the level summit of a hill about a mile from the camp. Having heard much of the habits and peculiarities of these little animals I determined to pay a visit to the community. The prairie dog is, in fact, one of the curiosities of the Far West, about which travellers delight to tell marvellous tales, endowing him at times, with something of the politic and social habits of a rational being, and giving him systems of civil government and domestic economy almost equal to what they used to bestow upon the beaver.

The Prairie Dog is an animal of the coney kind and about the size of a rabbit. He is of a sprightly, mercurial nature, quick, sensitive and somewhat petulant. He is very gregarious, living in large communities, sometimes of several acres in extent, where innumerable little heaps of earth shew the entrances to the subterranean cells of the inhabitants, and the well beaten tracks, like lanes and streets, shew their mobility and restlessness. According to the accounts given of them they would seem to be continually full of sport, business and public affairs; whisking about hither and thither, as if on gossipping visits to each other's houses, or congregating in the cool of the evening, or after a shower, and gambolling together in the open air. Sometimes, especially when the moon shines, they pass half the night in revelry, barking or yelping with short, quick yet weak tones, like those of very young puppies. While in the height of their playfulness and clamour, however, should there be the least alarm, they all vanish into their cells in an instant, and the village remains blank and silent. In case they are hard pressed by their pursuers, without any hope of escape, they will assume a pugnacious air, and a most whimsical look of impotent wrath and defiance.

The Prairie Dogs are not permittted to remain sole and undisturbed inhabitants of their own homes. Owls and rattlesnakes are said to take up their abodes with them, but whether as invited guests or unwelcome intruders, is a matter of controversy. The owls are of a peculiar kind and would seem to partake of the character of the hawk, for they are taller and more erect on their legs, more alert in their looks and rapid in their flight, than ordinary owls, and do not confine their excursions to the night, but sally forth in broad day.

Some say that they only inhabit cells which the prairie dogs have deserted and suffer to go to ruin, in consequence of the death in them of some relative, for they would make out this little animal to be endowed with keen sensibilities, that will not permit it to remain in the dwelling where it has witnessed the death of a friend. Other fanciful speculators represent the owl as a kind of housekeeper to the prairie dog, and, from having a note very similar, insinuate that it acts, in a manner, as family preceptor, and teaches the young litter to bark.

As to the rattle snake, nothing satisfactory has been ascertained of the part he plays in this most interesting household, though he is considered as little better than a sycophant and sharper, that winds himself into the concerns of the honest credulous little dog, and takes him in most sadly. Certain it is, if he acts as toad eater, he occasionally solaces himself with more than the usual perquisites of his order, as he is now and then detected with one of the younger members of the family in his maw.

Such are a few of the particulars that I could gather about the domestic economy of this little inhabitant of the prairies, who, with his pigmy republic, appears to be a subject of much whimsical speculation and burlesque remark among the hunters of the Far West.

It was towards evening that I set out with a companion to visit the village in question. Unluckily it had been invaded in the course of the day by some of the rangers, who had shot two or three of its inhabitants, and thrown the whole sensitive community in confusion. As we approached we could perceive numbers of the inhabitants seated at the entrances of their cells, while centinels seemed to have been posted on the outskirts, to keep a look out. At sight of us the picket guards scampered in and gave the alarm; whereupon every inhabitant gave a short yelp or bark and dived into his hole, his heels twinkling in the air as if he had thrown a summerset.

We traversed the whole village, or republic, which covered an area of about thirty acres, but not a whisker of an inhabitant was to be seen. We probed their cells as far as the ramrods of our rifles would reach, but could unearth neither dog, nor owl nor rattlesnake. Moving quietly to a little distance we lay down upon the ground and watched for a long time silent and motionless. By and bye a cautious old burgher would slowly put forth the end of his nose but instantly draw it in again. Another, at a greater distance would emerge entirely, but, catching a glance of us would throw a summerset and plunge back again into his hole. At length some who resided on the opposite side of the village, taking courage from the continued stillness, would steal forth and hurry off to a distant hole, the residence possibly of some family connexion or gossipping friend, about whose safety they were solicitous, or with whom they wished to compare notes about the late occurrences.

Others, still more bold, assembled in litttle knots, in the streets and public places, as if to discuss the recent outrages offered to the commonwealth, and the atrocious murders of their fellow burghers. We rose from the ground and moved forward to take a nearer view of these public proceedings when, yelp! yelp! yelp!—there was a shrill alarm passed from mouth to mouth; the meetings suddenly dispersed; feet twinkled in the air in every direction, and in an instant all had vanished into the earth.

The dusk of the evening put an end to our observations, but the train of whimsical comparisons produced in my brain by the moral attributes which I had heard given to these little politic animals, still continued after my return to camp; and late in the night, as I lay awake after all the camp was asleep, and heard in the stillness of the hour, a faint clamour of shrill voices from the distant village, I could not help picturing to myself the inhabitants gathered together in noisy assemblage, and windy debate, to devise plans for the public safety, and to vindicate the invaded rights and insulted dignity of the republic.

CHAPTER XXXIII

A council in the camp—Reasons for facing homewards—Horses lost—Departure with a detachment on the homeward route—Swamp—Wild horse—Camp scene by night—The owl the harbinger of dawn.

While breakfast was preparing a council was held as to our future movements. Symptoms of discontent had appeared for a day or two past among the rangers, most of whom, unaccustomed to the life of the prairies, had become impatient of its privations, as well as of the restraints of the camp. The want of bread had been felt severely, and they were wearied with constant travel. In fact the novelty and excitement of the expedition were at an end. They had hunted the deer, the bear, the elk, the buffalo and the wild horse, and had no further object of leading interest to look forward to. A general inclination prevailed, therefore, to turn homewards.

Grave reasons disposed the captain and his officers to adopt this resolution. Our horses were generally much jaded by the fatigues of travelling and hunting, and had fallen away sadly for want of good pasturage, and from being tethered at night, to protect them from Indian depredations. The late rains, too, seemed to have washed away the nourishment from the scanty herbage that remained, and since our encampment during the storm our horses had lost flesh and strength rapidly. With every possible care, horses, accustomed to grain, and to the regular and plentiful nourishment of the stable and the farm, lose heart and condition in travelling on the prairies. In all expeditions of the kind we were engaged in, the hardy Indian horses, which are generally mustangs, or a cross of the wild breed, are to be preferred. They can stand all fatigues, hardships and privations, and thrive on the grasses and wild herbage of the plains.

Our men, too, had acted with little fore thought; gallopping off whenever they had a chance, after the game that we encountered while on the march. In this way they had strained and wearied their horses, instead of husbanding their strength and spirits. On a tour of the kind, horses should as seldom as possible be put off of a quiet walk: and the average days journey should not exceed ten miles.

We had hoped by pushing forward, to reach the bottoms of the Red River, which abound with young cane, a most nourishing forage for cattle at this season of the year. It would now take us several days to arrive there, and in the meantime many of our horses would probably give out. It was the time, too, when the hunting parties of Indians set fire to the prairies; the herbage, throughout this part of the country, was in that parched state favorable to combustion, and there was daily more and more risk that the prairies between us and the fort would be set on fire by some of the return parties of Osages, and a scorched desert left for us to traverse. In a word we had started too late in the season or loitered too much in the early part of our march, to accomplish our originally intended tour; and there was imminent hazard, if we continued on, that we should lose the greater part of our horses, and, beside suffering various other inconveniences, be obliged to return on foot. It was determined, therefore, to give up all further progress, and turning our faces to the southeast, to make the best of our way back to Fort Gibson.

This resolution being taken there was an immediate eagerness to put it into operation. Several horses, however, were missing, and among others those of the captain and the Surgeon. Persons had gone in search of them, but the morning advanced without any tidings of them. Our party in the mean time, being all ready for a march, the commissioner, determined to set off in the advance, with his original escort of a lieutenant and fourteen rangers, leaving the captain to come on, at his convenience, with the main body. At ten o'clock, we accordingly started, under the guidance of Beatte; who had hunted over this part of the country and knew the direct route to the garrison.

For some distance we skirted the prairie, keeping a south east direction, and in the course of our ride we saw a variety of wild animals, deer, white and black wolves, Buffalos and wild horses. To the latter our half breeds and Tonish gave ineffectual chase, only serving to add to the weariness of their already jaded steeds. Indeed it is rarely that any but the weaker and least fleet of the wild horses are taken in these hard racings; while the horse of the huntsman is prone to be knocked up. The latter, in fact, risks a good horse to catch a bad one. On this occasion Tonish, who was a perfect imp on horseback, and noted for ruining every animal he bestrode, succeeded in laming and almost disabling the powerful grey, on which we had mounted him at the outset of our tour.

After proceeding a few miles we left the prairie and struck to the east, taking what Beatte pronounced an old Osage war track. This led us through a rugged tract of country, overgrown with scrubbed forests and entangled thickets, and intersected by deep ravines, and brisk running streams, the sources of Little River. About three o'clock we encamped by some pools of water in a small valley, having come about fourteen miles. We had brought on a supply of provisions from our last camp, and supped heartily upon stewed buffalo meat, roasted venison, beignets, or fritters of flour fried in bear's lard, and tea made of a species of the golden rod, which we had found, throughout our whole route, almost as grateful a beverage as coffee. Indeed our coffee, which, as long as it held out, had been served up with every meal, according to the custom of the West, was by no means a beverage to boast of. It was roasted in a frying pan, without much care, pounded in a leathern bag, with a round stone, and, boiled in our prime and almost only kitchen utensil, the camp kettle, in "branch" or brook water, which, on the prairies, is deeply coloured by the soil, of which it always holds abundant particles in a state of solution and suspension. In fact in the course of our tour we had tasted the quality of every variety of soil, and the draughts of water we had taken might vie in diversity of colour, if not of flavour, with the tinctures of an apothecary's shop. Pure, limpid water, is a rare luxury on the prairies, at least at this season of the year.

Supper over, we placed sentinels about our scanty and diminished camp, spread our skins and blankets under the trees, now nearly destitute of foliage, and slept soundly until morning.

We had a beautiful day break. The camp again resounded with cheerful voices; every one was animated with the thoughts of soon being at the fort; and revelling on bread and vegetables. Even our saturnine man Beatte seemed inspired on the occasion and, as he drove up the horses for the march, I heard him singing in nasal tones, a most forlorn Indian ditty. All this transient gaiety, however, soon died away amidst the fatigues of our march, which lay through the same kind of rough, hilly, thicketed country as that of yesterday. In the course of the morning we arrived at the valley of Little River where it wound through a broad bottom of alluvial soil. At present it had overflowed its banks and inundated a great part of the valley. The difficulty was to distinguish the stream from the broad sheets of water it had formed, and to find a place where it might be forded; for it was in general deep and miry, with abrupt crumbling banks. Under the pilotage of Beatte, therefore, we wandered for some time among the links made by this winding stream, in what appeared to us a trackless labyrinth of swamps, thickets and standing pools. Sometimes our jaded horses dragged their limbs forward with the utmost difficulty, having to toil for a great distance, with the water up to the stirrups, and beset at the bottom with roots and creeping plants. Sometimes we had to force our way through dense thickets of brambles and grape vines, which almost pulled us out of our saddles. In one place one of the pack horses sank in the mire and fell on his side, so as to be extricated with great difficulty. Wherever the soil was bare, or there was a sand bank, we beheld innumerable tracks of bears, wolves, buffaloes wild horses, turkeys and water fowl, shewing the abundant sport this valley might afford to the huntsman: our men, however, were sated with hunting, and too weary to be excited by these signs, which in the outset of our tour, would have put them in a fever of anticipation. Their only desire at present was to push on doggedly for the fortress.

At length we succeeded in finding a fording place where we all crossed Little River, with the water and mire to the saddle girths, and then halted for an hour and a half, to overhaul the wet baggage, and give the horses time to rest.

On resuming our march we came to a pleasant little meadow, surrounded by groves of elms and cotton wood trees, in the midst of which was a fine black horse grazing. Beatte, who was in the advance, beckoned us to halt, and, being mounted on a mare, approached the horse gently, step by step, imitating the whinny of the animal with admirable exactness. The noble courser of the prairie gazed for a time, snuffed the air, neighed, pricked up his ears, and pranced round and round the mare, in gallant style but keeping at too great a distance for Beatte to throw the lariat. He was a magnificent object, in all the pride and glory of his nature. It was admirable to see the lofty and airy carriage of his head; the freedom of every movement; the elasticity with which he trod the meadow. Finding it impossible to get within noosing distance, and seeing that the horse was receding and growing alarmed, Beatte slid down from his saddle, levelled his rifle across the back of his mare and took aim with the evident intention of creasing him. I felt a throb of anxiety for the safety of the noble animal, and called out to Beatte to desist. It was too late; he pulled the trigger as I spoke; luckily he did not shoot with his usual accuracy, and I had the satisfaction to see the coal black steed dash off unharmed into the forest.

On leaving this valley we again ascended among broken hills and rugged, ragged forests equally harassing to horse and rider. The ravines too were of red clay and often so steep that in descending the horses would put their feet together and fairly slide down, and then scramble up the opposite side like cats. Here and there among the thickets in the valleys, we met with sloes and persimmon, and the eagerness with which our men broke from the line of march, and ran to gather these poor fruits shewed how much they craved some vegetable condiment after living so long exclusively on animal food.

About half past three we encamped near a brook in a meadow where there was some scanty herbage for our half famished horses. As Beatte had killed a fat doe in the course of the day, and one of our company a fine turkey, we did not lack for provisions.

It was a splendid autumnal evening. The horizon after sunset, was of a clear apple green, rising into a delicate lake, which gradually lost itself in a deep purple blue. One narrow streak of cloud of a mahogany colour edged with amber and gold, floated in the west, and just beneath it was the evening star, shining with the pure brilliancy of a diamond. In unison with this scene there was an evening concert of insects of various kinds, all blended and harmonized into one sober and somewhat melancholy note, which I have always found to have a soothing effect upon the mind, disposing it to quiet musings.

The night that succeeded was calm and beautiful. There was a faint light from the moon, now in its second quarter, and after it had set, a fine star light, with shooting meteors. The wearied rangers after a little murmuring conversation round their fires sank to rest at an early hour, and I seemed to have the whole scene to myself. It is delightful, in thus bivouacking on the prairies, to lie awake and gaze at the stars; it is like watching them from the deck of a ship at sea, when at one view we have the whole cope of heaven. One realizes, in such lonely scenes, that companionship with these beautiful luminaries which made astronomers of the eastern shepherds, as they watched their flocks by night. How often, while contemplating their mild and benignant radiance, I have called to mind the exquisite text of Job: "Canst thou bind the sweet influences of the Pleiades, or loose the bands of Orion?" I do not know why it was, but I felt this night unusually affected by the solemn magnificence of the firmament, and seemed, as I lay thus under the open vault of heaven, to inhale with the pure untainted air, an exhilarating buoyancy of spirit, and as it were, an ecstasy of mind. I slept and waked alternately, and when I slept my dreams partook of the happy tone of my waking reveries. Towards morning one of the centinels, the oldest man in the troop, came and took a seat near me: he was weary and sleepy and impatient to be relieved. I found he had been gazing at the heavens also, but with different feelings.

"If the stars don't deceive me," said he, "it is near day break."

"There can be no doubt of that," said Beatte, who lay close by. "I heard an owl just now."

"Does the owl, then, hoot towards day break?" asked I.

"Aye, sir, just as the cock crows."

This was a useful habitude of the bird of wisdom of which I was not aware. Neither the stars nor owl deceived their votaries. In a short time there was a faint streak of light in the east.

CHAPTER XXXIV

Old Creek encampment—Scarcity of provisions—Bad weather—Weary marching—A hunter's bridge.

The country through which we passed this morning (Nov. 2) was less rugged, and of more agreeable aspect than that we had lately traversed. At eleven o'clock we came out upon an extensive prairie, and about six miles to our left, beheld a long line of green forest, marking the course of the north fork of the Canadian. On the edge of the prairie and in a spacious grove of noble trees which overshadowed a small brook, were the traces of an old Creek hunting camp. On the bark of the trees were rude delineations of hunters and squaws, scrawled with charcoal; together with various signs and hieroglyphics which our half breeds interpreted as indicating that from this encampment the hunters had returned home.

In this beautiful camping ground we made our midday halt. While reposing under the trees we heard a shouting at no great distance, and presently the Captain and the main body of rangers, whom we had left behind two days before, emerged from the thicket and, crossing the brook, were joyfully welcomed into the camp. The Captain and the Doctor had been unsuccessful in the search after their horses, and were obliged to march for the greater part of the time on foot; yet they had come on with more than ordinary speed.

We resumed our march about one o'clock, keeping easterly and approaching the north fork obliquely: it was late before we found a good camping place; the beds of the streams were dry, the prairies, too, had been burnt in various places by Indian hunting parties: at length we found water in a small alluvial bottom where there was tolerable pasturage.

On the following morning there were flashes of lightning in the east with low rumbling thunder, and clouds began to gather about the horizon. Beatte prognosticated rain, and that the wind would veer to the north. In the course of our march a flock of brant were seen over head, flying from the north. "There comes the wind!" said Beatte, and in fact it began to blow from that quarter almost immediately with occasional flurries of rain.

About half past nine o'clock we forded the north fork of the Canadian and encamped about one, that our hunters might have time to beat up the neighborhood for game. In fact a serious scarcity began to prevail in the camp. Most of the rangers were young, heedless and inexperienced, and could not be prevailed upon, while provisions abounded, to provide for the future, by jerking meat or carrying away any on their horses. On leaving an encampment they would leave quantities of meat lying about, trusting to providence and their rifles for a future supply. The consequence was that any temporary scarcity of game, or ill luck in hunting produced almost a famine in the camp. In the present instance they had left loads of buffalo meat at the camp on the great prairie, and having ever since been on a forced march, leaving no time for hunting, they were now destitute of supplies and pinched with hunger. Some had not eaten any thing since the morning of the preceding day. Nothing would have persuaded them when revelling in the abundance of the buffalo encampment, that they would so soon be in such famishing plight.

The hunters returned with indifferent success. The game had been frightened away from this part of the country by Indian hunting parties which had preceded us. Ten or a dozen wild turkeys were brought in, but not a deer had been seen. The rangers began to think turkeys and even prairie hens deserving of attention; game which they had hitherto considered unworthy of their rifles.

The night was cold and windy, with occasional sprinklings of rain, but we had roaring fires to keep us comfortable. In the night a flight of wild geese passed over the camp, making a great cackling in the air; symptoms of approaching winter.

We set forward at an early hour the next morning in a north east course and came upon the trace of a party of Creek Indians, which enabled our poor horses to travel with more ease. We entered upon a fine champaign country. From a rising ground we had a noble prospect over extensive prairies finely diversified by groves and tracts of wood land and bounded by long lines of distant hills all clothed with the rich mellow tints of autumn. Game too was more plenty. A fine buck sprang up from among the herbage on our right and dashed off at full speed; but a young ranger by the name of Childers who was on foot levelled his rifle, discharged a ball that broke the neck of the bounding deer and sent him tumbling head over heels forward. Another buck and a doe, beside several turkeys were killed before we came to a halt, so that the hungry mouths of the troop were once more supplied.

About three o'clock we encamped in a grove after a forced march of twenty five miles, that had proved a hard trial to the horses. For a long time after the head of the line had encamped the rest kept straggling in, two and three at a time; one of our pack horses had given out, about nine miles back, and a poney belonging to Beatte shortly after. Many of the other horses looked so gaunt and feeble that doubts were entertained of their being able to reach the fort. In the night there was heavy rain, and the morning dawned cloudy and dismal. The camp resounded, however, with something of its former gaiety. The rangers had supped well, and were renovated in spirits anticipating a speedy arrival at the garrison. Before we set forward on our march Beatte returned and brought his poney to the camp with great difficulty. The pack horse, however, was completely knocked up and had to be abandoned. The wild mare too had cast her foal, through exhaustion, and was not in a state to go forward. She and the poney, therefore, were left at this encampment, where there was water and good pasturage, and where there would be a chance of their reviving, and being afterwards sought out and brought to the garrison.

We set off about eight o'clock, and had a day of weary and harassing travel part of the time over rough hills, and part over rolling prairies. The rain had rendered the soil slippery and plashy so as to afford unsteady foot hold. Some of the rangers dismounted, their horses having no longer strength to bear them. We made a halt in the course of the morning, but the horses were too tired to graze. Several of them laid down, and there was some difficulty in getting them on their feet again. Our troop presented a forlorn appearance, straggling slowly along, in a broken and scattered line that extended over hill and dale for three miles and upwards, in groupes of three and four widely apart; some on horseback some on foot, with a few laggards far in the rear. About four o'clock we halted for the night in a spacious forest, beside a deep narrow river called the Little North Fork or Deep Creek. It was late before the main part of the troop straggled into the encampment: many of the horses having given out. As the stream was too deep to be forded we waited until the next day to devise means to cross it; but our half breeds swam the horses of our party to the other side in the evening as they would have better pasturage, and the stream was evidently swelling. The night was cold and unruly; the wind sounding hoarsely through the forest and whirling about the dry leaves. We made long fires of great trunks of trees, which diffused something of consolation, if not cheerfulness around.

The next morning there was general permission given to hunt until twelve o'clock, the camp being destitute of provisions. The rich woody bottom in which we were encamped abounded with wild turkeys, of which a considerable number were killed. In the mean time preparations were made for crossing the river, which had risen several feet during the night; and it was determined to fell trees for the purpose, to serve as bridges.

The captain and Doctor and one or two other leaders of the camp, versed in wood craft, examined with learned eye the trees growing on the river bank, until they singled out a couple of the largest size, and most suitable inclinations. The axe was then vigorously applied to their roots in such way as to ensure their falling directly across the stream. As they did not reach to the opposite bank, it was necessary for some of the men to swim across and fell trees on the other side to meet them. They at length succeeded in making a precarious foot way across the deep and rapid current, by which the baggage could be carried over: but it was necessary to grope our way, step by step, along the trunks and main branches of the trees, which for a part of the distance were completely submerged, so that we were to our waists in water. Most of the horses were then swam across, but some of them were too weak to brave the current; and evidently too much knocked up to bear any further travel.

Twelve men, therefore, were left at the encampment to guard these horses until by repose and good pasturage they should be sufficiently recovered to complete their journey, and the Captain engaged to send the men a supply of flour and other necessaries as soon as we should arrive at the fort.

CHAPTER XXXV

A look out for land—Hard travelling and hungry halting—A frontier farm house—Arrival at the garrison.

It was a little after one o'clock when we again resumed our weary wayfaring. The residue of that day and the whole of the next were spent in toilsome travel. Part of the way was over stoney hills, part across wide prairies, rendered spongy and mirey by the recent rain, and cut up by brooks swollen into torrents. Our poor horses were so feeble that it was with difficulty we could get them across the deep ravines and turbulent streams. In traversing the miry plains they slipped and staggered at every step, and most of us were obliged to dismount and walk for the greater part of the way. Hunger prevailed throughout the troop; every one began to look anxious and haggard; and to feel the growing length of each additional mile. At one time in crossing a hill Beatte climbed a high tree commanding a wide prospect, and took a look out like a mariner from the mast head at sea. He came down with cheering tidings. To the left he had beheld a line of forest stretching across the country which he knew to be the woody border of the Arkansas; and at a distance he had recognized certain land marks from which he concluded that we could not be above forty miles distant from the fort. It was like the welcome cry of land to tempest tost mariners.

In fact we soon after saw smoke rising from a woody glen at a distance. It was supposed to be made by a hunting party of Creek or Osage Indians from the neighborhood of the Fort, and was joyfully hailed as a harbinger of man. It was now confidently hoped that we would soon arrive among the frontier hamlets of Creek Indians, which are scattered along the skirts of the uninhabited wilderness; and our hungry rangers trudged forward with reviving spirit, regaling themselves with savory anticipations of farm house luxuries, and enumerating every article of good cheer, until their mouths fairly watered at the shadowy feasts thus conjured up.

A hungry night, however, closed in upon a toilsome day. We encamped on the border of one of the tributary streams of the Arkansas, amidst the ruins of a stately grove that had been riven by a hurricane. The blast had torn its way through the forest in a narrow column, and its course was marked by enormous trees shivered and splintered and upturned with their roots in the air: all lay in one direction, like so many brittle reeds broken and trodden down by the hunter.

Here was fuel in abundance without the labour of the axe: we had soon immense fires blazing and sparkling in the frosty air and lighting up the whole forest, but alas! we had no meat to cook at them. The scarcity in the camp almost amounted to famine. Happy was he who had a morsel of jerked meat, or even the half picked bones of a former repast. For our part, we were more lucky at our mess than our neighbors; one of our men having shot a turkey. We had no bread to eat with it, nor salt to season it withal. It was simply boiled in water; the latter was served up as soup, and we were fain to rub each morsel of the turkey on the empty salt bag, in hopes some saline particle might remain to relieve its insipidity.

The night was biting cold; the brilliant moon light sparkled on the

frosty chrystals which covered every object around us. The water froze
beside the skins on which we bivouacked, and in the morning I found
the blanket in which I was wrapped covered with a hoar frost; yet I
had never slept more comfortably.

After a shadow of a breakfast, consisting of turkey bones and a cup
of coffee without sugar, we decamped at an early hour, for hunger is
a sharp quickener on a journey. The prairies were all gemmed with
frost, that covered the tall weeds and glistened in the sun. We saw
great flights of prairie hens, or grouse, that hovered from tree to tree,
or sat in rows along the naked branches, waiting until the sun should
melt the frost from the weeds and herbage. Our rangers no longer
despised such humble game, but turned from the ranks in pursuit of
a prairie hen as eagerly as they formerly would go in pursuit of a deer.

Every one now pushed forward anxious to arrive at some human
habitation before night. The poor horses were urged beyond their
strength in the thought of soon being able to indemnify them for
present toil, by rest and ample provender. Still the distances seemed
to stretch out more than ever, and the blue hills pointed out as landmarks on the horizon to recede as we advanced. Every step became a
labour: every now and then a miserable horse would give out and
lie down. His owner would rouse him by main strength; force him
forward to the margin of some stream where there might be a scanty
border of herbage and then abandon him to his fate. Among those that
were thus left on the way was one of the led horses of the Count, a
prime hunter, that had taken the lead of every thing in the chase of the
wild horses. It was intended, however, as soon as we should arrive
at the fort, to send out a party provided with corn, to bring in such
of the horses as should survive.

In the course of the morning we came upon Indian tracks, crossing
each other in various directions, a proof that we must be in the neighborhood of human habitations. At length, on passing through a skirt
of woods we beheld two or three log houses, sheltered under lofty trees
on the border of a prairie, the habitations of Creek Indians, who had
small farms adjacent. Had they been sumptuous villas abounding with
the luxuries of civilization, they could not have been hailed with greater
delight.

Some of the rangers rode up to them in quest of food; the greater
part, however, pushed forward in search of the habitation of a white
settler, which we were told was at no great distance. The troop soon
disappeared among the trees and I followed slowly in their track,
for my once fleet and generous steed faltered under me and was just
able to drag one foot after the other, yet I was too weary and exhausted
to spare him.

In this way we crept feebly on until, on turning a thick clump of trees a frontier farm house suddenly presented itself to view. It was a low tenement of logs overshadowed by great forest trees, but it seemed as if a very region of Cocaigne prevailed around it. Here was a stable and barn and granaries teeming with abundance, while legions of grunting swine, gobbling turkeys, cackling hens and strutting roosters swarmed about the farm yard.

My poor jaded and half famished horse raised his head and pricked up his ears at the well known sights and sounds. He gave a chuckling inward sound, something like a dry laugh; whisked his tail, and made great lee way toward a corn crib, filled with golden ears of maize, and it was with some difficulty that I could control his course, and steer him up to the door of the cabin.

A single glance within was sufficient to rouse every gastronomic faculty. There sat the Captain of the rangers and his officers round a three legged table crowned by a broad and smoking dish of boiled beef and turnips. I sprang off of my horse in an instant, cast him loose to make his way to the corn crib, and entered this palace of plenty. A fat good humoured negress received me at the door. She was the mistress of the house, the spouse of the white man, who was absent. I hailed her as some swart fairy of the wild, that had suddenly conjured up a banquet in a desert: and a banquet was it in good sooth. In a twinkling she lugged from the fire a huge iron pot that might have rivalled one of the famous flesh pots of Egypt, or the witches' cauldron in Macbeth. Placing a brown earthen dish on the floor she inclined the corpulent cauldron on one side, and out leaped sundry great morsels of beef, with a regiment of turnips tumbling after them, and a rich cascade of broth overflowing the whole. This she handed me with an ivory smile that extended from ear to ear; apologizing for her humble fare and the humble style in which it was served up. Humble fare! humble style! Boiled beef and turnips—and an earthen dish to eat them from! To think of apologizing for such a treat to a half starved man from the prairies—and then such magnificent slices of bread and butter! Head of Apicius, what a banquet!

"The rage of hunger" being appeased I began to think of my horse. He, however, like an old campaigner, had taken good care of himself. I found him paying assiduous attention to the crib of Indian corn, and dexterously drawing forth and munching the ears that protruded between the bars. It was with great regret that I interrupted his repast, which he abandoned with a heavy sigh, or rather a rumbling groan. I was anxious, however, to rejoin my travelling companions, who had passed by the farm house without stopping, and proceeded to the banks of the Arkansas; being in the hopes of arriving before night at the Osage Agency. Leaving the Captain and his troop, therefore, amidst the abundance of the farm, where they had determined to quarter themselves for the night, I bade adieu to our sable hostess, and again pushed forward.

A ride of about a mile brought me to where my comrades were waiting on the banks of the Arkansas, which here poured along between beautiful forests. A number of Creek Indians, in their brightly coloured dresses, looking like so many gay tropical birds, were busy aiding our men to transport the baggage across the river in a canoe. While this was doing, our horses had another regale from two great cribs heaped up with ears of Indian corn, which stood near the edge of the river. We had to keep a check upon the poor half famished animals, lest they should injure themselves by their voracity.

The baggage being all carried to the opposite bank, we embarked in the canoe, and swam our horses across the river. I was fearful, lest in their enfeebled state, they should not be able to stem the current; but their banquet of Indian corn had already infused fresh life and spirit into them, and it would appear as if they were cheered by the instinctive consciousness of their approach to home, where they would soon be at rest and in plentiful quarters; for no sooner had we landed and resumed our route, than they set off on a hand gallop, and continued so for a great part of seven miles that we had to ride through the woods.

It was an early hour in the evening when we arrived at the Agency on the banks of the Verdigris river, whence we had set off about a month before. Here we passed the night comfortably quartered; yet, after having been accustomed to sleep in the open air, the confinement of a chamber was, in some respects, irksome. The atmosphere seemed close, and destitute of freshness; and when I woke in the night and gazed about me upon complete darkness, I missed the glorious companionship of the stars.

The next morning after breakfast, I again set forward in company with the worthy Commissioner for Fort Gibson where we arrived much tattered, travel stained and weather beaten, but in high health and spirits—and thus ended my foray into the Pawnee Hunting Grounds.

THE END

ABBOTSFORD

The Abbotsford Family in 1817

An engraving after the painting by David Wilkie, reproduced in *The Sketch-book of Geoffrey Crayon* (D. C. Heath, copyright 1907).

ABBOTSFORD

To ———— ————

I sit down to perform my promise of giving you an account of a visit made many years since to Abbotsford: I hope, however, that you do not expect much from me, for the travelling notes taken at the time are so scanty and vague, and my memory so extremely fallacious, that I fear I shall disappoint you with the meagreness and crudeness of my details.

Late in the evening of the 29th August 1817, I arrived at the ancient little border town of Selkirk, where I put up for the night. I had come down from Edinburgh partly to visit Melrose Abbey and its vicinity, but chiefly to get a sight of the "mighty minstrel of the north." I had a letter of introduction to him from Thomas Campbell the poet, and had reason to think, from the interest he had taken in some of my earlier scribblings, that a visit from me would not be deemed an intrusion.

On the following morning, after an early breakfast, I set off in a post chaise for the Abbey. On the way thither I stopped at the gate of Abbotsford and sent the postillion to the house with the letter of introduction and my card, on which I had written that I was on my way to the ruins of Melrose Abbey, and wished to know whether it would be agreeable to Mr. Scott (he had not yet been made a Baronet) to receive a visit from me in the course of the morning.

While the postillion was on his errand I had time to survey the mansion. It stood some short distance below the road, on the side of a hill sweeping down to the Tweed; and was as yet but a snug gentleman's cottage; with something rural and picturesque in its appearance. The whole front was overrun with evergreens, and immediately above the portal was a great pair of elk horns, branching out from beneath the foliage, and giving the cottage the look of a hunting lodge. The huge baronial pile, to which this modest mansion in a manner gave birth, was just emerging into existence: part of the walls, surrounded by scaffolding, already had risen to the height of the cottage, and the court yard in front, was encumbered by masses of hewn stone.

The noise of the chaise had disturbed the quiet of the establishment. Out sallied the warder of the castle, a black greyhound, and, leaping on one of the blocks of stone began a furious barking. His alarum brought out the whole garrison of dogs:

> Both mongrel, puppy, whelp and hound,
> And curs of low degree;

all open mouthed and vociferous.—I should correct my quotation—not a cur was to be seen on the premises: Scott was too true a sportsman, and had too high a veneration for pure blood, to tolerate a mongrel.

In a little while the "lord of the castle" himself made his appearance. I knew him at once by the descriptions I had read and heard, and the likenesses that had been published of him. He was tall, and of a large and powerful frame. His dress was simple and almost rustic. An old green shooting coat, with a dog whistle at the button hole, brown linen pantaloons, stout shoes that tied at the ankles, and a white hat that had evidently seen service. He came limping up the gravel walk, aiding himself by a stout walking staff, but moving rapidly and with vigour. By his side jogged along a large irongrey stag hound of a most grave demeanour, who took no part in the clamour of the canine rabble, but seemed to consider himself bound, for the dignity of the house, to give me a courteous reception.

Before Scott had reached the gate he called out in a hearty tone, welcoming me to Abbotsford, and asking news of Campbell. Arrived at the door of the chaise he grasped me warmly by the hand: "Come drive down, drive down to the house," said he, "ye're just in time for breakfast, and afterwards ye shall see all the wonders of the Abbey."

I would have excused myself on the plea of having already made my breakfast. "Hout man," cried he, "a ride in the morning in the keen air of the Scotch hills is warrant enough for a second breakfast."

I was accordingly whirled to the portal of the cottage, and in a few moments found myself seated at the breakfast table. There was no one present but the family, which consisted of Mrs. Scott, her eldest daughter Sophia, then a fine girl about seventeen, Miss Ann Scott, two or three years younger: Walter, a well grown stripling, and Charles a lively boy, eleven or twelve years of age. I soon felt myself quite at home, and my heart in a glow with the cordial welcome I experienced. I had thought to make a mere morning visit, but found I was not to be let off so lightly. "You must not think our neighborhood is to be read in a morning like a newspaper," said Scott, "it takes several days of study for an observant traveller that has a relish for auld world trumpery. After breakfast you shall make your visit to Melrose Abbey; I shall not be able to accompany you, as I have some household affairs to attend to, but I will put you in charge of my son Charles, who is very learned in all things touching the old ruin and the neighborhood it stands in, and he and my friend Johnny Bower will tell you the whole truth about it, with a good deal more that you are not called upon to believe

—unless you be a true and nothing-doubting antiquary. When you come back I'll take you out on a ramble about the neighborhood. Tomorrow we will take a look at the Yarrow, and the next day we will drive over to Dryburgh Abbey, which is a fine old ruin well worth your seeing"— in a word before Scott had got through with his plan I found myself committed for a visit of several days, and it seemed as if a little realm of romance was suddenly opened before me.

———

After breakfast I accordingly set off for the Abbey with my little friend Charles, whom I found a most sprightly and entertaining companion. He had an ample stock of anecdotes about the neighborhood, which he had learned from his father, and many quaint remarks and sly jokes, evidently derived from the same source, all which were uttered with a Scottish accent and a mixture of Scottish phraseology, that gave them additional flavour.

On our way to the Abbey he gave me some anecdotes of Johnny Bower, to whom his father had alluded. He was sexton of the parish and custodian of the ruin, employed to keep it in order and show it to strangers;—a worthy little man, not without ambition in his humble sphere. The death of his predecessor had been mentioned in the newspapers, so that his name had appeared in print throughout the land. When Johnny succeeded to the guardianship of the ruin, he stipulated that, on his death, his name should receive like honorable blazon; with this addition, that it should be from the pen of Scott. The latter gravely pledged himself to pay this tribute to his memory, and Johnny now lived in the proud anticipation of a poetic immortality.

I found Johnny Bower a decent looking little old man in blue coat and red waistcoat. He received us with much greeting and seemed delighted to see my young companion, who was full of merriment and waggery, drawing out his peculiarities for my amusement. The old man was one of the most authentic and particular of cicerones; he pointed out every thing in the Abbey that had been described by Scott in his Lay of the Last Minstrel: and would repeat, with broad Scottish accent, the passage which celebrated it. Thus, in passing through the cloisters, he made me remark the beautiful carvings of leaves and flowers wrought in stone with the most exquisite delicacy, and, notwithstanding the lapse of centuries, retaining their sharpness as if fresh from the chisel: rivalling, as Scott has said, the real objects of which they were imitations:

> Nor herb nor flowret glistened there
> But was carved in the cloister arches as fair.

He pointed out also among the carved work a nun's head of much beauty, which he said Scott always stopped to admire—"for the shirra' had a wonderful eye for all sic matters."

I would observe that Scott seemed to derive more consequence in the neighborhood from being sheriff of the county than from being poet.

In the interior of the Abbey Johnny Bower conducted me to the identical stone on which stout William of Deloraine and the monk took their seat on that memorable night when the wizard's book was to be rescued from the grave. Nay, Johnny had even gone beyond Scott in the minuteness of his antiquarian research, for he had discovered the very tomb of the wizard, the position of which had been left in doubt by the poet. This he boasted to have ascertained by the position of the oriel window, and the direction in which the moon beams fell at night, through the stained glass, casting the shadow to the red cross on the spot; as had all been specified in the poem. "I pointed out the whole to the shirra," said he, "and he could na' gainsay but it was varra clear." I found afterward that Scott used to amuse himself with the simplicity of the old man, and his zeal in verifying every passage of the poem, as though it had been authentic history, and that he always acquiesced in his deductions. I subjoin the description of the wizard's grave, which called forth the antiquarian research of Johnny Bower.

> Lo warrior! now the cross of red,
> Points to the grave of the mighty dead.
> Slow moved the monk to the broad flag stone
> Which the bloody cross was traced upon:
> He pointed to a secret nook:
> An iron bar the warrior took;
> And the monk made a sign with his withered hand
> The grave's huge portal to expand.
>
> It was by dint of passing strength,
> That he moved the massy stone at length.
> I would you had been there, to see
> How the light broke forth so gloriously,
> Streamed upward to the chancel roof
> And through the galleries far aloof
>   And, issuing from the tomb
> Showed the monk's cowl and visage pale,
> Danced on the dark-brown warrior's mail,
>   And kissed his waving plume.
>
> Before their eyes the wizard lay,
> As if he had not been dead a day.

> His hoary beard in silver rolled,
> He seemed some seventy winters old;
> A palmer's amice wrapped him round;
> With a wrought Spanish baldric bound,
>   Like a pilgrim from beyond the sea:
> His left hand held his book of might;
> A silver cross was in his right:
>   The lamp was placed beside his knee.

The fictions of Scott had become facts with honest Johnny Bower. From constantly living among the ruins of Melrose Abbey, and pointing out the scenes of the poem, the Lay of the Last Minstrel had, in a manner, become interwoven with his whole existence, and I doubt whether he did not now and then mix up his own identity with the personages of some of its cantos.

He could not bear that any other production of the poet should be preferred to the Lay of the Last Minstrel. "Faith," said he to me, "it's just e'en as gude a thing as Mr. Scott has written—an if he were stannin there I'd tell him so—an' then he'd lauf!"

He was loud in his praises of the affability of Scott. "He'll come here sometimes," said he, "with great folks in his company, an the first I know of it is his voice, calling out Johnny!—Johnny Bower!—and when I go out I am sure to be greeted with a joke or a pleasant word. He'll stand and crack and lauff wi' me, just like an auld wife—and to think that of a man that has such an awfu' knowledge o' history!"

One of the ingenious devices on which the worthy little man prided himself, was to place a visitor opposite to the Abbey, with his back to it and bid him bend down and look at it between his legs. This he said gave an entire different aspect to the ruin. Folks admired the plan amazingly, but as to the "leddies" they were dainty on the matter, and contented themselves with looking from under their arms.

As Johnny Bower piqued himself upon showing every thing laid down in the poem, there was one passage that perplexed him sadly. It was the opening of one of the cantos:

> If thou would'st view fair Melrose aright,
> Go visit it by the pale moonlight;
> For the gay beams of lightsome day,
> Gild but to flout the ruins gray, &c.

In consequence of this admonition, many of the most devout pilgrims to the ruin could not be contented with a day light inspection, and insisted it could be nothing, unless seen by the light of the moon. Now, unfortunately, the moon shines but for a part of the month; and what is still more unfortunate, is very apt in Scotland to be obscured by clouds and mists. Johnny was sorely puzzled, therefore, how to accommodate his poetry-struck visitors with this indispensable moonshine. At length, in a lucky moment, he devised a substitute. This was a great double tallow candle stuck upon the end of a pole, with which he would conduct his visitors about the ruins on dark nights; so much to their satisfaction that, at length, he began to think it even preferable to the moon itself. "It does na' light up a' the Abbey at ance to be sure," he would say, "but then you can shift it about and show the auld ruin bit by bit, whiles the moon only shines on one side."

Honest Johnny Bower! So many years have elapsed since the time I treat of, that it is more than probable his simple head lies beneath the walls of his favorite Abbey. It is to be hoped his humble ambition has been gratified, and his name recorded by the pen of the man he so loved and honored.

After my return from Melrose Abbey Scott proposed a ramble to shew me something of the surrounding country. As we sallied forth every dog in the establishment turned out to attend us. There was the old stag hound Maida that I have already mentioned, a noble animal, and a great favorite of Scott's, and Hamlet, the black greyhound, a wild thoughtless youngster, not yet arrived to the years of discretion. And Finette a beautiful setter, with soft silken hair, long pendant ears and a mild eye, the parlour favorite. When in front of the house we were joined by a superannuated grey hound who came from the kitchen wagging his tail; and was cheered by Scott as an old friend and comrade.

In our walks Scott would frequently pause in conversation to notice his dogs and speak to them as if rational companions; and indeed there appears to be a vast deal of rationality in these faithful attendants on man, derived from their close intimacy with him. Maida deported himself with a gravity becoming his age and size, and seemed to consider himself called upon to preserve a great degree of dignity and decorum in our society. As he jogged along a little distance ahead of us the young dogs would gambol about him, leap on his neck, worry at his ears and endeavour to teaze him into a frolic. The old dog would keep on for a long time with imperturbable solemnity, now and then seeming to rebuke the wantonness of his young companions. At length he would make a sudden turn, seize one of them and tumble him in the dust, then giving a glance at us, as much as to say, "You see gentlemen, I can't help giving way to this nonsense," would resume his gravity and jog on as before.

Scott amused himself with these peculiarities. "I make no doubt," said he, "when Maida is alone with these young dogs he throws gravity aside and plays the boy as much as any of them; but he is ashamed to do so in our company: and seems to say, 'Ha' done with your nonsense youngsters; what will the laird and that other gentleman think of me if I give way to such foolery.'"

Maida reminded him he said of a scene on board an armed yacht in which he made an excursion with his friend Adam Ferguson. They had taken much notice of the Boatswain, who was a fine sturdy seaman, and evidently felt flattered by their attention. On one occasion the crew were "piped to fun" and the sailors were dancing and cutting all kinds of capers to the music of the ship's band. The Boatswain looked on with a wistful eye as if he would like to join in, but a glance at Scott and Ferguson showed that there was a struggle with his dignity, fearing to lessen himself in their eyes. At length one of his messmates came up and seizing him by the arm challenged him to a jig. The Boatswain, continued Scott, after a little hesitation complied, made an awkward gambol or two, like our friend Maida, but soon gave it up. "It's of no use," said he jerking up his waistband and giving a side glance at us—"one can't dance always nouther."

Scott amused himself with the peculiarities of another of his dogs, a little shamefaced terrier, with large glassy eyes, one of the most sensitive little bodies to insult and indignity in the world. If ever he whipped him, he said, the little fellow would sneak off and hide himself from the light of day in a lumber garret from whence there was no drawing him forth but by the sound of the chopping knife, as if chopping up his victuals, when he would steal forth with humbled and down cast look, but would skulk away again if any one regarded him.

While we were discussing the humours and peculiarities of our canine companions, some object provoked their spleen and produced a sharp and petulant barking from the smaller fry, but it was some time before Maida was sufficiently aroused to ramp forward two or three bounds and join in the chorus, with a deep mouthed bow-wough!

It was but a transient outbreak, and he returned instantly, wagging his tail, and looking up dubiously in his master's face, uncertain whether he would censure or applaud.

"Aye aye, old boy!" cried Scott, "you have done wonders. You have shaken the Eildon hills with your roaring, you may now lay by your artillery for the rest of the day. Maida is like the great gun at Constantinople," continued he, "it takes so long to get it ready that the small guns can fire off a dozen times first, but when it does go off it plays the very d—l."

These simple anecdotes may serve to show the delightful play of

Scott's humours and feelings in private life. His domestic animals were his friends. Every thing about him seemed to rejoice in the light of his countenance: the face of the humblest dependant brightened at his approach, as if he anticipated a cordial and cheering word. I had occasion to observe this particularly in a visit which we paid to a quarry whence several men were cutting stone for the new edifice; who all paused from their labour to have a pleasant "crack wi' the laird." One of them was a burgess of Selkirk with whom Scott had some joke about the old song:

> Up with the Souters o' Selkirk
> And down with the Earl of Home.

Another was precentor at the Kirk, and, beside leading the psalmody on Sunday, taught the lads and lasses of the neighborhood dancing on week days, in the winter time, when out-of-door labor was scarce.

Among the rest was a tall straight old fellow, with a healthful complexion and silver hair, and a small, round crowned white hat. He had been about to shoulder a hod, but paused, and stood looking at Scott, with a slight sparkling of his blue eye, as if waiting his turn: for the old fellow knew himself to be a favorite.

Scott accosted him in an affable tone, and asked for a pinch of snuff. The old man drew forth a horn snuff box. "Hoot man," said Scott, "not that old mull, where's the bonnie French one that I brought you from Paris?"—"Troth, your honour," replied the old fellow, "sic a mull as that is nae for week days."

On leaving the quarry Scott informed me that when absent at Paris he had purchased several trifling articles as presents for his dependants, and among others the gay snuff box in question, which was so carefully reserved for Sundays by the veteran. "It was not so much the value of the gifts," said he, "that pleased them, as the idea that the laird should think of them when so far away."

The old man in question I found was a great favorite with Scott: if 1 recollect right he had been a soldier in early life, and his straight erect person, his ruddy yet rugged countenance, his grey hair, and an arch gleam in his blue eye, reminded me of the description of Edie Ochiltree. I find that the old fellow has since been introduced by Wilkie in his picture of the Scott family.

We rambled on among scenes which had been familiar in Scottish song and rendered classic by the pastoral muse long before Scott had thrown the rich mantle of his poetry over them. What a thrill of pleasure did I feel when I first saw the broom covered tops of the Cowden Knowes, peeping above the grey hills of the Tweed: and what touching associations were called up by the sight of Ettrick Vale, Galla Water and the Braes of Yarrow. Every turn brought to mind some household air, some almost forgotten song of the nursery, by which I had been lulled to sleep in my childhood, and with them the looks and voices of those who had sung them, and who were now no more. Scotland is eminently a land of song, and it is these melodies, chaunted in our ears in the days of infancy, and connected with the memory of those we have loved, and who have passed away, that clothe Scottish landscape with such tender associations. The Scottish songs, in general, have something intrinsically melancholy in them, owing in all probability to the pastoral and lonely life of those who composed them, who were often mere shepherds, tending their flocks in the solitary glens, or folding them among the naked hills. Many of these rustic bards have passed away without leaving a name behind them; nothing remains of them but their sweet and touching songs, which live like echoes about the places they once inhabited. Most of these simple effusions of pastoral poets are linked with some favorite haunt of the poet and in this way not a mountain, or valley, a town, or tower, green shaw or running stream, in Scotland but has some popular air connected with it, that makes its very name a key note to a whole train of delicious fancies and feelings.

Let me step forward in time, and mention how sensible I was to the power of these simple airs in a visit which I made to Ayr the birth place of Robert Burns. I passed a whole morning about "the banks and braes of Bonnie Doon," with his tender little love verses running in my head. I found a poor Scotch carpenter at work among the ruins of Kirk Alloway, which was to be converted into a school house. Finding the purpose of my visit he left his work, sat down with me on a grassy grave close by where Burns' father was buried, and talked of the poet whom he had known personally. He said his songs were familiar to the poorest and most illiterate of the country folk, *"and it seemed to him as if the country had grown more beautiful, since Burns had written his bonnie little songs about it."*

I found Scott was quite an enthusiast on the subject of the popular songs of his country and he seemed gratified to find me so alive to them. Their effect in calling up in my mind the recollections of early times and scenes in which I had first heard them reminded him he said of the lines of his poor friend Leyden to the Scottish muse—

> In youth's first morn, alert and gay,
> Ere rolling years had passed away,

Remembered like a morning dream,
I heard the dulcet measures float,
In many a liquid winding note,
    Along the bank of Teviot's stream.

Sweet sounds! that oft have soothed to rest
The sorrows of my guileless breast,
    And charmed away mine infant tears;
Fond memory shall your strains repeat,
Like distant echoes, doubly sweet,
    That on the wild the traveller hears.

Scott went on to expatiate on the popular songs of Scotland. "They are a part of our national inheritance," said he; "and something that we may truly call our own. They have no foreign taint; they have the pure breath of the heather and the mountain breeze. All the genuine legitimate races that have descended from the ancient Britons; such as the Scotch, the Welsh and the Irish, have national airs. The English have none, because they are not natives of the soil, or, at least, are mongrels. Their music is all made up of foreign scraps like a harlequin jacket, or a piece of mosaic. Even in Scotland, we have comparatively few national songs in the eastern part, where we have had most influx of strangers. A real old Scottish song is a cairn gorm, a gem of our own mountains: or rather, it is a precious relic of old times, that bears the national character stamped upon it: like a cameo, that shows what the national visage was in former days, before the breed was crossed."

While Scott was thus discoursing we were passing up a narrow glen, with the dogs beating about, to right and left, when suddenly a black cock burst upon the wing.

"Aha!" cried Scott, "there will be a good shot for master Walter, we must send him this way with his gun when we go home. Walter's the family sportsman now, and keeps us in game. I have pretty nigh resigned my gun to him, for I find I cannot trudge about as briskly as formerly."

Our ramble took us on the hills commanding an extensive prospect. "Now," said Scott, "I have brought you, like the pilgrim in the Pilgrim's Progress to the top of the Delectable Mountains, that I may show you all the goodly regions hereabouts. Yonder is Lammermuir, and Smallholm, and there you have Gallashiels, and Torwoodlie, and Gallawater: and in that direction you see Teviotdale, and the Braes of Yarrow, and Ettrick stream winding along like a silver thread, to throw itself into the Tweed."

He went on thus to call over names celebrated in Scottish song, and most of which had recently received a romantic interest from his own pen. In fact I saw a great part of the border country spread out before me, and could trace the scenes of those poems and romances which had in a manner bewitched the world. I gazed about me for a time with mute surprize, I may almost say with disappointment. I beheld a mere succession of gray waving hills, line beyond line, as far as my eye could reach, monotonous in their aspect, and so destitute of trees, that one could almost see a stout fly walking along their profile: and the far famed Tweed appeared a naked stream, flowing between bare hills, without a tree or a thicket on its banks; and yet, such had been the magic web of poetry and romance thrown over the whole, that it had a greater charm for me than the richest scenery I beheld in England.

I could not help giving utterance to my thoughts. Scott hummed for a moment to himself, and looked grave: he had no idea of having his muse complimented at the expense of his native hills. "It may be partiality," said he, at length; "but to my eye these grey hills and all this wild border country have beauties peculiar to themselves. I like the very nakedness of the land; it has something bold, and stern and solitary about it. When I have been for some time in the rich scenery about Edinburgh, which is like ornamented garden land, I begin to wish myself back again among my own honest gray hills; and if I did not see the heather at least once a year, *I think I should die!*"

The last words were said with an honest warmth, accompanied with a thump on the ground with his staff, by way of emphasis, that showed his heart was in his speech. He vindicated the Tweed, too, as a beautiful stream in itself, and observed that he did not dislike it for being bare of trees, probably from having been much of an angler in his time, and an angler does not like to have a stream overhung by trees, which embarrass him in the exercise of his rod and line.

I took occasion to plead, in like manner, the associations of early life for my disappointment in respect to the surrounding scenery. I had been so accustomed to hills crowned with forests and streams breaking their way through a wilderness of trees, that all my ideas of romantic landscape were apt to be well wooded.

"Aye, and that's the great charm of your country," cried Scott. "You love the forest as I do the heather—but I would not have you think I do not feel the glory of a great woodland prospect. There is nothing I should like more than to be in the midst of one of your grand wild original forests: with the idea of hundreds of miles of untrodden forest around me. I once saw at Leith, an immense stick of timber, just landed from America. It must have been an enormous tree when it stood on its native soil, at its full height and with all its branches. I gazed at it with admiration; it seemed like one of the gigantic obelisks which are now and then brought from Egypt, to shame the pigmy monuments of Europe: and, in fact, these vast aboriginal trees, that have sheltered the Indians before the intrusion of the white men are the monuments and antiquities of your country."

The conversation here turned upon Campbell's poem of Gertrude of Wyoming, as illustrative of the poetic materials furnished by American scenery. Scott spoke of it in that liberal style in which I always found him to speak of the writings of his cotemporaries. He cited several passages of it with great delight. "What a pity it is," said he, "that Campbell does not write more and oftener, and give full sweep to his genius. He has wings that would bear him to the skies; and he does now and then spread them grandly, but folds them up again and resumes his perch, as if he was afraid to launch away. He don't know or won't trust his own strength. Even when he has done a thing well he has often misgivings about it. He left out several fine passages of his Lochiel, but I got him to restore some of them." Here Scott repeated several passages in a magnificent style. "What a grand idea is that," said he, "about prophetic boding, or, in common parlance, second sight—

Coming events cast their shadows before.

It is a noble thought and nobly expressed. And there's that glorious little poem, too, of Hohenlinden; after he had written it he did not seem to think much of it, but considered some of it 'd—d drum and trumpet lines.' I got him to recite it to me, and I believe that the delight I felt and expressed had an effect in inducing him to print it. The fact is," added he, "Campbell is in a manner a bug bear to himself. The brightness of his early success is a detriment to all his further efforts. *He is afraid of the shadow that his own fame casts before him.*"

While we were thus chatting, we heard the report of a gun among the hills. "That's Walter I think," said Scott, "he has finished his morning's studies and is out with his gun. I should not be surprized if he had met with the black cock; if so, we shall have an addition to our larder, for Walter is a pretty sure shot."

I enquired into the nature of Walter's studies. "Faith," said Scott, "I can't say much on that head. I am not over bent upon making prodigies of any of my children. As to Walter I taught him, while a boy, to ride, and shoot and speak the truth, as to the other parts of his education I leave them to a very worthy young man, the son of one of our clergymen, who instructs all my children."

I afterwards became acquainted with the young man in question, George Thomson, son of the minister of Melrose, and found him

possessed of much learning, intelligence, and modest worth. He used
to come every day from his father's residence at Melrose to superintend
the studies of the young folks, and occasionally took his meals at
Abbotsford, where he was highly esteemed. Nature had cut him out,
Scott used to say, for a stalwart soldier, for he was tall, vigorous, active,
and fond of athletic exercises, but accident had marred her work, the
loss of a limb in boyhood having reduced him to a wooden leg. He was
brought up, therefore, for the church, whence he was occasionally
called the Dominie, and is supposed, by his mixture of learning, simplicity, and amiable eccentricity, to have furnished many traits for the
character of Dominie Sampson. I believe he often acted as Scott's
amanuensis, when composing his novels. With him the young people were
occupied, in general, during the early part of the day, after which they
took all kinds of healthful recreations in the open air; for Scott was as
solicitous to strengthen their bodies as their minds.

We had not walked much further before we saw the two Miss
Scotts advancing along the hill side to meet us. The mornings studies
being over, they had set off to take a ramble on the hills and gather
heather blossoms with which to decorate their hair for dinner. As they
came bounding lightly like young fawns, and their dresses fluttering in
the pure summer breeze, I was reminded of Scott's own description of
his children in his introduction to one of the cantos of Marmion.

> My imps, though hardy, bold, and wild,
> As best befits the mountain child
> Their summer gambols tell and mourn,
> And anxious ask will spring return,
> And birds and lambs again be gay
> And blossoms clothe the hawthorn spray?
>
> Yes, prattlers, yes, the daisy's flower
> Again shall paint your summer bower;
> Again the hawthorn shall supply
> The garlands you delight to tie:
> The lambs upon the lea shall bound,
> The wild birds carol to the round,
> And while you frolick light as they,
> Too short shall seem the summer day.

As they approached, the dogs all sprang forward and gambolled around
them. They played with them, for a time, and then joined us with
countenances full of health and glee. Sophia, the eldest, was the most
lively and joyous; having much of her father's varied spirit in conversa-

tion, and seeming to catch excitement from his words and looks. Ann was of quieter mood, rather silent, owing, in some measure, no doubt, to her being some years younger.

———

At dinner Scott had laid by his half rustic dress, and appeared clad in black. The girls, too, in completing their toilette, had twisted in their hair the sprigs of purple heather which they had gathered on the hillside, and looked all fresh and blooming from their breezy walk.

There was no guest at dinner but myself. Around the table were two or three dogs in attendance. Maida, the old stag hound took his seat at Scott's elbow looking up wistfully in his master's eye; while Finette, the pet spaniel, placed herself near Mrs. Scott, by whom I soon perceived she was completely spoiled.

The conversation happening to turn on the merits of his dogs, Scott spoke with great feeling and affection of his favorite terrier Camp, who is depicted by his side in the earlier engravings of him. He talked of him as of a real friend whom he had lost, and Sophia Scott, looking up archly in his face, observed that Papa shed a few tears when poor Camp died. I may here mention another testimonial of Scott's fondness for his dogs, and his humorous mode of showing it, which I subsequently met with. Rambling with him one morning about the grounds adjacent to the house I observed a small antique monument, on which was inscribed, in Gothic characters—

Cy git le preux Percy.
(Here lies the brave Percy.)

I paused supposing it to be the tomb of some stark warrior of the olden time, but Scott drew me on, "Pooh," cried he, "it's nothing but one of the monuments of my nonsense of which you'll find enough hereabouts." I learnt afterwards that it was the grave of a favorite greyhound.

Among the other important and privileged members of the household who figured in attendance at the dinner, was a large grey cat, who I observed was regaled from time to time with tit bits from the table. This sage grimalkin was a favorite of both master and mistress and slept at night in their room. And Scott laughingly observed that one of the least wise parts of their establishment was, that the window was left open at night for puss to go in and out. The cat assumed a kind of ascendancy among the quadrupeds; sitting in state in Scott's arm chair, and occasionally stationing himself on a chair beside the door as if to review his subjects as they passed, giving each dog a cuff beside the ears as he went by. This clapperclawing was always taken in good part; it appeared to be, in fact, a mere act of sovereignty on the part of grimalkin to remind the others of their vassalage; which they acknowledged, by the most perfect acquiescence. A general harmony prevailed between sovereign and subjects, and they would all sleep together in the sunshine.

Scott was full of anecdote and conversation during dinner. He made some admirable remarks upon the Scottish character, and spoke strongly in praise of the quiet, orderly, honest conduct of his neighbors, which one would hardly expect said he, from the descendants of moss troopers, and borderers, in a neighborhood famous in old times for brawl, and feud, and violence of all kinds. He said he had, in his official capacity of sheriff, administered the laws for a number of years during which there had been very few trials. The old feuds and local interests, and rivalries and animosities of the Scotch, however, still slept he said in their ashes, and might easily be roused. Their hereditary feeling for names was still great. It was not always safe to have even the game of football between villages, the old clannish spirit was too apt to break out. The Scotch he said, were more revengeful than the English; they carried their resentments longer, and would sometimes lay them by for years, but would be sure to gratify them in the end.

The ancient jealousy between the Highlanders and the Lowlanders still continued to a certain degree, the former looking upon the latter as an inferior race, less brave and hardy, but at the same time, suspecting them of a disposition to take airs upon themselves under the idea of superior refinement. This made them techy and ticklish company for a stranger on his first coming among them: ruffling up and putting themselves upon their mettle on the slightest occasion, so that he had in a manner to quarrel and fight his way into their good graces.

He instanced a case in point in a brother of Mungo Park who went to take up his residence in a wild neighborhood of the Highlands. He soon found himself considered as an intruder, and that there was a disposition among these cocks of the hills, to fix a quarrel on him, trusting that, being a Lowlander, he would shew the white feather.

For a time he bore their flings and taunts with great coolness, until one, presuming on his forbearance, drew forth a dirk, and, holding it before him, asked him if he had ever seen a weapon like that in his part of the country. Park, who was a Hercules in frame, seized the dirk and, with one blow, drove it through an oaken table:—"Yes," replied he, "and tell your friends that a man from the Lowlands drove it where the devil himself cannot draw it out again." All present were delighted with the feat and the words that accompanied it. They drank with Park to a better acquaintance and were staunch friends ever afterwards.

After dinner we adjourned to the drawing room, which served also for study and library. Against the wall on one side was a long writing table, with drawers; surmounted by a small cabinet of polished wood, with folding doors richly studded with brass ornaments, within which Scott kept his most valuable papers. Above the cabinet, in a kind of niche, was a complete corslet of glittering steel, with a closed helmet, and flanked by gauntlets and battle axes. Around were hung trophies and reliques of various kinds: a scymitar of Tippoo Saib; a Highland broadsword from Flodden field; a pair of Rippon spurs from Bannockburn; and above all a gun which had belonged to Rob Roy, and bore his initials, R. M. G. an object of peculiar interest to me at the time, as it was understood Scott was actually engaged in printing a novel founded on the story of that famous outlaw.

On each side of the cabinet were book cases, well stored with works of romantic fiction in various languages, many of them rare and antiquated. This however, was merely his cottage library, the principal part of his books being at that time at Edinburgh.

From this little cabinet of curiosities Scott drew forth a manuscript picked up on the field of Waterloo, containing copies of several songs popular at the time in France. The paper was dabbled with blood— "The life blood very possibly," said Scott, "of some gay young officer, who had cherished these songs as a keepsake from some lady love in Paris."

He adverted in a mellow and delightful manner to the little half gay, half melancholy campaigning song said to have been composed by General Wolfe, and sung by him at the mess table, on the eve of the Storming of Quebec, in which he fell so gloriously.

> Why soldiers why,
> Should we be melancholy boys?
> Why soldiers why,
> Whose business 'tis to die!
> For should next campaign,
> Send us to him who made us, boys,
> We're free from pain:
> But should we remain,
> A bottle and kind landlady
> Makes all well again.

"So," added he, "the poor lad who fell at Waterloo, in all probability had been singing these songs in his tent the night before the battle, and thinking of the fair dame who had taught him them, and promising himself, should he outlive the campaign, to return to her all glorious from the wars."

I find since that Scott published translations of these songs among some of his smaller poems.

The evening passed away delightfully in this quaint looking apartment, half study half drawing room. Scott read several passages from the old romance of Arthur, with a fine deep sonorous voice and a gravity of tone that seemed to suit the antiquated, black letter volume. It was a rich treat to hear such a work, read by such a person and in such a place; and his appearance as he sat reading, in a large armed chair, with his favorite hound Maida at his feet, and surrounded by books, and reliques and border trophies, would have formed an admirable and most characteristic picture.

While Scott was reading, the sage grimalkin already mentioned had taken his seat in a chair beside the fire, and remained with fixed eye and grave demeanour, as if listening to the reader. I observed to Scott that his cat seemed to have a black letter taste in literature.

"Ah," said he, "these cats are a very mysterious kind of folk. There is always more passing in their minds than we are aware of. It comes no doubt from their being so familiar with witches and warlocks." He went on to tell a little story about a gude man who was returning to his cottage one night, when in a lonely out of the way place he met with a funeral procession of cats all in mourning, bearing one of their race to the grave in a coffin covered with a black velvet pall. The worthy man, astonished and half frightened, at so strange a pageant, hastened home and told what he had seen to his wife and children. Scarce had he finished when a great black cat that sat beside the fire raised himself up, exclaimed, "Then am I king of the cats," and vanished up the chimney. The funeral seen by the gude man was of one of the cat dynasty.

"Our grimalkin, here," added Scott, "sometimes reminds me of the story by the airs of sovereignty which he assumes; and I am apt to treat him with respect from the idea that he may be a great prince incog: and may sometime or other come to the throne."

In this way Scott would make the habits and pecularities of even the dumb animals about him subjects for humorous remark or whimsical story.

Our evening was enlivened also by an occasional song from Sophia Scott, at the request of her father. She never waited to be asked twice, but complied frankly and cheerfully. Her songs were all Scotch, sung without any accompaniment, in a simple manner, but with great spirit and expression, and in their native dialects, which gave them an additional charm. It was delightful to hear her carol off in sprightly style and with an animated air, some of those generous spirited old Jacobite songs, once current among the adherents of the Pretender in Soctland, in which he is designated by the appellation of "the Young Chevalier."

These songs were much relished by Scott notwithstanding his loyalty; for the unfortunate "Chevalier" has always been a hero of romance with him; as he has with many other staunch adherents to the House of Hanover, now that the Stuart line has lost all its terrors. In speaking on the subject, Scott mentioned, as a curious fact that, among the papers of the "Chevalier," which had been submitted by government to his inspection, he had found a memorial to Charles, from some adherents in America, dated 1778, proposing to set up his standard in the back settlements. I regret that, at the time, I did not make more particular enquiries of Scott on the subject; the document in question, however, in all probability, still exists among the Pretender's papers, which are in the possession of the British Government.

In the course of the evening Scott related the story of a whimsical picture hanging in the room, which had been drawn for him by a lady of his acquaintance. It represented the doleful perplexity of a wealthy and handsome young English knight of the olden time, who in the course of a border foray, had been captured and carried off to the castle of a hardheaded and high handed old baron. The unfortunate youth was thrown into a dungeon and a tall gallows erected before the castle gate for his execution. When all was ready he was brought into the castle hall where the grim baron was seated in state, with his warriors armed to the teeth around him, and was given his choice either to swing on the gibbet or to marry the baron's daughter. The last may be thought an easy alternative, but unfortunately, the young lady was hideously ugly, with a mouth from ear to ear, so that not a suiter was to be had for her, either for love or money, and she was known through-out the border country by the name of Muckle mouthed Mag!

The picture in question represented the unhappy dilemma of the handsome youth. Before him sat the grim baron, with a face worthy of the father of such a daughter, and looking daggers and rat's bane. On one side of him was Muckle mouthed Mag, with an amorous smile across the whole breadth of her countenance, and a leer enough to turn a man to stone, on the other side was the father confessor, a sleek friar, jogging the youth's elbow, and pointing to the gallows, seen in per-spective through the open portal.

The story goes that after long balancing in mind between the altar and the halter, the love of life prevailed, and the youth resigned himself to the charms of Muckle mouthed Mag. Contrary to all the probabilities of romance, the match proved a happy one. The baron's daughter if not beautiful was a most exemplary wife; her husband was never troubled with any of those doubts and jealousies which sometimes mar the happiness of connubial life, and was made the father of a fair and undoubtedly legitimate line, that still flourishes on the border.

I give but a faint outline of the story from vague recollection; it may perchance be more richly related elsewhere, by some one who may retain something of the delightful humour with which Scott recounted it.

When I retired for the night, I found it almost impossible to sleep, the idea of being under the roof of Scott, of being on the borders of the Tweed, in the very centre of that region which had for some time past, been the favorite scene of romantic fiction, and above all the recollections of the ramble I had taken, the company in which I had taken it, and the conversation which had passed, all fermented in my mind and nearly drove sleep from my pillow.

On the following morning the sun darted his beams from over the hills through the low lattice window. I rose at an early hour and looked out between the branches of eglantine which overhung the casement. To my surprize Scott was already up and forth, seated on a fragment of stone, and chatting with the workmen employed on the new building. I had supposed, after the time he had wasted upon me yesterday, he would be closely occupied this morning: but he appeared like a man of leisure who had nothing to do but bask in the sunshine and amuse himself.

I soon dressed myself and joined him. He talked about his proposed plans of Abbotsford: happy would it have been for him could he have contented himself with his delightful little vine covered cottage, and the simple, yet hearty and hospitable style, in which he lived at the time of my visit. The great pile of Abbotsford with the huge expense it entailed upon him, of servants, retainers, guests and baronial style, was a drain upon his purse, a task upon his exertions and a weight upon his mind that finally crushed him.

As yet, however, all was in embryo and perspective, and Scott pleased himself with picturing out his future residence as he would one of the fanciful creations of his own romances. "It was one of his air castles," he said, "which he was reducing to solid stone and mortar." About the place were strewed various morsels from the ruins of Melrose Abbey, which were to be incorporated in his mansion. He had already constructed out of similar materials a kind of Gothic shrine over a spring, and had surmounted it by a small stone cross.

Among the reliques from the Abbey which lay scattered before us was a most quaint and antique little lion, either of red stone, or painted red; which hit my fancy. I forget whose cognizance it was; but I shall never forget the delightful observations concerning old Melrose to which it accidentally gave rise.

The Abbey was evidently a pile that called up all Scott's poetic and romantic feelings; and one to which he was enthusiastically attached by the most fanciful and delightful of his early associations. He spoke of it, I may say, with affection. "There is no telling," said he, "what treasures are hid in that glorious old pile. It is a famous place for antiquarian plunder. There are such rich bits of old time sculpture for the architect, and old time story for the poet. There is as rare picking in it as in a Stilton cheese, and in the same taste—the mouldier the better."

He went on to mention circumstances of "mighty import" connected with the Abbey which had never been touched, and which had even escaped the researches of honest Johnny Bower. The heart of Robert Bruce, the hero of Scotland, had been buried in it. He dwelt on the beautiful story of Bruce's pious and chivalrous request in his dying hour, that his heart might be carried to the Holy Land and placed in the Holy Sepulchre, in fulfilment of a vow of pilgrimage; and on the loyal expedition of Sir James Douglas to convey the glorious relique. Much might be made he said out of the adventures of Sir James in that adventurous age; of his fortunes in Spain and his death in a crusade against the Moors: with the subsequent fortunes of the heart of Robert Bruce, until it was brought back to its native land and enshrined within the holy walls of old Melrose.

As Scott sat on a stone talking in this way, and knocking with his staff against the little red lion which lay prostrate before him, his grey eyes kindled beneath his shagged eyebrows; scenes, images, incidents kept breaking upon his mind as he proceeded; mingled with touches of the mysterious and supernatural as connected with the heart of Bruce. It seemed as if a poem or romance were breaking vaguely on his imagination. That he subsequently contemplated something of the kind, as connected with this subject, and with his favorite ruin of Melrose is evident from his introduction to 'The Monastery'; and it is a pity that he never succeeded in following out these shadowy but enthusiastic conceptions.

A summons to breakfast broke off our conversation when I begged to recommend to Scott's attention my friend the little red lion, who had led to such an interesting topic, and hoped he might receive some niche or station in the future castle, worthy of his evident antiquity and apparent dignity. Scott assured me, with comic gravity, that the valiant little lion should be most honourably entertained. I hope, therefore that he still flourishes at Abbotsford.

Before dismissing the theme of the reliques from the Abbey I will mention another, illustrative of Scott's varied humours. This was a human scull, which had probably belonged of yore to one of those jovial friars, so honourably mentioned in the old border ballad.

> O the monks of Melrose made gude kale
>   On Fridays, when they fasted.
> They wanted neither beef nor ale,
>   As long as their neighbors' lasted.

This scull Scott had caused to be cleaned and varnished, and placed it on a chest of drawers in his chamber, immediately opposite his bed; where I have seen it, grinning most dismally. It was an object of great awe and horror to the superstitious housemaids, and Scott used to amuse himself with their apprehensions. Sometimes in changing his dress he would leave his neckcloth coiled around it like a turban, and none of the "lasses" dared to remove it. It was a matter of great wonder and speculation among them that the laird should have such an "awsome fancy for an auld girning scull."

At breakfast that morning Scott gave an amusing account of a little Highlander called Campbell of the North, who had a law suit of many years standing with a nobleman in his neighborhood about the boundaries of their estates. It was the leading object of the little man's life; the running theme of all his conversations; he used to detail all the circumstances at full length to every body he met and to aid him in his descriptions of the premises and make his story "mair preceese" he had a great map made of his estate, a huge roll several feet long which he used to carry about on his shoulder. Campbell was a long bodied, but short and bandy legged little man, always clad in the highland garb, and as he went about with this great roll on his shoulder and his little legs curving like a pair of parentheses below his kilt he was an odd figure to behold. He was like little David shouldering the spear of Goliath, which was like unto a weaver's beam.

Whenever sheep shearing was over Campbell used to set out for Edinburgh to attend to his law suit. At the inns he paid double for all his meals and his nights lodgings; telling the landlords to keep it in mind until his return, so that he might come back that way at free cost; for he knew, he said, that he would spend all his money among the lawyers at Edinburgh, so he thought it best to secure a retreat home again.

On one of his visits he called upon his lawyer but was told he was not at home but his lady was. "It is just the same thing," said little Campbell. On being shown into the parlour, he unrolled his map, stated his case at full length, and, having gone through with his story, gave her the customary fee. She would have declined it but he insisted on her taking it. "I ha' had just as much pleasure," said he, "in telling the whole tale to you, as I should have had in telling it to your husband—and I believe full as much profit."

The last time he saw Scott he told him he believed he and the laird were near a settlement, as they agreed to within a few miles of the boundary. If I recollect right Scott added that he advised the little man to consign his cause and his map to the care of "Slow Willie Mowbray" of tedious memory; an Edinburgh worthy, much employed by the country people, for he tired out every body in office by repeated visits and drawling endless prolixity; and gained every suit by dint of boring.

These little stories and anecdotes which abounded in Scott's conversation rose naturally out of the subject, and were perfectly unforced; though in thus relating them in a detached way without the observations or circumstances which led to them and which have passed from my recollection they want their setting to give them proper relief. They will serve however to shew the natural play of his mind, in its familiar moods, and its fecundity in graphic and characteristic detail.

His daughter Sophia and his son Charles were those of his family who seemed most to feel and understand his humours, and to take delight in his stories. Mrs. Scott did not always pay the same attention to them, and would now and then make a casual remark which would operate a little like a damper. Thus Scott was going on with great glee to relate an anecdote of the Laird of Macnab; "who, poor fellow!" premised he, "is dead and gone—" "Why, Mr. Scott," exclaimed the good lady, "Macnab's not dead, is he?" "Faith my dear," replied Scott with humorous gravity, "if he's not dead they've done him great injustice, for they've buried him!"

The joke passed harmless and unnoticed by Mrs. Scott, but hit the poor Dominie just as he had raised a cup of tea to his lips, causing a burst of laughter which sent half of the contents about the table.

After breakfast Scott was occupied for some time correcting proof sheets which he had received by the mail. The novel of Rob Roy, as I have already observed, was at that time in the press, and I supposed them to be the proof sheets of that work. The authorship of the Waverly novels was still a matter of conjecture and uncertainty; though few doubted their being, principally at least, written by Scott. One proof to me of his being the author, was that he never adverted to them. A man so fond of any thing Scottish and any thing relating to national history or local legend, could not have been mute respecting such productions had they been written by another. He was fond of quoting the works of his cotemporaries; he was continually reciting scraps of border songs, or relating anecdotes of border story. With respect to his own poems, and to these novels, however, he was mute, and while with him I observed a scrupulous silence on the subject.

I may here mention a singular fact, of which I was not aware at the time, that Scott was very reserved with his children respecting his own writings, and was even disinclined to their reading his romantic poems. I learnt this, some time after from a passage in one of his letters to me, adverting to a set of the American miniature edition of his poems, which on my return to England, I forwarded to one of the young ladies. "In my hurry," writes he, "I have not thanked you in Sophia's name, for the kind attention which furnished her with the American volumes. I am not quite sure I can add my own, since you have made her acquainted with much more of Papa's folly than she would otherwise have learned; for I have taken special care they should never see any of these things during their earlier years."

To return to the thread of my narrative. When Scott had got through his brief literary occupation we set out on a ramble. The young ladies started to accompany us but had not gone far when they met a poor old labourer and his distressed family and turned back to take them to the house and relieve them.

On passing the bounds of Abbotsford we came upon a bleak looking farm, with a forlorn crazy old manse or farm house standing in naked desolation. This, however, Scott told me was an ancient hereditary property called Lauckend, about as valuable as the patrimonial estate of Don Quixote, and which, in like manner, conferred a hereditary dignity upon its proprietor; who was a petty laird, and though poor as a rat, prided himself upon his ancient blood and the standing of his house. He was accordingly called Lauckend according to the Scottish custom of naming a man after his family estate, but he was more generally known through the country round, by the name of Lauckie Long Legs, from the length of his limbs. While Scott was giving this account of him we saw him at a distance striding along one of his fields with his plaid fluttering about him, and he seemed well to deserve his appellation, for he looked all legs and tartan.

Lauckie knew nothing of the world beyond his neighborhood. Scott told me that on returning to Abbotsford from his visit to France, immediately after the war, he was called on by his neighbors generally, to enquire after foreign parts. Among the number came Lauckie Long Legs and an old brother as ignorant as himself. They had many enquiries to make about the French, whom they seemed to consider some remote and semi barbarous horde—"And what like are thae Barbarians in their own country?" said Lauckie, "can they write?—can they cypher?" He was quite astonished to learn that they were nearly as much advanced in civilization as the gude folks of Abbotsford.

After living for a long time in single blessedness Lauckie all at once, and not long before my visit to the neighborhood, took it into his head to get married. The neighbors were all surprized; but the family connexion, who were as proud as they were poor, were grievously scandalized, for they thought the young woman on which he had set his mind, quite beneath him. It was in vain, however, that they remonstrated on the misalliance he was about to make: he was not to be swayed from his determination. Arraying himself in his best, and saddling a gaunt steed that might have rivalled Rosinante, and placing a pillion behind his saddle, he departed to wed and bring home the humble lassie who was to be made mistress of the venerable hovel of Lauckend, and who lived in a village on the opposite side of the Tweed.

A small event of the kind makes a great stir in a little quiet country neighborhood. The word soon circulated through the village of Melrose, and the cottages in its vicinity, that Lauckie Long Legs had gone over the Tweed to fetch home his bride. All the good folks assembled at the bridge to await his return. Lauckie, however, disappointed them; for he crossed the river at a distant ford, and conveyed his bride safe to his mansion, without being perceived.

Let me step forward in the course of events, and relate the fate of poor Lauckie as it was communicated to me a year or two afterwards in a letter by Scott. From the time of his marriage he had no longer any peace, owing to the constant intermeddlings of his relatives, who would not permit him to be happy in his own way, but endeavoured to set him at variance with his wife. Lauckie refused to credit any of their stories to her disadvantage; but the incessant warfare he had to wage, in defence of her good name wore out both flesh and spirit. His last conflict was with his own brothers in front of his paternal mansion. A furious scolding match took place between them; Lauckie made a vehement profession of faith in her immaculate honesty, and then fell dead at the threshold of his own door. His person, his character, his name, his story and his fate entitled him to be immortalized in one of Scott's novels, and I looked to recognize him in some of the succeeding works from his pen; but I looked in vain.

————

After passing by the domains of honest Lauckie Scott pointed out at a distance the Eildon stone. There in ancient days stood the Eildon tree, beneath which Thomas the Rhymer according to popular tradition, dealt forth his prophecies, some of which still exist in antiquated ballads.

Here we turned up a little glen with a small burn or brook whimpering and dashing along it making an occasional waterfall, and over hung, in some places with mountain ash and weeping birch. "We are now," said Scott, "treading classic; or rather Fairy ground. This is the haunted glen of Thomas the Rhymer where he met with the queen of Fairy land, and this the Bogle burn, or goblin brook along which she rode on her dapple grey palfrey, with silver bells ringing at the bridle."

"Here," said he, pausing, "is Huntley Bank on which Thomas the Rhymer lay musing and sleeping when he saw, or dreamt he saw, the queen of Elfland:

> True Thomas lay on Huntlie bank
>   A ferlie he spied wi' his e'e;
> And there he saw a ladye bright,
>   Come riding down by the Eildon Tree.
>
> Her skirt was o' the grass green silk,
>   Her mantle o' the velvet fyne;
> At ilka tett of her horse's mane
>   Hung fifty siller bells and nine.

Here Scott repeated several of the stanzas and recounted the circumstance of Thomas the Rhymer's interview with the fairy and his being transported by her to fairy land.

> And till seven years were gone and past,
> True Thomas on earth was never seen.

"It is a fine old story," said he, "and might be wrought up into a capital fairy tale."

Scott continued on, leading the way as usual, and limping up the wizard glen, talking as he went, but as his back was toward me, I could only hear the deep growling tones of his voice, like the low breathing of an organ, without distinguishing the words, until pausing and turning his face towards me, I found he was reciting some scrap of border minstrelsy about Thomas the Rhymer. This was continually the case in my ramblings with him about this storied neighborhood. His mind was fraught with the traditionary fictions connected with every object around him, and he would breathe it forth as he went, apparently as much for his own gratification as for that of his companion.

> Nor hill, nor brook, we paced along,
> But had its legend or its song.

His voice was deep and sonorous, he spoke with a Scottish accent, and with somewhat of the Northumbrian "burr," which, to my mind gave a doric strength and simplicity to his elocution. His recitation of poetry was at times magnificent.

I think it was in the course of this ramble that my friend Hamlet, the black greyhound, got into a sad scrape. The dogs were beating about the glens and fields as usual, and had been for some time out of sight, when we heard a barking at some distance to the left. Shortly after we saw some sheep scampering over the hills: with the dogs after them. Scott applied to his lips the ivory whistle always hanging at his button hole, and soon called in the culprits excepting Hamlet. Hastening up a bank which commanded a view along a fold or hollow of the hills, we beheld the sable prince of Denmark standing by the bleeding body of a sheep. The carcass was still warm, the throat bore marks of the fatal gripe, and Hamlet's muzzle was stained with blood. Never was culprit more completely caught in *flagrante delictu*. I supposed the doom of poor Hamlet to be sealed; for no higher offence can be committed by a dog in a country abounding with sheep walks. Scott, however, had a greater value for his dogs than for his sheep. They were his companions and friends. Hamlet too, though an irregular impertinent kind of youngster, was evidently a favorite. He would not for some time believe it could be he who had killed the sheep. It must have been some cur of the neighborhood, that had made off on our approach and left poor Hamlet in the lurch. Proofs, however, were too strong, and Hamlet was generally condemned. "Well! Well," said Scott, "it's partly my own fault. I have given up coursing for some time past and the poor dog has had no chance after game to take the fire edge off of him. If he was put after a hare occasionally he never would meddle with sheep."

I understood, afterwards, that Scott actually got a pony, and went out now and then coursing with Hamlet, who in consequence, shewed no further inclination for mutton.

———

A further stroll among the hills brought us to what Scott pronounced the remains of a Roman camp, and as we sat upon a hillock which had once formed a part of the ramparts he pointed out the traces of the lines and bulwarks and the prætorium and shewed a knowledge of castrametation that would not have disgraced the antiquarian Oldbuck himself. Indeed various circumstances that I observed about Scott during my visit concurred to persuade me that many of the antiquarian humours of Monkbarns were taken from his own richly compounded character, and that some of the scenes and personages of that admirable novel were furnished by his immediate neighborhood.

He gave me several anecdotes of a noted pauper named Andrew Gemmells or Gammell as it was pronounced, who had once flourished on the banks of Galla Water, immediately opposite Abbotsford, and whom he had seen and talked and joked with when a boy, and I instantly recognized the likeness of that mirror of philosophic vagabonds and Nestor of beggars Edie Ochiltree. I was on the point of pronouncing the name and recognizing the portrait, when I recollected the incognito observed by Scott with respect to the novels, and checked myself, but it was one among many things that tended to convince me of his authorship.

His picture of Andrew Gemmells exactly accorded with that of Edie as to his height, carriage and soldier like air, as well as his arch and sarcastic humour. His home, if home he had, was at Gallashiels but he went "daundering" about the country, along the green shaws and beside the burns, and was a kind of walking chronicle throughout the valleys of the Tweed the Ettrick and the Yarrow, carrying the gossip from house to house, commenting on the inhabitants and their concerns, and never hesitating to give them a dry rub as to any of their faults or follies.

A shrewd beggar like Andrew Gemmells, Scott added, who could sing the old Scotch airs, tell stories and traditions, and gossip away the long winter evenings, was by no means an unwelcome visitor at a lonely manse or cottage. The children would run to welcome him, and place his stool in a warm corner of the ingle nook, and the old folks would receive him as a privileged guest.

As to Andrew, he looked upon them all as a parson does upon his parishioners, and considered the alms he received as much his due as the other does his tythes. I rather think, added Scott, Andrew considered himself more of a gentleman than those who toiled for a living, and that he secretly looked down upon the painstaking peasants that fed and sheltered him.

He had derived his aristocratical notions in some degree from being admitted occasionally to a precarious sociability with some of the small country gentry, who were sometimes in want of company to help while away the time. With these Andrew would now and then play at

cards and dice, and he never lacked "siller in pouch" to stake on a
game, which he did with a perfect air of a man to whom money was
a matter of little moment, and no one could lose his money with more
gentlemanlike coolness.

Among those who occasionally admitted him to this familiarity was
old John Scott of Galla, a man of family who inhabited his paternal
mansion of Torwoodlee. Some distinction of rank however was still
kept up. The laird sat on the inside of the window and the beggar on
the outside, and they played cards on the sill.

Andrew now and then told the laird a piece of his mind very freely;
especially on one occasion, when he had sold some of his paternal lands
to build himself a larger house with the proceeds. The speech of honest
Andrew smacks of the shrewdness of Edie Ochiltree.

"It's a' varra weel—it's a' varra weel Torwoodlee," said he; "but who
would ha' thought that your father's son would ha' sold two gude estates
to build a shaw's (cuckoo's) nest on the side of a hill?"

That day there was an arrival at Abbotsford of two English tourists;
one a gentleman of fortune and landed estate, the other a young clergyman whom he appeared to have under his patronage, and to have brought
with him as a travelling companion.

The patron was one of those well bred, common place gentlemen
with which England is over run. He had great deference for Scott,
and endeavoured to acquit himself learnedly in his company aiming
continually at abstract disquisitions, for which Scott had little relish.
The conversation of the latter as usual was studded with anecdotes
and stories some of them of great pith and humour; the well bred
gentleman was either too dull to feel their point; or too decorous to
indulge in hearty merriment; the honest parson, on the contrary, who
was not too refined to be happy, laughed loud and long at every joke, and
enjoyed them with the zest of a man who has more merriment in his
heart than coin in his pocket.

After they were gone some comments were made upon their different
deportments. Scott spoke very respectfully of the good breeding and
measured manners of the man of wealth, but with a kindlier feeling of
the honest parson, and the homely but hearty enjoyment with which he
relished every pleasantry. "I doubt," said he, "whether the parson's lot
in life is not the best; if he cannot command as many of the good things
of this world by his own purse as his patron can, he beats him all hollow
in his enjoyment of them when set before him by others. Upon the
whole," added he, "I rather think I prefer the honest parson's good

humour to his patron's good breeding—I have a great regard for a hearty laugher."

He went on to speak of the great influx of English travellers, which of late years had inundated Scotland; and doubted whether they had not injured the old fashioned Scottish character. "Formerly, they came here occasionally as sportsmen," said he, "to shoot moor game, without any idea of looking at scenery; and they moved about the country in hardy simple style, coping with the country people in their own way; but now they come rolling about in their equipages, to see ruins and spend money, and their lavish extravagance has played the vengeance with the common people. It has made them rapacious in their dealings with strangers; greedy after money and extortionate in their demands for the most trivial services. Formerly," continued he, "the poorer classes of our people were comparatively disinterested; they offered their services gratuitously in promoting the amusement or aiding the curiosity of strangers, and were gratified by the smallest compensation; but now they make a trade of shewing rocks and ruins, and are as greedy as Italian cicerones. They look upon the English as so many walking money bags, the more they are shaken and poked the more they will leave behind them."

I told him that he had a great deal to answer for on that head, since it was the romantic associations he had thrown by his writings over so many out of the way places in Scotland, that had brought in the influx of curious travellers.

Scott laughed and said he believed I might be in some measure in the right, as he recollected a circumstance in point. Being one time at Glenross, an old woman who kept a small inn which had but little custom, was uncommonly officious in her attendance upon him, and absolutely incommoded him with her civilities. The secret at length came out. As he was about to depart she addressed him with many curtsies, and said she understood he was the gentleman that had written a bonnie book about Loch Katrine. She begged him to write a little about their lake also, for she understood his book had done the inn at Loch Katrine a muckle deal of good.

On the following day I made an excursion with Scott and the young ladies to Dryburgh Abbey. We went in an open carriage, drawn by two sleek old black horses, for which Scott seemed to have an affection, as he had for every dumb animal that belonged to him. Our road lay through a variety of scenes rich in poetical and historical associations, about most of which Scott had something to relate. In one part of the drive he pointed to an old border keep or fortress on the summit of a naked hill several miles off which he called Smallholm Tower, and a rocky knoll on which it stood, the "Sandy Knowe crags." It was a place, he said, peculiarly dear to him from the recollections of childhood. His grandfather had lived there in the old Smallholm Grange or farm house: and he had been sent there, when but two years old, on account of his lameness, that he might have the benefit of the pure air of the hills and be under the care of his grandmother and aunts.

In the introduction of one of the cantos of Marmion he has depicted his grandfather, and the fireside of the farm house; and has given an amusing picture of himself in his boyish years.

> Still with vain fondness could I trace
> Anew, each kind familiar face,
> That brightened at our evening fire;
> From the thatched mansion's gray-haired sire,
> Wise without learning, plain and good,
> And sprung of Scotland's gentler blood;
> Whose eye in age, quick, clear and keen,
> Showed what in youth its glance had been;
> Whose doom discording neighbours sought,
> Content with equity unbought;
> To him the venerable priest,
> Our frequent and familiar guest,
> Whose life and manners well could paint
> Alike the student and the saint;
> Alas! whose speech too oft I broke
> With gambol rude and timeless joke;
> For I was wayward, bold, and wild,
> A self-willed imp, a grandame's child;
> But half a plague, and half a jest,
> Was still endured, beloved, caress'd.

It was, he said, during his residence at Smallholm crags that he first imbibed his passion for legendary tales, border traditions, and old national songs and ballads. His grandmother and aunts were well versed in that kind of lore, so current in Scottish country life. They used to recount them in long gloomy winter days, and about the ingle nook at night, in conclave with their gossip visitors; and little Walter would sit and listen with greedy ear, thus, taking into his infant mind the seeds of many a splendid fiction.

There was an old shepherd, he said, in the service of the family, who used to sit under the sunny wall and tell marvellous stories and recite old time ballads as he knitted stockings. Scott used to be wheeled out in his chair in fine weather, and would sit beside the old man and listen to him for hours.

The situation of Sandy Knowe was favorable both for story teller and listener. It commanded a wide view over all the border country, with its feudal towers, its haunted glens and wizard streams. As the old shepherd told his tales he could point out the very scene of action. Thus, before Scott could walk, he was made familiar with the scenes of his future stories; they were all seen as through a magic medium, and took that tinge of romance which they ever after retained in his imagination. From the height of Sandy Knowe he may be said to have had the first look out upon the promised land of his future glory.

On referring to Scott's works I find many of the circumstances related in this conversation, about the old tower and the boyish scenes connected with it, recorded in the introduction to Marmion already cited. This was frequently the case with Scott; incidents and feelings that had appeared in his writings were apt to be mingled up in his conversation, for they had been taken from what he had witnessed and felt in real life, and were connected with those scenes among which he lived and moved and had his being. I make no scruple at quoting the passage relative to the tower, though it repeats much of the foregone imagery, and with vastly superior effect.

> Thus while I ape the measure wild
> Of tales that charmed me yet a child,
> Rude though they be, still with the chime
> Return the thoughts of early time;
> And feelings roused in life's first day,
> Glow in the line, and prompt the lay.
> Then rise those crags, that mountain tower,
> Which charmed my fancy's wakening hour,
> Though no broad river swept along
> To claim perchance heroic song;
> Though sighed no groves in summer gale
> To prompt of love a softer tale;
> Though scarce a puny streamlet's speed
> Claimed homage from a shepherd's reed;
> Yet was poetic impulse given,
> By the green hill and clear blue heaven.
> It was a barren scene, and wild,
> Where naked cliffs were rudely piled;
> But ever and anon between
> Lay velvet turfs of loveliest green;

And well the lonely infant knew
Recesses where the wall-flower grew,
And honey-suckle loved to crawl
Up the low crag and ruined wall.
I deemed such nooks the sweetest shade
The sun in all his round surveyed;
And still I thought that shattered tower
The mightiest work of human power;
And marvelled as the aged hind
With some strange tale bewitched my mind,
Of forayers, who, with headlong force,
Down from that strength had spurred their horse,
Their southern rapine to renew,
Far in the distant Cheviot's blue,
And, home returning, filled the hall
With revel, wassell-rout, and brawl—
Methought that still with tramp and clang
The gate-way's broken arches rang;
Methought grim features, seamed with scars,
Glared through the window's rusty bars.
And ever by the winter hearth,
Old tales I heard of woe or mirth,
Of lovers' slights, of ladies' charms,
Of witches' spells, of warriors' arms;
Of patriot battles, won of old
By Wallace wight and Bruce the bold;
Of later fields of feud and fight,
When, pouring from the highland height,
The Scottish clans, in headlong sway,
Had swept the scarlet ranks away.
While stretched at length upon the floor,
Again I fought each combat o'er,
Pebbles and shells, in order laid,
The mimic ranks of war displayed;
And onward still the Scottish Lion bore,
And still the scattered Southron fled before.

Scott eyed the distant height of Sandy Knowe with an earnest gaze as we rode along, and said he had often thought of buying the place, repairing the old tower and making it his residence. He has in some measure, however, paid off his early debt of gratitude in clothing it with poetic and romantic associations, by his tale of "The Eve of St. John." It is to be hoped that those who actually possess so interesting a monument of Scott's early days will preserve it from any further delapidation.

Not far from Sandy Knowe Scott pointed out another old border hold, standing on the summit of a hill, which had been a kind of enchanted castle to him in his boyhood. It was the tower of Bemerside, the baronial residence of the Haigs or De Hagas, one of the oldest families of the border. There had seemed to him, he said, almost a wizard spell hanging over it, in consequence of a prophecy of Thomas the Rhymer, in which in his young days he most potently believed:

> Betide, betide, whate'er betide,
> Haig shall be Haig of Bemerside.

Scott added some particulars which shewed that, in the present instance, the venerable Thomas had not proved a false prophet, for it was a noted fact that, amid all the changes and chances of the border; through all the feuds and forays, and sackings and burnings, which had reduced most of the castles to ruins, and the proud families that once possessed them, to poverty, the tower of Bemerside still remained unscathed, and was still the strong hold of the ancient family of Haig.

Prophecies, however, often ensure their own fulfilment. It is very probable that the prediction of Thomas the Rhymer has linked the Haigs to their tower as their rock of safety, and has induced them to cling to it almost superstitiously, through hardship and inconveniences that would, otherwise, have caused its abandonment.

I afterwards saw, at Dryburgh Abbey, the burying place of this predestinated and tenacious family, the inscription of which shewed the value they set upon their antiquity:

> Locus Sepulturæ
> Antiquessimæ Familiæ
> De Haga
> De Bemerside.

In reverting to the days of his childhood Scott observed that the lameness which had disabled him in infancy gradually decreased; he soon acquired strength in his limbs, and though he always limped, he became, even in boyhood, a great walker. He used frequently to stroll from home and wander about the country for days together, picking up all kinds of local gossip and observing popular scenes and characters. His father used to be vexed with him for this wandering propensity and, shaking his head would say he fancied the boy would make nothing but a pedlar. As he grew older he became a keen sportsman and passed much of his time hunting and shooting. His field sports led him into the most wild and unfrequented parts of the country, and in this way he picked up much of that local knowledge which he has since evinced in his writings.

His first visit to Loch Katrine, he said, was in his boyish days, on a shooting excursion. The island, which he has made the romantic residence of the Lady of the Lake, was then garrisoned by an old man and his wife. Their house was vacant: they had put the key under the door and were absent fishing. It was at that time a peaceful residence, but became afterwards a resort of smugglers, until they were ferreted out.

In after years, when Scott began to turn this local knowledge to literary account, he revisited many of those scenes of his early ramblings, and endeavoured to secure the fugitive remains of the traditions and songs that had charmed his boyhood. When collecting materials for his Border Minstrelsy he used, he said, to go from cottage to cottage and make the old wives repeat all they knew, if but two lines; and by putting these scraps together he retrieved many a fine characteristic old ballad or tradition from oblivion.

I regret to say that I can recollect scarce any thing of our visit to Dryburgh Abbey. It is on the estate of the Earl of Buchan. The religious edifice is a mere ruin, rich in Gothic antiquities, but especially interesting to Scott from containing the family vault, and the tombs and monuments of his ancestors. He appeared to feel much chagrin at their being in the possession and subject to the intermeddlings of the Earl, who was represented as a nobleman of an eccentric character. The latter, however, set great value on these sepulchral reliques, and had expressed a lively anticipation of one day or other having the honor of burying Scott and adding his monument to the collection, which he intended should be worthy of the "mighty minstrel of the north,"—a prospective compliment which was by no means relished by the object of it.

One of my pleasantest rambles with Scott about the neighborhood of Abbotsford, was taken in company with Mr. William Laidlaw the steward of his estate. This was a gentleman for whom Scott entertained a particular value. He had been born to a competency, had been well educated, his mind was richly stored with varied information and he was a man of sterling moral worth. Having been reduced by misfortune Scott had got him to take charge of his estate. He lived at a small farm on the hill side above Abbotsford, and was treated by Scott as a cherished and confidential friend, rather than a dependant.

As the day was showery, Scott was attended by one of his retainers, named Tommie Purdie, who carried his plaid, and who deserves especial mention. Sophia Scott used to call him her father's grand vizier, and she gave a playful account one evening, as she was hanging on her father's arm, of the consultations which he and Tommie used to have about matters relative to farming. Purdie was tenacious of his opinions, and he and Scott would have long disputes in front of the house as to something that was to be done on the estate, until the latter fairly tired out would abandon the ground and the argument, exclaiming, "Well, well Tom, have it your own way."

After a time, however, Purdie would present himself at the door of the parlour and observe, "I ha' been thinking over the matter, and upon the whole I think I'll take your honour's advice."

Scott laughed heartily when this anecdote was told of him. It was with him and Tom, he said, as it was with an old laird and a pet servant, whom he had indulged until he was positive beyond all endurance. "This won't do!" cried the old laird, in a passion, "we can't live together any longer—we must part." "An' where the deel does your honour mean to go?" replied the other.

I would moreover observe of Tom Purdie, that he was a firm believer in ghosts, and warlocks, and all kinds of old wives' fables. He was a religious man too, mingling a little degree of Scottish pride in his devotion, for though his salary was but twenty pounds a year, he had managed to afford seven pounds for a family Bible. It is true he had one hundred pounds clear of the world, and was looked up to by his comrades as a man of property.

In the course of our mornings walk we stopped at a small house belonging to one of the laborers on the estate. The object of Scott's visit was to inspect a relique which had been digged up in the Roman camp and which, if I recollect right, he pronounced to have been a tongs. It was produced by the cottager's wife, a ruddy healthy looking dame, whom Scott addressed by the name of Ailie. As he stood regarding the relique, turning it round and round, and making comments upon it half grave, half comic, with the cottage group around him, all joining occasionally in the colloquy, the inimitable character of Monkbarns was again brought to mind, and I seemed to see before me that prince of antiquarians and humourists holding forth to his unlearned and un-believing neighbors.

Whenever Scott touched, in this way, upon local antiquities, and in all his familiar conversations about local traditions and superstitions, there was always a sly and quiet humour running at the bottom of his discourse, and playing about his countenance, as if he sported with the subject. It seemed to me as if he distrusted his own enthusiasm and was disposed to droll upon his own humours and peculiarities, yet at the same time a poetic gleam in his eye, would shew that he really took a strong relish and interest in the theme. "It was a pity," he said, "that antiquarians were generally so dry, for the subjects they handled were rich in historical and poetic recollections, in picturesque details, in quaint and heroic characteristics, and in all kinds of curious and obsolete courtesies and ceremonials. They are always groping among the rarest materials for poetry, but they have no idea of turning them to poetic use. Now every fragment from old times has in some degree its story with it; or gives an inkling of something characteristic of the circumstances and manners of its day, and so sets the imagination at work."

For my own part I never met with antiquarian so delightful either in his writings or his conversation, and the quiet subacid humour that was prone to mingle in his disquisitions gave them, to me, a peculiar and an exquisite flavor. But he seemed, in fact, to undervalue every thing that concerned himself. The play of his genius was so easy that he was unconscious of its mighty power; and made light of those sports of intellect that shamed the efforts and labours of other minds.

Our ramble this morning took us again up the Rhymer's glen and by Huntley bank, and Huntley wood, and the silver waterfall overhung with weeping birches and mountain ash, those delicate and beautiful trees which grace the green shaws and burn sides of Scotland. The heather, too, that closely woven robe of Scottish landscape which covers the nakedness of its hills and mountains, tinted the neighborhood with soft and rich colours. As we ascended the glen the prospects opened upon us; Melrose, with its towers and pinnacles, lay below; beyond was the Eildon hills, the Cowden Knowes, the Tweed, Galla water; and all the storied vicinity; the whole landscape varied by gleams of sunshine and driving showers.

Scott, as usual, took the lead, limping along with great activity; and in joyous mood, giving scraps of border rhymes and border stories. Two or three times in the course of our walk there were drizzling showers which I supposed would put an end to our ramble, but my companions trudged on as unconcernedly as if it had been fine weather.

At length, I asked whether we had not better seek some shelter. "True," said Scott, "I did not recollect that you were not accustomed to our Scottish mists. This is a lachrymose climate ever more showering. We however are 'children of the mist' and must not mind a little whimpering of the clouds any more than a man must the weeping of an hysterical wife. As you are not accustomed to be wet through as a matter of course in a mornings walk, we will bide a bit under the lee of this bank until the shower is over." Taking his seat under shelter of a thicket he called to his man Tom for his tartan: then turning to me, "come," said he, "come under my plaidy as the old song goes;" so, making me nestle down beside him he wrapped a part of the plaid round me, and took me, as he said under his wing.

While we were thus nestled together he pointed to a hole in the opposite bank of the glen. That, he said, was the hole of an old grey badger, who was doubtless snugly housed in this bad weather. Sometimes he saw him at the entrance of his hole, like a hermit at the door of his cell, telling his beads, or reading a homily. He had a great respect for the venerable anchorite, and would not suffer him to be disturbed. He was a kind of successor to Thomas the Rhymer, and perhaps might be Thomas himself returned from Fairy land, but still under fairy spell.

Some accident turned the conversation upon Hogg the poet, in which Laidlaw, who was seated beside us took a part. Hogg had once been a shepherd in the service of his father, and Laidlaw gave many interesting anecdotes of him of which I now retain no recollection. They used to tend the sheep together when Laidlaw was a boy, and Hogg would recite the first struggling conceptions of his muse. At night when Laidlaw was quartered comfortably in bed in the farm house poor Hogg would take to the shepherd's hut, in the field on the hill side, and there lie awake for hours together, and look at the stars and make poetry, which he would repeat the next day to his companion.

Scott spoke in warm terms of Hogg, and repeated passages from his beautiful poem of Kelmeny, to which he gave great and well merited praize. He gave, also, some amusing anecdotes of Hogg and his publisher Blackwood who was at that time just rising into the bibliographical importance which he has since enjoyed.

Hogg in one of his poems I believe the Pilgrims of the Sun had dabbled a little in metaphysics, and like his heroes had got into the clouds. Blackwood, who began to affect criticism, argued stoutly with him as to the necessity of omitting or elucidating some obscure passage. Hogg was immoveable.

"But man—" said Blackwood, "I dinna ken what ye mean in this passage—" "Hout tout man," replied Hogg impatiently, "I dinna ken always what I mean mysel."

There is many a metaphysical poet in the same predicament with honest Hogg.

Scott promised to invite the Shepherd to Abbotsford during my visit, and I anticipated much gratification in meeting with him from the account I had received of his character and manners, and the great pleasure I had derived from his works. Circumstances, however, prevented Scott from performing his promise, and to my great regret I left Scotland without seeing one of its most original and national characters.

When the weather held up we continued our walk until we came to a beautiful sheet of water, in the bosom of the mountain, called (if I recollect right) the lake of Cauldshiel. Scott prided himself much upon this little Mediterranean Sea in his dominions, and hoped I was not too much spoiled by our great lakes in America to relish it. He proposed to take me out to the centre of it, to a fine point of view; for which purpose we embarked in a small boat, which had been put on the lake by his neighbor Lord Somerville. As I was about to step on board, I observed in large letters on one of the benches "Search No. 2." I paused for a moment and repeated the inscription aloud, trying to recollect something I had heard or read to which it alluded. "Pshaw," cried Scott, "it is only some of Lord Somerville's nonsense—get in!" In an instant scenes in the Antiquary connected with "Search No. 1" flashed upon my mind. "Ah I remember now!" said I—and with a laugh took my seat but adverted no more to the circumstance.

We had a pleasant row about the lake, which commanded some pretty scenery. The most interesting circumstance connected with it, however, according to Scott, was, that it was haunted by a bogle in the shape of a water bull, which lived in the deep parts and now and then came forth upon dry land and made a tremendous roaring that shook the very hills. This story had been current in the vicinity from time immemorial,—there was a man living who declared he had seen the bull,—and he was believed by many of his simple neighbors. "I don't choose to contradict the tale," said Scott, "for I am willing to have my lake stocked with any fish, flesh or fowl that my neighbors think proper to put into it; and these old wives' fables are a kind of property in Scotland that belong to the estates and go with the soil. Our streams and lochs are like the rivers and pools in Germany that have all their Wasser Nixe, or water witches, and I have a fancy for these kind of amphibious bogles and hobgoblins."

———

Scott went on after we had landed to make many remarks mingled with picturesque anecdotes concerning the fabulous beings with which the Scotch were apt to people the wild streams and lochs that occur in the solemn and lonely scenes of their mountains: and to compare them with similar superstitions among the northern nations of Europe; but Scotland he said, was above all other countries for this wild and vivid progeny of the fancy, from the nature of the scenery, the misty magnificence and vagueness of the climate, the wild and gloomy events of its history; the clannish divisions of its people; their local feelings, notions and prejudices; the individuality of their dialect, in which all kinds of odd and peculiar notions were incorporated; by the secluded life of their mountaineers; the lonely habits of their pastoral people; much of whose time was passed on the solitary hill sides; their traditional songs which clothed every rock and stream with old world stories, handed down from age to age and generation to generation. The Scottish mind he said was made up of poetry and strong common sense; and the very strength of the latter, gave perpetuity and luxuriance to the former. It was a strong tenacious soil, into which, when once a seed of poetry fell, it struck deep root and brought forth abundantly. "You will never weed these popular stories and songs and superstitions out of Scotland," said he. "It is not so much that the people believe in them, as that they delight in them. They belong to the native hills and streams of which they are fond, and to the history of their forefathers of which they are proud."

"It would do your heart good," continued he, "to see a number of our poor country people seated round the ingle nook, which is generally capacious enough, and passing the long dark dreary winter nights listening to some old wife, or strolling gaberlunzie, dealing out auld world stories, about bogles and warlocks, or about raids and forays, and border skirmishes, or reciting some ballad stuck full of those fighting names that stir up a true Scotchman's blood like the sound of a trumpet. These traditional tales and ballads have lived for ages in mere oral circulation, being passed from father to son, or rather from grandam to grandchild, and are a kind of hereditary property of the poor peasantry, of which it would be hard to deprive them, as they have not circulating libraries to supply them with works of fiction in their place."

I do not pretend to give the precise words, but, as nearly as I can from scanty memorandums and vague recollections, the leading ideas of Scott. I am constantly sensible, however, how far I fall short of his copiousness and richness.

He went on to speak of the elves and sprites so frequent in Scottish legend. "Our fairies, however," said he, "though they dress in green and gambol by moonlight about the banks and shaws and burn sides, are not such pleasant little folks as the English fairies, but are apt to bear more of the warlock in their natures, and to play spiteful tricks. When I was a boy I used to look wistfully at the green hillocks that were said to be haunted by fairies, and felt sometimes as if I should like to lie down by them and sleep, and be carried off to Fairy land, only that I did not like some of the cantrips which used now and then to be played off upon visitors."

Here Scott recounted, in graphic style and with much humour, a little story which used to be current in the neighborhood, of an honest burgess of Selkirk who being at work upon the hill of Peatlaw fell asleep upon one of these 'fairy knowes' or hillocks. When he awoke he rubbed his eyes and gazed about him with astonishment for he was in the market place of a great city, with a crowd of people bustling about him, not one of whom he knew. At length he accosted a byestander and asked him the name of the place. "Hout man," replied the other, "are ye in the heart o' Glasgow, and speer the name of it." The poor man was astonished and would not believe either ears or eyes; he insisted that he had laid down to sleep but half an hour before on the Peatlaw near Selkirk. He came well nigh being taken up for a mad man when fortunately a Selkirk man came by who knew him and took charge of him, and conducted him back to his native place. Here, however, he was likely to fare no better when he spoke of having been whisked in his sleep from the Peatlaw to Glasgow. The truth of the matter at length came out; his coat, which he had taken off when at work on the Peatlaw was found lying near a "fairy knowe," and his bonnet, which was missing, was discovered on the weathercock of Lanark steeple. So it was as clear as day that he had been carried through the air by the fairies while he was sleeping, and his bonnet had been blown off, by the way.

I give this little story but meagerly from a scanty memorandum; Scott has related it in somewhat different style in a note to one of his poems; but in narration these anecdotes derived their chief zest from the quiet but delightful humour, the bonhommie with which he seasoned them, and the sly glance of the eye from under his bushy eye brows; with which they were accompanied.

———

That day at dinner we had Mr. Laidlaw and his wife and a female friend who accompanied them. The latter was a very intelligent respectable person, about the middle age, and was treated with particular attention and courtesy by Scott. Our dinner was a most agreeable one; for the guests were evidently cherished visitors to the house, and felt that they were appreciated.

When they were gone Scott spoke of them in the most cordial manner. "I wished to shew you," said he, "some of our really excellent, plain Scotch people: not fine gentlemen and ladies, for such you can meet every where, and they are every where the same. The character of a nation is not to be learnt from its fine folks."

He then went on with a particular eulogium on the lady who had accompanied the Laidlaws. She was the daughter, he said, of a poor country clergyman who had died in debt, and left her an orphan and destitute. Having had a good plain education, she immediately set up a child's school and had soon a numerous flock under her care by which she earned a decent maintenance. That, however, was not her main object. Her first care was to pay off her father's debts, that no ill word or ill will might rest upon his memory. This, by dint of Scottish economy, backed by filial reverence and pride, she accomplished, though in the effort she subjected herself to every privation. Not content with this, she in certain instances refused to take pay for the tuition of the children of some of her neighbors, who had befriended her father in his need, and had since fallen into poverty. "In a word," added Scott, "she is a fine old Scotch girl; and I delight in her more than in many a fine lady I have known; and I have known many of the finest."

It is time, however, to draw this rambling narrative to a close. Several days were passed by me, in the way I have attempted to describe, in almost constant, familiar and joyous conversation with Scott. It was, as if I were admitted to a social communion with Shakspeare, for it was with one of a kindred, if not equal genius. Every night I retired with my mind filled with delightful recollections of the day, and every morning I rose with the certainty of new enjoyment. The days thus spent I shall ever look back to as among the very happiest of my life; for I was conscious at the time of being happy.

The only sad moment that I experienced at Abbotsford was that of my departure; but it was cheered with the prospect of soon returning; for I had promised, after making a tour in the Highlands, to come and pass a few more days on the banks of the Tweed, when Scott intended to invite Hogg the poet to meet me. I took a kind farewell of the family, with each of whom I had been highly pleased; if I have refrained from dwelling particularly on their several characters, and giving anecdotes of them individually, it is because I consider them shielded by the sanctity of domestic life: Scott, on the contrary, belongs to history. As he accompanied me on foot, however, to a small gate on the confines of his premises, I could not refrain from expressing the enjoyment I had experienced in his domestic circle, and passing some warm eulogiums on the young folks from whom I had just parted. I shall never forget his reply. "They have kind hearts," said he, "and that is the main point as to human happiness. They love one another, poor things, which is every thing in domestic life. The best wish I can make you my friend," added he, laying his hand upon my shoulder, "is that when you return to your own country, you may get married and have a family of young bairns about you. If you are happy there they are to share your happiness—and if you are otherwise—there they are to comfort you."

By this time we had reached the gate where he halted and took my hand. "I will not say farewell," said he, "for it is always a painful word; but I will say come again. When you have made your tour to the Highlands come here and give me a few more days—but come when you

please, you will always find Abbotsford open to you, and a hearty
welcome."

———

I have thus given, in a rude style, my main recollections of what
occurred during my sojourn at Abbotsford and I feel mortified that I
can give but such meagre scattered and colourless details of what was
so copious, rich and varied. During several days that I passed there
Scott was in admirable vein. From early morn until dinner time, he was
rambling about shewing me the neighborhood; and during dinner and
until late at night engaged in social conversation. No time was reserved
for himself, he seemed as if his only occupation was to entertain me. And
yet I was almost an entire stranger to him; one of whom he knew
nothing but an idle book I had written, and which, some years before,
had amused him. But such was Scott—he appeared to have nothing to do
but lavish his time, attention and conversation on those around him. It
was difficult to imagine what time he found to write those volumes
that were incessantly issuing from the press; all of which, too, were of a
nature to require reading and research. I could not find that his life
was ever otherwise than a life of leisure and haphazard recreation, such
as it was during my visit. He scarce ever balked a party of pleasure, or
a sporting excursion; and rarely pleaded his own concerns as an excuse
for rejecting those of others. During my visit I heard of other visitors
who had preceded me, and who must have kept him occupied for many
days, and I have had an opportunity of knowing the course of his daily
life for some time subsequently. Not long after my departure from
Abbotsford my friend Wilkie arrived there, to paint a picture of the
Scott family. He found the house full of guests. Scott's whole time was
taken up in riding and driving about the country, or in social conversation at home. "All this time," said Wilkie to me, "I did not presume to
ask Mr. Scott to sit for his portrait, for I saw he had not a moment to
spare; I waited for the guests to go away; but as fast as one set went
another arrived, and so it continued for several days: and with each
set he was completely occupied. At length all went off and we were
quiet. I thought, however, Mr. Scott will now shut himself up among his
books and papers; for he has to make up for lost time. It won't do for
me to ask him now to sit for his picture. Laidlaw, who managed his estate
came in, and Scott turned to him, as I supposed, to consult about business. 'Laidlaw,' said he, 'tomorrow morning we'll go across the water
and take the dogs with us—there's a place where I think we shall be
able to find a hare.'"
"In short," added Wilkie, "I found that instead of business he was

thinking only of amusement, as if he had nothing in the world to occupy him. So I no longer feared to intrude upon him."

The conversation of Scott was frank, hearty, picturesque and dramatic; during the time of my visit he inclined to the comic rather than the grave, in his anecdotes and stories. And such I was told was his general inclination. He relished a joke, or a trait of humour, in social intercourse, and laughed with right good will. He talked not for effect or display, but from the flow of his spirits the stores of his memory and the vigour of his imagination. He had a natural turn for narration, and his narratives and descriptions were without effort, yet wonderfully graphic. He placed the scene before you like a picture; he gave the dialogue with the appropriate dialect or peculiarities and described the appearance and characters of his personages with that spirit and felicity evinced in his writings. Indeed his conversation reminded me continually of his novels and it seemed to me that during the whole time I was with him he talked enough to fill volumes and that they could not have been filled more delightfully.

He was as good a listener as talker, appreciated every thing that others said, however humble might be their rank or pretensions, and was quick to testify his perception of any point in their discourse. He arrogated nothing to himself, but was perfectly unassuming and unpretending, entering with heart and soul into the business, or pleasure, or I had almost said folly, of the hour and the company. No one's concerns, no one's thoughts and opinions, no one's tastes and pleasures seemed beneath him. He made himself so thoroughly the companion of those with whom he happened to be, that they forgot for a time his vast superiority; and only recollected and wondered, when all was over, that it was Scott with whom they had been on such familiar terms, and in whose society they had felt so perfectly at their ease.

It was delightful to observe the generous spirit in which he spoke of all his literary cotemporaries; quoting the beauties of their works and pointing out their merits; and this too with respect to persons with whom he might have been supposed to be at variance in literature or politics. Jeffrey it was thought had ruffled his plumes in one of his reviews, yet Scott spoke of him in terms of high and warm eulogy both as an author and as a man.

His humour in conversation, as in his works, was genial and free from all causticity. He had a quick perception of faults and foibles, but he looked upon poor human nature with an indulgent eye; relishing what was good and pleasant, tolerating what was frail, and pitying what was evil. It is this beneficent spirit which gives such an air of bonhommie to Scott's humour throughout all his works. He played with the foibles and errors of his fellow beings, and presented them in a thousand whimsical and characteristic lights, but the kindness and generosity of his nature would not allow him to be a satirist. I do not recollect a sneer throughout his conversation any more than there is throughout his works.

Such is a rough sketch of Scott, as I saw him in private life, not merely at the time of the visit here narrated, but in the casual intercourse of subsequent years. Of his public character and merits all the world can judge. His works have incorporated themselves with the thoughts and concerns of the whole civilized world for a quarter of a century, and have had a controlling influence over the age in which he lived. But when did a human being ever exercise an influence more salutary and benignant. Who is there that, on looking back over a great portion of his life, does not find the genius of Scott administering to his pleasures, beguiling his cares and soothing his lonely sorrows. Who does not still guard his works as a treasury of pure enjoyment, an armoury to which to resort in time of need, to find weapons with which to fight off the evils and the griefs of life. For my own part, in periods of dejection, I have hailed the announcement of a new work from his pen as an earnest of certain pleasure in store for me, and have looked forward to it as a traveller on a waste looks to a green spot at a distance, where he feels assured of solace and refreshment. When I consider how much he has thus contributed to the better hours of my past existence, and how independent his works still make me, at times, of all the world for my enjoyment, I bless my stars that cast my lot in his days, to be thus cheered and gladdened by the outpourings of his genius. I consider it one of the greatest advantages that I have derived from my literary career, that it has elevated me into genial communion with such a spirit; and as a tribute of gratitude for his friendship, and veneration for his memory I cast this humble stone upon his cairn, which will soon, I trust, be piled aloft with the contributions of abler hands.

NEWSTEAD ABBEY

Newstead Abbey—West Front

Reproduced from *The Crayon Miscellany* (G. P. Putnam's Sons, Holly Edition, 1895).

HISTORICAL NOTICE

Being about to give a few sketches taken during a three weeks sojourn in the ancestral mansion of the late Lord Byron, I think it proper to premise some brief particulars concerning its history.

Newstead Abbey is one of the finest specimens in existence of those quaint and romantic piles, half castle half convent, which remain as monuments of the olden times of England. It stands too in the midst of a legendary neighborhood; being in the heart of Sherwood Forest, and surrounded by the haunts of Robin Hood and his band of outlaws, so famous in ancient ballad and nursery tale. It is true, the forest scarcely exists but in name, and the tract of country over which it once extended its broad solitudes and shades is now an open and smiling region, cultivated with parks, and farms and enlivened with villages.

Newstead, which probably once exerted a monastic sway over this region, and controlled the consciences of the rude foresters, was originally a priory founded in the latter part of the twelfth century, by Henry II, at the time when he sought, by building of shrines and convents, and by other acts of external piety, to expiate the murder of Thomas a Becket. The priory was dedicated to God and the Virgin, and was inhabited by a fraternity of canons regular of St. Augustine. This order was originally simple and abstemious in its mode of living, and exemplary in conduct; but, it would seem that it gradually lapsed into those abuses which disgraced too many of the wealthy monastic establishments; for there are documents among its archives which intimate the prevalence of gross misrule and dissolute sensuality among its members.

At tht time of the dissolution of the convents during the reign of Henry VIII, Newstead underwent a sudden reverse, being given, with the neighboring manor and rectory of Papelwick, to Sir John Byron, Steward of Manchester and Rochdale, and Lieutenant of Sherwood Forest. This ancient family worthy figures in the traditions of the Abbey, and in the ghost stories with which it abounds, under the quaint and graphic appellation of "Sir John Byron the little, with the great beard." He converted the saintly edifice into a castellated dwelling, making it his favorite residence and the seat of his forest jurisdiction.

The Byron family being subsequently ennobled by a baronial title, and enriched by various possessions, maintained great style and retinue at Newstead. The proud edifice partook, however, of the vicissitudes of the times, and Lord Byron, in one of his poems represents it as alternately the scene of lordly wassailing and of civil war.

171

Hark how the hall resounding to the strain
  Shakes with the martial music's novel din!
The heralds of a warrior's haughty reign
  High crested banners wave thy walls within.

Of changing centinels the distant hum
  The mirth of feasts, the clang of burnished arms,
The braying trumpet, and the hoarser drum
  Unite in concert with increased alarms.

About the middle of the last century the Abbey came into the possession of another noted character, who makes no less figure in its shadowy traditions than Sir John the little with the great beard. This was the grand uncle of the poet, familiarly known among the gossipping chroniclers of the Abbey as "The Wicked Lord Byron." He is represented as a man of irritable passions and vindictive temper, in the indulgence of which an incident occurred which gave a turn to his whole character and life, and in some measure affected the fortunes of the Abbey. In his neighborhood lived his kinsman and friend Mr. Chaworth proprietor of Annesley Hall. Being together in London in 1765, in a chamber of the Star and Garter tavern in Pall Mall a quarrel arose between them. Byron insisted upon settling it upon the spot by single combat. They fought without seconds, by the dim light of a candle, and Mr. Chaworth, although the most expert swordsman, received a mortal wound. With his dying breath he related such particulars of the contest as induced the coroner's jury to return a verdict of wilful murder. Lord Byron was sent to the tower and subsequently tried before the House of Peers, where an ultimate verdict was given of manslaughter.

He retired after this to the Abbey, where he shut himself up to brood over his disgraces; grew gloomy, morose and fantastical and indulged in fits of passion and caprice that made him the theme of rural wonder and scandal. No tale was too wild or too monstrous for vulgar belief. Like his successor the poet, he was accused of all kinds of vagaries and wickedness. It was said that he always went armed, as if prepared to commit murder on the least provocation. At one time when a gentleman of his neighborhood was to dine *tete a tete* with him, it is said a brace of pistols were gravely laid with the knives and forks upon the table, as part of the regular table furniture, and implements that might be needed in the course of the repast. Another rumour states that being exasperated at his coachman for disobedience to orders, he shot him on the spot, threw his body into the coach where Lady Byron was seated, and, mounting the box, officiated in his stead. At another time, according to the same vulgar rumors, he threw her Ladyship into the lake in front of the Abbey, where she would have been drowned but for the timely aid of the gardener. These stories are doubtless exaggerations of trivial incidents which may have occurred; but it is certain that the wayward passions of this unhappy man caused a separation from his wife and finally spread a solitude around him. Being displeased at the marriage of his son and heir, he displayed an inveterate malignancy towards him. Not being able to cut off his succession to the Abbey estate, which descended to him by entail, he endeavoured to injure it as much as possible, so that it might come a mere wreck into his hands. For this purpose he suffered the Abbey to fall out of repair and every thing to go to waste about it, and cut down all the timber on the estate, laying low many a tract of old Sherwood Forest, so that the Abbey lands lay stripped and bare of all their ancient honours. He was baffled in his unnatural revenge by the premature death of his son, and passed the remainder of his days in his deserted and dilapidated halls, a gloomy misanthrope, brooding amidst the scenes he had laid desolate.

His wayward humours drove from him all neighborly society, and for a part of the time he was almost without domestics. In his misanthropic mood, when at variance with all human kind, he took to feeding crickets, so that in process of time the Abbey was overrun with them, and its lonely halls made more lonely at night by their monotonous music. Tradition adds that, at his death, the crickets seemed aware that they had lost their patron and protector, for they one and all packed up bag and baggage and left the Abbey, trooping across its courts and corridors in all directions.

The death of the "Old Lord," or "The Wicked Lord Byron," for he is known by both appellations, occurred in 1798: and the Abbey then passed into the possession of the Poet. The latter was but eleven years of age and living in humble style with his mother in Scotland. They came soon after to England to take possession. Moore gives a simple but striking anecdote of the first arrival of the poet at the domains of his ancestors.

They had arrived at the Newstead toll bar and saw the woods of the Abbey stretching out to receive them, when Mrs. Byron, affecting to be ignorant of the place, asked the woman of the toll-house—to whom that seat belonged? She was told that the owner of it, Lord Byron, had been some months dead. "And who is the next heir?" asked the proud and happy mother. "They say," answered the old woman, "it is a little boy who lives at Aberdeen—" "And this is he, bless him!" exclaimed the nurse, no longer able to contain herself, and turning to kiss with delight the young lord who was seated on her lap.*

*Moore's Life of Lord Byron.

During Lord Byron's minority the Abbey was let to Lord Grey de Ruthen, but the poet visited it occasionally during the Harrow vacations when he resided with his mother at lodgings in Nottingham. It was treated little better by its present tenant than by the old lord who preceded him, so that, when, in the autumn of 1808, Lord Byron took up his abode there, it was in a ruinous condition. The following lines from his own pen may give some idea of its condition.

> Through thy battlements, Newstead, the hollow winds whistle.
>   Thou, the hall of my fathers, art gone to decay:
> In thy once smiling garden, the hemlock and thistle
>   Have choked up the rose which once bloomed in the way.
>
> Of the mail-covered barons who, proudly, to battle
>   Led thy vassals from Europe to Palestine's plain,
> The escutcheon and shield, which with every wind rattle,
>   Are the only sad vestiges now that remain.*

In another poem he expresses the melancholy feeling with which he took possession of his ancestral mansion.

> Newstead! what saddening scene of change is thine,
>   Thy yawning arch betokens sure decay:
> The last and youngest of a noble line
>   Now holds thy mouldering turrets in his sway.
>
> Deserted now, he scans thy gray-worn towers,
>   Thy vaults, where dead of feudal ages sleep,
> Thy cloysters, pervious to the wintry showers,
>   These—these he views, and views them but to weep.
>
> Yet he prefers thee to the gilded domes,
>   Or gew gaw grottoes of the vainly great;
> Yet lingers mid thy damp and mossy tombs,
>   Nor breathes a murmur 'gainst the will of fate.†

Lord Byron had not fortune sufficient to put the pile in extensive repair, or to maintain any thing like the state of his ancestors. He restored some of the apartments so as to furnish his mother with a comfortable habitation, and fitted up a quaint study for himself, in which among

*Lines on leaving Newstead Abbey.
†Elegy on Newstead Abbey.

books and busts and other library furniture were two sculls of the ancient friars, grinning on each side of an antique cross. One of his gay companions gives a picture of Newstead when thus repaired, and the picture is sufficiently desolate.

"There are two tiers of cloisters with a variety of cells and rooms about them, which, though not inhabited, nor in an inhabitable state, might easily be made so; and many of the original rooms, among which is a fine stone hall, are still in use. Of the Abbey church one end only remains; and the old kitchen with a long range of apartments, is reduced to a heap of rubbish. Leading from the Abbey to the modern part of the habitation is a noble room seventy feet in length and twenty three in breadth; but every part of the house displays neglect and decay, save those which the present lord has lately fitted up."*

Even the repairs thus made were but of transient benefit for, the roof being left in its dilapidated state, the rain soon penetrated into the apartments which Lord Byron had restored and decorated, and in a few years rendered them almost as desolate as the rest of the Abbey.

Still he felt a pride in the ruinous old edifice; its very dreary and dismantled state addressed itself to his poetical imagination, and to that love of the melancholy and the grand which is evinced in all his writings. "Come what may," said he in one of his letters, "Newstead and I stand or fall together. I have now lived on the spot. I have fixed my heart upon it, and no pressure, present or future, shall induce me to barter the last vestige of our inheritance. I have that pride within me which will enable me to support difficulties—Could I obtain in exchange for Newstead Abbey the first fortune in the country, I would reject the proposition."

His residence at the Abbey, however, was fitful and uncertain. He passed occasional portions of time there, sometimes studiously and alone, oftener idly and recklessly, and occasionally with young and gay companions in riot and revelry and the indulgence of all kinds of mad caprice. The Abbey was by no means benefited by these roystering inmates, who sometimes played off monkish mummeries about the cloysters, at other times turned the state chambers into schools for boxing and single stick and shot pistols in the great hall. The country people of the neighborhood were as much puzzled by these madcap vagaries of the new incumbent as by the gloomier habits of the "Old Lord" and began to think that madness was inherent in the Byron race, or that some wayward star ruled over the Abbey.

It is needless to enter into a detail of the circumstances which led his Lordship to sell his ancestral estate, notwithstanding the partial pre-

*Letter of the late Charles Skinner Mathews Esq.

dilections and hereditary feelings which he had so eloquently expressed. Fortunately it fell into the hands of a man who possessed something of a poetical temperament, and who cherished an enthusiastic admiration for Lord Byron. Colonel (at that time Major) Wildman had been a school mate of the poet, and sat with him on the same form at Harrow. He had subsequently distinguished himself in the war of the Peninsula and at the battle of Waterloo, and it was a great consolation to Lord Byron, in parting with his family estate, to know that it would be held by one capable of restoring its faded glories, and who would respect and preserve all the monuments and memorials of his line.*

The confidence of Lord Byron in the good feeling and good taste of Colonel Wildman has been justified by the event. Under his judicious eye and munificent hand the venerable and romantic pile has risen from its ruins in all its old monastic and baronial splendour, and additions have been made to it in perfect conformity of style. The groves and forests have been replanted; the lakes and fish ponds cleaned out and the gardens rescued from the "hemlock and thistle" and restored to their pristine and dignified formality.

The farms on the estate have been put in complete order, new farm houses built of stone in the picturesque and comfortable style of the old English granges; the hereditary tenants secured in their paternal

---

*The following letter, written in the course of the transfer of the estate, has never been published.

Venice Nov. 18th 1818.

My dear WILDMAN

Mr. Hanson is on the Eve of his return so that I have only time to return a few inadequate thanks for your very kind letter. I should regret to trouble you with any requests of mine in regard to the preservation of any signs of my family which may still exist at Newstead—and leave everything of that kind to your own feelings, present or future, upon the subject.—The portrait which you flatter me by desiring—would not be worth to you your trouble & expense of such an expedition—but you may rely upon your having the very first that may be painted and which may seem worth your acceptance.

I trust that Newstead will, being yours—remain so and that it may see you as happy as I am very sure that you will make your dependants—With regard to myself you may be sure that whether in the 4th or 5th or sixth form at Harrow, or in the fluctuations of after-life, I shall always remember with regard my old schoolfellow —fellow monitor—and friend; and recognise with respect the gallant soldier, who, with all the advantages of fortune and allurements of youth to a life of pleasure— devoted himself to duties of a nobler order—and will receive his reward in the esteem and admiration of his country.

Ever yours
most truly
& affectly,
BYRON.

homes and treated with the most considerate indulgence; every thing in a word gives happy indications of a liberal and beneficent landlord.

What most, however, will interest the visitors to the Abbey in favour of its present occupant, is the reverential care with which he has preserved and renovated every monument and relique of the Byron family, and every object in any wise connected with the memory of the poet. Eighty thousand pounds have already been expended upon the venerable pile, yet the work is still going on, and Newstead promises to realize the hope faintly breathed by the poet when bidding it a melancholy farewell.

> Haply thy sun emerging yet may shine,
>   Thee to irradiate with meridian ray;
> Hours splendid as the past may still be thine,
>   And bless thy future, as thy former day.

ARRIVAL AT THE ABBEY

I had been passing a merry Christmas in the good old style at a venerable family hall in Derbyshire, and set off to finish the holydays with the hospitable proprietor of Newstead Abbey. A drive of seventeen miles through a pleasant country, part of it the storied region of Sherwood Forest, brought me to the gate of Newstead Park. The aspect of the park was by no means imposing, the fine old trees that once adorned it having been laid low by Lord Byron's wayward predecessor.

Entering the gate, the post chaise rolled heavily along a sandy road, between naked declivities, gradually descending into one of those gentle and sheltered valleys, in which the sleek monks of old loved to nestle themselves. Here a sweep of the road round an angle of a garden wall brought us full in front of the venerable edifice, embosomed in the valley, with a beautiful sheet of water spreading out before it.

The irregular grey pile, of motley architecture, answered to the description given by Lord Byron:

> An old, old monastery once, and now
> Still older mansion, of a rich and rare
> Mixed Gothic——

One end was fortified by a castellated tower, bespeaking the baronial and warlike days of the edifice; the other end maintained its primitive monastic character. A ruined chapel flanked by a solemn grove, still reared its front entire. It is true, the threshold of the once frequented portal was grass grown, and the great lancet window, once glorious with painted glass, was now entwined and overhung with ivy, but the old convent cross still braved both time and tempest on the pinnacle of the chapel, and below, the blessed effigies of the Virgin and child, sculptured in grey stone, remained uninjured in their niche, giving a sanctified aspect to the pile.*

A flight of rooks, tenants of the adjacent grove, were hovering about the ruin and balancing themselves upon every airy projection, and looked down with curious eye and cawed as the post chaise rattled along below.

The chamberlain of the Abbey, a most decorous personage, dressed in black, received us at the portal. Here, too, we encountered a memento of Lord Byron, a great black and white Newfoundland dog, that had accompanied his remains from Greece. He was descended from the famous Boatswain and inherited his generous qualities. He was a cherished inmate of the Abbey, and honored and caressed by every visitor. Conducted by the chamberlain, and followed by the dog, who assisted in doing the honours of the house, we passed through a long low vaulted hall, supported by massive gothic arches, and not a little resembling the crypt of a cathedral, being the basement story of the Abbey.

From this we ascended a stone staircase, at the head of which a pair of folding doors admitted us into a broad corridor that ran round the interior of the Abbey. The windows of the corridor looked into a quadrangular grass grown court, forming the hollow centre of the pile. In the midst of it rose a lofty and fantastic fountain, wrought of the same grey stone as the main edifice, and which has been well described by Lord Byron.

> Amidst the court a gothic fountain play'd
>   Symmetrical, but decked with carvings quaint,
> Strange faces, like to men in masquerade,
>   And here perhaps a monster, there a saint:
> The spring gush'd through grim mouths of granite made,
>   And sparkled into basins, where it spent
> Its little torrent in a thousand bubbles,
> Like man's vain glory, and his vainer troubles.†

----

*——— in a higher niche, alone, but crowned,
  The Virgin Mother of the God-born child
With her son in her blessed arms, looked round,
  Spared by some chance, when all beside was spoiled:
She made the earth below seem holy ground.
                                    DON JUAN, Canto XIII.

†Don Juan, Canto XIII.

Around this quadrangle were low vaulted cloysters, with gothic arches, once the secluded walk of the monks: the corridor along which we were passing was built above these cloysters, and their hollow arches seemed to reverberate every footfall. Every thing thus far had a solemn monastic air; but, on arriving at an angle of the corridor, the eye, glancing along a shadowy gallery, caught a sight of two dark figures in plate armour, with closed visors, bucklers braced and swords drawn standing motionless against the wall. They seemed two phantoms of the chivalrous era of the Abbey.

Here the chamberlain, throwing open a folding door, ushered us at once into a spacious and lofty saloon; which offered a brilliant contrast to the quaint and sombre apartments we had traversed. It was elegantly furnished and the walls hung with paintings, yet something of its original architecture had been preserved and blended with modern embellishments. There were the stone-shafted casements and the deep bow window of former times. The carved and panelled wood work of the lofty ceiling had likewise been carefully restored, and its gothic and grotesque devices, painted and gilded in their ancient style. Here too were emblems of the former and latter days of the Abbey, in the effigies of the first and last of the Byron line that held sway over its destinies. At the upper end of the saloon, above the door, the dark gothic portrait of "Sir John Byron the little with the great beard" looked grimly down from his canvas, while, at the opposite end, a white marble bust of the *genius loci,* the noble poet, shone conspicuously from its pedestal.

The whole air and style of the apartment partook more of the palace than the monastery; and its windows looked forth on a suitable prospect, composed of beautiful groves, smooth verdant lawns, and silver sheets of water. Below the windows was a small flower garden, inclosed by stone ballustrades, on which were stately peacocks, sunning themselves and displaying their plumage. About the grass plots in front were gay cock pheasants, and plump partridges, and nimble footed water hens, feeding about in perfect security.

Such was the medley of objects presented to the eye on first visiting the Abbey, and I found the interior fully to answer the description of the poet.

> The mansion's self was vast and venerable,
>   With more of the monastic than has been
> Elsewhere preserved: the cloysters still were stable,
>   The cells too, and refectory, I ween:
> An exquisite small chapel had been able,
>   Still unimpaired, to decorate the scene;
> The rest had been reform'd, replaced or sunk
> And spoke more of the baron than the monk.

Huge halls, long galleries, spacious chambers, join'd
   By no quite lawful marriage of the arts,
Might shock a connoisseur; but when combin'd
   Form'd a whole which, irregular in parts,
Yet left a grand impression on the mind,
   At least of those whose eyes were in their hearts.

It is not my intention to lay open the scenes of domestic life at the Abbey, or to describe the festivities of which I was a partaker during my sojourn within its hospitable walls; I wish merely to present a picture of the edifice itself, and of those personages and circumstances about it, connected with the memory of Byron.

I forbear, therefore, to dwell on my reception by my excellent and amiable host and hostess, or to make my reader acquainted with the elegant inmates of the mansion that I met in the saloon; and I shall pass on at once with him to the chamber allotted me, and to which I was most respectfully conducted by the chamberlain.

It was one of a magnificent suite of rooms, extending between the court of the cloisters and the Abbey garden, the windows looking into the latter. The whole suite formed the ancient state apartment and had fallen into decay during the neglected days of the Abbey, so as to be in a ruinous condition in the time of Lord Byron. It had since been restored to its ancient splendour, of which my chamber may be cited as a specimen. It was lofty and well proportioned; the lower part of the walls was panelled with ancient oak, the upper part hung with Goblen tapestry, representing oriental hunting scenes, wherein the figures were of the size of life, and of great vivacity of attitude and colour.

The furniture was antique, dignified and cumbrous.—High backed chairs curiously carved, and wrought in needle work; a massive clothes press of dark oak, well polished, and inlaid with landscapes of variously tinted woods; a bed of state, ample and lofty, so as only to be ascended by a moveable flight of steps; the huge posts supporting a high tester with a towering tuft of crimson plumes at each corner and rich curtains of crimson damask hanging in broad and heavy folds.

A venerable mirror of plate glass stood on the toilette, in which belles of former centuries may have contemplated and decorated their charms. The floor of the chamber was of tessellated oak, shining with wax, and partly covered by a Turkey carpet. In the centre stood a massy oaken table, waxed and polished as smooth as glass, and furnished with a writing desk of perfumed rose wood.

A sober light was admitted into the room through gothic stone shafted casements, partly shaded by crimson curtains, and partly over shadowed by the trees of the garden. This solemnly tempered light added to the effect of the stately and antiquated interior.

Two portraits, suspended over the doors, were in keeping with the scene. They were in ancient Vandyke dresses; one was a cavalier, who may have occupied this apartment in days of yore the other a lady with a black velvet mask in her hand, who may once have arrayed herself for conquest at the very mirror I have described.

The most curious relique of old times, however, in this quaint but richly dight apartment, was a great chimney piece of panel work carved in high relief, with niches or compartments each containing a human bust, that protruded almost entirely from the wall. Some of the figures were in ancient gothic garb, the most striking among them was a female, who was earnestly regarded by a fierce Saracen from an adjoining niche.

This panel work is among the mysteries of the Abbey; and causes as much wide speculation as the Egyptian hyeroglyphics. Some suppose it to illustrate an adventure in the Holy Land, and that the lady in effigy has been rescued by some crusader of the family from the turbaned Turk who watches her so earnestly. What tends to give weight to these suppositions is, that similar pieces of panel work exist in other parts of the Abbey, in all of which are to be seen the Christian lady and her Saracen guardian or lover. At the bottom of these sculptures are emblazoned the armorial bearings of the Byrons.

I shall not detain the reader however, with any further description of my apartment, or of the mysteries connected with it. As he is to pass some days with me at the Abbey, we shall have time to examine the old edifice at our leisure and to make ourselves acquainted, not merely with its interior, but likewise with its environs.

THE ABBEY GARDEN

The morning after my arrival, I rose at an early hour. The daylight was peering brightly between the window curtains, and drawing them apart, I gazed through the gothic casement upon a scene that accorded in character with the interior of the ancient mansion. It was the old Abbey garden, but altered to suit the tastes of different times and occupants. In one direction were shady walks and alleys, broad terraces and lofty groves; in another, beneath a grey monastic looking angle of the edifice, overrun with ivy and surmounted by a cross, lay a small French garden, with formal flower pots, gravelled walks, and stately stone ballustrades.

The beauty of the morning, and the quiet of the hour, tempted me to an early stroll; for it is pleasant to enjoy such old time places alone, when one may indulge poetical reveries and spin cobweb fancies without interruption. Dressing myself, therefore, with all speed, I descended a small flight of steps from the state apartment into the long corridor over the cloisters, along which I passed to a door at the farther end. Here I emerged into the open air, and descending another flight of stone steps, found myself in the centre of what had once been the Abbey chapel.

Nothing of the sacred edifice remained, however, but the gothic front with its deep portal and grand lancet window, already described. The nave, the side walls, the choir, the sacristy, all had disappeared. The open sky was over my head, a smooth shaven grass plot beneath my feet. Gravel walks and shrubberies had succeeded to the shadowy aisles, and stately trees to the clustering columns.

> Where now the grass exhales a murky dew,
>   The humid pall of life extinguished clay,
> In sainted fame the sacred fathers grew
>   Nor raised their pious voices but to pray.
>
> Where now the bats their wavering wings extend
>   Soon as the gloaming spread her warning shade
> The choir did oft their mingling vespers blend
>   Or matin orizons to Mary paid.

Instead of the matin orizons of the monks, however, the ruined walls of the chapel now resounded to the cawing of innumerable rooks that were fluttering and hovering about the dark grove which they inhabited, and preparing for their morning flight.

My ramble led me along quiet alleys, bordered by shrubbery, where the solitary water hen would now and then scud across my path and take refuge among the bushes. From hence I entered upon a broad terraced walk, once a favorite resort of the friars, which extended the whole length of the old Abbey garden, passing along the ancient stone wall which bounded it. In the centre of the garden lay one of the monkish fish pools, an oblong sheet of water, deep set like a mirror, in green sloping banks of turf. In its glassy bosom was reflected the dark mass of a neighboring grove, one of the most important features of the garden.

This grove goes by the sinister name of "The Devil's Wood," and enjoys but an equivocal character in the neighborhood. It was planted by "The Wicked Lord Byron," during the early part of his residence at the Abbey, before his fatal duel with Mr. Chaworth. Having something of a foreign and classical taste he set up leaden statues of satyrs or fawns at each end of the grove. These statues, like every thing else about the old Lord, fell under the suspicion and obloquy that overshadowed him in the latter part of his life. The country people who knew nothing of heathen mythology and its sylvan deities, looked with horror at idols invested with the diabolical attributes of horns and cloven feet. They probably supposed them some object of secret worship of the gloomy and secluded misanthrope, and reputed murderer, and gave them the name of "The old lord's devils."

I penetrated the recesses of the mystic grove. There stood the ancient and much slandered statues, overshadowed by tall larches, and stained by dank green mould. It is not a matter of surprize that strange figures thus behoofed and behorned, and set up in a gloomy grove, should perplex the minds of the simple and superstitious yeomanry. There are many of the tastes and caprices of the rich that in the eyes of the uneducated must savor of insanity.

I was attracted to this grove, however, by memorials of a more touching character. It had been one of the favorite haunts of the late Lord Byron. In his farewell visit to the Abbey, after he had parted with the possession of it, he passed some time in this grove in company with his sister; and as a last memento, engraved their names on the bark of a tree.

The feelings that agitated his bosom during this farewell visit, when he beheld round him objects dear to his pride, and dear to his juvenile recollections, but of which the narrowness of his fortune would not permit him to retain possession, may be gathered from a passage in a poetical epistle, written to his sister in after years.

> I did remind you of our own dear lake
> By the old hall, *which may be mine no more:*
> Lemans is fair; but think not I forsake
> The sweet remembrance of a dearer shore:
> Sad havoc Time must with my memory make
> Ere *that* or *thou* can fade these eyes before;
> Though, like all things which I have loved, they are
> Resigned forever, or divided far.
>
> I feel almost at times as I have felt
> In happy childhood; trees and flowers and brooks
> Which do remember me of where I dwelt
> Ere my young mind was sacrificed to books,
> Come as of yore upon me, and can melt
> My heart with recognition of their looks;

And even at moments I would think I see
Some living things I love—but none like thee.

I searched the grove for some time before I found the tree on which
Lord Byron had left his frail memorial. It was an elm of peculiar form,
having two trunks, which sprang from the same root and, after growing
side by side, mingled their branches together. He had selected it,
doubtless, as emblematical of his sister and himself. The names of
BYRON and AUGUSTA were still visible. They had been deeply cut in the
bark, but the natural growth of the tree was gradually rendering them
illegible, and a few years hence, strangers will seek in vain for this
record of fraternal affection.

Leaving the grove I continued my ramble along a spacious terrace,
overlooking what had once been the kitchen garden of the Abbey.
Below me lay the monks' stew, or fish pond, a dark pool overhung by
gloomy cypresses, with a solitary water hen swimming about in it.

A little further on and the terrace looked down upon the stately
scene on the south side of the Abbey; the flower garden with its stone
ballustrades and stately peacocks, the lawn with its pheasants and
partridges, and the soft valley of Newstead beyond.

At a distance, on the border of the lawn, stood another memento of
Lord Byron: an oak planted by him in his boyhood, on his first visit to
the Abbey. With a superstitious feeling inherent in him he linked his
own destiny with that of the tree. "As it fares," said he, "so will fare
my fortunes." Several years elapsed, many of them passed in idleness
and dissipation. He returned to the Abbey a youth scarce grown to
manhood, but as he thought with vices and follies beyond his years. He
found his emblem oak almost choked by weeds and brambles and took
the lesson to himself.

Young oak when I planted thee deep in the ground,
    I hoped that thy days would be longer than mine,
That thy dark waving branches would flourish around,
    And ivy thy trunk with its mantle entwine.

Such, such was my hope—when in infancy's years
    On the land of my fathers I rear'd thee with pride;
They are past and I water thy stem with my tears—
    Thy decay not the weeds that surround thee can hide.

I leaned over the stone ballustrade of the terrace and gazed upon the
valley of Newstead, with its silver sheets of water gleaming in the
morning sun. It was a Sabbath morning which always seems to have a

hallowed influence over the landscape, probably from the quiet of the day, and the cessation of all sounds of week day labour. As I mused upon the mild and beautiful scene, and the wayward destinies of the man, whose stormy temperament forced him from this tranquil paradise to battle with the passions and perils of the world, the sweet chime of bells from a village a few miles distant, came stealing up the valley. Every sight and sound this morning seemed calculated to summon up touching recollections of poor Byron. The chime was from the village spire of Hucknall Torkard, beneath which his remains lie buried!

———— I have since visited his tomb. It is in an old grey country church, venerable with the lapse of centuries. He lies buried beneath the pavement, at one end of the principal aisle. A light falls on the spot through the stained glass of a gothic window, and a tablet on the adjacent wall announces the family vault of the Byrons. It had been the wayward intention of the poet to be entombed, with his faithful dog, in the monument erected by him in the garden of Newstead Abbey. His executors showed better judgment and feeling, in consigning his ashes to the family sepulchre, to mingle with those of his mother and his kindred. Here,

> After life's fitful fever, he sleeps well.
> Malice domestic, foreign levy, nothing
> Can touch him further!

How nearly did his dying hour realize the wish made by him but a few years previously in one of his fitful moods of melancholy and misanthropy:

> When Time, or soon or late, shall bring
>   The dreamless sleep that lulls the dead,
> Oblivion! may thy languid wing
>   Wave gently o'er my dying bed!
>
> No band of friends or heirs be there,
>   To weep or wish the coming blow:
> No maiden with dishevell'd hair,
>   To feel, or feign decorous woe.
>
> But silent let me sink to earth,
>   With no officious mourners near:
> I would not mar one hour of mirth,
>   Nor startle friendship with a fear.

He died among strangers; in a foreign land without a kindred hand to close his eyes, yet he did not die unwept. With all his faults and errors and passions and caprices, he had the gift of attaching his humble dependants warmly to him. One of them, a poor Greek accompanied his remains to England and followed them to the grave. I am told that, during the funeral ceremony, he stood holding on by a pew in an agony of grief, and when all was over, seemed as if he would have gone down into the tomb with the body of his master.—A nature that could inspire such attachments must have been generous and beneficent.

PLOUGH MONDAY

Sherwood Forest is a region that still retains much of the quaint customs and holyday games of the olden time. A day or two after my arrival at the Abbey, as I was walking in the cloisters, I heard the sound of rustic music, and now and then a burst of merriment, proceeding from the interior of the mansion. Presently the chamberlain came and informed me that a party of country lads were in the servants' hall, performing Plough Monday antics, and invited me to witness their mummery. I gladly assented, for I am somewhat curious about these reliques of popular usages. The servants' hall was a fit place for the exhibition of an old gothic game. It was a chamber of great extent which, in monkish times had been the refectory of the Abbey. A row of massive columns extended lengthwise through the centre, whence sprung gothic arches, supporting the low vaulted ceiling. Here was a set of rustics dressed up in something of the style represented in the books concerning popular antiquities. One was in a rough garb of frieze, with his head muffled in bear's skin, and a bell dangling behind him; that jingled at every movement. He was the clown or fool of the party, probably a traditional representative of the ancient satyr. The rest were decorated with riband and armed with wooden swords. The leader of the troop recited the old ballad of St. George and the dragon, which has been current among the country people for ages; his companions accompanied the recitation with some rude attempt at acting, while the clown cut all kinds of antics.

To these succeeded a set of morrice dancers gaily dressed up with ribands and hawks' bells. In this troop we had Robin Hood and Maid Marian, the latter represented by a smooth faced boy: also, Beelzebub, equipped with a broom, and accompanied by his wife Bessy, a termagant old beldame. These rude pageants are the lingering remains of the old customs of Plough Monday, when bands of rustics, fantastically dressed, and furnished with pipe and tabor, dragged what was called the "fool plough" from house to house, singing ballads and performing antics, for which they were rewarded with money and good cheer.

But it is not in "merry Sherwood Forest" alone that these remnants of old times prevail. They are to be met with in most of the counties north of the Trent, which classic stream seems to be the boundary line of primitive customs. During my recent Christmas sojourn at Barlboro' Hall, on the skirts of Derbyshire and Yorkshire, I had witnessed many of the rustic festivities peculiar to that joyous season, which have rashly been pronounced obsolete, by those who draw their experience merely from city life. I had seen the great Yule clog put on the fire on Christmas Eve, and the wassail bowl sent round, brimming with its spicy beverage. I had heard carols beneath my window by the choristers of the neighboring village, who went their rounds about the ancient Hall at midnight according to immemorial custom. We had mummers and mimers too with the story of St. George and the dragon and other ballads and traditional dialogues, together with the famous old interlude of the Hobby Horse, all represented in the antechamber and servants' hall by rustics, who inherited the custom and the poetry from preceding generations.

The boar's head, crowned with rosemary had taken its honoured station among the Christmas cheer; the festal board had been attended by glee singers and minstrels from the village to entertain the company with hereditary songs and catches during their repast; and the old Pyrrhic game of the sword dance, handed down since the time of the Romans, was admirably performed in the court yard of the mansion by a band of young men, lithe and supple in their forms and graceful in their movements, who I was told went the rounds of the villages and country seats during the Christmas holydays.

I specify these rural pageants and ceremonials, which I saw during my sojourn in this neighborhood, because it has been deemed that some of the anecdotes of holyday customs given in my preceding writings, related to usages which have entirely passed away. Critics who reside in cities have little idea of the primitive manners and observances, which still prevail in remote and rural neighborhoods.

In fact in crossing the Trent one seems to step back into old times: and in the villages of Sherwood Forest we are in a black letter region. The moss grown cottages, the lowly mansions of grey stone; the gothic crosses at each end of the villages and the tall may pole in the centre transport us in imagination to foregone centuries: every thing has a quaint and antiquated air.

The tenantry on the Abbey estate partake of this primitive character. Some of the families have rented farms there for nearly three hundred years, and, notwithstanding that their mansions fell to decay and every thing about them partook of the general waste and misrule of the Byron dynasty, yet nothing could uproot them from their native soil. I am happy to say that Colonel Wildman has taken these staunch loyal families under his peculiar care. He has favoured them in their rents, repaired, or rather rebuilt their farm houses, and has enabled families, that had almost sunk into the class of mere rustic laborers, once more to hold up their heads among the yeomanry of the land.

I visited one of these renovated establishments that had but lately been a mere ruin, and now was a substantial grange. It was inhabited by a young couple. The good woman shewed every part of the establishment with decent pride, exulting in its comfort and respectability. Her husband I understood had risen in consequence with the improvement of his mansion, and now began to be known among his rustic neighbors by the appellation of "The Young Squire."

OLD SERVANTS

In an old, time-worn, and mysterious looking mansion like Newstead Abbey, and one so haunted by monkish, and feudal, and poetical associations, it is a prize to meet with some ancient crone, who has passed a long life about the place, so as to have become a living chronicle of its fortunes and vicissitudes. Such a one is Nanny Smith, a worthy dame, near seventy years of age, who for a long time served as house-keeper to the Byrons. The Abbey and its domains comprize her world, beyond which she knows nothing, but within which she has ever conducted herself with native shrewdness and old fashioned honesty. When Lord Byron sold the Abbey her vocation was at an end, yet still she lingered about the place, having for it the local attachment of a cat. Abandoning her comfortable housekeeper's apartment, she took shelter in one of the "rock houses," which are nothing more than a little neighborhood of cabins excavated in the perpendicular walls of a stone quarry at no great distance from the Abbey. Three cells, cut in the living rock, formed her dwelling; these she fitted up humbly but comfortably; her son William labored in the neighborhood and aided to support her, and Nanny Smith maintained a cheerful aspect and an independent spirit. One of her gossips suggested to her that William should marry and bring home a young wife to help her and take care of her. "Nay! nay," replied Nanny, tartly, "I want no young mistress in *my house*." So much for the love of rule—poor Nanny's house was a hole in a rock!

Colonel Wildman on taking possession of the Abbey found Nanny Smith thus humbly nestled. With that active benevolence which charac-terizes him, he immediately set William up in a small farm on the estate, where Nanny Smith has a comfortable mansion in her old days. Her pride is roused by her son's advancement. She remarks with exultation that people treat William with much more respect now that he is a farmer, than they did when he was a laborer. A farmer of the neighborhood has even endeavored to make a match between him and his sister, but Nanny Smith has grown fastidious and interfered. The girl she said was too old for her son: besides she did not see that he was in any need of a wife.

"No," said William, "I ha' no great mind to marry the wench; but if the Colonel and his lady wish it, I am willing. They have been so kind to me I should think it my duty to please them." The Colonel and his lady, however, have not thought proper to put honest William's gratitude to so severe a test.

Another worthy whom Colonel Wildman found vegetating upon the place, and who had lived there for at least sixty years, was old Joe Murray. He had come there when a mere boy in the train of the "Old Lord," about the middle of the last century, and had continued with him until his death. Having been a cabin boy when very young Joe always fancied himself a bit of a sailor, and had charge of all the pleasure boats on the lake, though he afterwards rose to the dignity of butler. In the latter days of the old Lord Byron, when he shut himself up from all the world, Joe Murray was the only servant retained by him, excepting his housekeeper Betty Hardstaff; who was reputed to have an undue sway over him and was derisively called Lady Betty among the country folk.

When the Abbey came into the possession of the late Lord Byron Joe Murray accompanied it as a fixture. He was reinstated as butler in the Abbey, and High Admiral on the lake, and his sturdy honest mastiff qualities won so upon Lord Byron as even to rival his Newfoundland dog in his affections. Often when dining he would pour out a bumper of choice Madeira and hand it to Joe as he stood behind his chair. In fact when he built the monumental tomb which stands in the Abbey garden he intended it for himself, Joe Murray and the dog. The two latter were to lie on each side of him. Boatswain died not long afterwards and was regularly interred and the well known epitaph inscribed on one side of the monument. Lord Byron departed for Greece. During his absence a gentleman to whom Joe Murray was showing the tomb, observed, "Well, old boy you will take your place here some twenty years hence."

"I don't know that, sir," growled Joe in reply. "If I was sure his Lordship would come here I should like it well enough but I should not like to lie alone there with the dog."

Joe Murray was always extremely neat in his dress and attentive to his person, and made a most respectable appearance. A portrait of him still hangs in the Abbey representing him a hale fresh looking old fellow, in a flaxen wig, a blue coat and buff waistcoat, with a pipe in his hand. He discharged all the duties of his station with great fidelity, unquestionable honesty, and much outward decorum, but if we may believe his contemporary Nanny Smith, who as housekeeper shared the sway of the household with him, he was very lax in his minor morals, and used to sing loose and profane songs as he presided at the table in the servants' hall, or sat taking his ale and smoking his pipe by the evening fire. Joe had evidently derived his convivial notions from the race of English country squires who flourished in the days of his juvenility. Nanny Smith was scandalized at his ribald songs, but, being above harm herself, endured them in silence. At length on his singing them before a young girl of sixteen she could contain herself no longer but read him a lecture that made his ears ring, and then flounced off to bed. The lecture seems, by her account, to have staggered honest Joe, for he told her the next morning that he had had a terrible dream in the night. An Evangelist stood at the foot of his bed with a great Dutch Bible, which he held with the printed part towards him and after a while pushed it in his face. Nanny Smith undertook to interpret the vision, and read from it such a homily, and deduced such awful warnings, that Joe became quite serious, left off singing and took to reading good books for a month. "But after that," continued Nanny, "he relapsed and became as bad as ever, and continued to sing loose and profane songs to his dying day."

When Colonel Wildman became proprietor of the Abbey he found Joe Murray flourishing in a green old age though upwards of fourscore, and continued him in his station as butler. The old man was rejoiced at the extensive repairs that were immediately commenced, and anticipated with pride the day when the Abbey should rise out of its ruins with renovated splendor, its gates be thronged with trains and equipages and its halls once more echo to the sound of joyous hospitality.

What chiefly, however, concerned Joe's pride and ambition was a plan of the Colonel's, to have the ancient refectory of the convent, a great vaulted room supported by gothic columns, converted into a servants' hall. Here Joe looked forward to rule the roast at the head of the servants' table, and to make the gothic arches ring with those hunting and hard drinking ditties which were the horror of the discreet Nanny Smith. Time however was fast wearing away with him, and his great fear was that the hall would not be completed in his day. In his eagerness to hasten the repairs he used to get up early in the morning and ring up the workmen. Notwithstanding his great age, also, he would turn out, half dressed, in cold weather to cut sticks for the fire. Colonel Wildman kindly remonstrated with him for thus risking his health, as others would do the work for him.

"Lord sir," exclaimed the hale old fellow, "it's my air bath, I'm all the better for it."

Unluckily as he was thus employed one morning a splinter flew up and wounded one of his eyes. An inflammation took place; he lost the sight of that eye, and subsequently of the other. Poor Joe gradually pined away, and grew melancholy. Colonel Wildman kindly tried to cheer him up—"Come, come old boy," cried he, "be of good heart. You will yet take your place in the servants' hall."

"Nay, nay, sir," replied he, "I did hope once that I should live to see it—I looked forward to it with pride, I confess, but it is all over with me now. I shall soon go home!"

He died shortly afterwards at the advanced age of eighty six, seventy of which had been passed as an honest and faithful servant at the Abbey. Colonel Wildman had him decently interred in the church of Hucknall Torkard, near the vault of Lord Byron.

SUPERSTITIONS OF THE ABBEY

The anecdotes I had heard of the quondam housekeeper of Lord Byron, rendered me desirous of paying her a visit. I rode in company with Colonel Wildman, therefore, to the cottage of her son William where she resides, and found her seated by her fireside, with a favorite cat perched upon her shoulder and purring in her ear. Nanny Smith is a large good looking woman, a specimen of the old fashioned country housewife, combining antiquated notions and prejudices, and very limited information, with natural good sense. She loves to gossip about the Abbey and Lord Byron, and was soon drawn into a course of anecdotes, though mostly of a humble kind, such as suited the meridian of the housekeeper's room and servants' hall. She seemed to entertain a kind recollection of Lord Byron, though she had evidently been much perplexed by some of his vagaries; and especially by the means he adopted to counteract his tendency to corpulency. He used various modes to sweat himself down: sometimes he would lie for a long time in a warm bath, sometimes he would walk up the hills, in the park, wrapped up and loaded with great coats "a sad toil for the poor youth," added Nanny, "he being so lame."

His meals were scanty and irregular consisting of dishes which Nanny seemed to hold in great contempt, such as pilaw, maccaroni and light puddings.

She contradicted the report of the licentious life which he was reported to lead at the Abbey, and of the paramours said to have been brought with him from London. "A great part of his time used to be passed lying on a sopha reading. Sometimes he had young gentlemen of his acquaintance with him and they played some mad pranks, but nothing but what young gentlemen may do and no harm done."

"Once it is true," she added, "he had with him a beautiful boy as a page which the house maids said was a girl. For my part I know nothing about it. Poor soul he was so lame he could not go out much with the men, all the comfort he had was to be a little with the lasses. The housemaids, however, were very jealous; one of them, in particular, took the matter in great dudgeon. Her name was Lucy, she was a great favorite with Lord Byron and had been much noticed by him and began to have high notions. She had her fortune told by a man who squinted, to whom she gave two and sixpence. He told her to hold up her head and look high, for she would come to great things. Upon this," added Nanny, "the poor thing dreamt of nothing less than becoming a lady and mistress of the Abbey, and promised me, if such luck should happen to her, she would be a good friend to me. Ah well aday! Lucy never had the fine fortune she dreamt of; but she had better than I thought for; she is now married, and keeps a public house at Warwick."

Finding that we listened to her with great attention Nanny Smith went on with her gossipping. "One time," said she, "Lord Byron took a notion that there was a deal of money buried about the Abbey by the monks in old times and nothing would serve him but he must have the flagging taken up in the cloisters; and they digged and digged, but found nothing but stone coffins full of bones. Then he must needs have one of the coffins put in one end of the great hall, so that the servants were afraid to go there of nights. Several of the sculls were cleaned and put in frames in his room. I used to have to go into the room at night to shut the windows, and if I glanced an eye at them they all seemed to grin; which I believe sculls always do. I can't say but I was glad to get out of the room.

"There was at one time (and for that matter there is still) a good deal said about ghosts haunting about the Abbey. The keeper's wife said she saw two standing in a dark part of the cloisters just opposite the chapel, and one in the garden, by the lord's well. Then there was a young lady, a cousin of Lord Byron, who was staying in the Abbey and slept in the room next the clock; and she told me that one night when she was lying in bed, she saw a lady in white come out of the wall on one side of the room and go into the wall on the opposite side.

"Lord Byron one day said to me, 'Nanny, what nonsense they tell about ghosts, as if there ever were any such things. I have never seen any thing of the kind about the Abbey and I warrant you have not.' This was all done, do you see, to draw me out, but I said nothing but shook my head. However, they say his Lordship did once see something. It was in the great hall—something all black and hairy: he said it was the devil.

"For my part," continued Nanny Smith, "I never saw any thing of the kind—but I heard something once—I was one evening scrubbing the floor of the little dining room at the end of the long gallery; it was after dark; I expected every moment to be called to tea but wished to finish what I was about. All at once I heard heavy footsteps in the great hall. They sounded like the tramp of a horse. I took the light and went to see what it was. I heard the steps come from the lower end of the hall to the fire place in the centre, where they stopped: but I could see nothing. I returned to my work, and in a little time heard the same noise again. I went again with the light; the footsteps stopped by the fire place as before. Still I could see nothing. I returned to my work, when I heard the steps for a third time. I then went into the hall without a light, but they stopped just the same, by the fire place half way up the hall. I thought this rather odd, but returned to my work. When it was finished, I took the light and went through the hall, as that was my way to the kitchen. I heard no more footsteps and thought no more of the matter, when, on coming to the lower end of the hall I found the door locked, and then on one side of the door, I saw the stone coffin with the scull and bones that had been digged up in the cloisters."

Here Nanny paused: I asked her if she believed that the mysterious footsteps had any connexion with the skeleton in the coffin: but she shook her head, and would not commit herself. We took our leave of the good old dame shortly after, and the story she had related gave subject for conversation on our ride homeward. It was evident she had spoken the truth as to what she had heard, but had been deceived by some peculiar effect of sound. Noises are propagated about a huge irregular edifice of the kind in a very deceptive manner; footsteps are prolonged and reverberated by the vaulted cloisters and echoing halls; the creaking and slamming of distant gates, the rushing of the blast through the groves and among the ruined arches of the chapel, have all a strangely delusive effect at night.

Colonel Wildman gave an instance of the kind from his own experience. Not long after he had taken up his residence at the Abbey he heard one moonlight night a noise as if a carriage was passing at a distance. He opened the window and leaned out. It then seemed as if the great iron roller was dragged along the gravel walks and terrace, but there was nothing to be seen. When he saw the gardener, on the following morning, he questioned him about working so late at night. The gardener declared that no one had been at work, and the roller was chained up. He was sent to examine it, and came back with a countenance full of surprise. The roller had been moved in the night, but he declared no mortal hand could have moved it. "Well," replied the Colonel good humouredly, "I am glad to find I have a brownie to work for me."

Lord Byron did much to foster and give currency to the superstitious tales connected with the Abbey by believing or pretending to believe in them. Many have supposed that his mind was really tinged with superstition, and that this innate infirmity was increased by passing much of his time in a lonely way, about the empty halls and cloysters of the Abbey, then in a ruinous melancholy state, and brooding over the sculls and effigies of its former inmates. I should rather think that he found poetical enjoyment in these supernatural themes, and that his imagination delighted to people this gloomy and romantic pile with all kinds of shadowy inhabitants. Certain it is the aspect of the mansion under the varying influence of twilight and moonlight, and cloud and sunshine operating upon its halls, and galleries and monkish cloysters, is enough to breed all kinds of fancies in the minds of its inmates, especially if poetically or superstitiously inclined.

I have already mentioned some of the fabled visitants of the Abbey. The goblin friar however is the one to whom Lord Byron has given the greatest importance. It walked the cloysters by night, and sometimes glimpses of it were seen in other parts of the Abbey. Its appearance was said to portend some impending evil to the master of the mansion. Lord Byron pretended to have seen it about a month before he contracted his illstarred marriage with Miss Milbanke.

He has embodied this tradition in the following ballad, in which he represents the fryar as one of the ancient inmates of the Abbey, maintaining by night a kind of spectral possession of it, in right of the fraternity. Other traditions, however, represent him as one of the friars doomed to wander about the place in atonement for his crimes. But to the ballad—

> Beware! beware of the Black Friar,
>   Who sitteth by Norman stone,
> For he mutters his prayer in the midnight air,
>   And his mass of the days that are gone.
> When the Lord of the Hill, Amundeville
>   Made Norman Church his prey,
> And expell'd the friars, one friar still
>   Would not be driven away.
>
> Though he came in his might with King Henry's right,
>   To turn church lands to lay,
> With sword in hand, and torch to light
>   Their walls if they said nay,

A monk remain'd, unchased unchain'd,
  And he did not seem form'd of clay,
For he's seen in the porch, and he's seen in the church,
  Though he is not seen by day.

And whether for good, or whether for ill,
  It is not mine to say;
But still to the house of Amundeville
  He abideth night and day.
By the marriage-bed of their lords, 'tis said,
  He flits on the bridal eve;
And 'tis held as faith, to their bed of death
  He comes—but not to grieve.

When an heir is born he is heard to mourn,
  And when aught is to befall
That ancient line, in the pale moonshine
  He walks, from hall to hall.
His form you may trace, but not his face,
  'Tis shadow'd by his cowl;
But his eyes may be seen from the folds between,
  And they seem of a parted soul.

But beware! beware of the Black Friar
  He still retains his sway
For he is yet the church's heir
  Whoever may be the lay.
Amundeville is lord by day,
  But the monk is lord by night,
Nor wine nor wassail could raise a vassal
  To question that friar's right.

Say nought to him as he walks the hall,
  And he'll say nought to you;
He sweeps along in his dusky pall,
  As o'er the grass the dew.
Then gramercy! for the Black Friar;
  Heaven sain him! fair or foul,
And whatsoe'er may be his prayer
  Let ours be for his soul.

Such is the story of the goblin friar which partly through old tradition
and partly through the influence of Lord Byron's rhymes, has become

completely established in the Abbey, and threatens to hold possession as long as the old edifice shall endure. Various visitors have either fancied or pretended to have seen him, and a cousin of Lord Byron, Miss Kitty Parkins, is even said to have made a sketch of him from memory. As to the servants at the Abbey, they have become possessed with all kinds of superstitious fancies. The long corridors and gothic halls, with their ancient portraits and dark figures in armour, are all haunted regions to them; they even fear to sleep alone, and will scarce venture at night on any distant errand about the Abbey unless they go in couples.

Even the magnificent chamber in which I was lodged was subject to the supernatural influences which reigned over the Abbey, and was said to be haunted by "Sir John Byron the little with the great beard." The ancient black looking portrait of this family worthy, which hangs over the door of the great saloon, was said to descend occasionally at midnight from its frame, and walk the rounds of the state apartments. Nay, his visitations were not confined to the night, for a young lady, on a visit to the Abbey, some years since, declared that, in passing in broad day by the door of the identical chamber I have described, which stood partly open, she saw Sir John Byron the little seated by the fire place, reading out of a great black letter book. From this circumstance some have been led to suppose that the story of Sir John Byron may be in some measure connected with the mysterious sculptures of the chimney piece already mentioned; but this has no countenance from the most authentic antiquarians of the Abbey.

For my own part, the moment I learned the wonderful stories and strange suppositions connected with my apartment, it became an imaginary realm to me. As I lay in bed at night and gazed at the mysterious panel work, where gothic Knight and christian dame, and paynim lover glared upon me in effigy, I used to weave a thousand fancies concerning them. The great figures in the tapestry, also, were almost animated by the workings of my imagination, and the Vandyke portraits of the cavalier and lady that looked down with pale aspects from the wall, had almost a spectral effect, from their immoveable gaze and silent companionship.

> For by dim lights the portraits of the dead
> Have something ghastly, desolate, and dread.
> ——Their buried locks still wave
> Along the canvas; their eyes glance like dreams
> On ours, as spars within some dusky cave,
> But death is imaged in their shadowy beams.

In this way I used to conjure up fictions of the brain, and clothe the objects around me with ideal interest and import, until, as the Abbey clock tolled midnight, I almost looked to see Sir John Byron the little with the long beard stalk into the room with his book under his arm, and take his seat beside the mysterious chimney piece.

ANNESLEY HALL

At about three miles distance from Newstead Abbey, and contiguous to its lands, is situated Annesley Hall, the old family mansion of the Chaworths. The families, like the estates, of the Byrons and Chaworths were connected in former times, until the fatal duel between their two representatives. The feud, however, which prevailed for a time, promised to be cancelled by the attachment of two youthful hearts. While Lord Byron was yet a boy he beheld Mary Anne Chaworth, a beautiful girl, and the sole heiress of Annesley. With that susceptibility to female charms, which he evinced almost from childhood, he became almost immediately enamoured of her. According to one of his biographers it would appear that at first their attachment was mutual, yet clandestine. The father of Miss Chaworth was then living, and may have retained somewhat of the family hostility, for we are told that the interviews of Lord Byron and the young lady were private, at a gate which opened from her father's grounds to those of Newstead. However, they were so young at the time that these meetings could not have been regarded as of any importance: they were little more than children in years; but, as Lord Byron says of himself, his feelings were beyond his age.

The passion thus early conceived was blown into a flame, during a six weeks vacation which he passed with his mother at Nottingham. The father of Miss Chaworth was dead, and she resided with her mother at the old Hall of Annesley. During Byron's minority the estate of Newstead was let to Lord Grey de Ruthen, but its youthful Lord was always a welcome guest at the Abbey. He would pass days at a time there, and from thence make frequent visits to Annesley Hall. His visits were encouraged by Miss Chaworth's mother; she partook none of the family feud, and probably looked with complacency upon an attachment that might heal old differences and unite two neighboring estates.

The six weeks vacation passed as a dream amongst the beautiful bowers of Annesley. Byron was scarce fifteen years of age, Mary Chaworth was two years older, but his heart, as I have said was beyond his age, and his tenderness for her was deep and passionate. These early loves, like the first run of the uncrushed grape, are the sweetest and strongest gushings of the heart, and however they may be superseded by other attachments in after years, the memory will continually recur to them and fondly dwell upon their recollections.

His love for Miss Chaworth, to use Lord Byron's own expression, was "the romance of the most romantic period of his life," and I think we can trace the effect of it throughout the whole course of his writings; coming up, every now and then, like some lurking theme which runs through a complicated piece of music, and links it all in a pervading chain of melody.

How tenderly and mournfully does he recall in after years, the feelings awakened in his youthful and inexperienced bosom, by this impassioned yet innocent attachment; feelings, he says, lost or hardened in the intercourse of life:

> The love of higher things and better days;
>   The unbounded hope, and heavenly ignorance
> Of what is called the world, and the world's ways;
>   The moments when we gather from a glance
> More joy than from all future pride or praise,
>   Which kindle manhood, but can ne'er entrance
> The heart in an existence of its own,
> Of which another's bosom is the zone.

Whether this love was really responded to by the object is uncertain. Byron sometimes speaks as if he had met with kindness in return, at other times he acknowledges that she never gave him reason to believe she loved him. It is probable, however, that at first she experienced some flutterings of the heart. She was at a susceptible age; had as yet formed no other attachments; her lover, though boyish in years, was a man in intellect, a poet in imagination, and had a countenance of remarkable beauty.

With the six weeks vacation ended this brief romance. Byron returned to school deeply enamoured, but if he had really made any impression on Miss Chaworth's heart, it was too slight to stand the test of absence. She was at that age when a female soon changes from the girl to the woman, and leaves her boyish lovers far behind her. While Byron was pursuing his schoolboy studies, she was mingling with society and met with a gentleman of the name of Musters, remarkable it is said for manly beauty. A story is told of her having first seen him from the top of Annesley Hall, as he dashed through the park with hound and horn, taking the lead of the whole field in a fox chase, and that she was struck by the spirit of his appearance, and his admirable horsemanship. Under such favorable auspices he wooed and won her and when Lord Byron next met her, he learned to his dismay that she was the affianced bride of another.

With that pride of spirit which always distinguished him he controlled his feelings and maintained a serene countenance. He even affected to speak calmly on the subject of her approaching nuptials. "The next time I see you," said he, "I suppose you will be Mrs. Chaworth," (for she was to retain her family name.) Her reply was, "I hope so."

I have given these brief details preparatory to a sketch of a visit which I made to the scene of this youthful romance. Annesley Hall I understood was shut up, neglected and almost in a state of desolation, for Mr. Musters rarely visited it, residing with his family in the neighborhood of Nottingham. I set out for the Hall on horseback, in company with Colonel Wildman, and followed by the great Newfoundland dog Boatswain. In the course of our ride we visited a spot memorable in the love story I have cited. It was the scene of this parting interview between Byron and Miss Chaworth, prior to her marriage. A long ridge of upland advances into the valley of Newstead like a promontory into a lake, and was formerly crowned by a beautiful grove, a land mark to the neighboring country. The grove and promontory are graphically described by Lord Byron in his "Dream," and an exquisite picture given of himself and the lovely object of his boyish idolatry—

> I saw two beings in the hues of youth
> Standing upon a hill, a gentle hill,
> Green and of mild declivity, the last
> As 'twere the cape of a long ridge of such,
> Save that there was no sea to lave its base,
> But a most living landscape, and the wave
> Of woods and cornfields, and the abodes of men,
> Scatter'd at intervals, and wreathing smoke
> Arising from such rustic roofs;—the hill
> Was crown'd with a peculiar diadem
> Of trees, in circular array, so fix'd,
> Not by the sport of nature, but of man:
> These two, a maiden and a youth, were there
> Gazing—the one on all that was beneath
> Fair as herself—but the boy gazed on her;
> And both were fair, and one was beautiful:
> And both were young—yet not alike in youth.
> As the sweet moon on the horizon's verge
> The maid was on the verge of womanhood:
> The boy had fewer summers, but his heart

Had far outgrown his years, and to his eye
There was but one beloved face on earth,
And that was shining on him.

I stood upon the spot consecrated by this memorable interview. Below
me extended the "living landscape," once contemplated by the loving
pair; the gentle valley of Newstead, diversified by woods and cornfields,
and village spires and gleams of water, and the distant towers and pinnacles of the venerable Abbey. The "diadem of trees," however, was
gone. The attention drawn to it by the poet; and the romantic manner
in which he had associated it with his early passion for Mary Chaworth,
had nettled the irritable feelings of her husband, who but ill brooked
the poetic celebrity conferred on his wife by the enamoured verses of
another. The celebrated grove stood on his estate, and in a fit of spleen
he ordered it to be levelled with the dust. At the time of my visit the
mere roots of the trees were visible; but the hand that laid them low
is execrated by every poetical pilgrim.

Descending the hill we soon entered a part of what once was Annesley
Park, and rode among time worn and tempest riven oaks and elms, with
ivy clambering about their trunks, and rooks' nests among their branches.
The park had been cut up by a post road, crossing which we came to
the Gate House of Annesley Hall. It was an old brick building that
might have served as an outpost or barbican to the hall during the civil
wars, when every gentleman's house was liable to become a fortress.
Loopholes were still visible in its walls, but the peaceful ivy had mantled
the sides, overrun the roof, and almost buried the ancient clock in front,
that still marked the waning hours of its decay.

An arched way led through the centre of the gate house, secured by
grated doors of open iron work, wrought into flowers and flourishes.
These being thrown open we entered a paved court yard, decorated
with shrubs and antique flower pots, with a ruined stone fountain in
the centre. The whole approach resembled that of an old French chateau.

On one side of the court yard was a range of stables now tenantless,
but which bore traces of the fox hunting squire; for there were stalls
boxed up into which the hunters might be turned loose when they came
home from the chase.

At the lower end of the court, and immediately opposite the gate
house, extended the hall itself; a rambling, irregular pile, patched and
pieced at various times, and in various tastes, with gable ends, stone
ballustrades, and enormous chimneys, that strutted out like buttresses
from the walls. The whole front of the edifice was overrun with
evergreens.

We applied for admission at the front door, which was under a heavy porch. The portal was strongly barricadoed, and our knocking was echoed by waste and empty halls. Every thing bore an appearance of abandonment. After a time, however, our knocking summoned a solitary tenant from some remote corner of the pile. It was a decent looking little dame, who emerged from a side door at a distance, and seemed a worthy inmate of the antiquated mansion. She had, in fact, grown old with it. Her name she said was Nanny Marsden, if she lived until next August she would be seventy one: a great part of her life had been passed in the Hall, and, when the family removed to Nottingham, she had been left in charge of it. The front of the house had been thus warily barricadoed in consequence of the late riots at Nottingham; in the course of which the dwelling of her master had been sacked by the mob. To guard against any attempt of the kind upon the Hall, she had put it in this state of defence: though I rather think she and a superannuated gardener comprized the whole garrison. "You must be attached to the old building," said I, "after having lived so long in it." "Ah sir!" replied she, "I am *getting in years.* I have a furnished cottage of my own in Annesley Wood, and begin to feel as if I should like to go and live in my own home."

Guided by the worthy little custodian of the fortress, we entered through the sally port by which she had issued forth, and soon found ourselves in a spacious, but somewhat gloomy hall, where the light was partially admitted through square stone shafted windows, overhung with ivy. Every thing around us had the air of an old fashioned country squire's establishment. In the centre of the hall was a billiard table, and about the walls were hung portraits of race horses, hunters and favorite dogs mingled indiscriminately with family pictures.

Staircases led up from the hall to various apartments. In one of the rooms we were shown a couple of buff jerkins and a pair of ancient jack boots of the time of the cavaliers; reliques which are often to be met with in the old English family mansions. These, however, had peculiar value, for the good little dame assured us they had belonged to Robin Hood. As we were in the midst of the region over which that famous outlaw once bore ruffian sway it was not for us to gainsay his claim to any of these venerable reliques, though we might have demurred that the articles of dress here shewn were of a date much later than his time. Every antiquity, however, about Sherwood Forest is apt to be linked with the memory of Robin Hood and his gang.

As we were strolling about the mansion our fourfooted attendant Boatswain followed leisurely as if taking a survey of the premises. I turned to rebuke him for his intrusion, but the moment the old housekeeper understood he had belonged to Lord Byron, her heart seemed to yearn towards him.

"Nay, nay," exclaimed she, "let him alone, let him go where he pleases. He's welcome. Ah, dear me! If he lived here I should take great care of him. He should want for nothing.—Well!" continued she, fondling him, "who would have thought that I should see a dog of Lord Byron in Annesley Hall!"

"I suppose then," said I, "you recollect something of Lord Byron, when he used to visit here." "Ah bless him!" cried she, "that I do! He used to ride over here and stay three days at a time and sleep in the blue room. Ah! poor fellow! He was very much taken with my young mistress; he used to walk about the garden and the terraces with her, and seemed to love the very ground she trod on. He used to call her *his bright morning star of Annesley.*"

I felt the beautiful poetic phraze thrill through me.

"You appear to like the memory of Lord Byron," said I.

"Ah sir! why should not I? He was always main good to me when he came here. Well! well! they say it is a pity he and my young lady did not make a match. Her mother would have liked it. He was always a welcome guest, and some think it would have been well for him to have had her, but it was not to be! He went away to school, and then Mr. Musters saw her, and so things took their course."

The simple soul now showed us into the favorite sitting room of Miss Chaworth, with a small flower garden under the windows, in which she had delighted. In this room Byron used to sit and listen to her as she played and sang, gazing upon her with the passionate, and almost painful devotion of a love sick stripling. He himself gives us a glowing picture of his mute idolatry:

> He had no breath, no being, but in hers;
> She was his voice; he did not speak to her
> But trembled on her words; she was his sight,
> For his eye followed hers, and saw with hers,
> Which coloured all his objects;—he had ceased
> To live within himself; she was his life,
> The ocean to the river of his thoughts,
> Which terminated all: upon a tone,
> A touch of hers, his blood would ebb and flow,
> And his cheek change tempestuously—his heart
> Unknowing of its cause of agony.

There was a little Welsh air called Mary Anne, which, from bearing her own name, he associated with herself, and often persuaded her to sing it over and over for him.

The chamber, like all the other parts of the house, had a look of sadness and neglect; the flowerplots beneath the window, which once bloomed beneath the hand of Mary Chaworth, were overrun with weeds; and the piano, which had once vibrated to her touch, and thrilled the heart of her stripling lover, was now unstrung and out of tune.

We continued our stroll about waste apartments, of all shapes and sizes, and without much elegance of decoration. Some of these were hung with family portraits, among which was pointed out that of the Mr. Chaworth who was killed by the "wicked Lord Byron."

These dismal looking portraits had a powerful effect upon the imagination of the stripling poet on his first visit to the Hall. As they gazed down from the wall he thought they scowled upon him, as if they had taken a grudge against him on account of the duel of his ancestor. He even gave this as a reason, though probably in jest, for not sleeping at the Hall, declaring that he feared they would come down from their frames at night to haunt him.

A feeling of this kind he has embodied in one of his stanzas of Don Juan:

> The forms of the grim knights and pictured saints
>   Look living in the moon; and as you turn
> Backward and forward to the echoes faint
>   Of your own footsteps—voices from the urn
> Appear to wake, and shadows wild and quaint
>   Start from the frames which fence their aspects stern,
> As if to ask you how you dare to keep
> A vigil there, where all but death should sleep.

Nor was the youthful poet singular in these fancies; the Hall, like most old English mansions that have ancient family portraits hanging about their dusky galleries and waste apartments, had its ghost story connected with these pale memorials of the dead. Our simplehearted conductor stopped before the portrait of a lady who had been a beauty in her time, and inhabited the Hall in the heyday of her charms. Something mysterious or melancholy was connected with her story; she died young, but continued for a long time to haunt the ancient mansion, to the great dismay of the servants and the occasional disquiet of the visitors, and it was with much difficulty her troubled spirit was conjured down and put to rest.

From the rear of the Hall we walked out into the garden, about which Byron used to stroll and loiter in company with Miss Chaworth. It was laid out in the old French style. There was a long terraced walk, with heavy stone ballustrades and sculptured urns overrun with ivy and evergreens. A neglected shrubbery bordered one side of the terrace with a lofty grove inhabited by a venerable community of rooks. Great

flights of steps led down from the terrace to a flower garden laid out
in formal plots. The rear of the Hall which overlooked the garden had
the weather stains of centuries, and its stoneshafted casements and an
ancient sun dial against its walls, carried back the mind to days of yore.

The retired and quiet garden, once a little sequestered world of love
and romance, was now all matted and wild, yet was beautiful even in
its decay. Its air of neglect and desolation was in unison with the fortune
of the two beings who had once walked here in the freshness of youth,
and life, and beauty. The garden, like their young hearts, had gone to
waste and ruin.

Returning to the Hall we now visited a chamber built over the porch,
or grand entrance: it was in ruinous condition; the ceiling having fallen
in and the floor given way. This, however, is a chamber rendered interesting by poetical associations. It is supposed to be the oratory alluded
to by Lord Byron in his Dream, wherein he pictures his departure from
Annesley, after learning that Mary Chaworth was engaged to be married.

> There was an ancient mansion, and before
> Its walls there was a steed caparison'd:
> Within an antique Oratory stood
> The Boy of whom I spake;—he was alone,
> And pale and pacing to and fro: anon
> He sate him down, and seized a pen; and traced
> Words which I could not guess of; then he lean'd
> His bow'd head on his hands, and shook as 'twere
> With a convulsion—then arose again,
> And with his teeth and quivering hands did tear
> What he had written, but he shed no tears.
> And he did calm himself, and fix his brow
> Into a kind of quiet: as he paused,
> The Lady of his love re-enter'd there;
> She was serene and smiling then, and yet
> She knew she was by him beloved,—she knew,
> For quickly comes such knowledge, that his heart
> Was darken'd with her shadow, and she saw
> That he was wretched, but she saw not all.
> He rose, and with a cold and gentle grasp
> He took her hand; a moment o'er his face
> A tablet of unutterable thoughts
> Was traced, and then it faded, as it came;
> He dropp'd the hand he held, and with slow steps
> Retired, but not as bidding her adieu,
> For they did part with mutual smiles,—he pass'd

> From out the massy gate of that old Hall,
> And mounting on his steed he went his way;
> And ne'er repass'd that hoary threshold more.

In one of his journals Lord Byron describes his feelings after thus leaving the oratory. Arriving on the summit of a hill, which commanded the last view of Annesley, he checked his horse, and gazed back with mingled pain and fondness upon the groves which embowered the Hall, and thought upon the lovely being that dwelt there, until his feelings were quite dissolved in tenderness. The conviction at length recurred that she never could be his, when, rousing himself from his reverie he stuck his spurs into his steed and dashed forward as if, by rapid motion to leave reflection behind him.

Yet, notwithstanding what he asserts in the verses last quoted, he did pass the "hoary threshold" of Annesley again. It was, however, after the lapse of several years, during which he had grown up to manhood, had passed through the ordeal of pleasures and tumultuous passions, and had felt the influence of other charms. Miss Chaworth too had become a wife and a mother, and he dined at Annesley Hall at the invitation of her husband. He thus met the object of his early idolatry in the very scene of his tender devotions, which as he says, her smiles had once made a heaven to him. The scene was but little changed. He was in the very chamber where he had so often listened entranced to the witchery of her voice; there were the same instruments and music; there lay her flower garden beneath the window and the walks through which he had wandered with her in the intoxication of youthful love. Can we wonder that amidst the tender recollections which every object around him was calculated to awaken, the fond passion of his boyhood should rush back in full current to his heart. He was himself surprized at this sudden revulsion of his feelings, but he had acquired self possession and could command them. His firmness however was doomed to undergo a further trial. While seated by the object of his secret devotion, with all these recollections throbbing in his bosom, her infant daughter was brought into the room. At sight of the child he started; it dispelled the last lingerings of his dream, and he afterwards confessed that to repress his emotions at the moment was the severest part of his task.

The conflict of feelings that raged within his bosom throughout this fond and tender yet painful and embarrassing visit are touchingly depicted in lines which he wrote immediately afterwards, and which, though not addressed to her by name, are evidently intended for the eye and the heart of the fair lady of Annesley.

> Well! thou art happy, and I feel
> That I should thus be happy too;

For still my heart regards thy weal
  Warmly as it was wont to do.

Thy husband's blest—and 'twill impart
  Some pangs to view his happier lot:
But let them pass—Oh! how my heart
  Would hate him, if he loved thee not!

When late I saw thy favourite child
  I thought my jealous heart would break;
But when the unconscious infant smiled,
  I kiss'd it for its mother's sake.

I kiss'd it, and repress'd my sighs
  Its father in its face to see
But then it had its mother's eyes,
  And they were all to love and me.

Mary, adieu! I must away:
  While thou art blest I'll not repine;
But near thee I can never stay;
  My heart would soon again be thine.

I deem'd that time, I deem'd that pride
  Had quench'd at length my boyish flame;
Nor knew, till seated by thy side,
  My heart in all, save hope, the same.

Yet I was calm: I knew the time
  My breast would thrill before thy look;
But now to tremble were a crime
  We met, and not a nerve was shook.

I saw thee gaze upon my face
  Yet meet with no confusion there;
One only feeling could'st thou trace;
  The sullen calmness of despair.

Away! away! my early dream
  Remembrance never must awake
Oh! where is Lethe's fabled stream?
  My foolish heart, be still, or break.

The revival of this early passion, and the melancholy associations which it spread over those scenes in the neighborhood of Newstead, which would necessarily be the places of his frequent resort while in England, are alluded to by him as a principal cause of his first departure for the Continent:

When man expelled from Eden's bowers
  A moment lingered near the gate,
Each scene recalled the vanish'd hours
  And bade him curse his future fate.

But wandering on through distant climes,
  He learnt to bear his load of grief;
Just gave a sigh to other times,
  And found in busier scenes relief.

Thus Mary must it be with me
  And I must view thy charms no more;
For, while I linger near to thee,
  I sigh for all I knew before.

It was in the subsequent June that he set off on his pilgrimage by sea and land, which was to become the theme of his immortal poem. That the image of Mary Chaworth, as he saw and loved her in the days of his boyhood, followed him to the very shore, is shewn in the glowing stanzas addressed to her on the eve of embarcation—

'Tis done—and shivering in the gale
The bark unfurls her snowy sail;
And whistling o'er the bending mast,
Loud sings on high the fresh'ning blast;
And I must from this land be gone,
Because I cannot love but one.

And I will cross the whitening foam,
And I will seek a foreign home;
Till I forget a false fair face,
I ne'er shall find a resting place;
My own dark thoughts I cannot shun,
But ever love, and love but one.

To think of every early scene,
Of what we are, and what we've been,

Would whelm some softer hearts with woe—
But mine, alas! has stood the blow;
Yet still beats on as it begun,
And never truly loves but one.

And who that dear loved one may be
Is not for vulgar eyes to see,
And why that early love was crost,
Thou know'st the best, I feel the most;
But few that dwell beneath the sun
Have loved so long, and loved but one.

I've tried another's fetters too,
With charms, perchance, as fair to view;
And I would fain have loved as well,
But some unconquerable spell
Forbade my bleeding breast to own
A kindred care for aught but one.

'Twould soothe to take one lingering view,
And bless thee in my last adieu;
Yet wish I not those eyes to weep
For him that wanders o'er the deep;
His home, his hope, his youth are gone,
Yet still he loves, and loves but one.

The painful interview at Annesley Hall which revived with such intenseness his early passion, remained stamped upon his memory with singular force, and seems to have survived all his "wandering through distant climes" to which he trusted as an oblivious antidote. Upward of two years after the event, when, having made his famous pilgrimage he was once more an inmate of Newstead Abbey, his vicinity to Annesley Hall brought the whole scene vividly before him; and he thus recalls it in a poetic epistle to a friend.

I've seen my bride another's bride,—
Have seen her seated by his side,—
Have seen the infant which she bore,
Wear the sweet smile the mother wore,
When she and I in youth have smil'd
As fond and faultless as her child:—
Have seen her eyes, in cold disdain,
Ask if I felt no secret pain,

> And *I* have acted well my part,
> And made my cheek belie my heart,
> Return'd the freezing glance she gave,
> Yet felt the while *that* woman's slave;—
> Have kiss'd, as if without design,
> The babe which ought to have been mine,
> And show'd, alas! in each caress,
> Time had not made me love the less.

"It was about the time," says Moore in his life of Lord Byron, "when he was thus bitterly feeling and expressing the blight which his heart had suffered from a *real* object of affection, that his poems on an imaginary one, 'Thyrza,' were written." He was at the same time grieving over the loss of several of his earliest and dearest friends, the companions of his joyous schoolboy hours. To recur to the beautiful language of Moore, who writes with the kindred and kindling sympathies of a true poet: "All these recollections of the young and the dead mingled themselves in his mind with the image of her, who, though living, was, for him, as much lost as they, and diffused that general feeling of sadness and fondness through his soul, which found a vent in these poems. * * * It was the blending of the two affections, in his memory and imagination, that gave birth to an ideal object combining the best features of both, and drew from him those saddest and tenderest of love poems, in which we find all the depth and intensity of real feeling touched over with such a light as no reality ever wore."

An early, innocent and unfortunate passion, however fruitful of pain it may be to the man, is a lasting advantage to the poet. It is a well of sweet and bitter fancies; of refined and gentle sentiments; of elevated and ennobling thoughts; shut up in the deep recesses of the heart, keeping it green amidst the withering blights of the world, and, by its casual gushes and overflowings, recalling at times all the freshness and innocence and enthusiasm of youthful days. Lord Byron was conscious of this effect; and purposely cherished and brooded over the remembrance of his early passion and of all the scenes of Annesley Hall connected with it. It was this remembrance that allured his mind to some of its most elevated and virtuous strains, and shed an inexpressible grace and pathos over his best productions.

Being thus put upon the traces of this little love story, I cannot refrain from threading them out, as they appear from time to time in various passages of Lord Byron's works. During his subsequent rambles in the East, when time and distance had softened away his "early romance" almost into the remembrance of a pleasing and tender dream, he received accounts of the object of it, which represented her, still in her paternal

Hall, among her native bowers of Annesley; surrounded by a blooming
and beautiful family; yet a prey to secret and withering melancholy.

> ———In her home,
> A thousand leagues from his,—her native home,
> She dwelt, begirt with growing infancy,
> Daughters and sons of beauty, but—behold!
> Upon her face there was the tint of grief,
> The settled shadow of an inward strife,
> And an unquiet drooping of the eye,
> *As if its lid were charged with unshed tears.*

For an instant the buried tenderness of early youth and the fluttering
hopes which accompanied it, seem to have revived in his bosom, and
the idea to have flashed upon his mind, that his image might be connected with her secret woes—but he rejected the thought almost as soon
as formed.

> What could her grief be?—she had all she loved,
> And he who had so loved her was not there
> To trouble with bad hopes, or evil wish,
> Or ill repress'd affliction, her pure thoughts.
> What could her grief be?—she had loved him not,
> Nor given him cause to deem himself beloved,
> Nor could he be a part of that which prey'd
> Upon her mind—a spectre of the past.

The cause of her grief was a matter of rural comment in the neighborhood of Newstead and Annesley. It was disconnected from all idea
of Lord Byron, but attributed to the harsh and capricious conduct of
one to whose kindness and affection she had a sacred claim. The domestic
sorrows which had long preyed in secret on her heart, at length affected
her intellect, and the "bright morning star of Annesley," was eclipsed
for ever.

> The lady of his love,—oh! she was changed
> As by the sickness of the soul; her mind
> Had wandered from its dwelling, and her eyes,
> They had not their own lustre, but the look
> Which is not of the earth; she was become
> The queen of a fantastic realm: her thoughts
> Were combinations of disjointed things;
> And forms impalpable and unperceived

> Of others' sight, familiar were to hers.
> And this the world calls frenzy.

Notwithstanding lapse of time, change of place, and a succession of splendid and spirit stirring scenes in various countries, the quiet and gentle scene of his boyish love seems to have held a magic sway over the recollections of Lord Byron, and the image of Mary Chaworth to have unexpectedly obtruded itself upon his mind like some supernatural visitation. Such was the fact on the occasion of his marriage with Miss Milbanke; Annesley Hall and all its fond associations floated like a vision before his thoughts, even when at the altar and on the point of pronouncing the nuptial vows. The circumstance is related by him with a force and feeling that persuade us of its truth.

> A change came o'er the spirit of my dream;
> The wanderer was return'd.—I saw him stand
> Before an altar—with a gentle bride;
> Her face was fair, but was not that which made
> The star-light of his boyhood;—as he stood
> Even at the altar; o'er his brow there came
> The self same aspect, and the quivering shock
> That in the antique oratory shook
> His bosom in its solitude; and then—
> As in that hour—a moment o'er his face
> The tablet of unutterable thoughts
> Was traced,—and then it faded as it came,
> And he stood calm and quiet, and he spoke
> The fitting vows, but heard not his own words,
> And all things reel'd around him: he could see
> Not that which was, nor that which should have been—
> But the old mansion, and the accustomed hall,
> And the remember'd chambers, and the place,
> The day, the hour, the sunshine and the shade,
> All things pertaining to that place and hour,
> And her who was his destiny, came back,
> And thrust themselves between him and the light:
> What business had they there at such a time?

The history of Lord Byron's union is too well known to need narration. The errors, and humiliations, and heartburnings that followed upon it, gave additional effect to the remembrance of his early passion, and tormented him with the idea, that had he been successful in his suit to the lovely heiress of Annesley they might both have shared a happier destiny. In one of his manuscripts, written long after his marriage, having accidentally mentioned Miss Chaworth as "my M. A. C." "Alas!" exclaims he with a sudden burst of feeling, "why do I say *my?* Our union would have healed feuds in which blood had been shed by our fathers; it would have joined lands broad and rich, it would have joined at least *one* heart, and two persons not ill matched in years—and—and—and— what has been the result!"

But enough of Annesley Hall and the poetical themes connected with it. I felt as if I could linger for hours about its ruined oratory, and silent hall and neglected garden, and spin reveries and dream dreams, until all became an ideal world around me. The day, however, was fast declining and the shadows of evening throwing deeper shades of melancholy about the place. Taking our leave of the worthy old housekeeper, therefore, with a small compensation and many thanks for her civilities, we mounted our horses and pursued our way back to Newstead Abbey.

THE LAKE

Before the mansion lay a lucid lake
  Broad as transparent, deep, and freshly fed
By a river, which its softened way did take
  In currents through the calmer water spread
Around: the wild fowl nestled in the brake
  And sedges, brooding in their liquid bed:
The woods sloped downward to its brink, and stood
With their green faces fixed upon the flood.

Such is Lord Byron's description of one of a series of beautiful sheets of water, formed in old times by the monks by damming up the course of a small river. Here he used daily to enjoy his favorite recreations of swimming and sailing. The "wicked old Lord" in his scheme of rural devastation had cut down all the woods that once fringed the lake; Lord Byron, on coming of age, endeavoured to restore them, and a beautiful young wood, planted by him, now sweeps up from the water's edge, and clothes the hill side opposite to the Abbey. To this woody nook Colonel Wildman has given the appropriate title of "The Poet's Corner."

The lake has inherited its share of the traditions and fables connected with every thing in and about the Abbey. It was a petty mediterranean sea on which the "wicked old Lord" used to gratify his nautical tastes and humours. He had his mimic castles and fortresses along its shores, and his mimic fleets upon its waters, and used to get up mimic seafights. The remains of his petty fortifications still awaken the curious enquiries of visitors. In one of his vagaries he caused a large vessel to be brought on wheels from the sea coast and launched in the lake. The country people were surprized to see a ship thus sailing over dry land. They called to mind a saying of Mother Shipton the famous prophet of the vulgar, that whenever a ship freighted with ling should cross Sherwood Forest Newstead would pass out of the Byron family. The country people who detested the old Lord were anxious to verify the prophecy. Ling in the dialect of Nottingham is the name for heather, with this plant they heaped the fated barque as it passed, so that it arrived full freighted at Newstead.

The most important stories about the lake, however, relate to the treasures that are supposed to lie buried in its bosom. These may have taken their origin in a fact which actually occurred. There was one time fished up from the deep part of the lake a great eagle of molten brass, with expanded wings, standing on a pedestal or perch of the same metal. It had doubtless served as a stand or reading desk, in the Abbey chapel, to hold a folio Bible or missal.

The sacred relique was sent to a brazier to be cleaned. As he was at work upon it he discovered that the pedestal was hollow and composed of several pieces. Unscrewing these, he drew forth a number of parchment deeds and grants appertaining to the Abbey and bearing the seals of Edward III and Henry VIII which had thus been concealed, and ultimately sunk in the lake by the friars to substantiate their right and title to these domains at some future day.

One of the parchment scrolls thus discovered, throws rather an awkward light upon the kind of life led by the friars of Newstead. It is an indulgence granted to them for a certain number of months, in which plenary pardon is assured in advance for all kinds of crimes, among which, several of the most gross and sensual are specifically mentioned.

After inspecting these testimonials of monkish life, in the regions of Sherwood Forest, we cease to wonder at the virtuous indignation of Robin Hood and his outlaw crew at the sleek sensualists of the cloister:

> I never hurt the husbandman
>> That use to till the ground
> Nor spill their blood that range the wood
>> To follow hawk and hound.

> My chiefest spite to clergy is,
>> Who in these days bear sway;

With fryars and monks with their fine spunks,
I make my chiefest prey.

OLD BALLAD OF ROBIN HOOD.

The brazen Eagle has been transferred to the parochial and collegiate church of Southall, about twenty miles from Newstead, where it may still be seen in the centre of the chancel supporting, as of yore, a ponderous Bible. As to the documents it contained, they are carefully treasured up by Colonel Wildman among his other deeds and papers, in an iron chest secured by a patent lock of nine bolts, almost equal to a magic spell.

The fishing up of this brazen relique, as I have already hinted, has given rise to tales of treasure lying at the bottom of the lake thrown in there by the monks when they abandoned the Abbey. The favorite story is, that there is a great iron chest there filled with gold and jewels, and chalices and crucifixes. Nay, that it has been seen, when the water of the lake was unusually low. There were large iron rings at each end, but all attempts to move it were ineffectual; either the gold it contained was too ponderous, or what is more probable, it was secured by one of those magic spells usually laid upon hidden treasure. It remains, therefore, at the bottom of the lake to this day; and it is to be hoped, may one day or other be discovered by the present worthy proprietor.

ROBIN HOOD AND SHERWOOD FOREST

While at Newstead Abbey I took great delight in riding and rambling about the neighborhood, studying out the traces of merry Sherwood Forest, and visiting the haunts of Robin Hood. The reliques of the old Forest are few and scattered, but as to the bold outlaw that once held a kind of freebooting sway over it, there is scarce a hill or dale, a cliff or cavern, a well or fountain in this part of the country that is not connected with his memory. The very names of some of the tenants on the Newstead estate, such as Beardall and Hardstaff, sound as if they may have been borne in old times by some of the stalwart fellows of the outlaw gang.

One of the earliest books that captivated my fancy when a child was a collection of Robin Hood ballads "adorned with cuts," which I bought of an old Scotch pedlar, at the cost of all my holyday money. How I devoured its pages, and gazed upon its uncouth wood cuts. For a time my mind was filled with picturings of "merry Sherwood," and the exploits and revellings of the bold foresters; and Robin Hood,

Little John, Friar Tuck and their doughty compeers were my heroes of romance.

These early feelings were in some degree revived when I found myself in the very heart of the far famed forest, and, as I said before, I took a kind of schoolboy delight in hunting up all traces of old Sherwood and its sylvan chivalry. One of the first of my antiquarian rambles was on horseback, in company with Colonel Wildman and his lady, who undertook to guide me to some of the mouldering monuments of the forest. One of these stands in front of the very gate of Newstead Park, and is known throughout the country by the name of "The Pilgrim Oak." It is a venerable tree of great size, overshadowing a wide area of the road. Under its shade the rustics of the neighborhood have been accustomed to assemble on certain holydays and celebrate their rural festivals. This custom had been handed down from father to son for several generations, until the oak had acquired a kind of sacred character.

The "old Lord Byron," however, in whose eyes nothing was sacred, when he laid his desolating hand on the groves and forests of Newstead, doomed likewise this traditional tree to the axe. Fortunately the good people of Nottingham heard of the danger of their favorite oak, and hastened to ransom it from destruction. They afterwards made a present of it to the poet, when he came to the estate, and the Pilgrim Oak is likely to continue a rural gathering place for many coming generations.

From this magnificent and time honoured tree we continued on our sylvan research, in quest of another oak, of more ancient date and less flourishing condition. A ride of two or three miles, the latter part across open wastes, once clothed with forest, now bare and cheerless, brought us to the tree in question. It was the Oak of Ravenshead, one of the last survivors of old Sherwood, and which had evidently once held a high head in the forest, it was now a mere wreck, crazed by time, and blasted by lightning and standing alone on a naked waste, like a ruined column in a desert.

> The scenes are desert now, and bare,
> Where flourished once a forest fair,
> When these waste glens with copse were lined,
> And peopled with the hart and hind.
> Yon lonely 'oak,' would he could tell
> The changes of his parent dell,
> Since he, so gray and stubborn now,
> Waved in each breeze a sapling bough.
> Would he could tell how deep the shade
> A thousand mingled branches made.
> Here in my shade methinks he'd say

The mighty stag at noontide lay.
While doe and roe and red-deer good,
Have bounded by through gay green-wood.

At no great distance from the Ravenshead Oak is a small cave which goes by the name of Robin Hood's stable. It is in the breast of a hill, scooped out of brown freestone, with rude attempts at columns and arches. Within are two niches which served, it is said, as stalls for the bold outlaw's horses. To this retreat he retired when hotly pursued by the law, for the place was a secret even from his band. The cave is overshadowed by an oak and alder and is hardly discoverable even at the present day, but when the country was overrun with forest it must have been completely concealed.

There was an agreeable wildness and loneliness in a great part of our ride. Our devious road wound down, at one time, among rocky dells, by wandering streams, and lonely pools, haunted by shy water fowl. We passed through a skirt of woodland, of more modern planting, but considered a legitimate offspring of the ancient forest, and commonly called Jock of Sherwood. In riding through these quiet, solitary scenes, the partridge and the pheasant would now and then burst upon the wing, and the hare scud away before us.

Another of these rambling rides in quest of popular antiquities, was to a chain of rocky cliffs called the Kirkby Crags, which skirt the Robin Hood hills. Here leaving my horse at the foot of the crags, I scaled their rugged sides and seated myself in a niche of the rocks called Robin Hood's chair. It commands a wide prospect over the valley of Newstead, and here the bold outlaw is said to have taken his seat, and kept a look out upon the roads below, watching for merchants, and Bishops, and other wealthy travellers, upon whom to pounce down, like an eagle from his eyrie.

Descending from the cliffs and remounting my horse, a ride of a mile or two further along a narrow "robber path" as it was called, which wound up into the hills between perpendicular rocks, led to an artificial cavern cut in the face of a cliff, with a door and window, wrought through the living stone. This bears the name of Friar Tuck's cell, or hermitage, where, according to tradition, that jovial anchorite used to make good cheer and boisterous revel with his freebooting comrades.

Such were some of the vestiges of old Sherwood and its renowned "yeomandrie" which I visited in the neighborhood of Newstead. The worthy clergyman who officiated as chaplain at the Abbey, seeing my zeal in the cause informed me of a considerable tract of the ancient forest, still in existence about ten miles distant. There were many fine old oaks in it he said, that had stood for centuries, but were now shattered and "stag headed," that is to say their upper branches were bare, and blasted and straggling out like the antlers of a deer. Their trunks, too, were hollow, and full of crows and jack daws, who made them their nestling places. He occasionally rode over to the forest in the long summer evenings and pleased himself with loitering in the twilight about the green alleys and under the venerable trees.

The description given by the chaplain made me anxious to visit this remnant of old Sherwood, and he kindly offered to be my guide and companion. We accordingly sallied forth one morning on horseback on this sylvan expedition. Our ride took us through a part of the country where King John had once held a hunting seat; the ruins of which are still to be seen. At that time the whole neighborhood was an open royal forest, or Frank chase, as it was termed; for King John was an enemy to parks and warrens and other enclosures, by which game was fenced in for the private benefit and recreation of the nobles and the clergy.

Here on the brow of a gentle hill commanding an extensive prospect of what had once been forest, stood another of those monumental trees which, to my mind, gave a peculiar interest to this neighborhood. It was the Parliament Oak, so called in memory of an assemblage of the kind held by King John beneath its shade. The lapse of upwards of six centuries had reduced this once mighty tree to a mere crumbling fragment, yet, like a gigantic torso in ancient statuary, the grandeur of the mutilated trunk gave evidence of what it had been in the days of its glory. In contemplating its mouldering remains, the fancy busied itself in calling up the scene that must have been presented beneath its shade, when this sunny hill swarmed with the pageantry of a warlike and hunting court. When silken pavilions and warrior tents decked its crest, and royal standards and baronial banners, and knightly pennons rolled out to the breeze; when prelates, and courtiers, and steel clad chivalry thronged round the person of the monarch, while at a distance loitered the foresters in green, and all the rural and hunting train that waited upon his sylvan sports.

> A thousand vassals mustered round
> With horse, and hawk, and horn, and hound;
> And through the brake the rangers stalk
> And falc'ners hold the ready hawk;
> And foresters in green wood trim
> Lead in the leash the gazehound grim.

Such was the phantasmagoria that presented itself for a moment to my imagination, peopling the silent place before me with empty shadows of the past. The reverie however was transient; king, courtier, and steel clad warrior, and forester in green, with horn, and hawk, and hound, all faded again into oblivion, and I awoke to all that remained of this once stirring scene of human pomp and power—a mouldering oak and a tradition!

We are such stuff as dreams are made of!

A ride of a few miles further brought us at length among the venerable and classic shades of Sherwood. Here I was delighted to find myself in a genuine wild wood, of primitive and natural growth, so rarely to be met with in this thickly peopled and highly cultivated country. It reminded me of the aboriginal forests of my native land. I rode through natural alleys and green wood groves, carpeted with grass and shaded by lofty and beautiful birches. What most interested me, however, was to behold around me the mighty trunks of veteran oaks, old monumental trees, the patriarchs of Sherwood Forest. They were shattered, hollow and moss grown, it is true, and their "leafy honours" were nearly departed; but like mouldering towers they were noble and picturesque in their decay, and gave evidence even in their ruins, of their ancient grandeur.

As I gazed about me upon these vestiges of once "Merrie Sherwood" the picturings of my boyish fancy began to rise in my mind; and Robin Hood and his men to stand before me.

> He clothed himself in scarlet then,
>   His men were all in green;
> A finer show throughout the world
>   In no place could be seen.
>
> Good lord! it was a gallant sight
>   To see them all in a row;
> With every man a good broad sword
>   And eke a good yew bow.

The horn of Robin Hood again seemed to resound through the forest. I saw his sylvan chivalry, half huntsmen, half freebooters, trooping across the distant glades, or feasting and revelling beneath the trees; I was going on to embody, in this way, all the ballad scenes that had delighted me when a boy, when the distant sound of a wood cutter's axe roused me from my day dream.

The boding apprehensions which it awakened were too soon verified. I had not ridden much further when I came to an open space where the work of destruction was going on. Around me lay the prostrate trunks of venerable oaks, once the towering and magnificent lords of the forest, and a number of wood cutters were hacking and hewing at another gigantic tree, just tottering to its fall.

Alas! for old Sherwood Forest: it had fallen into the possession of a noble agriculturalist: a modern utilitarian, who had no feeling for poetry or forest scenery. In a little while and this glorious wood land will be laid low; its green glades turned into sheep walks; its legendary bowers supplanted by turnip fields; and "Merry Sherwood" will exist but in ballad and tradition.

"Oh, for the poetical superstitions," thought I, "of the olden time! that shed a sanctity over every grove; that gave to each tree its tutelar genius or nymph, and threatened disaster to all who should molest the hamadryads in their leafy abodes. Alas! for the sordid propensity of modern days, when every thing is coined into gold, and this once holyday planet of ours is turned into a mere 'working day world.'"

My cobweb fancies put to flight, and my feelings out of tune, I left the forest in a far different mood from that in which I had entered it, and rode silently along until on reaching the summit of a gentle eminence, the chime of evening bells came on the breeze across the heath from a distant village.

I paused to listen.

"They are merely the evening bells of Mansfield," said my companion.

"Of Mansfield!" Here was another of the legendary names of this storied neighborhood, that called up early and pleasant associations. The famous old ballad of the King and the Miller of Mansfield came at once to mind, and the chime of the bells put me again in good humour.

A little further on and we were again on the traces of Robin Hood. Here was Fountain dale where he had his encounter with that stalwart shaveling Friar Tuck, who was a kind of saint militant alternately wearing the casque and the cowl.

> The curtal fryar kept Fountain dale
>   Seven long years and more,
> There was neither lord, knight or earl
>   Could make him yield before.

The moat is still shewn which is said to have surrounded the strong hold of this jovial and fighting friar; and the place where he and Robin Hood had their sturdy trial of strength and prowess, in the memorable conflict which lasted

> From ten o'clock that very day
> Until four in the afternoon,

and ended in the treaty of fellowship. As to the hardy feats both of sword and trencher performed by this "curtal fryar," behold are they not recorded at length in the ancient ballads, and in the magic pages of Ivanhoe?

The evening was fast coming on and the twilight thickening as we rode through these haunts famous in outlaw story. A melancholy seemed to gather over the landscape as we proceeded, for our course lay by shadowy woods, and across naked heaths and along lonely roads, marked by some of those sinister names by which the country people in England are apt to make dreary places still more dreary. The horrors of "Thieves' Wood," and the "Murderers' Stone," and "the Hag Nook," had all to be encountered in the gathering gloom of evening, and threatened to beset our path with more than mortal peril. Happily, however, we passed all these ominous places unharmed and arrived in safety at the portal of Newstead Abbey highly satisfied with our greenwood foray.

THE ROOK CELL

In the course of my sojourn at the Abbey I changed my quarters from the magnificent old state apartment haunted by Sir John Byron the little, to another in a remote corner of the ancient edifice, immediately adjoining the ruined chapel. It possessed still more interest in my eyes, from having been the sleeping apartment of Lord Byron during his residence at the Abbey. The furniture remained the same. Here was the bed in which he slept, and which he had brought with him from college, its gilded posts surmounted by coronets, giving evidence of his aristocratical feelings. Here was likewise his college sopha; and about the walls were the portraits of his favorite butler, old Joe Murray, of his "fancy" acquaintance, Jackson the pugilist, together with pictures of Harrow School and the college at Cambridge, in which he was educated.

The bed chamber goes by the name of The Rook Cell, from its vicinity to the Rookery which, since time immemorial, has maintained possession of a solemn grove adjacent to the chapel. This venerable community afforded me much food for speculation during my residence in this apartment. In the morning I used to hear them gradually waking and seeming to call each other up. After a time the whole fraternity would be in a flutter: some balancing and swinging on the tree tops, others perched on the pinnacles of the Abbey church, or wheeling and hovering about in the air, and the ruined walls would reverberate with their incessant cawings. In this way they would linger about the rookery and its vicinity for the early part of the morning, when, having apparently mustered all their forces, called over the roll and determined upon their line of march, they one and all would sail off in a long straggling flight to maraud the distant fields. They would forage the country for miles and remain absent all day, excepting now and then a scout would come home, as if to see that all was well. Towards night the whole host might be seen like a dark cloud in the distance, winging their way homeward. They came, as it were, with whoop and halloo, wheeling high in the air above the Abbey, making various evolutions before they alighted and then keeping up an incessant cawing in the tree tops, until they gradually fell asleep.

It is remarked at the Abbey that the rooks, though they daily sally forth on forays throughout the week, yet keep about the venerable edifice on Sundays, as if they had inherited a reverence for the day from their ancient confreres, the monks. Indeed a believer in the metempsychosis might easily imagine these gothic looking birds to be the embodied souls of the ancient friars still hovering about their sanctified abode.

I dislike to disturb any point of popular and poetic faith and was loth, therefore, to question the authenticity of this mysterious reverence for the Sabbath on the part of the Newstead rooks; but certainly in the course of my sojourn in the rook cell, I detected them in a flagrant outbreak and foray on a bright Sunday morning.

Beside the occasional clamour of the rookery, this remote apartment was often greeted with sounds of a different kind; from the neighboring ruins. The great lancet window in front of the chapel adjoins the very wall of the chamber, and the mysterious sounds from it at night, have been well described by Lord Byron:

> ————Now loud, now fainter,
> The gale sweeps through its fretwork, and oft sings
> The owl his anthem, where the silenced quire
> Lie with their hallelujahs quenched like fire.
>
> But on the noontide of the moon, and when
> The wind is winged from one point of heaven,
> There moans a strange unearthly sound, which then
> Is musical—a dying accent driven
>
> Through the huge arch, which soars and sinks again.
> Some deem it but the distant echo given
> Back to the night wind by the waterfall,
> And harmonized by the old choral wall.

Others, that some original shape or form,
   Shaped by decay perchance, hath given the power
To this grey ruin, with a voice to charm.
   Sad, but serene, it sweeps o'er tree or tower:
The cause I know not, nor can solve; but such
The fact:—I've heard it,—once perhaps too much.

Never was a traveller in quest of the romantic in greater luck. I had, in sooth, got lodged in another haunted apartment of the Abbey; for in this chamber Lord Byron declared he had more than once been harassed at midnight by a mysterious visitor. A black shapeless form would sit cowering upon his bed, and after gazing at him for a time with glaring eyes would roll off and disappear. The same uncouth apparition is said to have disturbed the slumbers of a newly married couple that once passed their honeymoon in this apartment.

I would observe that the access to the Rook Cell is by a spiral stone staircase leading up into it, as into a turret, from the long shadowy corridor over the cloysters, one of the midnight walks of the goblin friar. Indeed to the fancies engendered in his brain in this remote and lonely apartment, incorporated with the floating superstitions of the Abbey, we are no doubt indebted for the spectral scene in Don Juan.

Then as the night was clear, though cold, he threw
   His chamber door wide open—and went forth
Into a gallery, of sombre hue,
   Long furnish'd with old pictures of great worth,
Of knights and dames heroic and chaste too
   As doubtless should be people of high birth.

   ❋   ❋   ❋   ❋   ❋   ❋   ❋

No sound except the echo of his sigh
   Or step ran sadly through that antique house,
When suddenly he heard, or thought so, nigh,
   A supernatural agent—or a mouse,
Whose little nibbling rustle will embarrass
Most people, as it plays along the arras.

It was no mouse, but lo! a monk, arrayed
   In cowl and beads, and dusky garb, appeared,
Now in the moonlight, and now lapsed in shade;
   With steps that trod as heavy, yet unheard;
His garments only a slight murmur made;
   He moved as shadowy as the sisters weird,

But slowly; and as he passed Juan by
Glared, without pausing, on him a bright eye.

Juan was petrified; he had heard a hint
   Of such a spirit in these halls of old,
But thought like most men, there was nothing in't
   Beyond the rumour which such spots unfold,
Coin'd from surviving superstition's mint,
   Which passes ghosts in currency like gold,
But rarely seen, like gold compared with paper.
And *did* he see this? or was it a vapour?

Once, twice, thrice pass'd, repass'd—the thing of air,
   Or earth beneath, or heaven, or t'other place;
And Juan gazed upon it with a stare,
   Yet could not speak or move; but, on its base
As stands a statue, stood: he felt his hair
   Twine like a knot of snakes around his face;
He tax'd his tongue for words, which were not granted,
To ask the reverend person what he wanted.

The third time after a still longer pause,
   The shadow pass'd away—but where? the hall
Was long, and thus far there was no great cause
   To think his vanishing unnatural:
Doors there were many, through which, by the laws
   Of physics, bodies, whether short or tall,
Might come or go; but Juan could not state
Through which the spectre seem'd to evaporate.

He stood, how long he knew not but it seem'd
   An age—expectant, powerless, with his eyes
Strain'd on the spot where first the figure gleam'd;
   Then by degrees recall'd his energies,
And would have pass'd the whole off as a dream,
   But could not wake; he was, he did surmise,
Waking already, and returned at length
Back to his chamber, shorn of half his strength.

As I have already observed, it is difficult to determine whether Lord Byron was really subject to the superstitious fancies which have been imputed to him, or whether he merely amused himself by giving currency to them among his domestics and dependants. He certainly never scrupled to express a belief in supernatural visitations, both verbally and in his correspondence. If such were his foible, the Rook Cell was an admirable place to engender these delusions. As I have lain awake at night I have heard all kinds of mysterious and sighing sounds from the neighboring ruin. Distant footsteps too, and the closing of doors in remote parts of the Abbey, would send hollow reverberations and echoes along the corridor and up the spiral staircase. Once, in fact, I was roused by a strange moaning sound at the very door of my chamber. I threw it open, and a form "black and shapeless with glaring eyes" stood before me. It proved, however, neither ghost nor goblin, but my friend Boatswain, the great Newfoundland dog, who had conceived a companionable liking for me, and occasionally sought me in my apartment. To the hauntings of even such a visitant as honest Boatswain may we attribute some of the marvellous stories about the Goblin Friar.

THE LITTLE WHITE LADY

In the course of a mornings ride, with Colonel Wildman, about the Abbey lands, we found ourselves in one of the prettiest little wild woods imaginable. The road to it had led us among rocky ravines overhung with thickets, and now wound through birchen dingles and among beautiful groves and clumps of elms and beeches. A limpid rill of sparkling water, winding and doubling in perplexed mazes, crossed our path repeatedly, so as to give the wood the appearance of being watered by numerous rivulets. The solitary and romantic look of this piece of wood land, and the frequent recurrence of its mazy stream, put him in mind, Colonel Wildman said, of the little German fairy tale of Undine, in which is recorded the adventures of a knight who had married a water nymph. As he rode with his bride through her native woods, every stream claimed her as a relative, one was a brother, another an uncle, another a cousin.

We rode on amusing ourselves with applying this fanciful tale to the charming scenery around us, until we came to a lowly grey stone farm house, of ancient date, situated in a solitary glen, on the margin of the brook and overshadowed by venerable trees. It went by the name, I was told, of the Weir Mill farm house. With this rustic mansion was connected a little tale of real life, some circumstances of which were related to me on the spot, and others I collected in the course of my sojourn at the Abbey.

Not long after Colonel Wildman had purchased the estate of Newstead he made it a visit for the purpose of planning repairs and alterations. As he was rambling one evening about dusk in company with his architect through this little piece of woodland, he was struck with its peculiar characteristics, and then for the first time compared it to the haunted wood of Undine. While he was making the remark a small female figure in white flitted by without speaking a word, or indeed appearing to notice them. Her step was scarcely heard as she passed, and her form was indistinct in the twilight.

"What a figure," exclaimed Colonel Wildman, "for a fairy or sprite! How much a poet or a romance writer would make of such an apparition, at such a time and in such a place."

He began to congratulate himself upon having some elfin inhabitant for his haunted wood, when, on proceeding a few paces, he found a white frill lying in the path, which had evidently fallen from the figure that had just passed.

"Well," said he, "after all, this is neither sprite nor fairy, but a being of flesh and blood and muslin."

Continuing on he came to where the road passed by an old mill in front of the Abbey. The people of the mill were at the door. He paused and enquired whether any visitor had been at the Abbey but was answered in the negative.

"Has nobody passed by here?"

"No one, sir."

"That's strange! Surely I met a female in white, who must have passed along this path."

"Oh, sir! you mean the little White Lady—oh yes, she went by here not long since."

"The little White Lady! And pray who is the little White Lady?"

"Why, sir, that nobody knows, she lives in the Weir Mill farm house, down in the skirts of the wood. She comes to the Abbey every morning, keeps about it all day, and goes away at night. She speaks to nobody, and we are rather shy of her, for we don't know what to make of her."

Colonel Wildman now concluded that it was some artist or amateur employed in making sketches of the Abbey, and thought no more about the matter. He went to London and was absent for some time. In the interim his sister, who was newly married, came with her husband to pass the honeymoon at the Abbey. The little White Lady still resided in the Weir Mill farm house, on the border of the haunted wood, and continued her daily visits to the Abbey. Her dress was always the same, a white gown with a little black spencer or boddice and a white hat with a short veil that screened the upper part of her countenance. Her habits were shy lonely and silent; she spoke to no one, and sought no companionship excepting with the Newfoundland dog, that had belonged to Lord Byron. His friendship she secured by caressing him and occasionally bringing him food and he became the companion of her solitary walks. She avoided all strangers, and wandered about the retired parts of the garden; sometimes sitting for hours, by the tree on which Lord Byron had carved his name, or at the foot of the monument, which he had erected among the ruins of the chapel. Sometimes she read, sometimes she wrote with a pencil on a small slate which she carried with her; but much of her time was passed in a kind of reverie.

The people about the place gradually became accustomed to her, and suffered her to wander about unmolested: their distrust of her subsided on discovering that most of her peculiar and lonely habits arose from the misfortune of being deaf and dumb. Still she was regarded with some degree of shyness, for it was the common opinion that she was not exactly in her right mind.

Colonel Wildman's sister was informed of all these circumstances by the servants of the Abbey, among whom the little White Lady was a theme of frequent discussion. The Abbey and its monastic environs being haunted ground it was natural that a mysterious visitant of the kind, and one supposed to be under the influence of mental hallucination, should inspire awe in a person unaccustomed to the place. As Colonel Wildman's sister was one day walking along a broad terrace of the garden she suddenly beheld the little White Lady coming towards her, and, in the surprize and agitation of the moment, turned and ran into the house.

Day after day now elapsed and nothing more was seen of this singular personage. Colonel Wildman at length arrived at the Abbey, and his sister mentioned to him her rencountre and fright in the garden. It brought to mind his own adventure with the little White Lady in the wood of Undine, and he was surprized to find that she still continued her mysterious wanderings about the Abbey. The mystery was soon explained. Immediately after his arrival he received a letter written in the most minute and delicate female hand, and in elegant and even eloquent language. It was from the little White Lady. She had noticed and been shocked by the abrupt retreat of Colonel Wildman's sister on seeing her in the garden walk, and expressed her unhappiness at being an object of alarm to any of his family. She explained the motives of her frequent and long visits to the Abbey which proved to be a singularly enthusiastic idolatry of the genius of Lord Byron, and a solitary and passionate delight in haunting the scenes he had once inhabited. She hinted at the infirmities which cut her off from all social communion with her fellow beings, and at her situation in life as desolate and bereaved, and concluded by hoping that he would not deprive her of her only comfort, the permission of visiting the Abbey occasionally and lingering about its walks and gardens.

Colonel Wildman now made further enquiries concerning her and found that she was a great favorite with the people of the farm house where she boarded, from the gentleness, quietude and innocence of her manners. When at home she passed the greater part of her time in a small sitting room reading and writing.

Colonel Wildman immediately called on her at the farm house. She received him with some agitation and embarrassment, but his frankness and urbanity soon put her at her ease. She was past the bloom of youth, a pale, fragile, nervous little being, and apparently deficient in most of her physical organs, for, in addition to being deaf and dumb she saw but imperfectly. They carried on a communication by means of a small slate which she drew out of her reticule, and on which they wrote their questions and replies. In writing or reading she always approached her eyes close to the written characters.

This defective organization was accompanied by a morbid sensibility almost amounting to disease. She had not been born deaf and dumb; but had lost her hearing in a fit of sickness, and with it the power of distinct articulation. Her life had evidently been checquered and unhappy; she was apparently without family or friend, a lonely desolate being, cut off from society by her infirmities.

"I am always amongst strangers," said she, "as much so in my native country, as I could be in the remotest parts of the world. By all I am considered as a stranger and an alien; no one will acknowledge any connexion with me. I seem not to belong to the human species."

Such were the circumstances that Colonel Wildman was able to draw forth in the course of his conversation, and they strongly interested him in favor of this poor enthusiast. He was too devout an admirer of Lord Byron himself not to sympathize in this extraordinary zeal of one of his votaries, and he entreated her to renew her visits to the Abbey, assuring her that the Edifice and its grounds should always be open to her.

The little White Lady now resumed her daily walks in the Monk's Garden, and her occasional seat at the foot of the monument: she was shy and diffident, however, and evidently fearful of intruding. If any persons were walking in the garden she would avoid them and seek the most remote parts; and was seen like a sprite, only by gleams and glimpses, as she glided among the groves and thickets. Many of her feelings and fancies during these lonely rambles, were embodied in verse, noted down on her tablet, and transferred to paper in the evening on her return to the farm house. Some of these verses now lie before me, written with considerable harmony of versification but chiefly curious as being illustrative of that singular and enthusiastic idolatry with which she almost worshipped the genius of Byron, or rather, the romantic image of him formed by her imagination.

Two or three extracts may not be unacceptable. The following are
from a long rhapsody addressed to Lord Byron:

> By what dread charm thou rulest the mind
>   It is not given for us to know;
> We glow with feelings undefined,
>   Nor can explain from whence they flow.
>
> Not that fond love which passion breathes
>   And youthful hearts enflame;
> The soul a nobler homage gives
>   That bows to thy great name.
>
> Oft have we own'd the muses' skill
>   And proved the power of song,
> But sweetest notes ne'er woke the thrill
>   That solely to thy verse belong.
>
> This—but far more, for thee we prove,
>   Something that bears a holier name,
> Than the pure dream of early love,
>   Or friendship's nobler flame.
>
> Something divine—Oh! what it is
>   *Thy* muse alone can tell,
> So sweet but so profound the bliss
>   We dread to break the spell.

This singular and romantic infatuation, for such it might truly be
called, was entirely spiritual and ideal, for, as she herself declares in
another of her rhapsodies, she had never beheld Lord Byron; he was,
to her, a mere phantom of the brain.

> I ne'er have drunk thy glance—Thy form
>   My earthly eye has never seen,
> Though oft, when fancy's visions warm,
>   It greets me in some blissful dream.
>
> Greets me, as greets the sainted seer
>   Some radiant visitant from high,
> When heaven's own strains break on his ear
>   And wrap his soul in ecstasy.

Her poetical wanderings and musings were not confined to the Abbey grounds, but extended to all parts of the neighborhood connected with the memory of Lord Byron, and among the rest to the groves and gardens of Annesley Hall, the seat of his early passion for Miss Chaworth. One of her poetical effusions mentions her having seen from Howet's Hill in Annesley Park a "sylph like form," in a car drawn by milk white horses, passing by the foot of the hill, who proved to be the "favorite child" seen by Lord Byron, in his memorable interview with Miss Chaworth after her marriage. That favorite child was now a blooming and beautiful girl approaching to womanhood, and seems to have understood something of the character and story of this singular visitant, and to have treated her with gentle sympathy. The little White Lady expresses in touching terms, in a note to her verses, her sense of this gentle courtesy. "The benevolent condescension," says she, "of that amiable and interesting young lady, to the unfortunate writer of these simple lines, will remain engraved upon a grateful memory, till the vital spark that now animates a heart that too sensibly feels, and too seldom experiences such kindness, is forever extinct."

In the meantime Colonel Wildman, in occasional interviews, had obtained further particulars of the story of the stranger, and found that poverty was added to the other evils of her forlorn and isolated state. Her name was Sophia Hyatt. She was the daughter of a country bookseller, but both her parents had died several years before. At their death her sole dependance was upon her brother, who allowed her a small annuity on her share of the property left by their father, and which remained in his hands. Her brother who was a captain of a merchant vessel removed with his family to America, leaving her almost alone in the world, for she had no other relative in England but a cousin, of whom she knew almost nothing. She received her annuity regularly for a time but unfortunately her brother died in the West Indies, leaving his affairs in confusion, and his estate overhung by several commercial claims which threatened to swallow up the whole. Under these disastrous circumstances her annuity suddenly ceased; she had in vain tried to obtain a renewal of it from the widow, or even an account of the state of her brother's affairs. Her letters for three years past had remained unanswered, and she would have been exposed to the horrors of the most abject want, but for a pittance quarterly doled out to her by her cousin in England.

Colonel Wildman entered with characteristic benevolence into the story of her troubles. He saw that she was a helpless, unprotected being, unable from her infirmities and her ignorance of the world, to prosecute her just claims. He obtained from her the addresses of her relatives in America, and of the commercial connexion of her brother; promised through the medium of his own agents in Liverpool, to institute an enquiry into the situation of her brother's affairs, and to forward any letters she might write, so as to ensure their reaching their place of destination.

Inspired with some faint hopes the little White Lady continued her wanderings about the Abbey and its neighborhood. The delicacy and timidity of her deportment increased the interest already felt for her by Mrs. Wildman. That lady, with her wonted kindness, sought to make acquaintance with her, and inspire her with confidence. She invited her into the Abbey; treated her with the most delicate attention, and seeing that she had a great turn for reading, offered her the loan of any books in her possession. She borrowed a few, particularly the works of Sir Walter Scott, but soon returned them; the writings of Lord Byron seemed to form the only study in which she delighted, and when not occupied in reading those, her time was passed in passionate meditations on his genius. Her enthusiasm spread an ideal world around her in which she moved and existed as in a dream, forgetful at times of the real miseries which beset her in her mortal state.

One of her rhapsodies is however of a very melancholy cast; anticipating her own death, which her fragile frame and growing infirmities rendered but too probable. It is headed by the following paragraph:

"Written beneath the tree on Crowholt Hill, where it is my wish to be interred, (if I should die in Newstead)."

I subjoin a few of the stanzas: they are addressed to Lord Byron:

> Thou, while thou stand'st beneath this tree,
>   While by thy foot this earth is press'd,
> Think, here the wanderer's ashes be—
>   And wilt thou say, sweet be thy rest!
> *   *   *   *   *   *   *
>
> 'Twould add even to a seraph's bliss,
>   Whose sacred charge thou then may be,
> To guide—to guard—yes, Byron! yes,
>   That glory is reserved for me.
>
> If woes below may plead above
>   A frail heart's errors, mine forgiven,
> To that "high world" I soar, where "love
>   Surviving" forms the bliss of Heaven.
>
> O wheresoe'er, in realms above,
>   Assign'd my spirit's new abode,

> 'Twill watch thee with a seraph's love
>   'Till thou too soar'st to meet thy God.
>
> And here, beneath this lonely tree—
>   Beneath the earth thy feet have press'd,
> My dust shall sleep—once dear to thee
>   These scenes—here may the wanderer rest!

In the midst of her reveries and rhapsodies, tidings reached Newstead of the untimely death of Lord Byron. How they were received by this humble but passionate devotee I could not ascertain; her life was too obscure and lonely to furnish much personal anecdote, but among her poetical effusions are several written in a broken and irregular manner and evidently under great agitation.

The following sonnet is the most coherent and most descriptive of her peculiar state of mind.

> Well, thou art gone—but what wert thou to me?
>   I never saw thee—never heard thy voice,
> Yet my soul seemed to claim affiance with thee.
>   The Roman bard has sung of fields Elysian
> Where the soul sojourns ere she visits earth,
>   Sure it was there my spirit knew thee, Byron!
> Thine image haunteth me like a past vision;
>   It hath enshrined itself in my heart's core:
> 'Tis my soul's soul—it fills the whole creation.
>   For I do live but in that world ideal
> Which the muse peopleth with her bright fancies,
>   And of that world thou art a monarch real
> Nor ever earthly sceptre ruled a kingdom,
>   With sway so potent as thy lyre the mind's dominion.

Taking all the circumstances here adduced into consideration it is evident that this strong excitement and exclusive occupation of the mind upon one subject, operating upon a system in a high state of morbid irritability, was in danger of producing that species of mental derangement called monomania. The poor little being was aware, herself, of the dangers of her case and alluded to it in the following passage of a letter to Colonel Wildman, which presents one of the most lamentable pictures of anticipated evil ever conjured up by the human mind.

"I have long," writes she, "too sensibly felt the decay of my mental faculties, which I consider as the certain indication of that dreaded calamity which I anticipate with such terror. A strange idea has long haunted my mind that Swift's dreadful fate will be mine—it is not ordinary insanity I so much apprehend but something worse—absolute idiotism.

"O Sir! think what I must suffer from such an idea without an earthly friend to look up to for protection in such a wretched state—exposed to the indecent insults which such spectacles always excite. But I dare not dwell upon the thought; it would facilitate the event I so much dread and contemplate with horror. Yet I cannot help thinking from people's behaviour to me at times, and from after reflections upon my conduct, that symptoms of the disease are already apparent."

Five months passed away but the letters written by her, and forwarded by Colonel Wildman to America relative to her brother's affairs remained unanswered; the enquiries instituted by the Colonel had as yet proved equally fruitless. A deeper gloom and despondency now seemed to gather upon her mind. She began to talk of leaving Newstead, and repairing to London in the vague hope of obtaining relief or redress by instituting some legal process to ascertain and enforce the will of her deceased brother. Weeks elapsed, however, before she could summon up sufficient resolution to tear herself away from the scene of poetical fascination. The following simple stanzas selected from a number written about the time, express in humble rhymes the melancholy that preyed upon her spirits.

> Farewell to thee, Newstead, thy time riven towers
>   Shall meet the fond gaze of the pilgrim no more;
> No more may she roam through thy walks and thy bowers
>   Nor muse in thy cloysters at eves pensive hour.
>
> Oh how shall I leave you, ye hills and ye dales,
>   Where lost in sad musing, though sad not unblest,
> A lone pilgrim I stray—Ah! in these lovely vales,
>   I hoped, vainly hoped that the pilgrim might rest.
>
> Yet rest is far distant—in the dark vale of death
>   Alone shall I find it, an outcast forlorn—
> But hence vain complaints though by fortune bereft
>   Of all that could solace in life's early morn.
>
> Is not man from his birth doomed a pilgrim to roam
>   O'er the world's dreary wilds, whence, by fortune's rude
>   gust,
> In his path if some flowret of joy chance to bloom
>   It is torn and its foliage laid low in the dust.

At length she fixed upon a day for her departure. On the day previous she paid a farewell visit to the Abbey: wandering over every part of the grounds and garden; pausing and lingering at every place particularly associated with the recollection of Lord Byron and passing a long time seated at the foot of the monument, which she used to call "her altar." Seeking Mrs. Wildman, she placed in her hands a sealed pacquet, with an earnest request that she would not open it until after her departure from the neighborhood. This done she took an affectionate leave of her, and with many bitter tears, bade farewell to the Abbey.

On retiring to her room that evening Mrs. Wildman could not refrain from inspecting the legacy of this singular being. On opening the pacquet, she found a number of fugitive poems, written in a most delicate and minute hand, and evidently the fruits of her reveries and meditations during her lonely rambles: from these the foregoing extracts have been made. These were accompanied by a voluminous letter, written with the pathos and eloquence of genuine feeling, and depicting her peculiar situation and singular state of mind in dark but powerful colours.

"The last time," says she, "that I had the pleasure of seeing you in the garden, you asked me why I leave Newstead; when I told you my circumstances obliged me, the expression of concern which I fancied I observed in your look and manner would have encouraged me to have been explicit at the time, but from my inability of expressing myself verbally."

She then goes on to detail precisely her pecuniary circumstances by which it appears that her whole dependance for subsistence was on an allowance of thirteen pounds a year from her cousin who bestowed it through a feeling of pride lest his relative should come upon the parish. During two years this pittance had been augmented, from other sources, to twenty three pounds, but the last year it had shrunk within its original bounds, and was yielded so grudgingly, that she could not feel sure of its continuance from one quarter to another. More than once it had been withheld on slight pretenses, and she was in constant dread lest it should be withdrawn entirely.

"It is with extreme reluctance," observes she, "that I have so far exposed my unfortunate situation but I thought you expected to know something more of it, and I feared that Colonel Wildman, deceived by appearances, might think that I am in no immediate want, and that the delay of a few weeks, or months respecting the enquiry can be of no material consequence. It is absolutely necessary to the success of the business that Colonel Wildman should know the exact state of my circumstances without reserve, that he may be enabled to make a correct representation of them to any gentlemen whom he intends to interest, who, I presume, if they are not of America themselves, have some

connexions there, through whom my friends may be convinced of the
reality of my distress, if they pretend to doubt it, as I suppose they do:
but to be more explicit is impossible, it would be too humiliating to
particularize the circumstances of the embarrassment in which I am
now unhappily involved—my utter destitution. To disclose all might, too,
be liable to an inference which I hope I am not so void of delicacy, of
natural pride, as to endure the thought of. Pardon me madam, for thus
giving trouble where I have no right to do—compelled to throw myself
upon Colonel Wildman's humanity to entreat his earnest exertions
in my behalf, for it is now my only resource. Yet do not too much
despise me for thus submitting to imperious necessity—it is not love
of life; believe me it is not, nor anxiety for its preservation. I cannot
say, "There are things that make the world dear to me"—for in the world
there is not an object to make *me* wish to linger here another hour, could
I find that rest and peace in the grave which I have never found on earth,
and I fear will be denied me there."

Another part of her letter developes more completely the dark despondency hinted at in the conclusion of the foregoing extract—and presents a
lamentable instance of a mind diseased, which sought in vain, amidst
sorrow and calamity, the sweet consolations of religious faith.

"That my existence has hitherto been prolonged," says she, "often
beyond what I have thought to have been its destined period, is astonish-
ing to myself. Often when my situation has been as desperate, as
hopeless, or more so, if possible, than it is at present, some unexpected
interposition of Providence has rescued me from a fate that has
appeared inevitable. I do not particularly allude to recent circumstances
or latter years, for from my earlier years I have been the child of
Providence—then why should I distrust its care now. I do not *dis*trust it
—neither do I trust it. I feel perfectly unanxious, unconcerned and indifferent to the future; but this is not trust in Providence—not that trust
which alone claims its protection. I know this is a blameable indifference
—it is more—for it reaches to the interminable future. It turns almost with
disgust from the bright prospects which religion offers for the consolation
and support of the wretched, and to which I was early taught, by an
almost adored mother, to look forward to with hope and joy, but to me
they can now afford no consolation. Not that I doubt the sacred
truths that religion inculcates. I cannot doubt—though I confess I have
somtimes tried to do so, because I no longer wish for that immortality
of which it assures us. My only wish now is for rest and peace—endless
rest. "For rest—but not to feel 'tis rest," but I cannot delude myself
with the hope that such rest will be my lot. I feel an internal evidence,
stronger than any arguments that reason or religion can enforce, that I
have that within me which is imperishable; that drew not its origin from

the "clod of the valley." With this conviction, but without a hope to brighten the prospect of that dread future:

> "I dare not look beyond the tomb
> Yet cannot hope for peace before."

Such an unhappy frame of mind, I am sure madam, must excite your commiseration. It is perhaps owing, in part at least, to the solitude in which I have lived I may say even in the midst of society, when I have mixed in it, as my infirmities entirely exclude me from that sweet intercourse of kindred spirits—that sweet solace of refined conversation; the little intercourse I have at any time with those around me cannot be termed conversation—they are not kindred spirits—and even where circumstances have associated me (but rarely indeed) with superior and cultivated minds who have not disdained to admit me to their society, they could not by all their generous efforts, even in early youth, lure from my dark soul the thoughts that loved to lie buried there, nor inspire me with the courage to attempt their disclosure; and yet of all the pleasures of polished life which fancy has often pictured to me in such vivid colours, there is not one that I have so ardently coveted as that sweet reciprocation of ideas, the supreme bliss of enlightened minds in the hour of social converse. But this I knew was not decreed for me—

> "Yet this was in my nature—"

but since the loss of my hearing I have always been incapable of verbal conversation. I need not, however, inform you madam of this. At the first interview with which you favored me, you quickly discovered my peculiar unhappiness in this respect: you perceived from my manner, that any attempt to draw me into conversation would be in vain—had it been otherwise perhaps you would not have disdained, now and then, to have soothed the lonely wanderer with yours. I have sometimes fancied, when I have seen you in the walk, that you seemed to wish to encourage me to throw myself in your way. Pardon me if my imagination, too apt to beguile me with such dear illusions, has deceived me into too presumptuous an idea here. You must have observed that I generally endeavoured to avoid both you and Colonel Wildman. It was to spare your generous hearts the pain of witnessing distress you could not alleviate. Thus cut off, as it were, from all human society, I have been compelled to live in a world of my own, and certainly with the beings with which my world is peopled I am at no loss to converse. But though I love solitude and am never in want of subjects to amuse my fancy, yet solitude too much indulged in must necessarily have an unhappy effect upon the mind, which, when left to seek for resources solely within itself, will unavoidably, in hours of gloom and despondency brood over corroding thoughts that prey upon the spirits, and sometimes terminate in confirmed misanthropy—especially with those who, from constitution, or early misfortunes, are inclined to melancholy, and to view human nature in its dark shades. And have I not cause for gloomy reflections? The utter loneliness of my lot would alone have rendered existence a curse to one whose heart nature has formed glowing with all the warmth of social affection, yet without an object on which to place it—without one natural connexion, one earthly friend to appeal to, to shield me from the contempt, indignities and insults to which my deserted situation continually exposes me."

I am giving long extracts from this letter, yet I cannot refrain from subjoining another, which depicts her feelings with respect to Newstead.

"Permit me, madam, again to request your and Colonel Wildman's acceptance of those acknowledgements which I cannot too often repeat for your unexampled goodness to a rude stranger. I know I ought not to have taken advantage of your extreme good nature so frequently as I have. I should have absented myself from your garden during the stay of the company at the Abbey, but, as I knew I must be gone long before they would leave it, I could not deny myself the indulgence, as you so freely gave me your permisson to continue my walks, but now they are at an end. I have taken my last farewell of every dear and interesting spot, which I now never hope to see again, unless my disembodied spirit may be permitted to revisit them.—Yet O! if Providence should enable me again to support myself with any degree of respectability, and you should grant me some little humble shed, with what joy shall I return and renew my delightful rambles. But dear as Newstead is to me, I will never again come under the same unhappy circumstances as I have this last time—never without the means of at least securing myself from contempt. How dear, how very dear Newstead is to me, how unconquerable the infatuation that possesses me I am now going to give a too convincing proof. In offering to your acceptance the worthless trifles that will accompany this I hope you will believe that I have no view to your amusement. I dare not hope that the consideration of their being the products of your own garden, and most of them written there, in my little tablet, while sitting at the foot of *my Altar*—I could not, I cannot resist the earnest desire of leaving this poor memorial of the many happy hours I have there enjoyed. Oh! do not reject them, madam, suffer them to remain with you, and if you should deign to honor them with a perusal, when you read them repress, if you can, the smile that I know will too naturally arise, when you recollect the appearance of the wretched being who has dared to devote her whole soul to the contemplation of such more than human excellence. Yet ridiculous as such devotion may appear to some I must take leave to say, that if the sentiments which I have entertained for that exalted being could be duly appreciated, I trust they would be found to be of such a nature as is no dishonor even for him to have inspired." * * *

"I am now coming to take a last, last view of scenes too deeply impressed upon my memory ever to be effaced even by madness itself. O madam! may you never know, nor be able to conceive the agony I endure in tearing myself from all that the world contains of dear and sacred to me: the only spot on earth where I can ever hope for peace or comfort—May every blessing the world has to bestow attend you, or rather, may you long, long live in the enjoyment of the delights of your own paradise, in sweet seclusion from a world that has no real blessings to bestow. Now I go—but O might I dare to hope that when you are enjoying these blissful scenes, a thought of the unhappy wanderer might sometimes cross your minds, how soothing would such an idea be, if I dared to indulge it—Could you see my heart at this moment, how needless would it be to assure you of the respectful gratitude, the affectionate esteem this heart must ever bear you both."

The effect of this letter upon the sensitive heart of Mrs. Wildman may be more readily conceived than expressed. Her first impulse was to give a home to this poor homeless being, and to fix her in the midst of those scenes which formed her earthly paradise. She communicated her wishes to Colonel Wildman and they met with an immediate response in his generous bosom. It was settled on the spot that an apartment should be fitted up for the little White Lady in one of the new farm houses, and every arrangement made for her comfortable and permanent maintenance on the estate. With a woman's prompt benevolence Mrs. Wildman, before she laid her head upon her pillow, wrote the following letter to the destitute stranger.

Newstead Abbey,
Tuesday night, Sept. 20th, 1825.

Dear Madam,

On retiring to my bed chamber this evening I have opened your letter and cannot lose a moment in expressing to you the strong interest which it has excited both in Colonel Wildman and myself, from the details of your peculiar situation, and the delicate, and let me add elegant language in which they are conveyed. I am anxious that my note should reach you previous to your intended departure from this neighborhood and should be truly happy if by any arrangement for your accommodation, I could prevent the necessity of your undertaking the journey. Colonel Wildman begs me to assure you that he will use his best exertion in the investigation of those matters which you have confided to him, and should you remain here at present, or return again after a short absence, I trust we shall find means to become better acquainted, and to convince you of the interest I feel, and the real satisfaction it would afford me to contribute in any way to your comfort and happiness. I will only now add my thanks for the little packet which I received with your letter, and I must confess that the letter has so entirely engrossed my attention, that I have not as yet had time for the attentive perusal of its companion.

                          Believe me, Dear Madam
                             with sincere good wishes
                                    Yours truly
                                 Louisa Wildman.

Early the next morning a servant was despatched with the letter to the Weir Mill farm, but returned with the information that the little White Lady had set off, before his arrival, in company with the farmer's wife, in a cart for Nottingham, to take her place in the coach for London. Mrs. Wildman ordered him to mount horse instantly, follow with all speed, and deliver the letter into her hands before the departure of the coach.

The bearer of good tidings spared neither whip nor spur and arrived at Nottingham on a gallop. On entering the town a crowd obstructed him in the principal street. He checked his horse to make his way through it quietly. As the crowd opened to the right and left he beheld a human body lying on the pavement.—It was the corpse of the little White Lady!

It seems that on arriving in town and dismounting from the cart the farmer's wife had parted with her to go on an errand, and the White Lady continued on toward the coach office. In crossing a street a cart came along driven at a rapid rate. The driver called out to her, but she was too deaf to hear his voice or the rattling of his cart. In an instant she was knocked down by the horse, the wheels passed over her body and she died without a groan.

                             THE END.

LEGENDS OF
THE CONQUEST OF SPAIN

Malaga

Redrawn from an old print for *The Crayon Miscellany* Spanish Papers (G. P. Putnam's Sons, Holly Edition, 1895).

PREFACE

Few events in history have been so signal and striking in their main circumstances, and so overwhelming and enduring in their consequences as that of the Conquest of Spain by the Saracens; yet there are few where the motives and characters and actions of the agents have been envelloped in more doubt and contradiction. As in the memorable story of the Fall of Troy, we have to make out, as well as we can, the veritable details through the mists of poetic fiction; yet poetry has so combined itself with, and lent its magic colouring to every fact, that, to strip it away, would be to reduce the story to a meagre skeleton and rob it of all its charms. The storm of Moslem invasion that swept so suddenly over the peninsula, silenced for a time the faint voice of the muse, and drove the sons of learning from their cells. The pen was thrown aside to grasp the sword and spear, and men were too much taken up with battling against the evils which beset them on every side, to find time or inclination to record them.

When the nation had recovered in some degree from the effects of this astounding blow, or rather, had become accustomed to the tremendous reverse which it produced; and sage men sought to enquire and write the particulars, it was too late to ascertain them in their exact verity. The gloom and melancholy that had overshadowed the land had given birth to a thousand superstitious fancies: the woes and terrors of the past were clothed with supernatural miracles and portents, and the actors in the fearful drama had already assumed the dubious characteristics of romance. Or if a writer from among the conquerors undertook to touch upon the theme, it was embellished with all the wild extravagancies of an Oriental imagination; which afterwards stole into the graver works of the monkish historians.

Hence the earliest chronicles which treat of the downfall of Spain are apt to be tinctured with those saintly miracles which savour of the pious labours of the cloister, or those fanciful fictions that betray their Arabian authors. Yet from these apocryphal sources the most legitimate and accredited Spanish histories have taken their rise, as pure rivers may be traced up to the fens and mantled pools of a morass. It is true the authors, with cautious discrimination, have discarded those particulars too startling for belief, and have culled only such as, from their probability and congruity, might be safely recorded as historical facts; yet scarce one of these but has been connected in the original with some romantic fiction, and, even in its divorced state, bears traces of its former alliance.

To discard, however, every thing wild and marvellous in this portion of Spanish history, is to discard some of its most beautiful, instructive and national features; it is to judge of Spain by the standard of probability suited to tamer and more prosaic countries. Spain is virtually a land of poetry and romance, where every-day life partakes of adventure, and where the least agitation or excitement carries every thing up into extravagant enterprize and daring exploit. The Spaniards, in all ages, have been of swelling and braggart spirit, soaring in thought, pompous in word and valiant, though vain glorious, in deed. Their heroic aims have transcended the cooler conceptions of their neighbors, and their reckless daring has borne them on to achievements which prudent enterprize could never have accomplished. Since the time too of the conquest and occupation of their country by the Arabs, a strong infusion of Oriental magnificence has entered into the national character, and rendered the Spaniard distinct from every other nation of Europe.

In the following pages, therefore, the author has ventured to dip more deeply into the enchanted fountains of old Spanish chronicle, than has usually been done by those who in modern times have treated of the eventful period of the conquest; but in so doing he trusts he will illustrate more fully the character of the people and the times. He has thought proper to throw these records into the form of legends, not claiming for them the authenticity of sober history, yet giving nothing that has not historical foundation. All the facts herein contained, however extravagant some of them may be deemed, will be found in the works of sage and reverend chroniclers of yore, growing side by side with long acknowledged truths, and might be supported by learned and imposing references in the margin.

THE LEGEND OF DON RODERICK*

CHAPTER I

Of the ancient inhabitants of Spain—Of the misrule of Witiza the Wicked.

Spain, or Iberia, as it was called in ancient days, has been a country harassed from the earliest times, by the invader. The Celts, the Greeks, the Phenecians, the Carthaginians by turns, or simultaneously, infringed its territories; drove the native Iberians from their rightful homes, and established colonies and founded cities in the land. It subsequently fell into the all grasping power of Rome remaining for some time a subjugated province, and when that gigantic empire crumbled into pieces the Suevi, the Alani and the Vandals, those barbarians of the north, overran and ravaged this devoted country and portioned out the soil among them.

Their sway was not of long duration. In the fifth century the goths, who were then the allies of Rome, undertook the reconquest of Iberia, and succeeded after a desperate struggle of three years duration. They drove before them the barbarous hordes, their predecessors, intermarried and incorporated themselves with the original inhabitants, and founded a powerful and splendid empire, comprizing the Iberian peninsula, the ancient Narbonnaise, afterwards called Gallia gotica, or Gothic gaul, and a part of the African coast called Tingitania.

A new nation was, in a manner, produced by this mixture of the goths and the Iberians. Sprang from a union of warrior races, reared and nurtured amidst the din of arms, the Gothic Spaniards, if they may so be termed, were a warlike, unquiet, yet high minded and heroic people. Their simple and abstemious habits, their contempt for toil and suffering, and their love of daring enterprize fitted them for a soldier's life. So addicted were they to war that, when they had no external foes to contend with, they fought with one another; and, when

*Many of the facts in this legend are taken from an old chronicle written in quaint and antiquated Spanish and professing to be a translation from the Arabian chronicle of the Moor Rasis by Mohammed a Moslem writer, and Gil Perez a Spanish priest. It is supposed to be a piece of literary mosaic work, made up from both Spanish and Arabian chronicles: yet from this work most of the Spanish historians have drawn their particulars relative to the fortunes of Don Roderick.

engaged in battle, says an old chronicler, the very thunders and lightnings of heaven could not separate them.*

For two centuries and a half the gothic power remained unshaken; and the sceptre was wielded by twenty five successive kings. The crown was elective, in a council of palatines, composed of the Bishops and the nobles, who, while they swore allegiance to the newly made sovereign, bound him by a reciprocal oath, to be faithful to his trust. Their choice was made from among the people, subject only to one condition, that the king should be of pure gothic blood. But though the crown was elective in principle it gradually became hereditary from usage, and the power of the sovereign grew to be almost absolute. The king was commander in chief of the armies; the whole patronage of the kingdom was in his hands; he summoned and dissolved the national councils; he made and revoked laws according to his pleasure, and, having ecclesiastical supremacy, he exercised a sway even over the consciences of his subjects.

The goths at the time of their inroad were stout adherents to the Arian doctrines, but after a time they embraced the Catholic faith, which was maintained by the native Spaniards free from many of the gross superstitions of the church at Rome, and this unity of faith contributed more than anything else, to blend and harmonize the two races into one. The Bishops and other clergy were exemplary in their lives, and aided to promote the influence of the laws and maintain the authority of the state. The fruits of regular and secure government were manifest in the advancement of agriculture, commerce and the peaceful arts, and in the encrease of wealth, of luxury and refinement, but there was a gradual decline of the simple, hardy, and warlike habits that had distinguished the nation in its semi barbarous days.

Such was the state of Spain when in the year of Redemption 701, Witiza was elected to the gothic throne. The beginning of his reign gave promise of happy days to Spain. He redressed grievances, moderated the tributes of his subjects, and conducted himself with mingled mildness and energy in the administration of the laws. In a little while, however, he threw off the mask, and shewed himself in his true nature, cruel and luxurious.

Two of his relatives, sons of a preceding king awakened his jealousy for the security of his throne. One of them named Favila, Duke of Cantabria he put to death and would have inflicted the same fate upon his son Pelayo, but that the youth was beyond his reach, being preserved by providence for the future salvation of Spain. The other object of

*Florian de Ocampo, lib. 3. c. 12. Justin Abrev. Pomp. L44 Bleda. Cronica L2. c. 3.

his suspicion was Theodofredo, who lived retired from court. The violence of Witiza reached him even in his retirement. His eyes were put out and he was immured within a castle at Cordova. Roderick, the youthful son of Theodofredo, escaped to Italy, where he received protection from the Romans.

Witiza now considering himself secure upon the throne gave the reins to his licentious passions and soon by his tyranny and sensuality acquired the appellation of Witiza the Wicked. Despising the old gothic continence, and yielding to the example of the sect of Mahomet, which suited his lascivious temperament, he indulged in a plurality of wives and concubines, encouraging his subjects to do the same. Nay he even sought to gain the sanction of the church to his excesses, promulgating a law by which the clergy were released from their vows of celibacy and permitted to marry and to entertain paramours.

The Sovereign Pontiff Constantine threatened to depose and excommunicate him unless he abrogated his licentious law, but Witiza set him at defiance, threatening, like his gothic predecessor Alaric, to assail the eternal city with his troops and make spoil of her accumulated treasures.* "We will adorn our damsels," said he, "with the jewels of Rome and replenish our coffers from the mint of St. Peter."

Some of the clergy opposed themselves to the innovating spirit of the monarch and endeavoured from the pulpits to rally the people to the pure doctrines of their faith, but they were deposed from their sacred office, and banished as seditious mischief makers. The church of Toledo continued refractory: the archbishop Sindaredo, it is true, was disposed to accommodate himself to the corruptions of the times, but the prebendaries battled intrepidly against the new laws of the monarch, and stood manfully in defence of their vows of chastity. "Since the church of Toledo will not yield itself to our will," said Witiza, "it shall have two husbands." So saying he appointed his own brother Oppas, at that time archbishop of Seville, to take a seat with Sindaredo in the Episcopal chair of Toledo, and made him primate of Spain. He was a priest after his own heart and seconded him in all his profligate abuses.

It was in vain the denunciations of the church were fulminated from the chair of St. Peter: Witiza threw off all allegiance to the Roman Pontiff, threatening with pain of death, those who should obey the Papal mandates. "We will suffer no foreign ecclesiastic, with triple crown," said he, "to domineer over our dominions."

The Jews had been banished from the country during the preceding reign, but Witiza permitted them to return, and even bestowed upon their synagogues privileges of which he had despoiled the churches.

*Chron. de Luitprando 709. Abarca. Anales de Aragon (el Mahometismo, Fol. 5.)

The children of Israel, when scattered throughout the earth by the fall of Jerusalem, had carried with them into other lands the gainful arcana of traffic, and were especially noted as opulent money changers and curious dealers in gold and silver and precious stones; on this occasion, therefore, they were enabled, it is said, to repay the monarch for his protection by bags of money and caskets of sparkling gems, the rich product of their Oriental commerce.

The kingdom at this time enjoyed external peace, but there were symptoms of internal discontent. Witiza took the alarm; he remembered the ancient turbulence of the nation and its proneness to internal feuds. Issuing secret orders, therefore, in all directions, he dismantled most of the cities; and demolished the castles and fortresses that might serve as rallying points for the factious. He disarmed the people also and converted the weapons of war into the implements of peace. It seemed, in fact, as if the millennium were dawning upon the land, for the sword was beaten into a plowshare and the spear into a pruning hook.

While thus the ancient martial fire of the nation was extinguished its morals likewise were corrupted. The altars were abandoned, the churches closed, wide disorder and sensuality prevailed throughout the land, so that, according to the old chroniclers, within the compass of a few short years "Witiza the Wicked taught all Spain to sin."

CHAPTER II

The rise of Don Roderick—His government.

Woe to the ruler who founds his hope of sway on the weakness or corruption of the people. The very measures taken by Witiza to perpetuate his power ensured his downfall. While the whole nation, under his licentious rule was sinking into vice and effeminacy, and the arm of war was unstrung, the youthful Roderick, son of Theodofredo, was training up for action in the stern but wholesome school of adversity. He instructed himself in the use of arms; became adroit and vigorous by varied exercises, learned to despise all danger, and enured himself to hunger and watchfulness and the rigour of the seasons.

His merits and misfortunes procured him many friends among the Romans; and when, being arrived at a fitting age, he undertook to revenge the wrongs of his father and his kindred, a host of brave and hardy soldiers flocked to his standard. With these he made his sudden appearance in Spain. The friends of his house and the disaffected of all classes hastened to join him, and he advanced rapidly and without opposition, through an unarmed and enervated land.

Witiza saw too late the evil he had brought upon himself. He made a hasty levy, and took the field with a scantily equipped and undisciplined host, but was easily routed and made prisoner, and the whole kingdom submitted to Don Roderick.

The ancient city of Toledo, the royal residence of the gothic kings was the scene of high festivity and solemn ceremonial on the coronation of the victor. Whether he was elected to the throne according to the gothic usage, or seized it by the right of conquest, is a matter of dispute among historians, but all agree that the nation submitted cheerfully to his sway, and looked forward to prosperity and happiness under their newly elevated monarch. His appearance and character seemed to justify the anticipation. He was in the splendour of youth and of a majestic presence. His soul was bold and daring and elevated by lofty desires. He had a sagacity that penetrated the thoughts of men and a magnificent spirit that won all hearts. Such is the picture which ancient writers give of Don Roderick, when, with all the stern and simple virtues unimpaired, which he had acquired in adversity and exile, and flushed with the triumph of a pious revenge, he ascended the gothic throne.

Prosperity, however, is the real touchstone of the human heart; no sooner did Roderick find himself in possession of the crown, than the love of power, and the jealousy of rule were awakened in his breast. His first measure was against Witiza who was brought in chains into his presence. Roderick beheld the captive monarch with an unpitying eye, remembering only his wrongs and cruelties to his father. "Let the evil he has inflicted on others be visited upon his own head," said he. "As he did unto Theodofredo even so be it done unto him." So the eyes of Witiza were put out, and he was thrown into the same dungeon at Cordova in which Theodofredo had languished. There he passed the brief remnant of his days in perpetual darkness a prey to wretchedness and remorse.

Roderick now cast an uneasy and suspicious eye upon Evan and Siseburto the two sons of Witiza. Fearful lest they should foment some secret rebellion he banished them the kingdom. They took refuge in the Spanish dominions in Africa, where they were received and harboured by Requila, Governor of Tangier, out of gratitude for favours which he had received from their late father. There they remained, to brood over their fallen fortunes and to aid in working out the future woes of Spain.

Their uncle Oppas, Bishop of Seville, who had been made co-partner, by Witiza, in the Archepiscopal chair at Toledo, would have likewise fallen under the suspicion of the king; but he was a man of consummate art, and vast exterior sanctity, and won upon the good graces of the monarch. He was suffered, therefore, to retain his sacred office at

Seville; but the See of Toledo was given in charge to the venerable Urbino; and the law of Witiza was revoked that dispensed the clergy from their vows of celibacy.

The jealousy of Roderick for the security of his crown was soon again aroused and his measures were prompt and severe. Having been informed that the governors of certain castles and fortresses in Castile and Andalusia had conspired against him he caused them to be put to death and their strong holds to be demolished. He now went on to imitate the pernicious policy of his predecessor, throwing down walls and towers, disarming the people and thus incapacitating them from rebellion. A few cities were permitted to retain their fortifications, but these were entrusted to alcaydes in whom he had especial confidence; the greater part of the kingdom was left defenceless; the nobles, who had been roused to temporary manhood during the recent stir of war, sunk back into the inglorious state of inaction which had disgraced them during the reign of Witiza, passing their time in feasting and dancing to to the sound of loose and wanton minstrelsy.* It was scarcely possible to recognize in these idle wassailers and soft voluptuaries the descendants of the stern and frugal warriors of the frozen North; who had braved flood and mountain, and heat and cold, and had battled their way to empire across half a world in arms.

They surrounded their youthful monarch, it is true, with a blaze of military pomp. Nothing could surpass the splendour of their arms, which were embossed and enamelled, and enriched with gold and jewels and curious devices; nothing could be more gallant and glorious than their array; it was all plume and pennon and silken pageantry, the gorgeous trappings for tilt and tourney and courtly revel; but the iron soul of war was wanting.

How rare it is to learn wisdom from the misfortunes of others. With the fate of Witiza full before his eyes Don Roderick indulged in the same pernicious errors, and was doomed, in like manner, to prepare the way for his own perdition.

CHAPTER III

Of the loves of Roderick and the Princess Elyata.

As yet the heart of Roderick, occupied by the struggles of his early life, by warlike enterprizes and by the inquietudes of newly gotten power, had been insensible to the charms of women, but in the present

*Mariana. Hist. Esp. L6. c. 21.

voluptuous calm the amorous propensities of his nature assumed their sway. There are divers accounts of the youthful beauty who first found favour in his eyes and was elevated by him to the throne. We follow in our legend the details of an Arabian chronicler,* authenticated by a Spanish poet.† Let those who dispute our facts produce better authority for their contradiction.

Among the few fortified places that had not been dismantled by Don Roderick was the ancient city of Denia, situated on the Mediterranean coast, and defended on a rock built castle that overlooked the sea.

The Alcayde of the castle with many of the people of Denia was one day on his knees in the chapel, imploring the Virgin to allay a tempest which was strewing the coast with wrecks, when a centinel brought word that a moorish cruiser was standing for the land. The Alcayde gave orders to ring the alarm bells and light signal fires on the hill tops and rouse the country, for the coast was subject to cruel maraudings from the Barbary cruisers.

In a little while the horsemen of the neighborhood were seen pricking along the beach, armed with such weapons as they could find, and the Alcayde and his scanty garrison descended from the hill. In the mean time the moorish bark came rolling and pitching towards the land. As it drew near, the rich carving and gilding with which it was decorated; its silken bandaroles and banks of crimson oars shewed it to be no warlike vessel, but a sumptuous galliot destined for state and ceremony. It bore the marks of the tempest; the masts were broken, the oars shattered and fragments of snowy sails and silken awnings were fluttering in the blast.

As the galliot grounded upon the the sand the impatient rabble rushed into the surf to capture and make spoil; but were awed into admiration and respect by the appearance of the illustrious company on board. There were moors of both sexes sumptuously arrayed, and adorned with precious jewels, bearing the demeanour of persons of lofty rank. Among them shone conspicuous a youthful beauty, magnificently attired, to whom all seemed to pay reverence.

Several of the moors surrounded her with drawn swords, threatening death to any that approached; others sprang from the bark and throwing themselves on their knees before the Alcayde, implored him by his honour and courtesy as a knight, to protect a royal virgin from injury and insult.

"You behold before you," said they, "the only daughter of the King of Algiers, the betrothed bride of the son of the King of Tunis. We

---

*Perdida de España por Abulcacim Tarif Abentarique, lib. 1.
†Lope de Vega.

were conducting her to the court of her expecting bridegroom, when a tempest drove us from our course, and compelled us to take refuge on your coast. Be not more cruel than the tempest but deal nobly with that which even sea and storm have spared."

The Alcayde listened to their prayers. He conducted the princess and her train to the castle, where every honour due to her rank was paid her. Some of her ancient attendants interceded for her liberation, promising countless sums to be paid by her father for her ransom; but the Alcayde turned a deaf ear to all their golden offers. "She is a royal captive," said he, "it belongs to my sovereign alone to dispose of her." After she had reposed, therefore, for some days at the castle, and recovered from the fatigue and terror of the seas, he caused her to be conducted, with all her train, in magnificent state to the court of Don Roderick.

The beautiful Elyata* entered Toledo more like a triumphant sovereign than a captive. A chosen band of christian horsemen splendidly armed, appeared to wait upon her as a mere guard of honour. She was surrounded by the moorish damsels of her train and followed by her own moslem guards, all attired with the magnificence that had been intended to grace her arrival at the court of Tunis. The princess was arrayed in bridal robes, woven in the most costly looms of the Orient; her diadem sparkled with diamonds and was decorated with the rarest plumes of the bird of paradise, and even the silken trappings of her palfrey, which swept the ground, were covered with pearls and precious stones. As this brilliant cavalcade crossed the bridge of the Tagus all Toledo poured forth to behold it, and nothing was heard throughout the city but praises of the wonderful beauty of the princess of Algiers.

King Roderick came forth, attended by the chivalry of his court, to receive the royal captive. His recent voluptuous life had disposed him for tender and amorous affections, and at the first sight of the beautiful Elyata he was enraptured with her charms. Seeing her face clouded with sorrow and anxiety he soothed her with gentle and courteous words, and conducting her to a royal palace, "Behold," said he, "thy habitation, where no one shall molest thee. Consider thyself at home in the mansion of thy father, and dispose of any thing according to thy will."

Here the princess passed her time with the female attendants who had accompanied her from Algiers, and no one but the king was permitted to visit her; who daily became more and more enamoured of his lovely captive; and sought by tender assiduity, to gain her affections. The distress of the princess at her captivity was soothed by this gentle treatment. She was of an age when sorrow cannot long hold sway over

*By some she is called Zara.

the heart. Accompanied by her youthful attendants she ranged the spacious apartments of the palace and sported among the groves and alleys of its garden. Every day the remembrance of the paternal home grew less and less painful and the king became more and more amiable in her eyes, and when at length he offered to share his heart and throne with her, she listened with down cast looks and kindling blushes, but with an air of resignation.

One obstacle remained to the complete fruition of the monarch's wishes, and this was the religion of the princess. Roderick forthwith employed the archbishop of Toledo to instruct the beautiful Elyata in the mysteries of the christian faith. The female intellect is quick at perceiving the merits of new doctrines; the archbishop, therefore, soon succeeded in converting, not merely the princess, but most of her attendants, and a day was appointed for their public baptism. The ceremony was performed with great pomp and solemnity, in the presence of all the nobility and chivalry of the court. The princess and her damsels, clad in white, walked on foot to the cathedral, while numerous beautiful children, arrayed as angels, strewed their path with flowers and the archbishop, meeting them at the portal, received them, as it were, into the bosom of the church. The princess abandoned her moorish appellation of Elyata, and was baptised by the name of Exilona, by which she was thenceforth called, and has generally been known in history.

The nuptials of Roderick and the beautiful convert took place shortly afterwards and were celebrated with great magnificence. There were jousts and tourneys and banquets and other rejoicings which lasted twenty days, and were attended by the principal nobles from all parts of Spain. After these were over such of the attendants of the princess as refused to embrace christianity and desired to return to Africa, were dismissed with munificent presents, and an embassy was sent to the King of Algiers to inform him of the nuptials of his daughter, and to proffer him the friendship of King Roderick.*

*"Como esta Infanta era muy hermosa, y el Rey [Don Rodrigo] dispuesto y gentil hombre, entro por medio el amor y aficion, y junto con el regalo, con que la avia mandado hospedar y servir ful causa que el Rey persuadio esta Infanta, quo si se tornava a su ley de christiano la tomaria por muger, y que la haria señora de sus Reynos. Con esta persuasion ella fue contenta, y aviendose vuelto christiana, se caso con ella, y se celebraron sus bodas con muchas fiestas y regozijos, como era razon."—Abulcassim, Conq'st de Espan. cap. 3.

CHAPTER IV

Of Count Julian.

For a time Don Roderick lived happily with his young and beautiful Queen, and Toledo was the seat of festivity and splendor. The principal nobles throughout the kingdom repaired to his court to pay him homage, and to receive his commands; and none were more devoted in their reverence than those who were obnoxious to suspicion from their connexions with the late king.

Among the foremost of these was Count Julian, a man destined to be infamously renowned in the dark story of his country's woes. He was of one of the proudest gothic families, lord of Consuegra and Algeziras, and connected by marriage with Witiza and the Bishop Oppas; his wife, the Countess Frandina being their sister. In consequence of this connexion, and of his own merits, he had enjoyed the highest dignities and commands, being one of the Espatorios or Royal sword bearers; an office of the greatest confidence about the person of the sovereign.* He had moreover been entrusted with the military government of the Spanish possessions on the African coast of the strait, which at that time were threatened by the Arabs of the East, the followers of Mahomet, who were advancing their victorious standard to the extremity of Western Africa. Count Julian established his seat of government at Ceuta, the frontier bulwark and one of the far famed gates of the Mediterranean Sea. Here he boldly faced and held in check the torrent of moslem invasion.

Don Julian was a man of an active but irregular genius, and a grasping ambition; he had a love for power and grandeur, in which he was joined by his haughty countess; and they could ill brook the downfall of their house as threatened by the fate of Witiza. They had hastened, therefore, to pay their court to the newly elevated monarch, and to assure him of their fidelity to his interests.

Roderick was readily persuaded of the sincerity of Count Julian; he was aware of his merits as a soldier and a governor and continued him in his important command: honouring him with many other marks of implicit confidence. Count Julian sought to confirm this confidence by every proof of devotion. It was a custom among the goths to rear many of the children of the most illustrious families in the royal household. They served as pages to the king and hand maids and ladies of honour

---

*Condes Espatorios; so called from the drawn swords of ample size and breadth, with which they kept guard in the antechambers of the gothic kings. Comes Spathariorum, custodum corporis Regis Profectus. Hunc et Propospatharium appellatum existimo.—Patr. Pant. de Offic. Goth.

to the queen, and were instructed in all manner of accomplishments befitting their gentle blood. When about to depart for Ceuta to resume his command Don Julian brought his daughter Florinda to present her to the sovereigns. She was a beautiful virgin that had not as yet attained to womanhood. "I confide her to your protection," said he to the king, "to be unto her as a father; and to have her trained in the paths of virtue. I can leave with you no dearer pledge of my loyalty."

King Roderick received the timid and blushing maiden into his paternal care; promising to watch over her happiness with a parent's eye, and that she should be enrolled among the most cherished attendants of the queen. With this assurance of the welfare of his child Count Julian departed well pleased, for his government at Ceuta.

CHAPTER V

The story of Florinda.

The beautiful daughter of Count Julian was received with great favour by the Queen Exilona and admitted among the noble damsels that attended upon her person. Here she lived in honour and apparent security, and surrounded by innocent delights. To gratify his Queen, Don Roderick had built for her rural recreation a palace without the walls of Toledo, on the banks of the Tagus. It stood in the midst of a garden adorned after the luxurious style of the East. The air was perfumed by fragrant shrubs and flowers; the groves resounded with the song of the nightingale while the gush of fountains and waterfalls, and the distant murmur of the Tagus, made it a delightful retreat during the sultry days of summer. The charm of perfect privacy also reigned throughout the place, for the garden walls were high, and numerous guards kept watch without to protect it from all intrusion.

In this delicious abode, more befitting an Oriental voluptuary than a gothic king, Don Roderick was accustomed to while away much of that time which should have been devoted to the toilsome cares of government. The very security and peace which he had produced throughout his dominions by his precautions to abolish the means and habitudes of war, had effected a disastrous change in his character. The hardy and heroic qualities which had conducted him to the throne, were softened in the lap of indulgence. Surrounded by the pleasures of an idle and effeminate court, and beguiled by the example of his degenerate nobles, he gave way to a fatal sensuality that had lain dormant in his nature during the virtuous days of his adversity. The mere love of female beauty had first enamoured him of Exilona and the same passion, fostered by voluptuous idleness, now betrayed him into the commission of an act, fatal to himself and Spain. The following is the story of his error as gathered from ancient chronicle and legend.

In a remote part of the palace was an apartment devoted to the Queen. It was like an Eastern harem, shut up from the foot of man, and where the king himself but rarely entered. It had its own courts, and gardens and fountains, where the Queen was wont to recreate herself with her damsels, as she had been accustomed to do in the jealous privacy of her father's palace.

One sultry day the king, instead of taking his siesta, or mid day slumber, repaired to this apartment to seek the society of the Queen. In passing through a small oratory he was drawn, by the sound of female voices to a casement overhung with myrtles and jessamines. It looked into an interior garden or court, set out with orange trees, in the midst of which was a marble fountain surrounded by a grassy bank enamelled with flowers.

It was the high noon tide of a summer day, when, in sultry Spain, the landscape trembles to the eye and all nature seeks repose except the grasshopper, that pipes his lulling note to the herdsman as he sleeps beneath the shade.

Around the fountain were several of the damsels of the Queen, who, confident of the sacred privacy of the place, were yielding in that cool retreat to the indulgence prompted by the season and the hour. Some lay asleep on the flowery bank; others sat on the margin of the fountain, talking and laughing, as they bathed their feet in its limpid waters, and King Roderick beheld delicate limbs shining through the wave, that might rival the marble in whiteness.

Among the damsels was one who had come from the Barbary coast with the Queen. Her complexion had the dark tinge of Mauritania, but it was clear and transparent and the deep rich rose blushed through the lovely brown. Her eyes were black and full of fire, and flashed from under long silken eyelashes.

A sportive contest arose among the maidens as to the comparative beauty of the Spanish and moorish forms; but the Mauritanian damsel revealed limbs of voluptuous symmetry that seemed to defy all rivalry.

The Spanish beauties were on the point of giving up the contest when they bethought themselves of the young Florinda, the daughter of Count Julian, who lay on the grassy bank, abandoned to a summer slumber. The soft glow of youth and health mantled on her cheek; her fringed eyelashes scarcely covered their sleeping orbs, her moist and ruby lips were lightly parted, just revealing a gleam of her ivory teeth, while her innocent bosom rose and fell beneath her boddice, like the gentle swelling and sinking of a tranquil sea. There was a breathing tenderness and beauty in the sleeping virgin, that seemed to send forth sweetness like the flowers around her.

"Behold," cried her companions exultingly, "the champion of Spanish beauty!"

In their playful eagerness they half disrobed the innocent Florinda before she was aware. She awoke in time, however, to escape from their busy hands; but enough of her charms had been revealed to convince the monarch that they were not to be rivalled by the rarest beauties of Mauritania.

From this day the heart of Roderick was inflamed with a fatal passion. He gazed on the beautiful Florinda with fervid desire and sought to read in her looks whether there was levity or wantonness in her bosom, but the eye of the damsel ever sunk beneath his gaze and remained bent on the earth in virgin modesty.

It was in vain he called to mind the sacred trust reposed in him by Count Julian, and the promise he had given to watch over his daughter with paternal care, his heart was vitiated by sensual indulgence, and the consciousness of power had rendered him selfish in his gratifications.

Being one evening in the garden where the Queen was diverting herself with her damsels, and coming to the fountain where he had beheld the innocent maidens at their sport, he could no longer restrain the passion that raged within his breast. Seating himself beside the fountain he called Florinda to him to draw forth a thorn which had pierced his hand. The maiden knelt at his feet; to examine his hand, and the touch of her slender fingers thrilled through his veins. As she knelt too her amber locks fell in rich ringlets about her beautiful head, her innocent bosom palpitated beneath the crimson boddice, and her timid blushes increased the effulgence of her charms.

Having examined the monarch's hand in vain she looked up in his face with artless perplexity.

"Señor," said she, "I can find no thorn, nor any sign of wound."

Don Roderick grasped her hand and pressed it to his heart. "It is here, lovely Florinda!" said he, "It is here! and thou alone canst pluck it forth!"

"My lord!" exclaimed the blushing and astonished maiden.

"Florinda!" said Don Roderick, "Dost thou love me?"

"Señor," replied she, "my father taught me to love and reverence you. He confided me to your care as one who would be as a parent to me, when he should be far distant, serving your majesty with life and loyalty. May God incline your majesty ever to protect me as a father." So saying the maiden dropped her eyes to the ground and continued kneeling; but her countenance had become deadly pale, and as she knelt she trembled.

"Florinda," said the king, "either thou dost not, or thou wilt not understand me. I would have thee love me, not as a father, nor as a monarch, but as one who adores thee. Why dost thou start? No one shall know our loves; and moreover, the love of a monarch inflicts no degradation like the love of a common man. Riches and honours attend upon it. I will advance thee to rank and dignity, and place thee above the proudest females of my court. Thy father too shall be more exalted and endowed than any noble in my realm."

The soft eye of Florinda kindled at these words. "Señor," said she, "the line I spring from can receive no dignity by means so vile; and my father would rather die than purchase rank and power by the dishonour of his child. But I see," continued she, "that your majesty speaks in this manner only to try me. You may have thought me light and simple and unworthy to attend upon the Queen. I pray your majesty to pardon me, that I have taken your pleasantry in such serious part."

In this way the agitated maiden sought to evade the addresses of the monarch, but still her cheek was blanched, and her lip quivered as she spake.

The king pressed her hand to his lips with fervour. "May ruin seize me," cried he, "if I speak to prove thee. My heart, my kingdom are at thy command. Only be mine, and thou shalt rule absolute mistress of myself and my domains."

The damsel rose from the earth where she had hitherto knelt and her whole countenance glowed with virtuous indignation. "My lord," said she, "I am your subject, and in your power, take my life if it be your pleasure, but nothing shall tempt me to commit a crime which would be treason to the Queen, disgrace to my father, agony to my mother and perdition to myself." With these words she left the garden, and the king, for the moment, was too much awed by her indignant virtue to oppose her departure.

We shall pass briefly over the succeeding events of the story of Florinda about which so much has been said and sung by chronicler and bard: for the sober page of history should be carefully chastened from all scenes that might inflame a wanton imagination, leaving them to poems and romances and such like highly seasoned works of fantasy and recreation.

Let it suffice to say that Don Roderick pursued his suit to the beautiful Florinda, his passion being more and more inflamed by the resistance of the virtuous damsel. At length, forgetting what was due to helpless beauty, to his own honour as a knight, and his word as a sovereign, he triumphed over her weakness by base and unmanly violence.

There are not wanting those who affirm that the hapless Florinda lent a yielding ear to the solicitations of the monarch, and her name has been treated with opprobrium in several of the ancient chronicles and legendary ballads that have transmitted, from generation to generation, the story of the woes of Spain. In very truth however she appears to have been a guiltless victim, resisting as far as helpless female could resist, the arts and intrigues of a powerful monarch, who had nought to check the indulgence of his will, and bewailing her disgrace with a poignancy that shews how dearly she had prized her honour.

In the first paroxysm of her grief she wrote a letter to her father, blotted with her tears and almost incoherent from her agitation. "Would to God my father," said she, "that the earth had opened and swallowed me ere I had been reduced to write these lines. I blush to tell thee, what it is not proper to conceal. Alas my father! Thou hast entrusted thy lamb to the guardianship of the lion. Thy daughter has been dishonoured, the royal cradle of the Goths polluted and our lineage insulted and disgraced. Hasten my father, to rescue your child from the power of the spoiler, and to vindicate the honour of your house."

When Florinda had written these lines she summoned a youthful esquire who had been a page in the service of her father. "Saddle thy steed," said she, "and if thou dost aspire to knightly honour or hope for lady's grace; if thou hast fealty for thy lord or devotion to his daughter, speed swiftly upon my errand. Rest not, halt not, spare not the spur, but hie thee day and night until thou reach the sea; take the first bark and haste with sail and oar to Ceuta, nor pause until thou give this letter to the count my father."

The youth put the letter in his bosom. "Trust me lady," said he, "I will neither halt, nor turn aside, nor cast a look behind until I reach Count Julian." He mounted his fleet steed, sped his way across the bridge and soon left behind him the verdant valley of the Tagus.

CHAPTER VI

Don Roderick receives an extraordinary embassy.

The heart of Roderick was not so depraved by sensuality but that the wrong he had been guilty of toward the innocent Florinda, and the disgrace he had inflicted on her house weighed heavy on his spirit, and a cloud began to gather on his once clear and unwrinkled brow.

Heaven at this time, say the old Spanish chronicles, permitted a marvellous intimation of the wrath with which it intended to visit the monarch and his people, in punishment of their sins; nor are we, say the same orthodox writers, to startle and withhold our faith when we meet in the page of discreet and sober history with these signs and portents which transcend the probabilities of ordinary life, for the revolutions of empires and the downfall of mighty kings are awful events that shake the physical as well as the moral world, and are often announced by forerunning marvels and prodigious omens. With such like cautious preliminaries do the wary but credulous historiographers of yore usher in a marvellous event of prophecy and enchantment linked in ancient story with the fortunes of Don Roderick, but which modern doubters would fain hold up as an apocryphal tradition of Arabian origin.

Now so it happened, according to the legend, that about this time, as King Roderick was seated one day on his throne surrounded by his nobles, in the ancient city of Toledo, two men of venerable appearance entered the hall of audience. Their snowy beards descended to their breasts and their gray hairs were bound with ivy. They were arrayed in white garments of foreign or antiquated fashion, which swept the ground, and were cinctured with girdles, wrought with the signs of the zodiac, from which were suspended enormous bunches of keys of every variety of form. Having approached the throne and made obeisance, "Know oh king," said one of the old men, "that in days of yore, when Hercules of Lybia, surnamed the Strong, had set up his pillars at the ocean strait, he erected a tower near to this ancient city of Toledo. He built it of prodigious strength and finished it with magic art, shutting up within it a fearful secret, never to be penetrated without peril and disaster. To protect this terrible mystery he closed the entrance to the edifice with a ponderous door of iron, secured by a great lock of steel, and he left a command that every king who should succeed him should add another lock to the portal; denouncing woe and destruction on him who should eventually unfold the secret of the tower.

The guardianship of the portal was given to our ancestors, and has continued in our family, from generation to generation, since the days of Hercules. Several kings, from time to time, have caused the gate to be thrown open, and have attempted to enter, but have paid dearly for their temerity. Some have perished within the threshold, others have been overwhelmed with horror at tremendous sounds, which shook the foundations of the earth, and have hastened to reclose the door and secure it with its thousand locks. Thus since the days of Hercules the inmost recesses of the pile have never been penetrated by mortal man, and a profound mystery continues to prevail over this great enchantment. This, O king, is all we have to relate; and our errand is to entreat thee to repair to the tower and affix thy lock to the portal, as has been done by all thy predecessors." Having thus said, the ancient men made a profound reverence and departed from the presence chamber.*

---

*Perdida de España por Abulcasim Tarif Abentarique l. 1, c. 6. Cronica del Rey Don Rodrigo por el moro Rasis, l. 1, c. 1. Bleda. cron. cap. vii.

Don Roderick remained for some time lost in thought after the departure of the men; he then dismissed all his court excepting the venerable Urbino, at that time archbishop of Toledo. The long white beard of this prelate bespoke his advanced age, and his overhanging eyebrows shewed him a man full of wary counsel.

"Father," said the king, "I have an earnest desire to penetrate the mystery of this tower."

The worthy prelate shook his hoary head. "Beware, my son!" said he. "There are secrets hidden from man for his good. Your predecessors for many generations have respected this mystery, and have encreased in might and empire. A knowledge of it, therefore, is not material to the welfare of your kingdom. Seek not then to indulge a rash and unprofitable curiosity, which is interdicted under such awful menaces."

"Of what importance," cried the king, "are the menaces of Hercules the Lybian? Was he not a pagan; and can his enchantments have ought avail against a believer in our holy faith? Doubtless in this tower are locked up treasures of gold and jewels, amassed in days of old, the spoils of mighty kings, the riches of the pagan world. My coffers are exhausted; I have need of supply: and surely it would be an acceptable act in the eyes of heaven, to draw forth this wealth which lies buried under profane and necromantic spells, and consecrate it to religious purposes."

The venerable archbishop still continued to remonstrate, but Don Roderick heeded not his counsel for he was led on by his malignant star. "Father," said he, "it is in vain you attempt to dissuade me. My resolution is fixed. Tomorrow I will explore the hidden mystery, or rather the hidden treasures of this tower."

CHAPTER VII

Story of the marvellous and portentous tower.

The morning sun shone brightly upon the cliff built towers of Toledo when King Roderick issued out of the gate of the city at the head of a numerous train of courtiers and cavaliers, and crossed the bridge that bestrides the deep rocky bed of the Tagus. The shining cavalcade wound up the road that leads among the mountains, and soon came in sight of the necromantic tower.

Of this renowned edifice marvels are related by the ancient Arabian and Spanish chroniclers, "and I doubt much," adds the venerable Agapida, "whether many readers will not consider the whole as a cunningly devised fable, sprung from an oriental imagination; but it is not for me to reject a fact which is recorded by all those writers who are the fathers of our national history; a fact too, which is as well attested as most of the remarkable events in the story of Don Roderick. None but light and inconsiderate minds," continues the good Friar, "do hastily reject the marvellous. To the thinking mind the whole world is envelloped in mystery, and every thing is full of type and portent. To such a mind the necromantic tower of Toledo will appear as one of those wondrous monuments of the olden time, one of those Egyptian and Chaldaic piles, storied with hidden wisdom and mystic prophecy, which have been devised in past ages, when man yet enjoyed an intercourse with high and spiritual natures, and when human foresight partook of divination."

This singular tower was round and of great height and grandeur, erected upon a lofty rock and surrounded by crags and precipices. The foundation was supported by four brazen lions, each taller than a cavalier on horseback. The walls were built of small pieces of jasper and various coloured marbles, not larger than a man's hand; so subtilely joined however that but for their different hues they might be taken for one entire stone. They were arranged with marvellous cunning so as to represent battles and warlike deeds of times and heroes long since passed away, and the whole surface was so admirably polished that the stones were as lustrous as glass, and reflected the rays of the sun with such resplendent brightness as to dazzle all beholders.*

King Roderick and his courtiers arrived wondering and amazed at the foot of the rock. Here there was a narrow arched way cut through the living stone; the only entrance to the tower. It was closed by a massive iron gate, covered with rusty locks, of divers workmanship and in the fashion of different centuries, which had been affixed by the predecessors of Don Roderick. On either side of the portal stood the two ancient guardians of the tower, laden with the keys appertaining to the locks.

The king alighted and approaching the portal ordered the guardians to unlock the gate. The hoary headed men drew back with terror. "Alas!" cried they, "what is it your majesty requires of us. Would you have the mischiefs of this tower unbound, and let loose to shake the earth to its foundations?"

The venerable archbishop Urbino likewise implored him not to disturb a mystery which had been held sacred from generation to generation within the memory of man, and which even Cæsar himself, when sovereign of Spain, had not ventured to invade. The youthful cavaliers,

*From the minute account of the good Friar, drawn from the ancient chronicles, it would appear that the walls of the tower were pictured in mosaic work.

however, were eager to pursue the adventure and encouraged him in his rash curiosity.

"Come what come may," exclaimed Don Roderick, "I am resolved to penetrate the mystery of this tower." So saying he again commanded the guardians to unlock the portal. The ancient men obeyed with fear and trembling, but their hands shook with age, and when they applied the keys the locks were so rusted by time, or of such strange workmanship, that they resisted their feeble efforts, whereupon the young cavaliers pressed forward and lent their aid. Still the locks were so numerous and difficult, that with all their eagerness and strength a great part of the day was exhausted before the whole of them could be mastered.

When the last bolt had yielded to the key the guardians and the reverend archbishop again entreated the king to pause and reflect. "Whatever is within this tower," said they, "is as yet harmless and lies bound under a mighty spell: venture not then to open a door which may let forth a flood of evil upon the land." But the anger of the king was roused and he ordered that the portal should be instantly thrown open. In vain, however, did one after another exert his strength, and equally in vain did the cavaliers unite their forces, and apply their shoulders to the gate; though there was neither bar nor bolt remaining it was perfectly immoveable.

The patience of the king was now exhausted and he advanced to apply his hand; scarcely, however, did he touch the iron gate when it swung slowly open, uttering as it were a dismal groan, as it turned reluctantly upon its hinges. A cold damp wind issued forth, accompanied by a tempestuous sound. The hearts of the ancient guardians quaked within them and their knees smote together; but several of the youthful cavaliers rushed in, eager to gratify their curiosity or to signalize themselves in this redoubtable enterprize. They had scarcely advanced a few paces, however, when they recoiled, overcome by the baleful air, or by some fearful vision.* Upon this the king ordered that fires should be kindled, to dispel the darkness and to correct the noxious and long imprisoned air; he then led the way into the interior; but though stout of heart, he advanced with awe and hesitation.

After proceeding a short distance he entered a hall or antechamber, on the opposite side of which was a door, and before it on a pedestal stood a gigantic figure of the colour of bronze, and of a terrible aspect. It held a huge mace which it whirled incessantly, giving such cruel and resounding blows upon the earth as to prevent all further entrance.

The king paused at sight of this appalling figure, for whether it were a living being, or a statue of magic artifice he could not tell. On its

*Bleda. cronica. cap. 7.

breast was a scroll, whereon was inscribed in large letters, "I do my duty."* After a little while Roderick plucked up heart, and addressed it with great solemnity. "Whatever thou be," said he, "know that I come not to violate this sanctuary, but to inquire into the mystery it contains; I conjure thee therefore to let me pass in safey."

Upon this the figure paused with uplifted mace and the king and his train passed unmolested through the door.

They now entered a vast chamber of a rare and sumptuous architecture, difficult to be described. The walls were encrusted with the most precious gems, so joined together as to form one smooth and perfect surface. The lofty dome appeared to be self supported and was studded with gems, lustrous as the stars of the firmament. There was neither wood nor any other common or base material to be seen throughout the edifice. There were no windows or other openings to admit the day, yet a radiant light was spread throughout the place, which seemed to shine from the walls, and to render every object distinctly visible.

In the centre of this hall stood a table of alabaster of the rarest work-manship, on which was inscribed in Greek characters, that Hercules Alcides the Theban Greek had founded this tower in the year of the world three thousand and six. Upon the table stood a golden casket, richly set round with precious stones, and closed with a lock of mother of pearl, and on the lid were inscribed the following words.

"In this coffer is contained the mystery of the tower. The hand of none but a king can open it; but let him beware!, for marvellous events will be revealed to him, which are to take place before his death."

King Roderick boldly seized upon the casket. The venerable arch-bishop laid his hand upon his arm, and made a last remonstrance. "For-bear my son!" said he. "Desist while there is yet time. Look not into the mysterious decrees of providence. God has hidden them in mercy from our sight, and it is impious to rend the veil by which they are concealed."

"What have I to dread from a knowledge of the future?" replied Roderick, with an air of haughty presumption. "If good be destined me I shall enjoy it by anticipation; if evil, I shall arm myself to meet it." So saying he rashly broke the lock.

Within the coffer he found nothing but a linen cloth folded between two tablets of copper. On unfolding it he beheld painted on it figures of men on horseback of fierce demeanour, clad in turbans and robes of various colours, after the fashion of the Arabs, with scymetars hanging from their necks and cross bows at their saddle backs, and they carried banners and pennons with divers devices. Above them was inscribed in

*Idem

Greek characters, "Rash monarch! behold the men, who are to hurl thee from thy throne and subdue thy kingdom!"

At sight of these things the king was troubled in spirit and dismay fell upon his attendants. While they were yet regarding the paintings it seemed as if the figures began to move, and a faint sound of warlike tumult arose from the cloth, with the clash of cymbal and bray of trumpet, the neigh of steed and shout of army; but all was heard indistinctly, as if afar off, or in a reverie or dream. The more they gazed the plainer became the motion and the louder the noise; and the linen cloth rolled forth, and amplified, and spread out as it were a mighty banner, and filled the hall, and mingled with the air, until its texture was no longer visible, or appeared as a transparent cloud. And the shadowy figures became all in motion, and the din and uproar became fiercer and fiercer; and whether the whole were an animated picture, or a vision or an array of embodied spirits, conjured up by supernatural power no one present could tell. They beheld before them a great field of battle where christians and moslems were engaged in deadly conflict. They heard the rush and tramp of steeds, the blast of trump and clarion, the clash of cymbal and the stormy din of a thousand drums. There was the clash of swords and maces and battle axes; with the whistling of arrows and the hurtling of darts and lances. The christians quailed before the foe; the infidels pressed upon them and put them to utter rout; the standard of the cross was cast down, the banner of Spain was trodden under foot, the air resounded with shouts of triumph, with yells of fury and with the groans of dying men. Amidst the flying squadrons King Roderick beheld a crowned warrior whose back was towards him, but whose armour and device were his own, and who was mounted on a white steed that resembled his own war horse Orelia. In the confusion of the flight the warrior was dismounted and was no longer to be seen, and Orelia galloped wildly through the field of battle without a rider.

Roderick staid to see no more but rushed from the fatal hall followed by his terrified attendants. They fled through the outer chamber where the gigantic figure with the whirling mace had disappeared from his pedestal, and on issuing into the open air, they found the two ancient guardians of the tower lying dead at the portal, as though they had been crushed by some mighty blow. All nature which had been clear and serene, was now in wild uproar. The heavens were darkened by heavy clouds, loud bursts of thunder rent the air, and the earth was deluged with rain and rattling hail.

The king ordered that the iron portal should be closed, but the door was immoveable and the cavaliers were dismayed by the tremendous turmoil and the mingled shouts and groans that continued to prevail within. The king and his train hastened back to Toledo pursued and pelted by the tempest. The mountains shook and echoed with the thunder, trees were uprooted and blown down, and the Tagus raged and roared and overflowed its banks. It seemed to the affrighted courtiers as if the phantom legions of the tower had issued forth and mingled with the storm, for amidst the claps of thunder and the howling of the wind, they fancied they heard the sound of drums and trumpets, the shouts of armies and the rush of steeds. Thus beaten by tempest and overwhelmed with horror the king and his courtiers arrived at Toledo, clattering across the bridge of the Tagus and entering the gate in headlong confusion as though they had been pursued by an enemy.

In the morning the heavens were again serene and all nature was restored to tranquility. The king, therefore, issued forth with his cavaliers and took the road to the tower, followed by a great multitude, for he was anxious once more to close the iron door, and shut up those evils that threatened to overwhelm the land. But lo, on coming in sight of the tower, a new wonder met their eyes. An eagle appeared high in the air, seeming to descend from heaven. He bore in his beak a burning brand, and lighting on the summit of the tower, fanned the fire with his wings. In a little while the edifice burst forth into a blaze as though it had been built of rosin, and the flames mounted into the air with a brilliancy more dazzling than the sun; nor did they cease until every stone was consumed and the whole was reduced to a heap of ashes. Then there came a vast flight of birds, small of size and sable of hue, darkening the sky like a cloud; and they descended and wheeled in circles round the ashes, causing so great a wind with their wings that the whole was borne up into the air, and scattered throughout all Spain, and wherever a particle of that ashes fell, it was as a stain of blood. It is furthermore recorded by ancient men and writers of former days, that all those on whom this dust fell were afterwards slain in battle, when the country was conquered by the Arabs, and that the destruction of this necromantic tower was a sign and token of the approaching perdition of Spain.

"Let all those," concludes the cautious Friar, "who question the verity of this most marvellous occurrence, consult those admirable sources of our history, the chronicle of the Moor Rasis, and the work entitled the Fall of Spain, written by the Moor Abulcasim Tarif Abentarique. Let them consult moreover the venerable historian Bleda and the cloud of other Catholic Spanish writers, who have treated of this event, and they will find I have related nothing that has not been printed and published under the inspection and sanction of our most holy mother church. God alone knoweth the truth of these things; I speak but what has been handed down to me from times of old."

CHAPTER VIII

Count Julian, his fortunes in Africa—He hears of the dishonour of his child—His conduct thereupon.

The course of our legendary narration now returns to notice the fortunes of Count Julian after his departure from Toledo to resume his government on the coast of Barbary. He left the Countess Frandina at Algeziras, his paternal domain, for the province under his command was threatened with invasion. In fact, when he arrived at Ceuta he found his post in imminent danger from the all conquering moslems. The Arabs of the East, the followers of Mahomet having subjugated several of the most potent oriental kingdoms, had established their seat of Empire at Damascus, where, at this time, it was filled by Walid Almanzor, surnamed "The Sword of God." From thence the tide of moslem conquest had rolled on to the shores of the Atlantic, so that all Almagreb, or Western Africa, had submitted to the standard of the prophet, with the exception of a portion of Tingitania lying along the straits, being the province held by the goths of Spain and commanded by Count Julian. The Arab invaders were a hundred thousand strong, most of them veteran troops, seasoned in warfare and accustomed to victory. They were led by an old Arab general Muza ben Noseir, to whom was confided the government of Almagreb, most of which he had himself conquered. The ambition of this veteran was to make the moslem conquest complete, by expelling the christians from the African shores; with this view his troops menaced the few remaining gothic fortresses of Tingitania, while he himself sat down in person before the walls of Ceuta. The Arab chieftain had been rendered confident by continual success, and thought nothing could resist his arms and the sacred standard of the prophet. Impatient of the tedious delays of a siege he led his troops boldly against the rock built towers of Ceuta and attempted to take the place by storm. The onset was fierce, and the struggle desperate; the swarthy sons of the desert were light and vigorous, and of fiery spirit, but the goths enured to danger on this frontier, retained the stubborn valour of their race, so impaired among their brethren in Spain. They were commanded too by one skilled in warfare and ambitious of renown. After a vehement conflict the moslem assailants were repulsed at all points and driven from the walls. Don Julian sallied forth and harrassed them in their retreat, and so severe was the carnage that the veteran Muza was fain to break up his camp and retire confounded from the siege.

The victory at Ceuta resounded throughout Tingitania and spread universal joy. On every side were heard shouts of exultation mingled with praises of Count Julian. He was hailed by the people, wherever he went, as their deliverer, and blessings were invoked upon his head. The heart of Count Julian was lifted up and his spirit swelled within him, but it was with noble and virtuous pride for he was conscious of having merited the blessings of his country.

In the midst of his exultation, and while the rejoycings of the people were yet sounding in his ears the page arrived who bore the letter from his unfortunate daughter.

"What tidings from the king?" said the count as the page knelt before him.

"None my lord," replied the youth, "but I bear a letter sent in all haste by the lady Florinda."

He took the letter from his bosom and presented it to his lord. As Count Julian read it his countenance darkened and fell. "This," said he bitterly, "is my reward for serving a tyrant; and these are the honours heaped on me by my country while fighting its battles in a foreign land. May evil overtake me and infamy rest upon my name if I cease until I have full measure of revenge."

Count Julian was vehement in his passions, and took no counsel in his wrath. His spirit was haughty in the extreme but destitute of true magnanimity, and when once wounded, turned to gall and venom. A dark and malignant hatred entered into his soul, not only against Don Roderick, but against all Spain: he looked upon it as the scene of his disgrace, a land in which his family was dishonoured, and, in seeking to avenge the wrongs he had suffered from his sovereign, he meditated against his native country one of the blackest schemes of treason that ever entered into the human heart.

The plan of Count Julian was to hurl King Roderick from his throne and to deliver all Spain into the hands of the Infidels. In concerting and executing this traitorous plot it seemed as if his whole nature was changed; every lofty and generous sentiment was stifled, and he stooped to the meanest dissimulation. His first object was to extricate his family from the power of the king, and to remove it from Spain before his treason should be known; his next to deprive the country of its remaining means of defence against an invader.

With these dark purposes at heart, but with an open and serene countenance, he crossed over to Spain and repaired to the court at Toledo. Wherever he came he was hailed with acclamation as a victorious general and appeared in the presence of his sovereign radiant with the victory at Ceuta. Concealing from King Roderick his knowledge of the outrage upon his house, he professed nothing but the most devoted loyalty and affection.

The king loaded him with favours, seeking to appease his own conscience by heaping honours upon the father in atonement of the deadly wrong inflicted upon his child. He regarded Count Julian, also, as a man able and experienced in warfare and took his advice in all matters relating to the military affairs of the kingdom. The count magnified the dangers that threatened the frontier under his command, and prevailed upon the king to send thither the best horses and arms remaining from the time of Witiza, there being no need of them in the centre of Spain in its present tranquil state. The residue, at his suggestion, was stationed on the frontiers of Gallia; so that the kingdom was left almost wholly without defence against any sudden irruption from the south.

Having thus artfully arranged his plans, and all things being prepared for his return to Africa, he obtained permission to withdraw his daughter from the court and leave her with her mother, the Countess Frandina, who he pretended lay dangerously ill at Algeziras. Count Julian issued out of the gate of the city followed by a shining band of chosen followers, while beside him on a palfrey rode the pale and weeping Florinda. The populace hailed and blessed him as he passed, but his heart turned from them with loathing. As he crossed the bridge of the Tagus he looked back with a dark brow upon Toledo and raised his mailed hand and shook it at the royal palace of King Roderick, which crested the rocky height. "A father's curse," said he, "be upon thee and thine! may desolation fall upon thy dwelling and confusion and defeat upon thy realm!"

In his journeyings through the country he looked round him with a malignant eye; the pipe of the shepherd and the song of the husbandman were as discord to his soul; every sight and sound of human happiness sickened him at heart, and in the bitterness of his spirit he prayed that he might see the whole scene of prosperity laid waste with fire and sword by the invader.

The story of domestic outrage and disgrace had already been made known to the Countess Frandina. When the hapless Florinda came in presence of her mother, she fell on her neck, and hid her face in her bosom and wept; but the countess shed never a tear, for she was a woman haughty of spirit and strong of heart. She looked her husband sternly in the face. "Perdition light upon thy head," said she, "if thou submit to this dishonour. For my own part, woman as I am, I will assemble the followers of my house, nor rest until rivers of blood have washed away this stain."

"Be pacified," replied the count. "Vengeance is on foot, and will be sure and ample."

Being now in his own domains, surrounded by his relatives and friends, Count Julian went on to complete his web of treason. In this he was aided by his brother in law Oppas, the bishop of Seville; a man dark and perfidious as the night, but devout in demeanour, and smooth and plausible in council. This artful prelate had contrived to work himself into the entire confidence of the king and had even prevailed upon him to permit his nephews Evan and Siseburto, the exiled sons of Witiza, to return into Spain. They resided in Andalusia, and were now looked to as fit instruments in the present traitorous conspiracy.

By the advice of the Bishop, Count Julian called a secret meeting of his relatives and adherents on a wild rocky mountain not far from Consuegra, and which still bears the moorish appellation of "La Sierra de Calderin," or the mountain of treason.* When all were assembled Count Julian appeared among them accompanied by the Bishop and by the Countess Frandina. Then gathering around him those who were of his blood and kindred he revealed the outrage that had been offered to their house. He represented to them that Roderick was their legitimate enemy; that he had dethroned Witiza their relative, and had now stained the honour of one of the most illustrious daughters of their line. The Countess Frandina seconded his words. She was a woman majestic in person and eloquent of tongue, and being inspired by a mother's feelings, her speech aroused the assembled cavaliers to fury.

The count took advantage of the excitement of the moment to unfold his plan. The main object was to dethrone Don Roderick and give the crown to the sons of the late King Witiza. By this means they would visit the sins of the tyrant upon his head and, at the same time, restore the regal honours to their line. For this purpose their own force would be insufficient, but they might procure the aid of Muza ben Noseir the Arabian general in Mauritania, who would no doubt gladly send a part of his troops into Spain to assist in the enterprize.

The plot thus suggested by Count Julian received the unholy sanction of Bishop Oppas, who engaged to aid it secretly with all his influence and means: for he had great wealth and possessions and many retainers. The example of the reverend prelate determined all who might otherwise have wavered, and they bound themselves by dreadful oaths to be true to the conspiracy. Count Julian undertook to proceed to Africa and seek the camp of Muza to negotiate for his aid, while the Bishop was to keep about the person of King Roderick, and lead him into the net prepared for him.

All things being thus arranged Count Julian gathered together his treasure and taking his wife and daughter and all his household, abandoned the country he meant to betray, embarking at Malaga for Ceuta. The gate in the wall of that city through which they went forth,

*Bleda. Cap. 5.

continued for ages to bear the name of *Puerta de la Cava,* or, the gate of the harlot; for such was the opprobrious and unmerited appellation bestowed by the moors on the unhappy Florinda.*

CHAPTER IX

Secret visit of Count Julian to the Arab camp—First expedition of Taric el Tuerto.

When Count Julian had placed his family in security in Ceuta surrounded by soldiery devoted to his fortunes, he took with him a few confidential followers and departed in secret for the camp of the Arabian Emir, Muza ben Noseir. The camp was spread out in one of those pastoral valleys which lie at the feet of the Barbary hills, with the great range of the Atlas mountains towering in the distance. In the motley army here assembled were warriors of every tribe and nation that had been united by pact or conquest in the cause of Islam. There were those who had followed Muza from the fertile regions of Egypt, across the deserts of Barca, and those who had joined his standard from among the sunburnt tribes of Mauritanea. There were Saracen and Tartar, Syrian and Copt and swarthy moor: sumptuous warriors from the civilized cities of the east and the gaunt and predatory rovers of the desert. The greater part of the army, however, was composed of Arabs; but differing greatly from the first rude hordes that enlisted under the banner of Mahomet. Almost a century of continual wars with the cultivated nations of the east had rendered them accomplished warriors; and the occasional sojourn in luxurious countries and populous cities had acquainted them with the arts and habits of civilized life. Still the roving, restless and predatory habits of the genuine son of Ishmael prevailed in defiance of every change of clime or situation.

Count Julian found the Arab conqueror Muza surrounded by somewhat of Oriental state and splendour. He was advanced in life, but of a noble presence and concealed his age by tinging his hair and beard with henna. The count assumed an air of soldierlike frankness and decision when he came into his presence. "Hitherto," said he, "we have been enemies, but I come to thee in peace, and it rests with thee to make me the most devoted of thy friends. I have no longer country or king. Roderick the goth is an usurper, and my deadly foe; he has wounded my honour in the tenderest point, and my country affords me no redress. Aid me in my vengeance and I will deliver all Spain into

*Bleda. Cap. 4.

thy hands: a land far exceeding in fertility and wealth all the vaunted régions thou hast conquered in Tingitania."

The heart of Muza leaped with joy at these words, for he was a bold and ambitious conqueror and having over run all western Africa had often cast a wistful eye to the mountains of Spain as he beheld them brightening beyond the waters of the Strait. Still he possessed the caution of a veteran and feared to engage in an enterprize of such moment, and to carry his arms into another division of the globe without the approbation of his sovereign. Having drawn from Count Julian the particulars of his plan, and of the means he possessed to carry it into effect, he laid them before his confidential counsellors and officers and demanded their opinion. "These words of Count Julian," said he, "may be false and deceitful; or he may not possess the power to fulfill his promises. The whole may be a pretended treason to draw us on to our destruction. It is more natural that he should be treacherous to us than to his country."

Among the generals of Muza was a gaunt swarthy veteran, scarred with wounds; a very Arab, whose great delight was roving and desperate enterprize, and who cared for nothing beyond his steed, his lance and scymetar. He was a native of Damascus; his name was Taric ben Zeyad, but, from having lost an eye, he was known among the Spaniards by the appellation of Taric el Tuerto, or Taric, the one-eyed.

The hot blood of this veteran Ishmaelite was in a ferment when he heard of a new country to invade, and vast regions to subdue, and he dreaded lest the cautious hesitation of Muza should permit the glorious prize to escape them. "You speak doubtingly," said he, "of the words of this christian cavalier, but their truth is easy to be ascertained. Give me four galleys and a handful of men, and I will depart with this Count Julian, skirt the christian coast, and bring thee back tidings of the land, and of his means to put it in our power."

The words of the veteran pleased Muza ben Noseir, and he gave his consent, and Taric departed with four galleys and five hundred men; guided by the traytor Julian.* This first expedition of the Arabs against Spain took place, according to certain historians in the year of our Lord seven hundred and twelve, though others differ on this point, as indeed they do upon almost every point in this early period of Spanish history. The date to which the judicious chroniclers incline is that of seven hundred and ten, in the month of July. It would appear from some authorities, also, that the galleys of Taric cruised along the coasts of Andalusia and Lusitania under the feigned character of merchant barks, nor is this at all improbable, while they were seeking

*Beuter, Cron. Gen. de España, L. 1. c. 28. Marmol. Descrip. de Africa, L. 2. c. 10.

merely to observe the land and get a knowledge of the harbours. Where-
ever they touched, Count Julian dispatched emissaries to assemble
his friends and adherents at an appointed place. They gathered together
secretly at el Gezira Alhadra, that is to say the Green Island, where
they held a conference with Count Julian in presence of Taric ben
Zeyad.* Here they again avowed their readiness to flock to his standard
whenever it should be openly raised, and made known their various
preparations for a rebellion. Taric was convinced, by all that he had
seen and heard, that Count Julian had not deceived them, either as
to his disposition or his means to betray his country. Indulging his
Arab inclinations he made an inroad into the land, collected great
spoil and many captives, and bore off his plunder in triumph to Muza,
as a specimen of the riches to be gained by the conquest of the
christian land.†

CHAPTER X

Letter of Muza to the caliph—Second expedition of Taric el Tuerto.

On hearing the tidings brought by Taric el Tuerto, and beholding
the spoil he had collected, Muza wrote a letter to the Caliph Walid
Almanzor, setting forth the traitorous proffer of Count Julian, and the
probability, through his means, of making a successful invasion of
Spain. "A new land," said he, "spreads itself out before our delighted
eyes and invites our conquest. A land too, that equals Syria in the
fertility of its soil, and the serenity of its sky; Yemen, or Arabia the
happy, in its delightful temperature; India in its flowers and spices;
Hegiaz in its fruits and flowers; Cathay in its precious minerals and
Aden in the excellence of its ports and harbours. It is populous also
and wealthy, having many splendid cities and majestic monuments of
ancient art. What is to prevent this glorious land from becoming the
inheritance of the faithful? Already we have overcome the tribes of
Berbery, of Zab, of Derar, of Zaara, Mazamuda and Sus, and the victorious
standard of Islam floats on the towers of Tangier. But four leagues of
sea separate us from the opposite coast. One word from my sovereign
and the conquerors of Africa will pour their legions into Andalusia,
rescue it from the domination of the unbeliever and subdue it to the
law of the Koran."‡

*Bleda. Cron. c. 5.
†Conde. Hist. Dom. Arab. part 1. c. 8.
‡Conde, part 1. c. 8.

The caliph was overjoyed with the contents of the letter. "God is great!" exclaimed he, "and Mahomet is his prophet! It has been foretold by the ambassador of God that his law should extend to the ultimate parts of the West, and be carried by the sword into new and unknown regions. Behold another land is opened for the triumphs of the faithful. It is the will of Allah, and be his sovereign will obeyed." So the caliph sent missives to Muza authorizing him to undertake the conquest.

Upon this there was a great stir of preparation and numerous vessels were assembled and equipped at Tangiers to convey the invading army across the straits. Twelve thousand men were chosen for this expedition, most of them light Arabian troops, seasoned in warfare, and fitted for hardy and rapid enterprize. Among them were many horsemen, mounted on fleet Arabian steeds. The whole was put under the command of the veteran Taric el Tuerto, or the one-eyed, in whom Muza reposed implicit confidence, as in a second self. Taric accepted the command with joy; his martial fire was roused at the idea of having such an army under his sole command, and such a country to overrun and he secretly determined never to return unless victorious.

He chose a dark night to convey his troops across the Straits of Hercules and by break of day they began to disembark at Tarifa, before the country had time to take the alarm. A few christians hastily assembled from the neighborhood opposed their landing but were easily put to flight. Taric stood on the sea side and watched until the last squadron had landed, and all the horses, armour and munitions of war were brought on shore; he then gave orders to set fire to the ships. The moslems were struck with terror when they beheld their fleet wrapped in flames and smoke and sinking beneath the waves. "How shall we escape," exclaimed they, "if the fortune of war should be against us." "There is no escape for the coward!" cried Taric. "The brave man thinks of none: your only chance is victory." "But how without ships shall we ever return to our homes?" "Your home," replied Taric, "is before you; but you must win it with your swords."

While Taric was yet talking with his followers, says one of the ancient chroniclers, a christian female was descried waving a white pennon on a reed, in signal of peace. On being brought into the presence of Taric she prostrated herself before him. "Señor," said she, "I am an ancient woman; and it is now full sixty years past and gone since, as I was keeping vigils one winter's night by the fire side, I heard my father, who was an exceeding old man, read a prophecy said to have been written by a holy friar: and this was the purport of the prophecy, that a time would arrive when our country would be invaded and conquered by people from Africa of a strange garb, a strange tongue and a strange religion. They

were to be led by a strong and valiant captain, who would be known
by these signs; on his right shoulder he would have a hairy mole, and
his right arm would be much longer than the left, and of such length as
to enable him to cover his knee with his hand, without bending his body."

Taric listened to the old beldame with grave attention, and when
she had concluded he laid bare his shoulder, and lo! there was the mole
as it had been described; his right arm, also, was in verity found to
exceed the other in length, though not to the degree that had been
mentioned. Upon this the Arab host shouted for joy and felt assured
of conquest.*

The discreet Antonio Agapida, though he records this circumstance
as it is set down in ancient chronicle, yet withholds his belief from
the pretended prophecy, considering the whole a cunning device of
Taric, to encrease the courage of his troops. "Doubtless," says he,
"there was a collusion between this ancient sybil and the crafty son of
Ishmael; for these infidel leaders were full of damnable inventions to
work upon the superstitious fancies of their followers, and to inspire
them with a blind confidence in the success of their arms."

Be this as it may, the veteran Taric took advantage of the excitement
of his soldiery and led them forward to gain possession of a strong
hold, which was, in a manner, the key to all the adjacent country. This
was a lofty mountain or promontory almost surrounded by the sea and
connected with the main land by a narrow isthmus. It was called the
rock of Calpe, and like the opposite rock of Ceuta commanded the
entrance to the Mediterranean Sea. Here in old times Hercules had
set up one of his pillars and the city of Heraclea had been built.

As Taric advanced against this promontory, he was opposed by
a hasty levy of the christians, who had assembled under the banner
of a gothic noble of great power and importance, whose domains lay
along the mountainous coast of the Mediterranean. The name of this
christian cavalier was Theodomir, but he has universally been called
Tadmir by the Arabian historians, and is renowned as being the first
commander that made any stand against the inroad of the moslems. He
was about forty years of age; hardy, prompt and sagacious, and had all the
gothic nobles been equally vigilant and shrewd in their defence, the
banner of Islam would never have triumphed over the land.

Theodomir had but seventeen hundred men under his command, and
these but rudely armed; yet he made a resolute stand against the army
of Taric and defended the pass to the promontory with great valour.
He was at length obliged to retreat and Taric advanced and planted
his standard on the rock of Calpe, and fortified it as his strong hold,

*Perdida de España por Abulcasim Tarif Abentarique, lib. 1, c. VII.

and as the means of securing an entrance into the land. To commemorate his first victory he changed the name of the promontory, and called it Gibel Taric, or the mountain of Taric, but in process of time the name has gradually been altered to Gibraltar.

In the mean time, the patriotic chieftain Theodomir, having collected his routed forces, encamped with them on the skirts of the mountains and summoned the country round to join his standard. He sent off missives in all speed to the king, imparting in brief and blunt terms the news of the invasion, and craving assistance with equal frankness. "Señor," said he, in his letter, "the legions of Africa are upon us, but whether they come from heaven or earth I know not. They seem to have fallen from the clouds for they have no ships. We have been taken by surprize, overpowered by numbers and obliged to retreat, and they have fortified themselves in our territory. Send us aid, Señor, with instant speed, or rather, come yourself to our assistance."[*]

CHAPTER XI

Measures of Don Roderick on hearing of the invasion—Expedition of Ataulpho—Vision of Taric.

When Don Roderick heard that legions of turbaned troops had poured into the land from Africa, he called to mind the visions and predictions of the necromantic tower and great fear came upon him. But, though sunk from his former hardihood and virtue, though enervated by indulgence and degraded in spirit by a consciousness of crime, he was resolute of soul and roused himself to meet the coming danger. He summoned a hasty levy of horse and foot amounting to forty thousand, but now was felt the effect of the crafty counsel of Count Julian, for the best of the horses and armour intended for the public service had been sent into Africa, and were really in possession of the traytors. Many nobles, it is true, took the field with the sumptuous array with which they had been accustomed to appear at tournaments and jousts, but most of their vassals were destitute of weapons, and cased in cuirasses of leather or suits of armour almost consumed by rust. They were without discipline or animation, and their horses like themselves, pampered by slothful peace, were little fitted to bear the heat, and dust and toils of long campaigns.

This army Don Roderick put under the command of his kinsman Ataulpho, a prince of the royal blood of the Goths, and of a noble and

*Conde. Part 1. c. 9.

generous nature, and he ordered him to march with all speed to meet the foe, and to recruit his forces on the way with the troops of Theodomir.

In the mean time Taric el Tuerto had received large reinforcements from Africa, and the adherents of Count Julian and all those discontented with the sway of Don Roderick had flocked to his standard; for many were deceived by the representations of Count Julian and thought that the Arabs had come to aid him in placing the sons of Witiza upon the throne. Guided by the count the troops of Taric penetrated into various parts of the country and laid waste the land; bringing back loads of spoil to their strong hold at the rock of Calpe.

The prince Ataulpho marched with his army through Andalusia and was joined by Theodomir with his troops; he met with various detachments of the enemy foraging the country, and had several bloody skirmishes, but he succeeded in driving them before him, and they retreated to the rock of Calpe, where Taric lay gathered up with the main body of his army.

The prince encamped not far from the bay which spreads itself out before the promontory. In the evening he dispatched the veteran Theodomir with a trumpet to demand a parley of the Arab chieftain, who received the envoy in his tent surrounded by his captains. Theodomir was frank and abrupt in speech for the most of his life had been passed far from courts. He delivered in round terms the message of the Prince Ataulpho, upbraiding the Arab general with his wanton invasion of the land, and summoning him to surrender his army, or to expect no mercy.

The single eye of Taric el Tuerto glowed like a coal of fire at this message. "Tell your commander," replied he, "that I have crossed the strait to conquer Spain, nor will I return until I have accomplished my purpose. Tell him I have men skilled in war, and armed in proof with whose aid I trust soon to give a good account of his rabble host."

A murmur of applause passed through the assemblage of moslem captains. Theodomir glanced on them a look of defiance, but his eye rested on a renegado christian, one of his own ancient comrades, and a relation of Count Julian. "As to you Don Greybeard," said he, "you who turn apostate in your declining age, I here pronounce you a traytor to your God, your king and country; and stand ready to prove it this instant upon your body if field be granted me."

The traytor knight was stung with rage at these words, for truth rendered them piercing to the heart. He would have immediately answered to the challenge, but Taric forbade it, and ordered that the christian envoy should be conducted from the camp. "'Tis well," replied Theodomir, "God will give me the field which you deny. Let yon hoary apostate look to himself tomorrow in the battle, for I pledge myself to use my lance upon no other foe until it has shed his blood upon the native soil he has betrayed." So saying he left the camp, nor could the moslem chieftains help admiring the honest indignation of this patriot knight, while they secretly despised his renegado adversary.

The ancient moorish chroniclers relate many awful portents and strange and mysterious visions which appeared to the commanders of either army during this anxious night. Certainly it was a night of fearful suspense, and moslem and christian looked forward with doubt to the fortune of the coming day. The Spanish centinel walked his pensive round, listening occasionally to the vague sounds from the distant rock of Calpe, and eying it as the mariner eyes the thunder cloud, pregnant with terror and destruction. The Arabs too from their lofty cliffs beheld the numerous camp fires of the christians gradually lighted up, and saw that they were a powerful host; at the same time the night breeze brought to their ears the sullen roar of the sea which separated them from Africa. When they considered their perilous situation, an army on one side, with a whole nation aroused to reinforce it, and on the other an impassable sea, the spirits of many of the warriors were cast down, and they repented the day when they had ventured into this hostile land.

Taric marked their despondency, but said nothing. Scarce had the first streak of morning light trembled along the sea, however, when he summoned his principal warriors to his tent. "Be of good cheer," said he, "Allah is with us and has sent his prophet to give assurance of his aid. Scarce had I retired to my tent last night when a man of a majestic and venerable presence stood before me. He was taller by a palm than the ordinary race of men, his flowing beard was of a golden hue and his eyes were so bright that they seemed to send forth flashes of fire. I have heard the Emir Bahamet, and other ancient men, describe the prophet, whom they had seen many times while on earth, and such was his form and lineament. 'Fear nothing O Taric from the morrow,' said he, 'I will be with thee in the fight. Strike boldly then and conquer. Those of thy followers who survive the battle will have this land for an inheritance, for those who fall a mansion in paradise is prepared and immortal Houris await their coming.' He spake and vanished; I heard a strain of celestial melody and my tent was filled with the odours of Arabia the happy." "Such," say the Spanish chroniclers, "was another of the arts by which this arch son of Ishmael sought to animate the hearts of his followers, and the pretended vision has been recorded by the Arabian writers as a veritable occurrence. Marvellous indeed was the effect produced by it upon the infidel soldiery, who now cried out with eagerness to be led against the foe."

CHAPTER XII

Battle of Calpe—Fate of Ataulpho.

The grey summits of the rock of Calpe brightened with the first rays of morning, as the christian army issued forth from its encampment. The prince Ataulpho rode from squadron to squadron animating his soldiers for the battle. "Never should we sheathe our swords," said he, "while these infidels have a footing in the land. They are pent up within yon rocky mountain, we must assail them in their rugged hold. We have a long day before us, let not the setting sun shine upon one of their host who is not a fugitive, a captive or a corpse."

The words of the prince were received with shouts and the army moved towards the promontory. As they advanced, they heard the clash of cymbals and the bray of trumpets, and the rocky bosom of the mountain glittered with helms and spears and scymetars, for the Arabs, inspired with fresh confidence by the words of Taric, were sallying forth with flaunting banners, to the combat.

The gaunt Arab chieftain stood upon a rock as his troops marched by; his buckler was at his back and he brandished in his hand a double pointed spear. Calling upon the several leaders by their names he exhorted them to direct their attacks against the christian captains, and especially against Ataulpho, "for the chiefs being slain," said he, "their followers will vanish from before us like the morning mist."

The gothic nobles were easily to be distinguished by the splendour of their arms, but the prince Ataulpho was conspicuous above all the rest for the youthful grace and majesty of his appearance and the bravery of his array. He was mounted on a superb Andalusian charger richly caparizoned with crimson velvet embroidered with gold. His surcoat was of like colour and adornment, and the plumes that waved above his burnished helmet were of the purest white. Ten mounted pages magnificently attired followed him to the field, but their duty was not so much to fight as to attend upon their lord and to furnish him with steed or weapon.

The christian troops though irregular and undisciplined were full of native courage; for the old warrior spirit of their Gothic sires still glowed in their bosoms. There were two battalions of infantry, but Ataulpho stationed them in the rear, "for God forbid," said he, "that footsoldiers should have the place of honour in the battle, when I have so many valiant cavaliers." As the armies drew nigh to each other, however, it was discovered that the advance of the Arabs was composed of infantry. Upon this the cavaliers checked their steeds, and requested that the footsoldiery might advance and disperse this losel crew, holding it beneath their dignity to contend with pedestrian foes. The prince, however, commanded them to charge; upon which, putting spurs to their steeds, they rushed upon the foe.

The Arabs stood the shock manfully, receiving the horses upon the points of their lances; many of the riders were shot down with bolts from cross bows, or stabbed with the poniards of the moslems. The cavaliers succeeded, however, in breaking into the midst of the battalion and throwing it into confusion, cutting down some with their swords, transpiercing others with their spears and trampling many under the hoofs of their horses. At this moment, they were attacked by a band of Spanish horsemen, the recreant partizans of Count Julian. Their assault bore hard upon their countrymen, who were disordered by the contest with the foot soldiers, and many a loyal christian knight fell beneath the sword of an unnatural foe.

The foremost among these recreant warriors was the renegado cavalier whom Theodomir had challenged in the tent of Taric. He dealt his blows about him with a powerful arm and with malignant fury, for nothing is more deadly than the hatred of an apostate. In the midst of his career he was espied by the hardy Theodomir, who came spurring to the encounter. "Traytor," cried he, "I have kept my vow. This lance has been held sacred from all other foes to make a passage for thy perjured soul." The Renegado had been renowned for prowess before he became a traitor to his country, but guilt will sap the courage of the stoutest heart. When he beheld Theodomir rushing upon him he would have turned and fled; pride alone withheld him, and, though an admirable master of defence, he lost all skill to ward the attack of his adversary. At the first assault the lance of Theodomir pierced him through and through; he fell to the earth, gnashed his teeth as he rolled in the dust, but yielded his breath without uttering a word.

The battle now became general and lasted throughout the morning with varying success. The stratagem of Taric however began to produce its effect. The christian leaders and most conspicuous cavaliers were singled out and severally assailed by overpowering numbers. They fought desperately and performed miracles of prowess, but fell, one by one, beneath a thousand wounds. Still the battle lingered on throughout a great part of the day, and as the declining sun shone through the clouds of dust, it seemed as if the conflicting hosts were wrapped in smoke and fire.

The prince Ataulpho saw that the fortune of battle was against him. He rode about the field calling out the names of the bravest of his knights, but few answered to his call; the rest lay mangled on the field. With this handful of warriors he endeavoured to retrieve the day, when he was assailed by Tenderos a partizan of Count Julian, at the head of a body of recreant christians. At sight of this new adversary fire flashed from the eyes of the prince, for Tenderos had been brought up in his father's palace. "Well dost thou, traytor!" cried he, "to attack the son of thy lord who gave thee bread; thou, who hast betrayed thy country and thy God!"

So saying he seized a lance from one of his pages and charged furiously upon the apostate; but Tenderos met him in mid career, and the lance of the prince was shivered upon his shield. Ataulpho then grasped his mace which hung at his saddle bow and a doubtful fight ensued. Tenderos was powerful of frame and superior in the use of his weapons, but the curse of treason seemed to paralyze his arm. He wounded Ataulpho slightly between the greaves of his armour, but the prince dealt a blow with his mace that crushed through helm and scull and reached the brains; and Tenderos fell dead to earth, his armour rattling as he fell.

At the same moment a javelin hurled by an Arab transpierced the horse of Ataulpho, which sunk beneath him. The prince seized the reins of the steed of Tenderos, but the faithful animal, as though he knew him to be the foe of his late lord, reared and plunged and refused to let him mount. The prince, however, used him as a shield to ward off the press of foes, while with his sword he defended himself against those in front of him. Taric ben Zeyad arrived at the scene of conflict, and paused for a moment in admiration of the surpassing prowess of the prince; recollecting, however, that his fall would be a death blow to his army, he spurred upon him, and wounded him severely with his scymetar. Before he could repeat his blow Theodomir led up a body of christian cavaliers to the rescue, and Taric was parted from his prey by the tumult of the fight. The prince sank to the earth, covered with wounds and exhausted by the loss of blood. A faithful page drew him from under the hoofs of the horses and aided by a veteran soldier an ancient vassal of Ataulpho, conveyed him to a short distance from the scene of battle, by the side of a small stream that gushed out from among rocks. They stanched the blood that flowed from his wounds, and washed the dust from his face, and lay him beside the fountain. The page sat at his head and supported it on his knees, and the veteran stood at his feet, with his brow bent and his eyes full of sorrow. The prince gradually revived and opened his eyes. "How fares the battle?" said he. "The struggle is hard," replied the soldier, "but the day may yet be ours."

The prince felt that the hour of his death was at hand and ordered that they should aid him to rise upon his knees. They supported him between them and he prayed fervently for a short time, when, finding his strength declining, he beckoned the veteran to sit down beside him on the rock. Continuing to kneel he confessed himself to that ancient soldier, having no priest or friar to perform that office in this hour of extremity. When he had so done he sunk again upon the earth and pressed it with his lips, as if he would take a fond farewell of his beloved country. The page would then have raised his head but found that his lord had yielded up the ghost.

A number of Arab warriors who came to the fountain to slake their thirst, cut off the head of the prince and bore it in triumph to Taric, crying, "Behold the head of the christian leader." Taric immediately ordered that the head should be put upon the end of a lance together with the surcoat of the prince, and borne about the field of battle, with the sound of trumpets, atabals and cymbals.

When the christians beheld the surcoat and knew the features of the prince they were struck with horror, and heart and hand failed them. Theodomir endeavoured in vain to rally them, they threw by their weapons and fled, and they continued to fly and the enemy to pursue and slay them until the darkness of the night. The moslems then returned and plundered the christian camp where they found abundant spoil.

CHAPTER XIII

Terror of the country—Roderick rouses himself to arms.

The scattered fugitives of the christian army spread terror throughout the land. The inhabitants of the towns and villages gathered around them as they applied at their gates for food, or lay themselves down faint and wounded beside the public fountains. When they related the tale of their defeat old men shook their heads and groaned, and the women uttered cries and lamentations. So strange and unlooked for a calamity filled them with consternation and despair; for it was long since the alarm of war had sounded in their land, and this was a warfare that carried chains and slavery and all kinds of horrors in its train.

Don Roderick was seated with his beauteous Queen Exilona in the royal palace which crowned the rocky summit of Toledo, when the bearer of ill tidings came gallopping over the bridge of the Tagus. "What tidings from the army?" demanded the king, as the panting messenger was brought into his presence. "Tidings of great woe," exclaimed the soldier. "The prince has fallen in battle. I saw his head and surcoat upon a moorish lance and the army was overthrown and fled."

At hearing these words Roderick covered his face with his hands and for some time sat in silence; and all his courtiers stood mute and aghast and no one dared to speak a word. In that awful space of time passed before his thoughts all his errors and his crimes, and all the evils that had been predicted in the necromantic tower. His mind was filled with horror and confusion, for the hour of his destruction seemed at hand. But he subdued his agitation by his strong and haughty spirit, and when he uncovered his face no one could read on his brow the trouble and agony of his heart. Still every hour brought fresh tidings of disaster. Messenger after messenger came spurring into the city distracting it with new alarms. The infidels, they said, were strengthening themselves in the land; host after host were pouring in from Africa; the sea board of Andalusia glittered with spears and scymetars. Bands of turbaned horsemen had over run the plains of Sidonia even to the banks of the Guadiana. Fields were laid waste, towns and cities plundered, the inhabitants carried into captivity, and the whole country lay in smoking desolation.

Roderick heard all these tidings with an undaunted aspect, nor did he ever again betray sign of consternation, but the anxiety of his soul was evident in his warlike preparations. He issued orders that every noble and prelate of his kingdom should put himself at the head of his retainers and take the field, and that every man capable of bearing arms should hasten to his standard, bringing whatever horse and mule and weapon he possessed; and he appointed the plain of Cordova for the place where the army was to assemble. Throwing by then all the trappings of his late slothful and voluptuous life and arming himself for warlike action, he departed from Toledo at the head of his guard, composed of the flower of the youthful nobility. His Queen Exilona accompanied him, for she craved permission to remain in one of the cities of Andalusia, that she might be near her lord in this time of peril.

Among the first who appeared to hail the arrival of the king at Cordova was the Bishop Oppas, the secret partizan of the traytor Julian. He brought with him his two nephews, Evan and Siseburto the sons of the late King Witiza, and a great host of vassals and retainers, all well armed and appointed; for they had been furnished by Count Julian with a part of the arms sent by the king to Africa. The Bishop was smooth of tongue and profound in his hypocrisy; his pretended zeal and devotion and the horror with which he spoke of the treachery of his kinsman, imposed upon the credulous spirit of the king, and he was readily admitted into his most secret councils.

The alarm of the infidel invasion had spread throughout the land and roused the gothic valour of the inhabitants. On receiving the orders of Roderick every town and hamlet, every mountain and valley, had sent forth its fighting men, and the whole country was on the march towards Andalusia. In a little while there were gathered together on the plain of Cordova near fifty thousand horsemen and a countless host of footsoldiers. The gothic nobles appeared in burnished armour curiously inlaid and adorned, with chains and jewels of gold, and ornaments of precious stones, and silken scarfs and surcoats of brocade, or velvet richly embroidered; betraying the luxury and ostentation into which they had declined from the iron hardihood of their warlike sires. As to the common people, some had lances and shields and swords and cross bows but the greater part were unarmed, or provided merely with slings, and clubs studded with nails, and with the iron implements of husbandry; and many had made shields for themselves from the doors and windows of their habitations. They were a prodigious host, and appeared, say the Arabian chroniclers, like an agitated sea, but though brave in spirit, they possessed no knowledge of warlike art, and were ineffectual through lack of arms and discipline.

Several of the most ancient and experienced cavaliers beholding the state of the army advised Don Roderick to await the arrival of more regular troops, which were stationed in Iberia, Cantabria and Gallia gothica; but this counsel was strenuously opposed by the Bishop Oppas; who urged the king to march immediately against the infidels. "As yet," said he, "their number is but limited, but every day new hosts arrive like flocks of locusts from Africa. They will augment faster than we; they are living too at our expense, and while we pause, both armies are consuming the substance of the land."

King Roderick listened to the crafty counsel of the Bishop and determined to advance without delay. He mounted his war horse Orelia and rode among his troops assembled on that spacious plain, and wherever he appeared he was received with acclamations, for nothing so arouses the spirit of the soldier as to behold his sovereign in arms. He addressed them in words calculated to touch their hearts and animate their courage. "The Saracens," said he, "are ravaging our land and their object is our conquest. Should they prevail, your very existence as a nation is at an end. They will overturn your altars; trample on the cross, lay waste your cities, carry off your wives and daughters, and doom yourselves and sons to hard and cruel slavery. No safety remains for you but in the prowess of your arms. For my own part, as I am your king, so will I be your leader, and will be the foremost to encounter every toil and danger."

The soldiery answered their youthful monarch with loud acclamations, and solemnly pledged themselves to fight to the last gasp in defence of their country and their faith. The king then arranged the order of their march: all those who were armed with cuirasses and coats of mail were placed in the front and rear; the centre of the army was composed of a promiscuous throng, without body armour, and but scantily provided with weapons.

When they were about to march the king called to him a noble cavalier named Ramiro and delivering him the royal standard, charged him to guard it well for the honour of Spain; scarcely however had the good knight received it in his hand, when he fell dead from his horse and the staff of the standard was broken in twain. Many ancient courtiers who were present looked upon this as an evil omen, and counselled the king not to set forward on his march that day; but disregarding all auguries and portents he ordered the royal banner to be put upon a lance and gave it in charge of another standard bearer: then commanding the trumpets to be sounded he departed at the head of his host to seek the enemy.

The field where this great army assembled was called, from the solemn pledge given by the nobles and the soldiery, *El campo de la verdad,* or, The field of Truth; a name, says the sage chronicler Abul Cassim, which it bears even to the present day.*

CHAPTER XIV

March of the gothic army—Encampment on the banks of the Guadalete—Mysterious predictions of a palmer—Conduct of Pelistes thereupon.

The hopes of Andalusia revived as this mighty host stretched in lengthening lines along its fertile plains; from morn until night it continued to pour along, with sound of drum and trumpet; it was led on by the proudest nobles and bravest cavaliers of the land, and, had it possessed arms and discipline, might have undertaken the conquest of the world.

After a few days march Don Roderick arrived in sight of the moslem army, encamped on the banks of the Guadalete,† where that beautiful stream winds through the fertile land of Xeres. The infidel host was far inferior in number to the christians, but then it was composed of hardy and dexterous troops, seasoned to war, and admirably armed. The camp shone gloriously in the setting sun; and resounded with the clash of cymbal, the note of the trumpet and the neighing of fiery Arabian steeds. There were swarthy troops from every nation of the African coast, together with legions from Syria and Egypt, while the light Bedouins were careering about the adjacent plain. What grieved and incensed the spirit of the christian warriors, however, was to behold, a little apart

*La Perdida de España, cap. 9. Bleda. Lib. 2. c. 8.
†This name was given to it subsequently by the Arabs. It signifies the River of Death. Vide Pedraza, Hist. Granad. p. 3. c. 1.

from the moslem host, an encampment of Spanish cavaliers with the banner of Count Julian waving above their tents. They were ten thousand in number, valiant and hardy men, the most experienced of Spanish soldiery, most of them having served in the African wars: they were well armed and appointed also, with the weapons of which the count had beguiled his sovereign; and it was a grievous sight to behold such good soldiers arrayed against their country and their faith.

The christians pitched their tents about the hour of vespers, at a short league distant from the enemy and remained gazing with anxiety and awe upon this barbaric host that had caused such terror and desolation in the land: for the first sight of hostile encampment in a country disused to war is terrible to the newly enlisted soldier. A marvellous occurrence is recorded by the Arabian chroniclers as having taken place in the christian camp, but discreet Spanish writers relate it with much modification and consider it a stratagem of the wily Bishop Oppas, to sound the loyalty of the christian cavaliers.

As several leaders of the army were seated with the Bishop in his tent, conversing on the dubious fortunes of the approaching contest, an ancient pilgrim appeared at the entrance. He was bowed down with years, his snowy beard descended to his girdle and he supported his tottering steps with a palmer's staff. The cavaliers rose and received him with great reverence as he advanced within the tent. Holding up his withered hand, "Woe, woe to Spain!" exclaimed he, "for the vial of the wrath of heaven is about to be poured out. Listen warriors and take warning. Four months since, having performed my pilgrimage to the sepulchre of our Lord in Palestine, I was on my return towards my native land. Wearied and way-worn I lay down one night to sleep beneath a palm tree, by the side of a fountain, when I was awakened by a voice saying unto me in soft accents, 'Son of sorrow, why sleepest thou?' I opened my eyes and beheld one of a fair and beauteous countenance, in shining apparel and with glorious wings, standing by the fountain; and I said, 'who art thou, who callest upon me in this deep hour of the night?' "

" 'Fear not,' replied the stranger. 'I am an angel from heaven, sent to reveal unto thee the fate of thy country. Behold the sins of Roderick have come up before God, and his anger is kindled against him, and he has given him up to be invaded and destroyed. Hasten then to Spain, and seek the camp of thy countrymen. Warn them that such only shall be saved as shall abandon Roderick; but those who adhere to him shall share his punishment and shall fall under the sword of the invader.' "

The pilgrim ceased, and passed forth from the tent; certain of the cavaliers followed him to detain him, that they might converse further with him about these matters, but he was no where to be found. The sentinel before the tent said, "I saw no one come forth, but it was as if a blast of wind passed by me and there was a rustling as of dry leaves."

The cavaliers remained looking upon each other with astonishment. The Bishop Oppas sat with his eyes fixed upon the ground and shadowed by his overhanging brow. At length breaking silence in a low and faltering voice, "Doubtless," said he, "this message is from God; and since he has taken compassion upon us and given us notice of his impending judgement, it behoves us to hold grave council and determine how best we may accomplish his will and avert his displeasure."

The chiefs still remained silent as men confounded. Among them was a veteran noble named Pelistes. He had distinguished himself in the African wars, fighting side by side with Count Julian, but the latter had never dared to tamper with his faith for he knew his stern integrity. Pelistes had brought with him to the camp his only son who had never drawn a sword except in tourney. When the young man saw that the veterans held their peace, the blood mantled in his cheek, and, over-coming his modesty, he broke forth with a generous warmth. "I know not, cavaliers," said he, "what is passing in your minds, but I believe this pilgrim to be an envoy from the devil; for none else would have given such dastard and perfidious counsel. For my own part, I stand ready to defend my king my country and my faith; I know no higher duty than this, and if God thinks fit to strike me dead in the performance of it, his sovereign will be done!"

When the young man had risen to speak his father had fixed his eyes upon him with a grave and stern demeanour, leaning upon a two handed sword. As soon as the youth had finished, Pelistes embraced him with a father's fondness. "Thou hast spoken well my son," said he. "If I held my peace at the counsel of this losel pilgrim, it was but to hear thy opinion and to learn whether thou wert worthy of thy lineage and of the training I had given thee. Hadst thou counselled otherwise than thou hast done, hadst thou shewn thyself craven and disloyal; so help me God I would have struck off thy head with this weapon which I hold in my hand. But thou hast counselled like a loyal and a christian knight and I thank God for having given me a son worthy to perpetuate the honours of my line. As to this pilgrim, be he saint or be he devil, I care not; this much I promise, that if I am to die in defence of my country and my king, my life shall be a costly purchase to the foe. Let each man make the same resolve and I trust we shall yet prove the pilgrim a lying prophet." The words of Pelistes roused the spirits of many of the cavaliers; others, however, remained full of anxious fore-bodings, and when this fearful prophecy was rumoured about the camp, as it presently was by the emissaries of the Bishop, it spread awe and dismay among the soldiery.

CHAPTER XV

Skirmishing of the armies—Pelistes and his son—Pelistes and the bishop.

On the following day the two armies remained regarding each other
with wary but menacing aspect. About noontide King Roderick sent
forth a chosen force of five hundred horse and two hundred foot, the
best armed of his host, to skirmish with the enemy, that, by gaining
some partial advantage, they might raise the spirits of the army. They
were led on by Theodomir, the same Gothic noble who had signalized
himself by first opposing the invasion of the moslems.

The christian squadrons paraded, with flying pennons, in the valley
which lay between the armies. The Arabs were not slow in answering
their defiance. A large body of horsemen sallied forth to the encounter,
together with three hundred of the followers of Count Julian. There
was hot skirmishing about the field and on the banks of the river; many
gallant feats were displayed on either side, and many valiant warriors
were slain. As the night closed in, the trumpets from either camp summoned the troops to retire from the combat. In this days action the
christians suffered greatly in the loss of their distinguished cavaliers;
for it is the noblest spirits who venture most and lay themselves open
to danger, and the moslem soldiers had instructions to single out the
leaders of the adverse host. All this is said to have been devised by
the perfidious Bishop Oppas, who had secret communications with the
enemy while he influenced the councils of the king, and who trusted
that by this skirmishing warfare, the flower of the christian troops
would be cut off and the rest disheartened.

On the following morning a larger force was ordered out to skirmish,
and such of the soldiery as were unarmed were commanded to stand
ready to seize the horses and strip off the armour of the killed and
wounded. Among the most illustrious of the warriors who fought that
day was Pelistes, the gothic noble who had so sternly checked the tongue
of the Bishop Oppas. He led to the field a large body of his own vassals
and retainers, and of cavaliers trained up in his house; who had followed
him to the wars in Africa and who looked up to him more as a father
than a chieftain. Beside him was his only son, who now for the first
time was flashing his sword in battle. The conflict that day was more
general and bloody than the day preceding; the slaughter of the christian
warriors was immense, from their lack of defensive armour, and as
nothing could prevent the flower of the gothic chivalry from spurring
to the combat, the field was strewed with the bodies of the youthful
nobles. None suffered more however than the warriors of Pelistes. Their
leader himself was bold and hardy, and prone to expose himself to

danger, but years and experience had moderated his early fire; his son, however, was eager to distinguish himself in this his first essay, and rushed with impetuous ardour into the hottest of the battle. In vain his father called to caution him; he was ever in the advance and seemed unconscious of the perils that surrounded him. The cavaliers and vassals of his father followed him with devoted zeal, and many of them paid for their loyalty with their lives. When the trumpets sounded in the evening for retreat the troops of Pelistes were the last to reach the camp. They came slowly and mournfully and much decreased in number. Their veteran commander was seated on his war horse, but the blood trickled from the greaves of his armour. His valiant son was borne on the shields of his vassals; when they laid him on the earth near to where the king was standing they found that the heroic youth had expired of his wounds. The cavaliers surrounded the body and gave utterance to their grief, but the father restrained his agony and looked on with the stern resignation of a soldier.

Don Roderick surveyed the field of battle with a rueful eye, for it was covered with the mangled bodies of his most illustrious warriors, he saw, too, with anxiety, that the common people, unused to war and unsustained by discipline, were harassed by incessant toils and dangers, and were cooling in their zeal and courage.

The crafty Bishop Oppas marked the internal trouble of the king and thought a favorable moment had arrived to sway him to his purpose. He called to his mind the various portents and prophecies which had forerun their present danger. "Let not my lord the king," said he, "make light of these mysterious revelations, which appear to be so disastrously fulfilling. The hand of heaven appears to be against us. Destruction is impending over our heads. Our troops are rude and unskillful; but slightly armed, and much cast down in spirit. Better is it that we should make a treaty with the enemy, and, by granting part of his demands, prevent the utter ruin of our country. If such counsel be acceptable to my lord the king, I stand ready to depart upon an embassy to the moslem camp."

Upon hearing these words Pelistes who had stood in mournful silence, regarding the dead body of his son, burst forth with honest indignation. "By this good sword," said he, "the man who yields such dastard counsel deserves death from the hand of his countrymen rather than from the foe; and, were it not for the presence of the king, may I forfeit salvation, if I would not strike him dead upon the spot."

The Bishop turned an eye of venom upon Pelistes. "My lord," said he, "I too bear a weapon and know how to wield it. Were the king not present you would not dare to menace, nor should you advance one step, without my hastening to meet you."

The king interposed between the jarring nobles and rebuked the impetuosity of Pelistes, but at the same time rejected the counsel of the Bishop. "The event of this conflict," said he, "is in the hand of God; but never shall my sword return to its scabbard while an infidel invader remains within the land."

He then held a council with his captains and it was determined to offer the enemy general battle on the following day. A herald was dispatched defying Taric ben Zeyad to the contest and the defiance was gladly accepted by the moslem chieftain.* Don Roderick then formed the plan of action and assigned to each commander his several station, after which he dismissed his officers, and each one sought his tent to prepare by diligence or repose for the next day's eventful contest.

CHAPTER XVI

Traitorous message of Count Julian.

Taric ben Zeyad had been surprized by the valour of the christian cavaliers in the recent battles, and at the number and apparent devotion of the troops which accompanied the king to the field. The confident defiance of Don Roderick encreased his surprise. When the herald had retired he turned an eye of suspicion on Count Julian. "Thou hast represented thy countrymen," said he, "as sunk in effeminacy and lost to all generous impulse; yet I find them fighting with the courage and the strength of lions. Thou hast represented thy king as detested by his subjects and surrounded by secret treason, but I behold his tents whitening the hills and dales, while thousands are hourly flocking to his standard. Woe unto thee if thou hast dealt deceitfully with us, or betrayed us with guileful words."

Don Julian retired to his tent in great trouble of mind, and fear came upon him that the bishop Oppas might play him false; for it is the lot of traytors ever to distrust each other. He called to him the same page who had brought him the letter from Florinda revealing the story of her dishonor.

"Thou knowest, my trusty page," said he, "that I have reared thee in my household and cherished thee above all thy companions. If thou hast loyalty and affection for thy Lord, now is the time to serve him. Hie thee to the christian camp and find thy way to the tent of the Bishop Oppas. If any one ask thee who thou art, tell them thou art

*Bleda, Cronica.

of the household of the Bishop, and bearer of missives from Cordova. When thou art admitted to the presence of the Bishop, shew him this ring and he will commune with thee in secret. Then tell him Count Julian greets him as a brother, and demands how the wrongs of his daughter Florinda are to be redressed. Mark well his reply and bring it word for word. Have thy lips closed, but thine eyes and ears open, and observe every thing of note in the camp of the king. So, speed thee on thy errand. Away—away!"

The page hastened to saddle a Barbary steed, fleet as the wind and of a jet black colour, so as not to be easily discernible in the night. He girded on a sword and dagger, slung an Arab bow with a quiver of arrows at his side, and a buckler at his shoulder. Issuing out of the camp, he sought the banks of the Guadalete and proceeded silently along its stream, which reflected the distant fires of the christian camp. As he passed by the place which had been the scene of the recent conflict, he heard, from time to time, the groan of some expiring warrior who had crawled among the reeds on the margin of the river, and sometimes his steed stepped cautiously over the mangled bodies of the slain. The young page was unused to the sights of war and his heart beat quick within him. He was hailed by the centinels as he approached the christian camp, and, on giving the reply taught him by Count Julian, was conducted to the tent of the Bishop Oppas.

The Bishop had not yet retired to his couch; when he beheld the ring of Count Julian and heard the words of his message he saw that the page was one in whom he might confide. "Hasten back to thy lord," said he, "and tell him to have faith in me and all shall go well. As yet I have kept my troops out of the combat. They are all fresh, well armed and well appointed. The king has confided to myself, aided by the princes Evan and Siseburto, the command of a wing of the army. To morrow, at the hour of noon, when both armies are in the heat of action, we will pass over with our forces to the moslems. But I claim the compact made with Taric ben Zeyad, that my nephews be placed in dominion over Spain, and tributary only to the Caliph of Damascus."

With this traitorous message the page departed. He led his black steed cautiously by the bridle to present less mark for observation, as he went stumbling along near the expiring fires of the camp. On passing the last outpost, where the guards were half slumbering on their arms, he was overheard and summoned, but leaped lightly into the saddle and put spurs to his steed. An arrow whistled by his ear and two more stuck in the target which he had thrown upon his back. The clatter of swift hoofs echoed behind him, but he had learnt of the Arabs to fight and fly. Plucking a shaft from his quiver and turning and rising in the stirrups as his courser gallopped at full speed, he drew the arrow to the

head and launched it at his pursuer. The twang of the bow string was
followed by the crash of armour and a deep groan as the horseman
tumbled to the earth. The page pursued his course without further
molestation, and arrived at the moslem camp before the break of day.

CHAPTER XVII

Last day of the battle.

A light had burned throughout the night in the tent of the king, and
anxious thoughts and dismal visions troubled his repose. If he fell
into a slumber he beheld in his dreams the shadowy phantoms of the
necromantic tower, or the injured Florinda, pale and dishevelled,
imprecating the vengeance of heaven upon his head. In the mid
watches of the night, when all was silent except the footstep of the
centinel, pacing before his tent, the king rose from his couch and walking forth looked thoughtfully upon the martial scene before him. The
pale crescent of the moon hung over the Moorish Camp, and dimly
lighted up the windings of the Guadalete. The heart of the king was
heavy and oppressed, but he felt only for himself, says Antonio Agapida,
he thought nothing of the perils impending over the thousands of
devoted subjects in the camp below him, sleeping as it were on the
margin of their graves. The faint clatter of distant hoofs as if in rapid
flight reached the monarch's ear, but the horsemen were not to be
descried. At that very hour and along the shadowy banks of that river,
here and there gleaming with the scanty moonlight, passed the fugitive
messenger of Count Julian, with the plan of the next days treason.

The day had not yet dawned when the sleepless and impatient monarch summoned his attendants and arrayed himself for the field. He
then sent for the venerable Bishop Urbino who had accompanied him
to the camp, and, laying aside his regal crown he knelt with head
uncovered, and confessed his sins before the holy man. After this a
solemn mass was performed in the royal tent and the Eucharist administered to the monarch. When these ceremonies were concluded, he
besought the archbishop to depart forthwith for Cordova, there to
await the issue of the battle, and to be ready to bring forward reinforcements and supplies. The archbishop saddled his mule and departed just as the faint blush of morning began to kindle in the east.
Already the camp resounded with the thrilling call of the trumpet, the
clank of armour and the tramp and neigh of steeds. As the archbishop
passed through the camp he looked with a compassionate heart on this

vast multitude, of whom so many were soon to perish. The warriors pressed to kiss his hand, and many a cavalier, full of youth and fire, received his benediction, who was to lie stiff and cold before the evening.

When the troops were marshalled for the field Don Roderick prepared to sally forth in the state and pomp with which the gothic kings were wont to go to battle. He was arrayed in robes of gold brocade; his sandals were embroidered with pearls and diamonds, he had a sceptre in his hand, and he wore a regal crown resplendent with inestimable jewels. Thus gorgeously apparelled, he ascended a lofty chariot of ivory, the axle trees of which were of silver, and the wheels and pole covered with plates of burnished gold. Above his head was a canopy of cloth of gold embossed with armorial devices, and studded with precious stones.* This sumptuous chariot was drawn by milk white horses, with caparisons of crimson velvet, embroidered with pearls. A thousand youthful cavaliers surrounded the car; all of the noblest blood and bravest spirit, all knighted by the king's own hand and sworn to defend him to the last.

When Roderick issued forth in this resplendent state, says an Arabian writer, surrounded by his guards in gilded armour and waving plumes and scarfs and surcoats of a thousand dyes, it was as if the sun were emerging in the dazzling chariot of the day from amidst the glorious clouds of morning.

As the royal car rolled along in front of the squadrons the soldiers shouted with admiration. Don Roderick waved his sceptre and addressed them from his lofty throne, reminding them of the horror and desolation which had already been spread through the land by the invaders. He called upon them to summon up the ancient valour of their race and avenge the blood of their brethren. "One day of glorious fighting," said he, "and this infidel horde will be driven into the sea or will perish beneath your swords. Forward bravely to the fight: your families are behind you praying for your success; the invaders of your country are before you; God is above to bless his holy cause, and your king leads you to the field." The army shouted with one accord, "Forward to the foe; and death be his portion who shuns the encounter!"

The rising sun began to shine along the glistening waters of the Guadalete as the Moorish army, squadron after squadron, came sweeping down a gentle declivity to the sound of martial music. Their turbans and robes of various dyes and fashions gave a splendid appearance to their host; as they marched, a cloud of dust arose and partly hid them from the sight, but still there would break forth flashes of

*Entrand. Chron. an. Chris. 714.

steel and gleams of burnished gold, like rays of vivid lightning; while the sound of drum and trumpet and the clash of moorish cymbal were as the warlike thunder within that stormy cloud of battle.

As the armies drew near each other the sun disappeared among gathering clouds, and the gloom of the day was increased by the columns of dust which rose from either host. At length the trumpets sounded for the encounter. The battle commenced with showers of arrows, stones and javelins. The christian footsoldiers fought to disadvantage, the greater part being destitute of helm or buckler. A battalion of light arabian horsemen, led by a greek renegado named Maguel el Rumi, careered in front of the christian line, launching their darts and then wheeling off beyond the reach of the missiles hurled after them. Theodomir now brought up his seasoned troops into the action, seconded by the veteran Pelistes, and in a little while the battle became furious and promiscuous. It was glorious to behold the old gothic valour shining forth in this hour of fearful trial. Wherever the moslems fell the christians rushed forward seized upon their horses and stripped them of their armour and their weapons. They fought desperately and successfully, for they fought for their country and their faith. The battle raged for several hours, the field was strown with slain, and the moors, overcome by the multitude and fury of their foes began to falter.

When Taric beheld his troops retreating before the enemy he threw himself before them, and, rising on his stirrups, "Oh moslems! conquerors of Africa!" cried he, "Whither would you fly? The sea is behind you, the enemy before: you have no hope but in your valour and the help of God. Do as I do and the day is ours!"

With these words he put spurs to his horse and sprang among the enemy, striking to right and left, cutting down and destroying, while his steed, fierce as himself, trampled upon the footsoldiers, and tore them with his teeth. At this moment a mighty shout arose in various parts of the field. The noontide hour had arrived. The Bishop Oppas with the two princes, who had hitherto kept their bands out of the fight suddenly went over to the enemy, and turned their weapons upon their astonished countrymen. From that moment the fortune of the day was changed, and the field of battle became a scene of wild confusion and bloody massacre. The christians knew not whom to contend with, or whom to trust. It seemed as if madness had seized upon their friends and kinsmen, and that their worst enemies were among themselves.

The courage of Don Roderick rose with his danger. Throwing off the cumbrous robes of royalty and descending from his car, he sprang upon his steed Orelia, grasped his lance and buckler and endeavoured to rally his retreating troops. He was surrounded and assailed by a multitude of his own traitorous subjects but defended himself with wondrous prowess. The enemy thickened around him; his loyal band of cavaliers were slain bravely fighting in his defence; the last that was seen of the king was in the midst of the enemy dealing death at every blow.

A complete panic fell upon the christians; they threw away their arms and fled in all directions. They were pursued with dreadful slaughter, until the darkness of the night rendered it impossible to distinguish friend from foe. Taric then called off his troops from the pursuit and took possession of the royal camp; and the couch which had been pressed so uneasily on the preceding night by Don Roderick, now yielded sound repose to his conqueror.*

CHAPTER XVIII

The field of battle after the defeat—The fate of Roderick.

On the morning after the battle the Arab leader Taric ben Zeyad rode over the bloody field of the Guadalete, strewed with the ruins of those splendid armies which had so lately passed like glorious pageants along the river banks. There moor and christian, horseman and horse, lay gashed with hideous wounds, and the river, still red with blood, was filled with the bodies of the slain. The gaunt Arab was as a wolf roaming through the fold he had laid waste. On every side his eye revelled on the ruin of the country, on the wrecks of haughty Spain. There lay the flower of her youthful chivalry, mangled and destroyed, and the strength of her yeomanry prostrated in the dust. The gothic noble lay confounded with his vassals; the peasant with the prince; all ranks and dignities were mingled in one bloody massacre.

When Taric had surveyed the field he caused the spoils of the dead and the plunder of the camp to be brought before him. The booty was immense. There were massy chains and rare jewels of gold, pearls and precious stones, rich silks and brocades, and all other luxurious decorations in which the gothic nobles had indulged in the latter times of their degeneracy. A vast amount of treasure was likewise found, which had been brought by Roderick for the expenses of the war.

Taric then ordered that the bodies of the moslem warriors should be interred; as for those of the christians, they were gathered in heaps and vast pyres of wood were formed on which they were consumed.

*This battle is called indiscriminately by historians the battle of Guadalete, or of Xeres, from the neighborhood of that city.

The flames of these pyres rose high in the air and were seen afar off in the night; and when the christians beheld them from the neighboring hills they beat their breasts and tore their hair, and lamented over them as over the funeral fires of their country. The carnage of that battle infected the air for two whole months, and bones were seen lying in heaps upon the field for more than forty years; nay, when ages had past and gone, the husbandman, turning up the soil, would still find fragments of gothic cuirasses and helms, and moorish scymetars, the reliques of that dreadful fight.

For three days the fleet Arabian horsemen pursued the flying christians, hunting them over the face of the country, so that but a scanty number of that mighty host escaped to tell the tale of their disaster.

Taric ben Zeyad considered his victory incomplete so long as the gothic monarch survived; he proclaimed great rewards, therefore, to whomsoever should bring Roderick to him dead or alive. A diligent search was accordingly made in every direction, but for a long time in vain; at length a soldier brought Taric the head of a christian warrior, on which was a cap decorated with feathers and precious stones. The Arab leader received it as the head of the unfortunate Roderick, and sent it, as a trophy of his victory, to Muza ben Noseir, who, in like manner, transmitted it to the caliph at Damascus. The Spanish historians, however, have always denied its identity.

A mystery has ever hung, and ever must continue to hang, over the fate of King Roderick, in that dark and doleful day of Spain. Whether he went down amidst the storm of battle, and atoned for his sins and errors by a patriot grave, or whether he survived to repent of them in hermit exile, must remain matter of conjecture and dispute. The learned archbishop Rodrigo, who has recorded the events of this disastrous field, affirms that Roderick fell beneath the vengeful blade of the traytor Julian, and thus expiated with his blood his crime against the hapless Florinda; but the archbishop stands alone in his record of the fact. It seems generally admitted that Orelia, the favorite war horse of Don Roderick, was found entangled in a marsh, on the borders of the Guadalete, with the sandals and mantle and royal insignia of the king lying close by him. The river, at this place, ran broad and deep and was encumbered with the dead bodies of warriors and steeds; it has been supposed, therefore, that he perished in the stream; but his body was not found within its waters.

When several years had passed away, and men's minds, being restored to some degree of tranquility, began to occupy themselves about the events of this dismal day, a rumor arose that Roderick had escaped from the carnage on the banks of the Guadalete, and was still alive. It was said that, having from a rising ground, caught a view of the whole field of battle, and seen that the day was lost and his army flying in all directions, he likewise sought his safety in flight. It is added that the Arab horseman, while scouring the mountains in quest of fugitives, found a shepherd arrayed in the royal robes, and brought him before the conqueror, believing him to be the king himself. Count Julian soon dispelled the error. On being questioned the trembling rustic declared, that, while tending his sheep in the folds of the mountains there came a cavalier on a horse wearied and spent and ready to sink beneath the spur. That the cavalier with an authoritative voice and menacing air commanded him to exchange garments with him, and clad himself in his rude garb of sheep skin, and took his crook, and his scrip of provisions, and continued up the rugged defiles of the mountains leading towards Castile, until he was lost to view.*

This tradition was fondly cherished by many, who clung to the belief in the existence of their monarch, as their main hope for the redemption of Spain. It was even affirmed that he had taken refuge, with many of his host, in an island of the "Ocean Sea," from whence he might yet return once more to elevate his standard and battle for the recovery of his throne.

Year after year, however, elapsed, and nothing was heard of Don Roderick; yet, like Sebastian of Portugal and Arthur of England, his name continued to be a rallying point for popular faith, and the mystery of his end to give rise to romantic fables. At length, when generation after generation had sunk into the grave, and nearly two centuries had passed and gone, traces were said to be discovered that threw a light on the final fortunes of the unfortunate Roderick. At that time, Don Alphonso the Great, King of Leon, had wrested the city of Viseo in Lusitania from the hands of the moslems. As his soldiers were ranging about the city and its environs, one of them discovered in a field, outside of the walls, a small chapel or hermitage, with a sepulchre in front, on which was inscribed this epitaph in Gothic characters.

HIC REQUIESCIT RUDERICUS,
ULTIMUS REX GOTHORUM.

Here lies Roderick,
The last king of the Goths.

It has been believed by many that this was the veritable tomb of the monarch, and that in this hermitage he had finished his days in solitary penance. The warrior as he contemplated the supposed tomb

*Bleda, Cron. L. 2. c. 9. Abulcasim Tarif Abentarique L. 1. c. 10.

of the once haughty Roderick forgot all his faults and errors, and shed a soldier's tear over his memory: but when his thoughts turned to Count Julian his patriotic indignation broke forth, and with his dagger he inscribed a rude malediction on the stone.

"Accursed," said he, "be the impious and headlong vengeance of the traytor Julian. He was a murderer of his king, a destroyer of his kindred, a betrayer of his country. May his name be bitter in every mouth and his memory infamous to all generations."

Here ends the legend of Don Roderick.

ILLUSTRATIONS OF THE FOREGOING LEGEND

THE TOMB OF RODERICK

The venerable Sebastiano, Bishop of Salamanca, declares that the inscription on the tomb at Viseo in Portugal existed in his time, and that he had seen it. A particular account of the exile and hermit life of Roderick is furnished by Berganza on the authority of Portuguese chronicles.

Algunos historiadores Portugueses asseguran, que el Rey Rodrigo, perdida la batalla, huyo a tierra de Merida, y se recogio en el monasterio de Cauliniano, en donde, arrepentido de sus culpas, procuró confessarlas con muchas lagrimas. Deseando mas retiro, y escogiendo por compañero a un monge llamado Roman, y elevando la Imagen de Nazareth, que Cyriaco monge de nacion griega avra traidode Jerusalem al monasterio de Cauliniano, se subio a un monte muy aspero, que estaba sobre el mar, junto al lugar de Pedernegra. Vivio Rodrigo en compania de el monge en el hueco de una gruta por espacio de un año; despues se passo á la ermita de San Miguel, que estaba cerca de Viseo, en donde murio y fue sepultado.

Puedese ver esta relacion en las notas de Don Thomas Tamayo sobre Paulo deacano. El chronicon de San Millan, que llega hasta el año 883, deze que hasta su tiempo, si ignora el fin del Rey Rodrigo. Pocos años despues, el Rey Don Alonzo el Magno, aviéndo ganado la ciudad de Viseo, encontro en una iglesia el epitafio que en Romance dize—aqui yaze Rodrigo, ultimo Rey de los Godos.—Berganza, L. 1. c. 13.

THE CAVE OF HERCULES

As the story of the necromantic tower is one of the most famous as well as least credible points in the history of Don Roderick, it may be well to fortify or buttress it by some account of another marvel of the city of Toledo. This ancient city, which dates its existence almost from the time of the flood, claiming as its founder Tubal, the son of Japhet, and grandson of Noah,* has been the warrior hold of many generations and a strange diversity of races. It bears traces of the artifices and devices of its various occupants, and is full of mysteries and subjects for antiquarian conjecture and perplexity. It is built upon a high rocky promontory with the Tagus brawling round its base, and is overlooked by cragged and precipitous hills. These hills abound with clefts and caverns, and the promontory itself on which the city is built bears traces of vaults and subterraneous habitations, which are occasionally discovered under the ruins of ancient houses, or beneath the churches and convents.

These are supposed by some to have been the habitations, or retreats of the primitive inhabitants, for it was the custom of the ancients, according to Pliny, to make caves in high and rocky places and live in them through fear of floods; and such a precaution, says the worthy Don Pedro de Roxas, in his history of Toledo, was natural enough among the first Toledans, seeing that they founded their city shortly after the deluge, while the memory of it was still fresh in their minds.

Some have supposed these secret caves and vaults, to have been places of concealment of the inhabitants and their treasure, during times of war and violence; or rude temples for the performance of religious ceremonies in times of persecution. There are not wanting other, and grave writers, who give them a still darker purpose. In these caves, say they, were taught the diabolical mysteries of magic, and here were performed those infernal ceremonies and incantations, horrible in the eyes of God and man. "History," says the worthy Don Pedro de Roxas, "is full of accounts that the magi taught and performed their magic and their superstitious rites in profound caves and secret places; because as this art of the devil was prohibited, from the very origin of christianity, they always sought for hidden places in which to practice it." In the time of the moors this art, we are told, was publicly taught at their universities, the same as Astronomy, Philosophy and Mathematics, and at no place was it cultivated with more success than at Toledo. Hence this city has ever been darkly renowned for mystic science, insomuch that the magic art was called by the French and by other nations the Arte Toledana.

Of all the marvels, however, of this ancient, picturesque, romantic and necromantic city, none in modern times surpass the Cave of Hercules, if we may take the account of Don Pedro de Roxas for authentic. The

*Salazar, Hist. Gran. Cardinal. Prologo, vol. 1. plan 1.

entrance to this cave is within the church of San Gines, situated in nearly the highest part of the city. The portal is secured by massy doors, opening within the walls of the church, but which are kept rigorously closed. The cavern extends under the city and beneath the bed of the Tagus, to the distance of three leagues beyond. It is, in some places, of rare architecture, built of small stones curiously wrought, and supported by columns and arches.

In the year 1546 an account of this cave was given to the archbishop and cardinal Don Juan Martinez Siliceo who, desirous of examining it, ordered the entrance to be cleaned. A number of persons furnished with provisions, lanterns and cords then went in, and, having proceeded about half a league came to a place where there was a kind of chapel or temple, having a table or altar with several statues of bronze in niches or on pedestals.

While they were regarding this mysterious scene of ancient worship or incantation one of the statues fell, with a noise that echoed through the cavern and smote the hearts of the adventurers with terror. Recovering from their alarm they proceeded onward but were soon again dismayed by a roaring and rushing sound that encreased as they advanced. It was made by a furious and turbulent steam, the dark waters of which were too deep and broad and rapid to be crossed. By this time their hearts were so chilled with awe, and their thoughts so bewildered, that they could not seek any other passage by which they might advance; so they turned back and hastened out of the cave. It was night fall when they sallied forth, and they were so much affected by the terror they had undergone, and by the cold and damp air of the cavern, to which they were the more sensible from its being in the summer, that all of them fell sick and several of them died. Whether the Archbishop was encouraged to pursue his research and gratify his curiosity, the history does not mention.

Alonzo Telles de Meneses, in his history of the world, records, that not long before his time a boy of Toledo, being threatened with punishment by his master, fled and took refuge in this cave. Fancying his pursuer at his heels he took no heed of the obscurity or coldness of the cave but kept groping and blundering forward, until he came forth at three leagues distance from the city.

Another and very popular story of this cave, current among the common people, was that in its remote recesses lay concealed a great treasure of gold, left there by the Romans. Whoever would reach this precious hoard must pass through several caves or grottoes; each having its particular terror, and all under the guardianship of a ferocious dog, who has the key of all the gates, and watches day and night. At the approach of any one he shews his teeth and makes a hideous growling, but no adventurer after wealth has had courage to brave a contest with this terrific cerberus.

The most intrepid candidate on record was a poor man who had lost his all, and had those grand incentives to desperate enterprize, a wife and a large family of children. Hearing the story of this cave he determined to venture alone in search of the treasure. He accordingly entered, and wandered many hours bewildered about the cave. Often would he have returned, but the thoughts of his wife and children urged him on. At length he arrived near to the place where he supposed the treasure lay hidden; but here, to his dismay, he beheld the floor of the cavern strewn with human bones; doubtless the remains of adventurers like himself who had been torn to pieces.

Losing all courage he now turned and sought his way out of the cave. Horrors thickened upon him as he fled. He beheld direful phantoms glaring and gibbering around him and heard the sound of pursuit in the echoes of his footsteps. He reached his home overcome with affright; several hours elapsed before he could recover speech to tell his story, and he died on the following day.

The judicious Don Pedro de Roxas holds the account of the buried treasure for fabulous, but the adventure of this unlucky man for very possible, being led on by avarice, or rather, the hope of retrieving a desperate fortune. He, moreover, pronounces his dying shortly after coming forth as very probable; because the darkness of the cave, its coldness, the fright at finding the bones, the dread of meeting the imaginary dog, all joining to operate upon a man, who was past the prime of his days, and enfeebled by poverty and scanty food, might easily cause his death.

Many have considered this cave as intended originally for a sally or retreat from the city in case it should be taken; an opinion rendered probable, it is thought, by its grandeur and great extent.

The learned Salazar de Mendoza, however, in his history of the grand cardinal of Spain affirms it as an established fact that it was first wrought out of the rock by Tubal, the son of Japhet and grandson of Noah, and afterwards repaired and greatly augmented by Hercules the Egyptian, who made it his habitation after he had erected his pillars at the straits of Gibraltar. Here, too, it is said he read magic to his followers, and taught them those supernatural arts by which he accomplished his vast achievements. Others think that it was a temple dedicated to Hercules, as was the case, according to Pomponius Mela, with the great cave in the rock of Gibraltar; certain it is, that it has always borne the name of "The Cave of Hercules."

There are not wanting some who have insinuated that it was a work dating from the time of the Romans and intended as a cloaca or sewer of the city, but such a grovelling insinuation will be treated with proper scorn by the reader, after the nobler purposes to which he has heard this marvellous cavern consecrated.

From all the circumstances here adduced from learned and reverend authors, it will be perceived that Toledo is a city fruitful of marvels, and that the necromantic tower of Hercules has more solid foundation than most edifices of similar import in ancient history.

The writer of these pages will venture to add the result of his personal researches respecting the far famed cavern in question. Rambling about Toledo in the year 1827, in company with a small knot of antiquity hunters, among whom was an eminent British painter* and an English nobleman† who has since distinguished himself in Spanish historical research, we directed our steps to the church of San Gines and enquired for the portal of the secret cavern. The sacristan was a voluble and communicative man, and one not likely to be niggard of his tongue about any thing he knew, or slow to boast of any marvel pertaining to his church, but he professed utter ignorance of the existence of any such portal. He remembered to have heard, however, that immediately under the entrance to the church there was an arch of mason work, apparently the upper part of some subterranean portal; but that all had been covered up and a pavement laid down thereon; so that, whether it led to the magic cave or the necromantic tower remains a mystery, and so must remain until some monarch or archbishop shall again have courage and authority to break the spell.

*Mr. D. W——kie.
†Lord Mah——n.

LEGEND OF
THE SUBJUGATION OF SPAIN*

CHAPTER I

Consternation of Spain—Conduct of the conquerors—Missives between Taric and Muza.

The overthrow of King Roderick and his army on the banks of the Guadalete, threw open all southern Spain to the inroads of the moslems. The whole country fled before them; villages and hamlets were hastily abandoned; the inhabitants placed their aged and infirm, their wives and children, and their most precious effects on mules and other beasts of burden, and, driving before them their flocks and herds, made for distant parts of the land, for the fastnesses of the mountains, and for such of the cities as yet possessed walls and bulwarks. Many gave out, faint and weary, by the way, and fell into the hands of the enemy; others at the distant sight of a turban or a moslem standard, or on hearing the clangour of a trumpet, abandoned their flocks and herds and hastened their flights with their families. If their pursuers gained upon them, they threw by their household goods and whatever was of burthen, and thought themselves fortunate to escape, naked and destitute, to a place of refuge. Thus the roads were covered with scattered flocks and herds, and with spoil of all kind.

The Arabs, however, were not guilty of wanton cruelty or ravage; on the contrary, they conducted themselves with a moderation but seldom witnessed in more civilized conquerors. Taric el Tuerto, though a thorough man of the sword, and one whose whole thoughts were warlike, yet evinced wonderful judgement and discretion. He checked the predatory habits of his troops with a rigorous hand. They were forbidden under pain of severe punishment, to molest any peaceable and unfortified towns, or any unarmed and unresisting people, who

---

*In this legend most of the facts respecting the Arab inroads into Spain are on the authority of Arabian writers, who had the most accurate means of information. Those relative to the Spaniards are chiefly from old Spanish chronicles. It is to be remarked that the Arab accounts have most the air of verity and the events as they relate them are in the ordinary course of common life. The Spanish accounts on the contrary, are full of the marvellous, for there were no greater romancers than the monkish chroniclers.

remained quiet in their homes. No spoil was permitted to be made excepting in fields of battle, in camps of routed foes, or in cities taken by the sword.

Taric had little need to exercise his severity; his orders were obeyed through love, rather than fear, for he was the idol of his soldiery. They admired his restless and daring spirit, which nothing could dismay. His gaunt and sinewy form, his fiery eye, his visage seamed with scars, were suited to the hardihood of his deeds; and when mounted on his foaming steed, careering the field of battle with quivering lance or flashing scymetar, his Arabs would greet him with shouts of enthusiasm. But what endeared him to them more than all was his soldierlike contempt of gain. Conquest was his only passion; glory the only reward he coveted. As to the spoil of the conquered, he shared it freely among his followers, and squandered his own portion with openhanded generosity.

While Taric was pushing his triumphant course through Andalusia, tidings of his stupendous victory on the banks of the Guadalete were carried to Muza ben Nozier. Messengers after messengers arrived, vying who should most extol the achievements of the conqueror and the grandeur of the conquest. "Taric," said they, "has overthrown the whole force of the unbelievers in one mighty battle. Their king is slain; thousands and tens of thousands of their warriors are destroyed; the whole land lies at our mercy; and city after city is surrendering to the victorious arms of Taric."

The heart of Muza ben Noseir sickened at these tidings, and instead of rejoicing at the success of the cause of Islam, he trembled with jealous fear lest the triumphs of Taric in Spain should eclipse his own victories in Africa. He despatched missives to the Caliph Walid Almanzor, informing him of these new conquests, but taking the whole glory to himself, and making no mention of the services of Taric; or at least, only mentioning him incidentally as a subordinate commander. "The battles," said he, "have been terrible as the day of judgement; but by the aid of Allah we have gained the victory."

He then prepared in all haste to cross over into Spain and assume the command of the conquering army; and he wrote a letter in advance to interrupt Taric in the midst of his career. "Wherever this letter may find thee," said he, "I charge thee halt with thy army and await my coming. Thy force is inadequate to the subjugation of the land, and by rashly venturing thou mayst lose every thing. I will be with thee speedily, with a reinforcement of troops, competent to so great an enterprize."

The letter overtook the veteran Taric while in the full glow of triumphant success, having over run some of the richest part of Andalusia and just received the surrender of the city of Ecija. As he read the letter the blood mantled in his sunburnt cheek, and fire kindled in his eye, for he penetrated the motives of Muza. He suppressed his wrath, however, and turning with a bitter expression of forced composure to his captains, "Unsaddle your steeds," said he, "and plant your lances in the earth. Set up your tents and take your repose; for we must await the coming of the Wali with a mighty force to assist us in our conquest."

The Arab warriors broke forth with loud murmurs at these words: "What need have we of aid," cried they, "when the whole country is flying before us; and what better commander can we have than Taric to lead us on to victory?"

Count Julian, also, who was present, now hastened to give his traitorous counsel.

"Why pause," cried he, "at this precious moment? The great army of the goths is vanquished, and their nobles are slaughtered or dispersed. Follow up your blow before the land can recover from its panic. Over run the provinces, seize upon the cities, make yourself master of the capital, and your conquest is complete."*

The advice of Julian was applauded by all the Arab chieftains, who were impatient of any interruption in their career of conquest. Taric was easily persuaded to what was the wish of his heart. Disregarding the letter of Muza, therefore, he prepared to pursue his victories. For this purpose he ordered a review of his troops on the plain of Ecija. Some were mounted on steeds which they had brought from Africa, the rest he supplied with horses taken from the christians. He repeated his general orders, that they should inflict no wanton injury, nor plunder any place that offered no resistance. They were forbidden also to encumber themselves with booty, or even with provisions; but were to scour the country with all speed, and seize upon all its fortresses and strong holds.

He then divided his host into three several armies. One he placed under the command of the greek renegado Magued el Rumi, a man of desperate courage, and sent it against the ancient city of Cordova. Another was sent against the city of Malaga, and was led by Zayd ben Kesadi, aided by the Bishop Oppas. The third was led by Taric himself, and with this he determined to make a wide sweep through the kingdom.†

*Conde. p. 1. c. 10.
†Cronica de España de Alonzo el Sabio. P. 3. c. 1.

CHAPTER II

Capture of Granada—Subjugation of the Alpuxarra Mountains.

The terror of the arms of Taric ben Zeyad went before him; and at the same time the report of his lenity to those who submitted without resistance. Wherever he appeared, the towns for the most part sent forth some of their principal inhabitants to proffer a surrender; for they were destitute of fortifications and their fighting men had perished in battle. They were all received into allegiance to the caliph, and were protected from pillage or molestation.

After marching some distance through the country, he entered one day a vast and beautiful plain, interspersed with villages, adorned with groves and gardens, watered by winding rivers and surrounded by lofty mountains. It was the famous vega or plain of Granada, destined to be for ages the favorite abode of the moslems. When the Arab conquerors beheld this delicious vega they were lost in admiration; for it seemed as if the prophet had given them a paradise on earth, as a reward for their services in his cause.

Taric approached the city of Granada, which had a formidable aspect, seated on lofty hills and fortified with gothic walls and towers, and with the red castle or citadel built in times of old by the Phœnicians or the Romans. As the Arab chieftain eyed the place he was pleased with its stern warrior look, contrasting with the smiling beauty of its vega, and the freshness and voluptuous abundance of its hills and valleys. He pitched his tents before its walls, and made preparations to attack it with all his force.

The city, however, bore but the semblance of power. The flower of its youth had perished in the battle of the Guadalete, many of the principal inhabitants had fled to the mountains, and few remained in the city excepting old men, women and children, and a number of Jews, which last were well disposed to take part with the conquerors. The city, therefore, readily capitulated, and was received into vassalage on favourable terms. The inhabitants were to retain their property, their laws and their religion; their churches and priests were to be respected; and no other tribute was required of them than such as they had been accustomed to pay to their gothic kings.

On taking possession of Granada Taric garrisoned the towers and castles, and left as alcayde or governor a chosen warrior named Betiz Aben Habuz, a native of Arabia Felix, who had distinguished himself by his valour and abilities. This alcayde subsequently made himself king of Granada, and built a palace on one of its hills, the remains of which may be seen at the present day.*

Even the delights of Granada had no power to detain the active and ardent Taric. To the east of the city he beheld a lofty chain of mountains, towering to the sky, and crowned with shining snow. These were the "Mountains of the Sun and Air," and the perpetual snows on their summits gave birth to streams that fertilized the plains. In their bosoms, shut up among cliffs and precipices were many small valleys of great beauty and abundance. The inhabitants were a bold and hardy race, who looked upon their mountains as everlasting fortresses that could never be taken. The inhabitants of the surrounding country had fled to these natural fastnesses for refuge and driven thither their flocks and herds.

Taric felt that the dominion he had acquired of the plains would be insecure until he had penetrated and subdued these haughty mountains. Leaving Aben Habuz, therefore, in command of Granada, he marched with his army across the vega and entered the folds of the Sierra, which stretch towards the south. The inhabitants fled with affright on hearing the moorish trumpets, or beholding the approach of the turbaned horsemen, and plunged deeper into the recesses of their mountains. As the army advanced the roads became more and more rugged and difficult, sometimes climbing great rocky heights, and at other times descending abruptly into deep ravines, the beds of winter torrents. The mountains were strangely wild and sterile, broken into cliffs and precipices of variegated marble. At their feet were little valleys, enameled with groves and gardens, interlaced with silver streams, and studded with villages and hamlets, but all deserted by their inhabitants. No one appeared to dispute the inroad of the moslems, who

---

*The house shewn as the ancient residence of Aben Habuz is called *la Casa del Gallo* or the house of the weathercock; so named, says Pedraza in his history of Granada, from a bronze figure of an Arab horseman armed with lance and buckler, which once surmounted it; and which varied with every wind. On this warlike weathercock was inscribed in Arabic characters

> Dice el sabio Aben Habuz
> Que asi se defiende el Andaluz.
>
> (In this way, says Aben Habuz the wise,
> The Andalusian his foe defies.)

The Casa del Gallo, even until within twenty years, possessed two great halls beautifully decorated with morisco reliefs. It then caught fire and was so damaged as to require to be nearly rebuilt. It is now a manufactory of coarse canvas, and has nothing of the moorish character remaining. It commands a beautiful view of the city and the vega.

continued their march with increasing confidence, their pennons fluttering from rock and cliff, and the valleys echoing to the din of trumpet,
drum and cymbal. At length they came to a defile where the mountains
seemed to have been rent asunder to make way for a foaming torrent.
The narrow and broken road wound along the dizzy edge of precipices,
until it came to where a bridge was thrown across the chasm. It was a
fearful and gloomy pass; great beetling cliffs overhung the road, and
the torrent roared below. This awful defile has ever been famous in
the warlike history of those mountains; by the name, in former times,
of the Barranco de Tocos, and at present of The Bridge of Tablete. The
Saracen army entered fearlessly into the pass, a part had already crossed
the bridge and was slowly toiling up the rugged road on the opposite
side, when great shouts arose and every cliff appeared suddenly peopled
with furious foes. In an instant a deluge of missiles of every sort was
rained upon the astonished moslems. Darts, arrows, javelins and stones
came whistling down, singling out the most conspicuous cavaliers; and
at times great masses of rock, bounding and thundering along the
mountain side, crushed whole ranks at once, or hurled horses and riders
over the edge of the precipices.

It was in vain to attempt to brave this mountain warfare. The enemy
were beyond the reach of missiles, and safe from pursuit; and the
horses of the Arabs were here an incumbrance rather than an aid. The
trumpets sounded a retreat, and the army retired in tumult and confusion, harassed by the enemy until extricated from the defile.

Taric who had beheld cities and castles surrendering without a blow,
was enraged at being braved by a mere horde of mountain boors, and
made another attempt to penetrate the mountains, but was again waylaid
and opposed with horrible slaughter.

The fiery son of Ishmael foamed with rage at being thus checked
in his career and foiled in his revenge. He was on the point of abandoning the attempt, and returning to the vega, when a christian boor sought
his camp and was admitted to his presence. The miserable wretch
possessed a cabin and a little patch of ground among the mountains,
and offered, if these should be protected from ravage, to inform the
Arab commander of a way by which troops of horse might be safely
introduced into the bosom of the Sierra, and the whole subdued. The
name of this caitiff was Fandino, and it deserves to be perpetually
recorded with ignominy. His case is an instance how much it is in the
power at times of the most insignificant being to do mischief, and how
all the valour of the magnanimous and the brave, may be defeated by
the treason of the selfish and the despicable.

Instructed by this traytor, the Arab commander caused ten thousand
footsoldiers and four thousand horsemen, commanded by a valiant

captain named Ibrahim Albuxarra, to be conveyed by sea to the little port of Adra, at the Mediterranean foot of the mountains. Here they landed, and, guided by the traytor, penetrated to the heart of the Sierra, laying every thing waste. The brave mountaineers, thus hemmed in between two armies, destitute of fortresses and without hope of succour, were obliged to capitulate, but their valour was not without avail, for never even in Spain, did vanquished people surrender on prouder or more honorable terms. We have named the wretch who betrayed his native mountains, let us equally record the name of him whose pious patriotism saved them from desolation. It was the reverend Bishop Centerio. While the warriors rested on their arms in grim and menacing tranquility among the cliffs, this venerable prelate descended to the Arab tents in the valley, to conduct the capitulation. In stipulating for the safety of his people, he did not forget that they were brave men, and that they still had weapons in their hands. He obtained conditions accordingly. It was agreed that they should be permitted to retain their houses, lands and personal effects; that they should be unmolested in their religion, and their temples and priests respected: and that they should pay no other tribute than such as they had been accustomed to render to their kings. Should they prefer to leave the country and remove to any part of christendom, they were to be allowed to sell their possessions and to take with them the money, and all their other effects.*

Ibrahim Albuxarra remained in command of the territory, and the whole sierra or chain of mountains took his name, which has since been slightly corrupted into that of the Alpuxarras. The subjugation of this rugged region, however, was for a long time incomplete; many of the christians maintained a wild and hostile independence, living in green glens and scanty valleys among the heights; and the sierra of the Alpuxarras, has, in all ages been one of the most difficult parts of Andalusia to be subdued.

CHAPTER III

Expedition of Magued against Cordova—Defence of the patriot Pelistes.

While the veteran Taric was making this wide circuit through the land, the expedition, under Magued the Renegado, proceeded against the city of Cordova. The inhabitants of that ancient place had beheld the great army of Don Roderick spreading like an inundation over the plain

*Pedraza, Hist. Granad. p. 3. c. 2. Bleda. cronica, L.2. c. 10.

of the Guadalquivir, and had felt confident that it must sweep the infidel invaders from the land. What then was their dismay, when scattered fugitives, wild with horror and affright, brought them tidings of the entire overthrow of that mighty host, and the disappearance of the king! In the midst of their consternation, the gothic noble Pelistes arrived at their gates, haggard with fatigue of body and anguish of mind, and leading a remnant of his devoted cavaliers, who had survived the dreadful battle of the Guadalete. The people of Cordova knew the valiant and steadfast spirit of Pelistes, and rallied round him as a last hope. "Roderick is fallen," cried they, "and we have neither king nor captain; be unto us as a sovereign, take command of our city and protect us in this hour of peril!"

The heart of Pelistes was free from ambition, and was too much broken by grief to be flattered by the offer of command, but he felt above every thing for the woes of his country and was ready to assume any desperate service in her cause. "Your city" said he, "is surrounded by walls and towers, and may yet check the progress of the foe. Promise to stand by me to the last, and I will undertake your defence." The inhabitants all promised implicit obedience and devoted zeal, for what will not the inhabitants of a wealthy city promise and profess in a moment of alarm. The instant, however, that they heard of the approach of the moslem troops the wealthier citizens packed up their effects and fled to the mountains or to the distant city of Toledo. Even the monks collected the riches of their convents and churches and fled. Pelistes, though he saw himself thus deserted by those who had the greatest interest in the safety of the city, yet determined not to abandon its defence. He had still his faithful though scanty band of cavaliers, and a number of fugitives of the army, in all amounting to about four hundred men. He stationed guards, therefore, at the gates and in the towers, and made every preparation for a desperate resistance.

In the mean time, the army of moslems and apostate christians advanced under the command of the greek renegado Magued, and guided by the traytor Julian. While they were yet at some distance from the city their scouts brought to them a shepherd, whom they had surprized on the banks of the Guadalquivir. The trembling hind was an inhabitant of Cordova, and revealed to them the state of the place and the weakness of its garrison.

"And the walls and gates," said Magued, "are they strong and well guarded?"

"The walls are high and of wondrous strength," replied the shepherd, "and soldiers hold watch at the gates by day and night. But there is one place where the city may be secretly entered. In a part of the wall, not far from the bridge; the battlements are broken, and there is a breach at some height from the ground. Hard by stands a fig tree by the aid of which the wall may easily be scaled."

Having received this information Magued halted with his army, and sent forward several renegado christians, partizans of Count Julian, who entered Cordova as if flying before the enemy. On a dark and tempestuous night the moslems approached to the end of the bridge which crosses the Guadalquivir, and remained in ambush. Magued took a small party of chosen men, and, guided by the shepherd, forded the stream and groped silently along the wall to the place where stood the fig tree. The traytors who had fraudulently entered the city were ready on the wall to render assistance. Magued ordered his followers to make use of the long folds of their turbans instead of cords, and succeeded without difficulty in clambering into the breach.

Drawing their scymetars, they now hastened to the gate which opened towards the bridge; the guards, suspecting no assault from within, were taken by surprize, and easily overpowered, the gate was thrown open and the army that had remained in ambush rushed over the bridge and entered without opposition.

The alarm had by this time spread throughout the city; but already a torrent of armed men was pouring through the streets. Pelistes sallied forth with his cavaliers and such of the soldiery as he could collect and endeavoured to repel the foe, but every effort was in vain. The christians were slowly driven from street to street and square to square, disputing every inch of ground; until, finding another body of the enemy approaching to attack them in rear, they took refuge in a convent and succeeded in throwing to and barring the ponderous doors. The moors attempted to force the gates, but were assailed with such showers of missiles from the windows and battlements that they were obliged to retire. Pelistes examined the convent, and found it admirably calculated for defence. It was of great extent, with spacious courts and cloisters. The gates were massive and secured with bolts and bars; the walls were of great thickness; the windows high and grated; there was a great tank or cistern of water, and the friars, who had fled from the city, had left behind a good supply of provisions. Here then Pelistes proposed to make a stand, and to endeavour to hold out until succour should arrive from some other city. His proposition was received with shouts by his loyal cavaliers, not one of whom but was ready to lay down his life in the service of his commander.

CHAPTER IV

Defence of the Convent of St. George by Pelistes.

For three long and anxious months did the good knight Pelistes and his cavaliers defend their sacred asylum, against the repeated assaults of the infidels. The standard of the true faith was constantly displayed from the loftiest tower, and a fire blazed there throughout the night, as signals of distress to the surrounding country. The watchman from his turret kept a wary look out over the land, hoping in every cloud of dust to descry the glittering helms of christian warriors. The country, however, was forlorn and abandoned, or if perchance a human being was perceived, it was some Arab horseman, careering the plain of the Guadalquivir as fearlessly as if it were his native desert.

By degrees the provisions of the convent were consumed, and the cavaliers had to slay their horses, one by one, for food. They suffered the wasting miseries of famine without a murmur, and always met their commander with a smile. Pelistes, however, read their sufferings in their wan and emaciated countenances, and felt more for them than for himself. He was grieved at heart that such loyalty and valour should only lead to slavery or death, and resolved to make one desperate attempt for their deliverance. Assembling them one day in the court of the convent, he disclosed to them his purpose.

"Comrades and brothers in arms," said he, "it is needless to conceal danger from brave men. Our case is desperate; our countrymen either know not or heed not our situation, or have not the means to help us. There is but one chance of escape, it is full of peril, and, as your leader I claim the right to brave it. Tomorrow at break of day I will sally forth and make for the city gates at the moment of their being opened. No one will suspect a solitary horseman; I shall be taken for one of those recreant christians who have basely mingled with the enemy. If I succeed in getting out of the city I will hasten to Toledo for assistance. In all events I shall be back in less than twenty days. Keep a vigilant look out toward the nearest mountain. If you behold five lights blazing upon its summit, be assured I am at hand with succour, and prepare yourselves to sally forth upon the city as I attack the gates. Should I fail in obtaining aid I will return to die with you."

When he had finished his warriors would fain have severally undertaken the enterprize, and they remonstrated against his exposing himself to such peril; but he was not to be shaken from his purpose. On the following morning ere the break of day, his horse was led forth caparisoned into the court of the convent, and Pelistes appeared in complete armour. Assembling his cavaliers in the chapel, he prayed with them for some time before the altar of the holy Virgin. Then rising and standing in the midst of them, "God knows, my companions," said he, "whether we have any longer a country; if not, better were we in our graves. Loyal and true have you been to me, and loyal have ye been to my son, even to the hour of his death; and grieved am I that I have no other means of proving my love for you, than by adventuring my worthless life for your deliverance. All I ask of you before I go, is a solemn promise to defend yourselves to the last like brave men and christian cavaliers, and never to renounce your faith or throw yourselves on the mercy of the renegado Magued or the traytor Julian." They all pledged their words and took a solemn oath to the same effect before the altar.

Pelistes then embraced them one by one, and gave them his benediction, and as he did so his heart yearned over them, for he felt towards them, not merely as a companion in arms and as a commander, but as a father; and he took leave of them as if he had been going to his death. The warriors, on their part, crowded round him in silence kissing his hands and the hem of his surcoat, and many of the sternest shed tears.

The grey of the dawning had just streaked the east when Pelistes took lance in hand, hung his shield about his neck, and, mounting his steed, issued quietly forth from a postern of the convent. He paced slowly through the vacant streets, and the tramp of his steed echoed afar in that silent hour, but no one suspected a warrior, moving thus singly and tranquilly in an armed city, to be an enemy. He arrived at the gate just at the hour of opening; a foraging party was entering with cattle and with beasts of burthen, and he passed unheeded through the throng. As soon as he was out of sight of the soldiers who guarded the gate he quickened his pace, and at length galloping at full speed, succeeded in gaining the mountains. Here he paused and alighted at a solitary farm house to breathe his panting steed, but had scarce put foot to ground when he heard the distant sound of pursuit, and beheld a horseman spurring up the mountain.

Throwing himself again upon his steed, he abandoned the road and galloped across the rugged heights. The deep dry channel of a torrent checked his career, and his horse stumbling upon the margin rolled with his rider to the bottom. Pelistes was sorely bruised by the fall and his whole visage was bathed in blood. His horse, too, was maimed and unable to stand so that there was no hope of escape. The enemy drew near and proved to be no other than Magued the renegado general, who had perceived him as he issued forth from the city and had followed singly in pursuit. "Well met Señor Alcayde!" exclaimed he, "and overtaken in good time. Surrender yourself my prisoner."

Pelistes made no other reply than by drawing his sword, bracing his shield and preparing for defence. Magued, though an apostate, and a fierce warrior, yet possessed some sparks of knightly magnanimity. Seeing his adversary dismounted, he disdained to take him at a disadvantage, but, alighting, tied his horse to a tree.

The conflict that ensued was desperate and doubtful, for seldom had two warriors met so well matched or of equal prowess. Their shields were hacked to pieces, the ground was strewed with fragments of their armour, and stained with their blood. They paused repeatedly to take breath, regarding each other with wonder and admiration. Pelistes, however, had been previously injured by his fall, and fought to great disadvantage. The renegado perceived it, and sought not to slay him, but to take him alive. Shifting his ground continually he wearied his antagonist, who was growing weaker and weaker from the loss of blood. At length Pelistes seemed to summon up all his remaining strength to make a signal blow, it was skillfully parried, and he fell prostrate upon the ground. The Renegado ran up, and putting his foot upon his sword, and the point of the scymetar to his throat, called upon him to ask his life; but Pelistes lay without sense, and as one dead.

Magued then unlaced the helmet of his vanquished enemy, and seated himself on a rock beside him, to recover breath. In this situation the warriors were found by certain moorish cavaliers, who marvelled much at the traces of that stern and bloody combat.

Finding there was yet life in the christian knight, they laid him upon one of their horses and aiding Magued to remount his steed, proceeded slowly to the city. As the convoy passed by the convent the cavaliers looked forth and beheld their commander borne along bleeding and a captive. Furious at the sight they sallied forth to the rescue; but were repulsed by a superior force and driven back to the great portal of the church. The enemy entered pell mell with them, fighting from aisle to aisle, from altar to altar and in the courts and cloisters of the convent. The greater part of the cavaliers died bravely sword in hand, the rest were disabled with wounds and made prisoners. The convent which was lately their castle was now made their prison, and in aftertimes, in commemoration of this event, was consecrated by the name of St. George of the Captives.

CHAPTER V

Meeting between the patriot Pelistes and the traitor Julian.

The loyalty and prowess of the good knight Pelistes had gained him the reverence even of his enemies. He was for a long time disabled by his wounds, during which he was kindly treated by the Arab chieftains, who strove by every courteous means, to cheer his sadness and make him forget that he was a captive. When he was recovered from his wounds they gave him a magnificent banquet to testify their admiration of his virtues.

Pelistes appeared at the banquet clad in sable armour and with a countenance pale and dejected, for the ills of his country ever more preyed upon his heart. Among the assembled guests was Count Julian, who held a high command in the moslem army, and was arrayed in garments of mingled christian and morisco fashion. Pelistes had been a close and bosom friend of Julian in former times, and had served with him in the wars in Africa, but when the count advanced to accost him with his wonted amity, he turned away in silence and deigned not to notice him; neither, during the whole of the repast, did he address to him ever a word, but treated him as one unknown.

When the banquet was nearly at a close the discourse turned upon the events of the war, and the moslem chieftains, in great courtesy, dwelt upon the merits of many of the christian cavaliers who had fallen in battle, and all extolled the valour of those who had recently perished in the defence of the convent. Pelistes remained silent for a time, and checked the grief which swelled within his bosom as he thought of his devoted cavaliers. At length lifting up his voice "Happy are the dead," said he, "for they rest in peace, and are gone to receive the reward of their piety and valour! I could mourn over the loss of my companions in arms, but they have fallen with honour, and are spared the wretchedness I feel in witnessing the thraldom of my country. I have seen my only son, the pride and hope of my age, cut down at my side. I have beheld kindred friends and followers falling one by one around me, and have become so seasoned to those losses that I have ceased to weep. Yet there is one man over whose loss I will never cease to grieve. He was the loved companion of my youth and the steadfast associate of my graver years. He was one of the most loyal of christian knights. As a friend he was loving and sincere; as a warrior his achievements were above all praise. What has become of him alas I know not! If fallen in battle, and I knew where his bones were laid, whether bleaching on the plains of Xeres, or buried in the waters of the Guadalete, I would seek them out and enshrine them as the reliques of a sainted patriot. Or if, like many of his companions in arms, he should be driven to wander in foreign lands I would join him in his hapless exile, and we would mourn together over the desolation of our country!"

Even the hearts of the Arab warriors were touched by the lament of the good Pelistes, and they said, "Who was this peerless friend in whose praise thou art so fervent?"

"His name," replied Pelistes, "was Count Julian."

The moslem warriors stared with surprize. "Noble cavalier!" exclaimed they, "has grief disordered thy senses? Behold thy friend living and standing before thee, and yet thou dost not know him! This, this is Count Julian!"

Upon this Pelistes turned his eyes upon the count, and regarded him for a time with a lofty and stern demeanour; and the countenance of Julian darkened and was troubled, and his eye sank beneath the regard of that loyal and honourable cavalier. And Pelistes said, "In the name of God I charge thee, man unknown! to answer. Dost thou presume to call thyself Count Julian?"

The Count reddened with anger at these words. "Pelistes," said he, "what means this mockery; thou knowest me well; thou knowest me for Count Julian."

"I know thee for a base impostor!" cried Pelistes. "Count Julian was a noble gothic knight, but thou appearest in mongrel moorish garb. Count Julian was a christian, faithful and devout; but I behold in thee a renegado and an infidel. Count Julian was ever loyal to his king and foremost in his country's cause; were he living he would be the first to put shield on neck and lance in rest to clear the land of her invaders; but thou art a hoary traytor! thy hands are stained with the royal blood of the goths, and thou hast betrayed thy country and thy God. Therefore I again repeat, man unknown! if thou sayest thou art Count Julian, thou liest! My friend, alas, is dead; and thou art some fiend from hell, which hast taken possession of his body to dishonour his memory and render him an abhorrence among men!" So saying, Pelistes turned his back upon the traytor, and went forth from the banquet, leaving Count Julian overwhelmed with confusion, and an object of scorn to all the moslem cavaliers.

CHAPTER VI

*How Taric el Tuerto captured the city of Toledo through the aid of
the Jews, and how he found the famous talismanic table of Solomon.*

While these events were passing in Cordova, the one eyed Arab
general, Taric el Tuerto, having subdued the city and vega of Granada
and the Mountains of the Sun and Air, directed his march into the
interior of the kingdom, to attack the ancient city of Toledo, the
capital of the gothic kings. So great was the terror caused by the rapid
conquests of the invaders, that at the very rumour of their approach
many of the inhabitants, though thus in the very citadel of the kingdom, abandoned it and fled to the mountains with their families.
Enough remained, however, to have made a formidable defence, and
as the city was seated on a lofty rock, surrounded by massive walls and
towers, and almost girdled by the Tagus, it threatened a long resistance.
The Arab warriors pitched their tents on the vega, on the borders of
the river, and prepared for a tedious siege.

One evening, as Taric was seated in his tent meditating on the mode
in which he should assail this rock built city, certain of the patroles of
the camp brought a stranger before him. "As we were going our
rounds," said they, "we beheld this man lowered down with cords
from a tower, and he delivered himself into our hands praying to be
conducted to thy presence, that he might reveal to thee certain things
important for thee to know."

Taric fixed his eyes upon the stranger: he was a Jewish rabbi, with
a long beard which spread upon his gabardine and descended even
to his girdle. "What hast thou to reveal?" said he to the Israelite. "What
I have to reveal," replied the other, "is for thee alone to hear, command
then I intreat thee that these men withdraw." When they were alone
he addressed Taric in Arabic. "Know, Oh leader of the host of Islam,"
said he, "that I am sent to thee on the part of the children of Israel,
resident in Toledo. We have been oppressed and insulted by the
christians in the time of their prosperity, and now that they are
threatened with siege, they have taken from us all our provisions and
our money; they have compelled us to work like slaves, in repairing
their walls, and they oblige us to bear arms and guard a part of the
towers. We abhor their yoke, and are ready, if thou wilt receive us as
subjects and permit us the free enjoyment of our religion and our
property, to deliver the towers we guard into thy hands, and to give
thee safe entrance into the city."

The Arab chief was overjoyed at this proposition, and he rendered
much honour to the Rabbi, and gave orders to clothe him in a costly

robe and to perfume his beard with essences of a pleasant odour, so that he was the most sweetsmelling of his tribe; and he said, "Make thy words good and put me in possession of the city and I will do all and more than thou hast required and will bestow countless wealth upon thee and thy brethren."

Then a plan was devised between them by which the city was to be betrayed and given up. "But how shall I be secured," said he, "that all thy tribe will fulfil what thou hast engaged, and that this is not a stratagem to get me and my people into your power?"

"This shall be thy assurance," replied the Rabbi. "Ten of the principal Israelites will come to this tent and remain as hostages."

"It is enough," said Taric, and he made oath to accomplish all that he had promised, and the Jewish hostages came and delivered themselves into his hands.

On a dark night a chosen band of moslem warriors approached the part of the walls guarded by the Jews, and were secretly admitted into a postern gate and concealed within a tower. Three thousand Arabs were at the same time placed in ambush among rocks and thickets in a place on the opposite side of the river, commanding a view of the city. On the following morning Taric ravaged the gardens of the valley and set fire to the farm houses, and then breaking up his camp, marched off as if abandoning the siege.

The people of Toledo gazed with astonishment from their walls at the retiring squadrons of the enemy, and scarcely could credit their unexpected deliverance, before night there was not a turban nor a hostile lance to be seen in the vega. They attributed it all to the special intervention of their patron Saint Leocadia, and the following day being Palm Sunday, they sallied forth in procession, man, woman, and child, to the church of that blessed saint, which is situated without the walls, that they might return thanks for her marvellous protection.

When all Toledo had thus poured itself forth, and was marching with cross, and relique and solemn chaunt towards the chapel, the Arabs who had been concealed in the tower rushed forth and barred the gates of the city. While some guarded the gates others dispersed themselves about the streets slaying all who made resistance and others kindled a fire and made a column of smoke on the top of the citadel. At sight of this signal the Arabs in ambush beyond the river rose with a great shout, and attacked the multitude who were thronging to the church of St. Leocadia. There was a great massacre, although the people were without arms and made no resistance, and it is said in ancient chronicles, that it was the apostate Bishop Oppas who guided the moslems to their prey and incited them to this slaughter.

The pious reader, says Fray Antonio Agapida, will be slow to believe such turpitude, but there is nothing more venomous than the rancour of an apostate priest; for the best things in this world, when corrupted, become the worst and most baneful.

Many of the christians had taken refuge within the church and had barred the doors, but Oppas commanded that fire should be set to the portals, threatening to put every one within to the sword. Happily the veteran Taric arrived just in time to stay the fury of this reverend renegado. He ordered the trumpets to call off the troops from the carnage, and extended grace to all the surviving inhabitants. They were permitted to remain in quiet possession of their homes and effects, paying only a moderate tribute; and they were allowed to exercise the rites of their religion in the existing churches, to the number of seven, but were prohibited from erecting any others. Those who preferred to leave the city were suffered to depart in safety, but not to take with them any of their wealth.

Immense spoil was found by Taric in the alcazar or royal castle, situated on a rocky eminence in the highest part of the city. Among the regalia treasured up in a secret chamber were twenty five regal crowns of fine gold, garnished with jacynths, amethysts, diamonds and other precious stones. These were the crowns of the different gothic kings who had reigned in Spain; it having been the usage, on the death of each king, to deposit his crown in this treasury, inscribing on it his name and age.*

When Taric was thus in possession of the city the Jews came to him in procession, with songs and dances and the sound of timbrel and psaltry, hailing him as their lord, and reminding him of his promises.

The son of Ishmael kept his word with the children of Israel; they were protected in the possession of all their wealth and the exercise of their religion, and were moreover rewarded with jewels of gold and jewels of silver, and much monies.†

A subsequent expedition was led by Taric against Guadalaxara, which surrendered without resistance; he moreover captured the city of Medina Celi, where he found an inestimable table which had formed a part of the spoil taken at Rome by Alaric, at the time that the sacred city was conquered by the goths. It was composed of one single and entire emerald, and possessed talismanic powers; for traditions affirm that it was the work of genii and had been wrought by them for King Solomon the wise, the son of David. This marvellous relique was care-

*Conde. Hist. de las Arabes en España, c. 12.
†The stratagem of the Jews of Toledo is recorded briefly by Bishop Lucas de Tuy in his chronicle, but is related at large in the chronicle of the Moor Rasis.

fully preserved by Taric as the most precious of all his spoils, being intended by him as a present to the caliph, and in commemoration of it the city was called by the Arabs Medina Almeyda; that is to say, "The City of the table."*

Having made these and other conquests of less importance, and having collected great quantities of gold and silver and rich stuffs and precious stones, Taric returned with his booty to the royal city of Toledo.

CHAPTER VII

Muza ben Noseir—His entrance into Spain and capture of Carmona.

Let us leave for a season the bold Taric in his triumphant progress from city to city, while we turn our eyes to Muza ben Nozier, the renowned Emir of Almagreb, and the commander in chief of the moslem forces of the west. When that jealous chieftain had dispatched his letter commanding Taric to pause and await his coming, he immediately made every preparation to enter Spain with a powerful reinforcement, and to take command of the conquering army. He left his eldest son, Abdalasis in Caervan, with authority over Almagreb or Western Africa. This Abdalasis was in the flower of his youth, and beloved by the soldiery for the magnanimity and the engaging affability which graced his courage.

Muza ben Nozier crossed the Strait of Hercules with a chosen force of ten thousand horse and eight thousand foot, Arabs and Africans. He was accompanied by his two sons Meruan and Abdelola and by numerous illustrious Arabian cavaliers of the tribe of the Koreish. He landed his shining legions on the coast of Andalusia, and pitched his tents near to the Guadiana. There first he received intelligence of the disobedience of Taric to his orders, and that, without waiting his arrival, the impetuous chieftain had continued his career, and with his light Arab squadrons had overrun and subdued the noblest provinces and cities of the kingdom.

The jealous spirit of Muza was still more exasperated by these

---

*According to Arabian legends this table was a mirror revealing all great events, insomuch that by looking on it the possessor might behold battles and sieges and feats of chivalry, and all actions worthy of renown, and might thus ascertain the truth of all historic transactions. It was a mirror of history, therefore, and had very probably aided King Solomon in acquiring that prodigious knowledge and wisdom, for which he was renowned.

tidings; he looked upon Taric no longer as a friend and coadjutor, but as an invidious rival, the decided enemy of his glory, and he determined on his ruin. His first consideration, however, was to secure to himself a share in the actual conquest of the land, before it should be entirely subjugated.

Taking guides, therefore, from among his christian captives, he set out to subdue such parts of the country as had not been visited by Taric. The first place which he assailed was the ancient city of Carmona; it was not of great magnitude, but was fortified with high walls and massive towers, and many of the fugitives of the late army had thrown themselves into it.

The goths had by this time recovered from their first panic, they had become accustomed to the sight of moslem troops and their native courage had been roused by danger. Shortly after the Arabs had encamped before their walls a band of cavaliers made a sudden sally one morning before the break of day, fell upon the enemy by surprize, killed above three hundred of them in their tents, and effected their retreat into the city, leaving twenty of their number dead, covered with honorable wounds, and in the very centre of the camp.

On the following day they made another sally, and fell on a different quarter of the encampment; but the Arabs were on their guard, and met them with superior numbers. After fighting fiercely for a time, they were routed and fled full speed for the city, with the Arabs hard upon their traces. The guards within feared to open the gates lest with their friends they should admit a torrent of enemies. Seeing themselves thus shut out the fugitives determined to die like brave soldiers rather than surrender. Wheeling suddenly round, they opened a path through the host of their pursuers, fought their way back to the camp and raged about it with desperate fury, until they were all slain, after having killed above eight hundred of the enemy.*

Muza now ordered that the place should be taken by storm. The moslems assailed it on all sides, but were vigorously resisted; many were slain by showers of stones, arrows and boiling pitch, and many who had mounted with scaling ladders were thrown headlong from the battlements. The alcayde, Galo, aided solely by two men, defended a tower and a portion of the wall, killing and wounding with a cross bow more than eighty of the enemy. The attack lasted above half a day, when the moslems were repulsed with the loss of fifteen hundred men.

Muza was astonished and exasperated at meeting with such formidable resistance from so small a city for it was one of the few places,

*Abulcasim. Perdida de España, L. 1. c. 13.

during that memorable conquest, where the gothic valour shone forth with its proper lustre. While the moslem army lay encamped before the place it was joined by Magued the Renegado, and Count Julian the traytor, with one thousand horsemen; most of them recreant christians, base betrayers of their country, and more savage in their warfare than the Arabs of the desert. To find favour in the eyes of Muza, and to evince his devotion to the cause, the count undertook, by wiley stratagem to put this gallant city in his power.

One evening, just at twilight, a number of christians, habited as travelling merchants arrived at one of the gates, conducting a train of mules laden with arms and warlike munitions. "Open the gate quickly," cried they, "we bring supplies for the garrison, but the Arabs have discovered and are in pursuit of us." The gate was thrown open, the merchants entered with their beasts of burden, and were joyfully received. Meat and drink were placed before them, and after they had refreshed themselves they retired to the quarters allotted to them.

These pretended merchants were Count Julian and a number of his partizans. At the hour of midnight they stole forth silently, and assembling together proceeded to what was called the Gate of Cordova. Here setting suddenly upon the unsuspecting guards they put them to the edge of the sword, and, throwing open the gates admitted a great body of the Arabs. The inhabitants were roused from their sleep by sound of drum and trumpet and the clattering of horses. The Arabs scoured the streets; a horrible massacre was commenced, in which none were spared but such of the females as were young and beautiful, and fitted to grace the harems of the conquerors. The arrival of Muza put an end to the pillage and the slaughter, and he granted favorable terms to the survivors. Thus the valiant little city of Carmona, after nobly resisting the open assaults of the infidels, fell a victim to the treachery of apostate christians.*

CHAPTER VIII

Muza marches against the city of Seville.

After the capture of Carmona, Muza descended into a noble plain, covered with fields of grain, with orchards and gardens, through which glided the soft flowing Guadalquivir. On the borders of the river stood the ancient city of Seville surrounded by Roman walls, and defended

*Cron. gen. de España, por Alonzo el Sabio. P. 3. c. 1.

by its golden tower. Understanding from his spies that the city had lost the flower of its youth in the battle of the Guadalete, Muza anticipated but a faint resistance. A considerable force however, still remained within the place, and what they wanted in numbers they made up in resolution. For some days they withstood the assaults of the enemy, and defended their walls with great courage. Their want of warlike munitions however, and the superior force and skill of the besieging army, left them no hope of being able to hold out long. There were two youthful cavaliers of uncommon valour in the city. They assembled the warriors and addressed them. "We cannot save the city," said they, "but at least we may save ourselves, and preserve so many strong arms for the service of our country. Let us cut our way through the infidel force, and gain some secure fortress, from whence we may return with augmented numbers for the rescue of the city."

The advice of the young cavaliers was adopted. In the dead of the night the garrison assembled to the number of about three thousand, the most part mounted on horseback. Suddenly sallying from one of the gates they rushed in a compact body upon the camp of the Saracens, which was negligently guarded, for the moslems expected no such act of desperation. The camp was a scene of great carnage and confusion; many were slain on both sides, the two valiant leaders of the christians fell covered with wounds, but the main body succeeded in forcing their way through the centre of the army, and in making their retreat to Beja in Lusitania.

Muza was at a loss to know the meaning of this desperate sally. In the morning he perceived the gates of the city wide open. A number of ancient and venerable men presented themselves at his tent offering submission and imploring mercy, for none were left in the place but the old the infirm and the miserable. Muza listened to them with compassion and granted their prayer, and the only tribute he exacted was three measures of wheat and three of barley from each house or family. He placed a garrison of Arabs in the city, and left there a number of Jews to form a body of population. Having thus secured two important places in Andalusia, he passed the boundaries of the province and advanced with great martial pomp into Lusitania.

CHAPTER IX

Muza beseiges the city of Merida.

The army of Muza was now augmented to about eighteen thousand horsemen, but he took with him but few footsoldiers, leaving them to garrison the conquered towns. He met with no resistance on his entrance into Lusitania. City after city laid its keys at his feet, and implored to be received in peaceful vassalage. One city alone prepared for vigorous defence, the ancient Merida, a place of great extent, uncounted riches and prodigious strength. A noble goth named Sacarus was the governor; a man of consummate wisdom, patriotism and valour. Hearing of the approach of the invaders he gathered within the walls all the people of the surrounding country with their horses and mules, their flocks and herds, and most precious effects. To insure for a long time a supply of bread he filled the magazines with grain and erected windmills on the churches. This done he laid waste the surrounding country to a great extent, so that a besieging army would have to encamp in a desert.

When Muza came in sight of this magnificent city he was struck with admiration. He remained for some time gazing in silence upon its mighty walls and lordly towers, its vast extent and the stately palaces and temples with which it was adorned. "Surely," cried he at length, "all the people of the earth have combined their power and skill to embellish and aggrandize this city. Allah Achbar! Happy will he be who shall have the glory of making such a conquest!"

Seeing that a place so populous and so strongly fortified would be likely to maintain a long and formidable resistance, he sent messengers to Africa to his son Abdalasis, to collect all the forces that could be spared from the garrisons of Mauritania and to hasten and reinforce him.

While Muza was forming his encampment deserters from the city brought him word that a chosen band intended to sally forth at midnight and surprize his camp. The Arab commander immediately took measures to receive them with a counter surprize. Having formed his plan, and communicated it to his principal officers, he ordered that, throughout the day, there should be kept up an appearance of negligent confusion in his encampment. The outposts were feebly guarded; fires were lighted in various places, as if preparing for feasting, bursts of music and shouts of revelry resounded from different quarters, and the whole camp seemed to be rioting in careless security on the plunder of the land. As the night advanced the fires were gradually extinguished and silence ensued, as if the soldiery had sunk into deep sleep after the carousal.

In the mean time bodies of troops had been secretly and silently marched to reinforce the outposts, and the renegado Magued with a numerous force had formed an ambuscade in a deep stone quarry by which the christians would have to pass. These preparations being made they awaited the approach of the enemy in breathless silence.

About midnight the chosen force intended for the sally assembled and the command was confided to Count Tendero a gothic cavalier of tried prowess. After having heard a solemn mass and received the benediction of the priest, they marched out of the gate with all possible silence. They were suffered to pass the ambuscade in the quarry without molestation: as they approached the moslem camp every thing appeared quiet, for the footsoldiers were concealed in slopes and hollows, and every Arab horseman lay in his armour beside his steed. The centinels on the outposts awaited until the christians were close at hand and then fled in apparent consternation.

Count Tendero gave the signal for assault and the christians rushed confidently forward. In an instant an uproar of drums, trumpets and shrill war cries burst forth from every side. An army seemed to spring up from the earth; squadrons of horse came thundering on them in front, while the quarry poured forth legions of armed warriors in their rear.

The noise of the terrific conflict that took place was heard on the city walls and answered by shouts of exultation, for the christians thought it rose from the terror and confusion of the Arab camp. In a little while however they were undeceived by fugitives from the fight, aghast with terror, and covered with wounds. "Hell itself," cried they, "is on the side of these infidels; the earth casts forth warriors and steeds to aid them. We have fought, not with men, but devils!"

The greater part of the chosen troops who had sallied, were cut to pieces in that scene of massacre, for they had been confounded by the tempest of battle which suddenly broke forth around them. Count Tendero fought with desperate valour and fell covered with wounds. His body was found the next morning, lying among the slain and transpierced with half a score of lances. The renegado Magued cut off his head and tied it to the tail of his horse, and repaired with this savage trophy to the tent of Muza; but the hostility of the Arab general was of a less malignant kind. He ordered that the head and body should be placed together upon a bier and treated with becoming reverence.

In the course of the day a train of priests and friars came forth from the city to request permission to seek for the body of the Count. Muza delivered it to them, with many soldierlike encomiums on the valour of that good cavalier. The priests covered it with a pall of cloth of gold, and bore it back in melancholy procession to the city where it was received with loud lamentations.

The siege was now pressed with great vigour and repeated assaults were made, but in vain. Muza saw at length, that the walls were too high to be scaled and the gates too strong to be burst open without the aid of engines, and he desisted from the attack until machines for the purpose could be constructed. The governor suspected from this cessation of active warfare, that the enemy flattered themselves to reduce the place by famine; he caused, therefore, large baskets of bread to be thrown from the wall, and sent a messenger to Muza to inform him that, if his army should be in want of bread he would supply it, having sufficient corn in his granaries for a ten years siege.*

The citizens, however, did not possess the undaunted spirit of their governor. When they found that the moslems were constructing tremendous engines for the destruction of their walls, they lost all courage, and surrounding the governor in a clamorous multitude compelled him to send forth persons to capitulate.

The ambassadors came into the presence of Muza with awe, for they expected to find a fierce and formidable warrior in one who had filled the land with terror, but to their astonishment they beheld an ancient and venerable man with white hair, a snowy beard, and a pale emaciated countenance. He had passed the previous night without sleep, and had been all day in the field; he was exhausted therefore by watchfulness and fatigue, and his garments were covered with dust.

"What a devil of a man is this," murmured the ambassadors one to another, "to undertake such a siege when on the verge of the grave. Let us defend our city the best way we can, surely we can hold out longer than the life of this greybeard."

They returned to the city, therefore, scoffing at an invader who seemed fitter to lean on a crutch than to wield a lance; and the terms offered by Muza, which would otherwise have been thought favourable, were scornfully rejected by the inhabitants. A few days put an end to this mistaken confidence. Abdalasis the son of Muza arrived from Africa at the head of his reinforcement; he brought seven thousand horsemen, and a host of Barbary archers and made a glorious display as he marched into the camp. The arrival of this youthful warrior was hailed with great acclamations, so much had he won the hearts of the soldiery by the frankness, the suavity and generosity of his conduct. Immediately after his arrival a grand assault was made upon the city, and several of the huge battering engines being finished, they were wheeled up and began to thunder against the walls.

*Bleda. cronica. L. 2. c. 11.

The unsteady populace were again seized with terror and surrounding their governor with fresh clamours, obliged him to send forth ambassadors a second time to treat of a surrender. When admitted to the presence of Muza the ambassadors could scarcely believe their eyes, or that this was the same withered, whiteheaded old man, of whom they had lately spoken with scoffing. His hair and beard were tinged of a ruddy brown; his countenance was refreshed by repose and flushed with indignation and he appeared a man in the matured vigour of his days. The ambassadors were struck with awe. "Surely," whispered they one to the other, "this must be either a devil or a magician who can thus make himself old and young at pleasure!"

Muza received them haughtily. "Hence," said he, "and tell your people I grant them the same terms I have already proffered, provided the city be instantly surrendered, but by the head of Mahomet, if there be any further delay not one mother's son of ye shall receive mercy at my hands!"

The deputies returned into the city pale and dismayed. "Go forth! go forth!" cried they, "and accept whatever terms are offered. Of what avail is it to fight against men who can renew their youth at pleasure. Behold we left the leader of the infidels an old and feeble man and to day we find him youthful and vigorous!"*

The place was therefore surrendered forthwith, and Muza entered it in triumph. His terms were merciful. Those who chose to remain were protected in persons, possessions and religion; he took the property of those only who abandoned the city or had fallen in battle; together with all arms and horses and the treasures and ornaments of the churches. Among these sacred spoils was found a cup made of a single pearl, which a king of Spain, in ancient times, had brought from the temple of Jerusalem, when it was destroyed by Nebucadonozer. This precious relique was sent by Muza to the caliph and was placed in the principal mosque of the city of Damascus.†

Muza knew how to esteem merit even in an enemy. When Sacarus the governor of Merida appeared before him he lauded him greatly for the skill and courage he had displayed in the defence of his city; and, taking off his own scymetar, which was of great value, girded it upon him with his own hands. "Wear this," said he, "as a poor memorial of my admiration; a soldier of such virtue and valour is worthy of far higher honours."

He would have engaged the governor in his service, or have persuaded him to remain in the city as an illustrious vassal of the caliph, but the

*Conde, p. 1. c. 13. Ambrosio de Morales. N. B.—In the chronicle of Spain composed by order of Alonzo the Wise this anecdote is given as having happened at the siege of Seville.

†Marmol. descrip. de Africa, T.1. L.2.

noble minded Sacarus refused to bend to the yoke of the conquerors; nor could he bring himself to reside contentedly in his country when subjected to the domination of the infidels. Gathering together all those who chose to accompany him into exile, he embarked to seek some country where he might live in peace and in the free exercise of his religion; what shore these ocean pilgrims landed upon has never been revealed, but tradition vaguely gives us to believe that it was some unknown island, far in the bosom of the Atlantic.*

CHAPTER X

Expedition of Abdalasis against Seville and the "Land of Tadmir."

After the capture of Merida, Muza gave a grand banquet to his captains and distinguished warriors, in that magnificent city. At this martial feast were many Arab cavaliers who had been present in various battles, and they vied with each other in recounting the daring enterprizes in which they had been engaged and the splendid triumphs they had witnessed. While they talked with ardour and exultation Abdalasis the son of Muza alone kept silence, and sat with a dejected countenance. At length, when there was a pause, he turned to his father and addressed him with modest earnestness. "My lord and father," said he, "I blush to hear your warriors recount the toils and dangers they have passed, while I have done nothing to entitle me to their companionship. When I return to Egypt and present myself before the caliph he will ask me of my services in Spain: what battle I have gained, what town or castle I have taken. How shall I answer him? If you love me then as your son, give me a command, entrust to me an enterprize, and let me acquire a name worthy to be mentioned among men."

The eyes of Muza kindled with joy at finding Abdelasis thus ambitious of renown in arms. "Allah be praised!" exclaimed he, "the heart of my son is in the right place. It is becoming in youth to look upward and be aspiring. Thy desire Abdelasis, shall be gratified."

An opportunity at that very time presented itself to prove the prowess and discretion of the youth. During the siege of Merida the christian troops which had taken refuge at Beja had reinforced themselves from Peñaflor and suddenly returning had presented themselves before the gates of the city of Seville.† Certain of the christian inhabitants threw

*Abulcasim, Perdida de España, L. 1. c. 13.
†Espinosa. Antq. y Grand. de Seville. L. 2. c. 3.

open the gates and admitted them. The troops rushed to the alcazar, took it by surprize and put many of the moslem garrison to the sword; the residue made their escape and fled to the Arab camp before Merida, leaving Seville in the hands of the christians.

The veteran Muza, now that the siege of Merida was at an end, was meditating the recapture and punishment of Seville, at the very time when Abdelasis addressed him. "Behold, my son," exclaimed he, "an enterprize worthy of thy ambition. Take with thee all the troops thou hast brought from Africa. Reduce the city of Seville again to subjection and plant thy standard upon its alcazar. But stop not there —carry thy conquering sword into the southern parts of Spain; thou wilt find there a harvest of glory yet to be reaped."

Abdelasis lost no time in departing upon this enterprize. He took with him Count Julian, Magued el Rumi and the Bishop Oppas, that he might benefit by their knowledge of the country. When he came in sight of the fair city of Seville, seated like a queen in the midst of its golden plain, with the Guadalquivir flowing beneath its walls, he gazed upon it with the admiration of a lover, and lamented in his soul that he had to visit it as an avenger. His troops, however, regarded it with wrathful eyes, thinking only of its rebellion and of the massacre of their countrymen in the alcazar.

The principal people of the city had taken no part in this gallant but fruitless insurrection; and now, when they beheld the army of Abdalasis encamped upon the banks of the Guadalquivir, would fain have gone forth to make explanations; and intercede for mercy. The populace, however, forbade any one to leave the city, and, barring the gates, prepared to defend themselves to the last.

The place was attacked with resistless fury. The gates were soon burst open; the moslems rushed in, panting for revenge. They confined not their slaughter to the soldiery in the alcazar, but roamed through every street, confounding the innocent with the guilty in one bloody massacre, and it was with the utmost difficulty that Abdalasis could at length succeed in staying their sanguinary career.*

The son of Muza proved himself as mild in conquest as he had been intrepid in assault. The moderation and benignity of his conduct soothed the terrors of the vanquished, and his wise precautions restored tranquility. Having made proper regulations for the protection of the inhabitants he left a strong garrison in the place to prevent any future insurrection, and then departed on the further prosecution of his enterprize.

Wherever he went his arms were victorious; and his victories were

*Conde, P. 1. c. 14.

always characterized by the same magnanimity. At length he arrived on the confines of that beautiful region, comprizing lofty and precipitous mountains and rich and delicious plains, afterwards known by the name of the Kingdom of Murcia. All this part of the country was defended by the veteran Theodomir, who by skillful management had saved a remnant of his forces after the defeat on the banks of the Guadalete.

Theodomir was a staunch warrior, but a wary and prudent man. He had experienced the folly of opposing the Arabs in open field, where their cavalry and armour gave them such superiority, on their approach, therefore, he assembled all his people, capable of bearing arms, and took possession of the cliffs and mountain passes. "Here," said he, "a simple goatherd who can hurl down rocks and stones, is as good as a warrior, armed in proof." In this way he checked and harassed the moslem army in all its movements; showering down missiles upon it from overhanging precipices, and waylaying it in narrow and rugged defiles, where a few raw troops could make stand against a host.

Theodomir was in a fair way to baffle his foes and oblige them to withdraw from his territories, unfortunately, however, the wary veteran had two sons with him, young men of hot and heady valour, who considered all this prudence of their father as savouring of cowardice, and who were anxious to try their prowess in the open field. "What glory," said they, "is to be gained by destroying an enemy in this way, from the covert of rocks and thickets?"

"You talk like young men," replied the veteran. "Glory is a prize one may fight for abroad, but safety is the object when the enemy is at the door."

One day, however, the young men succeeded in drawing down their father into the plain. Abdalasis immediately seized on the opportunity and threw himself between the goths and their mountain fastnesses. Theodomir saw too late the danger into which he was betrayed. "What can our raw troops do," said he, "against those squadrons of horse that move like castles? Let us make a rapid retreat to Orihuela and defend ourselves from behind its walls."

"Father," said the eldest son, "it is too late to retreat, remain here with the reserve while my brother and I advance. Fear nothing. Am not I your son, and would I not die to defend you?"

"In truth," replied the veteran, "I have my doubts whether you are my son. But if I remain here, and you should all be killed, where then would be my protection? Come," added he turning to the second son, "I trust thou art veritably my son, let us hasten to retreat before it is too late."

"Father," replied the youngest, "I have not a doubt that I am honestly and thoroughly your son, and as such I honour you; but I owe duty likewise to my mother, and when I sallied to the war she gave me her blessing as long as I should act with valour, but her curse should I prove craven and fly the field. Fear nothing father. I will defend you while living and even after you are dead. You shall never fail of an honourable sepulture among your kindred."

"A pestilence on ye both," cried Theodomir, "for a brace of misbegotten madmen! what care I, think ye, where ye lay my body when I am dead. One days existence in a hovel is worth an age of interment in a marble sepulchre. Come my friends," said he turning to his principal cavaliers, "let us leave these hotheaded striplings and make our retreat; if we tarry any longer the enemy will be upon us."

Upon this the cavaliers and proud hidalgoes drew up scornfully and tossed their heads: "What do you see in us," said they, "that you think we will show our backs to the enemy? Forward! was ever the good old gothic watchword, and with that will we live and die!"

While time was lost in these disputes the moslem army kept advancing, until retreat was no longer practicable. The battle was tumultuous and bloody. Theodomir fought like a lion, but it was all in vain; he saw his two sons cut down and the greater part of their rash companions, while his raw mountain troops fled in all directions.

Seeing there was no longer any hope he seized the bridle of a favorite page who was near him, and who was about spurring for the mountains. "Part not from me," said he, "but do thou at least attend to my counsel my son: and of a truth I believe thou art my son; for thou art the offspring of one of my handmaids who was kind unto me." And indeed the youth marvellously resembled him. Turning then the reins of his own steed and giving him the spur, he fled amain from the field, followed by the page, nor did he stop until he arrived within the walls of Orihuela.

Ordering the gates to be barred and bolted he prepared to receive the enemy. There were but few men in the city capable of bearing arms, most of the youth having fallen in the field. He caused the women therefore to clothe themselves in male attire, to put on hats and helmets, to take long reeds in their hands instead of lances, and to cross their hair upon their chins in semblance of beards. With these troops he lined the walls and towers.

It was about the hour of twilight that Abdelasis approached with his army, but he paused when he saw the walls so numerously garrisoned. Then Theodomir took a flag of truce in his hand, and put a herald's tabard on the page and they two sallied forth to capitulate, and were graciously received by Abdelasis.

"I come," said Theodomir, "on the behalf of the commander of this city to treat for terms worthy of your magnanimity and of his dignity.

You perceive that the city is capable of withstanding a long siege, but he is desirous of sparing the lives of his soldiers. Promise that the inhabitants shall be at liberty to depart unmolested with their property, and the city will be delivered up to you tomorrow morning without a blow; otherwise we are prepared to fight until not a man be left."

Abdelasis was well pleased to get so powerful a place upon such easy terms, but stipulated that the garrison should lay down their arms. To this Theodomir readily assented, with the exception, however, of the governor and his retinue, which was granted out of consideration for his dignity. The articles of capitulation were then drawn out, and, when Abdalasis had affixed his name and seal, Theodomir took the pen and wrote his signature. "Behold in me," said he, "the governor of the city!"

Abdelasis was pleased with the hardihood of the commander of the place in thus venturing personally into his power, and entertained the veteran with still greater honour. When Theodomir returned to the city, he made known the capitulation, and charged the inhabitants to pack up their effects during the night and be ready to sally forth in the morning.

At the dawn of day the gates were thrown open, and Abdelasis looked to see a great force issuing forth, but to his surprize beheld merely Theodomir and his page in battered armour, followed by a multitude of old men, women and children.

Abdelasis waited until the whole had come forth, then turning to Theodomir, "Where," cried he, "are the soldiers whom I saw last evening, lining the walls and towers?"

"Soldiers have I none," replied the veteran. "As to my garrison behold it before you. With these women did I man my walls, and this my page is my herald, guard and retinue."

Upon this the Bishop Oppas and Count Julian exclaimed that the capitulation was a base fraud and ought not to be complied with: but Abdelasis relished the stratagem of the old soldier, and ordered that the stipulations of the treaty should be faithfully performed. Nay, so high an opinion did he conceive of the subtle wisdom of this commander, that he permitted him to remain in authority over the surrounding country on his acknowledging allegiance and engaging to pay tribute to the caliph; and all that part of Spain, comprizing the beautiful provinces of Murcia and Valencia, was long afterward known by the Arabic name of its defender, and is still recorded in Arabian chronicles as "The land of Tadmir."*

*Conde. P.1. Cronica del moro Rasis. Cron. general de España por Alonzo el Sabio. P.3. c. 1.

Having succeeded in subduing this rich and fruitful region, and having gained great renown for his generosity as well as valour, Abdelasis returned with the chief part of his army to the city of Seville.

CHAPTER XI

Muza arrives at Toledo—Interview between him and Taric.

When Muza ben Nozier had sent his son Abdelasis to subdue Seville, he departed for Toledo to call Taric to account for his disobedience to his orders; for amidst all his own successes, the prosperous career of that commander preyed upon his mind. What can content the jealous and ambitious heart? As Muza passed through the land, towns and cities submitted to him without resistance; he was lost in wonder at the riches of the country and the noble monuments of art with which it was adorned; when he beheld the bridges, constructed in ancient times by the Romans, they seemed to him the work, not of men, but of genii. Yet all these admirable objects only made him repine the more, that he had not had the exclusive glory of invading and subduing the land; and exasperated him the more against Taric, for having apparently endeavoured to monopolize the conquest.

Taric heard of his approach and came forth to meet him at Talavera, accompanied by many of the most distinguished companions of his victories, and with a train of horses and mules laden with spoil, with which he trusted to propitiate the favour of his commander. Their meeting took place on the banks of the rapid river Tietar, which rises in the mountains of Placencia and throws itself into the Tagus. Muza, in former days, while Taric had acted as his subordinate and indefatigable officer, had cherished and considered him as a second self, but now that he had started up to be a rival, he could not conceal his jealousy. When the veteran came into his presence he regarded him for a moment with a stern and indignant aspect. "Why hast thou disobeyed my orders?" said he. "I commanded thee to await my arrival with reinforcements, but thou hast rashly overrun the country, endangering the loss of our armies and the ruin of our cause."

"I have acted," replied Taric, "in such manner as I thought would best serve the cause of Islam, and in so doing I thought to fulfil the wishes of Muza. Whatever I have done has been as your servant; behold your share, as commander in chief, of the spoils which I have collected." So saying he produced an immense treasure in silver and gold and costly stuffs and precious stones, and spread it before Muza.

The anger of the Arab commander was still more kindled at the sight of this booty, for it proved how splendid had been the victories of Taric; but he restrained his wrath for the present, and they proceeded together in moody silence to Toledo. When he entered this royal city, however, and ascended to the ancient palace of the gothic kings, and reflected that all this had been a scene of triumph to his rival, he could no longer repress his indignation. He demanded of Taric a strict account of all the riches he had gathered in Spain, even of the presents he had reserved for the caliph, and, above all, he made him yield up his favourite trophy, the talismanic table of Solomon. When all this was done he again upbraided him bitterly with his disobedience of orders, and with the rashness of his conduct. "What blind confidence in fortune hast thou shewn," said he, "in overrunning such a country and assailing such powerful cities, with thy scanty force! What madness, to venture every thing upon a desperate chance, when thou knewest I was coming with a force to make the victory secure. All thy success has been owing to mere luck, not to judgement or generalship."

He then bestowed high praises upon the other chieftains for their services in the cause of Islam, but they answered not a word, and their countenances were gloomy and discontented, for they felt the injustice done to their favourite leader. As to Taric, though his eye burned like fire, he kept his passion within bounds. "I have done the best I could to serve God and the caliph," said he, emphatically; "my conscience acquits me, and I trust my sovereign will do the same."

"Perhaps he may," replied Muza bitterly, "but in the mean time I cannot confide his interests to a desperado who is heedless of orders and throws every thing at hazard. Such a general is unworthy to be entrusted with the fate of armies."

So saying he divested Taric of his command and gave it to Magued the renegado. The gaunt Taric still maintained an air of stern composure. His only words were "The caliph will do me justice!" Muza was so transported with passion at this laconic defiance that he ordered him to be thrown into prison and even threatened his life.

Upon this Magued el Rumi, though he had risen by the disgrace of Taric, had the generosity to speak out warmly in his favour. "Consider," said he to Muza, "what may be the consequences of this severity. Taric has many friends in the army; his actions too have been signal and illustrious, and entitle him to the highest honours and rewards, instead of disgrace and imprisonment."

The anger of Muza however was not to be appeased; and he trusted to justify his measures by dispatching missives to the caliph complaining of the insubordination of Taric and his rash and headlong conduct. The result proved the wisdom of the caution given by Magued. In the course of a little while Muza received a humiliating letter from the caliph ordering him to restore Taric to the command of the soldiers "whom he had so gloriously conducted," and not to render useless "one of the best swords in Islam."*

It is thus the envious man brings humiliation and reproach upon himself, in endeavouring to degrade a meritorious rival. When the tidings came of the justice rendered by the caliph to the merits of the veteran there was general joy throughout the army, and Muza read in the smiling countenances of every one around him a severe censure upon his conduct. He concealed however, his deep humiliation, and affected to obey the orders of his sovereign with great alacrity; he released Taric from prison, feasted him at his own table, and then publicly replaced him at the head of his troops. The army received its favourite veteran with shouts of joy, and celebrated with rejoicings the reconciliation of the commanders, but the shouts of the soldiery were abhorrent to the ears of Muza.

CHAPTER XII

Muza prosecutes the scheme of conquest—Siege of Saragossa—Complete subjugation of Spain.

The dissensions, which for a time had distracted the conquering army, being appeased, and the Arabian generals being apparently once more reconciled, Muza as commander in chief, proceeded to complete the enterprize by subjugating the northern parts of Spain. The same expeditious mode of conquest that had been sagaciously adopted by Taric was still pursued. The troops were lightly armed, and freed from every superfluous incumbrance. Each horseman beside his arms carried a small sack of provisions, a copper vessel in which to cook them and a skin which served him for surcoat and for bed. The infantry carried nothing but their arms. To each regiment or squadron was allowed a limited number of sumpter mules and attendants; barely enough to carry their necessary baggage and supplies; nothing was permitted that could needlessly diminish the number of fighting men, delay their rapid movements, or consume their provisions. Strict orders were again issued prohibiting on pain of death all plunder excepting the camp of an enemy or cities given up to pillage.†

*Conde. Part 1. c. 15.
†Conde, P. 1. c. 15.

The armies now took their several lines of march. That under Taric departed towards the north east; beating up the country towards the source of the Tagus; traversing the chain of Iberian or Arragonian mountains and pouring down into the plains and valleys watered by the Ebro. It was wonderful to see, in so brief a space of time, such a vast and difficult country penetrated and subdued; and the invading army, like an inundating flood, pouring its streams into the most remote recesses.

While Taric was thus sweeping the country to the north east, Muza departed in an opposite direction, yet purposing to meet him and to join their forces in the north. Bending his course westwardly, he made a circuit behind the mountains and then advancing into the open country displayed his banners before Salamanca, which surrendered without resistance. From hence he continued on towards Astorga, receiving the terrified submission of the land, then turning up the valley of the Douro he ascended the course of that famous river towards the east; crossed the Sierra de Moncayo, and, arriving on the banks of the Ebro marched down along its stream until he approached the strong city of Saragossa, the citadel of all that part of Spain. In this place had taken refuge many of the most valiant of the gothic warriors, the remnants of armies, and fugitives from conquered cities. It was one of the last rallying points of the land. When Muza arrived, Taric had already been for some time before the place, laying close siege; the inhabitants were pressed by famine and had suffered great losses in repeated combats, but there was a spirit and obstinacy in their resistance surpassing any thing that had yet been witnessed by the invaders.

Muza now took command of the siege, and ordered a general assault upon the walls; the moslems planted their scaling ladders and mounted with their accustomed intrepidity, but were vigorously resisted; nor could all their efforts obtain them a footing upon the battlements. While they were thus assailing the walls Count Julian ordered a heap of combustibles to be placed against one of the gates, and set on fire. The inhabitants attempted in vain from the barbican to extinguish the flames. They burnt so fiercely that in a little while the gate fell from the hinges. Count Julian gallopped into the city mounted upon a powerful charger, himself and his steed all covered with mail. He was followed by three hundred of his partizans, and supported by Magued the renegado, with a troop of horse.

The inhabitants disputed every street and public square; they made barriers of dead bodies, fighting behind these ramparts of their slaughtered countrymen. Every window and roof was filled with combatants, the very women and children joined in the desperate fight, throwing down stones and missiles of all kinds and scalding water upon the enemy.

The battle raged until the hour of vespers, when the principal inhabitants held a parley, and capitulated for a surrender. Muza had been incensed at their obstinate resistance, which had cost the lives of so many of his soldiers; he knew also that in the city were collected the riches of many of the towns of Eastern Spain. He demanded therefore, beside the usual terms, a heavy sum to be paid down by the citizens, called the contribution of blood, as by this they redeemed themselves from the edge of the sword. The people were obliged to comply. They collected all the jewels of their richest families and all the ornaments of their temples and laid them at the feet of Muza; and placed in his power many of their noblest youths as hostages. A strong garrison was then appointed, and thus the fierce city of Saragossa was subdued to the yoke of the conqueror.

The Arab generals pursued their conquests even to the foot of the Pyrenees; Taric then descended along the course of the Ebro and continued along the Mediterranean coast, subduing the famous city of Valencia with its rich and beautiful domains and carrying the success of his arms even to Denia.

Muza undertook with his host a wider range of conquest. He overcame the cities of Barcelona, Gerona and others that lay on the skirts of the eastern mountains, then crossing into the land of the Franks he captured the city of Narbonne, in a temple of which he found seven equestrian images of silver, which he brought off as trophies of his victory.* Returning into Spain he scoured its northern regions along Gallicia and the Asturias, passed triumphantly through Lusitania and arrived once more in Andalusia, covered with laurels, and enriched with immense spoils.

Thus was completed the subjugation of unhappy Spain. All its cities and fortresses, and strong holds were in the hands of the Saracens, excepting some of the wild mountain tracts that bordered the Atlantic and extended towards the north. Here then the story of the conquest might conclude, but that the indefatigable Chronicler Fray Antonio Agapida, goes on to record the fate of those persons who were most renowned in the enterprize. We shall follow his steps and avail ourselves of his information, laboriously collected from various sources; and truly the story of each of the actors in this great historical drama bears with it its striking moral, and is full of admonition and instruction.

*Conde. P. 1. c. 16.

CHAPTER XIII

*Feud between the Arab generals—They are summoned to appear
before the caliph at Damascus—Reception of Taric.*

The heart of Muza ben Nozier was now lifted up for he considered his glory complete. He held a sway that might have gratified the ambition of the proudest sovereign, for all western Africa, and the newly acquired peninsula of Spain were obedient to his rule, and he was renowned throughout all the lands of Islam as the great conqueror of the West. But sudden humiliation awaited him in the very moment of his highest triumph.

Notwithstanding the outward reconciliation of Muza and Taric, a deep and implacable hostility continued to exist between them; and each had busy partizans who distracted the armies by their feuds. Letters were incessantly dispatched to Damascus, by either party, extolling the merits of their own leader and decrying his rival. Taric was represented as rash, arbitrary and prodigal, and as injuring the discipline of the army, by sometimes treating it with extreme rigour, and at other times giving way to licentiousness and profusion. Muza was lauded as prudent, sagacious, dignified and systematic in his dealings. The friends of Taric on the other hand, represented him as brave, generous and high minded; scrupulous in reserving to his sovereign his rightful share of the spoils, but distributing the rest bounteously among his soldiers, and thus encreasing their alacrity in the service. "Muza, on the contrary," said they, "is grasping and insatiable, he levies intolerable contributions and collects immense treasure, but sweeps it all into his own coffers."

The caliph was at length wearied out by these complaints and feared that the safety of the cause might be endangered by the dissensions of the rival generals. He sent letters therefore, ordering them to leave suitable persons in charge of their several commands, and appear, forthwith, before him at Damascus.

Such was the greeting from his sovereign that awaited Muza on his return from the conquest of Northern Spain. It was a grievous blow to a man of his pride and ambition but he prepared instantly to obey. He returned to Cordova, collecting by the way all the treasures he had deposited in various places. At that city he called a meeting of his principal officers, and of the leaders of the faction of apostate christians, and made them all do homage to his son Abdelasis, as Emir or Governor of Spain. He gave this favorite son much sage advice for the regulation of his conduct and left with him his nephew Ayub, a man greatly honoured by the moslems for his wisdom and discretion, exhorting Abdelasis to consult him on all occasions and consider him as his bosom counsellor. He made a parting address to his adherents, full of cheerful confidence; assuring them that he would soon return, loaded with new favours and honours by his sovereign, and enabled to reward them all for their faithful services.

When Muza sallied forth from Cordova to repair to Damascus his cavalgada appeared like the sumptuous pageant of some Oriental potentate, for he had numerous guards and attendants splendidly armed and arrayed together with four hundred hostages who were youthful cavaliers of the noblest families of the Goths, and a great number of captives of both sexes, chosen for their beauty and intended as presents for the caliph. Then there was a vast train of beasts of burden laden with the plunder of Spain, for he took with him all the wealth he had collected in his conquests, and all the share that had been set apart for his sovereign. With this display of trophies and spoils, shewing the magnificence of the land he had conquered, he looked forward with confidence to silence the calumnies of his foes.

As he traversed the valley of the Guadalquivir he often turned and looked back wistfully upon Cordova, and at the distance of a league, when about to lose sight of it, he checked his steed upon the summit of a hill and gazed for a long time upon its palaces and towers. "Oh Cordova!" exclaimed he, "great and glorious art thou among cities, and abundant in all delights. With grief and sorrow do I part from thee, for sure I am it would give me length of days to abide within thy pleasant walls!" When he had uttered these words, say the Arabian chronicles, he resumed his wayfaring but his eyes were bent upon the ground and frequent sighs bespoke the heaviness of his heart.

Embarking at Cadiz he passed over to Africa with all his people and effects, to regulate his government in that country. He divided the command between his sons Abdelola and Meruan, leaving the former in Tangier, and the latter in Cairvan; thus having secured, as he thought, the power and prosperity of his family, by placing all his sons as his lieutenants in the countries he had conquered, he departed for Syria, bearing with him the sumptuous spoils of the west.

While Muza was thus disposing of his commands, and moving cumbrously under the weight of wealth, the veteran Taric was more speedy and alert in obeying the summons of the caliph. He knew the importance, where complaints were to be heard, of being first in presence of the judge; beside, he was ever ready to march at a moment's warning, and had nothing to impede him in his movements. The spoils he had made in his conquests had either been shared among his soldiers, or yielded up to Muza, or squandered away with open handed profusion. He appeared in Syria with a small train of war worn followers, and had

no other trophies to show than his battered armour, and a body seamed
with scars. He was received, however, with rapture by the multitude,
who crowded to behold one of those conquerors of the West whose
wonderful achievements were the theme of every tongue. They were
charmed with his gaunt and martial air, his hard sun burnt features
and his scathed eye. "All hail," cried they, "to the sword of Islam, the
terror of the unbelievers! behold the true model of a warrior, who
despises gain and seeks for nought but glory!"

Taric was graciously received by the caliph, who asked tidings of
his victories. He gave a soldierlike account of his actions, frank, and
full, without any feigned modesty yet without vain glory. "Commander
of the faithful," said he, "I bring thee nor silver, nor gold, nor precious
stones, nor captives, for what spoil I did not share with my soldiers
I gave up to Muza as my commander. How I have conducted myself
the honourable warriors of thy host will tell thee; nay, let our enemies
the christians be asked if I have ever shewn myself cowardly or cruel
or rapacious."

"What kind of people are these christians?" demanded the caliph.

"The Spaniards," replied Taric, "are lions in their castles, eagles in
the saddle, but mere women when on foot. When vanquished they
escape like goats to the mountains for they need not see the ground
they tread."

"And tell me of the Moors of Barbary."

"They are like Arabs in the fierceness and dexterity of their attacks
and in their knowledge of the stratagems of war; they resemble them
too in feature, in fortitude and hospitality; but they are the most
perfidious people upon earth and never regard promise or plighted
faith."

"And the people of Afranc; what sayest thou of them?"

"They are infinite in number, rapid in the onset, fierce in battle, but
confused and headlong in flight."

"And how fared it with thee among these people? Did they sometimes vanquish thee?"

"Never, by Allah!" cried Taric with honest warmth. "Never did a
banner of mine fly the field. Though the enemy were two to one, my
moslems never shunned the combat!"

The caliph was well pleased with the martial bluntness of the veteran
and shewed him great honour; and wherever Taric appeared he was
the idol of the populace.

CHAPTER XIV

Muza arrives at Damascus—His interview with the caliph—The table of Solomon—A rigorous sentence.

Shortly after the arrival of Taric el Tuerto at Damascus the caliph fell dangerously ill insomuch that his life was despaired of: during his illness tidings were brought that Muza ben Nozier had entered Syria with a vast cavalcade bearing all the riches and trophies gained in the western conquests. Now Suleiman ben Abdelmelec, brother to the caliph, was successor to the throne, and he saw that his brother had not long to live, and wished to grace the commencement of his reign by this triumphant display of the spoils of christendom, he sent messengers, therefore, to Muza, saying, "The caliph is ill and cannot receive thee at present, I pray thee tarry on the road until his recovery." Muza, however, paid no attention to the messages of Suleiman, but rather hastened his march to arrive before the death of the caliph. And Suleiman treasured up his conduct in his heart.

Muza entered the city in a kind of triumph with a long train of horses, and mules and camels laden with treasure, and with the four hundred sons of gothic nobles as hostages, each decorated with a diadem and a girdle of gold; and with one hundred christian damsels whose beauty dazzled all beholders. As he passed through the streets he ordered purses of gold to be thrown among the populace, who rent the air with acclamations. "Behold," cried they, "the veritable conqueror of the unbelievers! Behold the true model of a conqueror, who brings home wealth to his country!" And they heaped benedictions on the head of Muza.

The caliph Walid Almanzor rose from his couch of illness to receive the Emir; who when he repaired to the palace, filled one of its great courts with treasures of all kinds, the halls too were thronged with the youthful hostages magnificently attired, and with christian damsels, lovely as the houris of paradise. When the caliph demanded an account of the conquest of Spain he gave it with great eloquence; but in describing the various victories he made no mention of the name of Taric, but spoke as if every thing had been effected by himself. He then presented the spoils of the christians as if they had been all taken by his own hands, and when he delivered to the caliph the miraculous table of Solomon, he dwelt with animation on the virtues of that inestimable talisman.

Upon this Taric, who was present, could no longer hold his peace. "Commander of the faithful," said he, "examine this precious table, if any part be wanting." The caliph examined the table, which was composed of a single emerald, and he found that one foot was supplied by a foot of gold. The caliph turned to Muza and said, "Where is the other foot of the table?" Muza answered, "I know not; one foot was wanting when it came into my hands." Upon this Taric drew from beneath his robe a foot of emerald, of like workmanship to the others, and fitting exactly to the table. "Behold, Oh commander of the faithful!" cried he, "a proof of the real finder of the table; and so is it with the greater part of the spoils exhibited by Muza as trophies of his achieve-ments. It was I who gained them, and who captured the cities in which they were found. If you want proof, demand of these christian cavaliers here present, most of whom I captured; demand of those moslem warriors who aided me in my battles."

Muza was confounded for a moment, but attempted to vindicate himself. "I spake," said he, "as the chief of your armies, under whose orders and banners this conquest was achieved. The actions of the soldiers are the actions of the commander. In a great victory it is not supposed that the chief of the army takes all the captives, or kills all the slain, or gathers all the booty, though all are enumerated in the records of his triumph." The caliph however was wroth and heeded not his words. "You have vaunted your own deserts," said he, "and have forgotten the deserts of others; nay, you have sought to debase another who has loyally served his sovereign; the reward of your envy and covetousness be upon your head!" So saying, he bestowed a great part of the spoils upon Taric and the other chiefs, but gave nothing to Muza; and the veteran retired amidst sneers and murmurs of those present.

In a few days the Caliph Walid died, and was succeeded by his brother Suleiman. The new sovereign cherished deep resentment against Muza for having presented himself at court contrary to his command, and he listened readily to the calumnies of his enemies; for Muza had been too illustrious in his deeds not to have many enemies. All now took courage when they found he was out of favour, and they heaped slanders on his head; charging him with embezzling much of the share of the booty belonging to the sovereign. The new caliph lent a willing ear to the accusation and commanded him to render up all that he had pillaged from Spain. The loss of his riches might have been borne with fortitude by Muza, but the stygma upon his fame filled his heart with bitterness. "I have been a faithful servant to the throne from my youth upwards," said he, "and now am I de-graded in my old age. I care not for wealth, I care not for life, but let me not be deprived of that honour which God has bestowed upon me!"

The caliph was still more exasperated at his repining and stripped him of his commands, confiscated his effects, fined him two hundred thousand pesants of gold, and ordered that he should be scourged and exposed to the noon tide sun, and afterwards thrown into prison.* The populace, also, reviled and scoffed at him in his misery and as they beheld him led forth to the public gaze and fainting in the sun they pointed at him with derision and exclaimed, "Behold the envious man and the impostor; this is he who pretended to have conquered the land of the unbelievers!"

CHAPTER XV

Conduct of Abdelasis as Emir of Spain.

While these events were happening in Syria the youthful Abdelasis, the son of Muza, remained as Emir or governor of Spain. He was of a generous and benignant disposition, but he was open and confiding, and easily led away by the opinions of those he loved. Fortunately his father had left with him as a bosom counsellor the discreet Ayub, the nephew of Muza; aided by his advice, he for some time administered the public affairs prudently and prosperously.

Not long after the departure of his father he received a letter from him written while on his journey to Syria: it was to the following purport.

"Beloved son; honour of thy lineage; Allah guard thee from all harm and peril! Listen to the words of thy father. Avoid all treachery though it should promise great advantage, and trust not in him who counsels it, even though he should be a brother. The company of traytors put far from thee, for how canst thou be certain that he who has proved false to others will prove true to thee? Beware Oh my son of the seductions of love. It is an idle passion which enfeebles the heart and blinds the judgement; it renders the mighty weak and makes slaves of princes. If thou shouldst discover any foible of a vicious kind springing up in thy nature, pluck it forth, whatever pang it cost thee. Every error, while new, may easily be weeded out, but if suffered to take root, it flourishes, and bears seed, and produces fruit an hundred fold. Follow these counsels, Oh son of my affections, and thou shalt live secure."

Abdelasis meditated upon this letter, for some part of it seemed to contain a mystery which he could not comprehend. He called to him his cousin and counsellor the discreet Ayub. "What means my father," said he, "in cautioning me against treachery and treason? Does he think my nature so base that it could descend to such means?"

*Conde, Part 1. c. 17.

Ayub read the letter attentively. "Thy father," said he, "would put thee on thy guard against the traytors Julian and Oppas, and those of their party who surround thee. What love canst thou expect from men who have been unnatural to their kindred, and what loyalty from wretches who have betrayed their country?"

Abdalasis was satisfied with the interpretation, and he acted accordingly. He had long loathed all communion with these men, for there is nothing which the open ingenuous nature so much abhors as duplicity and treason. Policy, too, no longer required their agency; they had rendered their infamous service, and had no longer a country to betray, but they might turn and betray their employers. Abdelasis, therefore, removed them to a distance from his court, and placed them in situations where they could do no harm, and he warned his commanders from being in any wise influenced by their counsels or aided by their arms.

He now confided entirely in his Arabian troops, and in the moorish squadrons from Africa, and with their aid he completed the conquest of Lusitania to the ultimate parts of the Algarbe, or west, even to the shores of the great Ocean Sea.* From hence he sent his generals to over run all those vast and rugged sierras, which rise like ramparts along the ocean borders of the peninsula, and they carried the standard of Islam in triumph even to the mountains of Biscay, collecting all manner of precious spoil.

"It is not enough, O Abdelasis," said Ayub, "that we conquer and rule this country with the sword, if we wish our dominion to be secure we must cultivate the arts of peace, and study to secure the confidence and promote the welfare of the people we have conquered." Abdelasis relished counsel which accorded so well with his own beneficent nature. He endeavoured, therefore, to allay the ferment and confusion of the conquest; forbade, under rigorous punishment, all wanton spoil or oppression and protected the native inhabitants in the enjoyment and cultivation of their lands, and the pursuit of all useful occupations. By the advice of Ayub also he encouraged great numbers of industrious Moors and Arabs to emigrate from Africa and gave them houses and lands, thus introducing a peaceful mahometan population into the conquered provinces.

The good effect of the counsels of Ayub were soon apparent. Instead of a sudden but transient influx of wealth, made by the ruin of the land, which left the country desolate, a regular and permanent revenue sprang

---

*Algarbe, or Algarbia in Arabic, signifies the West, as Axarkia is the East, Algufia the North, and Aquibla the South. This will serve to explain some of the geographical names on the peninsula, which are of Arabian origin.

up, produced by reviving prosperity, and gathered without violence. Abdalasis ordered it to be faithfully collected and deposited in coffers by public officers appointed in each province for the purpose; and the whole was sent by ten deputies to Damascus to be laid at the feet of the caliph, not as the spoils of a vanquished country, but as the peaceful trophies of a wisely administered government.

The common herd of warlike adventurers, the mere men of the sword, who had thronged to Spain for the purpose of ravage and rapine were disappointed at being thus checked in their career and at seeing the reign of terror and violence drawing to a close. "What manner of leader is this," said they, "who forbids us to make spoil of the enemies of Islam and to enjoy the land we have wrested from the unbelievers?" The partizans of Julian, also, whispered their calumnies. "Behold," said they, "with what kindness he treats the enemies of your faith; all the christians who have borne arms against you, and withstood your entrance into the land are favoured and protected; but it is enough for a christian to have befriended the cause of the moslems, to be singled out by Abdelasis for persecution and to be driven with scorn from his presence."

These insinuations fermented the discontent of the turbulent and rapacious among the moslems, but all the friends of peace and order and good government applauded the moderation of the youthful Emir.

CHAPTER XVI

Loves of Abdelasis and Exilona.

Abdelasis had fixed his seat of government at Seville, as permitting easy and frequent communications with the coast of Africa. His palace was of noble architecture, with delightful gardens extending to the banks of the Guadalquivir. In a part of this palace resided many of the most beautiful christian females, who were detained as captives, or rather hostages to ensure the tranquility of the country. Those who were of noble rank were entertained in luxury and magnificence; slaves were appointed to attend upon them and they were arrayed in the richest apparel and decorated with the most precious jewels. Those of tender age were taught all graceful accomplishments, and even where tasks were imposed, they were of the most elegant and agreeable kind. They embroidered, they sang, they danced, and passed their times in pleasing revelry. Many were lulled by this easy and voluptuous existence; the scenes of horror through which they had passed were gradually effaced from their minds, and a desire was often awakened, of rendering themselves pleasing in the eyes of their conquerors.

After his return from his campaign in Lusitania, and during the intervals of public duty, Abdelasis solaced himself in the repose of this palace, and in the society of these christian captives. He remarked one among them who ever sat apart, and neither joined in the labours or sports of her companions. She was lofty in her demeanour and the others always paid her reverence, yet sorrow had given a softness to her charms, and rendered her beauty touching to the heart. Abdelasis found her one day in the garden with her companions; they had adorned their heads with flowers and were singing the songs of their country, but she sat by herself and wept. The youthful Emir was moved by her tears and accosted her in gentle accents. "Oh fairest of women!" said he, "why dost thou weep, and why is thy heart troubled?"

"Alas!" replied she, "have I not cause to weep, seeing how sad is my condition, and how great the height from which I have fallen? In me you behold the wretched Exilona, but lately the wife of Roderick and the queen of Spain, now a captive and a slave!" and having said these words she cast her eyes upon the earth and her tears began to flow afresh.

The generous feelings of Abdelasis were aroused at the sight of beauty and royalty in tears. He gave orders that Exilona should be entertained in a style befitting her former rank, he appointed a train of female attendants to wait upon her, and a guard of honour to protect her from all intrusion. All the time that he could spare from public concerns was passed in her society, and he even neglected his divan and suffered his counsellors to attend in vain, while he lingered in the apartments and gardens of the palace listening to the voice of Exilona.

The discreet Ayub saw the danger into which he was falling. "Oh Abdelasis," said he, "remember the words of thy father. 'Beware my son,' said he, 'of the seductions of love. It renders the mighty weak, and makes slaves of princes!'" A blush kindled on the cheek of Abdelasis, and he was silent for a moment. "Why," said he at length, "do you seek to charge me with such weakness. It is one thing to be infatuated by the charms of a woman; and another to be touched by her misfortunes. It is the duty of my station to console a princess who has been reduced to the lowest humiliation by the triumphs of our arms. In doing so I do but listen to the dictates of true magnanimity."

Ayub was silent, but his brow was clouded, and for once Abdelasis parted in discontent from his counsellor. In proportion as he was dissatisfied with others or with himself he sought the society of Exilona, for there was a charm in her conversation that banished every care. He daily became more and more enamoured, and Exilona gradually ceased to weep and began to listen with secret pleasure to the words of her Arab lover. When, however, he sought to urge his passion, she recollected the light estimation in which her sex was held by the followers of Mahomet, and assumed a countenance grave and severe.

"Fortune," said she, "has cast me at thy feet, behold I am thy captive and thy spoil. But though my person is in thy power, my soul is unsubdued; and know that, should I lack force to defend my honour, I have resolution to wash out all stain upon it with my blood. I trust, however, in thy courtesy as a cavalier to respect me in my reverses, remembering what I have been, and that though the crown has been wrested from my brow, the royal blood still warms within my veins.[*]

The lofty spirit of Exilona, and her proud repulse served but to encrease the passion of Abdelasis. He besought her to unite her destiny with his, and share his state and power, promising that she should have no rival nor copartner in his heart. Whatever scruples the captive queen might originally have felt to a union with one of the conquerors of her lord, and an enemy of her adopted faith, they were easily vanquished and she became the bride of Abdelasis. He would fain have persuaded her to return to the faith of her fathers; but though of moorish origin, and brought up in the doctrines of Islam, she was too thorough a convert to christianity to consent, and looked back with disgust upon a religion that admitted a plurality of wives.

When the sage Ayub heard of the resolution of Abdelasis to espouse Exilona he was in despair. "Alas my cousin!" said he, "what infatuation possesses thee? Hast thou then entirely forgotten the letter of thy father. 'Beware my son,' said he, 'of love. It is an idle passion which enfeebles the heart and blinds the judgment.' "

But Abdelasis interrupted him with impatience. "My father," said he, "spake but of the blandishments of wanton love; against these I am secured by my virtuous passion for Exilona."

Ayub would fain have impressed upon him the dangers he ran of awakening suspicion in the caliph, and discontent among the moslems, by wedding the queen of the conquered Roderick, and one who was an enemy to the religion of Mahomet; but the youthful lover only listened to his passion. Their nuptials were celebrated at Seville with great pomp and rejoicings, and he gave his bride the name of Omalisam; that is to say "She of the precious jewels;"[†] but she continued to be known among christians by the name of Exilona.

[*]Faxardo. corona, Gothica. T. 1. P. 492. Joan. Mar. de reb. Hisp. L. 6. c. 27.
[†]Conde, P. 1. c. 17.

CHAPTER XVII

Fate of Abdelasis and Exilona—Death of Muza.

Possession instead of cooling the passion of Abdelasis, only added to its force; he became blindly enamoured of his beautiful bride, and consulted her will in all things; nay, having lost all relish for the advice of the discreet Ayub, he was even guided by the counsels of his wife in the affairs of government. Exilona, unfortunately, had once been a queen, and she could not remember her regal glories without regret. She saw that Abdelasis had great power in the land; greater even than had been possessed by the gothic kings; but she considered it as wanting in true splendour until his brows should be encircled with the outward badge of royalty. One day when they were alone in the palace of Seville and the heart of Abdelasis was given up to tenderness, she addressed him in fond yet timid accents. "Will not my lord be offended," said she, "if I make an unwelcome request?" Abdelasis regarded her with a smile. "What canst thou ask of me Exilona," said he, "that it would not be a happiness for me to grant?" Then Exilona produced a crown of gold, sparkling with jewels, which had belonged to the king Don Roderick, and said, "Behold thou art king in authority, be so in thy outward state. There is majesty and glory in a crown; it gives a sanctity to power."

Then putting the crown upon his head she held a mirror before him that he might behold the majesty of his appearance. Abdelasis chid her fondly and put the crown away from him, but Exilona persisted in her prayer. "Never," said she, "has there been a king in Spain that did not wear a crown." So Abdelasis suffered himself to be beguiled by the blandishments of his wife, and to be invested with the crown and sceptre and other signs of royalty.[*]

It is affirmed by ancient and discreet chroniclers that Abdelasis only assumed this royal state in the privacy of his palace, and to gratify the eye of his youthful bride, but when was a secret ever confined within the walls of a palace? The assumption of the insignia of the ancient gothic kings was soon rumoured about, and caused the most violent suspicions. The moslems had already felt jealous of the ascendancy of this beautiful woman; and it was now confidently asserted that Abdelasis, won by her persuasions, had secretly turned christian.

The enemies of Abdelasis, those whose rapacious spirits had been kept in check by the beneficence of his rule, seized upon this occasion to ruin him. They sent letters to Damascus accusing him of apostacy and of an intention to seize upon the throne in right of his wife Exilona,

---

[*]Cron. gen. de Alonzo el Sabio. p. 3. Joan. mar. de reb Hisp. lib. 6. c. 27. Conde. p. 1. c. 19.

as widow of the late King Roderick. It was added that the christians were prepared to flock to his standard, as the only means of regaining ascendancy in their country.

These accusations arrived at Damascus just after the accession of the sanguinary Suleiman to the throne, and in the height of his persecution of the unfortunate Muza. The caliph waited for no proofs in confirmation, he immediately sent private orders that Abdelasis should be put to death, and that the same fate should be dealt to his two brothers, who governed in Africa, as a sure means of crushing the conspiracy of this ambitious family.

The mandate for the death of Abdalasis was sent to Abhilbar ben Obeidah and Zeyd ben Nabegat, both of whom had been cherished friends of Muza, and had lived in intimate favour and companionship with his son. When they read the fatal parchment, the scroll fell from their trembling hands. "Can such hostility exist against the family of Muza?" exclaimed they. "Is this the reward for such great and glorious services?" The cavaliers remained for some time plunged in horror and consternation. The order, however, was absolute, and left them no discretion. "Allah is great," said they, "and commands us to obey our sovereign." So they prepared to execute the bloody mandate with the blind fidelity of moslems.

It was necessary to proceed with caution. The open and magnanimous character of Abdelasis had won the hearts of a great part of the soldiery and his magnificence pleased the cavaliers who formed his guard, it was feared, therefore, that a sanguinary opposition would be made to any attempt upon his person. The rabble, however, had been embittered against him from his having restrained their depredations, and because they thought him an apostate in his heart, secretly bent upon betraying them to the christians. While, therefore, the two officers made vigilant dispositions to check any movement on the part of the soldiery, they let loose the blind fury of the populace, by publishing the fatal mandate. In a moment the city was in a ferment, and there was a ferocious emulation who should be first to execute the orders of the caliph.

Abdelasis was at this time at a palace in the country not far from Seville; commanding a delightful view of the fertile plain of the Guadalquivir. Hither he was accustomed to retire from the tumult of the court and to pass his time among groves and fountains and the sweet repose of gardens, in the society of Exilona. It was the dawn of day, the hour of early prayer, when the furious populace arrived at this retreat. Abdalasis was offering up his orizons in a small mosque which he had erected for the use of the neighboring peasantry. Exilona was in a chapel in the interior of the palace, where her confessor, a holy friar, was performing mass. They were both surprized at their devotions and dragged forth by the hands of the rabble. A few guards who attended at the palace would have made defence, but they were overawed by the sight of the written mandate of the caliph.

The captives were borne in triumph to Seville. All the beneficent virtues of Abdelasis were forgotten, nor had the charms of Exilona any effect in softening the hearts of the populace. The brutal eagerness to shed blood, which seems inherent in human nature, was awakened, and woe to the victims when that eagerness is quickened by religious hate. The illustrious couple adorned with all the graces of youth and beauty, were hurried to a scaffold in the great square of Seville, and there beheaded amidst the shouts and execrations of an infatuated multitude. Their bodies were left exposed upon the ground, and would have been devoured by dogs, had they not been gathered at night by some friendly hand, and poorly interred in one of the courts of their late dwelling.

Thus terminated the loves and lives of Abdelasis and Exilona, in the year of the incarnation seven hundred and fourteen. Their names were held sacred as martyrs to the christian faith; but many read in their untimely fate, a lesson against ambition and vain glory; having sacrificed real power and substantial rule, to the glittering bawble of a crown.

The head of Abdelasis was embalmed and inclosed in a casket and sent to Syria to the cruel Suleiman. The messenger, who bore it, overtook the caliph as he was performing a pilgrimage to Mecca. Muza was among the courtiers in his train, having been released from prison. On opening the casket and regarding its contents the eyes of the tyrant sparkled with malignant satisfaction. Calling the unhappy father to his side: "Muza," said he, "dost thou know this head?" The veteran recognized the features of his beloved son and turned his face away with anguish. "Yes! well do I know it," replied he, "and may the curse of God light upon him who has destroyed a better man than himself."

Without adding another word he retired to Mount Deran, a prey to devouring melancholy. He shortly after received tidings of the death of his two sons, whom he had left in the government of western Africa, and who had fallen victims to the jealous suspicions of the caliph. His advanced age was not proof against these repeated blows, and this utter ruin of his late prosperous family, and he sank into his grave sorrowing and broken hearted.

Such was the lamentable end of the conqueror of Spain, whose great achievements were not sufficient to atone in the eye of his sovereign for a weakness to which all men ambitious of renown are subject; and whose triumphs eventually brought persecution upon himself and untimely death upon his children.

Here ends the legend of the Subjugation of Spain.

LEGEND OF
COUNT JULIAN AND HIS FAMILY

In the preceding legends is darkly shadowed out a true story of the woes of Spain. It is a story full of wholesome admonition, rebuking the insolence of human pride and the vanity of human ambition, and shewing the futility of all greatness that is not strongly based on virtue. We have seen, in brief space of time, most of the actors in this historic drama, disappearing one by one from the scene, and going down, conquerors and conquered, to gloomy and unhonored graves. It remains, to close this eventful history, by holding up, as a signal warning, the fate of the traitor, whose perfidious scheme of vengeance brought ruin on his native land.

Many and various are the accounts given in ancient chronicle of the fortunes of Count Julian and his family, and many are the traditions on the subject still extant among the populace of Spain, and prepetuated in those countless ballads sung by peasants and muleteers, which spread a singular charm over the whole of this romantic land.

He who has travelled in Spain in the true way in which the country ought to be travelled; sojourning in its remote provinces; rambling among the rugged defiles and secluded valleys of its mountains, and making himself familiar with the people in their out of the way hamlets, and rarely visited neighborhoods, will remember many a group of travellers and muleteers, gathered of an evening round the door or the spacious hearth of a mountain venta, wrapped in their brown cloaks, and listening with grave and profound attention to the long historic ballad of some rustic troubadour, either recited with the true *ore rotundo* and modulated cadences of Spanish elocution, or chanted to the tinkling of a guitar. In this way he may have heard the doleful end of Count Julian and his family recounted in traditionary rhymes, that have been handed down from generation to generation. The particulars, however, of the following wild legend are chiefly gathered from the writings of the pseudo Moor Rasis; how far they may be safely taken as historic facts it is impossible now to ascertain, we must content ourselves, therefore, with their answering to the exactions of poetic justice.

As yet every thing had prospered with Count Julian. He had gratified his vengeance, he had been successful in his treason, and had acquired countless riches from the ruin of his country. But it is not outward success that constitutes prosperity. The tree flourishes with fruit and foliage while blasted and withering at the heart. Wherever he went Count Julian read hatred in every eye. The christians cursed him as the cause of all their woe; the moslems despised and distrusted him as a traytor. Men whispered together as he approached and then turned away in scorn, and mothers snatched away their children with horror if he offered to caress them. He withered under the execration of his fellow men, and, last and worst of all, he began to loathe himself. He tried in vain to persuade himself that he had but taken a justifiable vengeance; he felt that no personal wrong can justify the crime of treason to one's country.

For a time he sought in luxurious indulgence to soothe or forget the miseries of the mind. He assembled round him every pleasure and gratification that boundless wealth could purchase, but all in vain. He had no relish for the dainties of his board, music had no charm wherewith to lull his soul, and remorse drove slumber from his pillow. He sent to Ceuta for his wife Frandina his daughter Florinda and his youthful son Alarbot, hoping in the bosom of his family to find that sympathy and kindness which he could no longer meet with in the world. Their presence, however, brought him no alleviation. Florinda, the daughter of his heart, for whose sake he had undertaken this signal vengeance, was sinking a victim to its effects. Wherever she went, she found herself a byeword of shame and reproach. The outrage she had suffered was imputed to her as wantonness, and her calamity was magnified into a crime. The christians never mentioned her name without a curse, and the moslems, the gainers by her misfortune, spake of her only by the appellation of Cava, the vilest epithet they could apply to woman.

But the opprobrium of the world was nothing to the upbraiding of her own heart. She charged herself with all the miseries of these disastrous wars; the deaths of so many gallant cavaliers; the conquest and perdition of her country. The anguish of her mind preyed upon the beauty of her person. Her eye, once soft and tender in its expression, became wild and haggard; her cheek lost its bloom, and became hollow and pallid, and at times there was desperation in her words. When her father sought to embrace her she withdrew with shuddering from his arms, for she thought of his treason and the ruin it had brought upon Spain. Her wretchedness encreased after her return to her native country until it rose to a degree of frenzy. One day when she was walking with her parents in the garden of their palace she entered a tower and, having barred the door, ascended to the battlements. From thence she called to them in piercing accents, expressive of her insupportable anguish and desperate determination. "Let this city," said she, "be henceforth called Malacca, in memorial of the most wretched of women, who therein put an end to her days." So saying she threw herself headlong from the tower and was dashed to pieces. The city, adds the ancient chronicler, received the name thus given it though afterwards softened to Malaga, which it still retains in memory of the tragical end of Florinda.

The Countess Frandina abandoned this scene of woe and returned to Ceuta accompanied by her infant son. She took with her the remains of her unfortunate daughter, and gave them honourable sepulture in a mausoleum of the chapel belonging to the citadel. Count Julian departed for Carthagena, where he remained plunged in horror at this doleful event.

About this time the cruel Suleiman, having destroyed the family of Muza had sent an Arab general named Alahor to succeed Abdalasis as Emir or governor of Spain. The new Emir was of a cruel and suspicious nature and commenced his sway with a stern severity that soon made those under his command look back with regret to the easy rule of Abdalasis. He regarded with an eye of distrust the renegado christians who had aided in the conquest, and who bore arms in the service of the moslems; but his deepest suspicions fell upon Count Julian. "He has been a traitor to his own countrymen," siad he, "how can we be sure that he will not prove traitor to us."

A sudden insurrection of the christians who had taken refuge in the Asturian mountains, quickened his suspicions, and inspired him with fears of some dangerous conspiracy against his power. In the height of his anxiety he bethought him of an Arabian sage named Yuza who had accompanied him from Africa. This son of science was withered in form and looked as if he had outlived the usual term of mortal life. In the course of his studies and travels in the east he had collected the knowledge and experience of ages; being skilled in astrology, and, it is said, in necromancy and possessing the marvellous gift of prophecy or divination. To this expounder of mysteries Alahor applied to learn whether any secret treason menaced his safety.

The astrologer listened with deep attention and overwhelming brow, to all the surmises and suspicions of the Emir, then shut himself up to consult his books and commune with those supernatural intelligences subservient to his wisdom. At an appointed hour the Emir sought him in his cell. It was filled with the smoke of perfumes; squares and circles and various diagrams were described upon the floor, and the astrologer was poring over a scroll of parchment, covered with cabalistic characters. He received Alahor with a gloomy and sinister aspect; pretending to have discovered fearful portents in the heavens and to have had strange dreams and mystic visions.

"Oh Emir," said he, "be on your guard! treason is around you and in your path. Your life is in peril. Beware of Count Julian and his family."

"Enough," said the Emir. "They shall all die! Parents and children—all shall die!"

He forthwith sent a summons to Count Julian to attend him in Cordova. The messenger found him plunged in affliction for the recent death of his daughter. The count excused himself, on account of this misfortune, from obeying the commands of the Emir in person, but sent several of his adherents. His hesitation, and the circumstance of his having sent his family across the straits to Africa, were construed by the jealous mind of the Emir into proofs of guilt. He no longer doubted his being concerned in the recent insurrections, and that he had sent his family away, preparatory to an attempt, by force of arms, to subvert the moslem domination. In his fury he put to death Siseburto and Evan, the nephews of Bishop Oppas and sons of the former King Witiza, suspecting them of taking part in the treason. Thus did they expiate their treachery to their country in the fatal battle of the Guadalete.

Alahor next hastened to Carthagena to seize upon Count Julian; so rapid were his movements that the count had barely time to escape with fifteen cavaliers; with whom he took refuge in the strong castle of Marcuello, among the mountains of Arragon. The Emir, enraged to be disappointed of his prey, embarked at Carthagena and crossed the straits to Ceuta to make captives of the Countess Frandina and her son.

The old chronicle from which we take this part of our legend, presents a gloomy picture of the countess in the stern fortress to which she had fled for refuge, a picture heightened by supernatural horrors. These latter the sagacious reader will admit or reject according to the measure of his faith and judgement; always remembering that in dark and eventful times like those in question, involving the destinies of nations, the downfall of kingdoms and the crimes of rulers and mighty men, the hand of fate is sometimes strangely visible, and confounds the wisdom of the worldly wise, by intimations and portents above the ordinary course of things. With this proviso, we make no scruple to follow the venerable chronicler in his narration.

Now so it happened that the Countess Frandina was seated late at night in her chamber in the citadel of Ceuta, which stands on a lofty rock, overlooking the sea. She was revolving in gloomy thought the late disasters of her family when she heard a mournful noise like that of the sea breeze moaning about the castle walls. Raising her eyes she beheld her brother the Bishop Oppas at the entrance of the chamber. She advanced to embrace him, but he forbade her with a motion of his hand, and she observed that he was ghastly pale, and that his eyes glared as with lambent flames.

"Touch me not, sister," said he, with a mournful voice, "lest thou be consumed by the fire which rages within me. Guard well thy son, for blood hounds are upon his track. His innocence might have secured him the protection of heaven but our crimes have involved him in our common ruin." He ceased to speak and was no longer to be seen. His coming and going were alike without noise, and the door of the chamber remained fast bolted.

On the following morning a messenger arrived with tidings that the Bishop Oppas had been made prisoner in battle by the insurgent christians of the Asturias, and had died in fetters in a tower of the mountains. The same messenger brought word that the Emir Alahor had put to death several of the friends of Count Julian, had obliged him to fly for his life to a castle in Arragon, and was embarking with a formidable force for Ceuta.

The Countess Frandina, as has already been shown, was of courageous heart, and danger made her desperate. There were fifty moorish soldiers in the garrison; she feared that they would prove treacherous, and take part with their countrymen. Summoning her officers, therefore, she informed them of their danger, and commanded them to put those moors to death. The guards sallied forth to obey her orders. Thirty five of the moors were in the great square, unsuspicious of any danger, when they were severally singled out by their executioners, and, at a concerted signal, killed on the spot. The remaining fifteen took refuge in a tower. They saw the armada of the Emir at a distance and hoped to be able to hold out until its arrival. The soldiers of the countess saw it also, and made extraordinary efforts to destroy these internal enemies before they should be attacked from without. They made repeated attempts to storm the tower, but were as often repulsed with severe loss. They then undermined it, supporting its foundations by stanchions of wood. To these they set fire and withdrew to a distance, keeping up a constant shower of missiles to prevent the moors from sallying forth to extinguish the flames. The stanchions were rapidly consumed, and when they gave way the tower fell to the ground. Some of the moors were crushed among the ruins; others were flung to a distance and dashed among the rocks; those who survived were instantly put to the sword.

The fleet of the Emir arrived at Ceuta about the hour of vespers. He landed but found the gates closed against him. The countess, herself, spoke to him from a tower; and set him at defiance. The Emir immediately laid siege to the city. He consulted the astrologer Yuza, who told him that for seven days his star would have the ascendant over that of the youth Alarbot, but after that time the youth would be safe from his power, and would effect his ruin.

Alahor immediately ordered the city to be assailed on every side and at length carried it by storm. The countess took refuge with her forces in the citadel, and made desperate defence, but the walls were sapped and mined and she saw that all resistance would soon be unavailing. Her only thoughts now were to conceal her child. "Surely," said she, "they will not think of seeking him among the dead." She led him therefore into the dark and dismal chapel. "Thou art not afraid to be alone in this darkness my child?" said she.

"No mother," replied the boy, "darkness gives silence and sleep." She conducted him to the tomb of Florinda. "Fearest thou the dead, my child?" "No mother, the dead can do no harm, and what should I fear from my sister?"

The countess opened the sepulchre. "Listen my son," said she. "There are fierce and cruel people who have come hither to murder thee. Stay here in company with thy sister, and be quiet as thou dost value thy life!" The boy, who was of a courageous nature, did as he was bid, and remained there all that day, and all the night, and the next day until the third hour.

In the mean time the walls of the citadel were sapped, the troops of the Emir poured in at the breach and a great part of the garrison was put to the sword. The countess was taken prisoner and brought before the Emir. She appeared in his presence with a haughty demeanour, as if she had been a queen receiving homage; but when he demanded her son she faltered, and turned pale, and replied, "My son is with the dead."

"Countess," said the Emir, "I am not to be deceived; tell me where you have concealed the boy or tortures shall wring from you the secret."

"Emir," replied the countess, "may the greatest torments be my portion, both here and hereafter, if what I speak be not the truth. My darling child lies buried with the dead."

The Emir was confounded by the solemnity of her words; but the withered astrologer Yuza, who stood by his side regarding the countess from beneath his bushed eyebrows, perceived trouble in her countenance and equivocation in her words. "Leave this matter to me," whispered he to Alahor, "I will produce the child."

He ordered strict search to be made by the soldiery and he obliged the countess to be always present. When they came to the chapel her cheek turned pale and her lip quivered. "This," said the subtile astrologer to himself, "is the place of concealment!"

The search throughout the chapel, however, was equally vain, and the soldiers were about to depart, when Yuza remarked a slight gleam of joy in the eye of the countess. "We are leaving our prey behind," thought he, "the countess is exulting."

He now called to mind the words of her asseveration that her child was with the dead. Turning suddenly to the soldiers he ordered them to search the sepulchres. "If you find him not," said he, "drag forth the bones of that wanton Cava, that they may be burnt and the ashes scattered to the winds."

The soldiers searched among the tombs and found that of Florinda partly open. Within lay the boy in the sound sleep of childhood, and one of the soldiers took him gently into his arms to bear him to the Emir.

When the countess beheld that her child was discovered, she rushed into the presence of Alahor and, forgetting all her pride, threw herself upon her knees before him.

"Mercy! mercy!" cried she in piercing accents, "mercy on my son— my only child! Oh Emir! listen to a mother's prayer, and my lips shall kiss thy feet. As thou art merciful to him so may the most high God have mercy upon thee, and heap blessings on thy head."

"Bear that frantic woman hence," said the Emir, "but guard her well."

The countess was dragged away by the soldiery without regard to her struggles and her cries, and confined in a dungeon of the citadel.

The child was now brought to the Emir. He had been awakened by the tumult, but gazed fearlessly on the stern countenances of the soldiers. Had the heart of the Emir been capable of pity it would have been touched by the tender youth and innocent beauty of the child; but his heart was as the nether millstone, and he was bent upon the destruction of the whole family of Julian. Calling to him the astrologer he gave the child into his charge with a secret command. The withered son of the desert took the boy by the hand, and led him up the winding stair case of a tower. When they reached the summit Yuza placed him on the battlements.

"Cling not to me, my child," said he, "there is no danger." "Father, I fear not," said the undaunted boy, "yet it is a wondrous height!"

The child looked around with delighted eyes. The breeze blew his curling locks from about his face and his cheek glowed at the boundless prospect; for the tower was reared upon that lofty promontory on which Hercules founded one of his pillars. The surges of the sea were heard far below, beating upon the rocks, the sea gull screamed and wheeled about the foundations of the tower, and the sails of lofty caraccas were as mere specks on the bosom of the deep.

"Dost thou know yonder land beyond the blue water?" said Yuza.

"It is Spain"; replied the boy, "it is the land of my father and my mother."

"Then stretch forth thy hands and bless it, my child," said the astrologer.

The boy let go his hold of the wall and as he stretched forth his hands, the aged son of Ishmael, exerting all the strength of his withered limbs, suddenly pushed him over the battlements. He fell headlong from the top of that tall tower, and not a bone in his tender frame but was crushed upon the rocks beneath.

Alahor came to the foot of the winding stairs. "Is the boy safe?" cried he.

"He is safe," replied Yuza, "come and behold the truth with thine own eyes."

The Emir ascended the tower, and looked over the battlements, and beheld the body of the child a shapeless mass on the rocks far below, and the sea gulls hovering about it; and he gave orders that it should be thrown into the sea, which was done.

On the following morning the countess was led forth from her dungeon into the public square. She knew of the death of her child, and that her own death was at hand, but she neither wept nor supplicated. Her hair was disheveled, her eyes were haggard with watching and her cheek was as the monumental stone; but there were the remains of commanding beauty in her countenance, and the majesty of her presence awed even the rabble into respect.

A multitude of christian prisoners were then brought forth; and Alahor cried out, "Behold the wife of Count Julian; behold one of that traytorous family which has brought ruin upon yourselves and upon your country." And he ordered that they should stone her to death. But the christians drew back with horror from the deed, and said, "In the hand of God is vengeance, let not her blood be upon our heads." Upon this the Emir swore with horrid imprecations that whoever of the captives refused should himself be stoned to death. So the cruel order was executed, and the Countess Frandina perished by the hands of her countrymen. Having thus accomplished his barbarous errand the Emir embarked for Spain, and ordered the citadel of Ceuta to be set on fire, and crossed the straits at night by the light of its towering flames.

The death of Count Julian, which took place not long after, closed the tragic story of his family. How he died remains involved in doubt. Some assert that the cruel Alahor pursued him to his retreat among the mountains, and, having taken him prisoner, beheaded him; others that the moors confined him in a dungeon and put an end to his life with lingering torments; while others affirm that the tower of the castle of Marcuello, near Huesca in Arragon, in which he took refuge fell on him and crushed him to pieces. All agree that his latter end was miserable in the extreme, and his death violent. The curse of heaven, which had thus pursued him to the grave, was extended to the very place which had given him shelter; for we are told that the castle is no longer inhabited on account of the strange and horrible noises that are heard in it; and that visions of armed men are seen above it in the air; which are supposed to be the troubled spirits of the apostate christians who favoured the cause of the traitor.

In after times a stone sepulchre was shewn, outside of the chapel of the castle, as the tomb of Count Julian; but the traveller and the pilgrim avoided it, or bestowed upon it a malediction; and the name of Julian has remained a byeword and a scorn in the land for the warning of all generations. Such ever be the lot of him who betrays his country.

Here end the legends of the conquest of Spain.

Written in the Alhambra, June 10, 1829.

NOTE TO THE PRECEDING LEGEND

El licenciado Ardevines (Lib. 2. c. 8.) dize que dichos Duendos caseros o los del aire, hazen aparacer exercitos y peleas, como lo que se cuenta por tradicion (y aun algunos personas lo deponen como testigos de vista) de la torre y castello de Marcuello, lugar al pie de las montañas de Aragon (aora inhabitable, por las grandes y espantables ruidos, que en el se oyen) donde se retraxo el Conde Don Julian, causa de la perdicion de España; sobre el qual castillo, deze se ven en el aire ciertas visiones, como de soldados, que el vulgo dize son los cavalleros y gente que le favorecian.

Vide "el Ente Dislucidado, por Fray Antonio de Fuentolapeña capuchin. Seccion 3. Subseccion 5. Instancia 8. Num. 644.

As readers unversed in the Spanish language may wish to know the testimony of the worthy and discreet capuchin friar, Antonio de Fuentalapeña, we subjoin a translation of it.

"The licentiate Ardevines, (Book 2, chap. 8.) says, that the said house fairies, (or familiar spirits,) or those of the air, cause the apparitions of armies and battles; such as those which are related in tradition, (and some persons even depose to the truth of them as eye witnesses) of the tower and castle of Marcuello, a fortress at the foot of the mountains of Aragon, (at present uninhabitable, on account of the great and frightful noises heard in it) the place of retreat of Count Don Julian the cause of the perdition of Spain. It is said that certain apparitions of soldiers are seen in the air; which the vulgar say are those of the courtiers and people who aided him."

EDITORIAL APPENDIX

Textual Commentary,
Discussions, Lists, and Index by
Dahlia Kirby Terrell

LIST OF ABBREVIATIONS

The following symbols have been used in the editorial apparatus to designate the manuscripts and previously published texts of *The Crayon Miscellany*.

MSA   Manuscript used as printer's copy for the first American editions of *A Tour on the Prairies, Abbotsford and Newstead Abbey,* and *Legends of the Conquest of Spain*

MSE   Manuscript used as printer's copy for the first English editions of *A Tour on the Prairies* and of *Abbotsford and Newstead Abbey*

MS   Manuscript used as printer's copy for the first American edition and for the stereotyped sheets used for the first English edition of *Legends of the Conquest of Spain*

1A   First American editions of *A Tour on the Prairies, Abbotsford and Newstead Abbey,* and *Legends of the Conquest of Spain* (Philadelphia: Carey, Lea, and Blanchard, 1835)

2A   Second American edition, printed by Putnam's in 1849 as Volume IX of the Author's Revised Edition and including *A Tour on the Prairies,* and *Abbotsford and Newstead Abbey*

1E   First English editions (London: John Murray, 1835)

T   Twayne edition

EXPLANATORY NOTES

Records of the War Department and of the Office of Indian Affairs in the National Archives, as well as Irving's letters and Western journals and Latrobe's account in *The Rambler in North America* (1835), all aid in identifying or explaining references in *A Tour on the Prairies*. In addition, twentieth-century publications relating to the 1832 tour generally include cross references and various annotations. See especially Stanley T. Williams' and Barbara D. Simison's 1937 edition of Ellsworth's account in *Washington Irving on the Prairie or A Narrative of A Tour of the Southwest in the Year 1832*; *The Western Journals of Washington Irving*, ed. John Francis McDermott (1944); *A Tour on the Prairies*, ed. Joseph B. Thoburn and George C. Wells with additional footnote references by Muriel Wright (1955); *The Rambler in Oklahoma*, ed. Muriel H. Wright and George H. Shirk (1955); *A Tour on the Prairies*, ed. John Francis McDermott (1956); and *On the Western Tour with Washington Irving: The Journal and Letters of Count de Pourtalès*, ed. George F. Spaulding (1968).

The numbers before each note indicate the page and line in the Twayne edition. Chapter numbers, chapter or section titles, author's chapter or section summaries, texts, quotations, and footnotes are included in the line count. Only running heads and rules added to separate running heads from the text are omitted from the count.

5.2–10   "As ... childhood!] From "The Voyage" in *The Sketch Book* (1819).

5.12–13   voyage to Europe] Irving embarked from New York on the ship Mexico on May 25, 1815, for Liverpool, unaware that it would be seventeen years before he would return to America.

5.14   "world's geer"] Irving was using the Scottish word "geer" (now obsolete) meaning possesions in general.

6.2   "treading the primrose path of dalliance,"] In *Hamlet*, I, iii Ophelia says to Laertes,

> Do not, as some ungracious pastors do,
> Show me the steep and thorny way to heaven,

> Whiles, like a puffed and reckless libertine,
> Himself the primrose path of dalliance treads
> And recks not his own rede.

8.4	welcome me] On the evening of May 30, 1832, Irving was honored at a public dinner at the City Hotel in New York.
8.29	Having] Beginning of the preface to 2A.
9.9–10	extensive tour] Immediately before his tour in Oklahoma, Irving visited parts of New York, Ohio, Pennsylvania, New Hampshire, Kentucky, Missouri, and Kansas; and following the excursion he went to Alabama, Georgia, South Carolina, North Carolina, Virginia, and Washington, D.C.
9.16	"Story! . . . sir"] From Stanza 6 of "The Friend of Humanity and the Knife-Grinder" by the British statesman and poet George Canning (1770–1827).
10.17	Fort Gibson] Established in 1824 with Colonel Arbuckle as commander.
10.22–23	one of the commissioners] Henry L. Ellsworth (1791–1858) from Hartford, Connecticut.
10.24	settlement of the Indian tribes] The Indian Removal Act of June 30, 1830, provided all of the Indians living east of the Mississippi River might be moved west of it.
10.28	one of the towns of Connecticut] Windsor
10.36	Mr. L ———] Charles Joseph Latrobe (1801–1875), nephew of Benjamin Henry Latrobe, chief architect of the United States capitol.
11.4	third fellow traveller] Count Albert-Alexandre de Pourtalès (1812–1861).
11.5	Telemachus] Son of Penelope and Odysseus who helped his father slay Penelope's suitors.
11.15	Tonish] Antoine Deshetres (1791–1854).
11.15	Gil Blas] Hero of *Histoire de Gil Blas de Santillane*, a romance by Alaine René Le Sage, published in 1715.
12.19	Osage Agency] Actually the trading post of Auguste Pierre Choteau about four miles west of Fort Gibson.
12.34	rangers] The company, numbering one hundred and ten, was authorized by Congress on June 15, 1832, as part of a battalion of six hundred to serve on the frontiers. In late July and in August this company was recruited in Arkansas.

13.6–7   commander of Fort Gibson]   Colonel Matthew Arbuckle
                  (1776–1851).
13.11   lieutenant]   First Lieutenant Joseph Pentecost.
14.34   Col. Choteau]   A. P. Choteau, Jr. (1787–1838), who
                  had traveled with Irving's group from Independence,
                  was United States Indian agent to the Osages.
16.6   Antoine]   Antoine Lombard
16.11   Adonis]   Handsome young man loved by Aphrodite,
                  Greek goddess of love and beauty.
16.18   Pierre Beatte]   Written as "Billett" or "Bilyet" in Irv-
                  ing's journals; apparently a Frenchman rather than
                  of mixed parentage. (See J. F. McDermott's note,
                  p. 24, in A Tour on the Prairies [Norman: University
                  of Oklahoma Press, 1956]).
17.9   en Cavalier]   like royalty; literally "as a Royalist."
17.10   "a beggar on horseback"]   He will never alight, ride a
                  gallop, ride to the devil, ride to the gallows, run his
                  horse to death. See Burton, Anatomy of Melancholy,
                  II, iii, 2 and The Third Part of King Henry the Sixth,
                  I, iv, 127.
17.24   Berryhill]   Ellsworth referred to him as "a half breed
                  Indian"; Irving's journal lists only the name and makes
                  reference to the illness.
18.36   west]   It should read "east."
19.35   white man, ... frontier]   Ellsworth identified the place
                  as "(Mr. Hardrigers) a Creek"; the name may have
                  been "Hardage."
20.7   the hero of La Mancha]   Don Quixote
20.36   "Lynch's Law"]   Named for Captain William Lynch
                  (1742–1820), member of a vigilance committee in
                  Pittsylvania, Virginia, in 1780.
21.5   Lycurgus]   Real or legendary Spartan lawgiver of about
                  the ninth century B.C.
21.5   Draco]   Athenian statesman of the seventh century
                  B.C. noted for the severity of his code of laws.
24.7   preux chevalier]   valiant knight.
24.16   bandaleer]   A "bandoleer" or "bandolier" is a belt worn
                  over one shoulder and across the chest with pockets
                  for ammunition.
28.36   Capt. Bean]   Jesse Bean, native of Tennessee, had taken
                  part in engagements at New Orleans in 1814–1815
                  and in the Indian wars in Florida before he was
                  chosen to raise this company of rangers.

29.13   Old Ryan] John Ryan, native of Virginia and father of ranger William Ryan (whom Irving never mentioned), migrated with his family in 1829 to Arkansas where he was living when Captain Bean recruited his company. (Ryan is identified in an 1892 manuscript dictated by his daughter Irene to her son John Ryan Lewis and made available to this editor by a family descendant, the late Professor Quanah Lewis of Texas Tech University.)

30.11   "a land flowing with milk and honey"] Exod. 3:8, 33:3; Jer. 11:5, 33:22.

32.1   "Melancholy Jacques"] Contributor of sour philosophy in Shakespeare's comedy *As You Like It*.

32.25   Doctor] David Holt, civilian doctor assigned by Colonel Arbuckle to the rangers.

32.29   Red Fork] The Cimarron

32.31   Cross Timber] The difficult timber-covered areas were along early trails, but the timber was not continuous as Irving and other early travelers believed.

34.32   Covenanters] Members of a religious group in Scotland who bound themselves by a series of covenants to uphold the Presbyterian faith.

34.35   Praise-God Barebones] Praisegod Barbon, or Barebone, a London leatherseller and Anabaptist preacher of long sermons, served in Cromwell's parliament of 1653 and thus gave the parliament his name.

34.40   Charley] Charles Nelson of Batesville, Arkansas.

37.27   M'Lellan] Probably Willis McClenden of Batesville, Arkansas.

40.36   Gotham] Legendary English city whose inhabitants were noted for their foolishness.

41.24   Claude Lorraine] French painter (1600–1682).

41.34   rocky dell] According to Latrobe this site was "Bear's Glen."

42.31–32   Pawnees . . . entering.] In 1832 the Pawnees lived in what is now the state of Nebraska and seldom went as far south as Kansas, even in war parties; "Pawnee" was the term applied on the frontier to several Plains tribes, including the Comanches, the Wichita, and the Kiowas.

42.42   sons of Ishmael] An epithet for social outcasts from the biblical story of Sarah's casting out Ishmael, son

of Abraham and Hagar, in fear of the rights of her
son Isaac.

44.33–34   sacrifice . . . it]   Irving's nephew, John Treat Irving, Jr.,
recorded the story of a Pawnee sacrifice he heard about
in 1833 in his *Indian Sketches, Taken During an Expedition to the Pawnee Tribes* (ed. John Francis McDermott [Norman: University of Oklahoma Press, 1955]).

44.36   sergeant]   Isaac Bean, the captain's brother.

54.22   Sawyer]   William Sawyers of Spadra, Arkansas.

56.12   Nestor]   Wise old counselor who fought with the Greeks
at Troy.

57.7   "skir"]   Usually "skirr"; to cover in searching.

59.17   Konza]   A mispronunciation or variation of "Kansa,"
or "Kaw," a southwestern Siouan tribe that lived west
of the Osage River, south of the Omaha River, and
along the Kansas River.

61.14   Cliff Castle]   Ellsworth wrote that Doctor Holt called it
"Irvings castle."

62.43   King's party]   Second Lieutenant Robert King.

63.36   laso]   "lasso" in modern usage; *lazo* in Spanish.

66.33   Brasis]   Brazos

67.15   Mahomet]   Mohammed, founder of the Moslem religion.

68.18   green horns]   beginners; novices.

76.42   Clements]   Jeremiah C. Clements of Batesville, Arkansas.

77.33   Cock of the Woods]   In 1832 in Volume II of *Westward
Ho*, James Kirke Paulding used a similar expression,
"cock of the wood," to refer to the hero of his novel.

78.28   beaver dam]   Almost certainly on Bear Creek.

79.10   Leatherstocking]   Irving knew James Fenimore Cooper's
hero, Natty Bumppo, from having read *The Pioneers*
(1823) and possibly *The Prairie* (1827), though he
had not read of the younger Natty in *The Last of the
Mohicans* (1826).

81.2–3   little more . . Texas]   Actually they were several days
away from Texas, since the Red River (the boundary
line between Oklahoma and Texas) was more than
one hundred miles to the south.

81.7   the morning]   October 24

82.12   my book]   Irving was reading the French Bible which
Pourtalès had brought with him, one of the two books
among the men, the other being Ellsworth's pocket
testament, according to the commissioner.

82.34   his former rider]   Private Jeremiah C. Clements.

83.19	eight o'clock] October 25
83.27–28	north fork of the Red river] Actually the North Fork of the Canadian.
86.1	Scaramouch] A braggart and poltroon; stock character in old Italian comedy.
86.37	*stampedo*] stampede
87.12	daybreak] October 26
88.12–18	Fancying . . . stealing!] Of this incident Ellsworth wrote his wife that "Mr Irving has added a little here to make a good story, and says the Osages listened with attention to what I said but remarked 'they go and steal some horses before peace was made as they must not steal any afterwards'—but this is certainly by way of addenda."
90.31–91.19	A hunter . . . for life.] Ellsworth wrote that Captain Bean told this story (with more details) on October 18, the captain's having known the characters personally in Missouri explorations with William Ashley a fur trader; also told of Hugh Glass (deserted by companions in 1823) in several versions which have passed into oral tradition as a part of frontier lore.
92.1	Requa] William Requa (1795–1886).
92.3–4	had visited . . . frontier] Irving, Ellsworth, Latrobe, and Pourtalès had dinner at noon on October 6 at Hopefield Mission with Mr. Requa.
92.35	Surgeon] Dr. David Holt
93.21–25	At . . . spirits] Irving's journal notation of October 4 is the source for this story.
93.26	story] Colonel Choteau told the story on October 4, according to Irving's journal.
93.29	Nick a nansa] This stream, written "Nickanansa" at 93.26, is unidentified; according to Irving's journal it is "next to" Wagrushka.
93.43	Wagrushka] Recorded in Irving's journal on October 4 "*Wagrushka e abbe*—creek—"; it is Irving's spelling of the Osage name for Labette Creek which flows into the Neosho River near the present Kansas-Oklahoma line.
94.29	morning] October 28
96.15	fourteen] Irving's journal (in the undated notes at the end of the notebook for October 31–November 10 where this incident is recorded) gives Tonish's age as "about fifteen."

97.29–30   "close dungeon of innumerous boughs"]   From Milton's
                Comus, line 349.

102.33   Virtuoso]   Latrobe

103.12   Amateur]   Irving's word, referring here to Latrobe, had
                a favorable connotation in the 1830's meaning "a lover
                of a particular art or science."

108.22–23   coney . . . rabbit.]   Except for his classification of the
                prairie dog, Irving's observations are generally accu-
                rate; the prairie dogs burrow as do some rabbits, but
                they are rodents.

110.30   breakfast]   October 31

111.35   southeast]   At 112.3 Irving clarifies what seems to be an
                error here, since the route to Fort Gibson lay in a
                northeasterly direction; they "skirted the prairie" for
                a few miles to pick up an old wartrack to the east.

114.38–39   "Canst . . . Orion?"]   Job 38:31.

117.3   Childers]   Alexander C. Childers, bugler, from Bates-
                ville, Arkansas.

118.36   that day . . . next]   November 6 and 7

121.4   Cocaigne]   Cockaigne; an imaginary land of luxurious
                and idle living.

121.20   mistress of the house]   Ellsworth identifies her as Madam
                Bradley.

121.24   flesh pots of Egypt]   See *Don Quixote,* pt. 1, bk. 3,
                chap. 7 (p. 160 in the Modern Library Giant Edition).

121.34   Apicius]   A gourmet in the reign of Tiberius, Roman
                emperor 14–37 A.D.

122.23   Agency]   Colonel Choteau's trading post.

Abbotsford

125.12   "mighty minstrel of the north"]   An honorific title for
                the popular Border minstrel Walter Scott (1771–1832).

125.13   Thomas Campbell]   British poet and critic (1777–1844).

125.19   Abbotsford]   Scott's home on the Tweed about three
                miles from Melrose, bought as a hundred-acre farm in
                1811 and enlarged and renamed by Scott for the ford
                used by the abbots of Melrose; the building was under
                way during Irving's visit.

125.22   he . . . Baronet]   He was made a baronet in 1820.

126.1–2   Both . . . degree;]   From Goldsmith's *Elegy on the Death
                of a Mad Dog.*

127.38–39   Nor . . . fair.]   *The Lay of the Last Minstrel,* canto 2,
                st. 8.

128.22–129.8   Lo ... knee.]   *The Lay of the Last Minstrel*, canto 2,
st. 17, lines 1–2, 7–12; st. 18, lines 5–10, 13–16; st. 19,
lines 1–10.

129.33   one of the cantos]   canto 2.

131.8   Adam Ferguson]   Son of Professor Fergusson and Scott's
friend since early school days.

131.38   Eildon Hills]   A Roman road ran from Eildon Hills down
to the ford. References to "Eildon stone," "Eildon
tree," etc. are famous in "Border Minstrelsy"; here was
a favorite spot of Scott's, the site of the haunted glen
of Thomas the Rhymer.

132.34   Edie Ochiltree]   Beggar in Scott's novel *The Antiquary*
published in 1815.

132.35–36   Wilkie ... family]   Painting by David Wilkie in 1817.

133.4   Ettrick Vale]   Valley of the Ettrick River in Selkirk-
shire; birthplace of James Hogg, the poet, sometimes
called the "Ettrick Shepherd."

133.5   Braes of Yarrow]   The Yarrow is a small river flowing
into the Ettrick before its junction with the Tweed
near Selkirk. Burns uses the phrases "Yarrow Braes"
and "Ettrick Shaws" in a poem called "Braw Lads o'
Galla Water."

133.40   Leyden]   Dr. John Leyden, M.D., who had assisted
Scott in the preparation of the Border Minstrelsy in
1805 and who died in Java in 1811.

134.21   cairn gorm]   From the name of a mountain, meaning
blue cairn, between the shores of Aberdeen, Banff,
and Inverness: a precious stone of yellow or wine
color.

134.33–34   Pilgrim's Progress]   Religious allegory by John Bunyan
(1678).

135.41   Leith]   Former burgh in Scotland; now a port section
of Edinburgh.

136.20   Coming ... before.]   A line from Thomas Campbell's
Lochiel which Scott apparently "got him to restore."

137.22   one of the cantos]   Canto 1; Irving used two of Scott's
lines then omitted the following lines: "Feel the sad
influence of the hour, / And wail the daisy's vanished
flower."

139.29   Mungo Park]   Scottish explorer in Africa (1771–1806);
Scott's neighbor.

140.8   Saib]   Sahib

140.10–11   Rob Roy]   Rob Roy MacGregor.

140.19	Waterloo] Scene of Napoleon's defeat in 1815.
140.26	General Wolfe] James Wolfe (1727–1759), English general who defeated the French forces under Montcalm at Quebec in 1759.
142.2	Pretender in Scotland] Charles Edward Stuart.
144.15–16	Robert Bruce] (1274–1329) King of Scotland 1306–1329; won independence of Scotland from England.
145.5–8	O ... lasted.] The old words of *Galashiels*, a favorite Scottish air.
145.13–14	David ... beam.] 1 Sam. 17:7.
147.31	Don Quixote] Hero of Miguel de Cervantes' romance published in 1605 (first part) and 1615 (second part).
148.16	Rosinante] Don Quixote's thin, worn-out horse.
149.3	Thomas the Rhymer] Thomas Learmont of Ercildoune to whom Scott attributed the metrical romance *Sir Tristrem* which he inferred must have been written in the thirteenth century.
149.15–22	True ... nine.] The first two stanzas of the first part of Scott's "Thomas the Rhymer" in *Imitations of the Ancient Ballad.*
149.26–27	And ... seen.] The last two lines of the first part of Scott's "Thomas the Rhymer."
150.17	sable prince of Denmark] Reference to Shakespeare's Hamlet; Scott's greyhound was first named "Marmion" but later renamed because of his black coat.
150.20	*flagrante delictu*] *flagrante delicto*; red-handed; in the offense.
151.3	Oldbuck] Jonathan Oldbuck of Monkbarns, the title character of Scott's novel *The Antiquary* published in 1815.
151.14	Nestor] Wise old counselor who fought with the Greeks at Troy.
151.32	ingle] fireplace
153.32	Loch Katrine] Scene of Scott's *Lady of the Lake.*
153.34	muckle] much
153.36	Dryburgh Abbey] A part of the patrimonial estate of the wife of Scott's grandfather which would have descendel to Scott's father had not the grand uncle who owned it become bankrupt and sold it. Right of burial in the resting place of the family was retained.
154.3	"Sandy Knowe crags"] Robert Scott, Walter's grandfather, held the farm of Sandy Knowe, including Smallholm Tower, by lease.

154.9   one of the cantos]   Canto 3.
154.40   old shepherd]   His name was Hogg, and he had loaned
                 all of his savings to Robert Scott to buy stock for
                 Sandy Knowe; the story of how the money was fool-
                 ishly spent for a high spirited horse is told in Scott's
                 autobiography.
155.23–156.36 Thus . . . before.]   Introduction to canto 3 of *Marmion*.
156.41–42   "The Eve of St. John"] Written in the autumn of 1799.
157.10–11   Betide . . . Bemerside.]   Quoted by Scott in his ballad
                 "Thomas the Rhymer."
158.20   Earl of Buchan]   David Erskine Buchan.
158.32   Mr. William Laidlaw]   A friend since 1799, the year of
                 Scott's appointment as sheriff of Selkirkshire, and
                 Scott's neighbor and estate manager since 1815.
161.12   Hogg]   James Hogg (1770–1835).
161.25   Blackwood]   William Blackwood (1776–1834).
162.7   Lord Somerville]   John Somerville, with whom Scott
                 shared an interest in hunting and fishing.
163.15   gaberlunzie]   a wandering beggar.
166.12–13   book . . . him.]   In 1813 he and Mrs. Scott made their
                 sides sore laughing at *Diedrich Knickerbocker's His-
                 tory of New York* which Henry Brevoort sent Scott.
166.25–26   picture of the Scott family.]   "The Abbotsford Family,"
                 painted by David Wilkie in 1817 and exhibited in
                 1818, represents Scott and his family, Adam Fergusson
                 (for whom the portrait was painted), and an old
                 dependent, all masquerading in the garb of country
                 peasants (page 124 in this edition). See 132.35–36.
167.34   Jeffrey]   Francis Jeffrey, one of the founders of the
                 Edinburgh Review in 1802 and its editor from 1803
                 until 1820.

                                Newstead Abbey

171.2   three weeks sojourn]   In January, 1832.
171.3   Lord Byron]   George Gordon Byron (1788–1824).
171.5   Newstead Abbey]   Home of Lord Byron's family from
                 1540 until 1818 when Byron sold it to pay his debts;
                 founded in 1170 by Henry II and converted by Sir
                 John Byron into a house in 1540; reconstructed in the
                 nineteenth century in Gothic style to designs by John
                 Shaw.
171.8   Sherwood Forest]   In Nottinghamshire, England, four-

	teen miles north of Nottingham; principal scene of the legendary exploits of Robin Hood.
171.9	Robin Hood] English outlaw and hero said to have been born at Locksley, Nottinghamshire, about 1160.
171.16	Henry II] (1133–1189), first Plantagenet king; ruled from 1154–1189.
171.18	Thomas a Becket] Born in London 1118; murdered in Canterbury Cathedral December 29, 1170, because he opposed the curtailment of clerical privileges by Henry II.
171.20	Saint Augustine] Great Christian theologian (354–430).
171.26–27	Henry VIII] King 1509–1547; the Act of Supremacy in 1534 declared the king the supreme head of the church and clergy in England.
172.1–8	Hark . . . alarms.] "Elegy on Newstead Abbey," lines 49–56.
173.30	Moore] Thomas Moore (1779–1852) published a biography of Byron in 1830, the source of much of Irving's material for this essay.
174.2	Harrow] Famous school about twelve miles from London; founded 1571.
174.8–15	Through . . . remain.*] "On Leaving Newstead Abbey," lines 1–8.
174.18–19	Newstead! . . . fate!*] "Elegy on Newstead Abbey," lines 137–44, 149–52.
175.42	Charles Skinner Mathews, Esq.] Fellow of Downing College, Cambridge.
177.11–14	Haply . . . day.] Final stanza of "Elegy on Newstead Abbey."
177.16–17	venerable . . . Derbyshire,] Barlborough Hall owned by the Reverend C. R. Reaston Rodes.
177.31–33	An . . . Gothic—] *Don Juan,* canto 13, st. 55, lines 2, 3, 4.
178.28–35	Amidst . . . troubles.*] St. 65.
178.36–40	—in . . . ground.] First 5 of 8 lines in st. 61.
179.36–180.6	The mansion's . . . hearts.] *Don Juan,* canto 13, st. 66; st. 67, lines 1–6.
181.4	Vandyke] Of the style of the Flemish painter Anthony Van Dyck (1599–1641).
182.16–23	Where . . . paid.] "Elegy on Newstead Abbey," lines 28–36.
182.21	warning] It probably should read "waning."
183.28–184.2	I did . . . thee.] "Epistle to Augusta," sts. 10, 7.
184.29–36	Young . . . hide.] "To An Oak at Newstead," lines 1–8.

185.9	Hucknall Torkard] Fourteenth-century church where the tomb of Byron is located.
185.20–22	After . . . further!] Macbeth, III, ii, 23, 25–26.
185.26–37	When . . . fear.] "Euthanasia," lines 1–12.
186.30	ballad of St. George and the dragon] Legend about Saint George's using his magic sword to kill a dragon to which the king's daughter was being sacrificed.
186.34–35	Maid Marian] Robin Hood's sweetheart.
186.35	Beelzebub] Called "prince of the devils" (Matt. 12:24).
187.16–17	Hobby Horse] Part of the morris–dance in which a man dances about disguised in a pasteboard horse.
194.23	Miss Milbanke] Annabella Milbanke whom Byron married in 1815.
194.30–195.36	Beware! . . . soul.] Don Juan, canto 16, st. 40.
196.4	Kitty Parkins] The reference here may be to Margaret Parker.
196.36–41	For . . . beams.] Don Juan, canto 16, st. 17, lines 7–8. st. 19, lines 3–6.
198.15–22	The love . . . zone.] Don Juan, canto 16, st. 108.
198.37	Musters] John Musters.
202.26–36	He . . . agony.] "The Dream," sec. 2, lines 51–60.
203.17–24	The forms . . . sleep.] canto 16, st. 18.
205.41–206.34	Well! . . . break.] "Well Thou Art Happy."
207.6–17	When . . . before.] "To A Lady on Being Asked My Reason for Quitting England in the Spring," lines 1–12.
207.23–208.22	'Tis . . . one.] "Stanzas to a Lady, on Leaving England," sts. 1, 5, 8, 9, 10, 11.
208.25–26	"wandering through distant climes"] "To a Lady on Being Asked My Reason for Quitting England in the Spring," line 5.
208.32–209.8	I've . . . less.] "Epistle to a Friend," lines 25–40.
209.12	'Thyrza'] Published as "To Thyrza" October 11, 1811.
210.3–10	—In . . . tears.] "The Dream," sec. 5, lines 128–35.
210.16–23	What . . past.] "The Dream," sec. 5, lines 136–43.
210.31–211.2	The lady . . . frenzy.] "The Dream," sec. 7, lines 168–77.
211.13–35	A change . . . time?] "The Dream," sec. 6, lines 144–66.
212.2–7	"my M.A.C." . . . result!"] This is one of a number of passages that Irving took almost verbatim from Thomas Moore's Letters and Journals of Lord Byron: with Notices of His Life (London: John Murray, 1833).
212.17–24	Before . . . flood.] Don Juan, canto 13, st. 57.
213.6	Mother Shipton] Prophetess said to have lived in the reign of Henry VIII.

215.1 Little John] One of Robin Hood's followers who was over seven feet tall and who was named "Little John" in jest.

215.1 Friar Tuck] A jolly friar who joined Robin Hood's band.

215.32–216.3 The scenes . . . green-wood.] *Marmion*, canto 2, introduction, lines 1–4, 8–13, 22–23, 30–31.

217.12 King John] Ruler from 1199 to 1216; forced to sign the Magna Carta in 1215.

217.35–40 A thousand . . . grim.] *Marmion*, canto 2, introduction, lines 34–35, 38–40.

218.6 We . . . of!] *The Tempest*, IV, i, 156–57, reads ". . . dreams are made on."

218.16 "leafy honours"] Irving's phrase is reminiscent of language of the Neo-Classic Period. See, for example, Dryden's *Aeneid*, II, line 851 and Pope's pastoral poem, "Winter," line 32.

219.15 'working day world'] *As You Like It*, I, ii, 2.

219.25 ballad of the King and the Miller of Mansfield] John Cockle, a good-natured miller of Mansfield, gave a night's lodging to King Henry II who became lost on a hunting expedition and the next morning, to his surprise, was knighted and given a salary for his courtesy.

221.29–222.6 – – Now . . . much.] *Don Juan*, canto 13, st. 62, lines 5–8; st. 63; st. 64, lines 1–2, 5–8.

222.20–223.34 Then . . . strength.] *Don Juan*, canto 16, st. 17, lines 1–6; st. 20, lines 3–8; sts. 21–25.

229.7–8 "favorite child"] "Well! Thou Art Happy," line 9.

231.8 death of Lord Byron] In Greece in 1824.

232.1 Swift's dreadful fate] insanity

235.1 "clod of the valley"] a quotation from Byron's drama, "The Deformed Transformed," pt. 1, sc. 1, line 347, published in 1824.

237.6–19 "I am . . . both."] One of a number of passages quoted from letters now in the library of the University of Virginia. This letter is dated September 20, 1825.

Legends of the Conquest of Spain

259.37–38 the venerable Agapida] Fray Antonio Agapida, fictitious narrator of *The Conquest of Granada*.

260.41 Friar] Agapida.

264.33 Friar] Agapida.

300.25   Mr. D. W——kie] David Wilkie (1785–1841), Scot-
          tish painter who did the well-known Irving portrait in
          Seville in April, 1828, and who was knighted in 1836.
300.26   Lord Mah-n] Lord P. H. Stanhope Mahon (1805–1875)
          with whom Irving enjoyed a long friendship.
325.28   Nebucadonozer] The reference must be to Nebuchad-
          nezzar II who ruled 605–562 B.C. and who captured
          Jerusalem in 586 B.C. and destroyed the city.
351.9   Carthagena] Reference here and at 352.16 is to Carta-
          gena, seaport in Southeast Spain on the Mediterranean.

TEXTUAL COMMENTARY

Manuscript prepared as printer's copy for each of the first American editions in *The Crayon Miscellany* series still exists. Of more than eleven hundred pages originally used in setting the first American impressions of the four writings which came out in three volumes in 1835, fewer than two dozen pages are lacking, the greater number including those for the Advertisement and for the eight printed pages of Introduction in *A Tour on the Prairies*. In addition, printer's copy manuscript for the first English editions also exists for three of the works (*A Tour on the Prairies, Abbotsford*, and *Newstead Abbey*); and, in some instances, notes and earlier drafts are extant.[1] For *Legends of the Conquest of Spain* no British manuscript was written; instead sheets printed from the stereotyped plates prepared in America from the printer's copy manuscript were sent to England.

Through the generosity of individuals and institutions identified in the Acknowledgments, all of the manuscript materials and extant copies of notebooks, notes, and early drafts have been made available to the editor for use in determining Irving's original intentions and in establishing the definitive texts. Since no proof sheets survive, the American printer's copy manuscripts, which Irving worked on latest and which he saw through the press, are closest to his final intentions for the works. These serve as copy-texts for the Twayne edition.

For the following portions of text where such manuscript copy is lacking (*Tour* from the beginning through "men" 10.16 and from "crowned" 121.16 through "forward" 122.4; *Abbotsford* from "We" 132.37 through "more" 133.8, from "He" 167.17 through "concerns, no"

---

1. Journals Irving kept on the journey and later used in writing *A Tour on the Prairies* are in the New York Public Library (lacking the journal for the period of October 18–30, inclusive) and are available in *The Western Journals of Washington Irving*, ed. John Francis McDermott (Norman: University of Oklahoma Press, 1944); for *Abbotsford* two volumes of Irving's manuscript notes about his visit to Scotland in 1817 are located in the Rare Book Room of the Louis Round Wilson Library at the University of North Carolina and are in print in *Tour in Scotland 1817*, ed. Stanley T. Williams (New Haven: Yale University Press, 1927); and one page of *Abbotsford* (earlier state of manuscript numbered 19 and corresponding to 133.24–133.35, dated April 6, 1835) is in the Barrett Library at the University of Virginia; for *Newstead Abbey* the Barrett Library at Virginia has four letters from Sophia Hyatt (twenty-five pages measuring 10 x 16 inches each) and approximately one hundred pages of rough notes.

167.23–24 and from "Who" 168.12 through "as" 168.18; *Newstead* from the beginning through "Byron" 171.32 and from "I trust" 176.34 through "Byron" 176.45) the English printer's copy serve as copy-text. For the Advertisement and Introduction in *A Tour on the Prairies* and for the mission portion of manuscript for *Legends of the Conquest of Spain* (from "that" 295.25 through "Roderick" 296.9), copy-texts are the first impressions of the first American editions corresponding to Blanck's listings 10140, first or earlier state, and 10144, designated setting A.

Both the English and the American manuscripts for *A Tour on the Prairies*, *Abbotsford*, and *Newstead Abbey* have importance in the establishment of definitive texts. It seems clear that printer's manuscripts to go to London were being prepared by copyists at the same time that Irving continued to revise the material he was to send to the American printer. Frequently he made on the copied pages the same insertions, corrections, and deletions that appear on the American pages. Occasionally a portion of what appears to be the earlier draft will be pasted on the copied page in the English printer's manuscript, though more often the cutting and rearranging of materials appears in the American printer's copy. For the English edition of *A Tour on the Prairies*, Irving prepared a Preface of two brief paragraphs announcing the possibility of future numbers in the series and explaining the account as "a simple statement of facts" instead of the Advertisement and long Introduction to appear in the first American printing.[2] Later attention to the American forms continued even after British manuscripts and sheets had been sent to England, as evidenced by a number of substantive variations.

2. See the discussion of the writing of the American Introduction in the Introduction to the Twayne edition of *Tour*. A copy of the English Preface is included here.

"Preface" in the First English Edition of
A Tour on the Prairies

PREFACE.

It is the intention of the author to give the accumulated contents of his portfolio, as well as the casual lucubrations of his brain, in occasional numbers, published as circumstances may permit.

He has been much importuned to write an account of a tour, which he made to the Far West, and various publications on the subject have been announced as forthcoming from his pen, when, in truth, he had not as yet put pen to paper. To meet, in some degree, the expectations thus excited, he now furnishes a portion of that tour, comprising a visit to the Buffalo Prairies. It is a simple statement of facts, pretending to no high-wrought effect. Should it give satisfaction, however, he may be tempted to give further sketches of American scenes in some future numbers.

Lacking American copy, however, the editor selecting a basis for a definitive text must consider the English printer's copy in which Irving had a hand. Though the English manuscripts introduce new errors and lack Irving's latest additions and changes and his full authority for accidentals such as punctuation, spelling, capitalization, and paragraphing which sometimes varied with each copyist, they, nevertheless, are nearer his original intentions than printed forms set by compositors unfamiliar with his material.

Substantives which the American compositors misread and thus misset in the first American editions can often be verified by checking the British printer's copies. Numerous examples appear in the List of Rejected Substantives for each of the works. For instance, for *A Tour on the Prairies* see "invincible" set as "invisible" (50.13), "universal" as "unusual" (54.33), "level" as "lure" (63.16), "right" as "sight" (72.9), "stepping" as "stopping" (76.14), "relatives" as "relations" (92.13), "alive" as "alone" (94.19), "brawling" as "bawling" (96.38), "loading" as "leading" (96.41), "sweet" as "secret" (114.38), "rouse" as "raise" (120.21 and 121.14); for *Abbotsford,* "moon" as "morn" (130.8), "famous" as "famed" (139.10), "present" as "persons" (139.40), "balancing" as "labouring" (142.39), "where" as "when" (165.37), "green" as "given" (168.20); for *Newstead Abbey,* "moss grown" as "moss green" (187.36), "glared" as "gazed" (196.30), "Retired" as "Return'd" (204.41), "allured" as "attuned" (209.34), "gazehound" as "greyhound" (217.40), "Where" as "When" (232.28), "lovely" as "lonely" (232.29), "powerful" as "painful" (233.17), "sweet" as "secret" (237.13), and "engrossed" as "engaged" (238.7).

Surviving are the complete English manuscript of 424 pages of *A Tour on the Prairies* in the Hanley Collection at the University of Texas; all of the 145 pages of *Abbotsford* in the files of John Murray Publishing House in London; and 182 pages of *Newstead Abbey* (lacking 43 pages or the portions of the text from "were" 197.24 through "marked" 200.26, "vessel" 213.3 through "proprietor" 214.20, "The Rook Cell" 220.16 through "his" 229.27, "lying" 238.24 through "groan" 238.32) also in the Murray files. Leaves of the manuscripts sometimes consist of fragments pasted together; now in bound form they have been trimmed to measure generally 4 3/4 x 8 inches, but some are folded up slightly and some folded up as much as 5 inches. The manuscripts are written in a number of different hands; an occasional section or brief fragment is Irving's and corrections more often seem to be his. Compositors's signatures are on all of the manuscripts with portions of the names sometimes caught in the bindings. The *Tour* manuscript was bound by a London company in two volumes with a hardback cover of blue simulated leather. Compositors signed their names, usually at eight-page intervals and in the upper left corner: "Watson" (8 times); "Bagshaw" or "Bajshaw" or "Bayshaw" (11 times); "Hogg" (6 times); "Williams" (5 times); "Lindsay" (3 times); "Lewis" (7 times); and "Achcrill" (2 times). *Abbotsford* and *Newstead Abbey* are bound together; pages are numbered consecutively 1–[358], though repetition of numbers for several pages in *Abbotsford* and the use of as many as three numbers on one page where fragments were pasted together (122/123/124) make the final count meaningless. Missing from *Newstead Abbey* are pages 211, 233–241, 294–326, and 358. The essay "The Lake" comes after "Robin Hood and Sherwood Forest" instead of before it as in the American manuscript. Compositors' signatures which were not lost in the binding are either in the upper left corner or directly on the manuscript page with a number indicating the English edition page set from the copy. They include "Watson" (5 times); "Williams" (7 times); "Bagshaw" (2 times); "Sloane" (2 times); "[P]aine" (2 times); "[E]llison" (once); "E. Lindsay" (once); and "D. Lindsay" (once). Variations between the American and English manuscripts (307 for *A Tour on the Prairies*, 129 for *Abbotsford* and 88 for *Newstead Abbey*) are recorded in a separate list entitled Substantive Variants in Manuscripts for American and English First Editions.

Collations for the four writings of all forms which could have been altered by the author (manuscripts and all printed versions) reveal numerous passages with differences in substantives: more than 525 for *A Tour on the Prairies*, nearly 200 for *Abbotsford*, around 175 for *Newstead Abbey*, and almost 200 for *Legends of the Conquest of Spain*, even though the last volume appeared only in the first edition during Irving's lifetime. The Lists of Rejected Substantives for *Tour*, *Abbotsford*, and *Newstead* also include 244 substantives considered nonauthorial but appearing in the first and second American editions (146 in *Tour*, 27 in *Abbotsford*, and 71 in *Newstead*). In addition, the lists record a total of sixty-five substantives which should have been printed in the American publications but which compositors overlooked and omitted in setting from the printer's copies or, in the case of the second American edition, in setting from the first edition. The list for *Legends of the Conquest of Spain* has thirty-four nonauthorial substantives which appeared in the single edition and seven omissions. Differences in accidentals are much more numerous, varying in the British manuscripts partly because of the carelessness, or perhaps preferences, of copyists and in the American printed editions because of the house style of the publisher imposed on the works. Between the American manuscripts and the printed forms set from them there are an estimated nine thousand variations in accidentals.

The corruption of texts continued with each additional printing.

Though the 1849 revised edition made important corrections and additions, including the proper identification of the Scott children's tutor and of one of Scott's friendly retainers in *Abbotsford*, it also increased the errors. Among the examples are two in *A Tour on the Prairies* at 96.38 and at 97.31. In Irving's description of a bustling scene of preparation to leave camp on October 29, the 1849 volume, set from the first edition, repeats "brawling" which the earlier form had printed for "bawling" and errs further in making the succeeding phrase "after their horses" instead of "after the horses." In the other instance, in the phrase "pointed out to us" in the American manuscript, Irving had written over "me" to make it "us." The first compositor in 1835 apparently took the change for a cancellation and printed "out to"; the later edition attempted to correct this by shortening to "out."

The manuscripts themselves have errors which sometimes account for flaws in printed forms. Irving at times failed to delete all of a passage or he inadvertently deleted too much; in rewriting a phrase he often failed to alter the punctuation appropriately or occasionally to make a verb or a pronoun agree with a new subject or an antecedent; he misspelled, sometimes wrote a word or phrase twice, at times failed to pick up his pen at the end of a word and wrote two words together, and he was inconsistent in his use of capitals. Frequently he omitted punctuation to set off material inserted above the line, omitted punctuation at the end of his line, and failed to indent for a new paragraph when beginning a new page. In addition he pasted together fragments of earlier drafts at times obscuring a word or line or inserted a page or portion of a page without matching words exactly. Certain habits, such as marking over a comma to make it a period or marking over "this" to make it "the," were confusing to compositors.

THE AMERICAN MANUSCRIPTS

The greater portion of *The Crayon Miscellany* manuscripts used in setting print for American first editions of the three volumes in which the four writings appeared are in the Berg Collection of the New York Public Library, and one is in the possession of a New York descendant of Washington Irving. In the New York Public Library are *A Tour on the Prairies* (lacking the first three pages and pages 368 and 369), *Newstead Abbey* (lacking the first five pages and the last thirteen lines of Byron's letter to Wildman included in the first essay), and *Legends of the Conquest of Spain* (lacking the final copy for the last two pages of Chapter XVIII of "The Legend of Don Roderick"). In the possession of Irving B. Kingsford is the *Abbotsford* manuscript (lacking approximately two pages in three omissions). A single page of *Abbotsford* manuscript (corresponding to 133.24 from "Let" through 133.35 "it.") in the Barrett Collection of the University of Virginia, and three pages of *Newstead Abbey* in the possession of Helen Kingsford Preston (corresponding to 171.1 from "Historical Notice" through 171.21 "conduct;") are earlier state not used in setting copy for the first editions. The *Newstead Abbey* and *Legends of the Conquest of Spain* manuscripts in New York Public Library have been available to scholars for some time.[3] The manuscript for *A Tour on the Prairies* was discovered in clearing out an old house in Wilkes-Barre, Pennsylvania, in 1964 and was purchased for the Berg Collection by the curator, the late Dr. John D. Gordan. *Abbotsford* was originally in the possession of Irving's great niece, Julia Bowdoin, and has passed subsequently to her descendants, becoming the property of Irving B. Kingsford, its present owner, in 1951.

The manuscripts have a number of features in common: (1) small and at times difficult-to-read handwriting; (2) many deletions and interlineations; (3) worn pages, torn corners, varying colors of ink, especially in corrections; (4) foxing; (5) both pencil and ink mark-outs and revisions; (6) some cut sheets and cut sheets or fragments pasted together; (7) smudges; (8) erratic pagination, alteration of numbers, or the addition of subnumbers; (9) typesetters' signatures in the margins; and (10) numbers in the margins at intervals indicating pages in the first American printed texts. Each of the manuscripts includes portions of earlier drafts. Generally writing is on one side of the paper only, but sometimes the author made a false start on one side then turned the page over and wrote on the other side. All of the manuscripts are bound in hardback volumes with most sheets pasted down on larger sheets. Paper is wove and of similar quality, though some sheets in *A Tour on the Prairies* are higher quality stationery with rough edges, and sheets of *Legends of the Conquest of Spain* are more worn, stained, and brittle. No watermarks are perceptible.

A Tour on the Prairies

Generally the pages are 5 x 7 3/4 inches, sometimes consisting of as many as four fragments pasted together. Forty-two of the 382 leaves exceed 7 3/4 inches in length and are folded up at the bottom.

Erratic pagination includes the repetition of two numbers (5 and 26) and the omission of one (336) which later was penciled on 337 without

3. Both are described in H. L. Kleinfield's census of Washington Irving manuscripts which appeared in the *Bulletin of the New York Public Library* (68 [January, 1964]), 25, 26 and was reprinted as a supplement to William R. Langfeld's *Bibliography of Washington Irving* (Port Washington, N. Y., 1968).

alteration of numbers following. Subnumbers designate fifteen pages where material was inserted or redone without the renumbering of pages (55/2 and 55/3; 151/2 and 151/3; 272/2, 272/3, 272/4, 272/5, 272/6, 272/7, 272/8, and 272/9; 328/2, 328/3, 328/4). Pages 1, 2, 3, 368, and 369 are missing.

The clearest evidence that the manuscript served as printer's copy is the designation of beginnings of the first American edition pages appearing in the margins forty-one times, more often marking three-page intervals (20 times) but sometimes at 6, 9, 12, or 15-page intervals, possibly indicating longer stints for the compositors. Three compositors' signatures appear on pages 335 (Hal [ton?], 350 (Finerty), and 365 (Finerty).

Many of Irving's revisions throughout the manuscript are like those made in early drafts. He replaced "enjoy" with "see, and do and enjoy," first wrote "adventures" then "enterprizes" and finally "undertakings," deleted "took our departure" and substituted "left," frequently marked out a word or phrase then wrote it again and continued his sentence. His interest was in achieving the precise, clear, simple expression, in avoiding repetition, and in arranging his material in an orderly manner. Sometimes deleted passages appear later in the narrative, a synonym replaces a word used earlier, or an interlined phrase qualifies a word ("medley" becomes "medley of figures and faces"). Some corrections in different ink suggest that in a rereading of his work the author may have focused further attention on his panoramic sketches of the travelers and of the country they traversed. He first wrote of the appearance of the group "straggling along in a line" then replaced it with "stretching along in a line" (36.21–22); instead of "There was something almost melancholy in the change" describing the effect of the quiet forest scene after their departure he added the reference to "the rustling of the yellow leaves which the lightest breath of air brought down in wavering showers; a sign of the departing glories of the year" (46.20–22). Many of the same alterations are here that are on the copied English manuscript pages.

In addition, numerous variations reflect further work Irving did on his American copy after the English had been mailed to Aspinwall. The most conspicuous revisions came in Chapter XXXII, "Republic of Prairie Dogs," and in the last chapter, XXXV, about the return to Fort Gibson, where intermittently he added sentences totaling almost two hundred words and rewrote a number of sentences and paragraphs. Throughout the manuscript, in addition, he made many other substantive changes ranging from such a slight one as changing "make arrangements" to "make an arrangement" in referring to negotiating with Pierre Beatte in Chapter III to the more drastic alteration of the phrase "to the discomposure of the hectoring little Tonish" to read "to the discomposure of some of the troop" at the end of Chapter XVI.

Differences in paragraphing, in pointing, and in the changing of a single word ("The Ranger's Camp" to "The Honey Camp" in Chapter VIII, for example) indicate Irving's interest in form, in specificity, and in the achievement of a particular effect. Some alterations seem designed to reenforce the personal impressions Irving was recalling. In the last paragraph of Chapter XXXII he changed "we" to "I" in telling of listening to the prairie dogs "late in the night." In Chapter XXXIII to a description of a night scene where the weary rangers soon "sunk to rest" he added the clause "and I seemed to have the whole scene to myself." Through the manuscript fewer than a half dozen pages are free from deletions, interlineations, or corrections showing Irving's persistent revision.

Abbotsford

Of the 120 leaves stored together in a red leather binding, only 116 were used as text for the first American printing. Others are earlier notes and abortive fragments. Several torn sheets have been repaired and pasted down on larger sheets, some edges are worn or torn off, and a number of leaves are composed of several fragments pasted together, some extending to twice the usual size of 5 x 7 3/4 inches. Pagination is regular (1–116) except for 26 which is lacking. A portion of the manuscript for page 91 in the printed text (approximately three-fourths of a page which should be a part of MS page 114) is pasted on near the top of the last page (116) where ninety-two words are missing from the manuscript.

Printer's marks designating the beginning of pages in the first American volume appear 20 times (16 times at 3-page intervals, twice at 6-page intervals, once after 8 pages, once after 9, and once after 12). Compositors' signatures are on eleven pages: "Hall" (once), "Wood" (5 times), and "Buchanan" (5 times).

Scarcely a page is free from revisions revealing Irving's reticence in writing about an experience nearly two decades earlier, his desire to do justice to the "mighty minstrel of the north," and his usual interest in avoiding repetition and in writing clearly. Explaining his reluctance, he deleted "notes" which he said would be the basis for his narrative and wrote instead "travelling notes" and along with "meagreness" to describe his efforts he inserted "and crudeness." What he first called "a literary pilgrimage to the ruins of Melrose Abbey" he recast as "partly to visit Melrose Abbey and its vicinity, but chiefly to get a sight of the 'mighty minstrel of the north.'" A statement about his regret that he

remembered "little more than the outline" of Scott's Muckle mouthed
Mag story was deleted in one position to be brought in after he
had given full treatment to the anecdote in more than two pages in
order to apologize for his "vague recollection" in comparison to Scott's
"delightful humour" (142–143). Insertions and changes throughout
show his efforts to add dignity and grace to his description of Abbotsford and to make Scott's conversation simple and direct. Marking out
his lengthy reference to *Pilgrim's Progress* and to Scott's promise to
show his guest "all the good religion hereabouts," Irving recorded instead
Scott's promise to "take [him] out on a ramble about the neighborhood"
(127.2).

Irving's memory, however, served him poorly, as the frequent substitutions of names of Scott's poems indicate; and his errors in giving
1816 as the year of his visit rather than 1817 and of referring to Scott's
retainer as "George" rather than "Tommie Purdie" were not corrected
until 1849. These flaws, as well as several instances of writing two
                                          conversations
words, one above the other (for example, stories   ), without marking out either one, indicate his haste in preparing the copy. Furthermore, he did not take time to copy into the American manuscript two of
the longest quotations from Scott's poetry. On page 83 of the manuscript he wrote in pencil "quotation to come in here p. 92 of Marmion"
and noted the beginnings of the first and last of twenty lines to be
included. On the following page he wrote "See Marmion p. 90" and
copied only the first of fifty-six lines to be used. He could have sent a
copy of the poem with his manuscript. It is not likely that Irving
intended his directions for the printer, however; he probably was in-
structing a copyist. Since these pages seem to be earlier draft, they
could have been pasted on the other surviving manuscript pages later
and may not have been used as printer's copy at all. See the List of
Emendations for 154.31 and 156.23 for errors in MSE pages which
probably were also in copied MSA pages no longer available, since the
errors were printed in 1A exactly as they appear in MSE.

More than a hundred substantive changes made after the English
manuscript was finished indicate the author's continued nervousness
about his essay. In haste he failed to correct many errors, but nevertheless he inserted words or phrases that continued to show his concern
over his ability to treat his subject adequately or to give Scott's stories
the "proper" relief (for *Abbotsford* see Substantive Variants in Manuscripts for American and English First Editions, 146.20). To Scott's
story about the bogle who came on land in the shape of a water bull
he added "and made a tremendous roaring that shook the very hills"
(162.19). On the last pages particularly he seemed to be concerned

about simplicity and effective expression in such substitutions as "one
of the greatest advantages" for the more stilted "one of the few un-
mingled gratifications" (168.26).

Newstead Abbey

The 205-page manuscript bound many years ago into a large hardback
volume, has more worn and soiled pages, torn corners, and smudges
that either *A Tour on the Prairies* or *Abbotsford.*[4] Much of the handwriting is small and difficult to read, especially the long quotations
from Byron's poetry which are sometimes copied on both sides of the
sheets. (For example, on the back of page 11 in "Superstitions of the
Abbey" are three stanzas or twenty-four lines). Many sheets consist of
fragments pasted together. Irving numbered pages separately for each
of the eleven essays, renumbering some of the pages as many as five
times. Some sheets are without numbers, original pagination sometimes appears on the fragments (in several places on some sheets), and
at times the author skipped numbers.

Both the numbers in the margins to indicate American first edition
pages and four compositors' signatures prove the manuscript to be
printer's copy. Thirteen page indications come at 3-page intervals, 5 at
6-page intervals, and 5 at 9-page intervals. Signatures are "Wood" (once)
and "Hunt" (3 times).

Few of the pages, except for some of those quoting poetry, are
entirely free from cancellations and insertions, though the last essay,
"The Little White Lady," has fewer changes than earlier essays. All
of those about the Abbey and the one entitled "Annesley Hall" are full
of minor changes of words and phrases. Irving's indecision concerning
his quotations is reflected in his frequent cancellations of stanzas for
which he substituted others and in his using both sides of pages for
poetry several times, though his usual writing habit was to use only
one side. Frequently he cancelled a selection, then turned the sheet
over and wrote on the other side. The revisions seem to be those of an
early draft ("the heir to" is altered to "inherited"; "was struck with
the sight" becomes "caught a sight"; "landscape" is deleted for "scene").
In several instances minor alterations appear in a different ink (possibly
also in another hand) to change "said" to "added" or to insert the
phrases "as before" and "in a little time." Again after the English manu-

---

4. A note with the manuscript in the New York Public Library tells of Irving's
giving it to Adoniram Chandler, the printer, and of its passing in 1854 to his
son Franklin. The latter wrote a note explaining that the manuscript "was loaned
to a lady friend, who returned it with the first four leaves missing—saying 'the
baby got hold of it, and tore them up.'"

script was gone, Irving made additions and alterations before the printer's copy went to be stereotyped for Carey, Lea, and Blanchard. In one instance he deleted some thirty-five words he must have recognized as being repetitious (for *Newstead Abbey* see Substantive Variants, 181.23); at others he added words to reenforce what he was saying, to clarify, or to create an effect (see Substantive Variants, 196.24, 203.25–35, and 218.14, for example).

Legends of the Conquest of Spain

Leaves of the 396-page manuscript are partially attached on larger sheets and bound in a hardback volume with a dark green cover. The paper is the same kind used for other volumes but sheets are more discolored and edges are worn.[5] Some sheets consist of several fragments pasted together, but none are folded up at the bottom. Writing on the reverse side of several pages consists of false starts and cancelled material. Approximately half of the writing is Irving's hand. First the pages were numbered separately for each of the three legends and for the Preface, then Irving or someone else renumbered the first two legends consecutively, leaving the Preface ([1]–7 at the beginning) and "Legend of Count Julian & His Family" (1–24) at the end with the original numbers. Fragments pasted together with one number at the top and another lower on the page and the addition of pages (33 1/2, 42 1/2, 131 1/2), sometimes to add a footnote, indicate the kind of reworking of his material in which Irving engaged.

The note "Alhambra June 10th 1829" at the end of the "Legend of the Subjugation of Spain" indicates that Irving decided to add the last narrative, "Legend of Count Julian and His Family," later and finished it sometime between 1829 and 1835. At its conclusion he wrote "Alhambra (See the date at the end of the preceding legend)."[6] To the chapters he had written earlier for the first two legends, in 1835 he added synoptic headings, some in pencil, and several footnotes, sometimes turning the page and writing the information up the left side and sometimes scribbling it on a fragment or an extra page. In addition, through the pages here and there he made such insertions as "also" or "therefore," and added a qualifying phrase such as "of foreign or antiquated fashion" after "garments." He continued to preoccupy himself with Fray Antonio Agapida as a voice for his legends, sometimes deleting the

5. This manuscript, too, was given by Irving to A. Chandler, who stereotyped it, and it remained in his family until it was purchased by Mr. Hearst and finally became a part of the New York Public Library collection.

6. See Introduction for *Legends of the Conquest of Spain* for a discussion of Irving's writing of "The Legend of Don Roderick" and its "finishing touches."

reference and sometimes adding it. Once he altered "adds the devout Antonio Agapida" to "adds a venerable Friar," but the first American edition printed "adds the venerable Agapida," apparently Irving's revision in proof. His indecisiveness concerning the use of Agapida in *Legends* bothered him early and late.

The manuscript includes both the earlier draft submitted to the printer for the last pages of "Don Roderick" (two and one-half manuscript pages) and five of the seven pages Irving wrote to substitute for them as the volume was being stereotyped. At the top of the first page of the revision he wrote "to come in at p. 128"; and the new material was used for the portions of text from that point (294.13 in this edition) "Taric" to the end of the chapter. Lines from 295.25 "that" to the end of the chapter (approximately two manuscript pages) are missing.

Besides the page number designated on the rewritten portion of "The Legend of Don Roderick," several numbers in the margins throughout the manuscript mark beginnings of the first American edition pages; and twenty compositors' signatures appear at irregular intervals either at the top of the sheets or in the left hand margins. Names include "Farris" (11 times), "Howard" (6 times), and "Mitchell" (3 times).

Before the stereotyped proof sheets went to England, Irving made changes to serve for both the American and English printings, such as corrections in spelling and several stylistic alterations for conciseness and exactness. The two editions, for the most part, are alike except for variations in accidentals resulting from differing house styles. Irving's addition of a footnote at 273.42 on the English proof sheets but not on the American forms seems to be an isolated instance of his oversight in preparing duplicate sheets (see for *Legends* the List of Emendations, 273.42). After the English forms were mailed he continued to be interested in style as shown by a few minor changes that appear in 1A. One interesting revision made only in the American publication exemplifies attention to language and tone in referring in Chapter I of "Roderick" to the Jews' "gainful arcana of traffic" and their reputation "as opulent money changers" rather than the manuscript reading alluding to "the time when they borrowed the jewels of gold and jewels of silver from their neighbors." Overall, however, checking of proof failed to note incorrect compositorial settings of names such as Muza ben Noseir, misspelled "Nosier," for example, and certain errors in usage.

All of the American manuscripts have numerous alterations, partly because Irving continued to revise, but even more because he used sections of rough-draft manuscript in preparing his printer's copy. Sometimes an alteration helps to explain a textual problem; if so it another of my fellow travellers was Mr. L—; an Englishman by birth, but descended from

a foreign stock; and who had all the buoyancy and accommodating spirit of a native of the Continent. Having rambled over many countries he had become, to a certain degree, a citizen of the world, easily adapting himself to every ~~~ he was a man of a thousand occupations; a botanist, a geologist, a hunter of beetles and butterflies, a musical amateur, a sketcher of no mean pretensions, in short a complete Virtuoso; added to which he was a very indefatigable, though I ~~~ to say, of not always a very successful sportsman. Never had a man more irons in the fire, and, consequently, never was man more busy or more cheerful.

My third fellow traveller was one who had accompanied the former from Europe, and travelled with him as his Telemachus; being apt, like his prototype, to give occasional perplexity and disquiet to his Mentor. He was a young Swiss Count, scarce twenty one years of age, full of talent and spirit, but galliard in the extreme prone to every kind of wild adven—

[Transcription of MSA for *A Tour* corresponding to 10.36–11.9]

⟨One⟩ ↓Another↑ of my fellow travellers was Mr L——, /
an Englishman by birth, but descended from / a foreign stock;
and who had all the / buoyancy and accommodating spirit of
a / native of the Continent. ⟨He was, in fact, a⟩ ↑Having
rambled over / many countries he had become to a certain degree,
a /↓ citizen of the world, ⟨who had rambled over many /coun-
tries and⟩ ↑easily adapting himself to every change. [*illegible*] He was / ↓ a man of a thousand occupa- / -tions; a
botanist, a geologist, a hunter of / beetles and butterflies,
⟨a draughtsman⟩ a / musical amateur, a sketcher of no mean /
pretensions, ⟨and though last, not least,⟩ ↑in short a
complete virtuoso; added to which he was↓ a very / indefatigable, ⟨though I grieve to say⟩ . ⟨a⟩ ↑if not always a very↓
⟨very indifferent⟩ ↑successful↓ sportsman. Never had a / man
more irons in the fire, and consequently, / never was man
more busy or more cheerful.
    My third fellow traveller was one who had / accompanied
the former from Europe, and / travelled with him as his ⟨tel⟩
Telemachus; ⟨it / proves,⟩ ↑being apt,↓ like his prototype,
to give occasional / perplexity and disquiet to his mentor.
He / was a young Swiss Count, scarce twenty / one years of age,
full of talent a[n]d / spirit, but galliard in the extreme /
prone to every kind of wild adven [ture]

19

After my return from Melrose abbey
Scott proposed a ramble to shew me some.
thing of the surrounding country. As we
sallied forth every dog in the establishment
turned out to attend us. There was the old
stag hound Maida, that I have already mentioned
~~mountain hound Maida,~~ a noble
animal, ~~of the~~ ~~with fine slender limbs,~~ a great
favorite of Scotts; and Hamlet, the black
grey hound, a wild thoughtless youngster,
not yet arrived at the years of discretion.
And Finette a beautiful setter, with soft
silken hair, long pendant ears and a
mild eye, the parlour favorite. When we
in front of the house we were joined by a
superannuated grey hound, who came from
the kitchen wagging his tail; and was
cheered by Scott as an old friend and
comrade.
    In our walks Scott would frequently

[Transcription of MSE for *Abbotsford*
Corresponding to 130.17–130.27]

After my return from Melrose Abbey / Scott proposed a
ramble to shew me some- / thing of the surrounding country.
As we / sallied forth every dog in the establishment / turned
out to attend us. There was the old / ⟨mountain hound
Maida⟩, ↑[s]tag hound Maida, that I have already mentioned↓
a noble / animal ↑⟨of the mountain breed⟩,↓ ⟨with fine
clean limbs⟩ ↑and↓ a great / favorite of Scotts; and Hamlet,
the black / grey hound, a wild thoughtless youngster, / not
yet arrived ⟨at⟩ ↑to↓ the years of discretion. And Finette
a beautiful setter, with soft / silken hair, long pendant
ears and a / mild eye, the parlour favorite. When ⟨we⟩ / in
front of the house we were joined by a / superannuated grey
hound, who came from / the kitchen wagging his tail; and was /
cheered by Scott as an old friend and / comrade.
In our walks Scott would frequently

Editorial symbols used in transcriptions: ⟨ ⟩ restored cancellations;
↑ ↓ interlinear insertions above the line; ↓ ↑ interlinear insertion below
the line; / end of line in the manuscript; [ ] lost or illegible.

may be included in the Discussions of Adopted Readings for that text. (See, for example, Discussions at 97.31 for *A Tour*; 126.27 and 153.39 for *Abbotsford*; 199.13 for *Newstead*; and 265.36 for *Legends*.) It is also true that for *A Tour on the Prairies, Abbotsford,* and *Newstead Abbey* for which British manuscripts were prepared, those forms are full of changes, and the alterations within them may be relevant in the solution of a textual problem. (As examples, see the Discussions of Adopted Readings, 176.4 for *Newstead* and 133.8–9 for *Abbotsford*.) To list all of the changes in more than eighteen hundred pages of manuscript (more than eleven hundred for American printings and over seven hundred and fifty for the British), however, would require more space in an appendix or in the Textual Commentary than would be practical. Instead, facsimile leaves from the American manuscript of *A Tour on the Prairies* with its transcription and from the English manuscript of *Abbotsford* with its transcription are included in this edition as examples; and complete information for all of *The Crayon Miscellany* manuscripts has been deposited in the files at the University of Texas.[7]

TEXTS

For the two volumes, *A Tour on the Prairies* issued separately, and *Abbotsford* and *Newstead Abbey* published together in one volume, two printed editions appeared in Irving's lifetime and were revised by him. The first editions (hereafter called 1A) were printed by Carey, Lea, and Blanchard (Philadelphia, 1835) in two definable text states for each volume and, in the case of *A Tour on the Prairies*, in at least two impressions.[8] Though no proof sheets for either volume survived,

7. Neither the tightly bound English manuscript pages of *A Tour on the Prairies* in the Hanley Collection in the Miriam Lutcher Stark Library at the University of Texas or the privately owned American manuscript pages of *Abbotsford* can be photographed. The *Tour* American copy here is a part of the Berg Collection in the New York Public Library and the English *Abbotsford* copy is in the files of John Murray Publishing Co. in London.

8. It seems almost certain that *A Tour on the Prairies* went through at least three impressions, but the evidence is ambiguous and does not lead to sure chronological ordering of later impressions. A first and a second state may be defined with certainty; the number and sequence of impressions must be left to interpretation of the available evidence. Letters in the Carey and Lea manuscript letter books, now in the Historical Society of Pennsylvania, show that the original order was for five thousand copies. Pierre M. Irving in *Life and Letters* (III, 68) reports that by November 10, 1835, the publishers had paid Irving for eight thousand copies. The addition of three thousand copies, plus any more that may have been printed, would account for the later impressions but would not help in determining the exact number.

the 1A publications included a number of substantive revisions of one kind or another (more than fifty in *A Tour*, at least a half dozen in *Abbotsford*, and more than a dozen in *Newstead Abbey*), all recorded in the Lists of Emendations.[9] Changes apparently were for stylistic reasons in order to avoid repetition or to try to achieve a sharper, more effective expression (see, for example, the List of Emendations, 13.28–30 for *A Tour*, 168.29 for *Abbotsford*, and 191.9–10 for *Newstead Abbey*).

For the second edition (2A), George P. Putnam in New York printed all three writings in one volume in 1849 under the title *The Crayon Miscellany* as Volume IX of the Author's Revised Edition (ARE).[10]

Jacob Blanck's *Bibliography of American Literature* (New Haven, 1969), V, 41 and 42, numbers 10140 and 10142 listing *Tour* and *Abbotsford and Newstead Abbey*, notes (1) two "states" for *Tour* with "binger of dawn" in the last line of the synoptic heading on page 247 in the first and "harbinger of dawn" in the same position in the second state and (2) two "printings" for *Abbotsford and Newstead Abbey* with a copyright notice on both pages [2] and [4] in the first and a copyright notice on page [2] with page [4] blank in the second. Additional differences in the two states of *Tour*, not pointed out by Blanck, will be given in subsequent discussion in the Textual Commentary.

The copy of *A Tour on the Prairies* used in the Twayne edition for copy-text where manuscript is lacking can be described as follows: A/TOUR ON THE PRAIRIES./ [rule]/ BY THE AUTHOR OF THE SKETCH BOOK./ [rule]/ Philadelphia: [fancy type]/ CAREY, LEA, & BLANCHARD./ [rule of 21 dots]/ 1835. (17.8 x 11.1): [1]⁶ 2–23⁶. 23₆ is a blank. 12 pp. of ads in publisher's catalog. Page [3] begins with THE MAGDALEN AND OTHER TALES. [i]–[ii], series title, on verso copyright [1835] and printer; [iii]–[iv], Advertisement promising a future number of The Crayon Miscellany, verso blank; [v]–[vi], title, on verso same copyright and printer; [vii]–xv, Introduction; [xvi], blank; [17]–274, text. Series title: THE/CRAYON MISCELLANY./ [double rule]/ BY THE AUTHOR OF THE SKETCH BOOK./ [double rule]/ No. 1./ CONTAINING/ A Tour on the Prairies. [fancy type]/ [double rule]/ Philadelphia: [fancy type]/ CAREY, LEA & BLANCHARD. [rule of 15 dots]/ 1835. Printer: Stereotyped by A. Chandler. Binding: Blue-green or green vellum cloth. Sides blank. White paper label on spine: [rule]/ THE/CRAYON MISCELLANY/ No. 1./ [rule]/ A/ TOUR/ ON THE/PRAIRIES./BY THE AUTHOR OF/ THE/ SKETCH BOOK./ [rule].

9. Irving must have made his own proof corrections. Though Pierre Munro Irving was with his uncle in New York at the time, having already gone to work on material for *Astoria*, and therefore could have assisted Irving with the proofs, it is not likely that he did so. Pierre was engaged in a project to which Irving had committed himself but for which he could find little time until *A Tour* and the other numbers in the series were out of his way. Therefore, he probably was anxious that Pierre get the Astor materials in hand for his use as soon as he could turn to them.

10. The editor's personal copy of *The Crayon Miscellany* (2A) collates as follows: 12° (7 7/16 x 5 1/16): Preceded by two leaves (1–2)¹² 3–16¹², 2 leaves of ads integral with the book [signed on 1 and 5, 5 with added asterisk; signature 7

The texts were the 1835 Carey, Lea, and Blanchard printings. Though new errors were introduced and others overlooked, an effort was made to correct old ones. A *Tour on the Prairies* experienced such minor changes as "would" to "could" or of a singular verb to a plural for agreement and minor stylistic alterations for conciseness ("that we might arrive" to "to arrive"). From the long Introduction Irving retained only the last four paragraphs; and the Advertisement was omitted. In *Newstead Abbey* similar attention was directed toward correcting of spelling, being more specific, or adding to the nostalgia and sentimental effect (see, for example, the List of Emendations, 186.35, 219.19, 233.8). For *Abbotsford* Irving corrected the date of his visit from 1816 to 1817 and straightened out the confusion which resulted in 1A when he could not recall the name of one of Scott's retainers and referred to him instead as "George," the name he should have remembered as belonging to the tutor of the Scott children (see the List of Emendations, 136.41–137.1 and entries 159.1 through 159.19. Additional impressions of the 2A edition including these three writings were made in 1850, 1851, 1853, 1854, 1856, and 1859. The only change in the later impressions is that the title page for *Abbotsford* appears correctly on page 199 instead of on page 200 as the ARE or 2A edition printed it in 1849.

During Irving's lifetime *Legends of the Conquest of Spain* was published only in the first edition (1A) by Carey, Lea, and Blanchard in 1835.[11] In 1866 Pierre M. Irving included these three legends along with other legends that had not previously been published, in Volume I of *Spanish Papers* (New York: G. P. Putnam).

The process of discovering all substantive and accidental variants required examination and comparison of all relevant forms of the

---

belonging on p. 145 lacking], 192 leaves; pp. ⟨i–ii blank⟩ ⟨iii edition title page⟩ ⟨iv blank⟩ ⟨v title page⟩ ⟨vi copyright notice and printer's imprint⟩ ⟨vii Contents⟩ viii–xii ⟨xiii Introduction⟩ xiv ⟨15 *A Tour on the Prairies* title page⟩ ⟨16 blank⟩ ⟨17⟩–198 text ⟨199 blank⟩ ⟨200 *Abbotsford* title page⟩ ⟨201⟩–269 text ⟨270 blank⟩ ⟨271 *Newstead Abbey* title page⟩ ⟨272 blank⟩ ⟨273⟩–379 text ⟨380 blank⟩ ⟨381–382 ads⟩. It corresponds to Blanck 10171. Other copies examined are identical.

11. The copy used in the Twayne edition for copy-text for the two pages where manuscript is lacking corresponds to Blanck 10144 and has the Setting A as identified by "advertised" appearing in the last line of the first paragraph of "Beauties of Washington Irving" printed as front matter rather than "vertised" designated as Setting B. It collates as follows: 12° (7 1/16 x 4 1/4): ⟨–⟩², ⟨17–23⟩⁶, plus ⟨24⟩⁴ [leaves 1 and 3 signed, 3 with added asterisk], 138 leaves; ⟨blank⟩ "Beauties of Washington Irving", ⟨blank⟩ ⟨i comprehensive title⟩ ⟨ii copyright⟩ ⟨iii title page⟩ ⟨iv copyright⟩ ⟨v Preface⟩ vi–ix ⟨x blank⟩ ⟨11 text⟩ 12–276, plus 4 pages of ads not integral with the book. Other copies examined are identical except that "Beauties of Washington" appears opposite comprehensive title page (Setting B as designated in BAL).

writings which might throw light on any textual problem, involving both sight reading and machine collating. Lateral collations of copies of the same impression (to detect resettings or changes within editions) were made with the aid of the Hinman collating machine—for both American and British editions, though the latter were unauthorized. Vertical collations (including a copy of every form in which Irving might have had a hand plus a copy from the British printings) were made by sight reading, and all variations were recorded. Second collations and additional spot checks were made to substantiate findings.

Forms used for sight collations for *A Tour on the Prairies*, *Abbotsford*, and *Newstead Abbey* included printer's copies of the American manuscripts,[12] printer's copies of the English manuscripts, the first American printings, the first English printings, and the 2A printed in 1849.[13] For *Legends of the Conquest of Spain* forms used were printer's copy of the American manuscript,[14] the first American printing, and the first three legends in Volume I of *Spanish Papers*, though the last work was not published until seven years after Irving's death.[15] A search for an 1836 printing of *A Tour on the Prairies* by Carey, Lea, and Blanchard which Williams and Edge listed (but which they did not see) leads to the conclusion that the publication does not exist. There is no Library of Congress listing and no record in the cost book of Carey and Lea; furthermore, a survey of major libraries and repositories in the United States and Canada reveals no information. Williams and Edge apparently picked up the erroneous listing from Sabin.[16]

Machine collations to detect possible hidden impressions included seventeen full collations of authorized American printings and, in

12. Copies of the manuscripts used in sight readings were carefully read against the original manuscripts in the New York Public Library and in the files of Mr. Irving B. Kingsford for accuracy both before the collations were done and again before the establishment of texts was completed.

13. Specific printed copies used for *Tour* were (1) the editor's personal copy of 1A (BAL 10140), (2) the University of Texas copy of 1E (call no. TX 8cra, BAL 10139), and (3) the editor's personal copy of 2A (BAL 10171); for *Abbotsford and Newstead Abbey* the copies were (1), the editor's copy of 1A (BAL 10142), (2) the editor's copy of 1E (BAL 10141), and (3) the editor's copy of 2A (BAL 10171).

14. Again the copy of the manuscript was read twice against the original in the Berg Collection in the New York Public Library.

15. Specific printed copies used were (1) the editor's personal copy of 1A (BAL 10144), (2) the University of Texas uncatalogued copy of 1E in the Bartfield Collection (BAL 10287), and (3) the University of Texas copy of *Spanish Papers*, vol. 1, call no. Ir8spl (BAL 10201).

16. *A Dictionary of Books Relating to America* (New York: J. Sabin and Sons, 1877), IX, 146.

addition, thirteen of British publications, five of the three legends as reprinted in Volume I of *Spanish Papers* (1866, 1867, 1869, 1872), and spot readings in additional copies of American publications for each of the works.[17] No extensive resettings were found. The later state in *Tour* 1A has several corrections: (1) At 9.34 "regions" was altered to "region"; (2) "in in" at 13.37 was made "in"; (3) "casewith" at 42.34–35 was divided into two words; (4) at 54.32 an "h" was added to "wit"; (5) the comma after "Tonish" at 70.37 was removed; (6) quotation marks turned the wrong way before "and" at 76.32 were changed; (7) a hyphen was added to "forebod" at 93.5 at the end of the line; (8) a period was added at the end of the sentence after "missed" at 96.20; (9) "binger" in the synoptic heading at 110.29 was made "harbinger"; and (10) a comma ending a sentence after "view" at 121.2 was altered to a period. In a copy in the second text state, the printer's imprint on the verso of the series title has been noted in a variant state: the rules above and below the imprint are 3.35 centi-

17. The patterns for collations were as follows: *Tour* 1Aa (DT copy without cover) vs. 1Aa (DT copy with cover) and vs. Texas 1Ab (Ir8cr/1835a) and vs. Wisconsin 1Aa (Rare Book Dept. 972203) and vs. Wisconsin 1Aa (PS/2060/.A1); *Tour* Texas 1Ab (Ir8cr/1835a) vs. Haverford College 1Ab (PS2060/A1); *Tour* Wisconsin 1Aa (PS2060/.A1) vs. Minnesota 1Aa (Z81Ir8/ocbv.1) and vs. Texas Tech 1Aa (F/786.2/I72/5w); *Tour* 1Eb Wisconsin Hist Soc. (G83W/.172/2) vs. Texas 1Ea (Ir8cra) and vs. Duke 1Eb (817.24/I72TOB) and vs. Cincinnati 1Eb (PS 2070/T7/1835/R.B); *Abbts–News* 1Ab (DT copy) vs. Wisconsin 1Ab (DA/890/.A1/I67) and vs. Texas 1Aa (Ir8cr/V2/cop. 1); *Abbts–News* Texas 1Aa (Ir8cr3/V2) vs. Texas 1Aa (Ir8cr/V2/cop. 1) and vs. Wisconsin 1Aa (Rare Book Dept. 972204); *Abbts–News* 1Ea (DT copy) vs. Johns Hopkins 1Ea (PQ/2056/ A2/1835) and vs. Wisconsin 1Ea (DA/890/.A1/I67) and vs. Texas 1Eb (Ir8crb); *Abbts–News* Texas 1Eb (Ir8crb) vs. Wisconsin 1Eb (Rare Book Dept. CA 1900) and vs. Wisconsin 1Eb (DA/890/.A1/I67); *Abbts–News* Wisconsin 1EB (DA/ 890/.A1/I67) vs Library of Congress 1Eb (DA/890/.A1/I67); *Legends* 1Aa (DT copy) vs. Texas 1Ab (TX/60–1591) and vs. Wisconsin 1Aa (Rare Book Dept. 972205) and vs. Virginia 1Aa (PS2060/A1/1835/no.3/529932); *Legends* Texas 1E (uncatalogued Bartfield Collection) vs. Southern California 1E (810/ I724/r6/v. 3) and vs. Texas 1836 (Ww/Ir86/8351 ba): *Legends* Texas 1836 (Ww/Ir86/8351ba) vs. California Berkeley 1836 (952/I72/lege); *Crayon Miscellany* 1849 (2A) (DT copy) vs. Texas 2A (Ir8crw/1849) and vs. Texas 2A (Ir8crw/1851) and vs. 1850 Aderman 2A; *Crayon Miscellany* Texas 2A (Ir8crw/ 1849) vs. 1850 Aderman; *Spanish Papers* I, Putnam, 1866, Texas (Ir8spl/v. 1) vs. Putnam, 1866, St. Benedicts College (PS/2062/A1/1866) and vs. Putnam, 1866, Denver Pub. Lib. (946.02/I7251/v.1/102378) and vs. Putnam, 1866, Texas (Ir8sp); *Spanish Papers*, vol. 1, Putnam, 1866, Texas (Ir8sp) vs. Putnam, 1867, Wisconsin (PS/2052/.17/1); *Spanish Papers* I, Putnam, 1869 "Riverside Edition," Texas (Ir8sp/1869) vs. Lippincott, 1872, "Riverside Edition," Wisconsin (Y/Ir8/SP/ 1872). (Use of "a" and "b" with 1A printings refers to later states in which one or more corrections of spacing, spelling, or omission of hyphen or period were made.)

meters long, extending well past the printing, rather than 3.0 centimeters long, approximately coterminous with the printing.

Copies in the second text state have been noted on two papers;
sequence undetermined: (A) the sheets, exclusive of the publisher's
catalog, bulk 1.4 centimeters; (B) the sheets, exclusive of the publisher's catalog, bulk 1.8 centimeters. In addition to these differences
in 1A, two sets of labels on the spines can be described as follows:
(A) [double rule]/ THE/CRAYON/MISCELLANY./ [rule]/ A/TOUR/
ON THE/PRAIRIES./ BY THE AUTHOR OF/THE/SKETCH BOOK./
[double rule]. (B) [rule]/ THE/CRAYON MISCELLANY/NO. 1./
[rule]/ A/TOUR/ON THE/PRAIRIES./ BY THE AUTHOR OF/THE/
SKETCH BOOK./ [rule]. No sequence of labels is determined: both
states of the label have been noted on both text states. The publisher's
catalog bound at the end has been noted in six different states. All are
undated and lack page numbers, and all begin on p. [1] with DR. BIRD'S
NEW NOVEL–CALAVAR: (A1) 12 pp. Page [3] begins with THE/
WONDROUS TALE OF ALROY. (A2) 12 pp. Page [3] begins with
THE MAGDALEN AND OTHER TALES. (B1) 24 pp. Page [3] begins
with THE/WONDROUS TALE OF ALROY. (B2) 24 pp. Page [3]
begins with Cooper's New Novel/ THE HEADSMAN. (C1) 36 pp.
Page [36] devoted to NATIONAL SCHOOL MANUAL. (C2) 36 pp.
Page [25] devoted to NATIONAL SCHOOL MANUAL. There appears
to be no discernible sequence to the six states of the catalog. Although
not all states have been seen in both text states (or combined with both
states of the label on the spine), no pattern emerges from those seen,
and the suspicion is strong that if only enough copies could be examined, almost every combination would eventually appear.

The first and second English editions of A Tour on the Prairies are
so nearly alike in appearence and in title that they are more easily
described, and the distinctions between them defined, in one entry
than in two separate ones. The relationship of the two editions is complicated by the fact that the disguised second edition is not reset in
its entirety, and those signatures that are retained in their original
setting are often redressed (that is, they demonstrate minor shifts
within the forme and occasionally a change of position of running head
or signature mark) and in some instances show textual changes or the
resetting of a line or two. As a rule, the resetting is a line-for-line
reproduction of the first edition.

The general pattern of resetting the second edition is as follows:
signature [A]: the two titles are reset and substituted in the signature
as cancels. The remaining leaves are in the original setting, although
one number was accidentally lost in the table of contents (in a second
state of the series title of the second edition, an extraneous THE is

removed from the identification of the author); signature A: this singleton remains unchanged; signatures B–F: reset throughout; signature G:
reset except for one page; signature H: two pages are entirely reset;
seven pages reset in two lines or more; fifteen pages redressed, of
which several show textual changes; signature I: one page is reset; the
remainder redressed with several showing textual changes; signatures
K–L: occasional redressing or lines reset, with a very few textual changes;
signatures M–P: generally unchanged except for a few pages redressed.

The pattern of complete resetting in the early signatures of the text,
through partial resetting and redressing in the middle signatures, to
almost no change in the late signatures would suggest that when Spottiswoode discovered that more copies would be required than originally
planned, he reset and "corrected" the signatures whose type had already
been distributed; saved, redressed, and occasionally corrected the middle signatures which had been used for printing and taken from the
press but whose type had not yet been distributed; and simply reprinted
from the last signature. Ledger C in the Murray archives records that
Spottiswoode printed for Murray two thousand copies first and then
an additional one thousand. The addition was almost certainly the
second edition.

There is no question of the chronology of the two text states, even
without appeal to internal evidence. Thirty textual variants discovered
in signatures B–H (not including such matters as page numbers and
running heads) were compared with the readings in the setting manuscript for the edition. Of the thirty changes, six differ from the manuscript
in both editions, indicating that in the process of house styling by the
printer the text was changed immediately and then later changed again
to remove it still further from the manuscript. But of the twenty-four
remaining variants, the first edition follows the manuscript in twenty-
one instances. Presumably the three instances in which the second
edition follows the manuscript but the first edition does not are examples of house-styling "corrections" made in the first edition and later,
ironically enough, changed back to the manuscript readings, probably
without awareness of the correspondence. All of the changes are in
spelling or punctuation only, and none suggests authorial revision.[18]

18. The English editions can be described as follows: A/TOUR/ON/THE PRAI-
RIES./BY/THE AUTHOR OF "THE SKETCHBOOK./ [rule]/ LONDON: JOHN
MURRAY, ALBERMARLE STREET./MDCCXXXV. *First Edition.* (20.2 x 12.3):
[A]⁶ a¹ B–1¹² K–P¹². In some copies the stub of the singleton a protrudes between
signatures. B–C, pp. 24–25. Laid paper. *Second Edition.* (20.0 x 12.2): [A]⁶
(±[A] 1–2) a¹ B–1¹² K–P¹². A copy in the University of Texas in original binding
but loose in the boards allows certainty about sig. [A]: the first two leaves (the
titles) are cancels made before binding. Signature A is pasted to the verso of [A].

In *Abbotsford and Newstead Abbey* 1A in what becomes a second state, two periods were added at 157.30 after "Bemerside" and at 197.5 after "piece," and the comprehensive title page was omitted. The only change in *Legends* 1A in what Blanck refers to as the "b" state was the printing of the notice about "Beauties of Washington Irving" opposite the comprehensive title page rather than opposite a blank page with an additional blank leaf following to separate it from the title page. In the 1849 Putnam printing of *The Crayon Miscellany* (2A) the divisional title page for "Abbotsford" appeared incorrectly on page 200; the 1850 printing from the same plates corrected the error and put the title on page 199. Other differences discovered in machine collations are

---

Laid paper. [i]–[ii], series title, on verso printer; [iii]–[iv], title, verso blank; [v] – vi, Preface; [vii] – xiii, table of contents; [xiv], blank; [i] – 335, text; [336], printer. In one copy of the second edition noted, the two titles are reversed: the title precedes the series title. Series title: MISCELLANIES./BY/THE AU-THOR OF THE "THE SKETCH-BOOK."/ No.1./ CONTAINING/A TOUR ON THE PRAIRIES./ [rule]/ LONDON:/ JOHN MURRAY, ALBEMARLE STREET./ MDCCCXXXV. A second state of the series title of the second edition omits the superfluous THE in the third line. Printer: A. Spottiswoode, New-Street-Square, London. Binding: Gray-brown paper boards. White endpapers. White paper label on spine. The label appears in two states; no sequence apparent; both states appear on both editions: (A). [double rule]/ TOUR/ON THE/ PRAIRIES./ BY/THE AUTHOR/OF THE/SKETCH BOOK./ [double rule]. Approximately 6.1 centimeters tall. (B). With hyphen in SKETCH-BOOK. Approximately 5.1 centimeters tall. Also noted one reported in gray-brown boards with brown cloth shelfback; blue-black cloth; green cloth; purple cloth. All with paper label on spine in one of the two states. The cloth bindings are more common on second edition copies.

Representative variants in the first and second editions:

Signature page and Line	First Edition	Second Edition
(A) Series Title	Vertical extent of type, from top of A to baseline of date: 12.35 centimeters.	Vertical extent of type: 11.3 centimeters. (Second state: same, except extra THE omitted in line 3)
(A) Title	Vertical extent of type: 11.1 centimeters.	Vertical extent of type: 11.5 centimeters.
B 5.4$_F$	fire, and	fire; and
13.9	hunter's	hunters'
C 29.2$_F$	boned old	boned, old
41.6	blind!"	blind?"

The first edition, apparently of two thousand copies, was published March 2, 1835. The second edition, apparently of one thousand copies, may have been issued at the same time.

in accidentals, usually dropped punctuation at the end of a line as the result of type batter or plate wear rather than of deliberate change.

There is no evidence that Irving read the proof sheets of any of the English editions, though he read the sheets made of *Legends* from the stereotyped plates in America before they went to England and added a footnote not included in the sheets for 1A (see Discussions of Adopted Readings, 273.42). At the time of the English printings he was in America and arrangements for British publications by John Murray were made by Colonel Thomas Aspinwall. For *A Tour on the Prairies*, *Abbotsford*, and *Newstead Abbey* he sent manuscripts varying in some details from the American printer's copy manuscripts and lacking his last revisions. Additional variants were introduced by the English printers, thirty-eight new substantive errors in *A Tour on the Prairies*, seventeen in *Abbotsford*, and fifteen in *Newstead Abbey*. Findings from machine collations of copies of British printings are of interest in a history of the publication of the series but are not of specific relevance in the establishment of the texts, since changes within them are nonauthorial.[19]

Neither are the 2A editions of *A Tour on the Prairies*, *Abbotsford*, and *Newstead Abbey* after Irving's death or the numerous foreign language editions of these works or of *Legends of the Conquest of Spain* authoritative. Most of the translations were made from the British editions which lacked Irving's revisions.[20] Both the reprintings and the translations contain further corruptions of texts.

TREATMENT OF SUBSTANTIVES

Irving made a number of revisions in the proofs of all the works in *The Crayon Miscellany* for the first American editions.[21] Thereafter none of them experienced major changes. *Legends* did not reappear in print during Irving's lifetime. For the 2A volume containing *Tour*, *Abbotsford*, and *Newstead*, Irving seemed satisfied generally with the 1A texts; in *Tour* and *Newstead* he made only minor alterations; in *Abbotsford* he corrected the date of his visit to Scott, identified the retainer Tommie Purdie and the tutor George Thomson, and added 123

19. Identification of copies collated and recordings of variations will be on file with other information at the University of Texas.

20. See, for example, *Un Tour Dans Les Prairies, à L'Ouest Des États Unis*, trans. Ernest W**** (Tours, 1845) and *Walter Scott et Lord Byron, ou Voyages à Abbotsford et à Newstead*, trans. A. Sobry (Paris: Fournier jeune, 1835).

21. See the Textual Commentary to *Mahomet and His Successors* (Madison: University of Wisconsin Press, 1970), pp. 595–96 for a discussion of Irving's habits of revising proofs.

words in three sentences at 137.1–11 to describe the tutor and forty words in a one-sentence paragraph at 146.33–35 telling of the effect of Scott's anecdote on the young man visiting in Scott's home.

Yet the 1849 edition recovered none of the unintentional omissions in 1A; it retained many errors (for example, the reference to buffaloes "visible to our sight" rather than "to our right" in Chapter XXI and an error in time—"eight" rather than "three" o'clock—in Chapter XI of *Tour*); and it introduced new substantive errors. (For example, see the List of Rejected Substantives for *Tour*, 10.32, 37.12, and 81.27; for *Abbotsford*, 126.14; and for *Newstead*, 186.33 and 214.35).

In determining authorial substantive variants between the manuscript and 1A, Irving's earlier notes or his source—when either was available—was sometimes helpful (as was the journal recording of "three" rather than "eight" for *Tour* 37.5 and the *Newstead* notes and the poem reading "hope" like the printer's copy of the American manuscript (MSA) rather than "love" like 1A for 206.22, for example. In such instances, the more favorable manuscript readings were further validated as the author's intentions by their agreement with the source, with Irving's notes, or with earlier state of manuscript. For those works for which both English and American manuscripts exist, a comparison of the two readings at times could strengthen a decision concerning the possibility of a misreading of Irving's manuscript by the 1A compositor. Poor handwriting, numerous interlineations, and Irving's habit of writing over a word or of altering a letter or a punctuation mark all combined to make the job of reading a difficult one for the compositor. At times an examination of deleted material, of Irving's writing of the same kind elsewhere, or of his interlineation and placement of words can aid in determining how differences between the manuscript and 1A might have originated. For *Legends,* for which only one manuscript was prepared, as well as for the other three writings, the editorial procedure was to choose the MS reading over the 1A variant when the 1A was obviously a misreading (for example, "relation" for "relative" at 268.16, "nor" for "or" at 332.17, and "town" for "tower" at 357.30 in *Legends*). Another procedure was to adopt the reading required in context, as with the MSA and 1A "lea" versus 2A "lee" in *Tour* at 103.32 and the rendering of Scott's novel *The Monastery* in *Abbotsford* at 144.34 (see the List of Emendations).

Substantives in Irving's quotations from Scott's and Byron's poetry copied into the manuscripts generally agree with readings in standard editions. For two of the exceptions this edition corrects the instances in *Newstead Abbey* where the author miscopied "rush'd" for "gush'd" in Stanza LXV of Canto XIII from *Don Juan* and wrote "better" for "higher" in Stanza CVIII from Canto XVI and where both 1A and 2A printed his errors (see Discussions of Adopted Readings, 178.32 and 198.15). In a portion of *Abbotsford* for which there is no MSA available, the 1A errors in a quotation from the Introduction to Canto III of *Marmion* are corrected for clarity from "carest" to "caress'd" and from "sleights" to "slights," probably not Irving's errors (see Discussions of Adopted Readings, 154.31). Other variations are retained (see *Newstead* Discussions of Adopted Readings, 174.18), and Irving's accidentals in spelling and punctuation in the quotations are followed.

TREATMENT OF ACCIDENTALS

The vast number of variations between Irving's accidentals in the American manuscripts and those printed in the first editions are largely the result of the printer's house style. Carey, Lea, and Blanchard imposed a heavier system of pointing on Irving's text. Though he occasionally wrote a sentence with an inordinate number of commas, Irving generally disapproved of high pointing which, he felt, could "injure the fluency of style."[22] The insertion of six commas in one sentence in *A Tour on the Prairies* in 1A at 41.24–28 in addition to the two Irving had written in MSA is an extreme, but not an isolated, instance of the kind of changes that could occur.

No attempt has been made to achieve. consistency in Irving's accidentals or to "Americanize" his spelling. A form or usage is acceptable if justified by any of the dictionaries which might have been available to Irving as he wrote the works in 1834 and 1835 or by general nineteenth-century usage as recorded in the *Oxford English Dictionary*.[23] Variants in accidentals are emended only whenever it is clear that the variation is a slip. For example, in *Legends of the Conquest of Spain* the single instance in which he failed to alter "Tadmir" to "Theodomir" is obviously an oversight, as it was in *A Tour on the Prairies* twice when he neglected to change "Bilyet" to "Beatte." Variants in spelling, such as "savory–savoury," "gray–grey," "inflections–inflexions," Irving's older spellings such as "shew," "relique," "lanthorn," and "chrystals,"

22. See his 1819 letter to Henry Brevoort quoted in Pierre M. Irving's *The Life and Letters of Washington Irving* (New York: G. P. Putnam, 1863), I, 425. Also see Richard D. Rust's Textual Commentary in his edition of *Astoria* for a discussion of Irving's habits in punctuation and of the effect of the printer's changes.

23. For a discussion of dictionaries available to Irving see the Twayne edition of *Mahomet*, pp. 607–9. In addition to the *OED*, the dictionaries consulted in relation to *The Crayon Miscellany* were *Webster's Dictionary* (New York, 1828) and *Walker's Critical Pronouncing Dictionary* (London, 1815).

and such spellings as "bruize," "centinels," and "enured" are all retained as acceptable nineteenth-century usage. Many of Irving's inconsistencies in proper nouns are attributable to his sources, especially
for the Moorish histories, where he found varied spellings. Though
evidence within his manuscripts indicates his concern over names,
especially of major figures in *A Tour on the Prairies*, he, too, varied in
many of his spellings.

Many emendations of accidentals were necessary because Irving
unintentionally neglected to supply punctuation as he frequently did at
the end of a line or after an interlineation. Apparently he felt that the
pause usually indicated by a comma or semicolon was implied by the
position of the word or phrase at the end of the line or above it. Frequently he did not indent for a paragraph which he began on a new
page; his splicing together portions of manuscript for printer's copy
sometimes obscured punctuation or created errors; he rarely canceled
the punctuation mark belonging to a canceled passage; and he often
failed to alter his pointing when he revised a portion of his sentence.[24]
His interest in proper or effective punctuation, on the other hand, is
evidenced many times through his manuscripts by his marking over a
comma to make a period, a period to make a comma, or a semicolon
to make a comma, all alterations that could confuse the compositors.

Decisions concerning capitalization are difficult both because of Irving's inconsistencies and because his formation of letters often makes
lowercase and capital form indistinguishable. Especially is this true for
c, m, n, o, r, s, and *w.* Irving wrote as capitals both *k* and *K, g* and *G.*
In *A Tour on the Prairies* when he was writing of the major figures in
his story, his practice usually seemed to be to use lowercase for a word
in the generic sense and capitalized form to refer to a specific person
("a doctor" but "Doctor" in alluding to Doctor Holt, for example);
but he did not capitalize "lieutenant" and "sergeant," nor was he con-
sistent throughout the *Miscellany* series. Some of his *c*'s in writing the
references to Count Pourtalès, to Commissioner Ellsworth and to Captain Bean seem clearly to be capitalized; others are clearly lowercase.
Both these inconsistencies and Irving's eccentricities in sometimes capi-
talizing such nouns as "Bear," "Elk," "Oriental," "Edifice," and "Barbarians" are retained for this edition. Revisions of "bible" and of "christmas" to capitalized form as in 2A are accepted as possibly authorial and
each instance is noted in the List of Emendations. No emendations are
made silently.

Decisions concerning compounds and hyphenated words are fre-

24. See the Twayne edition of *Mahomet,* pp. 573, 580–81, 603–12 for a discussion of Irving's eccentricities in accidentals.

quently difficult ones also. Lists of Irving's practices in *Goldsmith*, *Mahomet*, and *Astoria*, as well as those for *The Crayon Miscellany*, have helped to serve as guides in questionable instances. Sometimes Irving ran words together, such as "pistolshot," "whiteman," "pockethandkerchief," or he separated parts of a word ordinarily written together, such as "to morrow" and "re load." He rarely hyphenated, though several times he wrote "a-head" and at other times wrote "ahead" (most frequently) and occasionally "a head." His usual practice was to write as two words those that the printers commonly hyphenated. In this edition of *The Crayon Miscellany* his compounds have been emended only whenever necessary for clarity, as in making Irving's "grey hound" read "greyhound" (see Discussions of Adopted Readings for *Abbotsford*, 125.36).

Certain omissions such as periods after abbreviations or at the ends of sentences, apostrophes to show possession or to indicate a contraction, and one of a set of quotation marks, are all supplied in this edition as they were in the 1A printings and all are noted in Lists of Emendations. Irving's rendering of *t* in "St." by a flourish, such as in "S'Louis" in *A Tour on the Prairies* and "S'Peter," "S'George" and "S'Leocardia" in *Legends of the Conquest of Spain* are all regularized for clarity as printed in 1A, and the changese are noted. Irving's footnotes for *Newstead Abbey* and for *Legends* are printed as he wrote them with no attempt to regularize punctuation or abbreviations except for clarity, each instance of which is noted in the Lists of Emendations.

Titles, Synoptic Headings, and Chapter Numbers

For this edition, titles of the four works, separate titles for the essays of *Newstead Abbey*, titles of the three legends, "Illustrations of the Foregoing Legend" at the end of the first legend, titles of the two illustrations, and "Note to the Preceding Legend" at the end of the final legend are all revised to the Twayne form without end punctuation and with the first word and all words except prepositions, articles, and conjunctions captialized. For *A Tour on the Prairies* three chapter titles which Irving underlined in the manuscripts (XIII, XV, and XX) appear in this form also as general titles above the synoptic headings. The 1A compositor printed the superior heading for XIII and XX but apparently overlooked the underlined title "The Elk Camp" for XV.

In the synoptic headings in *A Tour on the Prairies* and the first two legends of *Legends of the Conquest of Spain* for this edition the first word in each phrase is capitalized and other words which are not proper nouns are in lowercase in accordance with Irving's general habits.

Phrases are separated by dashes and a period placed at the end of the headings. In *A Tour* the single phrase headings for chapters are treated the same as longer synoptic headings as Irving usually wrote them in MSA; the two exceptions, chapters XXII and XXV, which he underlined in MSA are revised to this form. For *A Tour* and *Legends* all chapter numbers are revised to the Twayne form with Irving's Arabic numerals altered to Roman and the complete word replacing the abbreviation for chapter. No separate emendations are recorded in Lists of Emendations for any of these forms.

SEE MAP FOLLOWING PAGE 3
SHOWING IRVING'S ROUTE ON THE PRAIRIES OF OKLAHOMA
OCTOBER 8–NOVEMBER 9, 1832

Using the landscape description and chronology in Irving's Western journals and in the four separate accounts by him, Charles Joseph Latrobe, Henry L. Ellsworth, and Count de Pourtalés (see the Introduction for *A Tour on the Prairies*), the route was plotted on the United States Geological Survey Topographical Maps at a scale of 1:24000. Then the compilation was transferred to the Survey's Oklahoma base map at the scale of 1:500000 (approximately one inch equals eight miles) from which the route only with important streams and rivers and some present-day towns were traced at the same scale and the whole reduced to its present size for this volume. The route and camp sites have been determined as nearly accurately as possible, though variations in the accounts and lack of specific informaion in some instances make some locations necessarily approximate. Geographic names are those used by the United States Geological Survey.

Although Irving's text is faithfully and critically rendered, the Twayne press is responsible for the so-called appurtenances of the text—such typographical details as the precise arrangement of the comprehensive title page and half-title pages and other preliminary matter, pagination and lineation, footnote symbols, and the typography of chapter titles, running heads, table of contents, synoptic chapter headings and footnotes.

Except for the details just enumerated, then, the Introduction, the Textual Commentary, and the accompanying Discussions of Adopted Readings, together with the Lists of Emendations, of Rejected Substantives, of Substantive Variants in Manuscripts for American and English First Editions, and of End-of-Line Hyphenation, are designed to provide the reader with all of the data needed to reconstruct the copy-text and to follow the steps by which the Twayne text of *The*

Crayon Miscellany was established. Beyond this, the assembled evidence
is designed not only to enable the reader so minded to examine and
consider the bases on which all editorial decisions were made but to
reconsider them, if he chooses, and in the process to see the relation-
ships that exist among the several texts from Irving's manuscripts to a
reasonably close approximation of the printed book the author intended
it to be.

DISCUSSIONS OF ADOPTED READINGS

In these discussions of decisions to emend or not to emend, the symbols used to designate manuscripts and previously published editions are those given in the List of Abbreviations, page 361.

The page and line figures are keyed in each case to a word or words in the text to which the discussion or comment refers. A bracket separates the key word or words from the comment that follows.

A Tour on the Prairies

7.6	recognize] Here and at 9.31 and 10.4 where MSA is lacking, this edition emends to the spellings Irving used consistently in MSA.
18.36	west] Irving may have erred in writing "west" for "east" here since they were traveling northwest and the Arkansas was on their left.
19.39	trail] For clarity this edition adopts the 1A deletion here and in the following instances (all noted in the List of Emendations) where the author failed in MSA to delete the punctuation which belonged to a canceled passage: 21.24, 25.37, 45.34, 77.3, 93.5, 99.26, 113.2, and 113.6.
23.25	protegee] Irving erred in writing the feminine form, consistently printed in authorized editions. Correction seems unwarranted, however, since context makes his reference clear.
29.13	Old Ryan] Since Irving wrote over the *o* several times apparently to make it a capital and enclosed the epithet "Old Ryan" in quotation marks in two instances in MSA, we can assume that this term which he heard from Captain Bean and which he recorded in his notebooks is the one he meant to use. Therefore doubtful instances of "old" are emended to "Old."
34.36	In] When he began a new page, Irving frequently neglected to indent for a new paragraph. If space remains on the preceding pages, his intentions for paragraphing are clear; if not, as in this instance and at 64.33, context could have directed the indenting. This edition,

in these cases, assumes the paragraphing to be Irving's intention.

40.25   a half]   The addition of "a" in Irving's expressions of distance ("mile and a half") and of time ("hour and a half) in 1A in the instances cited could have been nonauthorial; however, they are adopted as possible authorial proof corrections since the readings are more idiomatic.

52.22   foot,]   Here and at 62.16, 84.22, 111.17, and 117.29 (all noted in the List of Emendations) the commas inserted in 1A are adopted for clarity.

54.3   which]   Here and in the five additional instances noted in the List of Emendations the 2A change from "that" is adopted since the decision could have been Irving's effort to improve style or euphony, or, as at 114.35, to avoid repetition.

60.6   at full speed]   Either a desire to elevate his style or a distaste for the phrase "like mad" by 1849 may have caused Irving to omit the phrase at 85.14 and to change it to "at full speed" here and at 104.17 and to "at headlong speed" at 72.36.

67.18   prairies]   The 1A compositor could have set "prairies" from habit rather than the MSA "plains"; more likely, however, Irving wrote "plains" unintentionally from having used it in the preceding paragraph and then corrected his error in reading proof.

76.27   Distant]   The 1A capitalization corrected Irving's error that occurred when he marked out "Several" in MSA without altering "distant" to capitalized form

95.29   shot]   Though the MSE "range" here seems a more logical reading, it is not in Irving's hand. See "pistolshot" at 98.38 and 101.34 also.

97.31   out to us]   In MSA Irving wrote over "me" to make the word "us," and the 1A compositor apparently believed it a cancellation. In 2A the confusing 1A reading "out to" was shortened to "out."

99.4   the tufted end]   The supposition is that the 1A compositor misread "end" as "and" and adjusted Irving's sentence by omitting "the" before "tufted" to make "erect," "tufted," and "whisking" all predicate adjectives to modify "tail."

115.21   Canadian]   Irving wrote "Arkansas" for "Canadian" here, but he used the correct name at 116.11; therefore this editor emends his slip. But see 83.28 where he misused "Red river" for "Canadian."

121.17   off of] The 1A compositor must have followed printer's copy MSA no longer extant here in using "off of" as MSA reads at 55.40, and 111.18. Therefore this reading is adopted rather than the MSE and 2A "off" since neither of the latter forms show consistency in the three "off of—off" uses.

Abbotsford

125.36   greyhound] Irving's writing of "greyhound" and "grey hound" is altered only in instances where confusion results from the use of what appears to be "black grey" as adjectives modifying "hound," as is the case here and at 130.21 and 150.10.

126.27   table.] This is the first of several instances in which the author apparently changed his mind about ending or continuing his sentence without altering the punctuation accordingly. Other examples, all noted, appear at 127.16, 165.10, and 166.34. Comparison of the MSE readings, when they are available, can be helpful in determining Irving's intentions.

129.27   and] Irving's punctuation in MSA belongs to a canceled passage here and at 142.5 and 154.2, both noted.

130.13   of,] Commas added for clarity in 1A are adopted here and at 137.37, 141.10, 148.39, and 164.30.

133.3   Knowes] Irving's erratic spelling of Scottish names ("Knows—Knowes," "Lammermuir—Lammer muir," "Smallholm—Smallyholme," "Etterick—Ettrick," "Teviotdale—Teviot dale") in his notes and in his manuscripts, which he sometimes tried to correct, are adopted in the accepted form for the reader's convenience.

133.8–9   Scotland . . . and] The strongest reason for accepting this MSE reading and the three words added in MSE at 140.17 but omitted in MSA is that the latter clearly seems an earlier draft with the interlineation in MSE likely representing an addition Irving intended for both as he prepared the two manuscripts but neglected to insert in the American form.

138.23   Cy . . . Percy.] Irving's habit was to omit punctuation of an inset quotation. Therefore his quotation marks here and 145.5 and 149.26–27 are considered slips and are emended.

142.27   young lady]   In MSE "Baron's daughter" is marked out and "young lady" written above the line in what appears to be the author's hand; therefore this reading is presumed Irving's choice.

144.34   'The Monastery';]   The single quotation marks probably were added for clarity when "the novel of" was deleted in proof, though the semicolon printed before the final single quotation mark in both 1A and 2A may or may not have been Irving's decision. This edition simplifies the 1A revision by placing the semicolon after the last mark.

153.39   associations,]   In MSA the word "Scott" after the comma is a false start which Irving neglected to delete.

154.31   caress'd]   The 1A "carest" here and "sleights" for "slights" at 156.23 were likely set from material no longer extant but prepared by the same copier who prepared MSE with the same errors. Irving's MSA, apparently early draft, instructs "quotation to come in here p. 92 of Marmion" and "See Marmion p. 90." Therefore this edition emends the errors.

156.23   lovers']   For MSE which serves as copy-text for the passages of poetry indicated in MSA only by the note "See Marmion p. 90," the singular possessives probably were miscopied here and at 156.24 for the plural possessives. See also Discussions of Adopted Readings, 154.31.

160.43   Tom]   This edition corrects this single instance in 2A where the author failed to alter "George" to "Tom" or "Tom Purdie."

167.4–7   during . . .will.]   Irving may have decided not to include in MSA the additional details (approximately 122 words) he wrote for MSE pointing out the gravity combined with the humor in Scott's talk because the addition is overly apologetic and it makes his comments less unified.

167.31–32   and . . . merits]   Since this phrase was written above the line in MSA, the assumption is that the compositor overlooked it.

168.15   guard]   In 2A the substitution of "regard" here for "guard" is less effective with Irving's image of Scott's work as a "treasury" or "armoury" where one "find[s] weapons with which to fight off the evils and the griefs of life." The change could have been the compositor's in setting from memory. Therefore the original reading is retained.

Newstead Abbey

171.8   neighborhood] Irving consistently spelled "or" in his American manuscripts; therefore the two instances of copy-text "our" in MSE here and at 171.28 are emended to the MSA spellings.

171.32   little] In six of seven uses, Irving wrote "Sir John Byron the little" (at 171.32, 179.22, 196.13, 196.20, 197.3, and 220.18–19); therefore the single instance in which he capitalized "Little" is considered a slip and emended to lowercase.

172.21   candle,] Commas added for clarity in 1A are adopted here and at 175.15, 178.8, 179.26, 196.17, and 236.11.

174.18   scene of change] Irving could have transposed "change of scene" as some Byron editions read here; however, several variations (174.11 "once" instead of "late," 174.13 "thy" for "their," 174.14 "wind" for "blast," and 174.19 "sure" for "slow," for example) probably indicate readings his source had, different from standard or definitive texts.

176.4   Colonel] Irving altered "Col." to "Colonel" here in MSE, probably indicating his preference. The change in 1A to "Colonel" also could have been his decision; therefore the full form is adopted for this edition.

176.31   &] Byron's eccentricities in his personal letter rather than the 1A revisions dictated by house style are presumed to be Irving's intentions. See the List of Rejected Substantives, entries 176.24–44.

178.32   gush'd] This edition corrects what was obviously an error in miscopying *r* for *g* from *Don Juan* both in MSA and MSE, corrected only in Murray's 1E but not in 1A or 2A. See also Discussions of Adopted Readings, 178.42 and 198.15.

178.42   XIII] Here in both MSA and MSE Irving erred in writing "Canto III" as his source, though in another instance at 178.41 he corrected the error in MSE. (See Substantive Variants.) Only the English edition corrected to XIII here, on authority other than the author's. This edition corrects this error the author overlooked.

180.24   Goblen]   Irving meant "Gobelin" to refer to the material made by the Gobelin family in Paris.

182.21   warning]   Irving may have miscopied from his source, adding an *r* to make "waning" "warning."

184.2   things I]   Irving probably miscopied "things I love" for Byron's "things to love."

186.28   riband]   Irving meant to use "riband" meaning "ribbon" but instead wrote "ribband," a term for the flexible piece which holds the ribs of a ship for plating. 1A corrected the spelling but made his word plural.

197.35   bowers]   Irving could have revised to "flowers" in 2A here, but the context suggests the broader reference to the dwelling since Annesley Hall is Irving's subject. Therefore a supposition is that the compositor could have inadvertently set "flowers" for "bowers."

198.15   higher]   Both in MSA and MSE "better" was written for "higher," probably in anticipation of "better" modifying "days" in the same line in *Don Juan*. Therefore it is emended as unintentional.

199.13   Hall]   Irving intended to capitalize the term referring to Annesley Hall, as indicated by his correcting "hall" to "Hall" three times in MSA and his writing it in seven instances with capital *H*. Therefore his slips are emended.

202.26–36   He ... agony]   Emended as unintentional since it is the single instance in which the author punctuated an inset quotation in *Newstead Abbey*.

207.14   Mary must]   Irving altered Byron's "Lady will" to "Mary must."

215.36–216.3 'oak,' ... greenwood.]   Irving made a fourteen-line stanza by selecting lines 1–4 and 8–13 from Stanza I of Scott's "Introduction to Canto Second" from *Marmion* and lines 22, 23, 30, and 31 of Stanza II. For Scott's "thorn" he wrote "oak."

217.35–40   A thousand ... grim.]   From "Introduction to Canto Second" Irving chose lines 34–40, altering Scott's punctuation and changing "gaze-hounds" to "gaze-hound."

224.32   trees.]   Irving wrote "It was evidently a" after his sentence at the bottom of the page in MSA, then began another sentence on the next page without deleting his false start.

226.14 little] In twelve of thirteen instances Irving wrote "little White Lady"; therefore this single example of his capitalization of "little" is considered a slip and is emended to lowercase.

235.3–4 "I . . . before."] Though he habitually omitted quotation marks for inset quotations in his own text, Irving copied them here and at 235.21 as they appeared in Sophia Hyatt's letter, still extant. With Irving, this edition follows his source here as the printed texts did.

237.16 minds] Irving copied from Sophia Hyatt's letter what appears to be an erroneous plural since her letter is addressed only to Colonel Wildman's sister. However, the reference throughout is to both of them, and the word here anticipates the end of her paragraph expressing gratitude to both. The 1A revision to "mind" is not likely Irving's; therefore the MSA plural from the letter is retained.

Legends of the Conquest of Spain

244.30 Witiza] Though his sources spelled "Wittiza," Irving consistently wrote and his publishers printed the ruler's name with one *t*.

255.32 Señor] This edition corrects Irving's misuse of "Senior" for "Señor" since the latter represents his intention.

259.5 counsel] For clarity this edition corrects "council" used for "counsel." See the List of Emendations, 282.17 and 341.21 for 1A corrections and the List of Rejected Substantives, 259.24 for correct MS usage.

216.35 antechamber] At 252.39 Irving spelled with *e* rather than *i* and wrote "antechambers" as one word.

265.20 Noseir] The spelling of names troubled Irving consistently. He wrote the name of the Arabian general "Noseir" in the five instances cited here and "Nozier" at 302.18, 318.12, 318.22, 331.6, 336.4, and 339.6. This edition prints both forms, as it also prints two spellings for the son of Noseir, "Abdelasis" as Irving wrote it in forty-eight instances and "Abdalasis" in ten. At 343.2 this edition emends the MS "Abdalesis" to "Abdalasis" as in 1A.

265.36 at all points] Irving attempted to alter "from all points" to read "at all points" but inadvertently marked out "all" and wrote "at" above it rather than above "from" which he should have deleted.

273.42   *Perdida . . . vii*] This footnote and the asterisk after "conquest" at 273.10 appear only in the English printing, probably an addition which Irving made in the stereotyped sheets to go to London but neglected to add in the duplicate sheets for the American printing.

275.2   Theodomir] Originally Irving wrote "Tadmir" in the manuscript but later altered it in every instance but this one to "Theodomir," his Anglicizing of "Teodomiro" in his sources. This edition emends the slip here but retains the phrase "Land of Tadmir" as Irving wrote it at 326.10 and 330.40.

283.14   Abul Cassim] Irving's reference is to the same source he lists elsewhere as Abulcacim Tarif Abentarique, but here in the manuscript he marked out the last name and wrote the first part as two words. According to Pidal (*Crónicas Generales de España*) the name should be "Abulcácim" and D. Eduardo Saavedra's *Estudio Sobre La Invasión de Los Arabes en España* (1892) gives the name as Abulcacín Tarif Abentarique.

283.20   host] This edition adopts the 1A revision of Irving's punctuation in instances (all noted in the List of Emendations) where he deleted without altering the punctuation accordingly, as is the case here and at 292.7, where clarity requires punctuation, as at 298.31, and where the comma clearly seems a slip of the pen as at 289.37.

292.10   Maguel el Rumi] Conde, Irving's source here, gave the name "Magueiz." Irving used both "Maguel" and "Magued," an inconsistency this edition follows.

300.10   1827] Irving altered his MS sentence but erred in writing "1826" rather than "1827" as the year of his visit.

300.22   led] Irving could have intended "lead" here as the subjunctive to express possibility in the continuous present; more likely, however, "lead" resulted from his thinking of the noun pronounced "led." The altering to led in 1E probably was not Irving's change on the English duplicate pages, but it is possible that the change represents his intent.

318.13   Emir] Irving consistently capitalized "Emir" in thirty uses and 1A printed "emir."

318.25   tribe of the Koreish] Irving's reference is to the idol
                  worshippers who opposed Mahomet, a group about
                  whom he wrote more at length in *Mahomet and His
                  Successors*. (See Chapter XI in H. A. Pochmann's and
                  E. N. Feltskog's edition published by the University
                  of Wisconsin Press in 1970).

326.24   taken . . . him?] Irving probably wrote a question mark
                  after "taken" in anticipation of the question he was
                  about to write.

350.8–9   to loathe . . . to] These eight words on one line in the
                  manuscript apparently were covered in the process of
                  pasting together fragments of pages. Either the com-
                  positor in 1835 saw them before the pasting of a later
                  date or the words were recovered in reading proof.

356.20   yourselves] Irving first wrote "your country" on sep-
                  arate lines, then deleted "country" and wrote "selves,"
                  omitting the necessary hyphen.

LISTS OF EMENDATIONS

In these lists of changes in the copy-texts, the symbols used to designate manuscripts and previously published editions are those given in the List of Abbreviations, page 361.

The numbers before each note indicate the page and line. Chapter numbers, chapter or section titles, author's chapter or section summaries, texts, quotations, and footnotes are included in the line count. Only running heads and rules added by the printer to separate running heads from the text are omitted from the count.

These notes identify emendations of the copy-texts. Substantive variants in the two manuscripts prepared for the American and English first editions for *Tour, Abbotsford,* and *Newstead* will appear here only when the unacceptable MSA reading which varies from MSE also varies from the 1A accepable reading or when the unacceptable MSA and 1A variation from MSE differs from the acceptable 2A reading.

The reading to the left of the bracket is the portion of the text under consideration and represents an accepted reading that differs from the copy-text. After the bracket a symbol identifies the source of the reading; after the semicolon is the rejected reading of the copy-text and any other authorized text in which that reading appears; then any other alternative reading with its source identified. In all cases where a difference between MSA and 1A is not specifically noted, the two are to be presumed identical; the same holds true for 1A and 2A and in the listing of emendations in accidentals for MSA and MSE.

The swung (wavy) dash ~ represents the same word, words, or characters that appear before the bracket, and is used in recording punctuation variants; the caret ‸ indicates that a mark of punctuation is omitted. T signifies that a decision to emend or not to emend has been made on the authority of the editor of the Twayne edition. An asterisk * before the page and line number indicates an explanation among the Discussions of Adopted Readings, which include decisions to emend as well as some decisions not to emend.

A number of errors or omissions calling for emendations are attributable to certain aspects of Irving's holographs or to the physical makeup of the manuscript leaves. (See the Textual Commentary, pages 376–406). Occurring frequently is Irving's neglect to place a needed punctuation mark after a word which came at the end of the line in the manuscript. This cause for emendation is signified in the List of Emendations by

end of line. Errors or lapses in punctuation associated with the interlineation of words or phrases in the manuscript or with Irving's marking
out and rewriting are all noted, the authority for emending in such
instances at times being the Twayne editor rather than the source cited
since printed editions lack authority for accidentals.

A Tour on the Prairies

*7.6	recognize] T; recognise 1A [*MSS lacking*]
9.20	man's] T; mans MSE; *Man's* 1A [*MSA lacking here and at 272.2*]. *Apostrophes to show possession inserted also at* 12.15, 13.26, 15.31–2, 18.31, 19.12, 20.36, 27.41, 28.36, 29.17, 32.11, 33.13, 33.22, 33.31, 33.43, 34.38, 35.21, 35.25, 39.18, 40.39, 41.31, 42.43, 43.42, 46.24, 50.32, 51.5, 52.37, 53.13, 53.19, 54.36, 55.35, 57.37, 59.31, 62.43, 63.26, 63.29, 66.16, 66.23, 66.25, 66.34, 67.26, 75.8, 76.25, 77.43, 81.12, 90.20, 92.17, 93.1, 93.27, 95.33, 95.39, 103.41, 104.33, 106.3, 108.30, 112.22, 112.34, 115.16, *and* 121.24. *MSE has an apostrophe at* 13.26.
9.30	Osage,] 1A; ~$_\wedge$ MSE. *End of line.* [*MSA lacking*]
9.31	civilization] 1A; civilisation MSE [*MSA lacking*]
9.38–10.1	hunting . . . bark] 1A; encampments formed of light bowers, branches MSE [*MSA lacking*]
10.2	sad havoc] 1A; hasty slaughter MSE [*MSA lacking*]
10.3	warily retire] 1A; retreat rapidly MSE [*MSA lacking*]
10.4	neighborhood] 2A; neighbourhood MSE, 1A [*MSA lacking*]
10.5	all] 1A; always MSE [*MSA lacking*]
10.6	incessant] 1A; practice incessant MSE [*MSA lacking*]
10.15	through . . . country] 1A; a part of MSE [*MSA lacking*]
10.20	St.] 1A; S' MSA; St$_\wedge$ MSE. *Emended also at* 93.33.
10.36	Mr.] MSE, 1A; Mr$_\wedge$ MSA. *Periods inserted after abbreviations also at* 12.21, 13.12, 18.33, 23.32, 40.23, 56.28, 78.17, 92.9, 92.12, 101.38, *and* 105.27. *MSE has a period at* 10.36 *and* 92.12 *only.*
10.40	any] 1A; every MSA.
11.23	creed,] 1A; creed$_\wedge$ and MSA.
11.24	Osage.] 1A; ~$_\wedge$ MSA. *Periods supplied at the end of sentences also at* 15.17, 17.4 [*end of line*], 17.5 [*end of line*], 17.10 [*end of line*], 24.42 [*end of line*], 27.5, 29.8 [*end of line*], 32.4, 34.11 [*end of line*], 36.1 [*end of line*], 36.33, 43.27, 44.1, 44.7 [*end of line*], 48.43

	[*end of line*], 53.13, 55.32 [*end of line*], 55.33, 56.29 [*end of line*], 57.38, 61.10, 62.22, 64.43, 65.36 [*end of line*], 66.35, 69.22, 70.28 [*end of line*], 72.26 [*end of line*], 74.26, 75.4 [*end of line*], 75.11 [*end of line*], 77.15 [*end of line*], 77.34, 78.1 [*end of line*], 78.20, 79.2, 80.26 [*end of line*], 80.38 [*end of line*], 81.18 [*end of line*], 86.35, 87.35, 87.43, 88.11, 90.7, 91.3, 93.2, 93.5, 93.25, 93.41, 93.42, 94.8, 95.23, 100.35, 102.17, 104.28, 107.28 [*end of line*], 108.24, 110.11, 112.39, 113.12, *and* 120.11.
11.28	seized] MSE, 1A; siezed MSA. *Emended also at* 35.3, 74.17, *and* 85.35.
11.35	cover] 1A; shelter MSA
13.4	connected . . . mission.] 1A; *omitted* MSA
13.18	grieved] 1A; groaned MSA
13.24	rivers,] MSE, 1A; ∼∧ MSA. *End of line.*
13.28–30	A pair . . . carried] 1A; Each one bestowed his scanty wardrobe in a pair of saddlebags, and those by no means crammed: these with his great coat were bestowed MSA
13.34	ourselves . . . together] 1A; a tolerable stock of flour, of coffee and sugar, MSA
13.35–36	for . . . upon] 1A; as we were to depend, for our main subsistence on MSA
13.37–38	journey, were taken] 1A; journey∧ we took MSA
14.17	French,] 1A; ∼∧ MSA. *End of line.*
14.20	reconnoitre] 1A; recconnoitre MSA. *Emended also at* 65.19 *and* 73.27.
15.13–14	ever seen] 1A; seen MSA
15.25	handkerchiefs] 1A; handkerchief MSA
16.11	worse] 1A; more MSA
16.16	full] MSE, 1A; ful MSA
16.23	presented] 1A; pointed out MSA
16.27	and] 1A; & MSA. *Emended also at* 17.5, 17.18, 38.27, 58.19, 97.4, 97.9, 99.4, 100.3, 104.18, 105.27, *and* 112.16.
17.2	evening's] 1A; Evenings MSA
17.4	yet] 1A; *omitted* MSA
17.10	"a . . . horseback."] 1A; ∧∼ . . . ∼·∧ MSA
17.27	accommodation, for] 1A; accomodation∧ for, MSA
17.28	himself] MSE, 1A; him self MSA
17.30	whiffling] 1A; wiffling MSA
18.4	animal,] 1A; ∼∧ MSA. *End of line.*
18.34	o'clock] 1A; oclock MSA. *Emended also at* 23.11,

| | 24.33, 28.13, 35.19, 45.26, 58.21, 66.3, 77.39, 81.19, 83.19, 83.26, 96.35, 97.1, 111.43, 112.18, 115.36, 116.11, 117.26, 117.37, 118.6, *and* 118.35. |

18.36   parallel] MSE, 1A; parrallel MSA. *Emended also at* 36.9, 47.37, 61.30, 75.43, 78.37, 81.21, 98.41, *and* 101.14.

19.5   their] 1A; those MSA

19.19   was sure] 1A; swore MSA

19.29   had] MSE, 1A; *omitted* MSA

19.29   the Indians] 1A; the fault of the Indians MSA

39.38   launched] MSE, 1A; lanched MSA

*39.39   trail] MSE, 1A; ~, MSA

20.8   enterprize] T; enterprise 1A; emprize MSA. *See the List of Rejected Substantives,* 22.16.

20.40   end] 2A; eventuate 1A

21.24   who] MSE, 1A; ~, MSA

22.8   besides, . . . number,] MSE, 1A; ~ₐ . . . ~, MSA

22.11   prairies] 1A; praries MSA. Prarie(s) *corrected also at* 24.42, 25.27, 27.29, 30.8, 30.12, 33.1, 33.30, 34.2, 35.15, 36.19, 42.26, 42.36, 42.38, 43.5, 43.22, 44.18, 50.20, 51.28, 54.3, 55.38, 58.16, 58.22, 59.5, 59.13, 59.17, 59.22, 61.6, 61.15, 61.27, 61.28, 62.6, 62.34, 62.35, 65.5, 65.8, 66.30, 66.34, 67.25, 67.27, 69.12, 70.20, 71.26, 71.40, 72.29, 74,18, 75.31, 76.37, 77.25, 79.28, 80.31, 84.13, 86.28, 90.23, 90.42, 91.5, 94.35, 94.37, 96.7, 99.24, 99.36, 99.42, *and* 106.35. *MSE spells* "*praries*" *and* "*prairies.*" *MSA emended to lowercase at* 61.28, 65.5, 71.26, 74.18, 79.28, 82.13, 88.11, 107.37, 108.16, 110.33, *and* 116.32.

22.39   had] 1A; *omitted* MSA

23.2   foremost] 1A; formost MSA

23.5   blind!"] MSE, 1A; ~!ₐ MSA. *One of a set of omitted quotation marks supplied also at* 29.13 ("That's), 32.9, 33.8, 44.35, 52.14 ("The), 68.12 (now"), 73.35 (horses"), 74.36 (buffalos"), 75.4 ("Where), 76.42 ("It), 91.38 ("However), 94.13 (sad"), 94.16 (Alas"), 94.16 ("since), 94.20, 96.24 (deer"), *and* 116.8 (wind").

23.9   affording] 1A; being MSA

24.2   his] 1A; his his MSA

24.11   Indian] 1A; and well cut MSA

24.29   dam;] 1A; ~, MSA. *For clarity.*

24.40   Beatte] 1A; Bilyet MSA

25.3   tree,] MSE, 1A; ~: MSA

25.12   feeling]   2A; feeling that 1A
25.14   occasionally]   1A; occasionly MSA
25.16   to arrive]   2A; that we might arrive 1A
25.34   chattering]   1A; and chattering MSA
25.37   Commissioner]   1A; ∼, MSA
25.40   not to]   MSE, 1A; to not to MSA
25.43   disturbed;]   MSE, 1A; ∼∧ MSA
26.39   Indians]   MSE, 1A; indians MSA
27.35   his]   1A; their MSA
28.7   his patron]   1A; the Count MSA
28.19   some]   2A; and some 1A
28.21   whence]   2A; from whence 1A. *Emended also at* 31.41,
                    38.26, 39.3, 59.23, 59.29, 105.35, 108.2, *and* 122.24.
28.23   branches]   1A; branches of trees MSA
28.34   arrival]   2A; arrival at the camp 1A
29.8   Captain,]   MSE, 1A; ∼∧ MSA. *End of line.*
29.13   "That's]   1A; Thats MSA. *Apostrophes inserted in con-*
                    tractions also at 29.13 (There's), 33.14, 43.39, 43.42,
                    44.1, 44.29, 44.29, 44.31, 44.38, 73.23, 80.15, 95.31,
                    and 115.6.
*29.13   Old]   T; "Old MSA; ∧old 1A. *Emended to capitalized*
                    form also at 33.13, 74.34, 74.35, 77.31, 78.17, 80.8, *and*
                    95.30.
30.22   others,]   MSE, 1A; ∼∧ MSA
30.29   into]   1A; up in MSA
30.29   a]   1A; one MSA
30.40   disturbing]   1A; agitating MSA
31.32   hands]   MSE, 1A; hand MSA
31.38   in the air]   1A; the air MSA
31.39   it all]   1A; all MSA
32.4   varmint,]   1A; ∼∧ MSA. *Comma inserted to separate*
                    quotation from speaker also at 35.15, 35.17, 43.38, 44.6
                    (few,), 44.23, 51.19 (hereabout,), 51.19 (Captain,),
                    91.38, 94.12, 94.12, 95.24 (hunter,), 96.24 (he,).
33.23   which ... perpendicularly]   2A; the ends of which were
                    thrust 1A
33.25   tickled]   1A; tickeled MSA
33.40–41   two ... and]   2A; the ribs of a fat buck, which stood
                    impaled on two wooden spits, and broiling before the
                    fire were 1A
34.18   enlisted,] 1A; ∼∧ MSA. *For clarity.*
*34.36   In *paragraph*]   1A; *no paragraph* MSA
36.24   kind]   1A; variety MSA

37.38	mess] 1A; lodge MSA
37.40	hunting lore.] MSE; hunting lore, MSA; hunting; 1A
40.10	eyelet] 2A; eylet 1A
°40.25	a half] 1A; half MSA. *Emended also at* 41.28, 52.26, *and* 113.27.
40.33	saddles,] MSE, 1A; ∼∧ MSA. *End of line.*
41.18	raccoons,] MSE, 1A; ∼∧ MSA. *End of line.*
42.34	was] 1A; is MSA
42.36	were] 1A; are MSA
42.40	Rocky Mountains] MSE, 1A; rocky mountains MSA. *Emended also at* 79.29.
44.32	recollect] 1A; reccollect MSA
44.33	sacrifice] 1A; sacrafice MSA
44.36	"Well"] MSE, 1A; ∧Well∧ MSA
44.39–40	Tombigbee] 1A; Tombigbe MSA
45.34	Captain] 1A; ∼, MSA
47.15	Tonish] 1A; our Tonish MSA
47.19	curiosity] 1A; vanity MSA
47.38	reconnoitering] 1A; recconnoitering MSA. *Emended also at* 48.1.
48.8	temperate,] MSE, 1A; ∼∧ MSA. *End of line.*
48.41	and,] MSE, 1A; *omitted* MSA
48.42	it] 1A; *omitted* MSA
49.5	any] 1A; any any MSA
49.9	we] 1A; you MSA
50.11	sacrifices] 1A; sacrafices MSA
50.14	sovereign] 1A; sovreign MSA. *Emended also at* 54.13.
50.21	sacrificed] 1A; sacraficed MSA
50.21	enormous] MSE, 1A; Enormous MSA
°52.22	foot,] 1A; ∼∧ MSA
53.22	turkeys] 1A; turkies MSA. *Emended also at* 117.6.
°54.3	which] 2A; that 1A. *Emended also at* 67.5, 67.9, 69.35, 86.4, *and* 114.35.
54.14	that] 1A; what MSA
54.36	steed] 1A; horse MSA
54.36	The . . . rode] 1A; I had the weakness to be a little proud of the one I rode; he MSA
55.2–3	was . . . until, in] 1A; soon learnt the imprudence of indulging him in such exertions. In MSA
55.8–9	Nobody, . . . him] 1A; But now a new difficulty presented itself. Nobody seemed disposed to lead the horse MSA
55.42	generally] 1A; oftener MSA

55.43   gallopping]   T; galloping 1A; gallopping or curvetting
                        MSA
55.43–56.1   Many . . . travelling,]   1A; With us, however, many of
                        the party MSA
56.6   hunters]   1A; Nimrods MSA
57.34   of the kind]   1A; *omitted* MSA
57.34   already mentioned,]   1A; *omitted* MSA
58.37   gloom]   MSE, 1A; gleam MSA
59.21   was astride of]   1A; had bestrode MSA
*60.6   at full speed]   2A; like mad 1A
60.17   sunrise]   MSE, 1A; sunrize MSA
60.22   a noble park]   1A; noble parks MSA
60.32   their appearance]   1A; these appearances MSA
62.5   advanced,]   1A; ∼∧ MSA. *For clarity.*
62.16   down,]   MSE, 1A; ∼∧ MSA
63.30   from]   1A; from the MSA
63.35   coil.]   1A; lariat or coil MSA
63.37   dexterous]   MSE, 1A; dextrous MSA
64.26   over]   1A; down MSA
64.26–27   interrupted]   MSE, 1A; interupted MSA
64.30   injury,]   MSE, 1A; ∼∧ MSA. *End of line.*
64.33   It *paragraph*]   MSE, 1A; It *no paragraph* MSA
65.20   was an]   1A; is an MSA
66.33   black]   1A; Black MSA
*67.18   prairies]   1A; plains MSA
67.23   brethren]   1A; bretheren MSA
69.31   was, as before,]   MSE, 1A; ∼∧∼ ∼∧ MSA
69.41   discipline]   MSE, 1A; dicipline MSA. *Emended also at*
                        75.36.
70.24   Timber]   MSE, 1A; timber MSA
71.21   approach]   2A; approach   toward   MSA;   approach
                        towards 1A
71.30   black jack]   T; black Jack MSA; black-jack 1A
72.14   preserved]   1A; pursued MSA
72.36   at headlong speed]   2A; like mad 1A
73.16   appeased]   1A; apeased MSA
73.35   "Look . . . horses!"]   MSE, 2A; ∧∼ . . . ∼!∧ MSA;
                        ∧∼ . . . ∼!" 1A
73.37–38   some of]   1A; *omitted* MSA
73.40   comrades]   1A; comerades MSA
74.4   which]   2A; whence 1A
74.27   description]   1A; discreption MSA
75.6   ball?]   MSE, 1A; ball. MSA

75.8	God's] 1A; gods MSA
75.15	had] 1A; has MSA
75.31	prairies] T; praries MSA; prairie 1A
76.13	then] 1A; now MSA
*76.27	Distant] MSE, 1A; distant MSA
77.3	chase] 1A; ~, MSA
77.10	attacked] 1A; has attacked MSA
78.23	the prairies] 1A; the the prairies MSA
78.30	this] MSE, 1A; in MSA
78.36	passed] MSE, 1A; past MSA
79.3	wore] 1A; had worn MSA
79.10	Leatherstocking] MSE, 1A; leatherstocking MSA
79.18	reconnoitered] 1A; recconnoitered MSA
79.29	foot] 1A; feet MSA
80.36	east] 1A; East MSA
82.6	a situation] 1A; situations MSA
82.33	entrapped] 1A; entangled MSA
84.22	speed,] MSE, 1A; ~∧ MSA
85.14	and yelling] 2A; like mad and yelling 1A. *See Discussions of Adopted Readings,* 60.6.
86.6	his] MSE, 1A; his his MSA
86.6	colt] 1A; the two colts MSA
86.17	North Fork] 1A; north fork MSA; North fork MSE
86.27	To the left] 1A; To the left To the left MSA
87.22	mien] MSE, 1A; mein MSA
88.2	made] 1A; made them MSA
88.17	them.] 1A; them—" MSA
89.13	Beatte] MSE, 1A; Bilyet MSA
89.21	swelled] MSE, 1A; swilled MSA
90.10	swollen] MSE, 1A; swoln MSA
90.12	display] MSE, 1A; desplay MSA
90.19	grizzly] 1A; grizly MSA; grizley MSE
90.25	grizzly] 1A; grizley MSA. *Emended also at* 90.35.
91.16	perished] 1A; have perished MSA
91.38	after] MSE, 1A; "after MSA
91.43	superintendence] MSE, 1A; superintendance MSA
92.5	produce] 2A; eventuate in 1A
92.19	the precarious] 1A; their precarious MSA
93.5	prone.] 1A; ~: MSA
93.19	these] 1A; their MSA
93.21	habitudes] MSE, 1A; habitutudes MSA
93.26	which I] MSE, 1A; which MSA
96.38	their horses] 2A; the horses 1A

97.2	labyrinths] 1A; labarynths MSA
97.10	smouldering] 1A; smouldring MSA
97.36–37	troop defiled] 1A; troops filed MSA
99.26	grounds] T; grounds, MSA; ground₍∧₎ 1A
100.7	useless,] MSE, 1A; ～₍∧₎ MSA. *End of line.*
100.8	the windings] MSE, 1A; its windings MSA
101.31	venomously] MSE, 1A; venimously MSA
104.13	frightened] 1A; frightned MSA
104.14	which] 1A; who MSA
104.17	at full speed] 2A; like mad 1A
105.18–20	what . . . and] 1A; in his case he had no provisions with him; was totally unversed in "wood craft," and was MSA
106.4	our] MSE, 1A; *omitted* MSA
106.12	horsemen] MSE, 1A; horseman MSA
107.10	had] 1A; *omitted* MSA
107.21	horse,] MSE, 1A; ～₍∧₎ MSA. *End of line.*
108.6	comrades] MSE, 1A; comrads MSA

See Substantive Variants in Manuscripts for American and English First Editions from this point to the end of A Tour on the Prairies.

108.17	curiosities] 1A; wonders MSA
108.18	something of] 1A; almost MSA
108.19	being, and] 1A; being, MSA
108.26	to] 1A; *omitted* MSA
108.31	congregating] 1A; congregating together MSA
109.27	hunters] 1A; wits MSA
111.17	kind,] 1A; ～₍∧₎ MSA
111.36	there] 1A; t[*illegible*] MSA
112.5	Buffalos] T; Buffalo's MSA; buffaloes 1A
112.14	east] MSE, 1A; East MSA
112.23	whole] 2A; *omitted* 1A
112.34	apothecary's] 1A; apothecaries MSA
113.2	which] MSE, 1A; ～, MSA
113.6	stream] 1A; ～, MSA
113.35	neighed] MSE, 1A; neighted MSA
114.26	musings] MSE, 1A; [*MS LOST*] MSA
114.36–37	How often] MSE, 1A; How often How often MSA
114.39	bands] 2A; bonds 1A
114.40–41	exhilarating] MSE, 1A; exhiliarating MSA
114.41	and . . . ecstasy] 1A; yet a delightful tranquility MSA
115.7	who] 1A; "who MSA

*115.21   Canadian]   T; Arkansas 1A
116.4   lightning]   1A; lightening MSA
116.7   brant]   2A; brandt 1A
116.30   turkeys]   1A; Turkies MSA
116.41   champaign]   MSE, 1A; champain MSA
117.24   there]   MSE, 1A; they MSA
117.29   dismounted,]   MSE, 1A; ~∧ MSA
117.31   but]   1A; when MSA
119.5   troop;]   1A; ~∧ MSA
119.6   each]   1A; every MSA
120.9   or grouse,]   2A; *omitted* 1A
120.12   the ranks]   1A; their ranks MSA
121.8   head and]   MSE, 1A; head MSA
*121.17   off of]   1A; off MSE, 2A [*MSA lacking*]
121.35–122.4   horse. . . . forward.]   1A; horse, but found he had taken
                 good care of himself, being assiduously employed
                 about the corn crib, nibbling the ears of Indian corn
                 that protruded between the bars. The Captain
                 and his troop halted for the night amidst the abun-
                 dance of the farm house; but my immediate fellow
                 travellers were anxious to arrive at the Osage Agency.
                 MSE [*MSA lacking*]
122.5   about]   1A; *omitted* MSA
122.5–7   me . . . forests.]   1A; us to the banks of the Arkansas
                 MSA
122.7–9   A number . . . canoe.]   1A; Here we found a canoe and
                 a number of Creek Indians: who assisted us in ferry-
                 ing our baggage and swimming our horses across the
                 stream. MSA
122.9–15   While . . . across the river.]   1A; *omitted* MSA
122.15–19   fearful, . . . consciousness]   1A; fearful∧ the poor ani-
                 mals would not have strength to stem the current;
                 but a feed of Indian corn had infused fresh life and
                 spirit into them, and it was evident they were aware
                 of MSA
122.20–23   quarters; . . . *paragraph* It]   1A; quarters. They abso-
                 lutely went on a handgallop for a great part of seven
                 miles that we had to ride through the woods, and it
                 MSA
122.25   comfortably quartered]   1A; in comfortable quarters
                 MSA
122.25–27   yet, . . . irksome.]   1A; yet∧ we had been for some
                 weeks past so accustomed to sleep entirely in the

open air, that at first the confinement of a chamber incommoded us. MSA

122.27–30   The atmosphere . . . stars.] 1A; *omitted* MSA

122.31–32   after breakfast, . . . for] 1A; I returned in company with my worthy companion the Commissioner to MSA

122.34   Grounds] 1A; grounds MSA

Abbotsford

125.9   1817] 2A; 1816 1A

125.22   Mr.] 1A; Mr_∧ MSA. *Periods inserted after abbreviations also at* 126.28, 129.17, 138.11, 146.25, 146.29, 156.41, 158.32, 162.8, 162.12, 164.22, 166.29, *and* 166.33.

*125.36   greyhound] 1A; grey hound MSA. *Emended also at* 130.21 *and* 150.10.

126.21   he,] MSE, 1A; ∼_∧ MSA. *Comma inserted to separate quotation from speaker also at* 129.16, 131.4, 131.18, 132.23 (honour,), 134.12 (inheritance,), 140.21 (Scott,), 141.18 (he,), 141.28 (exclaimed,), 146.6 (he,), 146.30, 152.36 (he,), 159.11, 160.36, 160.43 (he,), 162.10 (Pshaw,), 162.10 (Scott,), 165.5 (word,). *MSE has a comma at* 126.21 *only.*

*126.27   table.] 1A; ∼; MSA [*MSE lacking*]

126.41   Johnny] 1A; Johnnie MSA

127.2   I'll] MSE, 1A; Ill MSA. *Apostrophes inserted in contractions also at* 130.9 (na'), 130.40, 131.18, 132.22, 135.36, 136.14, 136.14, 136.21, 136.30, 136.35, 138.27, 146.29–30, 150.30, 152.14 (It's, it's, a'), 157.10, 159.16, (can't), *and* 166.38. *MSE has an apostrophe at* 127.2 *only.*

127.16   alluded. He] MSE; alluded; He MSA; alluded; he 1A

127.18   a worthy] MSE, 1A; was a worthy MSA

128.1   nun's] 1A; nuns MSA. *Apostrophes to show possession inserted also at* 128.8, 128.20, 128.29, 128.37, 129.3, 130.21, 131.12, 131.35, 132.1, 133.31, 133.41, 134.4, 134.33, 136.6, 136.34, 137.11, 137.21, 137.40, 138.10, 138.10, 138.18, 138.36, 142.26, 142.33, 142.37, 142.42, 144.4, 144.17, 144.38, 145.2, 145.21, 146.16, 147.19, 149.21, 149.24, 150.19, 152.16, 152.16, 152.36, 152.40, 155.13, 155.27, 156.20, 157.1, 159.2, 159.3, 159.12, 159.20, 159.27, 159.30, 160.19, 161.19, 162.11, 162.25,

163.18, 164.37, 164.39, 166.26, 167.23, 167.24, 167.24, *and* 167.42.

128.16   "and]   1A; _∧and MSA. *One of a set of omitted quotation marks supplied also at* 129.18, 131.19, 131.37 ("You), 131.40–41, 131.41, 132.23 ("Troth), 132.23 ("sic), 134.11, 134.33 (Now"), 134.33 ("I), 135.17 ("but), 136.17, 140.23, 146.2 (thing"), 146.6 ("in), 146.29 ("Why), 146.30 (he"), 146.31, 146.32, 152.36 ("I), 153.2, 153.5, 153.6 (sportsmen"), 153.13 ("the), 153.20, 154.3, 160.42, 162.12 (1"), 162.23 ("for), 163.7, 163.8 ("It), 163.12 (good"), 163.12 ("to), 163.23, 163.29 ("Our), 163.29 ("though), 164.32, 165.7, 165.32, 165.38 ("for), *and* 166.2. *MSE omitted quotation marks only at* 129.18, 131.19, 131.40–41, 131.41, 132.23, 146.29, 154.3, *and* 160.42.

128.22   the]   MSE, 1A; ∼, MSA

129.21   of]   MSE, 1A; if MSA

*129.27   and bid]   MSE, 1A; ∼, ∼ MSA

130.5   substitute]   1A; substitute for the moon MSA

130.8   the moon]   MSE, 2A; moon MSA; morn 1A

130.9   the Abbey]   1A; *omitted* MSA

130.10   ruin]   1A; Abbey MSA

*130.13   of,]   MSE, 1A; ∼_∧ MSA

130.21   greyhound]   1A; grey hound MSA

130.35   frolic]   1A; gambol MSA

131.7   an armed yacht]   1A; a ship of war MSA

131.16–17   continued Scott]   1A; *omitted* MSA

*133.3   Knowes]   1A; Knows MSE [*MSA lacking here only*]. *Emended also at* 160.27.

133.4   Ettrick]   1A; Etterick MSE [*MSA lacking here only*]. *Emended also at* 134.37 *and* 151.24.

133.23   feelings.]   MSE, 1A; ∼_∧ MSA. *Periods supplied at the end of sentences also at* 135.5, 142.7, 144.43, 145.17, 147.41, 149.18, 149.27, 154.39, 156.42, 158.18, 163.23, 167.6, *and* 168.10.

134.20   eastern]   1A; Eastern MSA

134.33–34   Pilgrim's Progress]   1A; pilgrims progress MSA

134.35   Lammermuir]   1A; Lammer muir MSA

134.35   Smallholm]   T; Smallyholme MSA; Smalholme 1A

134.37   Teviotdale]   MSE, 1A; Teviot dale MSA

135.7   could]   1A; can MSA

135.9   a stout]   MSE, 1A; stout MSA

135.11   England]   1A; ∼" MSA

136.20   before] T; ~" MSA; ~' 1A
136.23   'd——d] 1A; "~ MSA
136.41–137.1   George . . . intelligence,] 2A; who acted as private
                    tutor in the family, and whom I found possessed
                    of much intelligence∧ 1A
137.1–11   He used . . . Dominie Sampson.] 2A; *omitted* 1A
137.37   approached,] 1A; ~∧ MSA
137.39   joyous; having] MSE; joyous; and having MSA;
                    joyous, having 1A
*138.23   Cy . . . Percy.] MSE; "~ . . . ~." MSA
139.2   sovereignty] MSE, 1A; sovreignity MSA
139.3   acknowledged] MSE, 1A; acknowledged admitted
                    MSA
139.5   sovereign] MSE, 1A; sovreign MSA
139.37   Hercules] 1A; hercules MSA
140.21   gay] 1A; wild MSA
140.26   on the eve] MSE, 2A; in the air MSA, 1A
140.31   die!] 1A; ~!" MSA
140.40   who] 2A; that 1A
141.10   reading,] 1A; ~∧ MSA
141.28   sovereignty] MSE, 1A; sovreignty MSA
142.3   of] 1A; of and MSA
142.5   Chevalier] MSE, 1A; ~, MSA
142.32   sat] MSE, 2A; set MSA, 1A
*144.34   'The Monastery";] T; the novel of The Monastery
                    MSA; 'The Monastery;' 1A
145.5   O] T; "~ MSA
146.28   premised] 2A; said 1A
146.33–35   The joke . . . table.] 2A; *omitted* 1A
147.36–37   Long Legs] MSE, 1A; long legs MSA
148.2   Legs] 1A; legs MSA
148.3   whom] 2A; who 1A
148.22   Long Legs] 1A; Longlegs MSA
148.39   name,] MSE, 1A; ~∧ MSA
149.7–11   "We . . . now," . . . "treading . . . bridle."] MSE;
                    ∧We . . . now∧∧ . . . ∧treading . . . bridle.∧ MSA
149.15   True] 1A; Then MSA
149.16   wi'] MSE, 1A; 'wi MSA
149.20   fyne;] 1A; fine; MSE; ~∧ MSA. *End of line.*
149.26–27   And . . . seen.] T; "~ . . . ~." MSA
149.28–29   "It . . . story," . . . "and . . . tale."] MSE;
                    ∧It . . . story,∧ . . . ∧and . . . tale.∧ MSA

150.10   greyhound]   1A; grey hound MSA; grey-hound MSE.
                  End of line.
150.20   *flagrante delictu*]   1A; ~ ~ *no underlining* MSA
151.2   praetorium]   MSE, 1A; Praetorium MSA
151.3   Oldbuck]   1A; Old buck MSA; Old-buck MSE. *End
                  of line.*
151.32   would]   1A; ~, MSA
151.42   sometimes]   1A; now and then MSA; *omitted* MSE
153.18   cicerones]   2A; cicerone 1A
*153.59   associations,]   MSE, 1A; associations, Scott MSA
154.2   off]   MSE; ~: MSA; ~, 1A
*154.31   caress'd]   T; carest MSE, 1A [*MSA lacking*]
155.4   Knowe]   1A; Knows MSA
155.11   Knowe]   1A; Know MSA. *Emended also at* 156.37 *and*
                  157.3.
*156.23   lovers']   1A; lover's MSE [*MSA lacking*]
156.23   slights]   T; sleights MSE [*MSA lacking*]. See Discus-
                  sions of Adopted Readings, 154.31.
156.24   warriors']   1A; warrior's MSE [*MSA lacking*]
156.41   St.]   1A; S' MSA
157.32   which]   2A; that 1A
159.1   named Tommie Purdie,]   2A; *omitted* 1A
159.1   and who]   2A; This man, whose name, I think, was
                  George, 1A
159.4   Tommie]   2A; George 1A
159.5   Purdie]   2A; George 1A
159.8   Tom]   2A; George 1A
159.10   Purdie]   2A; George 1A
159.14   Tom]   2A; George 1A
159.19   Tom Purdie]   2A; George 1A
159.23   Bible]   2A; bible 1A
160.1   time]   MSE; *omitted* MSA; ~, 1A
*160.43   Tom]   T; George 2A
163.12–23   "It ... good," ... "to ... place."]   MSE, 1A;
                  ∧It ... good,∧ ... ∧to ... place∧ MSA
163.15   gaberlunzie,]   2A; gaberlunzie beggar, 1A
163.41   knowes]   1A; knows MSA
164.30   ladies,]   MSE, 1A; ~∧ MSA
165.10   Scott. It]   MSE; ~, it MSA; ~; it 1A
165.19   Highlands]   1A; highlands MSA
165.34   young]   1A; *omitted* MSA
166.34   time. It]   MSE; ~; It MSA; ~; it 1A
166.37–39   'Laidlaw,' ... 'tomorrow ... hare.' "]   T;

'~," ... "~ ... ~." MSA; "~∧" ... "~ ... ~." MSE;
'~,' ... 'to-morrow ... ~.' 1A

166.38	there's] 2A; theres MSA; thre's 1A
167.2	him] 1A; his time MSA
167.15	whole] 1A; *omitted* MSA
167.19	or] 1A; and MSE [*MSA lacking*]
167.30	spirit] 2A; mode 1A
168.11	a human] 2A; a human human MSA, 1A; human MSE
168.17	the griefs] 1A; griefs MSE [*MSA lacking*]
168.17	dejection, I] 1A; dejection, when everything around me was joyless, I MSE [*MSA lacking*]
168.29	cast] 1A; throw MSA

Newstead Abbey

*171.8	neighborhood] 1A; neighbourhood MSE [*MSA lacking*]
171.12	broad] 1A; *omitted* MSE [*MSA lacking*]
171.14	exerted] 1A; exirted MSE (*MSA lacking*]
171.20	canons] 1A; Canons MSE [*MSA lacking*]
171.20	St.] 1A; St∧ MSE [*MSA lacking here only*]. *Periods inserted after abbreviations also at* 172.17, 172.21, 173.34, 175.42, 176.25, 182.40, 186.30, 187.15, 199.7, 199.12, 202.19, 203.7, 230.8, 233.6, 233.10, 237.20, 237.29, *and* 238.17.
171.27	neighboring] 2A; neighbouring MSE, 1A [*MSA lacking*]
*171.31	little] T; Little 1A
172.3	warrior's] 1A; warriors MSA. *Apostrophes to show possession inserted also at* 172.24, 174.1, 174.13, 177.22, 178.35, 179.36, 182.37, 183.9, 184.14, 184.33, 186.16, 186.19, 186.26, 186.34, 187.17, 187.19, 188.26, 189.2, 189.12, 190.7, 190.31, 190.32, 190.33, 190.34, 191.8, 191.27, 192.33, 192.35, 195.28, 195.38, 197.21, 197.28, 197.32, 198.5, 198.22, 198.33, 200.19, 200.23, 206.3, 206.10, 206.13, 207.6, 208.31, 209.4, 209.39, 211.1, 211.36, 212.25, 212.31, 212.33, 216.5, 216.25, 216.34, 218.34, 220.10, 220.11, 223.7, 226.13, 226.19, 226.32, 227.31, 228.11, 228.18, 228.33, 229.5, 229.35, 230.2, 230.27, 230.29, 230.34, 230.38, 231.1, 231.22, 231.23, 231.28, 232.1, 232.12, 232.34, 232.36, 234.9, 236.15, 237.28, 238.15, *and* 238.27.
*172.21	candle,] MSE, 1A; ~∧ MSA

172.34	*tete a tete*] 1A; ∼ ∼ ∼ *no underlining* MSA
174.6	condition.] MSE, 1A; ∼∧ MSA. *Periods supplied at the end of sentences also at* 177.10, 181.23, 182.4, 189.11, 200.28, 204.27, 208.4, 232.3, *and* 232.22. *MSE has a variant reading at* 181.23.
175.5	"There] MSE, 1A; ∧There MSA. *One of a set of omitted quotation marks supplied also at* 190.23, 191.9 ("I), 192.15, 192.32, 192.42 (not'), 199.6, 196.7 (Chaworth"), 200.8 (trees"), 202.14, 212.2 (C"), *and* 225.20 (here").
175.15	state,] MSE, 1A; ∼∧ MSA
175.21	may,] 1A; ∼∧ MSA. *Comma inserted to separate quotation from speaker also at* 189.37 [*end of line*], 191.1 (sir,), 191.9 (sir,), 191.34 (Nanny,), 192.5 (true,), 192.5 (added,), 192.40, 193.3 (Smith,), 202.5 (I,), 202.13, 209.9 (Byron,), 219.22, 225.7 (Wildman,), 227.20 (strangers,), *and* 234.13. *MSE has a comma at* 209.9 *only.*
*176.4	Colonel] MSE, 1A; Col. MSA. *Also emended to full form at* 176.12, 188.2, 188.37, 189.14, 190.24, 190.41, 191.6, 191.14, 191.19, 193.34, 199.14, 212.33, 214.8, 215.7, 224.24, 224.37, 225.7, 225.31, 226.13, 226.18, 226.24, 226.32, 226.43, 227.5, 227.24, 229.19, 229.39, 231.35, 232.12, 233.36, 233.40, 234.9, 235.33, 236.15, 237.24, 237.36, *and* 237.42. *MSE abbreviated in all instances listed except* 176.4; *both MSS used periods erratically.*
177.16	Christmas] 2A; christmas 1A. *Also emended at* 187.6, 187.20, *and* 187.27.
177.20	Park] 2A; park 1A
178.8	rooks,] MSE, 1A; ∼∧ MSA
*178.32	gush'd] T; rush'd MSA
*178.41	XIII] T; III MSA
179.26	prospect,] MSE, 1A; ∼: MSA
179.27	beautiful] 1A; Beautiful MSA
180.37	Turkey] 1A; turkey MSA
181.17	Land] 1A; land MSA
181.19	Turk] 1A; turk MSA
181.21	Christian] MSE, 1A; christian MSA
182.39	"The] 1A; "the MSA
184.7–11	The ... affection.] 1A; *omitted* MSA
186.15	came] 2A; came to me 1A
186.22	whence] 2A; from whence 1A

*186.28   riband]   T; ribband MSA; ribbands MSE; ribands 1A
186.34   ribands]   1A; ribbands MSA
186.35   Beelzebub]   2A; Belzebub 1A
187.7   Derbyshire]   MSE, 1A; Derby shire MSA
187.14   custom]   2A; christmas custom 1A
187.17   antechamber]   2A; antichamber 1A
187.17   servants' hall]   1A; Servants∧ Hall MSA
187.24   Romans]   1A; romans MSA
189.1   mansion]   1A; fireside MSA
189.34   interred]   1A; entombed MSA
189.39   don't]   1A; dont MSA. *Apostrophes inserted in contrac-*
              tions also at 191.1 (it's), 195.3, 195.17 ('Tis), 198.20,
              205.3 (ne'er), 206.4 (husband's), 206.29, 207.32, 211.13,
              225.22, 225.30, 228.27, 230.25, 230.29, 230.37, *and*
              232.36. *MSE has an apostrophe at* 195.3, 195.18, 205.3,
              206.4, *and* 207.32.
190.2   and]   MSE, 1A; & MSA. *Also emended as in 1A at*
              214.21, 217.16 (and recreation), *and* 232.25.
190.15–16   Joe, ... morning]   1A; Joe. He told her the next morn-
              ing, she said, MSA
190.17   Bible]   2A; bible 1A. *Also emended at* 213.19 *and* 214.7.
191.9.10   to see it—]   1A; to see it finished and to take my seat
              at the head of it. MSA
191.10   pride]   1A; some pride MSA
192.9   jealous;]   MSE, 1A; ∼∧ MSA *End of line.*
192.14   Upon]   MSE, 1A; "∼ MSA
192.39   opposite]   1A; other MSA
193.2   devil]   1A; ∼" MSA
193.40   gardener]   1A; gardner MSA
194.9   effigies]   1A; coffins MSA
194.17   the Abbey]   1A; the rest of the Abbey MSA
196.17   night,]   MSE, 1A; ∼∧ MSA
196.21   book.]   MSE, 1A; ∼; MSA
198.8   which]   2A; that 1A [*MSE lacking*]
*198.15   higher]   T; better MSA [*MSE lacking*]
*199.13   Hall]   1A; hall MSA [*MSE lacking here only*].
              Emended also at 203.9, 203.13, 204.2, 205.7, *and* 210.1.
200.5   loving]   1A; youthful MSA [*MSE lacking*]
200.31   of]   1A; to MSA
200.39   chimneys]   1A; chimnies MSA
202.6   do]   1A; ∼" MSA
*202.26–36   He ... agony.]   T; "He ... agony." 1A
203.15   this]   MSE, 2A; the 1A

204.4	ancient] 1A; old time MSA
204.15	Dream] 1A; dream MSA
204.32	she knew] MSE, 1A; and she knew MSA
205.34	and he afterwards] MSE, 1A; and afterwards MSA
208.25	seems] MSE, 1A; *omitted* MSA
209.22	love] 1A; his MSA
213.8	Forest] 1A; forest MSA. *Emended also at* 213.33, 214.21, 214.24, 218.15, *and* 219.4. [*MSE lacking here and at* 213.33].
213.40	bear] 1A; have MSA [*MSE lacking*]
215.29	forest;] 1A; ~, MSA. *For clarity.*
216.42	existence] 1A; existance MSA
218.12	groves] 1A; glades MSA
218.14	around me] 2A; around 1A
218.30	resound] 2A; sound 1A
219.12	should molest] 1A; molested MSA
219.15	'working day world'"] 1A "~ ~ ~" MSA
219.17	had] 1A; *omitted* MSA
219.19	the heath] MSE, 2A; a heath 1A
220.4	Ivanhoe?] MSE, 1A; ~?" MSA
220.22–23	Here was the] 1A; The MSA [*MSE lacking*]
220.25–26	and . . . were] 1A; *omitted* MSA [*MSE lacking*]
221.16	metempsychosis] 2A; metemsychosis 1A [*MSE lacking*]
222.10	a mysterious] 1A; mysterious MSA [*MSE lacking*]
222.31	will] 1A; might MSA [*MSE lacking*]
*224.32	trees.] 1A; trees. It was evidently a MSA [*MSE lacking*]
224.33	house. With . . . mansion] 1A; house & with this rustic mansion and the wild wood adjacent MSA [*MSE lacking*]
226.8	unmolested] 1A; unnoticed MSA [*MSE lacking*]
*226.14	little] T; Little 1A [*MSE lacking*]
227.4	writing.] 1A; ~; MSA [*MSE lacking*]
227.8	deficient] 1A; defective MSA (*MSE lacking*]
227.10	communication] 1A; conversation MSA [*MSE lacking*]
227.18	friend] 1A; friends MSA
227.23	belong] 1A; belong, nor to be regarded as belonging MSA [*MSE lacking*]
227.35	remote] 1A; retired MSA [*MSE lacking*]
227.35	and was] 1A; *omitted* MSA [*MSE lacking*]
227.42	worshipped] 1A; worshiped MSA (*MSE lacking*]
228.2	rhapsody] 1A; raphsody MSA (*MSE lacking*]

228.25   rhapsodies]   1A; raphsodies MSA [*MSE lacking here
                  only*]. *Emended also at* 230.19 *and* 231.7.
229.4   seat]   1A; scene MSA
230.17   which]   2A; that 1A
231.19   ere]   1A; er'e MSA
232.2   worse]   1A; more horrible MSA; more terrible MSE
233.8   affectionate]   2A; affecting 1A
233.25   whole]   1A; main MSA
233.40   Wildman]   1A; W∧ MSA; W. MSE. *Emended to full
                  form also at* 235.33.
234.19   diseased]   MSE, 1A; deseased MSA
236.11   contempt,]   1A; ∼∧ MSA [*end of line*]; ∼∧ MSE

                            Legends of the Conquest of Spain

241.2   Few . . . been]   1A; There are few events in history MS
241.6   As in]   1A; Like MS
241.10   would be]   1A; is MS
241.16   or inclination]   1A; *omitted* MS
241.19   produced]   1A; had produced MS
241.20   and write]   1A; into MS
241.36   startling for]   1A; repugnant to MS
242.14   Since]   1A; From MS
242.19   enchanted . . . old]   1A; old enchanted fountains of MS
243.1   Roderick*]   T; Roderick∧ MS
243.13   and]   1A; and and MS
243.28   soldier's]   1A; soldier∧s MS. *Apostrophes to show pos-
                  session inserted also at* 251.8, 252.10, 253.9, 254.10,
                  255.30, 260.18, 267.21, 268.20, 272.39, 279.3, 284.21,
                  285.27, 290.21, 291.17, 294.39, 296.2, 325.15, 329.39,
                  350.11, *and* 355.10.
243.32   Mohammed]   1A; Mohamed MS
244.6   sovereign]   1A; sovreign MS. *Emended also at* 244.11,
                  250.10, 250.15, 252.16, 256.41, 260.40, 266.25, 266.39,
                  270.9, 271.32, 272.6, 282.27, 284.6, 285.23, 308.11,
                  332.24, 333.11, 336.6, 336.21, 336.32, 337.4, 337.15,
                  340.22, 340.27, 340.33, 347.20 *and* 348.39.
244.24   were]   1A; was MS
244.26–27   there was a]   1A; also in the MS
244.41   *lib.*]   1A; lib∧ MS. *Periods inserted after abbreviations
                  also at* 248.38, 252,41, 258.42, 258.43, 261.42, 262.42,
                  268.42, 270.42, 271.36, 283.36, 283.38, 295.39, 297.42,
                  300.25, 303.37, 307.37, 317.40, 319.42, 320.37, 325.40,
                  325.43, 364.41, 346.42, 357.12 *and* 357.26.

245.8   Despising]   1A; Dispising MS
245.10   temperament]   1A; temprament MS
245.15   Sovereign]   T; Sovreign MS; sovereign 1A
245.20   St. Peter]   1A; S'Peters MS *Emended also at* 245.35.
245.38   dominions.]   1A; ∼∧ MS. *Periods supplied at the end
               of sentences also at* 246.9, 248.28, 248.32, 252.4,
               257.3, 269.3, 270.2, 275.29, 285.27, 287.21, 291.28,
               293.18, 305.37, 305.16, 305.39, 307.10, 310.12, 324.17,
               324.24, 325.42, 328.6, 338.6, 341.16, 345.36, 354.30,
               356.6, *and* 356.23.
246.1–3   when ... changers and]   1A; ever since the time when
               they borrowed the jewels of gold and jewels of silver
               from their neighbors, on preparing for their mem-
               orable flight out of Egypt have been MS
246.15   millennium]   T; millenium MS, 1A
246.37   and]   1A; & MS. *Emended also at* 336.25, 342.31
               (*oppression* &), 354.4, 349.2 *and* 355.12.
246.39   enervated]   1A; ennervated MS
247.2   undisciplined]   1A; undiciplined MS. *Emended also
               at* 277.33.
247.25   head,]   1A; ∼∧ MS. *Comma inserted to separate quo-
               tation from speaker also at* 255.32 (she,), 256.9 (she,),
               269.32 (Hitherto,), 270.12 (he,), 270.26 (he,), 271.21
               (he,), 273.14 (he,), 275.33 (Greybeard,), 275.41,
               276.31, 276.36 (Such,), 277.6 (he,), 279.38 (hard,),
               280.34, 282.19, 282.29 (he,), 284.29, 285.1, 285.27,
               288.32 (he,), 289.26, 291.30 (fighting,), 291.30 (he,),
               291.34, 302.20 (they,), 308.10 (fallen,), 308.39
               (strength,), 314.6 (said,), 314.16, 325.17, 327.7 (he,),
               328.21, 328.24, 328.31 (do,), 328.39 (son,), 329.10,
               329.42 (Theodomir,), 331.33 (Taric,), 340.2, 340.3,
               341.5, 345.26 (father,), 352.42, 354.24 (countess,),
               354.42 (he,), *and* 356.5 (safe,).
247.25   head"]   1A; head∧ MS. *One of a set of omitted quota-
               tion marks supplied also at* 250.4, 251.32, 259.14
               ("are), 259.36 ("and), 259.37 ("whether), 260.5
               (minds"), 260.5 (do"), 262.28 ("Desist), 266.18,
               275.26 ("that), 277.6, 277.7, 277.36 ("for), 277.36
               (forbid"), 277.38, 279.38 ("but), 282.18, 288.32
               ("that), 291.30 (fighting"), 292.24 ("Whither), 296.9,
               297.28 ("History"), 297.29, 302.24, 316.7 ("that),
               321.10 ("We), 321.10 (city"), 321.11, 325.17 ("and),
               326.28 (praised"), 328.21 (glory"), 328.31 ("against),

330.12 ("Behold), 330.25 ("Where), 330.27 ("As),
332.17, 337.21, 338.18 (christians"), 338.19 ("are),
338.31, 338.33, 339.12, 343.14 ("with), 343.18, 347.16,
348.27 ("dost), 354.3 (dead"), *and* 357.35.

249.2	divers] 1A; Divers MS
249.14	and] T; & MS; *omitted* 1A
249.21	near,] 1A; ~∧ MSA. *For clarity.*
250.4	which] 1A; which which MS
250.35	any] 1A; every MS
251.2	apartments] 1A; appartments MS
252.33	every] 1A; *omitted* MS
253.4	sovereigns] 1A; sovreigns MS
253.6	trained] 1A; trained trained MS
253.33	disastrous] 1A; disasterous MS
*255.32	Señor] T; Senior MS, 1A. *Emended also at* 255.37, 256.9, 272.37, 274.10, *and* 274.14.
255.42	her countenance] 1A; the countenance MS
256.19	seize] 1A; sieze MS. *Emended also at* 286.28, 303.16, 303.31, *and* 352.16.
257.5	intrigues] 1A; enterprize MS
257.37	and his people] 1A; in his people MS
258.15	zodiac] 1A; Zodiac MS
258.17	obeisance,] T; ~∧ MS [*end of line*]; ~; 1A
258.42	España] 1A; Espana MS. *Emended also at* 283.36, 320.37, *and* 326.36.
*259.5	counsel] T; council MS, 1A. *Emended also at* 259.24 *and* 274.26.
259.21	religious] 1A; christian MS
261.32	dispel] 1A; dispell MS
*261.35	antechamber] T; anti-chamber MS [*end of line*]; anti-chamber 1A
262.26	seized] 1A; siezed MS. *Emended also at* 279.6, 279.17, 292.17, *and* 329.21.
262.41	+ Idem.] 1A; *omitted* MS
263.22	rout] 1A; route MS
*265.36	at all points] T; from all points 1A; from at points MS
266.15	bitterly] 1A; to himself MS
268.1–2	devout...council.] 1A; smooth and plausible in council and devout in demeanour. MS
268.15	represented to] 1A; reminded MS
268.19	person...tongue, and] 1A; ~, eloquent of tongue∧ and intrepid of spirit, and, MS
268.42	Bleda.] 1A; ~∧ MS. *Period supplied in footnote after*

	author also at 270.42, 283.36, 303.37, 307.37, 317.40, 324.42, 325.40, 345.37, *and* 346.41.
269.5–6	*Secret . . . Tuerto.*] 1A; *omitted* MS
269.16	deserts] 1A; desarts MS
271.16	Muza] 1A; Musa MS
271.16	Second] 1A; *omitted* MS
273.10	conquest*] T; conquest∧ MS, 1A. *See Discussions of Adopted Readings,* 273.42.
*273.42	*Perdida de España por Abulcasim Tarif Abentarique, lib. 1, c. vii.*] T; *omitted* MS, 1A
274.15	assistance*] 1A; assistance∧ MS
274.33	discipline] 1A; dicipline MS. *Emended also at* 287.20 *and* 336.17.
274.38	*Conde. Part 1. c. 9.*] 1A; *omitted* MS
*275.2	Theodomir] 1A; Tadmir MS
275.40	'Tis] 1A; Tis MS
276.30	'Fear . . . morrow,' . . . 'I . . . coming.'] 1A; "Fear . . . morrow," . . . "I . . . coming." MS. *Double quotation marks emended to single also at* 284.29–30, 284.32–40, 344.28–30, *and* 345.24–25.
276.36	say] 1A; says MS
277.41	losel] 1A; lossel MS
278.7	battalion] 1A; batallion MS
278.19	career] 1A; carreer MS. *Emended also at* 279.7, 302.36, 303.19, 306.30, 311.36, 327.33, 331.8, *and* 343.9.
279.24	recollecting] 1A; reccollecting MS
281.3	destruction] 1A; distruction MS
281.4	But] 1A; but MS
282.17	counsel] 1A; council MS. *Emended also at* 282.23, 285.20, 285.28, 287.31, 287.36, 288.2, 303.12, *and* 329.24.
*283.20	host] 1A; ∼, MS
283.29	dexterous] 1A; dextrous MS
284.13	taken place] 1A; occurred MS
284.21	received] 1A; recieved MS. *Emended also at* 351.3.
285.21	I know] 1A; and I know of MS
285.30	counselled] 1A; counciled MS
287.26	disastrously] T; disasterously MS, 1A
288.37	*Cronica.*] 1A; Cronica∧ MS. *Periods supplied at end of footnotes also at* 326.36, 327.42, 330.42, *and* 333.36.
289.6	thine eyes] 1A; thy eyes MS
289.10	discernible] T; descernable MS; discernable 1A
289.29	Evan and Siseburto] 1A; Eban and Sisiburto MS

289.37	guards] 1A; ~, MS
290.22	descried] 1A; discried MS
291.10	apparelled] 1A; apparreled MS
291.29	brethren] 1A; bretheren MS
292.2	were] 1A; *omitted* MS
292.7	arrows,] 1A; ~∧ MS
293.16	bloody ... Guadalete] 1A; field of the late bloody contest MS
293.17	had ... passed] 1A; the day before had passed MS
293.28–30	The booty ... brocades,] 1A; There was immense booty; in massy chains and rare jewels of gold, in pearls and precious stones, in rich silks and brocades∧ MS
294.39–40	being ... tranquility] 1A; relieved from the fear for personal safety MS
295.6–7	being ... rustic] 1A; questioning the trembling rustic he MS
295.9	That] 1A; And MS
295.39	10] 1A; X MS

For entries 295.25 through 296.9 two pages of Irving's eight pages of rewritten printer's copy are lacking; these entries record variations, therefore, in the earlier draft which is copy-text here even though it did not serve as printer's copy.

295.25–26	that ... Roderick.] 1A; *omitted* MS
296.26–30	At ... walls,] 1A; Many years afterwards, when Don Alfonso of Leon conquered the city of Viseo in Lusitania one of his warriors, wandering in a field without the walls, discovered MS
295.32–35	*HIC ... Goths.*] 1A; *Hic jacet Rodericus ultimus rex gothorum.* (Here lies Roderick the last king of the Goths) MS
295.36	believed] 1A; supposed MS
295.38	supposed] 1A; humble MS
296.5–6	impious ... Julian] 1A; malice of the traytor Julian, so impious and persevering. He was headlong in his vengeance, forgetful of his loyalty, his religion and his god. MS
296.8	infamous] 1A; accursed MS
296.9	Here ... Roderick.] 1A; *omitted* MS
296.19	el] 1A; la MS

296.24	Cauliniano] 1A; Cautiana MS
296.35	The Cave of Hercules] 1A; Illustration of the Legend of Don Roderick / The Cave of Hercules MS
297.42	plan 1] 1A; plan 1 & 2 MS
298.20–21	the . . . which] 1A; where dark waters MS
298.30	history] 1A; histry MS
298.31	world,] 1A; ~∧ MS
298.40	hoard] 1A; horde MS
299.37	them] 1A; him MS
300.7	history] 1A; story MS
*300.10	1827] T; 1826 MS, 1A
300.15	be] 1A; *omitted* MS
*300.22	led] T; lead MS, 1A
302.9	foaming] 1A; fiery MS
304.32	to retain] 1A; to be protected in MS
305.6	"Mountains of the Sun and Air"] 1A; ∧mountains of the sun and air∧ MS
306.5	the] 1A; the the MS
307.1	Ibrahim] 1A; Joseph MS
307.37	*Bleda. cronica, L. 2. c.* 10.] 1A; *omittted* MS
308.16–18	"Your . . . defence."] 1A; "Promise to stand by me to the last," said he, "and I will undertake your defence. Your city is surounded by walls and towers, and may yet check the progress of the foe." MS
310.2	St.] 1A; S' MS. *Emended also at* 312.37 *and* 316.40.
310.12	Guadalquivir] 1A; guadalquivir MS. *Emended also at* 327.17, *and* 343.27.
311.2	knows] 1A; ~" MS
311.30	alighted] 1A; allighted MS
312.12	perceived] 1A; percieved MS
312.26–27	steed, proceeded] 1A; steed. And they proceeded MS
314.26	country's] 1A; countries MS
315.23	thee] 1A; the MS
315.36	thou wilt] 1A; you will MS
315.38	thy] 1A; your MS
315.39	thee] 1A; you MS
316.34	Arabs] 1A; moors MS
317.19	twenty] 1A; Twenty MS
317.26	timbrel] 1A; timbral MS
317.40	España,] 1A; Espan. MS
*318.25	Koreish] 1A; Ceraishtes MS
320.33	Carmona,] 1A; ~∧ MSA. *For clarity.*
321.17	the most part] 1A; they were for the most part MS

324.15	they] 1A; *omitted* MS
324.18–19	The . . . one] 1A; When the ambassadors came into the presence of Muza they expected to find a fierce and formidable looking warrior in this man MS
325.18	renew . . . pleasure.] 1A; restore themselves from age to youth. MS
326.11	Merida,] 1A; ~∧ MSA. *For clarity.*
*326.24	taken . . . him?] 1A; ~? . . . ~. MS
327.22	principal] 1A; principle MS
327.26	leave the city] 1A; go forth MS
328.15	in] 1A; *omitted* MS
330.17	city, he] 1A; ~∧ ~, MS
331.19	Taric . . . and] 1A; When Taric heard of his approach he MS
332.7	repress] 1A; contain MS
332.22–23	"I . . . emphatically;] 1A; "I have done the best I could," said he emphatically, "to serve God and the caliph; MS
333.5	humiliation and reproach] 1A; shame MS
333.10	and] 1A; *omitted* MS
333.20	dissensions] 1A; dissentions MS
333.29	To] 1A; to MS
333.32	fighting men] 1A; the troops MS
334.3	or Arragonian] 1A; *omitted* MS
334.4	down] 1A; down its legions MS
334.17	de] 1A; of MS
335.5	their . . . resistance] 1A; the obstinate resistance of the inhabitants MS
335.19	Valencia] 1A; Valentia MS
336.11	reconciliation] 1A; recconciliation MS
336.23–26	"Muza, . . . contrary," . . . "is . . . coffers."] 1A; ∧Muza, . . . contrary,∧ . . . ∧is . . . coffers.∧ MS
336.33	grievous] 1A; grievious MS
337.36–37	was . . . alert] 1A; had been more speedy MS
337.37–40	He . . . warnings, and] 1A; He was ever ready for the march at a moment's warning; he knew the importance, where complaints were to be heard, to be first in presence of the judge, and he MS
338.10	He] 1A; Taric MS
338.36	the combat] 1A; thee combat MS
339.39	Taric] 1A; Tarif MS
340.1	emerald] 1A; emrald MS. *Emended also at* 340.5.

341.21   counsels] 1A; councils MS. *Emended also at* 341.31,
                   342.14, *and* 342.37.
343.2   Abdalasis] 1A; Abdalesis MS
343.10–12   "What . . . this," . . . "who . . . unbelievers?"] T;
                   ∧What . . . this,∧ . . . ∧who . . . unbelievers?" MS;
                   ∧What . . . this,∧ . . . ∧who . . . unbelievers?∧ 1A
343.26   was] 1A; *omitted* MS
345.4–9   spoil. But . . . veins.*] 1A; spoil, subject to thy will.
                   I trust, however, in thy courtesy as a cavalier, that
                   thou wilt respect my person, remembering who I was,
                   and that the crown has been wrested from my brow,
                   the royal blood still warms within my veins. Thou
                   mayst conquer my person, but not my will. If I
                   want force to defend my honour, I have resolution
                   to wash out all stain upon it with my blood.* MS
345.10   repulse] 1A; resistance MS
346.41–42   Conde. p. 1. c. 19.] 1A; *omitted* MS
348.7   which] 1A; that MS
348.43   Here . . . Spain.] 1A; Alhambra. June 10th 1829. MS
349.3–4   is . . . admonition,] 1A; of the perdition of Spain is
                   darkly shadowed out a true history, rife with whole-
                   some lessons, MS
349.10   history] 1A; story MS
349.15   Spain, and perpetuated in] 1A; Spain. The events of
                   Spanish history are so wild and picturesque in them-
                   selves as to render unnecessary the invention of the
                   poet and furnish themes for MS
349.21   the people] 1A; its people MS
349.26   rustic] 1A; unpretending MS
349.28–30   the doleful . . . generation. The] 1A; recounted the
                   doleful end of Count Julian and his family; the MS
349.33   safely taken] 1A; taken MS
349.33   facts] 1A; fact MS
*350.8–9   to loathe . . . to] 1A; *covered in pasting* MS
350.24   wantonness] 1A; wantoness MS
351.2–3   city, . . . chronicler, received] 1A; city∧ received MS
351.10   event] 1A; evint MS
352.28   downfall] 1A; downfal MS
354.21   faltered] 1A; faultered MS
354.34   subtile] 1A; subtil MS
355.27   wondrous] 1A; wonderous MS
355.28   around with delighted eyes. The] 1A; around, the MS
355.30   the tower . . . that] 1A; Ceuta stands on a MS

*356.20   yourselves]   1A; your selves MS

356.38–357.7   All ... generations.]   1A; A stone sepulchre is shewn,
                 outside of the chapel of the castle, in which it is
                 said his remains were interred; and a curse remains
                 upon the place for having given him refuge; for we
                 are told that the castle is no longer inhabited, on
                 account of the strange and horrible noises that are
                 heard in it; and that visions of armed men are seen
                 above it in the air; which are supposed to be the
                 troubled spirits of the apostate christians who favored
                 the cause of the traitor.*

                 All agree that the latter end of Julian was miserable
                 in the extreme. He became an outcast among men;
                 he was despoiled of his wealth and power; he heard
                 of the destruction of his family and he suffered worse
                 than a thousand deaths in the horrors of his con-
                 science. A violent and dismal death at length closed
                 his career, and his name remained a byeword and a
                 scorn, for the warning of future generations. MS

357.10   *Written in the Alhambra, June 10, 1829.*]   1A; Alham-
                 bra—(See the date at the end of the preceding legend)
                 MS

357.12   8.)]   1A; 8. MS. *End of line.*

357.22   Subseccion 5. Instancia 8. Num.]   1A; ~5ᴧ ~8ᴧ~: MS

LISTS OF REJECTED SUBSTANTIVES

These lists identify all substantive variants in the authorized printed texts that appeared during Irving's lifetime but that were not adopted for the Twayne text. With the lists of Substantive Variants in Manuscripts for American and English First Editions for the three works which had two manuscripts, they provide a historical record of all substantive variants in which the author could have had a hand.

The symbols used to designate manuscripts and previously published editions are those given in the List of Abbreviations, page 361.

The numbers before each note indicate the page and line. Chapter numbers, chapter or section titles, author's chapter or section summaries, texts, quotations, and footnotes are included in the line count. Only running heads and rules added by the printer to separate running heads from the text are omitted from the count.

These notes identify all 1A and 2A substantives not accepted in the Twayne edition. The reading to the left of the bracket represents the accepted reading, with the source identified by symbol after the bracket. Any reading after the semicolon is a rejected reading. Readings identified by an asterisk * are explained among the Discussions of Adopted Readings. Where a difference between MSA and 1A is not specifically noted, the two are presumed identical; the same is true for 1A and 2A.

A Tour on the Prairies

9.26	all] MSE, 1A; *omitted* 2A [*MSA lacking*]
9.27–28	Elk, the Buffalo] MSE, 1A; elk, the buffalo 2A [*MSA lacking*]
9.29	Thither] MSE; hither 1A [*MSA lacking*]
9.34	region] MSE: regions 1A [*MSA lacking*]
9.35	forms] MSE, 1A; form 2A [*MSA lacking*]
9.35	debateable] MSE, 1A; debatable 2A [*MSA lacking*]
9.36	None] MSE; none 1A [*MSA lacking*]
9.37	braves] MSE; Braves 1A [*MSA lacking*]
10.3	Buffalo] MSE; buffalo 1A [*MSA lacking here only*]. *Lowercase "buffalo" of 1A rejected for* Buffalo *of MSS also at* 16.1, 33.8, 58.5, 65.6, 65.6, 71.12, 72.7, 72.7, 72.17, 72.22, 72.33, 72.38, 77.23, 77.23, 81.27, 82.41, 83.3, 96.7, 97.11, 98.34, 98.38, 98.43, 99.18, 101.35, 104.23, *and* 103.25. *MSA and MSE agree.*

10.22–23	commissioners] 1A; Commissioners 2A
10.24–25	East . . . West] MSA; east . . . west 1A
10.32	select men] 1A; selectmen 2A
10.34	back woodsmen] 1A; backwoodsmen 2A
10.36	L——] 1A; L. 2A
10.43	virtuoso] MSA; Virtuoso 1A
11.2	or] 1A; nor 2A
11.6	mentor] MSA; Mentor 1A. *Capitalized form of 1A rejected also at* 13.18.
11.11–12	all prevalent] MSA; prevalent 1A
11.14	wiry] MSA; *omitted* 1A
11.14	Creole] 1A; creole 2A
11.17	Sometimes] MSA; sometimes 1A
11.37	Buffalo] 1A; buffalo 2A. *Capitalized form as in 1A and MSS also at* 22.13, 23.27, 29.32, *and* 29.33.
12.6	horse] MSA, 2A; horses 1A
12.8	gar] 1A; Gar 2A
12.17	buffalo] MSA, 2A; Buffalo 1A
12.17	young] MSA; *omitted* 1A
12.20	enquiries] MSA; inquiries 1A. *Spelled with* e *as in MSA also at* 73.13.
12.30	Buffalos] MSA; buffaloes 1A. *MSA* Buffalos *rather than 1A* buffaloes *also at* 85.20, 85.28, 88.20, *and* 112.5.
12.35	river] 1A; River 2A. *Lowercase of 1A and MSS retained also at* 21.33, 32.32, 44.40, 83.28, *and* 122.24.
13.1	protected too by privilege,] MSA; *omitted* 1A
13.3	very] MSA; *omitted* 1A
13.23	waggon] MSA; wagon 1A. *MSA spelling with* gg *retained also at* 14.13.
13.27	encumbrance] MSA; incumbrance 1A
13.37	in] MSA, 2A; in in 1A
14.36	loghouses] MSA; log houses 1A
15.5	groupe] MSA; group 1A. *Spelled with* e *as in MSA also at* 27.9, 46.19, 58.26, 58.37, *and* 95.16.
15.6	and] MSA; *omitted* 1A
15.7	leggings] MSA; leggins 1A. *MSA spelling* leggings *retained also at* 15.22, 16.25, 29.2, *and* 29.9.
15.7	moccasins] MSA; moccasons 1A. *MSA spelling* moccasins *retained also at* 15.23–24, 15.35, 24.15, 59.27, *and* 79.3.
15.9	on top] MSA; on the top 1A

15.14	West] MSA; west 1A. *Capitalized MSA form retained also at* 25.11, 25.39, 30.1, 38.10, 54.32, *and* 112.26.
15.32	A strapping] MSA; a strapping 1A
16.7	jack of all work] MSA; Jack-of-all-work 1A
16.31	woolen] MSA; woollen 1A
16.34	nor] MSA; or 1A
16.36	shewed] MSA; showed 1A. *MSA* shewed *retained also at* 25.24, 51.15, 56.14, 64.39, 78.30, 91.28, 107.26, *and* 114.12.
16.38	whiteman] MSA; white man 1A
17.3	prairies] MSA; Prairies 1A
17.8	extacies] MSA; ecstasies 1A
17.18	bedevilling] MSA; bedeviling 1A
18.38	Rangers] MSA; rangers 1A
19.14	sumach] MSA; Sumach 1A
19.15	enquire] MSA; inquire 1A. *Spelled with* e *as in MSA also at* 28.35.
19.17	lanthorn] MSA; lantern 1A
19.40	bush] MSA; brush 1A
20.7	descriptions] MSA; description 1A
20.14	recognized] MSA; recognised 1A. Z *spelling of MSA retained also at* 100.37, 119.11, *and in entries following as listed.*
20.28	surprize] MSA; surprise 1A. *Also at* 30.3, 65.34, 67.35, *and* 92.39.
20.33	surprized] MSA; surprised 1A. *Also at* 86.9.
20.36	plaintiff] MSA; plantiff 1A
21.34	Hunters] MSA; hunters 1A
22.16	enterprize] MSA; enterprise 1A. *Also at* 26.25, 48.15–16, *and* 95.3.
23.5	it] MSA; It 1A
23.12	were] MSA, 2A; was 1A
23.15	pea vine] MSA; pea-vines 1A
23.30	visitors] MSA, 2A; visiters 1A. *MSA and 2A* visitors *also at* 26.11, *and* 27.27.
24.9	caracolling] MSA; caracoling 1A
24.41	buffalos] MSA; buffaloes 1A. *MSA* os *rather than 1A* oes *also at* 61.30, 64.42, 65.1, 74.16, 74.36, 77.5, 78.32, 83.14, 86.25, 97.13, 99.39, 105.31, 105.38, *and* 106.34.
25.3	gossipped] MSA; gossiped 1A
25.4	banquetted] MSA; banqueted 1A
25.19	had] MSA, 2A; *omitted* 1A
25.30	They] MSA; they 1A

25.30	further] MSA; farther 1A
25.34	groupes] MSA; groups 1A. *MSA spelling with* e *also at* 28.25, 42.2, 42.9, 57.14, 69.25, *and* 117.35.
25.37–38	from horseback] MSA; from on horseback 1A
25.39	lay] MSA, 2A; ay 1A
26.3	encampment] MSA; camp 1A
26.18	chaunt] MSA; chant 1A. *MSA* u *spelling also at* 26.19, 26.22, 26.29, 27.23, 34.30, *and* 38.21.
26.19	accompanyment] MSA; accompaniment 1A
26.27	merryment] MSA; merriment 1A. *MSA spelling with* y *retained also at* 27.8.
27.13	for] MSA; *omitted* 1A
27.17	neighborhood of] MSA; neighbourhood of 1A; neighboring 2A
27.20	shepherd] MSA, 2A; Shepherd 1A
27.34	on] MSE; *omitted* MSA; in 1A
28.26	huge] MSA; large 1A
28.27	deer skins] MSA, 2A; deerskins 1A
28.32	horses] MSA; the horses 1A
29.9	deer skin] MSA, 2A; deerskin 1A. *Also* bear skin *of MSA and 2A at* 35.23 *rather than the 1A* bearskin.
29.13	There's] T; Theres MSA; there's 1A
29.14	He's] MSA; he's 1A
29.22	extacy] MSA; ecstasy 1A
29.29	surprizing] MSA; surprising 1A. *MSA spelling with* z *retained also at* 59.7.
29.30	Far West] MSA; far west 1A
29.33	the Buffalo] MSA; buffalo 1A
29.34	the flower] MSA; flower 1A
30.12	calculated] MSA, 2A; calcuated 1A
30.23	fire arms] MSA; his fire-arms 1A
30.37	Bee] 1A; bee 2A
31.26	cheerily] MSA; cheerfully 1A
31.27	banquetting] MSA; banqueting 1A. *MSA* tt *spelling retained also at* 34.5.
32.1	Melancholy] MSA; melancholy 1A
32.4	be all] MSA; all be 1A
32.6	Bears] MSA; bears 1A
33.6–7	tomorrow] MSA; to-morrow 1A
33.14	Nor] MSA; nor 1A
33.22	The meat] MSA; the meat 1A
33.38	slips] MSA; slices 1A
34.4	drank] MSA; drunk 1A

34.8	centinels] MSA; sentinels 1A. *MSA* c *spelling retained also at* 34.40, 54.8, 76.9, 77.40, 78.1, 78.5, 109.33, *and* 115.2.
34.12	around] MSA; round 1A
34.25	one] MSA; some 1A
34.30	methodist] 1A; Methodist 2A
35.20	East] MSA; east 1A
36.1	When] MSA; when 1A
36.8	that pure] 1A; a pure 2A
36.13	Sometimes] MSA; sometimes 1A
36.28	vollies] MSA; volleys 1A. *MSA spelling* vollies *retained also at* 39.20.
36.31	descriptions] MSA; description 1A
37.5	three] MSA; eight 1A
37.8	"hobbled"] MSA; ∧hobbled∧ 1A
37.10	far] MSA; *omitted* 1A
37.10	they] MSA; They 1A
37.12	or] 1A; nor 2A
37.16	after] MSA; afterwards 1A
37.27	M'Lellan] MSA; McLellan 1A
37.29	Elk] MSA; elk 1A. *Capitalized form of MSA retained also at* 37.33, 49.17, 50.36, *and* 52.40.
37.29	soon] MSA; seen 1A
37.35	re entered] MSA; re-entered 1A
37.40	woodmen] MSA; woodsmen 1A
37.40	lore] MSA; *omitted* 1A
37.40	They] MSA; they 1A
38.3	vein] MSA; kind 1A
38.9	barreled] MSA; barrelled 1A. *But see* 63.30.
38.20	chanticleer] MSA, 2A; chantcileer 1A
38.22	gobbling] MSA; gabbling 1A
38.29	tint] MSA; tuft 1A
38.34	enormous] MSA; *omitted* 1A
38.41	of voices] MSA; *omitted* 1A
38.42	A bear! A bear!] MSA; A bear! a bear! 1A
39.1	pole cat] MSA; polecat 1A. *Two words as in MSA also at* 39.15, 39.27, *and* 49.3.
39.5	jeers] MSA; jokes 1A
40.3	the baggage] MSA; their baggage 1A
40.8	dried] MSA; dry 1A
40.17	foot hold] MSA; foothold 1A. *Two words as in MSA also at* 117.29.
40.26	ferry men] MSA; ferrymen 1A; ferryman 2A

40.29	where it sank] MSA; when it sunk 1A
40.34	at least] MSA; *omitted* 1A
40.36	embarcation] 1A; embarkation 2A
41.20	cotton wood] MSA; cottonwood 1A; cotton-wood 2A. *Two words as in MSA also at* 83.31, 84.2, 86.23, *and* 113.30.
40.42	and propelled] MSA; *omitted* 1A
41.35	lime stone] MSA; limestone 1A
41.37	from among] 1A; among 2A
42.23	gossipping] MSA; gossiping 1A. *Spelled with* pp *as in MSA also at* 46.13, 53.17, 59.10, 108.30, *and* 110.7.
42.26	it] MSA; It 1A
42.34–35	case with] MSA, 2A; casewith 1A
43.2	to day] MSA; to-day 1A
43.14	woodman] MSA; woodsman 1A. *Omission of* s *as in MSA also at* 44.36.
43.39	It's] MSA; it's 1A
44.13	no body] MSA; nobody 1A
44.29	some how] MSA; somehow 1A. *Two words as in MSA also at* 72.39.
45.22	and baggage] 1A; *omitted* 2A
45.26	both] MSA; the 1A
45.27	green horn] MSA; greenhorn 1A. *Also* green horns *as in MSA at* 68.18.
45.36	the greatest] MSA; The greatest 1A
46.19	tones] MSA; tone 1A
46.19	the pensive] MSA; or the pensive 1A
46.28	at times] MSA; *omitted* 1A
46.33	tranquility] MSA; tranquillity 1A
46.36	skreen] MSA; screen 1A
47.5	gallopping] MSA; galloping 1A. *Spelled with* pp *as in MSA also at* 55.43, 59.36, 85.14, 102.2, *and* 111.14.
47.24	slipt] MSA; slipped 1A
47.28	part] MSA; place 1A
48.32	then] MSA; *omitted* 1A
48.34	the branches of] MSA; *omitted* 1A
49.23	that] MSA; *omitted* 1A
49.37	dem] MSA; the 1A
50.13	invincible] MSA; invisible 1A
50.16	Delawares] MSA; the Delawares 1A
50.16	incursion] MSA; excursion 1A
50.28	The Elk Camp] MSA; *omitted* 1A
51.42	Elks] MSA; elks 1A

53.29	often] MSA; *omitted* 1A
54.21	meazles] MSA; measles 1A
54.27	other wise] MSA; otherwise 1A
54.32	with] MSA, 2A; wit 1A
54.33	universal] MSA; unusual 1A
54.33	checquered] MSA; chequered 1A
55.30	depends] MSA; depended 1A
55.34	in] MSA; on 1A
56.10–11	mid day] MSA; mid-day 1A. *But see* 115.28.
56.12	"Old Ryan"] MSA; ₍old Ryan₎ 1A. *Also at* 162.8.
56.24	beside] 1A; besides 2A
58.19	tost] MSA; tossed 1A. *1A tossed rejected for the MSA tost also at* 119.14.
58.1	thundershowers] MSA; thunder showers 1A
58.11	thundergust] MSA; thunder-gust 1A
58.19	driven] MSE; driving 1A
58.23	rung] 1A; rang 2A
58.30	burthens] 1A; burdens 2A
58.38	tethered] MSA; the tethered 1A
59.9	great spirit] MSA; Great Spirit 1A
59.19	thunder bolt] MSA; thunderbolt 1A
59.27	moccasin] MSA; moccason 1A
59.42	mounted and] MSA; *omitted* 1A
60.31	Bugle] MSA; bugle 1A
61.18	Buffalo] 1A; buffalo 2A
61.23	The] MSA; the 1A
61.40	foot print] MSA; footprint 1A
62.12–13	gallopped] MSA; galloped 1A. *Spelled with* pp *as in MSA also at* 63.5, 72.36, *and* 98.30.
62.36	Encampment] MSA; encampment 1A
62.37	shewing] MSA; showing 1A. *MSA shewing retained also at* 113.20.
62.39	shewed] MSA; proved 1A
63.16	level] MSA; lure 1A
63.19	wonderful] MSA; *omitted* 1A
63.29	cracking off of] 1A; cracking of 2A
63.30	barrelled] MSA; barreled 1A
64.7	for us] MSA; *omitted* 1A
64.8	Creoles] MSA; creoles 1A
64.9	check] MSA; to check 1A
65.5	farfamed] MSA; far famed 1A. *See also* 104.3.
65.32	a head] MSA; ahead 1A. *Two words as in MSA also at* 106.43.

66.6	underwood] MSA; under wood 1A
67.23	North] MSE; north 1A
67.27	these] MSA; those 1A
67.38	imperturbable] MSA, 2A; imperturable 1A
68.18	wood craft] MSA; woodcraft 1A. *Two words as in MSA also at* 118.13.
69.16	offers] MSA; Offers 1A
70.20	One] MSA; one 1A
70.25	Camp of the Wild Horse] MSA; camp of the wild horse 1A
71.11	briar] MSA; brier 1A. Briar *as in MSA also at* 81.34.
71.19	Western Prairie] MSA; western prairie 1A
71.21	forest] 1A; the forest 2A
71.28	cross timber] MSA; Cross Timber 1A. *Lowercase form as in MSA also at* 72.3.
72.3	thence] MSA; these are 1A
72.9	right] MSA; sight 1A
72.26	The rest] MSA; the rest 1A
73.20	buffalo] MSA; buffaloes 1A
73.21	Apprehensions] MSA; apprehensions 1A
72.22	waylayed] 1A; waylaid 2A
73.29–30	in the adjacent fields] 1A; *omitted* 2A
73.39	mean time] MSA; Meantime 1A. *But see* 111.23.
74.31	Kangaroo] MSA; kangaroo 1A
75.4	"Where] MSA, 2A; ∧Where 1A
75.11	Others] MSA; others 1A
76.14	Stepping] MSA; Stopping 1A
76.25	narrative] MSA; narration 1A
76.37	Aye] MSA; Ay 1A
77.15	cried] MSA; said 1A
77.25	Bull] MSA; bull 1A
77.32	we] MSA; We 1A
77.33	Cock of the Woods] MSA; cock of the woods 1A
78.12	gossippers] MSA; gossipers 1A
78.24	the wind] MSA; The wind 1A
78.24	north west] MSA; northwest 1A
78.32	now were] MSA; were now 1A
78.35	high way] MSA; highway 1A
79.2	"trail"] MSA; ∧trail∧ 1A
79.7	after them] MSA; *omitted* 1A
79.13	We] MSA; we 1A
79.22	was] MSA, 2A; were 1A
80.17	should] MSA; would 1A

80.23	larger] MSA; large 1A
80.25	Bear] MSA; bear 1A
80.34	woefully] MSA; wofully 1A
81.5	buffalos] MSA; Buffaloes 1A
81.11	some] MSA; Some 1A
81.22	was] MSA; were 1A
81.26	brush wood] MSA; brushwood 1A. *See also* 88.24.
81.27	huge] 1A; large huge 2A
81.30	hills] MSA; hill 1A
81.33	bush] MSA; birch 1A
81.35	rejoined] MSA; joined 1A
82.1	to be] 1A; *omitted* 2A
82.28	Buffaloes] MSA; buffaloes 1A. *Capitalized MSA form retained also at* 97.32.
83.16	much] 1A; *omitted* 2A
83.19	Buffalo Camp] MSA; buffalo camp 1A
83.23–24	cross timbers] MSA; Cross Timber 1A
83.24	abound] MSA; abounds 1A
83.28	enameled] MSA; enamelled 1A
83.35	disposed] MSA; dispersed 1A
84.8	maneuvre] MSA; manoeuvre 1A
84.15	hunters] MSA; *omitted* 1A
84.16	Wherever] MSA; Whenever 1A
84.28	woods] MSA; wood 1A
84.30	to advance] MSA; advance 1A
84.30	shew] MSA; show 1A. *MSA* shew *retained also at* 105.27, 108.26, *and* 108.27.
85.6	Jack o lantern] MSA; Jack-o'-lantern 1A
85.31	on] MSA; upon 1A
85.37	forefeet] MSA; fore feet 1A
86.7	while] MSA; when 1A
86.35	mistletoe] MSE; misletoe 1A
87.23	his] MSA; His 1A
87.42	somewhat] MSA; *omitted* 1A
88.1	Pacificator] MSA; pacificator 1A
88.3	Father] MSA; father 1A. *Capitalized form as in MSA retained also at* 88.15.
88.4	Red] MSA; red 1A
88.13	enquired] MSA; inquired 1A
88.24	brush wood] MSA; brush-wood 1A; brushwood 2A
88.32	follow] MSA; have followed 1A
89.4–5	wood land] MSA; woodland 1A
89.10	Our] MSA; our 1A

89.15	penthouse] MSA; pent-house 1A
89.27	head] MSA; heads 1A
90.17	His] MSA; This 1A
90.22	rarely] MSA; scarcely 1A
90.28	withstanding] MSA; notwithstanding 1A
90.31	enured] MSA; inured 1A
91.7	had] 1A; *omitted* 2A
91.33	bruizes] MSA; bruises 1A
92.13	great] MSE; *omitted* 1A
92.13	relatives] MSA; relations 1A. *Corrected as in MSA also at 92.30, 94.11, 94.17, and 96.14.*
92.35	Surgeon] MSA; surgeon 1A
92.37	procure] MSA, 2A; promise 1A
92.40	Dat] MSA; dat 1A
92.43	Doctor] MSA; doctor 1A
93.23	play things] MSA; playthings 1A
93.29	Nick a nansa] MSA; Nickanansa 1A
94.19	alive] MSA; alone 1A
94.19	Come] MSA; come 1A
94.34	homewards] MSA; homeward 1A
95.20	faun] MSA; fawn 1A. *MSA faun retained also at 95.22.*
95.30	for] MSA; For 1A
96.24–25	"These . . . deer" . . . "have . . . kind."] MSA; ∧These . . . deer∧ . . . ∧have . . . kind.∧ 1A
96.34	29.th] MSA; 29. 1A
96.38	bawling] MSA; brawling 1A
96.41	loading] MSA, 2A; leading 1A
97.11	on] MSA; in 1A
97.24	The Great] MSA; the great 1A
*97.31	out to us] MSA; out to 1A; out 2A
98.8	maneuvres] MSA; maneouvres 1A
98.30	missed] 1A; it missed 2A
98.38	pistolshot] MSA; pistol shot 1A. *One word as in MSA retained also at 101.34.*
*99.4	the tufted end] MSA; tufted and 1A
99.14	horses] MSA; horse 1A
99.14	out of reach] MSA; out of the reach 1A
99.25	grounds] MSA; ground 1A
99.33	fet lock] MSA; fetlock 1A
100.2	he] MSE; *omitted* MSA; we 1A
100.3	laying] MSA; leaving 1A
100.6	off] MSA; *omitted* 1A

100.14–15	land marks] MSA; landmarks 1A. *Two words as in MSA also at* 103.24 *and* 119.12.
100.31	Sometimes] MSA; sometimes 1A
100.34	whine] MSA, 1A *setting b*, 2A; wine 1A *setting a*
101.3	farmhouse] MSA, 2A; farm house 1A. *But* farm house *at* 121.42.
101.7	nightfall] MSA, 2A; night-fall 1A
101.28	heave] MSA; bear 1A
101.30	queue] 1A; cue 2A
101.30	pantomime] MSA; pantomine 1A
101.38	L——] MSA; L. 1A. *MSA usage retained also at* 105.27.
102.4	could] MSA, 2A; would 1A
102.20–21	piece meal] MSA; piecemeal 1A
102.23	and croaking] MSA; croaking 1A
103.12	Amateur] MSA; amateur 1A
103.20	cruizing] MSA; cruising 1A
103.26	woodsman] 1A; woodman 2A
103.29	We] MSA; we 1A
103.32	lea] 1A; lee 2A
103.34	fire wood] MSA; firewood 1A
103.38	upon] MSA; on 1A
104.1	Roaring] MSA; roaring 1A
104.3	farfamed] MSA; far-famed 1A
104.22	broad side] MSA; broadside 1A
104.40	there] MSA; There 1A
104.43	day break] MSA; daybreak 1A. *Two words as in MSA also at* 112.39 *and* 115.6.
105.23	cruize] MSA; cruise 1A
105.28	late] MSA; little 1A
106.23	Indians] MSA; the Indians 1A
107.16	dinted] MSA; dented 1A
107.34	cool] MSA; cold 1A
107.36	pockethandkerchief] MSA; pocket handerchief 1A
107.43	day light] MSA; daylight 1A
107.42	awake] MSA; wake 1A
108.22	Prairie Dog] MSA; prairie dog 1A
109.1	Prairie Dogs] MSA; prairie dogs 1A
109.10	suffer] MSA; suffered 1A
109.17	rattle snake] MSA; rattlesnake 1A. *But* rattlesnakes *at* 109.2.
109.27	remark] MSA; remarks 1A

109.37   summerset] MSA; somerset 1A. *MSA* summerset *re-*
                tained also at 110.3.
110.29   *the harbinger*] T; ~ ~ *no underlining* MSA; *binger*
                1A
110.33   as of] MSA; as 1A
111.14   fore thought] MSA; forethought 1A
111.21   River] MSA; river 1A
111.23   meantime] MSA, 2A; mean time 1A
111.32   beside] MSA; besides 1A
111.35   southeast] MSA, 2A; south-east 1A. *But* south east *at*
                111.3.
113.4   Little] MSA; the Little 1A
113.17   sank] MSA; sunk 1A
113.19   buffaloes] MSA; *omitted* 1A
113.21   our] MSA; Our 1A
113.36   keeping] MSA; kept 1A
114.5   again] MSA; *omitted* 1A
114.38   sweet] MSA; secret 1A
115.28   midday] MSA; mid-day 1A
115.31   before] MSA; since 1A
115.31   thicket] MSA; thickets 1A
116.1   at] MSA; At 1A
116.7–8   over head] MSA; over-head 1A [*end of line*];
                overhead 2A.
116.13   game. In fact] 1A; game; for 2A
116.18   providence] MSA; Providence 1A
117.6   beside] MSA, 2A; besides 1A
117.12   poney] MSA; pony 1A. *MSA spelling* ey *retained also*
                at 117.19 *and* 117.22.
117.40   the stream] MSA; this stream 1A
118.31   fort] MSA; Fort 1A. *But see* 119.17.
118.36   wayfaring] MSA, 2A; way-faring 1A
118.37   stoney] MSA; stony 1A
118.38   mirey] MSA; miry 1A. *But see* 119.2.
119.14   tempest tost] MSA; tempest-tossed 1A
119.17   Fort] MSA; fort 1A
119.43   moon light] MSA; moon-light 1A [*end of line*];
                moonlight 2A
120.1   chrystals] MSA; crystals 1A
120.21   rouse] MSA; raise 1A. *MSA* rouse *retained also at*
                121.14.
120.32   woods] MSA; wood 1A
121.1   feebly] MSA; *omitted* 1A

121.11   lee way]   MSA; leeway 1A
121.24   cauldron]   MSA; caldron 1A. *MSA spelling with* u
              retained also at 121.26.
121.29   her]   MSA; our 1A
122.24   river]   1A; River 2A

                              Abbotsford

125.2   To _____ _____]   MSA; *omitted* 1A
125.18   post chaise]   MSA; postchaise 1A
126.14   irongrey]   MSA; iron-grey 1A; iron-gray 2A [*MSE
              lacking*]
126.14   of a most]   1A; of most 2A [*MSE lacking*]
126.35   it]   MSA; It 1A
127.2   Tomorrow]   MSA; To-morrow 1A. Tomorrow *as in
              MSA retained also at* 166.37.
127.10   anecdotes]   MSA; anecdote 1A
127.16   He]   MSA; he 1A
128.7   stout]   MSA; Stout 1A
128.7   monk]   MSA; Monk 1A
128.13   oriel]   MSA; Oriel 1A
128.17   afterward]   MSA; afterwards 1A
129.26   visitor]   MSA; visiter 1A. Visitor *as in MSA retained
              also at* 151.30.
130.4   visitors]   MSA; visiters 1A. Visitors *as in MSA retained
              also at* 103.7, 154.37, 163.37, 164.26, *and* 166.21.
130.8   the moon]   MSE; moon MSA; morn 1A.
130.9   na']   MSA; na$_\wedge$ 1A
130.9   ance]   MSA; aince 1A
130.12   So]   MSA; so 1A
130.18   shew]   MSA; show 1A. *Spelled with* e *as in MSA also
              at* 139.33, 146.21, 160.1, *and* 164.29.
130.22   And]   MSA; and 1A
131.9   Boatswain]   MSA; boatswain 1A. *Capitalized as in
              MSA also at* 131.12 *and* 131.16.
131.28   down cast]   MSA; downcast 1A
132.2   Every]   MSA; every 1A
132.3   dependant]   1A; dependent 2A
132.31   if]   MSA; If 1A
133.2   I first]   MSA; first I 1A [*MSE lacking*]
*133.8–9   Scotland . . . it]   MSE; It 1A
133.9   chaunted]   MSA; chanted 1A
133.27   Bonnie]   MSA; bonnie 1A

135.6	surprize] MSA; surprise 1A. Z *spelling of MSA re-tained also at* 143.17.
136.26	bug bear] MSA; bugbear 1A
136.31	surprized] MSA; surprised 1A. Z *spelling of MSA re-tained also at* 148.10.
136.34	enquired] MSA; inquired 1A
137.35	frolick] MSA; frolic 1A
138.5	toilette] MSA; toilet 1A
138.6	hillside] MSA; hill side 1A
138.14	terrier] MSA; *omitted* 1A
138.33	And] MSA; and 1A
138.35	ascendancy] MSA; ascendency 1A
139.10	famous] MSA; famed 1A
139.17	clannish] MSA, 2A; clanish 1A. *MSA spelling with* nn *retained also at* 162.37.
139.40	present] MSA; persons 1A
140.8	reliques] MSA; relics 1A. *MSA also at* 141.12, 143.39, 145.1, *and* 158.26.
140.8	scymitar] MSA; cimeter 1A
140.9	Flodden field] MSA; Floddenfield 1A
140.17	that time at] MSE; *omitted* 1A
141.28	king] MSA; King 1A
141.39	waited] MSE; wanted 1A
142.13	enquiries] MSA; inquiries 1A
142.21	hardheaded] MSA; hard-headed 1A
*142.27	young lady] MSE; Barons young lady MSA; baron's young lady 1A
142.39	balancing] MSA; labouring 1A
144.9	There] MSA; there 1A
114.15	honest] MSA; *omitted* 1A
144.19	on] MSE; of 1A
144.20	relique] MSA; relic 1A. *MSA spelling retained also at* 159.28 *and* 159.32.
144.28	kindled] 1A; twinkled 2A
145.8	neighbors'] MSE; neighbors∧ 1A
145.19	law suit] MSA; lawsuit 1A
145.24	descriptions] MSA; description 1A
146.25	stories] MSE; stories conversation MSA; conversation 1A
146.25	to them] MSE; *omitted* 1A
146.28	Laird] MSA; laird 1A
147.1	at least] MSA; *omitted* 1A
147.8	to these novels] MSE; their merits 1A

147.19	Papa's] T; Papa‸s MSA; papa's 1A
147.31	a hereditary] 1A; an hereditary 2A
147.32	petty] MSA; *omitted* 1A
148.1	enquire] MSA; inquire 1A
148.4	Barbarians] MSA; barbarians 1A
148.29	in a letter] MSE; in letter 1A
148.30	relatives] MSA; relations 1A
148.40	recognize] MSA; recognise 1A
149.8	Fairy] MSA; fairy 1A. *Capitalized MSA form also at* 149.9 *and* 161.11.
149.10	Bogle] MSA; bogle 1A
149.18	Tree] MSA; tree 1A
149.26	till] MSA; til 1A
149.29	fairy] MSA; *omitted* 1A
150.13	over] MSA; on 1A
150.19	gripe] MSA; grip 1A
150.29	Well! Well] MSA; Well, well 1A
150.35	shewed] MSA; showed 1A. *MSA* shewed *retained also at* 151.2, 157.12, *and* 157.25.
151.3	castrametation] MSA; castramatation 1A
151.10	Gammell] MSA; Gammel 1A
151.13	recognized] MSA; recognised 1A
151.15	recognizing] MSA; recognising 1A
152.21	common place] MSA; commonplace 1A
152.22	over run] MSA; overrun 1A
153.17	shewing] MSA; showing 1A. *MSA* shewing *retained also at* 166.8.
156.16	wassell] MSE, 1A; wassail 2A [*MSA lacking*]
156.22	woe] MSE, 2A; wo 1A [*MSA lacking*]
157.1	any] MSE; and 1A; *omitted* 2A
157.22	hardship] 1A; hardships 2A
157.39	pedlar] MSA; pedler 1A
158.31	pleasantest] 1A; pleasant 2A
159.20	fables] MSE; fable 1A
160.2	the theme] MSE; them 1A
160.6	courtesies and] MSE; *omitted* 1A
160.21	ash] MSE; ashes 1A
160.27	Galla water] MSA; the Galla water 1A
160.31	Two] MSE; two 1A
161.24	praize] MSA; praise 1A
161.31	immoveable] 1A; immovable 2A
162.3	Sea] MSA; sea 1A
164.1	byestander] MSA; bystander 1A

164.20	eye brows] MSA; eyebrows 1A
165.10	It] MSE; it 1A
165.37	where] MSA; when 1A
166.5	meagre] MSA; meager 1A
166.10	And] MSA; and 1A
166.14	him] MSA; *omitted* 1A
166.18	haphazard] MSA; hap-hazard 1A
166.30	set] 1A; *omitted* 2A
166.34	It] MSA; it 1A
167.2	So] MSA; so 1A
167.4	during] MSA; During 1A
167.5	And] MSA; and 1A
167.18	appreciated] MSE, 1A; appreciating 2A [*MSA lacking*]
167.24	and opinions] MSA; no one's opinions 1A
*167.31–32	and . . . merits] MSA; *omitted* 1A
*168.15	guard] MSE, 1A; regard 2A [*MSA lacking*]
168.20	on] MSA; in 1A
168.20	green] MSA, 2A; given 1A

Newstead Abbey

For Newstead Abbey MSE is lacking for entries 197.35 through 200.22, 213.20 through 214.11, and 220.25 through 229.10.

171.21	conduct] MSE; its conduct 1A [*MSA lacking*]
171.32	beard] MSA; Beard 1A. *Lowercase as in MSA retained also at* 172.11, 179.22, 196.13, *and* 197.4.
172.5	centinels] MSA; sentinels 1A
172.6	burnished] MSA; burnish'd 1A
172.11	little] MSA; Little 1A. *Lowercase as in MSA retained also at* 179.22, 196.13, 196.20, 197.3, *and* 220.19.
172.12	gossipping] MSA; gossiping 1A. *Spelled with* pp *as in MSA also at* 192.21.
172.13	The] MSA; the 1A
172.39	Lady] MSA, 2A; lady 1A
172.41	Ladyship] MSA; ladyship 1A
173.28	Poet] MSA; poet 1A
174.22	gray-worn] MSA, 2A; gray worn 1A
174.24	cloysters] MSA; cloisters 1A. *MSA* cloysters *retained also at* 175.33–34, 179.1, 179.3, 179.38, 194.7, 194.14, 194.19, 222.17, *and* 232.26.
174.27	gew gaw] MSA; gewgaw 1A

175.37	Old Lord] MSA; old lord 1A
176.1	feelings] MSA; feeling 1A
176.4–5	school mate] MSA; schoolmate 1A
176.24	18th] MSA; 18 1A
176.25	dear] MSA; Dear 1A
176.26	Eve] MSA; eve 1A
*176.31	&] MSA; and 1A
176.32	your] MSA; *omitted* 1A
176.36	4th or 5th] MSA; fourth or fifth 1A
176.37	after-life] MSE; after life 1A [*MSA lacking*]
176.37	schoolfellow] MSE, 2A; school-fellow 1A [*MSA lacking*]
176.44	& affectly] MSA; and affectionately 1A
177.3	visitors] MSA, 2A; visiters 1A. *Corrected as in MSA and 2A also at* 196.2, 203.34, *and* 213.3.
177.5	relique] MSA; relic 1A. *MSA spelling retained also at* 181.8, 213.20, *and* 214.10.
177.6	any wise] MSA, 2A; anywise 1A
177.17	holydays] 1A; holidays 2A
177.23	post chaise] MSA; postchaise 1A. *Two words as in MSA also at* 178.10.
178.16	visitor] MSA, 2A; visiter 1A. *Corrected as in MSA and 2A also at* 222.10, *and* 225.18.
178.39	Spared] MSA; Spar'd 1A
179.2	walk] MSA; walks 1A
179.21	gothic] MSA; Gothic 1A
179.23	canvas] MSA, 2A; canvass 1A
179.28	inclosed] MSA, 2A; enclosed 1A
179.29	ballustrades] MSA; balustrades 1A. *MSA ll spelling retained* also at 181.39, 184.18, 200.39, *and* 203.39.
179.32	about] MSA; almost 1A
179.43	baron] MSA; friar 1A
180.1	join'd] MSA; joined 1A
180.3	combin'd] MSA; combined 1A
180.4	Form'd] MSA; Formed 1A
*180.24	Goblen] MSE; goblen MSA; goblin 1A
180.29	variously] MSA; various 1A
180.31	moveable] 1A; movable 2A
180.32	towering] MSA; *omitted* 1A
180.34	toilette] MSA; toilet 1A
181.5	other a lady] MSA; other was a lady 1A
181.16	hyeroglyphics] MSA; hieroglyphics 1A
182.21	spread] MSA; spreads 1A

182.23	orizons] MSA; orisons 1A. *MSA spelling retained also at* 182.23.
182.37	"The] MSA; "the 1A
183.2	These] 1A; The 2A
183.9	lord's devils] T; lord‸s devils MSA; Lord‸s devils MSE; Lord's Devils 1A
183.12	surprize] MSA; surprise 1A. *MSA spelling retained* also at 193.43 *and* 226.21.
183.35	forever] MSA; for ever 1A. *One word as in MSA also at* 229.18.
184.34	rear'd] MSA; reared 1A
184.37	ballustrade] MSA; balustrade 1A
185.2	sounds] MSA; kinds 1A
185.26	Time] MSA; time 1A
185.32	dishevell'd] MSA; dishevelled 1A
185.33	woe] MSA, 2A; wo 1A
186.4	dependants] MSA; dependents 1A
186.6	funeral] MSA; *omitted* 1A
186.18	reliques] MSA; relics 1A. *MSA spelling retained also at* 201.29, 201.34, *and* 214.24.
186.26	bear's skin] T; bears skin MSA; bearskin 1A
186.30	dragon] MSA; Dragon 1A. *Lowercase as in MSA retrained also at* 187.15.
186.30	has] 1A; had 2A
186.33	morrice dancers] 1A; morris-dancers 2A
186.33	gaily] 1A; gayly 2A
187.36	grown] MSA; green 1A
187.37	may] MSA; May 1A
188.9	shewed] MSA; showed 1A
188.13	The Young] MSA; the young 1A
118.21	comprize] MSA; comprise 1A
188.24	yet] 1A; *omitted* 2A
189.11	I] MSA; that I 1A
189.16–17	Old Lord] MSA; old lord 1A
189.27	High Admiral] MSA; high admiral 1A
189.35	During] MSA; during 1A
189.39	If] MSA; if 1A
189.41	there] MSA; *omitted* 1A
190.1	old] MSA; *omitted* 1A
190.15	honest] 1A; *omitted* 2A
190.22	But] MSA; but 1A
191.7	You] MSA; you 1A
191.26	a humble] MSA; an humble 1A

192.2	sopha] 1A; sofa 2A. *But see the List of Rejected Substantives,* 220.25.
192.17	well aday] MSA; well-a-day 1A
193.1	Lordship] MSA; lordship 1A
193.10	fire place] MSA; fire-place 1A; fireplace 2A. *Two words as in MSA also at 193.13, 193.15, and 196.20–21.*
193.13	Still] MSA; still 1A
194.16	superstitiously] MSA, 2A; stuperstitiously 1A
194.23	illstarred] MSA; ill-starred 1A
194.23	marriage] MSA, 2A; marrage 1A
194.25	fryar] MSA; friar 1A. *Also* fryars *as in MSA at* 214.1.
196.4	Kitty] MSA; Sally 1A
196.16	its] MSA; the 1A
196.18	in passing] MSA; on passing 1A
196.29	Knight and christian dame, and paynim] MSA; knight and Christian dame, and Paynim 1A
196.30	glared] MSA; gazed 1A
196.38	locks] MSA; looks 1A
196.39	canvas] MSA, 2A; canvass 1A
196.41	imaged] MSA; mingled 1A
197.13	Anne] MSA; Ann 1A. *Corrected to MSA spelling also at* 202.37.
*197.35	bowers] 1A; flowers 2A
198.27	at a] 1A; of a 2A
198.36	schoolboy] MSA; school-boy 1A
199.19	land mark] MSA; landmark 1A
199.29	cornfields] MSA; corn fields 1A; corn-fields 2A
199.33	fix'd] MSA; fixed 1A
199.40	on] MSA; in 1A
200.7	towers] MSA; towns 1A
200.21	Gate House] MSA; gate house 1A
200.22	barbican] MSA; barbacan 1A
201.9	removed] MSA; had removed 1A
201.14–15	comprized] MSA; comprised 1A
201.17	*years.* I] MSA; *years,* and 1A
201.27	hall] MSA; Hall 1A
201.28	jerkins] MSA, 2A; jerkens 1A
201.35	shewn] MSA; shown 1A. *MSA* shewn *retained also at* 207.21 *and* 219.36.
201.38	fourfooted] MSA; four-footed 1A
202.2	He] MSA; he 1A
202.12	phraze] MSA; phrase 1A
202.41	flowerplots] MSA; flower plots 1A

203.4	waste] MSA; the waste 1A
203.5	these] MSA; them 1A
203.28	simplehearted] MSA; simple hearted 1A
204.12	ruinous] MSA; a ruinous 1A
204.30	Lady] MSA; lady 1A
204.30	re-enter'd] MSA; re-entered 1A
204.41	Retired] MSA; Return'd 1A
205.28	surprized] MSA; surprised 1A. *MSA spelling retained also at* 213.5 *and* 226.27.
205.31	devotion] 1A; devotions 2A
205.34	dream] MSA; Dream 1A
205.35	emotions] MSA; emotion 1A
206.22	hope] MSA; love 1A
206.33	fabled] MSA, 2A; flabled 1A
207.6	expelled] MSA; expell'd 1A
207.7	moment] MSA, 2A; monent 1A
208.1	woe] MSA; wo 1A
208.7	crost] MSA; cross'd 1A
208.20	that] 1A; who 2A
208.26	Upward] MSA; Upwards 1A
208.35	smil'd] MSA; smiled 1A
209.1	*I*] MSA; I 1A
209.34	allured] MSA; attuned 1A
210.10	*lid*] MSA; *lids* 1A
210.36	her] MSA; but her 1A
211.37	heartburnings] MSA; heart burnings 1A
212.33	The] MSA; the 1A
212.36	mediterranean] MSA; Mediterranean 1A
213.2	enquiries] MSA; inquiries 1A. *Spelled with* e *as in MSA also at* 226.43, *and* 232.13
213.11	barque] MSA; bark 1A
213.20	brazier] MSA; brasier 1A
214.4	Eagle] MSA; eagle 1A
214.11	tales] 1A; the tales 2A
214.25	Forest] MSA; forest 1A
214.34	pedlar] MSA; pedler 1A
214.35	its uncouth] 1A; is uncouth 2A
214.37	revellings] MSA; revelling 1A
215.10	The Pilgrim] MSA; the Pilgrim 1A
215.28	survivors] MSA; survivers 1A
216.4	the Ravenshead] 1A; Ravenshead 2A
216.19	the pheasant] MSA; pheasant 1A
216.27	Bishops] MSA; bishops 1A

217.4	jack daws] MSA; jackdaws 1A
217.15	enclosures] 1A; inclosures 2A
217.22	held] 1A; keld 2A
217.31	when] MSA; When 1A
217.40	gazehound] MSA; greyhound 1A
218.31	his] 1A; this 2A
219.5	agriculturalist] MSA; agriculturist 1A
219.6	wood land] MSA; woodland 1A. *Two words as in MSA also at* 224.23.
219.7	turned] 1A; be turned 2A
219.8	Merry] MSA; Merrie 1A
219.10	Oh] MSA; O 1A
219.13	propensity] MSA; propensities 1A
219.29	stalwart] MSA, 2A; stalworth 1A
220.14	all] MSA; *omitted* 1A
220.25	sopha] MSA; sofa 1A
220.27	"fancy"] MSA; ₍fancy₎ 1A
220.28	in] MSA; at 1A
220.30	bed chamber] MSA; bedchamber 1A
220.30	The Rook] MSA; the Rook 1A
220.37	pinnacles] 1A; pinnacle 2A
221.12	daily] 1A; *omitted* 2A
221.20	loth] MSA, 2A; loath 1A
221.29	fainter] MSA; frantic 1A
221.31	where] MSA; when 1A
221.31	silenced] MSA; silent 1A
222.14	honeymoon] MSA; honey-moon 1A. *MSA reading* honeymoon *retained also at* 225.35.
224.7	moaning] MSA; *omitted* 1A
224.32–33	name, I] MSA; name, as I 1A
225.18	enquired] MSA; inquired 1A
225.24	little] MSA; Little 1A. *Lowercase* little *as in MSA also at* 225.26, 225.26, 225.35, 226.14, 226.20, 226.26, 226.31, 227.31, 229.12, 230.5, 237.26, 238.14, *and* 238.24.
225.24	went] MSA; passed 1A
225.37	daily visits] MSA; visits daily 1A
225.38	boddice] MSA; bodice 1A
226.25	rencountre] MSA; rencounter 1A
226.35	which] 1A; whhich 2A
226.42	its] 1A; the 2A
227.8	fragile] MSA; *omitted* 1A
227.17	checquered] MSA; chequered 1A
227.29	Edifice] MSA; edifice 1A

228.8	enflame] MSA; inflame 1A
228.10	That] MSA; And 1A
229.10	and beautiful] MSA; *omitted* 1A
229.42	addresses of her relatives] MSA; address of her relations 1A
230.2	enquiry] MSA; inquiry 1A. *MSA* e *spelling retained also at* 233.38 *and* 234.30.
230.3	ensure] MSA; insure 1A
232.1	it] MSA; It 1A
232.4	Sir] MSA; sir 1A
232.28	Where] MSA; When 1A
232.29	lovely] MSA; lonely 1A
232.38	chance] MSA; chanced 1A
232.39	foliage] MSA, 2A; foilage 1A
233.6	pacquet] MSA; packet 1A. *MSA* pacquet *retained also at* 233.11
233.17	powerful] MSA; painful 1A
233.32	pretenses] MSA; pretences 1A
233.33	withdrawn entirely] MSA; entirely withdrawn 1A
234.5	now] MSA; *omitted* 1A
234.40	to] 1A; as to 2A
234.31	blameable] 1A; blamable 2A
234.35	forward to] 1A; forward 2A
234.36	now] MSA; *omitted* 1A
235.34	generous] MSA, 2A; geneorus 1A
236.12	exposes] MSA; exposed 1A
236.14	another] 1A; another letter 2A
236.38	poor] MSA; *omitted* 1A
237.13	sweet] MSA; secret 1A
*237.16	minds] MSA; mind 1A
237.17	Could] MSA; could 1A
237.33	Dear Madam,] MSA; *omitted* 1A
237.39	intended] MSA; *omitted* 1A
237.40–41	accommodation] MSA, 2A; accomodation 1A
238.7	engrossed] MSA; engaged 1A
238.9	Dear Madam] MSA; dear madam 1A
238.13	despatched] 1A; dispatched 2A
238.18	hands] MSA; hand 1A

Legends of the Conquest of Spain

241.4	Conquest] MS; conquest 1A
241.6	envelloped] MS; enveloped 1A. *MS form retained also at* 260.7.

241.19   enquire]   MS; inquire 1A
241.27   Oriental]   MS; oriental 1A. *Capitalized form as in MS*
                also at 242.16, 246.7, 253.28, 269.29, *and* 337.7.
242.9   enterprize]   MS; enterprise. 1A. Z *spelling of MS re-*
                tained also at 242.14, 243.27, 268.28, 270.19, 272.13,
                299.4, 302.40, 310.37, 326.25, 327.8, 327.13, 327.40,
                333.23, *and* 335.36.
242.28   acknowledged]   MS; acknowleged 1A
243.7   Carthaginians]   MS; Carthagenians 1A
243.14   goths]   MS; Goths 1A. *Lowercase* goths *as in MS re-*
                tained also at 243.23, 244.17, 252.35, 265.17, 265.32,
                303.14, 314.29, 317.36, 319.12, *and* 328.29.
243.19   comprizing]   MS; comprising 1A. Z *Spelling as in MS*
                retained also at 328.2 *and* 330.37.
243.20   gotica]   MS; Gotica 1A
243.20   gaul]   MS; Gaul 1A
243.23   the Iberians]   MS; Iberians 1A
244.3   gothic]   MS; Gothic 1A. *Lowercase* gothic *as in MS*
                retained also at 244.9, 244.30, 245.9, 245.17, 247.5,
                247.8, 247.18, 252.11, 252.39, 253.29, 265.24, 273.29,
                273.35, 277.23, 281.39, 282.1, 286.30, 286.38, 291.6,
                292.15, 293.24, 293.31, 294.8, 294.14, 304.19, 304.35,
                and 308.5.
244.5   Bishops]   MS; bishops 1A. *Capitalized form as in MS*
                also at 244.22
244.6   the nobles]   MS; nobles 1A
244.26   encrease]   MS; increase 1A. *MS* e *spelling retained also*
                at 273.14 *and* 345.10.
244.34   shewed]   MS; showed 1A. *MS* shewed *retained also at*
                249.22, 259.5, *and* 338.38.
244.37   Duke]   MS; duke 1A
244.40   providence]   MS; Providence 1A. *Lowercase as in MS*
                also at 262.29.
245.31   Episcopal]   MS; episcopal 1A
245.36   Papal]   MS; papal 1A
246.16   plowshare]   MS; plough-share 1A. *End of line.*
246.23   government]   MS; Government 1A
246.31   enured]   MS; inured 1A
247.24   evil]   MS; evils 1A
247.35   Governor]   MS; governor 1A. *Capitalized MS form re-*
                tained also at 336.38.
247.39   Bishop]   MS; bishop 1A. *Capitalized   MS   form   re-*

tained also at 268.8 268.12, 268.36, 281.33, 282.23, 284.17, 285.42, 287.40, 288.3, 289.1, 289.2, *and* 289.23.

247.40   Archepiscopal]   MS; archepiscopal 1A

248.1   See]   MS; see 1A

248.12   entrusted]   MS; intrusted 1A. *MS* e *spelling retained also at* 332.28.

248.19   North]   MS; north 1A. *Capitalized MS form retained also at* 342.41.

248.26   pennon]   MS; banner 1A

248.36   enterprizes]   MS; enterprises 1A. Z *spelling as in MS retained also at* 326.14–15.

249.4   chronicler]   MS; Chronicler 1A

249.13   moorish]   MS; Moorish 1A. *Lowercase form as in MS also at* 249.20, 250.18, 251.20, 254.35, *and* 268.10.

249.23   galliot]   MS; galiot 1A. *MS* ll *retained also at* 249.27.

249.30   moors]   MS; Moors 1A. *Lowercase form as in* **MS** *retained also at* 249.34, 269.3, 292.20, 297.33, 309.26, 353.18, 353.19, 353.29, 353.31, *and* 356.35.

249.39   King]   MS; king 1A. *Capitalized form as in MS retained also at* 249.40, 251.29, *and* 281.31.

250.21   Orient]   MS; orient 1A

250.23   palfrey]   MS; palfry 1A

250.33   Behold]   MS; behold 1A

250.34   Consider]   MS; consider 1A

251.6   down cast]   MS; downcast 1A

251.11   at]   MS; in 1A

251.32   dispuesto]   MS; dispuesta 1A

251.34   Rey]   MS; rey 1A

251.38   Conq'st]   MS; conq'st 1A

252.4   Queen]   MS; queen 1A. *Capitalized form as in MS retained also at* 253.16, 254.5, 254.8, 254.12, 254.22, 254.30, 255.20, 256.14, 256.27, 280.30, *and*   281.25.

252.4   splendor]   MS; splendour 1A

252.7–8   connexions]   MS; connexion 1A

252.15   Royal]   MS; royal 1A

252.39   antechambers]   MS; anti-chambers 1A

252.39   kings]   MS; Kings 1A

254.4   ancient]   MS; an old 1A

254.6   Eastern]   MS; eastern 1A. *Capitalized form as in MS retained also at* 335.7

254.30   Mauritania]   MS; Mauritanea 1A. *MS spelling retained also at* 255.10.

255.29	encreased] MS; increased 1A. *Spelled with* e *as in MS also at* 259.10, 288.18, 298.19, *and* 350.37.
255.36	Dost] MS; dost 1A
256.5	Riches] MS; riches 1A
257.7	shews] MS; shows 1A. *MSA* shews *retained also at* 298.43.
257.31	Roderick] MS; Don Roderick 1A
257.33	spirit] MS; spirits 1A
258.15	cinctured] MS; cintured 1A
258.17	oh] MS; O 1A
258.19	Strong] MS; strong 1A
259.1	some time] MS; sometime 1A
259.8	Beware] MS; beware 1A
259.9	There] MS; there 1A
259.15	Was] MS; was 1A
259.24	counsel] MS; council 1A. *MS* counsel *retained also at* 266.19.
260.5	Friar] MS; friar 1A. *Capitalized MS form retained also at* 260.41 *and* 264.33.
260.30	portal] MS; portals 1A
261.21	immoveable] MS; immovable 1A. *MS* immoveable *retained also at* 263.41.
262.9	encrusted] MS; incrusted 1A
262.28	Desist] MS; desist 1A
262.39	scymetars] MS; scimitars 1A. *Spelled* scymetars *as in MS also at* 277.14, 281.10, 294.8, *and* 309.14.
264.3	overflowed] MS; flowed above 1A
264.6	of drums] MS; of the drums 1A
264.40	most] MS; *omitted* 1A
264.41	speak out] MS; speak nothing but 1A
265.10	East] MS; east 1A. *Capitalized MS form retained also at* 342.40.
265.11	Empire] MS; empire 1A
265.12	Walid] MS; Waled 1A. *MS* i *spelling retained also at* 271.18, 302.28, 339.27, *and* 340.26.
265.20	general] MS; General 1A
*265.20	Noseir] MS; Nosier 1A. *MS* ei *spelling retained also at* 268.26, 269.10, 270.31, *and* 294.20.
265.25	sat] MS; set 1A
266.6	rejoycings] MS; rejoicings 1A
266.12	lady] MS; Lady 1A
266.29	Infidels] MS; infidels 1A
266.37	over] MS; *omitted* 1A

267.39   pacified]   MS; satisfied 1A
267.39   Vengeance]   MS; vengeance 1A
268.16   relative]   MS; relation 1A
268.26   insufficient]   MS; sufficient 1A
269.18   moor]   MS; Moor 1A. *Lowercase form as in MS re-
                tained also at 293.18.*
269.35   goth]   MS; Goth 1A. *Lowercase form as in MS retained
                also at 322.9.*
270.6   Strait]   MS; strait 1A. *Capitalized form as in MS re-
                tained also at 318.22.*
270.20   scymetar]   MS; scimitar 1A. *MS spelling* scymetar *re-
                tained also* at 279.26, 302.10, 312.18, *and* 325.34.
270.27   easy]   MS; easily 1A
270.33   traytor]   MS; traitor 1A. *MS y spelling retained also
                at* 275.34, 275.37, 278.20, 279.3, 281.29, 294.30, 296.6,
                306.42, 307.3, 308.33, 311.10, 314.28, 314.34, 320.4, *and*
                350.5.
271.2   dispatched]   MS; despatched 1A. *MS i spelling re-
                tained also at* 275.18, 288.8, 318.14, *and* 336.14.
271.4   el]   MS; *omitted* 1A
272.4   West]   MS; west 1A. *Capitalized form as in MS re-
                tained also at* 336.9, 338.3, *and* 342.40.
272.10   Tangiers]   MS; Tangier 1A
272.20   Straits]   MS; straits 1A
272.23   opposed]   MS; and opposed 1A
272.30   The]   MS; the 1A
272.42   by people]   MS; by a people 1A
274.13   surprize]   MS; surprise 1A. *MS z spelling retained also
                at* 309.16, 314.9, 319.16, 322.31, 322.32, 327.2, *and*
                330.21.
274.26   was . . . effect]   MS; were . . . effects 1A
274.28   traytors]   MS; traitors 1A. *MS y spelling retained also
                at* 288.29, 309.10, 341.22, *and* 342.2.
274.35   toils]   MS; toil 1A
276.8   centinel]   MS; sentinel 1A. *MS c spelling retained also
                at* 290.13.
276.10   eying]   MS; eyeing 1A
276.34   Houris]   MS; houries 1A
277.3   grey]   MS; gray 1A. *MS e spelling retained also at*
                311.20.
277.5   prince]   MS; Prince 1A. *Lowercase form as in MS re-
                tained also at* 277.24 *and* 278.39.
277.6   sheathe]   MS; sheath 1A

277.27   caparizoned]   MS; caparisoned 1A
278.11   partizans]   MS; partisans 1A. *MS z spelling retained also at* 309.4, 320.18, 334.38, 336.13, *and* 343.13.
278.22   Renegado]   MS; renegado 1A. *Capitalized form as in MS retained also at* 307.34, 312.17, *and* 320.3.
278.43   partizan]   MS; partisan 1A. *MS z spelling retained also at* 281.29.
279.11   paralyze]   MS; paralyse 1A
280.32   gallopping]   MS; galloping 1A
282.17   gothica]   MS; Gothica 1A. *But* gotica *at* 243.20.
282.37   youthful]   MS; *omitted* 1A
283.35   spirit]   MS; spirits 1A
283.38   Pedraza]   MS; Pedruza 1A
284.23   Woe]   MS; woe 1A
285.8   judgement]   MS; judgment 1A. *Spelled with additional e as in MS also at* 301.26, 302.32, 332.17, 341.25, *and* 352.26.
285.19   would]   MS; could 1A
285.31   shewn]   MS; shown 1A. *MS spelling* shewn *retained also at* 305.29, 332.13, 338.16, *and* 357.3.
285.40–41   forebodings]   MS; foreboding 1A
286.24   flower]   MS; power 1A
287.23   favorable]   MS; favourable 1A. *MS or form retained also at* 320.27.
287.21   unskillful]   MS; unskilful 1A
288.15   surprized]   MS; surprised 1A. *MS z spelling retained also at* 308.35 *and* 347.43.
288.28   bishop]   MS; Bishop 1A
288.31   dishonor]   MS; dishonour 1A
288.34   Lord]   MS; lord 1A
289.2   shew]   MS; show 1A
289.13   silently]   MS; sliently 1A
289.20   centinels]   MS; sentinels 1A. *MS c spelling retained also at* 323.13.
289.23   when]   MS; When 1A
289.29–30   To morrow]   MS; Tomorrow 1A
289.37   where]   MS; when 1A
289.43   gallopped]   MS; galloped 1A. *Spelled with pp as in MS also at* 334.36.
290.15   Moorish Camp]   MS; moorish camp 1A
290.30   Eucharist]   MS; eucharist 1A
292.2   clash]   MS; lash 1A
292.10   arabian]   MS; Arabian 1A

292.10   greek]   MS; Greek 1A. *Lowercase form as in MS re-*
            tained also at 303.31, *and* 308.32.
292.23   on]   MS; in 1A
292.24   Whither]   MS; whither 1A
292.27   sprang]   MS; sprung 1A
292.31   The noontide]   MS; the noontide 1A
294.9   reliques]   MS; relics 1A. *MS spelling* reliques *retained*
            also at 314.1.
294.10   fleet]   MS; *omitted* 1A
294.17   Taric]   MS; to Taric 1A
294.28   archbishop]   MS; Archbishop 1A
294.32   favorite]   MS; favourite 1A. *MS or spelling retained*
            also at 304.14, 329.22, *and* 336.39.
294.41   rumor]   MS; rumour 1A
295.17   Sea]   MS; sea 1A. *Capitalized form as in MS retained*
            also at 342.19.
295.24   nearly]   MS; near 1A
296.19   batalla]   MS; battalla 1A
296.20   procuró]   MS; procuro 1A
296.23   griega]   MS; griego 1A
296.25   Pedernegra]   MS; Pederneyra 1A
296.27   San]   MS; san 1A. *Capitalized form as in MS retained*
            also at 296.30.
296.33   Romance]   MS; romance 1A
297.6   devices]   MS; divices 1A
297.32   practice]   MS; practise 1A
297.34   Astronomy, Philosophy and Mathematics]   MS; astron-
            omy, philosophy, and mathematics 1A
297.40   Cave]   MS; cave 1A
298.8   cave]   MS; cavern 1A
298.29   Archbishop]   MS; archbishop 1A
299.11   strewn]   MS; strown 1A
300.14   enquired]   MS; inquired 1A
301.17   flights]   MS; flight 1A
302.18   vying]   MS; vieing 1A
302.25   Noseir]   MS; Nozier 1A. *MS* s *spelling retained also at*
            318.10. *See also* 265.20.
303.5   Set]   MS; set 1A
304.37   governor]   MS; governour 1A
305.26   enameled]   MS; enamelled 1A
306.10   The Bridge]   MS; the bridge 1A
307.2   Mediterranean]   MS; Mediteranean 1A

307.8	honorable] MS; honourable 1A. *MS* or *spelling retained also at* 319.18.
310.27	No] MS; no 1A
311.4	you] MS; ye 1A
311.27	burthen] MS; burden 1A
311.42	Señor Alcayde] MS; señor alcayde 1A
312.3	yet] MS; *omitted* 1A
312.16	skillfully] MS; skilfully 1A
313.16	count] MS; Count 1A
314.19	Count] MS; count 1A. *Capitalized form as in MS retained also at* 323.41.
314.29	hast] MS; has 1A
315.15	on the vega] MS; in the vega 1A
315.29	Oh] MS; O 1A. *MS spelling* Oh *retained also at* 337.21, 340.6, 341.24, 341.31, 344.11, 351.42, *and* 355.10.
315.34	in] MS; *omitted* 1A.
315.41	Rabbi] MS; rabbi 1A. *Capitalized form as in MS retained also at* 316.10.
316.27	Saint] MS; saint 1A
316.28	Palm] MS; palm 1A
316.33	relique] MS; relic 1A. *MS spelling* relique *retained also at* 317.39 *and* 325.29.
318.4	table] MS; Table 1A
*318.13	Emir] MS; emir 1A
323.14	awaited] MS; waited 1A
324.3	siege] MS; seige 1A. *Error in 1A corrected to MS spelling also at* 324.12, 324.26, 326.32, *and* 327.5.
324.36	to wield] MS; wield 1A
325.9	Surely] MS; surely 1A
325.17	Of] MS; of 1A
325.29	principal] MS; principle 1A
326.6	what] MS; What 1A
326.25	entrust] MS; intrust 1A
327.9	Reduce] MS; reduce 1A
328.1	characterized] MS; characterised 1A
328.4	Kingdom] MS; kingdom 1A
328.5	skillful] MS; skilful 1A
328.7	staunch] MS; stanch 1A
328.35	Am] MS; am 1A
328.40	thou] MS; that thou 1A
328.40	veritably] MS; virtually 1A
330.38	afterward] MS; after 1A
330.41	general de] MS; *gen.* 1A

331.21	spoil] MS; spoils 1A. *But see* 331.36.
332.17	or] MS; nor 1A. *MS or retained also at* 344.4.
332.41	dispatching] MS; despatching 1A
334.29	the moslems] MS; The moslems 1A
335.34	Chronicler] MS; chronicler 1A
336.15	extolling] MS; exalting 1A
336.17	rigour] MS; rigor 1A
336.23	encreasing] MS; increasing 1A
336.33	Northern] MS; northern 1A
337.16	shewing] MS; showing 1A. *MS* shewing *retained also at* 349.5.
337.31	thus] MS; Thus 1A
337.33	countries] MS; country 1A
337.39	moment's] MSA; moments 1A
338.7	behold] MS; Behold 1A
338.12	nor silver] MS; no silver 1A
338.13	spoil] MS; spoils 1A
338.20	the saddle] MS; their saddles 1A
338.22	tread.] MS; tread on. 1A
338.34	Never] MS; never 1A
339.5	during] MS; During 1A
339.31	houris] MS; houries 1A
340.25	sneers] MS; the sneers 1A
340.36	stygma] MS; stigma 1A
341.38	Part] MS; P. 1A
342.41	South] MS; south 1A
343.29	ensure] MS; insure 1A
343.29	tranquility] MS; tranquillity 1A
345.16	Abdelasis] MS; Abadalasis 1A. *MS spelling* Abdelasis *retained also at* 345.21.
345.35	She] MS; she 1A
345.36	christians] MS; the christians 1A
345.37	P] MS; p 1A
346.31	when] MS; where 1A
347.26	embittered] MS; imbittered 1A
347.40	orizons] MS; orisons 1A
348.21	inclosed] MS; enclosed 1A
349.8	conquerors] MS; conqueror 1A
349.9	unhonored] MS; unhonoured 1A
349.13	chronicle] MS; chronicles 1A
349.23	round] MS; around 1A
349.27	chanted] MS; chaunted 1A
351.43	Your] MS; your 1A

352.16	so] MS; So 1A
352.33	Countess] MS; countess 1A
354.13	bid] MS; bidden 1A
354.35	to himself] MS; *omitted* 1A
356.14	disheveled] MS; dishevelled 1A
356.20	traytorous] MS; traitorous 1A
356.29	straits] MS; straights 1A
357.6	byeword] MS; bye-word 1A
357.26	2] MS; II 1A
357.30	tower] MS; town 1A
357.31	Aragon] MS; Arragon 1A. *But see* Arragon at 352.19, 353.11, *and* 356.37.

SUBSTANTIVE VARIANTS IN MANUSCRIPTS FOR AMERICAN AND ENGLISH FIRST EDITIONS

For each of the three works having two manuscripts (*A Tour on the Prairies*, *Abbotsford*, and *Newstead Abbey*), all substantive variants are listed in two columns, headed MSA and MSE (see List of Abbreviations, page 361).

The numbers indicate the relevant page and line in the Twayne edition. In most instances the readings for this edition are those of the MSA; a double asterisk ** indicates adoption of the MSE reading. Usually the adopted MSE reading agrees with 1A and for that reason is listed also in the List of Emendations; if not, it appears as the acceptable reading in the List of Rejected Substantives to reflect the rejected 1A reading. In instances when neither the MSA nor the MSE provides the adopted reading, that reading can be found in the entry designated by the page and line number listed here in the appropriate List of Emendations. A single asterisk * identifies readings explained among the Discussions of Adopted Readings for each work.

A Tour on the Prairies

	MSA	MSE
10.20	S'	St
10.21	extends	extend
10.23	government	Government
10.26	civilization	civilisation
11.23	and without country	**without country
11.24	jargon	Babilonysh jargon
11.26	hear	*omitted*
11.28	siezed	**seized
12.6	horse	horses
12.9	Frenchman	frenchman
12.11	Anticipations	Anticipation
12.15	Counts	Count's
12.29	spake	spoke
13.2	service	services
13.23	on	in

	MSA	MSE
13.26	hunters	hunter's
13.28–30	bestowed	placed
13.31	placed	put
14.4	these	the
15.8	excepting	except
15.9	top	the top
15.26	Beside	Besides
15.40	process	progress
16.15	us	*omitted*
16.16	ful	**full
16.24	metasses	metusses
16.25	japanned	jappanned
16.29	aided	added to
16.31	sullen	sallow
16.36	shewed	he shewed
16.42	an	*omitted*
17.8	Tonish	little Tonish
17.10	a beggar	the beggar
17.22	thridding	threading
17.23	dusk we	dusk when we
17.24	of the	by the
17.28	him self	**himself
18.36	parrallel	parralel
19.9	gipsey	gypsey
19.22	his	the
19.24	forth	*omitted*
19.29	he the	**he had the
19.38	lanched	**launched
20.2	narrow well trampled	well trampled narrow
21.6	homeward	homewards
21.29	&	**and
22.7	are	were
22.15	calmer	calm
22.37	a warlike	warlike
23.30	visitors	visiters
23.32	In the	In this
24.20	bust	breast
24.23	foray	forage
24.38	this	that
25.11	awaken	awakens
25.22	farther	further

	MSA	MSE
25.40	to not to	**not to
26.19	accompanyment	accompaniment
26.39	indians	**Indians
27.8	merryment	merriment
27.27	Indian	three Indian
27.34	*omitted*	**on
27.40	had had	had
28.11	Honey Camp	Rangers' Camp
28.27	feet	foot
31.7	whisp	wisp
31.32	hand	**hands
32.1	Melancholy	melancholy
32.6	raccoons	racoons
32.31	the Cross	The Cross
33.21	provision	provisions
33.23	dogwood	Dog wood
34.5	this	the
35.3	siezed	**seized
35.36	brush	bush
36.8	pure	*omitted*
36.9	parrallel	**parallel
36.15	in	on
36.32	on	in
38.7	these	the
38.35	and limb	and from limb
40.1	rangers	Rangers
40.29	river	River
41.1	buffalo	Buffalo
41.34	for	*omitted*
42.35	rove	roam
42.40	rocky mountains	**Rocky Mountains
43.18	screened	secured
44.6	There's	Theres
44.19	He's . . . is.	*omitted*
45.11	glaring	flaring
46.7	off	of
46.36	skreen	grove
47.29	sculls	skulls
47.37	parrallel	**parallel
48.38	turkey	Turkey
48.41	style,	**style, and,
50.21	Enormous	**enormous

	MSA	MSE
51.36	lie	be
51.42	Elks	elks
52.23	had	they had
53.21	one	or
53.33	once	*omitted*
54.32	with a poor hungry soil	the soil poor and hungry
55.18	his	its
55.40	of	*omitted*
57.20	on	in
57.27	some of the troop	the hectoring little Tonish
58.2	draggled	dragged
58.17	in	into
58.19	driving	**driven
58.37	gleam	**gloom
58.38	tethered	the tethered
60.17	sunrize	**sunrise
61.30	on	*omitted*
61.30	parrallel	**parallel
61.33	the tracks	tracks
62.13	to a	on
62.22	grounds	ground
62.29	ornamented	ornamental
62.35	skirts	skirt
63.2	lieutenant	Lieutenant
63.37	dextrous	**dexterous
64.26–27	interupted	**interrupted
65.7	**in**	into
65.26	companions	companion
65.36	mane	main
66.31	every	any
67.23	north	**North
68.12	be sorry, and	*omitted*
68.17	them	the young rangers
69.40	burthen	burden
69.41	dicipline	**discipline
70.24	timber	**Timber
71.27	rugged	ragged
71.39	on	in
71.42	calcining	charring
72.30	grew	grow

	MSA	MSE
72.35	camp	the camp
73.22	waylayed	waylaid
74.4	on	in
74.17	siezed	**seized
74.28	field	fields
74.37	beyond	behind
75.9	and worry	*omitted*
75.31	in	upon
75.36	dicipline	**discipline
75.43	parrallel	**parallel
*76.27	distant	**Distant
76.37	in the	at
77.29	cookery	cooking
77.31–32	companion	companions
78.16	Change of route.	*omitted*
78.19	woodsman	woodman
78.30–31	in amphibious	*this amphibious
78.36	past	**passed
78.37	parrallel	**parallel
79.10	leatherstocking	**Leatherstocking
79.22	to the	to our
79.27	border	borders
79.29	rocky mountains	**Rocky Mountains
80.3–4	wildness and darkness	darkness and wildness
80.23	larger	large
80.34	woefully	wofully
80.39	further	farther
81.21	parrallel	**parallel
83.15	flesh of which	whose flesh
83.28	enameled	enamelled
85.4	back	*omitted*
85.8	toward	towards
85.14	Frenchman	Frenchmen
85.30	them	these
85.35	siezed	**seized
86.1	little	that little
86.4	its	his
86.6	his his	**his
86.17	north	**North
86.18	the rivers of	*omitted*
86.35	misletoe	mistletoe

	MSA	MSE
87.15	could descry	descried
87.22	mein	**mien
87.29	would	should
89.13	Bilyet	**Beatte
89.21	swilled	**swelled
89.23	cowering	cowring
90.10	swoln	**swollen
90.12	desplay	**display
90.19	grizly	grizley
90.23	Rocky Mountains	rocky mountains
90.28	withstanding	notwithstanding
90.31	enured	inured
91.17	fort	Fort
91.23	is	was
91.28	shewed	showed
91.33	bruizes	bruises
91.35	crushed	broken
91.43	superintendance	**superintendence
92.5	advantages	advantage
92.13	zeal	**great zeal
92.34	sculls	skulls
92.40	heart	a heart
93.16	prophet	Prophet
93.21	habitutudes	**habitudes
93.26	which	**which I
93.33	S'	St
94.3	hasten	haste
94.17	relatives	relations
95.20	faun	fawn
95.22	faun	fawn
*95.29	shot	range
98.8	maneuvres	manouvres
98.38	pistolshot	pistol shot
98.40	chase	chace
98.41	parrallel	**parallel
99.15	horses	horse
100.2	*omitted*	**he
100.7	further	farther
100.8	its windings	**the windings
101.3	farmhouse	farm house
101.14	parrallel	**parallel
101.31	venimously	**venomously

	MSA	MSE
101.34	pistolshot	pistol shot
104.18	whither he would not	whether he would or not
105.38	trampings	tramplings
106.4	*omitted*	* *our
106.12	horseman	* *horsemen
106.27	wide	*omitted*
106.42	as staunch	staunch
107.17–18	discerned	descried
107.36	pockethandker-chief	pocket handkerchief
107.37	in the fork	on the fork
108.6	comrads	* *comrades
108.13	burrow	great burrow
108.13	Prairie	* *prairie
108.15–16	Having . . . community.	Late in the afternoon I set out with a companion to visit it.
108.16–21	The prairie . . . wonders of . . . with almost the . . . being, giving him . . . beaver.	*omitted*
108.22–23	The Prairie . . . sensitive	The prairie dog is a little animal of the cony kind about the size of a rabbit, of a sprightly nature, quick, sensitive, mercurial
108.25–28	innumerable . . . restlessness.	the well beaten tracks show the constant mobility and restlessness of the inhabitants.
108.28–29	According . . . to be	They seem in fact
108.30	gossipping	*omitted*
108.30–32	houses, or congre-gating together . . . air	holes; congregating in the open air and gambolling together in the cool evenings after showers.
108.32–33	especially . . . shines	*omitted*
108.33–36	or . . . instant,	and yelping with weak tones, like very young puppies; but on the least alarm they all vanish into their cells,

	MSA	MSE
108.37–38	In case . . . will	Should they be surprised, and have no means of escape they
109.1–2	Prairie . . . homes	prairie dogs are not, however, the sole inhabitants of these villages.
109.3	as	*omitted*
109.4–8	and would . . . sally	more alert in their looks, tall on their legs, and rapid in flight than the ordinary species, and a bird that sallies
109.9–16	cells . . . bark.	the ruinous habitations of the prairie dogs, which the latter have deserted in consequence of the death of some relative: **for it** would seem that the sensibilities of these very singular little dogs will not permit them to remain in a dwelling in which they have lost a friend. Others affirm that the owl is a kind of housekeeper to the prairie dog, and, from having a note very similar, it is even insinuated that it teaches the young litter to bark, being employed as a family preceptor.
109.17–23	ascertained . . . maw.	learnt of the part he takes in the domestic economy of this most interesting household. Some insinuate that he is a mere sycophant and sharper, and takes in the honest credulous little prairie dogs most sadly: certain it is, that, from being now and then detected with one of the young ones of the family in his maw, he evidently solaces himself in private with more than the usual perquisites of a toad-eater.
109.24–27	Such . . . the wits of the Far West.	The accounts I had received of these very social and politic little animals made me approach the village with great interest.
109.28–29	It . . . question.	*omitted*

	MSA	MSE
109.29–36	Unluckily . . . air	Unfortunately it had been visited in the course of the day by some of the rangers who had even shot two or three of the citizens. The whole community, therefore, was outraged and incensed; centinels seemed to have been posted on the outskirts; on our approach there appeared to be a scampering in of the picket guards to give the alarm. Whereupon the wary citizens, who were seated at the entrances to their holes, gave each a short yelp or bark, and dived into the earth, his heels twinkling in the air as he descended,
109.38	or republic	*omitted*
109.39	but . . . an	Not a single
109.40–41	We . . . rattlesnake.	There were innumerable holes, each having a small hillock of earth about it, thrown out by the little animal in burrowing: these holes were empty as far as we could probe them with the ramrods of our rifles; nor could we unearth either dog, or owl or rattle snake.
109.41	quietly	off quietly
109.43	By . . . burgher	By degrees some cautious old citizen, near at hand
110.1	draw . . . again.	withdraw it.
110.2	Another, . . . distance	Others farther off,
110.3–4	plunge . . . hole.	dive back into their holes.
110.4	some . . . on	the inhabitants of
110.6–7	the residence . . . about	as if to the residence of some relative, or gossipping friend, where they might compare notes on
110.10	as if	*omitted*
110.11	burghers	citizens
110.12–15	to take . . . direction,	softly to reconnoitre them more distinctly, when yelp! yelp! yelp!

	MSA	MSE
		passed from mouth to mouth. There was a sudden dispersal. We caught glimpses of twinkling feet in every direction,
110.17–20	the train . . . camp; and	*omitted*
110.20–25	as I . . . republic.	after our return to the camp, we could hear a faint clamour from the distant village, as if the inhabitants were lamenting in general assemblage some great personage that had fallen in their commonwealth.
110.37	elk	Elk
110.22–24	It . . . out.	*omitted*
111.27	fort	Fort
111.32	beside	besides
111.42	lieutenant	Lieutenant
112.3	prairie	prairies
112.14	East	**east
112.17	brisk	fresh
112.36	sentinels	sentinals
112.41	fort	Fort
113.1	amidst	under
113.10	for	*omitted*
113.11	labyrinth	labrynth
113.27	for	*omitted*
113.27	half	**a half
113.34	prairie	Prairie
113.35	neighted	**neighed
114.10	persimmon	the persimmon
114.16	doe	Doe
114.17	for	*omitted*
114.22	a diamond	the diamond
114.27–31	The night . . . myself.	We had again a beautiful night. The tired rangers after a little murmuring conversation around their fires soon sank to rest. There was a faint light from the moon, now in its second quarter, and after it had set a fine star light with shooting meteors.

	MSA	MSE
114.32	awake	*omitted*
114.33–34	when . . . heaven	*omitted*
114.36	eastern shepherds	Eastern Shepherds
114.36–37	How often How often	**How often
114.38	sweet	secret
114.42–43	exhiliarating	**exhiliarating
115.2	centinels	sentinels
115.34	yet	but
115.36	resumed	commenced
116.41	champain	**champaign
117.24	they would	**there would
118.7	in	on
118.15	inclinations	inclination
118.37	stoney	stony
119.19	would	should
119.30	lay	lying
120.17	distances	distance
121.8	head	**head and
121.9	the	these

Abbotsford

	MSA	MSE
126.42	good	great
172.17	employed . . . show	keeping it in order and showing
127.18	was a worthy	**a worthy
127.26	in blue coat	in a blue coat
127.32	Scottish	Scotch
128.14	to	of
128.16	varra clear	all varra clear
129.20	an	and
129.20	I	I∧ll
129.21	if	**of
129.21	his voice	hearing his voice
129.21	and	an'
129.22	I am	I'm
129.23	and lauff	an' lauff
130.8	moon	**the moon
131.32	aroused	roused
131.36	censure or applaud	receive censure or applause

	MSA	MSE
131.39–40	Maida . . . he	Maida, continued he, is like the great gun at Constantinople
132.7	them	these
132.11	And	An'
132.33	grey	gray
*133.8–9	It	**Scotland is eminently a land of song, and it
133.17	their	these
133.19	of pastoral poets	*omitted*
133.32	songs	writings
134.22	relic	relique
134.37	Teviot dale	**Teviotdale
135.9	stout	**a stout
135.10	a naked . . . hills	*omitted*
135.13	beheld	had beheld
135.24	with	by
135.33	to hills	to see hills
137.38	They played with them, for a time, and then	They
137.40	joyous; and having	**joyous; having
138.2	measure	manner
138.31	regaled . . . to time	from time to time regaled
139.2	sovreignity	**sovereignty
139.3	acknowledged admitted	**acknowledged
139.5	sovreign	**sovereign
139.21	the Lowlanders	Lowlanders
140.17	*omitted*	**that time at
140.18	this	his
140.25	in the air	**on the eve
141.32	sovreignty	**sovereignty
141.39	wanted	**waited
142.11	1778	in 1778
142.21	hardheaded	hard headed
*142.27	Barons young lady	**young lady
142.32	set	**sat
143.18	on	in
144.19	of	**on
144.27	before him	at his feet

	MSA	MSE
145.8	neighbors	neighbors'
145.19	law suit	lawsuit
145.32	Campbell	he
145.34	landlords	Landlord
146.19	or	and
146.20	proper	*omitted*
146.25	stories conversation	**stories
146.25	*omitted*	**to them
146.39	them	these
147.3	any thing	every thing
147.8	their merits	**to these novels
147.19	would	could
147.24	but had	but they had
147.24	met	met with
147.36–37	long legs	**Long Legs
148.6	learn	hear
148.29	in letter	**in a letter
149.16	'wi	**wi'
149.17	there	then
149.18	Tree	tree
149.20	fyne	fine
149.23–24	circumstance	circumstances
150.10	grey hound	grey-hound *end of line*
150.26	had killed	killed
150.27	on	at
151.2	Praetorium	praetorium
151.3	Old buck	Old-buck *end of line*
151.13	philosophic	philosophical
151.43	now and then	*omitted*
152.5	occasionally	now and then
*153.39	associations, Scott	**associations,
157.1	and	**any
157.22	hardship	hardships
157.38	fancied	feared
159.13	of	*omitted*
159.20	fable	**fables
160.1	*omitted*	**time
160.2	them	**the theme
160.6	*omitted*	**courtesies and
160.13	subacid	subdued

	MSA	MSE
160.21	ashes	**ash
160.25	prospects	prospect
160.27	the storied	that storied
160.31	two	**Two
160.34	as unconcernedly	unconcernedly
161.7	of his hole	*omitted*
161.31	immoveable	immovable
161.32	this	the
162.3	in	of
162.11	scenes	the scenes
162.19	and made . . . hills.	*omitted*
162.27	these	those
162.30	were	are
163.3	mind . . . was	minds . . . were
163.20	passed	passed on
163.29	legend	legends
163.31	bear	have
163.41	these	their
164.3	speer	speir
164.4	ears or eyes	eyes or ears
164.20	glance	gleam
164.20	eye brows	eye-brows
164.40	Scottish	Scotch
165.5	she is	she's
165.10	it	**It
165.11	Shakspeare	Shakespeare
165.30	hearts	good hearts
166.12	book I	book that I
166.21	rejecting	neglecting
*167.4–7	during . . . will.	a vein of strong, shrewd common-sense [*one word*] ran throughout it, as it does throughout all his writings, but was enriched and enlivened by incessant touches of feeling, of fancy and humour. I have not done justice to the copious flow of grave thought that often mingled in his conversations, for at this distance of time little remains in my memory but salient points and light whimsical

	MSA	MSE
		and characteristic anecdotes. Indeed during the whole time of my visit he seemed in a lively playful mood, and his remarks and stories inclined to the comic rather than grave. Such, however, I was told was the usual habit of his mind in social intercourse. He relished a joke, or a trait of humour and laughed with right good will.
167.7	He . . . effect	Scott never talked for not for effect
167.10	effort	effect
167.14	conversation	conversations
167.41	beneficient	benignant
168.2	nature	nature tempered the sharpness of his wit and
168.11	a human human	human
168.26	greatest advantages	few unmingled gratifications

Newstead Abbey

	MSA	MSE
172.2	novel	revel
172.12	gossipping	gossiping
173.3	this	the
173.7	estate	estates
173.15	laid	made
173.19	mood	moods
173.31	poet	Poet
175.16–17	a few years	after years
*176.4	Col.	**Colonel
176.6	war	wars
178.20	being	being in
178.41	III	**XIII
179.1	this	the
179.4	seemed to reverberate	reverberated
180.14	I shall	shall
180.18	the windows	and
*180.24	goblen	**Goblen
181.19–20	give . . .	confirm the belief in some occult

	MSA	MSE
	suppositions	meaning connected with these figures
181.21	christian	**Christian
181.23	Byrons	Byrons, and a date carrying them back to the days of "Sir John Byron the little with the great beard," a traditional personage of some shadowy importance about the venerable mansion as will hereafter be shewn
183.9	lords	Lords
183.12	surprize	surprise
185.11	lies	is
*186.28	ribband	ribbands
187.7	Derby shire	**Derbyshire
187.15–16	the story . . . together with	ballads and traditional dialogues and
187.19	boars	boars'
187.23	since	from
188.15–20	In . . . who	One of the living chronicles of Newstead Abbey is an old dame, nearly seventy years of age, named Nanny Smith, who has passed her life on the place, and
188.21	comprize	comprise
188.37–38	Nanny Smith	the poor woman
190.2	&	**and
191.26	such as suited the	suited to
192.11	with	of
192.41	were	are
193.12	by	at
194.25	fryar	friar
196.5	at the Abbey	of the Abbey
196.23	sculptures	sculpture
196.24	already mentioned	*omitted*
197.14	that	the
210.14–15	comprized	comprised
202.12	phraze	phrase
203.15	the	**this
203.15	has embodied	has since embodied
203.15	his stanzas	the cantos
203.25–35	Nor . . . rest.	*omitted*

	MSA	MSE
204.4	its	the
204.9	life	hope
204.30	re-enter'd	re-entered
204.32	and she knew	**she knew
205.23	witchery	witching
205.28	surprized	surprised
205.34	and afterwards	**and he afterwards
208.25	*omitted*	**seems
208.25	wandering	wanderings
208.26	Upward	Upwards
210.11	fluttering	flattering
211.12	persuade	persuades
214.22	While	During my sojourn
215.14	had	has
215.34–35	When . . . hind.	*omitted*
216.4	oak	**Oak
217.14	King	*omitted*
217.25	the mutilated	its mutilated
217.31	when	When
218.13	birches	beeches
218.14	old monumental trees	*omitted*
219.6	wood land	woodland
219.19	a heath	**the heath
219.28	were	came
220.9	sinister	dismal
220.9	by which	with which
230.15	those	them
230.30	then	there
231.28	minds	worlds
232.2	horrible	terrible
232.4	Sir	sir
233.6	Seeking	At length seeking
234.19	deseased	**diseased
234.35	forward to	forward
234.36	sacred	sound
235.12	me	*omitted*
236.16	those	these
237.39	this	the
237.42	exertion	exertions
238.6	letter	latter

LIST OF COMPOUND WORDS
HYPHENATED
AT END OF LINE

List I for the four writings includes compound and possible compound words that are hyphenated at the end of the line in the copy-text. In deciding whether these words should be printed in the T text as hyphenated, one word, or two words, the editor has made the decision first on the use of each compound word elsewhere in the copy-text; or second, when the word does not appear elsewhere in the copy-text, on Irving's practice in other writings of this period; or finally, if the word does not appear in Irving's other writings of the period, on contemporary American usage. Each word is listed in its editorially accepted form after the page and line numbers of its appearance in the T text.

List II presents compounds or possible compounds that are hyphenated at the end of the line in the T text. They are listed in the form in which they would have appeared in the T text had they come in midline.

LIST I

7.41	outgrown	95.2–3	undertaking
9.15–16	knifegrinder	96.23	marksman
11.17	Sometimes	100.21	something
15.25	tastefully	101.7	nightfall
15.31–32	blacksmith's	102.28	foreshoulder
17.15	horseback	109.2	rattlesnakes
34.29	schoolmaster	114.24–25	somewhat
49.10	henceforth	119.30	upturned
62.26	woodland	121.10	something
72.6	woodland	126.4	sportsman
82.37	Frenchman	135.29	overhung
83.5	whenever	154.34	grandmother
84.4	gentleman	172.22	swordsman
85.5	however	179.13	something
87.24	something	185.1	landscape
89.11	saddlebags	191.31	sometimes
90.15	hamstring	193.23	footsteps

196.12	supernatural	276.21	however
198.36	schoolboy	282.2	inlaid
207.2	neighborhood	287.37	countrymen
209.14	schoolboy	290.34	archbishop
215.11	overshadowing	306.9	warlike
237.39	neighborhood	309.16	overpowered
243.15	undertook	310.23	countrymen
253.23	waterfalls	312.36	aftertimes
259.4	overhanging	330.5	otherwise
261.35	antechamber	322.17	generalship
268.33	otherwise	350.22	byeword
272.18	overrun		

LIST II

9.15	knifegrinder	120.18	landmarks
13.27	underwent	125.26	gentleman's
13.29	wardrobe	127.19	newspapers
15.31	blacksmith's	135.21	myself
18.34	overgrown	140.8	Highland
18.37	overtake	142.29	throughout
22.19	haphazard	152.18	clergyman
22.28	uplands	160.37	however
25.37	horseback	161.41	without
28.38	warfare	172.33	gentleman
42.41	counterparts	176.35	myself
47.17	whenever	183.3	overshadowed
62.17	horsemen	188.20	housekeeper
64.40	overtaken	199.10	understood
65.20	marksman	201.40	housekeeper
66.24	throughout	203.30	Something
71.10	horseman	209.16	themselves
71.19	something	226.4	sometimes
73.13	something	229.10	understood
75.42	something	229.22	bookseller
89.25	woodland	242.25	however
95.2	undertaking	244.33	however
95.14	woodman	245.36	mandates
98.37	horseback	261.7	workmanship
109.21	himself	261.13	Whatever
111.14	whenever	262.17	workmanship
114.24	somewhat	262.26	archbishop
119.21	themselves	264.9	headlong

269.28	somewhat	311.9	yourselves
271.1	Wherever	316.13	themselves
278.35	throughout	316.29	without
285.16	overcoming	332.30	midnight
285.40	forebodings	331.35	behold
303.2	however	335.21	overcame
310.36	undertaken	338.32	sometimes
310.37	himself		

OWNERSHIP OR LOCATION OF EXTANT MANUSCRIPTS USED AS COPY-TEXT FOR THE CRAYON MISCELLANY

The following symbols will identify the owner or location of manuscripts serving as copy-text for the portions of established text indicated:

B   The Berg Collection of the New York Public Library
H   The Hanley Collection of the Miriam Lutcher Stark Library at the University of Texas
K   Irving B. Kingsford
M   The John Murray Publishing House of London

A Tour on the Prairies

9.17	("Chapter I") − − 10.16 ("men.")	H
10.17	("It") − − 121.16 ("table")	B
121.16	("crowned") − − 122.4 ("forward.")	H
122.5	("A ride") − − 122.34 ('Grounds.")	B

Abbotsford

125.1	("To _____ _____") − − 132.36 ("family.")	K
132.37	("We") − − 133.8 ("more.")	M
133.8	("Scotland") − − 154.11 ("years.")	K
154.12	("Still") − − 154.31 ("caress'd.")	M
154.32	("It") − − 155.23 ("wild")	K
155.24	("Of") − − 156.36 ("before.")	M
156.37	("Scott") − − 167.17 ("delightfully.")	K
167.18	("He") − − 167.23–24 ("concerns, no")	M
167.24	("one's thoughts") − − 168.12 ("benignant.")	K
168.12	("Who") − − 168.18 ("as")	M
168.18	("an") − − 168.30 ("hands.")	K

Newstead Abbey

171.1	("Historical Notice") − − 171.32 ("Byron")	M
171.32	("the little") − − 176.33 ("acceptance.")	B

| 176.34 | ("I trust") — — 176.45 ("Byron.") | M |
| 177.1 | ("homes") — — 238.32 ("groan.") | B |

Legends of the Conquest of Spain

| 241.1 | ("Preface") — — 295.25 ("discovered") | B |
| 133.1 | ("Illustrations") — — 357.35 ("him.") | B |

PARTS OF PRINTED EDITIONS
USED AS COPY-TEXT

The symbol 1A will identify the printed texts or first American editions used as copy-texts for the portions of established texts indicated. Specific copies used are personal copies of the editor corresponding to Blanck's listings 10140, first or earlier state, and 10144, designated Setting A.

A Tour on the Prairies

5.1	("Introduction") − − 9.16 ("sir.")	1A

Legends of the Conquest of Spain

295.25	("that") − − 296.9 ("Roderick.")	1A

SEGMENTS OF MANUSCRIPTS NOT USED
AS COPY-TEXT

The following symbols will identify the location or owner of extant manuscripts or segments not used as copy-text:

NYPL   The New York Public Library (MS Division)
B   The Berg Collection of the New York Public Library
H   The Hanley Collection of the Miriam Lutcher Stark
       Library of the University of Texas
M   The John Murray Publishing House
K   Irving B. Kingsford
P   Helen Kingsford Preston
V   The Barrett Library at the University of Virginia
NC   The University of North Carolina (Louis Round Wilson
       Library)

A Tour on the Prairies

Portions of Journals II, III, IV of Irving's Western Journals   NYPL
    [Published in John Francis McDermott's *The Western
    Journals of Washington Irving* (Norman: University
    of Oklahoma Press, 1944.)]
424 pages of printer's copy for the 1835 John Murray
    publication   H
    [Except for approximately 4 pages which serve as
    copy-text]

Abbotsford

145 pages of printer's copy for the 1835 John Murray
    publication   M
    [Except for portions of 5 pages or approximately
    108 lines which serve as copy-text]
1 leaf (earlier draft) corresponding to 133.24–133.35   V
Approximately 4 leaves of notes and abortive fragments   K
Two small volumes of notes about Irving's visit to Scotland   NC
    [Published in Stanley Williams' *A Tour in Scotland*
    (New Haven: Yale University Press, 1927).]

Newstead Abbey

182 pages of printer's copy for the 1835 John Murray publication, lacking 43 pages	M
[Except for approximately 2 1/2 pages which serve as copy-text]	
3 Pages of Historical Notice	P
25 pages or four letters from Sophia Hyatt	V
Rough notes (approximately 100 pages)	V

Legends of the Conquest of Spain

2 1/2 pages of earlier draft remaining with the 5 surviving pages of the 7 Irving wrote to replace them	B

INDEX